THE HUMAN RESOURCE
PROBLEM-SOLVER'S HANDBOOK

THE HUMAN RESOURCE PROBLEM-SOLVER'S HANDBOOK

Joseph D. Levesque, CMC/SPHR

McGraw-Hill, Inc.
New York   St. Louis   San Francisco   Auckland   Bogotá
Caracas   Lisbon   London   Madrid   Mexico   Milan
Montreal   New Delhi   Paris   San Juan   São Paulo
Singapore   Sydney   Tokyo   Toronto

Library of Congress Cataloging-in-Publication Data

Levesque, Joseph D.
    The human resource problem-solver's handbook / Joseph D. Levesque.
        p.   cm.
    Includes index.
    ISBN 0-07-037531-3 :
    1. Supervision of employees. 2. Personnel management—United
States. 3. Labor laws and legislation—United States. I. Title.
    HF5549. 12.L49   1991
    658.3—dc20   91-31233
                                                                    CIP

1 2 3 4 5 6 7 8 9 0   DOC/DOC   9 7 6 5 4 3 2 1

ISBN   0-07-037531-3

The sponsoring editor for this book was Theodore Nardin, and the production supervisor was Pamela Pelton.

Printed and bound by R. R. Donnelley & Sons Company.

ACKNOWLEDGEMENTS

I have often commented that writing a book is analogous to birthing in terms of the tedious, demanding, yet creative nature of the effort. Thoughts give way to words, words to chapters, and eventually chapters to the more developed body of a book. It is a very private, personal experience, but it is by no means the result of a single contributor.

Indeed, many people contributed a substantial effort in this book, and I wish to acknowledge their toil as well as their belief in sharing my vision of this book. Special praise goes to:

Jean L. Hyner; manager of The Executive Office Center and good friend who spent untold hours preparing and making countless editorial changes to the lengthy manuscript.

Michelle L. Daggett; staff analyst for the firm who spent many hours at the California State University, Sacramento library conducting, summarizing, and organizing research material, as well as the laborious task of preparing an extensive index so that the multitude of topic references can be easily found.

Ellen R. Levesque; author, columnist, and (conveniently) my mother who has worked with the written word for many years, served as one of the editors of this book.

Prem Hunji Turner; labor law attorney and special counsel to the California Labor Law Council for her review and critique of the manuscript in an effort to assure the proficiency of technical legal points illustrated herein.

DEDICATION

This book is gratefully dedicated to my clients, students, colleagues, and mentors; all of whom have provided me the continuing opportunity to search for and find the methods, insights, and answers that help make our workplaces a more productive life experience.

PREFACE

What This Book Is About,
Why It Will Help You Manage People Better,
And How To Get The Most From This Book

What This Book Is About

This book is about managing and solving some of the more difficult, often critical people problems we all confront each day in our workplaces. As managers and supervisors of our organization's human resources, we have a professional, legal, and moral obligation to handle each decision we make with skill and accuracy. Yet, when it comes to dealing effectively with the myriad of workplace events that occur each day, we make some very serious, usually unintentional mistakes because we lack the necessary background knowledge and decision making skills.

As most of us have learned—frequently the hard way through our mistakes—understanding and dealing effectively with people in an organizational setting is no easy task. Each person we deal with is very different in many respects, and then there are the dynamics of human interaction under unique workplace conditions, expectations, and standards. To make matters even more complex, we must contend with an ever-increasing body of law that serves to protect employee interests, and in doing so sets limitations on the actions of managers with severe liabilities that can cost our employers plenty. Managerial and supervisorial decision making error—and equally important, the way we handle any given situation—is not only a costly company liability, but it also damages and sometimes destroys the delicate nature of work relationships. This cost can eventually be greater than the threat of legal costs to which most of us have become so atuned.

So, what this book is about is learning more about the forces that shape human issues in the workplace—giving them social, economic, historical, and legal significance—and the practical methods of solving critical issues before they become problems, as well as dealing with them when they do become problems. Specifically, this book takes a contemporary look at many of the most crucial problems related to employment discrimination, romance in the workplace, child care, employee privacy rights, wrongful discharge, human behavior traits, dealing with behaviorally difficult employees, and developing personnel policies, performance appraisal, and other control systems to better guide people toward productive work relations. It is written in a clear, easily understood fashion so that you can read chapters for the more in-depth background leading to a fuller understanding of issue solving, or it can be used as a quick reference guide when these situations emerge. Once you begin using it more frequently, I think you'll find yourself reading it more and more thoroughly. After all, it contains the answers you've been looking for, so why not make your job easier by reading for depth rather than a quick fix.

Why This Book Will Help You Manage People Better

Most managers and supervisors I've worked with over the years have been very intelligent, well intentioned people. But, first and foremost, managers are trained to carry out a primary occupational role; to do very particular, often technical work be it accounting, engineering, nursing, marketing, data processing or an endless variety of other specialty vocations. For many people who move into the supervisory or management ranks, dealing with people issues has never been an emphasis in their professional development (thus it becomes about as easy as learning a second language), nor is it a well developed body of new knowledge offered to new managers before assuming these responsibilities.

Learning about human behavior and dealing effectively with people issues in the workplace is often treated with the same abandonment that is given to parenting; anyone can do it, and since I'm as smart or smarter (or better at something) then the next person, I can do it too. Ask any person who has completed the parenting cycle of life if they wish they had the wisdom that experience taught them and listen to their reply about mistakes made, the effects of those mistakes, and what advice they'd give to new parents. So it goes with managing. Like parenting, we must become lifelong students. We can never know too much, and we can ill afford to close our minds to the different aspects of becoming good, well rounded managers. The more we learn, the more professional we become as managers, the job becomes more second nature, and our contribution to our organization becomes greater.

This book is intended to be one of many such contributors to your professional growth as a manager of people. Its sole purpose is to help you understand, handle, and solve many of those stomach twisting problems that have become legally and behaviorally intense in today's workplace. It will help you become a better manager of people because it provides you with the necessary background to make informed decisions, it points out important aspects of problems, it deals only with relevant, real-life issues, and it succinctly gives you practical problem solving approaches, decision factors, and application suggestions. Moreover, it is written *by a practitioner for the practitioner*, so you are assured that this information is not of a purely theoretical nature. It is the experience, insight, and training from one who has completed—but never stops learning—the parenting life cycle. Use it to your advantage and be a better manager of people for it.

How To Get The Most From This Book
There are two ways to use this book; read it thoroughly, chapter by chapter, even if you read only selected chapters of most interest to you; or use it as a reference source relying on the table of contents and index to find different aspects of your interest topic. Obviously, the more you read, the better informed you become. As the old saying goes, a little knowledge can become dangerous. For this reason, I caution you not to rely solely on the table of contents to locate a particular topic—use the index as well. The reason is that any one topic in the human resource/human behavior field can be discussed from many reference points. For example, employee performance can be a matter of conduct, productivity, pay, privacy, discrimination, wrongful discharge, discipline, policy, and the like. The matter of performance, then, can be contained in several different chapters depending on the issue, so it may be important to read parts of a few chapters to obtain a fuller perspective of any singular problem you're trying to resolve.

Second, this book is not a "quick fix, simplistic, just do the following three things to solve all your problems on a given matter" answer to workplace dilemmas. It is a reader, designed to give full background, explanations, factors to consider, and approaches. If you regard a little reading now and then as troublesome, or you require that the world be explained in simple answers, you've bought the wrong book. Far too often a difficult problem has become much more complex because of oversimplified diagnosis or perfunctory thought toward its solution. This book was written to achieve greater depth on critical matters of people problems in the workplace, not for the faint of heart.

Finally, you will quickly observe in reading most parts of this book that considerable emphasis has been given to legal aspects of each problem area. Legal aspects stem from statutory, regulatory, and case law whether from federal or state sources. The reason for somewhat of a legal emphasis, although far from exclusive, throughout this book is because legal liabilities now permeate virtually every aspect of employment decisions and actions. It is a fact we must learn to cope with, and it is a major influence in problem solving decisions. It thus becomes an imperative body of knowledge with which all managers and supervisors should develop at least fundamental familiarity. In this regard, I've attempted to consolidate much of the legally oriented information in an easily understood fashion, and to draw out legal trends (rather then a definitive treatise) on many issues by illustrating the thinking of the courts on most problem issues.

I think you'll find the summaries of these cases both interesting and enlightening. After reading several of them, you should begin to better understand much of the common sense theory used by these courts. The real payoff comes when you can begin evaluating legal issues to the extent of anticipating how a court might view one of your workplace decisions that advances to legal scrutiny. As a final word of caution, keep the legal liability of human resource decisions in perspective. Legal factors are very significant, but they are not always the most beneficial to the greater welfare of the organization in all situations. Sometimes we must make a conscious decision to proceed at legal risk. When this is done it should only be on the basis of being well informed about the degree of risk.

Joseph D. Levesque

CONTENTS

PART I.
PROBLEMS INVOLVING DISCRIMINATORY ACTIONS

Contents

PART II.
SOLVING PROBLEMS RELATED TO EMPLOYMENT RIGHTS

PART III.
SOLVING PROBLEMS INVOLVING DIFFICULT EMPLOYEES AND WORKPLACE CONTROL MECHANISMS

Contents

TABLE OF PROBLEM DISCRIMINATION QUESTIONS, THEIR ANALYSIS, AND SOLUTIONS

Chapter I: 3. Gender Discrimination, Sexual Harassment, and Workplace Romance

THE HUMAN RESOURCE
PROBLEM-SOLVER'S HANDBOOK

PART I. SOLVING PROBLEMS INVOLVING DISCRIMINATORY CONDUCT

Since enactment of the 1935 National Labor Relations Act and the Fair Labor Standards Act in 1938 following the nation's tumultuous depression era, no other legislation has had such a profound effect upon the employer-employee relationship than the 1964 Civil Rights Act and its resultant administrative interpretations and legal decisions. Nor did it end there. Following the 1972 Equal Employment Opportunity Act which broadened the authority and scope of the 1964 Act and the powers of the Equal Employment Opportunity Commission (EEOC), there began to emerge an unparalleled sequence of federal and state statutes to bring type-specific personal characteristics within the meaning of discrimination. Having recognized more than racially-oriented inequities as a pervasive condition barring employment and employment related opportunities across the country, legislation began to systematically address inequities occurring in the workplace associated with one's age, physical disability, marital status, childbirth condition, religious beliefs, political affiliation, sex, sexually-oriented conduct (harassment), and sexual orientation (homosexuality).

Presently, it would appear that the greatest impact of these voluminous laws, regulations, and procedural guidelines has been little more than to deter some employers from the more obvious forms of discriminatory practices—a rather shallow consequence for one of the most advanced societies in the world! While laws may serve their purpose as a deterent, or as a source of notariety to reshape public opinion, the core of discrimination remains as bias and prejudice. Implanted from one generation to the next, prejudice in our society has long been reinforced by cultural, economic, regional, and social value systems that then become the basis of perceptions and their resultant behavior by each successive generation.

In a broad sense, it is a sad state of events that leads a government to mandate prohibitions against what is really a form of social injustice when we know that these actions are inhumane in the first place. Is it changing? Is prejudice—the indiscriminate adverse conduct toward others based on fallacious beliefs—fading with each successive and more enlightened generation? Those who remember the demonstrations at Selma, Alabama, Little Rock, Arkansas, Berkeley, and Kent State during the 1960's may think so; that is, until we open our eyes to see that nearly three decades has not changed much. The media reports events almost daily that reminds us of the inequalities and inhumanities that persist.

- In Cummings, Georgia (January 1986), 20,000 marchers had to be protected by 2,200 National Guardsmen from an all-white town embittered by the 1912 rape and murder of a white girl. No blacks have been allowed to live there since.

- In the Soviet Union, Jews continue their attempts through public demonstration for the end to their oppression.

- In Ireland, the Protestants and Catholics remain fused in their battle for religious domination, as do the Moslems, Palestenians, and Jews of the Middle East.

We continue to hear about female workers being denied a resumption of their job after childbirth, being sexually harassed and threatened, and being denied employment opportunities because of their marital status or the fact that they have (or may want) children. The elderly and youthful, too, are pushed aside as if they have overstayed their usefulness or have too little to contribute. Many of our older, more experienced workers are being coaxed, coerced, and in other ways pushed out with early or mandatory retirements only to face an unfriendly economy and often an unwelcome existence. Are these actions fair, are they right, are they truly necessary for the successful operation of our business organizations, or are they merely a pretextual manifestation of our fears? The chapters in Part I will examine not only some of those issues, but will address particular employment laws, exemplary court cases, difficult situations encountered by managers, case studies, and solutions to several common problems faced by managers every day in the workplace setting.

The employment practices most vulnerable and under greatest scrutiny in the past have been what we might call "active" practices; those where the act has a clearly adverse effect on a particular person or class of persons. Primary are those practices connected to the acquisition and continuation of employment—hiring and terminations. Secondary are those practices affecting maintenance of the employment relationship such as training, promotion, pay, benefits, and discipline. As we proceed into future developments of fair employment law, we can expect the courts to become less forgiving about many of our "passive" practices. They tend to have an equivalent discriminatory effect against many people, but less intentionally than active practices, therefore they become less obvious to even those of us in the human resource profession. These passive practices, as some evidence is already beginning to indicate, receiving greatest attention will be those based on systematic and programmatic operations including such matters as job assignments and work content, organizational development programs, benefit plans, performance appraisal systems, and workforce forecasting methods.

We should remember that employment laws—through administrative enforcement of regulations, and their associated legal decisions through judicial interpretation—are merely the government's way of bringing to our attention those conditions determined to be a manifest inequity in the employment relationship. We are being told by legal authority how to, or not to, conduct business with our employees because they possess inalienable rights and protections. Like any form of law, we have the choice of obeying it (or making a legitimate effort to do so), or disregarding it (because we don't agree with it) because it causes us operational headaches—or whatever our reasons might be. When we knowingly disobey laws, we most certainly operate at considerable risk. With regard to employment laws, we risk violating more than the intent of law; we violate fair and reasonable treatment of our employees, their dignity and human rights, our own ethics, and the effectiveness of our businesses.

One might assume, then, so long as we don't violate the laws, regulations, and practices of fair employment—presuming we are knowledgeable about them—we have nothing to be concerned about. Not so; it's regretably not that easy. We must always remain cognizant (a degree of being on-guard) for the *potential* of illegal or improper actions that can result from routine interactions and decisions so common to the operations of any business. Employment laws, particularly those protecting constitutional rights, are changing and expanding into new realms of employee protectionism. We should not take the laws or trends in judicial thinking lightly lest we wish to tease Golieth, nor should we remain naive about our ability to avoid allegations or substantiation of our wrongdoing. The law journals are filled with cases of surprised employers, and probably many more have not been published because they were settled out of court much to the disdain of the employer even if that be a better choice of two evils.

So, while the systemmatic order of the chapters in Part I is on those type-specific kinds of discrimination, the real issue to be dealt with becomes much more basic; it is the way we as managers deal with people—all people—under our supervision and generally all other employees with whom we have contact at work. It has to do with our value systems, our perceptions, our heritages, our methods of communicating, our procedures and rituals, and it has a great deal to do with our maturity and the ability to self-examine our motives and fears. In other words, sometimes the resolution to any problem lies in our ability to deal with our own human frailties first, and second to examine our responsibility to the organization as managers—that is, being entrusted with the obligation to make sound decisions and be a credible source of leadership for others to follow.

CHAPTER I: 1.0
PROBLEMS CHARACTERIZED BY WORKFORCE
AGE AND AGE DISCRIMINATION

One of the most apparent features of our work environments is the diversity of our workforce age composition. The age of our employees carries many connotations, some positive and some not so positive. What is commonly found is that positive connotations form the basis of perceived age attributes while negative connotations shape age prejudice. Both are problems when they become the predominant foundation of employment decisions. Too, there are other dimensions of the age of our employees that can become problematic for the manager. The issues of workforce age, the problems associated with age bias, and approaches to solving these problems are the primary topics of this chapter. Solutions will be found within general discussions, case law question analysis, and at the end of the chapter. This reading will help sharpen your background in behavioral and other discrimination-related issues raised throughout this book.

The fact that people pass through many life stages throughout the course of their adult years has been the subject of considerable study by psychologists and sociologists for many years. What has become most evident in this research has been that people are likely to experience certain kinds of events, will react differently to those events, and they will undergo considerable, sometimes predictable change in the way they behave, the way they view themselves and their environment, and the way they attempt to influence the course of their life through each life stage. For the personnelist or manager whose charge is to maintain productive relations with an age-diverse workforce, the task can become very complicated when we consider all of the possible influences that tend to shape individual behavior. Some of the more pertinent influences consist of adolescent development and value systems, personality traits, genetic differences, reinforcement experiences, and the whole complex that influences, controls, and restrains human behavior.

While it may not be our place as managers of people to burden our minds with such complexities of human behavior, we should at least concede that behavior is the single most important part of the work environment—it is what people do and how they do it. For that reason, it is worth examining even if only in a very general way. The fact that much of our behavior is intricately connected to age as a measure of our role, productivity, and overall performance at work, makes the topic fair game—and a highly influential ingredient—in any discussion of age. In this case, the focus is on discrimination due to age, but the real underlying issues are much greater.

From a more pure business operations point of view, recognition must be given to a few hard facts about the age of our workforce. First, most employers cannot hire those under the age of 18 due to state child labor laws. Second, federal and state law prohibit employment-related discrimination against those who are over the age of 40. Third, it is not reasonable to assume that all people are equally able (or disabled) to continue meeting work demands forever, and certainly not the way they could when they were younger.

Last, and perhaps most confronting, is the fact that the American workforce will see the greatest number of employees over the age of 40 during the next two decades than during any other period in history due to the aging of the "baby boom" generation.

For managers and human resource professionals, the crux of the problem thus becomes one of maintaining productive balances between employee skills, experience, accountabilities, lifestyle needs, and adaptation to changing business conditions. This chapter explores those problems and provides specific ideas and approaches to their resolution.

1.10   SOME UNDERLYING ISSUES ABOUT EMPLOYEE AGE

Perhaps the largest, most pervasive influence upon age discrimination in employment has to do with our socio-economic orientation toward people in certain age groups, and in particular the elderly. It is interesting to note that the United States is one of the few countries having a *negative* stigma attached to societal usefulness of both its elderly and its young, yet we are very much attached to what Harry Levinson referred to as "youth worship" in his profile of corporate America's attitudes toward middle-age managers.

In employment circles, age discrimination has tended to mean one thing: the adverse employment decision or act where the basis was age, and the person(s) affected are in the "protected class" of persons aged 40 or over. Why? Because employment decisions are made on conditions of 1) *controls* exerted on the organization (primarily that of laws and regulations), *or* 2) *discretion*, meaning free choice, by top executives who frame policy and guide decisions.

In other words, we have become sensitive to this 40+ age group not because of a new moral attitude, nor a change in organizational orientation toward one's productivity during these years, but because we want to avoid the implications of violating laws prohibiting such action. Also, few would probably argue that most age related employment problems don't begin to occur with existing employees until around age 55 when workers are often characterized as unable to change with new trends and ideas, keep pace with younger workers, pose medical problems, and the like. Yet the protected group starts at age 40 to account for those individuals who frequently encounter employment barriers in obtaining new employment (the selection process), and surface again about age 60 as a retirement issue.

For example, in the period of 1950-1983, the percentage of employed men over 65 years of age dropped from 45.8 to 17.8 percent, while men in the 55-64 age group went from 87 to 70 percent. Other than World War II, women have not participated in the workforce heavily until the late 1960's (less than 10 percent are over 65). Women in the 55-64 age group peaked at 43 percent in 1970, while total participation in the workforce is now slightly greater by women than by men.

Conversely, there are three significant conditions that may begin to reverse the past trend toward retirement prior to age 65: increased age levels for Social Security eligibility; the cost-of-living (inflation) deteriorating effect upon fixed incomes; and increased life expectancy. When the Social Security Act was passed in 1935, the eligible age for retirement income benefits was 62 until 1983 when it was raised to 65, and is scheduled to change to 67 around the year 2000. Second, while cost-of-living increases vary from year-to-year, they are persistent and usually highest in many of the categories needed most by the elderly (e.g., housing, transportation, and medical care). Last, life expectancy has also remained on the rise. In the period 1960-83, men increased their average life from 75.9 years to 77.8 years, while women increased from 79.6 years to 82.7 years. It is estimated based on past trends that by the year 2000, men will average 79.2 years and women 84.7 years. The implications of living longer on a fixed income reaching retirement benefit eligibility later, and an inflation-driven decline in prosperity become very powerful influences upon the (voluntary) retirement decision of employees—one which we will all face in our time.

For employers contemplating the age composition of its workforce, hiring and placement strategies, and effects upon such operating costs as contributory retirement plans and other demographically induced considerations, the over age 55 group is going to become a reckoning force. In 1980, the total population over age 55 was 47.4 million. According to the U.S. Census Bureau estimates, this age group will rise to roughly 58.8 million by the year 2000, to 74.1 million by 2010 (a 64 percent increase in only a 30 year period), and to 88 million by the year 2025.

If we look at the issue of age discrimination in a broader sense, we should recognize that, while the 40 to retirement age group have historically experienced the most systemic form of discrimination, there are in fact other age groups who experience different kinds of discriminatory conditions in employment. Because these conditions have not captured the attention or notoriety received by the protected age group, they are not protected by law as a compelling force to correct a similar type of workplace inequity, and have been taken rather matter-of-factly by managers and policy decision makers. These "unprotected" age groups are, for reasons of age patterns discussion, those in what might be called the Aspiring Years (18-25 years of age) and the Career Development Years (26-39 years of age).

It is in these earlier age groups where the work related issues underlying certain kinds of problems take on an entirely different complexion, set of conditions, and ultimately a relatively undetected form of age discrimination—or at the very least a bias. They are often confronted with barriers as being viewed as too young, inexperienced, unstable, immature, and unreliable, or during later employment years as too aggressive, impulsive, unorthodox, complacent, independent, or staid. To the employer considering them, or the manager supervising them, they may well be these things and more which are appropriate considerations in rendering employment decisions. But, when such decisions as hiring, promotion, pay setting, and the like are made on the basis of perceptions linking these conditions to age is where managers are most likely to run afoul. In the long run, we will no doubt be better off if we simply focus on using our managerial skills and basic knowledge of human behavior (and development) to make decisions about, and attempt to work with, people regardless of their apparent age.

Since employees at any age can present various problems to their supervisor, other employees, and work unit operations, it seems more fitting to discuss each age group in the context of their employment characteristics, problems, and prospective solutions. However, most attention will be given to those protected or otherwise influenced by law as a practical matter, since it is here where the manager is most vulnerable to serious consequence of error.

1.11 THE ASPIRING YEARS, AGE 18-25

The Fair Labor Standards Act[1] of 1938 (as amended) restricts the employment of persons under the age of 18, both in response to the abuse of child labor during the early American industrial period at the turn of the century, and to encourage a high school education as the minimum standard across the country. Even now, as a remnant

---

[1] Failure to comply with minimum age hiring, particularly where work hazards exist, can turn into criminal charges of negligence due to the serious disability or wrongful death of a minor. Such was the situation in the case of *Blancato v. Feldspar Corp.* (1987).

of the economic bearing of our laws and agrarian heritage, there are exceptions to the 18 year old rule in agricultural industries.

So, does life begin in the real world at 18, and if so, how does one go about getting that first opportunity? Moreover, is it appropriate for employers to reject applicants because of their youthful inexperience? Most of us would probably agree, largely based on our own retrospective youth, that many young people lack basic skills, have little concept of monetary worth, are undisciplined about work routine and self-responsibility, and are often resistant to authority. We could likewise find exceptions to these characteristics within this age group, as well as find examples of them in older age groups.

The Aspiring Years tend to be those in which many major decisions and lifestyle choices are made that can have a rather profound effect upon future directions and behavioral orientation. Such early choices as living away from home (with or without a living companion), buying a car and household furnishings, social pursuits, marriage, child rearing, and vocational interests are among the most personally demanding decisions of human existence. Depending on the outcomes of these decisions as they begin to unfold, they can positively reinforce earlier ideals about life and work that are usually established in the family environment during adolescence; or they can become the breeding ground for negative behavior associated with fear, intimidation, a sense of inadequacy, anger (resentment at a milder level), disappointment, failure, injustice, and disillusionment. These are just a few manifestations of decisions or experiences that didn't pan out to their expectation.

On the surface these early vocational/life decisions and experiences may not seem significant issues to those in their more established working years—the decision makers. We often make light of the fact that those in this age group are supposed to "pay their dues", that their tough experiences "build character", and we may even be interacting with them in a way that fosters a weak self-image—and are later confused by their negative, misguided behavior! To managers and human resource professionals who prefer to avoid problems rather than dealing with them after they occur, you should ponder this point more thoroughly in light of your own orientation toward these workers.

The Aspiring Years are also fragile ones. Consider two very different (admittedly stereotyped) tracks, then all that lies between them. First is the case of the high school graduate or drop-out who is not academically motivated, lacks readily usable skills for the real world job market, has marginal verbal, reading, and writing skills. This person is of blue-collar parents who have been divorced for 10 years, but the father earned a sizable wage from a semi-skilled unionized trade, worked steadily for many years where the earnings provided him with every visible sign of material success and enjoyment of life. The 18 year old, now an emancipated minor and ready to enter the workforce, not surprisingly wants that which parents have achieved—and more—but wants it faster and better, usually meaning without as much effort or undergoing as many obstacles as have been observed.

Our second case is that of an 18 year old, raised by both parents who have professional careers and some college background, and who was given a salient orientation about a wide range of vocational, social, and other life matters during earlier years. This person did well throughout school and views college as a natural extension of this stage in life, along with part-time employment of nearly any kind that will serve a temporary need for money to acquire basic necessities.

Neither have a particular job in mind since both are lacking many usable skills and possess little knowledge of what goes on (what jobs entail and are called) in the work-world, let alone how to find them. One wants full-time employment; the other wants full-time followed by part-time employment during the school terms. As the two of them commence these separate tracks, they will encounter many different experiences that will continue to shape each successive decision for many years to come— either reinforcing their behavior in a positive manner or slowly but progressively building experiences that become manifest to negative behavior. The college student could fail classes due to inattention or poor study discipline; could have difficulty adjusting socially to people in a new environment; or could remain indecisive about which field to study. The other aspirant may likewise not fare so well during the first few years. This individual may encounter a fiercely competitive job market because of the vast number of equals and a declining demand in unskilled or semi-skilled occupations; may not understand the influence of a sensitive economy on such jobs; may be rejected in a rather brisk manner on a number of occasions; and may become painfully surprised at the nature of working conditions, co-workers, and promotional limitations once employed.

Whatever vocational choices are made and experiences encountered during these initial adult years, they are not likely to change dramatically in the years to follow. The Aspiring Years will tend to establish and solidify not only the general course of one's vocational pursuit, but also the individual's ability to accept, adjust, and cope with attendant conditions thereafter. Those who struggle with career choice will probably continue to make vocational changes; those who lack motivation or fail to embrace self-responsibility (want things handed to them or done for them) will likely become marginal performers; and those who possess illusions or false values about the work-world will be inclined toward negative behavior.

What is required of managers and supervisors in their dealings with those in their Aspiring Years? Understanding for one thing. Understanding, that is, within the context of the job or type of business being applied to, and hiring or operating restraints placed upon those in authority to employ and supervise these workers. They themselves need to be understood better if the employer-employee relationship is to be a fruitful one for both. This requires that there be some level of acceptance by managers of their range (or limitation) of particular skills, their present and future vocational interests, and particular approaches to getting work done once a selection decision has been made. If these traits prove unsatisfactory following an adequate amount of time, opportunity, and supervision, they should be carefully counseled in a positive manner about the conditions that worked against them before they are terminated. These are learning and adjustment years for this age group, they should be dealt with accordingly, and with no less respect or dignity than that afforded to other, perhaps more settled employees.

Another important consideration in managing those in the Aspiring Years, as Ken Blanchard (One Minute Manager) suggests, is to catch them doing something right and recognize them for it. These individuals are not very distant from home and school where they received the greatest amount of encouragement to succeed. Because supervisors often become something akin to a "parental" source of approval, many employees in this age group try hard to please an admired supervisor. If they are to continue such dedicated effort, even though the visible result might be less than what would be ultimately desired, they should be given recognition for each successive level of achievement.

Some will undoubtedly fail to adjust again and again. They will have difficulty in understanding and accepting organizational structures, supervisory authority, company policy, and requisite work habits. They may seek out the short-cuts, conspire with other employees, bend rules, perform at minimal levels, and in other respects just get by any way they can. Such a behavioral orientation to work usually signifies an incomplete learning process. In these cases, the employer may find it necessary to enlighten through counseling, discipline, and when necessary termination. Let's face it, getting fired can be a very educational experience, and one that results in growth if it is done in a skilled manner. Dr. Morris Massey refers to such behaviorally changing circumstances as a "significant emotional event"; i.e., some event that materially changes the way we behave or react to something based on earlier perceptions.

So, while those in the Aspiring Years do not presently constitute a legally protected age group in terms of discrimination, they do represent a very diverse class of employees that require yet a different set of managerial practices, skills, and understanding to either avoid or effectively handle the kinds of problems that this group tends to raise as a direct result of their age. Too, it might do well for managers to bear in mind that these individuals will eventually reach an age of legal protection, and their adjustment or lack thereof to the work-world as determined by earlier experiences will have a considerable influence on how they perceive the actions of their employer henceforth. We are what we were, plus what we will be. If we as managers can develop better ways to understand our employees, and we can control the course of present conditions in a positive way, then perhaps we can become more effective at influencing what our employees "will be".

1.12   THE CAREER DEVELOPMENT YEARS, AGE 26-39

Those employees in their Development Years tend to be distinguished from their younger co-workers by making major career and lifestyle decisions, and usually a commitment to those decisions. Most major aspects of life develop in this period, but the experiences and process individuals undergo in the development of each component of their life are likely to be handled with varying degrees of desired result. It can be a very confusing and stressful period; it can be a very rewarding and stabilizing time; and it is often both. Those who have the capacity to tackle career and personal decisions with resound assurance—regardless of whether such decisions prove to be right or wrong—will tend to demonstrate consistent behavior, a positive outlook, and remain goal oriented. Those having lower thresholds of dealing with such things as pressure, change, or disappointments can be highly prone to become difficult employees. Largely associated with their inability to adjust or feel in control of conditions as they occur (a form of personal power and inner strength), these individuals are likely candidates for such workplace problems as substance abuse, absenteeism, anti-social and perhaps antagonistic behavior, insubordination, lack of concentration (performance decline), and sexual harassment.

Typically, the Development Years relative to employment are the most progressive. Their focus is upon performance, ambition that produces the desire for advancement, and productivity in terms of working diligently toward new challenges with a sense of sound purpose in life. These are the years for the "fast-trackers", and during which many will advance to the ranks of supervisors and line-to-upper level managers. Some will achieve the executive ranks, but these cases are few in proportion to all others in this age group.

Others are going to come to the realization that their jobs are dead-ended. Their vocational paths are short with little opportunity to make lateral job-path moves due to the specialization or limitation of their skills. Also, there can emerge the realization that there are few promotional opportunities with their employer. In these cases, an employer change might be impractical due to their accumulated seniority, benefits vesting, and/or insufficient gain compared to risks associated with changing employers. Stagnation of this type may be acceptable to a few, but probably not to a majority of workers. It leads to frustration and sometimes even a very deep sense of (self) incompetence, thereby overreacting in such common situations as the criticism of a supervisor, ratings on their performance appraisal report, and in other ways unduly sensitive to anything they perceive to be diminishing them personally, their work result, or the importance of their work to that of others. When such a pattern of behavior *begins* to emerge, the supervisor would be well advised to consult with higher management to discuss the situation and a counseling approach with the employee.

Alternatively, management should additionally consider other solution approaches such as job rotation, enhancement or redesign, along with retraining or providing advanced training in conjunction with job enhancement. In the absence of something new, something more challenging or worth looking forward to, some of these workers will eventually become either so frustrated that they'll quit to seek a new work environment, or they become a behavioral nemesis to their supervisor.

Yet another emergent group in their Development Years has come to light during the last two decades. They are more experiential about work and career. Like the college student who becomes confused about so many choices and their own diverse interests, these individuals make vocational changes every two to five years. They often pursue jobs with entirely different skills, exposures, and working conditions. However, because of their rather eclectic approach to learning and performing new kinds of jobs, they frequently bring a refreshing level of enthusiasm, imagination, and insightful manner of pointing out new methods and opportunities.

If not provided with a consistent flow of challenging work, training and promotional opportunities, recognition, and change, these individuals move quickly and usually without fanfare to other endeavors. They are less tied to traditional values of pursuing a singular career and the investment of long term service rewards by staying with one employer. They thrive on change and are often very effective change agents, but they can become equally impatient when change or other job conditions fail to match their expectations of how things should be. For this reason, they tend not to do well or last long in the larger, more bureaucratically structured organization, and therefore they tend to move about small to medium size organizations where their direct impact would be more visible, faster, and probably (so they believe) more recognized for their individual achievement.

In addition to the pressures of advancing in position and learning new skills, the Development Years are usually those in which individuals assume a major role in family life. These are the most active years for marriage, child bearing and rearing, and personal problems associated with both, not the least of which can and often does become financial, as well as the burden of child care when the parent(s) work.

This is likewise the period in which many experience spousal separations, divorce, single parenting, childless parent living, and remarriages. Such special circumstances can add monumental adjustment demands on the otherwise productive employee. The result can be a disasterous one for both the employee and supervisor if only the *effect* of the employee's situation is addressed (absenteeism, lack of concentration, personal telephone calls, depression, missing deadlines, and the like) rather than trying to accommodate and otherwise help the employee work through the underlying *causes* of what are probably temporary circumstances.

Taking into account the number of hours, months, and years people are engaged in work—through many difference life cycles and events—it is not reasonable to believe that our employees will not be affected on the job by the personal impact of difficult life events; nor our own performance for that matter. The difference lies in the manner in which it is handled. Many an employee going through difficult personal experiences with the aid and support of an understanding supervisor and an accommodating employer has become the most faithful, reliable, and productive person on the company's payroll. Conversely, harsh or insensitive handling of these types of circumstances will certainly incline employees toward basic self-preservation (defensive) or defiant (resentful) behavior. You can count on it. Why? Because this age group, and to an increasing extent the next higher age group, have by this stage in life developed a very profound sense of principles, of right and wrong, and of the(ir) definition of what is fair and reasonable. Moreover, they're willing to make you aware of it in one way or another.

The attitudes that establish guiding principles for employees are not commonly held in the same perspective or regard by upper management—it's easier to get a clear view of the entire valley from the top of the mountain than it is to see the top of the mountain from the valley. Nevertheless, the principles of fair and reasonable treatment are embraced sometimes passionately by employees of this age group (and well into their 40's). They will fight back with equal determination based on the strength of their convictions for what they believe to be unjust, inequitable, and yes even unethical practices.

Unlike their more obedient counterparts of say 20 or 30 years ago, these employees are less afraid to access administrative means of redress or legal remedies. Indeed, they represent the most likely age group to file grievances and claims of discrimination, wrongful terminations, wage and hour violations, and allegations of other managerial wrongdoing (e.g., whistleblowing). After reading a sufficient number of various employment related court cases, you may begin to see that employees in this age group are neither ignorant, naive, nor passive about employment matters; that they're frequently right (they win); and that employers can do some incredibly foolish things in their *deliberate* handling of personnel matters. Consequently, those in the Development Years need employment conditions and leadership that is far more precise, fair and opportunistic than in years past.

1.13   THE STABILIZING MIDDLE YEARS, AGE 40-60

Usually referred to as Middle Age, this group of individuals begin early signs of stabilizing personal and career life development as they pass through their 40's. This becomes a time when marriages and remarriages take on either a settling effect or else some form of single lifestyle is found to work best. Their children are more independent and beginning to shape their own future, thereby leaving their parents more time to pursue what they choose—most often it shifts to career and leisure.

The mid 30's to 40's is also a time of spousal reentry into the labor force for those electing the course of full-time child care through adolescence or early teenage of their children. It is a time for them to nurture their children toward their own beginnings, watching their children transcend into adulthood, assuming the role of grandparent, and slowly but progressively change lifestyle back to that of a couple. If an alternative course is taken, usually through divorce or early spousal death, it becomes a time of acceptance and adjustment to that which life has handed them. This does not necessarily mean resignation and attendant loss of hope for a fulfilling, enjoyable life. It means that they are mature and responsible enough to go forward the way things are, even if they would have preferred some things to have been different. The emotional struggles of earlier years begin to fade, and a calmer, more predicable future lies ahead.

Career-wise, this group works on slower, long range refinements to their skills. They have either reached, or very close to reaching, the pinnacle of their field, be it a pipefitter, executive secretary, communications specialist, salesperson, or administrator. They reach the level of their competence or other career controls that inhibit or cease further advances; some prefer and accept it, some merely adjust to it, yet some deeply resent it finding adjustment difficult indeed (they may blame everyone and everything except themselves in light of a much larger picture).

This is a period for most workers to have highly developed skills and a keen awareness of how organizations operate. They are generally well attuned to business practices, efficient work procedures, organizational roles and relationships, and matters of policy—they are seasoned so to speak. They typically represent our journey level workers, supervisors, managers, and top administrators; and because of holding such positions, they are in a position of controlling (the in-power group) the work of younger subordinates, and thereby represent a sharp division of labor, trust, and common interest/orientation toward workplace activities.

The Stabilizing Middle years are also those that have historically been the most troublesome with regard to age discrimination. It is at this stage when conflicts arise between the positive attributes of one's age (experience, maturity, advanced skills, etc.) and the preconceived negative biases toward this age group (slow, unimaginative, health risk, inflexible, etc.). Anyone who has spent a reasonable amount of time working with people of all ages should have discovered by now that most preconceived notions about the skills, abilities, and behaviors of those in the 40-60 age group are no more or less of a problem than those negative characteristics of earlier age groups. Somewhere along the line, many people who are in managerial, decision making positions have been mislead to believe that specific workplace problems or employee traits are indigenous to age alone. Even if such were proven, we should expect the same problems from each and every person in that age group. These beliefs are rarely reinforced to any appreciable level by the experienced manager who has come to realize that employee problems are not as simple as the age factor.

It is however, at this age threshold when fair employment laws become a factor to protect this and the next higher age group against traditionally inhibiting barriers to employment based on age discrimination, or bias if you prefer. A word of caution here. One should not infer that those over 40 years of age are troublemakers or even particularly prone to sue their employer simply because of the legal illustrations that follow. It is because they are legally protected and therefore have access to legal remedy that these cases exist, and because some employment related wrongdoing has occurred pertaining to their hiring, training, promotion, benefits, discipline, termination, mandatory retirement, or some other employment decision where their age was a compelling influence. There is little doubt that if the same protections against age discrimination were lowered to say age 21, we would see a virtual flood of new cases from these younger employees claiming their employer to be age biased in their decisions.

1.14   THE EXPERIENCED ELDERLY, AGE 60+

It was pointed out earlier that 1) the bulk of litigation pertaining to age discrimination has been in the age 40-60 group due no doubt to the fact that these are the most prevalent ages for protected discrimination to take place; 2) that the percentage of people in the workforce drops dramatically after age 65; and 3), that many workers over age 60 tend to avoid lodging complaints for fear of retaliation, its effect on their working conditions, and/or the need to work a certain number of additional years to maximize pension benefits. However, because it may well be necessary during the coming years for employees to work longer to achieve eligibility for Social Security income benefits and as an economic hedge against inflation that continuously devalues fixed incomes, employees in the over 60 age group may become more openly expressive about the manner in which they are subjected to age discrimination. It's their right, they've earned it, the laws are in place to protect them, and those that enforce laws and regulations will surely see to it that employers comply to both the letter as well as the spirit of law.

There is probably no more natural event than each of us going through our life stages and ultimately reaching our elderly years—the Elderly Experienced as I prefer to refer to this stage with emphasis on the positive of this human resource group who elects to continue an active workforce contribution. Yet there continues to exist in this Age of Enlightenment, as we like to think of our contemporary society, a pervasive, pretextual set of myths and culturally ingrained biases that have served to stereotype older workers as feeble, simple-minded, inflexible, and overly sensitive people as a whole. This idea has been heavily reinforced through the years in American society by the media, in literature, and through motion picture characterizations.

Like all other characteristics that distinguish people—be it age, color, sex, height, and so forth—we have this cultural propensity to over-generalize with the result being *individually* false values and therefore adverse *group* discrimination. We see each member of any group as stereotypical of our notions about those characteristics provided for us about the group. Other beliefs held about older workers are that "they" (group) cost more to keep, are absent more due to frequent illness, become accident prone, have declining productivity, less adaptive to change, have poor memories, are less trainable, and lose their creative abilities. When I hear comments or implied notions such as these, I am immediately moved to think to myself, "Why then do we have throughout history such a vast number of people who have made exceptional contributions after the age of 70?" Consider, for example:

Benjamin Franklin; invented bi-focals at age 78
Pablo Casals; a master celloist at age 90
Carl Sandburg; wrote "Rememberance Rock" at age 70
"Colonel Sanders"; started national chicken franchise at age 67
Ronald Reagan; 40th U.S. President up to age 77
Titian; completed masterpiece "The Battle of Leponto" at 95

If people such as these are exceptions, then how do we dismiss such people as Congressman Claude Pepper (86), Chief Justice Florence Murray (74) of the Rhode Island Supreme Court, CEO of Occidental Petroleum Corporation Armand Hammer (88), and the list goes on and on. Are all of these exceptions, or are more of the elderly using their experience longer to mark their contributions to organizations, to law, and to our society? It's a point we as managers of our human resources should ponder with greater depth and insight.

In the workplace throughout America, the two decade period spanning the mid 1960's to mid 1980's there was a marked deemphasis of retaining older workers in employment. The qualities of experience, business wisdom and maturity, and advanced skills gave way to a new management philosophy that favored youth, energy, and adaptiveness to a rapidly changing economy and technology. We began to summarily discard those we perceived as unable or unwilling to change, keep pace, or innovate with the movement. Why is that trend reversing as we advance into the 1990's? Perhaps it is because business has learned that too much youth can mean excessive inexperience, that unharnessed (impatient and underdeveloped) energy has a way of getting out of control, and adaptiveness has been found to be a personal, not an age, trait. With the rapid decline in older workers, business began to loose internal continuity and balance in the operational makeup of its workforce. It lost that fundamental, succession-development advantage of mentorship—the intrinsic ability to impart advanced skills, knowledge, methods, and styles of work from seniors to their proteges.

The opportunity to regain the balance of experienced employees will shortly emerge demographically as the nation begins a rather sharp increase in the number of current "baby-boomers" during the next two decades. As they begin to enter their Experienced Elderly years, they will displace the more modest number of this age group presently participating in the workforce, but there is likely to be a major difference. The new Experienced Elderly will be coming from a more health conscious, educated, and technologically advanced era. They are therefore more likely to possess much the same productivity and creativity value to business as what we presently associate with the contributions of employees in their 40's and 50's.

Employers may have also begun to recognize that a major cost factor of productivity is turnover and absenteeism, neither of which has ever been proven to be characteristic of the Experienced Elderly as a worker group. In fact, the contrary may be more accurate by virtue of studies showing those over age 55 where only 5 percent are institutionalized or unable to care for themselves, and only 10-15 percent have some degree of physical or health limitation. We may want to additionally consider such other workplace attributes of the Experienced Elderly as being more quickly functional and contributory, needing less trial-and-error learning, less inclined to change employment for promotional opportunities, more realistic about business operations and employment conditions, and more inclined to share an established or desirable organizational culture once it's identified.

For those managers who fear permanence more than turnover, they should recognize that permanence can have the positive result of stability, or the negative result of dormancy; the difference lies in the manner in which upper management orchestrates the use of existing talent at all levels of its human resource pool. In my own experience, I have worked with both dormant and stabilizing older workers; directly as a manager of support staff, and indirectly as a consultant to various organizations where interaction with their employees and familiarity with operational problems was required. Many of them still adhere to a strong work ethic, a tireless and reliable work routine, and are keen at catching and correcting the errors of others. They present no risk or problem to management, for they will depart from the workforce on their own accord even before management wants them to. I should interject here that this very manuscript, and its nearly 800 page predecessor, was prepared by my workaholic 62 year old secretary who had the additional duties of keeping up with an endless stream of client and other work.

Yet, admittedly, there are also those permanent fixtures in every organization representing the dormant older worker who does not subscribe to a work ethic; who feels they have paid their dues and now wants to collect (get paid while others take up the slack); and who become obstructive behavioral problems. The point to be made is that people begin to decline—in health, skills, thinking, accuracy, output, and other workplace necessities—at a variable rate, not at a particular age. Challenging and meaningful work, training, and new opportunities have a way of revitalizing an otherwise declining worker. But when decline becomes apparent beyond workplace accommodations, it may become necessary for management to objectively pursue the problem solving avenue of employment separation—preferably with dignity, preparation, and mutual understanding.

1.20 THE LAWS AFFECTING EMPLOYMENT AGE

Age discrimination became a prohibited employment activity in 1967 when the Age Discrimination In Employment Act (ADEA) was signed into law.[2] The original act covered job applicants and employees in the 40 to 60 age group, and its provisions were enforced by the Department of Labor. In 1975, the Act was amended to extend the age to 65, and again in 1978 to age 70. In 1979, regulatory and enforcement authority was shifted to the Equal Employment Opportunity Commission (EEOC) who was given broad authority to receive, investigate, and either conciliate settlements, conduct administrative hearings, initiate court action, or abandon claims due to lack of sufficient evidence to support the allegation.

The ADEA is intended to protect this age group from arbitrary and age-biased discrimination in hiring, promotions, training, fringe benefits, compensation, discipline, and terminations. It is applicable to private employers with 20 or more employees; governmental employers; employment agencies; and labor unions with 25 or more members. Since 1979, the number of cases filed has increased markedly as indicated below, and the trend is likely to continue due to the EEOC's 1981 regulations that make age bias litigation more favorable to claimants.

ADEA Cases Filed With EEOC

Fiscal Year	*Number of Cases*
1979	3,000
1980	9,000
1981	12,700
1982	16,100

In October 1986, President Reagan signed into law the Omnibus Budget Reconciliation Act (OBRA) which carried a provision for the ultimate amendment to the ADEA. The OBRA effectively lifted the former upper age limit of 70 years, and makes it an additional age related discriminatory practice to provide any different medical program to older workers than what the employer offers to younger workers. Although a startling measure to most employers who perhaps see the government engaged in a "cradle-to-grave" mentality of regulating employment, some states have had such an "infinite" age provision contained in their state fair employment statutes for a number of years.

The federal move to an infinite age was inevitable, and it was met with very mixed

---

[2] A summary of the ADEA is contained in Levesque, Joseph D.; *Manual Of Personnel Policies, Procedures, And Operations*, pp. 314-321. Employers should also note that there is a fine of $100 for failure to post ADEA notices (29 USC ss:627), and that the normal two year statute of limitations for an employee's filing a claim can be extended one year due to the employer's failure to provide such posted notice; *Zipes v. Trans World Airlines, Inc.* (1982).

reactions, new litigation prospects, and further changes in employment practices—particularly those related to elderly hiring, mandatory retirement, leaves of absence, healthcare and life insurance plans, and substantiation of inadequate job performance. There is also the likelihood that the existence of an infinite age in employment discrimination may be almost entirely academic when one considers the studies that conclude people are retiring earlier than in past years. This is due in part to employer-sponsored pension plans with early retirement incentives, and that people in general simply tire of the rigors, complications, and aggravations of working.

The EEOC, too, continues to exert legal influence on age discrimination matters by ever-changing regulations, policy, and interpretive decisions. Although these administrative sources of opinion do not, in themselves, carry legal weight per se, they can be highly influential to the courts when they're grappling with an untested or obscure issue. A good example of the type of legal volley between courts and administrative compliance agencies was the issue of whether or not it was age discrimination to discontinue pension plan contributions after normal retirement age—as defined in a bona fide retirement plan. While under the DOL's jurisdiction, an interpretation was released to the effect that employers were exempt from continuing pension plan contributions and benefit accruals once an employee reached normal retirement age, providing it was a bona fide retirement plan. After jurisdiction shifted to the EEOC, two attempts were made without final action to rescind this exemption. The issue remained something of a legal controversy until the case of *American Association of Retired Persons v. EEOC* (1987) wherein the plaintiff organization alleged that the EEOC acted improperly by not rescinding the exemption. The court agreed and so ordered the EEOC. This means that employers can no longer use the exemption as a reason to contribute differently to pension plans, nor reduce benefit accruals, for employees who continue to work beyond the plan's normal retirement age.

Similarly, in an uncoerced move on the part of the EEOC, a new policy position was released by the Commission in 1987 having to do with "age harassment". Here the EEOC's position is that age harassment is to age discrimination in the same way that sexual harassment is to sex discrimination—a position of theory difficult to argue. The essence of the EEOC policy, then, is to bring any form of age related harassment into the fold of prohibited discriminatory employer conduct, even where the harassment is being conducted between employees—but especially by managers and supervisors. It is now highly probable that the EEOC and courts will follow the same principles in examining particular cases as those used in sexual harassment complaints. Specific prohibitions will include:

- Age inferred remarks having derogatory connotation

- Comments that attribute a person's health, attendance, performance, attitudes, and the like to their age

- Age jokes

- Use of age related terms such as pops, the old man, goat, and so forth.

1.21   CASE LAW SOLUTIONS TO AGE DISCRIMINATION PROBLEMS

As we transition here from the social to the legal aspects of age, let us bear in mind that legal case history is merely a sort of guidance system for management; it establishes the principles of lawful conduct, employer and employee rights, fair and reasonable activities, and that which is prohibited. Court cases tell us of trends in legal thinking as interpretations of law based on a given set of circumstances. Although it is not at all uncommon for various state courts, or state versus federal courts, to decide differently on very similar cases, there eventually emerges a fairly reliable set of legal principles in each area of employment law that serves to shape and reshape employer practices. One must therefore remain flexible and stay abreast of these developments.

The number and topical variety of age discrimination cases are much too voluminous for comprehensive treatment in a single book. Given this limitation, the illustrative cases that follow have been selected for five reasons.

1. They involve topics of vital, difficult, or sensitive concern to employers.

2. They have common if not universal occurrance.

3. They are typical or at least representative of a significant age-related problem.

4. They were decided by a court of higher authority.

5. They were precedent or landmark decisions of importance to employers.

Now let's examine some age related discrimination problems and deal with the practical aspects of their solution. In order of discussion, the topics selected are:

- Inferences of Age
- Waivers and Executive Exemption
- Partnerships
- Mandatory And Other Retirement Policies
- Performance Terminations

- Layoffs
- Collateral Estoppel
- Willfulness of Violation
- Repeated Violations

Do Age-Inferred Remarks Constitute Discrimination?
If So, Can They Overshadow Good Cause Termination?

According to a jury decision in the case of *Smith v. Consolidated Mutual Water Company* (1986) age inferred remarks are a form of age discrimination. In this case the plaintiff's supervisor often referred to him as "an old goat". Smith was terminated for allegedly falsifying water meter tests, but was never confronted by the employer on the allegation, and he was subsequently replaced by a younger worker. Smith wins.

The fact that Smith was fired in relation to being called an old goat, coupled with being replaced by a younger employee, will generally be held to be sufficient evidence of a prima facie (surface validity) case of age discrimination. Additionally, and particularly with jury trials, the termination of an employee based on mere allegation (absent evidence, discussion with the employee, or other pre-termination measures—perhaps lesser discipline) is suggestive of a pretextual discharge, i.e., that the real reason for termination was the employee's age, but the employer used the pretext of allegedly falsifying meters.

If, in fact, the real problem with "an old goat" employee is their behavior, then the employer should more closely examine the specific behavior and become very clear about the ways in which it is a problem—and is the problem(s) job related. Is this employee resistent to following supervisory instructions? Is the employee disruptive to the working relationship of other employees? Is this person inefficient in his work, or rude to customers? These are the kinds of performance and job related behavior questions that should be examined in order to determine the basis of a course of action, not the employee's age. If you think you have a supervisor using age-inference names with employees, point out why it's a poor practice, then order them to stop doing it.

Will An Employee's Signed Waiver Against Filing An Age-Based Claim Legally Relieve The Employer? Can Executives Be Held Exempt From Age Discrimination Law?

In the case of employee waivers, the answer is not necessarily. There have been numerous cases of this heard in federal and state courts with a considerable number of such waivers held to be invalid on the basis of it being unlawful to negotiate away a sanction against age discrimination, or the prospect of it. Although it is a strong temptation to try to get employees to waive legal action in a negotiated employment separation (usually termination or early retirement "golden handshakes"), it must be done in accordance with EEOC regulations. Otherwise, such waivers can imply an element of coersion on the part of the employer and yield punitive and/or higher amounts of other damage awards than might have otherwise been the judgment.

The case that started courts taking a closer look at whether employees knew what rights they were waiving was where a federal appeals court ruled in the case of *Runyan v. National Cash Register Corp.* (1986) that the waiver of a 59 year old (expert in labor law) lawyer was valid, and that such waivers would only be held valid by employees "like him"; meaning those educated and knowledgeable about their legal rights regardless of any form, contract, or waiver agreement they were asked or required to sign. The implication of this case is that only such "educated and knowledgeable" employees as labor lawyers, personnel administrators, and labor relations professionals could be held responsible for waiving their rights.

Concerning the question of executive exemption, yes, the ADEA specifically exempts "bona fide executives" and those in "high executive positions", providing they receive substantial pensions. To be exempt, such executives need be top-level executives, not merely the highest ranking according to *Colby v. The Graniteville Co.* (1986). Here, the court dismissed the complaint of a former senior vice president of a textile manufacturer who was forced to retire under a mandatory age 65 company policy. In claiming that he was not an exempt executive, he asserted that it was the president who made policy and held veto authority over his decisions affecting his subordinates. The court summarily rejected his arguments as rather shallow characterizations of his responsible decision making job.

A case in direct contravention to this was decided by the Second Circuit Court in *Whittlesey v. Union Carbide Corp.* (1984) when it determined that a highly paid chief labor counsel was not exempt within the meaning of the ADEA. Here, the court held that attorneys, when acting as counsel, are typically not in high policy-making positions. Having been retired by the company at age 65, the court awarded four years front pay to age 70.

Employers would be well advised to openly designate, and communicate to incumbents and new hires, those positions meeting the definition of exempt as applied to the ADEA. The guidelines are contained in EEOC regulations, and to a large extent parallel those of the Fair Labor Standards Act. They require that the employee:

1. Has the primary duty of management,

2. Customarily direct the work of at least two employees,

3. Have some authority or voice in hiring and firing employees,

4. Customarily and regularly exercise discretionary powers, and

5. They spend at least 80 percent of their time performing those functions.

In so categorizing and informing ADEA exempt employees in advance, future problems related to claims litigation may be averted entirely.

Can Partners Of A Company Be Treated As "Employees" And Thereby Held Liable For Age Discrimination Violations?

In some cases, yes, according to a federal appeals court decision in *EEOC v. Peat, Martwick, Mitchell, & Co.* (1985) where partners were held to be "employees" of their own firm with respect to the company's retirement policies. The distinction that makes this determination has to do with the structure of the company and whether or not the EEOC finds that the structure has an inherently discriminatory effect upon the partners. In these matters, the EEOC is empowered to subpeona partnership records relating to the partnership structure as a means of making its determination.

Companys held by partnership arrangements should have legal counsel examine its retirement and any other age related policies of either the company or any partnership agreements. Of particular concern might be differential accruals, vesting, and contributions to retirement and benefit plans based directly or indirectly on age.

Can Older Employees In Certain Occupations Be Treated Differently Concerning Mandatory Retirement Policies?

There were three unanimous U.S. Supreme Court decisions with different circumstances, and all with mandatory retirement age implications that point to a resounding no to the question. The first two involve airline flight officers, and the third municipal firefighters.

In *Trans World Airlines, Inc. v. Thurston*, the employment practice in dispute relates to the bumping rights of captains to the lower position of flight engineer. According to Federal Aviation Administration (FAA) regulations, captains are not permitted to continue in that capacity beyond age 60, however flight engineers were. Upon or prior to reaching age 60, captains could automatically bump less senior flight engineers if they were disqualified from their capacity for reasons other than age. If their disqualification was due to age (involuntary, mandatory retirement), the captains were denied the right to bump flight engineers and were required to use bidding procedures to acquire engineer positions. Since the engineer position did not have a mandatory retirement age under FAA regulations, the court concluded that the differential treatment under age versus non-age related disqualification as captains constituted a discriminatory transfer practice.

In the related case of *Western Airlines, Inc. v. Criswell* (1985), the U.S. Supreme Court upheld jury instructions that an employer must be able to show that it is "highly impractical" to evaluate each person occupying a particular safety-sensitive job in support of its mandatory age 60 retirement policy. Here, the company required flight engineers to retire at age 60. Using the bona-fide occupational qualification (BFOQ) of safety-sensitive job, the company argued that it was impractical to evaluate each and every flight engineer. The jury disagreed. The consequence of this case is that employers wishing to establish mandatory retirement age requirements must be able to demonstrate either 1) the performance related basis for each job, or 2) the basis of such evaluations being highly impractical to ensure that individual employees possess or do not possess the necessary qualifications to continue in the job.

The third case on mandatory retirement involves municipal firefighters. In *Johnson v. Mayor and City Council of Baltimore* (1985), the city established a policy of mandatory retirement between age 55-70 depending on length of service, using the requirement of age 55 retirement for federal firefighters as the basis for establishing the lowest age and using this as its BFOQ defense. The court rejected the city's argument stating that the ADEA does not imply that federal rules, applicable only to federal employees, are adequate sources of authority for state or local governments to establish a mandatory retirement age. In other words, the BFOQ of federal rules was a weak defense and employers have a much more substantial burden of proof in justifying "blanket" mandatory retirement age requirements—directly correlated to inadequacy of job performance.

In a similar "public safety" case, such a BFOQ test was accepted by a federal district court in *EEOC v. New Jersey* (1985) wherein the mandatory age 55 retirement requirement for police officers was held not to be a violation of the ADEA. Here, the employer produced sufficient evidence to show that a person's endurance (a job related condition of performance) is diminished after age 55, and that "adequate aerobic activity" is a reasonable BFOQ since people in this occupation must be able to withstand more strain on their heart and lungs than do other occupations.

Following this line of judicial interpretation of the employer's burden of BFOQ proof, there may be at least some latitude for an employer's defense in jobs where there exists substantial evidence of abnormal respiratory or other strenuous physical job demands. However, based on the 1986 federal lifting of the upper age 70 on protected discrimination claims, employers may be required to conduct more frequent job related evaluations to determine performance adequacy in all aspects of a job.

Can An Employer Use Poor Performance Rather Than Age As A Reason To Terminate?

Yes, presuming the nature of the employee's performance deficiencies are job related, thoroughly documented, and efforts to correct specific deficiencies by management can be demonstrated, including communication to the employee and sufficient time to allow correction. If, on the other hand, the termination for alleged and undocumented poor performance is used by the employer as a pretext to get rid of older, long service employees for superficial reasons, the answer is absolutely not. The situation could not be more clearly demonstrated than the Supreme Court of Montana case in *Flanigan v. Prudential Federal Saving & Loan Association* (1986) in which the plaintiff, a 28 year service employee, was awarded $1.5 million in damages ($1.3 million punitive, $94,000 compensatory, and $100,000 for emotional distress). The employee was hired in 1952 as a teller and received three promotions with the last one being in 1976 to Assistant Loan Counselor. In 1980, she was advised that her position was being eliminated but she could resume a teller position. One month after her retraining she was fired without notice, given six months severance pay, and offered a part-time teller position which she declined. She was told both that her performance was poor, unknowlingly to her, and, alternatively, that the move was part of a cost cutting measure. Here's what the court concluded about the employer's actions.

1. Evidence indicated that the workforce had not been reduced. In fact, younger and less paid employees (tellers) had been retained.

2. The employer failed to comply with its own policy of progressive discipline established as a warning mechanism to identify and correct performance problems. By terminating without notice, the employer denied her access to a (contractual) "due process" employment right.

3. The company president was known to refer to older employees as "deadwood" and "ballast", which the court considered callous remarks and further testimony that the reason of alleged poor performance was a mere pretext for otherwise contemptuous treatment of a higher paid employee—which someone in the organization had progressively authorized as a result of her continued contributions to the business; ironic at least, foolish result at best! No doubt the employer was alarmed to learn that their business insurance policy does not cover punitive damages, nor would the shareholders be any too pleased!

Can An Employer Lay Off Older Employees In Favor Of Younger Employees During A Reduction-In-Force?

During the mid-1980's, several courts dealt with this age impacting question which can be problematic to a variety of related human resource matters (e.g., seniority, pension plans, succession planning, etc.) and business types. Most litigation during this period focused on what would constitute prima facie evidence to establish a case that the layoff was age biased, and some elements of an employer's defense if its intentions were to avoid age impacted layoffs.

It has already been shown in the preceding analysis that the mere expression of a legitimate nondiscriminatory reason for age 60 retirement of airline captains for a BFOQ defense will not suffice (see also *Trans World Airlines v. Thurston*, 1985). The same principle holds true for reduction-in-force decisions. That is, the employer must be able to demonstrate its business or performance related reason for each protected person laid off in the utmost objective terms (such as statistical age analyses). When dealing with performance as a determinant, the employer should be very exact about specific differences in such areas as knowledge, skill, timeliness, quality and accuracy, and any other performance related results between the person laid off and retained employees doing the same job.

A major danger for employers is in the case of an age protected employee layoff who is subsequently replaced by a younger worker, even if the replacement is within age protection as in the constructive discharge case of *Williams v. Caterpiller Tractor Co.* (1985). Three notable cases have established at least fundamental criteria for an employee to make a prima facie claim of age discrimination, and they are:

1. The employee was in the protected age group.

2. The employee was fired or demoted (or in some other manner adversely affected).

3. The employee had been performing the job well enough to meet the employer's legitimate expectations.

4. The employee was qualified to assume an available position at the time of the action.

5. Convincing evidence is available pointing to the employer's intentional decision on the basis of age, or that the employee was disadvantaged in favor of a younger worker.

Coburn v. Pan American World Airways, Inc. (1983), *Williams v. General Motors* (1982), and *Oxman v. WLS-TV* (1985); see also *Starrojev v. Ebasco Services, Inc.* (1981)

However, there have been other cases in which the courts have concluded that a protected employee who has been subjected to a layoff or other adverse action must show more than cursory evidence (e.g., replacement by a younger worker) in order to establish a case sufficient to shift the burden of nondiscriminatory proof to the employer. For example, in *Holley v. Sanyo Manufacturing, Inc.* (1985), the court rejected this very claim stating that more direct, statistical, or circumstantial evidence would be required for the court's acceptance of prima facie age discrimination. Such might consist of demonstrating the company's pattern of forced early retirements, failure to promote older workers, reduction of duties for older workers, anti-older worker philosophy of management through testimonials, or proof of preferential treatment of younger workers.

An example of a solid defense was seen in Graff v. Bendix Corp. (1986) where two senior engineer positions were eliminated in the automotive controls division due to declines in car sales. Despite the company's use of subjective factors to determine whom would be laid off, the federal district court determined that age itself was not the reason for layoff, and that the company's actions were not discriminatory. The specific measures taken by Bendix prior to layoff were:

1. Gave effected employees ample notice of layoff in accordance with company policy.

2. Gave affected employees the option of transfer to another division or early retirement.

3. If they chose early retirement, each would receive a $1,000 per month pension and $6,000 severence pay.

4. Prepared an "age impact" statement (including the fact that the mean and median workforce age actually went up slightly after the layoff).

Similarly, in *Arnell v. Pan American World Airways, Inc.* (1986) the court found no age discrimination to exist as alleged by 11 supervisors who were laid off due to reductions at Pan Am's Kennedy Airport operation. The reasoning of the court here was that Pan Am used a peer comparison evaluation system in which each employee subject to layoff was scored on their qualifications, abilities, and performance. Neither age nor salary was considered. Even though evidence pointed to prima facie age discrimination (laid off employees were older than those retained), Pan Am's evaluation system—although not terribly objective—was accepted by the court as a legitimate nondiscriminatory bases for its decision, and therefore not a pretext. In other words, so long as an employer can show a reasonably legitimate method of evaluating who should and should not be retained, and that such factors are related to their jobs, objectively evaluated, and do not consider age or salary (payroll cost savings), then the defense of such claims are materially strengthened. See also *Zick v. Verson Allsteel Press Co.* (1986).

While employers should not use these as absolute defense guidelines, they do serve well as illustrations of the kind of effort, thought, and measures that should be considered in a reduction-in-force action. In other words, consciousness is one thing, intent (to discriminate) is quite another.

Can A State Unemployment Insurance Decision Bar A Federal Age Discrimination Suit?

Yes, if the unemployment insurance board's decision is reviewed (on appeal) by a state court. The legal theory is called collateral estoppel meaning that a particular action cannot be relitigated. In the case of *Robert v. Jefferson Federal Savings And Loan Association* (1985), the protected employee worked as a mortgage processing officer who was offered a transfer to another office when the company decided to change her position to that of a loan consultant (a younger worker). After protesting her transfer to no avail, she resigned and filed an unemployment insurance claim. Her claim was denied on the basis of insufficient cause for resigning. She filed suit in superior court who also rejected her claim. It was then that she filed a constructive discharge age discrimination action under the ADEA in federal court. Generally, a constructive discharge occurs when the employer deliberately makes the employee's job conditions sufficiently intolerable so as to force the employee to resign. Not finding this to be the case (there was a sincere offer of a transfer), the federal district court rejected the claim of constructive discharge. Also, the federal court disallowed the ADEA claim on the basis of the U.S. Supreme Court decision in *Kremer v. Chemical Construction Co.* (1982) wherein a state court dismissal of an employment discrimination claim would bar relitigation in the same state.

As a word of caution, this case could have gone in the opposite direction had circumstances been slightly different. For example, had this employee been able to convince the unemployment insurance board that she was in fact constructively discharged, and thereby granted benefits, she may have prevailed in federal (or state) court under a separate age discrimination action using transcripts of the unemployment insurance board's decision as evidence supporting her contention that the discharge was based on age (or even that it was a factor). It is for this reason that many employers either do not contest unemployment insurance claims, or they contest them with the same evidenciary thoroughness as a litigated case in those states that do not apply the theory of collateral estoppel. In any case, where a former employee has filed for unemployment insurance benefits, the employer's acceptance or rejection of the reason(s) for employment separation should be given careful consideration in light of prospective secondary litigation.

Under What Circumstances Will The Courts Find An Employer In Willful Violation Of Age Discrimination?

There were two particular 1986 cases in which the courts addressed the issue of an employer's willful violation of the ADEA. As defined, willfulness means that the employer's action was done "knowingly, intentionally, deliberately and not accidentally, mistakenly, or inadvertently."

In *Weems v. INA Corp.*, the fourth circuit court of appeals found that a 59 year old office manager had been (age) intentionally denied the same position when INA merged with Aetna in 1982. Their Charlotte, North Carolina claims offices were combined into one office, and the 44 year old Aetna manager was selected to head the consolidated office. The older manager was given the option of taking the assistant manager position or a one year furlough at full pay and pension credit. The district court determined his denial of the promotion to manager of the larger consolidated office was directly related to his age, and awarded him double damages. It was only the double damages that was reversed by the appeals court who stated, on the basis of *Trans World Airways, Inc. v. Thurston* (1985), "whether an act is willful for the purposes of the ADEA requires some inquiry into the defendant's knowledge regarding the Act." Since the district court gave no such instructions to the jury, the appeals court remanded the case back for a new trial on damages only.

In EEOC v. Westinghouse, an entirely different set of circumstances existed, but the effect of Westinghouse's layoff policy moved a federal district court to determine that their action was "blatant, willful age discrimination" and characterized their practice as "heartless corporate policy." The policy specified that laid-off employees who were eligible for pension benefits were given the option of severence or pension benefits, but not both. The court noted that the two benefits are vastly different in principle, and that the essence of denying severence to eligible pensioners could not present a more clear example of willful age discrimination.

1.22   EMPLOYER DEFENSES

Many of the cases during the early to mid 1980's dealt with procedural matters under the ADEA as district from Title VII litigation after its 1978 amendments including enforcement authority transfer to the EEOC. Under the ADEA, there are two legal theories in which a plaintiff can attempt to establish a prima facie case of age discrimination.

1. **Disparate Treatment:** a showing that the employer's action was intentional and purposeful treatment toward older workers that resulted in less favorable employment conditions.

2. **Disparate Impact:** a showing that the employer's practices, whether intentional or not, tend to have an adverse differential effect on older workers, regardless of the employer's motivation. This is normally the course sought by class action suits, however, such suits are not available under the ADEA which has caused some to believe that disparate impact cannot therefore be a cause of action under the ADEA. The EEOC disagrees stating that "Employment criteria that are age-neutral on their face but which nevertheless have a disparate impact on members of the protected age group must be justified as a business necessity" (EEOC, 181, p. 47725).

Either as a consequence of the validity of disparate impact application or the nature of the more common workplace events on older workers, most litigation has been developed under the disparate treatment action. Here, direct or indirect evidence is necessary for the plaintiff to establish employer intent.

Direct evidence can consist of such policies and practices as mandatory retirement at a particular age, declining retirement or life insurance benefits after a specific age, or refusal to hire after a certain age. Indirect evidence, on the other hand, is by intent, inference, or its practical implication such as verbal statements implying age was a factor in an employment decision or action, using age related remarks like "don't be such an old hen", and the use of statistical data to demonstrate the employer's less favorable treatment among older workers (e.g., hiring, promotions, pay increases) including marked fluctuations in the average age of the employer's workforce.

However, statistical evidence in itself is not the caveat for age discrimination. Some courts have found statistical data to be of "probative" value but not necessarily conclusive. From these cases it would appear that there should be a much more direct, conclusive inference that can be drawn from the data to point to the employer's age preferences.

Although limited and seemingly becoming less reliable since early 1980 age litigation, there are five basic defense rationales for employers to oppose age discrimination cases or claims, and they are:

1. **Bona Fide Occupational Qualification (BFOQ):** The valid need to establish age criteria to a particular job due to unique conditions of the job where age can be established as a detriment (to the employee(s), public, customers, other workers, etc.). The Act itself states that it shall not be an unlawful act for employers to base certain of its age decisions on age "where age is a bona fide occupational qualification reasonably necessary to the normal operation of the particular business" [29 U.S.C. S 623 (f) (1)]. A few of the illustrative cases presented in this chapter suggest that the courts—particularly juries— see the application of BFOQ defenses as having rare justification and narrow circumstances of legitimacy.

2. **Business Necessity:** Similar to the BFOQ rationale, this defense focuses on the employer's need to deliberately discriminate against older workers in some way due to very specific conditions associated with the nature of their business. Examples, although not arguably of particular merit, might be youth counselors, teen fashion sales clerks, and cocktail servers in an establishment catering to young professionals. Admittedly weak examples, but the defense lies in the strength of association of employing other than older workers as a matter of business survival such as targeted clientele, trademark representation (Playboy Clubs), or product.

3. **Factor Other Than Age (FOA):** Always based on circumstances related to an individual employee, this defense requires the employer to clearly articulate the justification of its action with the protected worker based on the determining factor that gave rise to the employer's action. Such other (than age) factors can include violation of company policy, misconduct, absenteeism, poor performance, lack of cooperation, and layoffs. Once the employer shows a reasonable FOA justification, the burden of proof shifts to the employee who will then have to demonstrate that the FOA is a mere pretext of the employer's age discrimination.

4. **Bona Fide Seniority System:** Typically, a "bona fide" seniority system is one in which the employer has given certain preferences (benefit accruals, promotion, layoff) and other time-in-grade or service length advantages to workers through collective bargaining agreements or its own policies. The employer's defense is then one of treating the effected employee in accordance with established agreement or policy—as it has done or would do for similarly situated persons regardless of their age.

5. **Good Cause:** Usually associated with demotions, discipline, and discharge actions, this defense only necessitates that the employer justify its action on the basis of incriminating evidence demonstrating a reasonable breach by the employee of the employment relationship. Examples might include overt insubordination, falsification, poor judgment, theft, absence of necessary leadership, and the like. Evidence that should be available to demonstrate the employer's good cause action is, in almost all cases, well documented written records or accounts of events. These consist of records of counseling sessions, written warnings, discussions of policy or particular prohibitions, and performance appraisal reports where deficiencies were described including the effect on operations, relationships, and/or productivity. If, on the other hand, you happen to be unfortunate enough to lose an age discrimination case involving damages, you should try to avoid lump-sum payments and withhold proper income tax on amounts paid. For example, in the case of *Gelof v. Papineau* (1986) a planner in Delaware's Office of Management, Budget, and Planning was awarded over $100,000 in back pay, pension and health benefits, *plus* $85,000 to pay the additional taxes created by the lump-sum award (as opposed to earning the award amount over her normal work life). There seems to be no end to the legal twists of fate for employers.

1.30   SOLUTIONS MANAGEMENT SHOULD CONSIDER

Most business operations require a variety of different jobs to carry out the enterprise, and for this reason business requires different kinds of people and skills—be they young, middle aged, or elderly. Each person contributes based on the application of their skills and other traits required by the job for suitable performance. The young need opportunities to get started, learn, and make career selections. As career choices are made, employees need development to refine, upgrade, and learn additional new skills for advancement. When workers reach the height of their careers, they may require other innovations in their employer's human resource program that provides stability and a productive conclusion to their work life. Each worker needs, and has the right to expect, that throughout their employment years they will be recognized and rewarded for their contributions, treated fairly and with dignity, and given some voice in those employment matters that affect them. It just makes good business and managerial sense to do so as a matter of practice. With a more narrow view toward age discrimination litigation—the cost of ascertaining what is right and who was wrong—two separate analyses of ADEA litigation between 1980-1983 (301 and 152 cases respectively) found the following:

- Seventy-five percent of the suits were filed by professional and managerial employees.

- Over seventy percent of the cases dealt with termination actions, including mandatory retirement.

- The most frequently sued business organizations were manufacturing, service, and government.

- Most litigants were over age 50. Common claimants were white, middle-class males which presently consist of 30 percent of the labor force (over age 39), often characterized by their employers as "malingerers" or "disruptive boat-rockers."

- The chances of an employer winning are 50 percent, with an additional 18 percent split between employer and employee.

- The use of a reasonable "business necessity" defense will slightly increase the employer's chance of winning.

- Mandatory retirement and pension-related cases favored the employee more often than other issues.

- The use of performance data as evidence by employers for their termination or demotion decisions improved the employer's chances of winning.

- Most cases of willful and blatant employer actions (stereotype remarks, innuendos, overt efforts, and coercion) were handsomely won by employees.

With the 1978 amendments to the ADEA, the balance of power shifted from employers winning more suits on procedural grounds to employees winning on substantive grounds. The most significant changes in the amendments producing this win-lose record were:

1. Unlike race and sex discrimination cases under Title VII of the Civil Rights Act, age discrimination cases may be heard by jury trials. Since juries are typically composed of wage earners, there tends to be greater inherent empathy for the claimant.

2. The amendments removed many of the preexisting procedural conditions that served as roadblocks to claimants establishing their case, and was the basis of employers winning about half of the suits filed.

3. The amendments had the effect of nullifying many previous court decisions and legal theory developed during the prior decade such as a reversal of the U.S. Supreme Court's decision in *United Airlines v. McMann* where the court established bona fide retirement plan parameters.

4. Enforcement for ADEA violations was shifted on July 1, 1979 from the DOL to the EEOC, but the EEO didn't release its final regulations until September 29, 1981, thereby creating considerable confusion for employers over a two-year period as to compliance standards.

One of the more interesting reasons for increased activity in age law suits has to do with the courts' practice of awarding both attorney fees and liquidated damages at sometimes twice the amount of actual loss by the claimant, and this presents an encouraging atmosphere for both plaintiff attorneys and claimants. Also, the hidden costs associated with such conditions as publicity and internal morale can be extensive as was the case for I. Magnin (*Chancellier v. Federated Department Stores,* 1981) when 300 irate customers heard about the firing of three long term employees and decided to return their charge cards.

The legal case illustrations used in this chapter are by no means intended to be conclusive to the nature of the issue. There can be considerable variation in the decisions of different court jurisdictions even on the same or substantially similar circumstances. Like many employment laws, the ADEA leaves a good deal of interpretive latitude for the EEOC and the courts to draw new conclusions. When such a realm of decision making latitude exists for the courts, the determination of which party prevails often rests on the soundness of evidence and the nature of interplay between the parties that gave rise to the action. Clearly, authoritative counsel should be sought before taking any action with an employee that would reasonably be seen as having age discrimination implications.

Perhaps more important than even the law and what has often become our managerial game of changing policy and practices to give the image of compliance, we ought to begin rethinking and reshaping the values, perceptions, and myths held by our employees, particularly those managerial decision makers with fixed notions about elderly workers. Based on the previous case discussions, it should be clear that the courts are telling us that age discrimination will not be tolerated absent an employer's reasonably sound job related proof that a particular individual cannot perform their job in an acceptable manner given its requirements. So, first it seems that we ought to rid ourselves of those notions about older workers that precipitates discriminatory practices and conduct; second, to begin examining outdated human resource practices that disadvantage and underutilize older workers; and third, to develop much clearer standards of measuring the continued fitness of employees based on all aspects of job conditions.

When the decline in job performance begins (an unfortunate but inevitable condition for us all), it will be necessary for management to begin dealing with its workplace effect, including some degree of accommodation when it is appropriate to the nature of decline (e.g., a certain level of physical or health limitation may be more acceptable than the complete loss of the employee's talent). Management must become more open to the *proper* utilization of its elderly workforce changes in its practices and policies, as well as clearer about the means to objectify job requirements, measuring critical levels of performance in order to distinguish the acceptable from the unacceptable, and to transition (not trash) those that decline beyond the threshold of operational needs.

Here are two itemized preventative approaches for the manager to take in initiating constructive measures within their organizations concerning age discrimination and utilization matters. The first takes a human resource management approach that creates a more equitable set of conditions that allows more effective use of the Experienced Elderly, while the second approach is more preventative when the employer is called on to defend against an age claim or legal action.

Human Resource Approach

1. Provide ongoing training opportunities to update or provide new skills to all employees, but targeting those over age 40.

2. Conduct a minimum of five year forecasts to project changes in the number, type, and nature of jobs including attrition and the need for new skills.

3. Use older workers to teach training programs and to assume a mentorship role with designated other workers.

4. Remove or ease pension and other benefit plan provisions that discourage continued employment past a specific age or service length. Continue to contribute the same amount for older worker pension plans and benefit insurance premiums as for younger workers.

5. Adopt flexible benefit programs that allow employees to select a variable arrangement of benefits that meet their changing life circumstances.

6. Adopt a flexible income plan permitting employees to place some of their income into tax-deferred savings, annuities, or other income yielding (supplemental retirement income) investment plans; or to place pre-tax earnings into a benefit expense account (IRS 125 account).

7. Change policies on part-time employment to allow flexible hours and job assignments, even if employment benefits are reduced accordingly.

8. Open up opportunities for older workers to work as-needed (intermittent or consultant), special assignments, or to fill in during periods of peak workloads, vacations, and other casual employment situations rather than paying exorbitant fees to temporary help agencies.

Prevent-Defense Approach

1. Acquaint all management personnel with the basics of EEOC guidelines and stress the importance of using valid, job related decisions in all their personnel actions including the avoidance of inappropriate comments or conversations with employees.

2. Collect and keep current all data related to workforce age. Use this data to determine age-impact of decisions related to hiring, demotion, promotion, layoff, and terminations.

3. Develop job related dimensions of performance inclusive of worker traits and working conditions rather than generic task-oriented performance dimensions. Develop other means of documenting and tracking ongoing performance changes to allow timely identification, notice, correction, and follow-up action (see Chapters III: 2 and 4).

4. Prepare policies prohibiting age discrimination in employment matters including jokes or age related comments, and provide a complaint mechanism and disciplinary action for offenders (see Chapters III:2.25 and III:3.31). Disseminate the policy to all workers and provide follow-up communications such as periodic training sessions, films, or discussion groups.

5. Keep current of professional literature and court decisions affecting age discrimination, and initiate internal policy, training, and other changes as the issues unfold.

6. If an older worker is being replaced, select the replacement on the basis of having at least equal skill, knowledge, experience, or other traits as the older worker. Be prepared to demonstrate this by supportive documentation.

7. Heavily document any instance in which an older worker is offered an alternative to layoff such as demotion or transfer, or in which an older worker is offered severance pay or early retirement credit as part of a separation agreement. In the latter event, such a waiver does not fully protect the employer from an ADEA suit, and waivers can be held jurisdictionally invalid in some states.

8. Avoid defending claims and suits on the basis of economic savings by layoffs or retirements of older, higher paid workers. Not only does the ADEA prohibit personnel actions which could save costs to the employers benefit plans, but the courts have determined that employment cost is relative to performance output rather than absolute in terms of pay.

9. Effectuate changes in the perception of older workers from that of a potential liability to one of an experienced human resource which is to be measured by the same performance criteria as any other worker. As with other workers, declines in performance should initially be examined for such non-age related causes as boredom with routine, frustration due to a lack of challenging job content, and the objectivity of superiors.

Ideally, the Human Resources and Prevent-Defense approach should be carried out concurrently as a matter of thorough human resource administration. While we must never lose sight of the imminent possibility of compliance or legal problems, we ought not let these matters distort the very principles upon which management [must learn to] strive. Namely, these consist of the most effective utilization of our human resources, fair and reasonable treatment of all employees, developing skills and new methods to be more effective, and making sound decisions through objective evaluation of each situation. The choice is ours, but rest assured that today's employees, unions, compliance agencies, and the courts stand prepared to keep us honest about our intentions.

CHAPTER I: 2.0
PROBLEMS BASED ON THE RACE, COLOR, OR
NATIONAL ORIGIN OF EMPLOYEES

The oldest form of societal discrimination is that based on the differences in our physical appearances, yet it is just such differences that created the American heritage and have made the United States unique among all nations. In spite of a civil war over the issue of racial prejudice and a resurgence of the same problem 100 years later as demonstrated by nationwide civil disobedience, the problem of racial and ethnic discrimination in the workplace persists.

The workplace problems associated with race and ethnic discrimination can be solved. As presented in this chapter, solving the problem requires a better understanding of its nature, changes in attitudes and management practices, compliance with the laws that govern ethical business decisions, and improving our human resource management skills. Consequently, it should be mandatory reading for every manager who must make decisions about diverse workforce members.

If one thing stands out more than any other about the American workplace or its societal structure, it is its cultural, racial, and ethnic diversity. Clearly, this is the singular characteristic and hallmark that distinguishes us, along with democratic doctrines of justice, from virtually all other nations. From the arrival of the first European settlers in the 14th century who discovered native inhabitants of the land, the 16th century arrival of black slaves from Africa, the 18th century arrival of 17 million European immigrants through Ellis Island, and continuing through the 20th century with people seeking new opportunities from other lands, the United States has continuously fostered an open-arms policy to any person or group desirous of freedom and opportunity. Yet there is another part of our culturally diverse history that is not as egalitarian as our immigration policies have led the unsuspecting to believe, and that is the history of what happened to these newcomers once they arrived and began their pursuit of our prophetic and lauded opportunities of democracy. Here, history conveys a dramatically different set of circumstances filled with accounts of rejection, degradation, humiliation, prejudice, denial of rights and privileges, unlawful treatment, and, yes, even brutality including lynchings.

This is hardly the portrayal of a free, equal society but it is true and it is, however regrettably, a matter of recorded history. There remains the more present question of what future history will record in the way of this contrast between external policy and internal experience of those hopeful cultural groups who come to this country in search of job opportunities and a prosperous, fulfilling new life. Indeed, each of us play a significant role in what the annals of cultural, racial, and ethnic history will recount for this country during the 20th century, and whether or not its society can overcome those conditions that have divided its people for six centuries.

2.10 THE EVOLUTION OF SOCIAL ORDER AND CHANGE

For those wonderng about the utility of a discussion on the evolution of cultural history in America, the answer lies in regaining perspective as to current conditions and how they came to be. It is hoped that through this brief examination of our diversity that managers gain better perspective or some added clarity about the issue of race and cultural differences among those that compete for jobs, seek advancement, and otherwise present themselves in the workplace. After all, it is one's occupation and place of employment, or lack thereof, that exerts one of the most profound influences on our economic and social well being, and upon social order.

When people are treated unequally or excluded in connection with such an influential determinant of their well being as employment, and thereby threaten their basic survival, unpleasant events are destined to emerge. At the very core of this exclusion and differential treatment are those beliefs and value systems held by one group toward another that results in prejudice. The term attached to such interaction is ethnocentrism meaning ethnic superiority and the ability to amass various resources to gain a dominant position over others (another group). Our history is replete with this type of behavior, not the least of which was the 622,000 men that died in the Civil War between northern and southern states over the abolition of slavery. Even today, the mention of minorities leads people to think primarily of Black Americans rather than the much broader variation of race and ethnic groups that make up the diversity that is, has been, and will always be America.

2.11   THE EMERGENCE OF MINORITIES IN AMERICA

Fundamentally, minorities consist of those people who are not of Anglo-American (Caucasian) descent nor English speaking as their native language. In this regard, the definition of minority group by social scientist Louis Wirth remains a valid one:

> A minority group is any group of people who, because of their physical or cultural characteristics, are singled out from others in a society in which they live, for differential and unequal treatment, and who therefore regard themselves as objects of collective discrimination.[1]

Within the United States there are eight distinctive minority groups, all of whom are Americans but whose extraction from another land and culture is different and more recent than the Anglo-American. These eight groups are distinguished by race, ancestry, length of U.S. residency, and their geographic distribution. They consist of Native Americans (Indians), Blacks, Mexicans, Puerto Ricans, Cubans, Japanese, Chinese, and Filipinos.

American Indians represent the smallest minority group with a population of approximately one million people which is believed to be a reduction of one to two million people when the land was first settled by Europeans. Tribal competition for land and the American-Indian War reduced their numbers while governmental policy confiscated their land holdings, dispursing their population to just a few hundred tribes located on as many reservations across the entire nation. Presently, only about half of our native Americans live in urban areas, and nearly one-third of them remain on government controlled reservations as a means of protecting the lifestyle of their cultural heritage.

Unemployment, literacy, and healthcare problems are as poor if not worse for this minority group than any other, and these conditions are representative of the injustice and outrageously differential treatment exerted to a group historically having insufficient resources to neutralize the power of another. Even during the 1960's when social equality moved many Americans to take up the cause of individual rights, the concerted efforts of several Indian tribes to regain water and mineral rights on their land, and payment from the government for the land taken, met with failure and further persecution.

Black Americans first arrived in 1619 as slaves to southern landowners and servants to Anglos in northern states. From this early history of the presence of people with a different skin color, slavery and race has become inextricably synonymous with the perceived right to treat people who look different or behave differently than whites in a manner that supports a caste system rather than an egalitarian system of society. As Elizabeth McTaggart Alquist notes:

> There have been many different systems of slavery in the world, and they have all been harsh and debilitating to some degree. The system which prevailed in the United

---

[1] Wirth, Louis; "The Problem of Minority Groups", in Ralph Linten, ed., *The Science of Man In World Crisis*; N.Y.: Columbia University Press, 1945.

States has been called the harshest, most destructive one known to exist...Not only was enslavement a permanent, hereditary, and legal status in the United States, as elsewhere, but in addition slaves were confined to a limited array of work rules, exploited in a capitalist system of agriculture, viewed as property rather than persons, and widely prevented from securing any release from slave status.[2]

As a result of the Civil War, four million slaves were freed but little change followed for many years after Reconstruction since most slaves were without money, education (educating slaves was held to be illegal), or skills other than agricultural labor. Those that were provided with land leases by their former masters found the differences in their freedom to be only slight, and their economic opportunity to be negligible. In many parts of the country, primarily the southern and southwestern states, whenever blacks made any attempt to exercise their right to freedom, whites were quick to react through collective ostracizing such as the activities of the Klu Klux Klan, sometimes brutally beating or killing blacks for suspicion of crimes.

Another example are the equal-but-separate, or "Jim Crow", laws established by most southern states by 1885 requiring separate water fountains, restroom facilities, and public transportation. In order to justify the treatment of blacks separately and less than whites, many began to attach themselves to the beliefs of social Darwinism which held that there are measurable and profound biological differences among various races due to the amount of time lapse in their evolution as a learned species. This theory advocated that blacks were physically and intellectually inferior to Caucasians, Asians, and Indians because blacks were believed to have evolved in Africa some 200,000 years after these other races. It was also held that more than 95 percent of the biological makeup of human beings is identical with all other human beings. How much difference the other 5 percent makes is probably a matter of inconsequential research.

In other words, a pure race simply does not exist. In the example of the Black American, 80 percent of this group are of mixed white and Indian ancestry according to anthropologist Melvin Herehovits. Following persistent pursuit of the debates over anthropological and biological differences in race that might further justify the belief in racial superiority, there has never been one source of unequivocal scientific evidence to support an intellectual difference between the races. The most convincing evidence for differences in intelligence and ability point to such other factors as educational opportunities, economic status, and value system held by individuals.

Of the approximately 28 million Black Americans populating the United States, most reside in urban areas throughout the country. Despite being the largest, second oldest, and most geographically dispersed minority group, black men and women are

---

[2] Almquist, Eliz. McTaggart; *Minorities, Gender, and Work*. Lexington, Mass: Lexington Books, 1979, pp. 45-46.

ranked as one of the lowest groups based on individual income whose occupational concentration remains in a secondary labor market (unskilled and semi-skilled occupations). It is perhaps interesting here to note that it has taken 100 years from Reconstruction for four blacks to reach the ranks of senior executive within 1,000 of the nation's largest companies according to a 1985 survey, which is one more than there was in 1979.

Mexican Americans today, like blacks, are also of mixed white and Indian ancestry, and to some degree were also involuntarily dispersed—throughout the southwest in their case. Most Mexican-Americans became descendents of early settlers who then became U.S. Citizens when Mexico seceded the Southwest Territory, and later when Texas joined the Union. Now, it is sometimes difficult to determine the population size and locale of this minority group due to second, third, and fourth generation intermarriage who often list themselves as white with the Census Bureau.

The plight of Mexican-Americans to gain economic opportunity continues to be difficult due to language, education, and social barriers that has constrained advancement in these areas. Similar to southern blacks, most Mexicans were used as laborers in agricultural communities throughout the southwest and west. Whether citizens or illegal aliens from Mexico, those that were given regular employment for subsistence wages were encouraged to have large families (and they were devout Catholics whereby birth control was disapproved) so that the children could eventually participate in field labor. With unending exploitation and a worsening of the economic advantage in farm labor, by the 1960's, Caesar Chavez came to be to Mexican-Americans what Martin Luther King, Jr. came to represent to Black Americans—a leader providing hope for economic opportunities and a proletariat of minority rights. Although known to be less inclined toward mass forms of civil disobedience, the 21 month strike against Farah Manufacturing Company in Texas by Mexican-Americans for the company's refusal to recognize their labor union in the mid 1970's is perhaps a good example of the contemporary struggle for equal rights and treatment among minorities.

Puerto Ricans and Cubans represent the other two Spanish heritage minority groups. Of the current 2 million Puerto Ricans now living in New York and other eastern cities, their largest migrations were in the 1920's as contract farm laborers, and in the 1940's as defense industry workers. Of the slightly less than one million Cubans, most of the original immigrants arrived in the 1950's when many affluent Cubans sought to escape the Castro regime. Following the failure of the Bay of Pigs invasion in the early 1960's, these immigrants were given citizenship and politically sympathetic permanence in the United States as did many Vietnamese fleeing the communist takeover of their country in the mid 1970's. Most of the original Cuban immigrants have remained in Florida, but subsequent generations have moved to eastern and western cities in hopes of finding new career and lifestyle opportunities.

Chinese Americans first began to arrive in the western states in the 1870's to work in mining, construction, lumbering, and the railroad. They worked as laborers, cooks, carpenters, laundry workers, and servants. Most were easily and frequently exploited because of their unfamiliarity with the English language, monetary system, and customs of an altogether foreign land. Chinese women were not allowed to immigrate to the U.S. until after World War II. Todate, the one-half million or so female population has yet to reach gender parity. Most reside in California with a secondary populous in eastern cities. Tending to be more entreprenurial than some minority groups, the Asian (Chinese and Japanese) Americans now represent one of the least economically, socially, or educationally deprived minority groups due to their acquisition of land, small businesses, and frugal ancestors who worked hard and saved money for future investments in their new homeland.

Japanese Americans originally immigrated to Hawaii and California in 1900. Initially, like the Chinese, it was the men who came to work as truck farmers, gardeners, fishermen, and servants. Some women followed when money was sufficient, and others came as mail-order brides. Japanese, like Chinese and other "foreign" immigrants were prohibited from joining labor unions or leasing farm land. Of the present one-half plus million American Japanese, about three-fourths still reside in Hawaii and California due to their prevalence of agriculture and, no doubt, due to World War II internment of Japanese Americans in those states. The land and other possessions held by Japanese Americans at the time of internment was hastily confiscated by an overacting, if not racially provoked, government and who subjected these citizens to degradation surpassed only by slavery in the southern states. Historically, this event stands as a more contemporary reminder that the American government and its majority Anglo owned and operated economic power sources have been pitifully unfaithful to the principles of the nation's Constitution. Worse yet, it has been consistent in its deprivation, in one form or another, of each and every minority group within its borders. Was it intentional? Probably not, but history has a way of recounting only factual reality.

American Filipinos began to arrive in 1946 at the conclusion of World War II seeking citizenship and with it better jobs, education, and the abundance for which the U.S. had become known. Like the Japanese, their island was nearest the American west coast, their economy based on agriculture, and their principal immigration was in Hawaii and California. Similar to Puerto Rico, their homeland was acquired by the United States in the war against Spain. Since this early tie to the Phillippines introduced the English language, most of the difficulty encountered by the original and successive American Filipinos has been based on differences in culture and custom. As a people, they have long been accustomed to the internal strife and economic hardship of an underdeveloped, often politically exploited country.

In an effort to gain some cultural distinction in the U.S., several Filipino organizations filed a class action suit against the EEOC in 1974, asking that they be listed separately from other ethnic groups on employer affirmative action reports.

For most minority groups of significant population in the United States, the original lure was for jobs and to earn more money than was available in their own lands. Most of these initial minority immigrants were men who intended to return to their homeland once enough money had been accumulated. This is particularly true of Puerto Ricans, Mexicans, and Chinese. Either through exploitation preventing their return, or enduring conditions of prosperity which changed their inclination to return, most have remained in the United States to become aliens and naturalized citizens.

Immigration also meant the knowingly difficult process of assimation into a new culture. Invariably, the infusion of one culture into another is often a painful one for both groups. For the immigrant, it is the learning of a new language, customs, foods, dress, and socio-economic system. It is the desire for acceptance, the cultural need to obtain individual dignity, and the prestige associated with the social and economic function of employment. For it to be successful, the assimilation process must be two-way: the minority must learn to adapt to the values, methods, and customs of the majority; and the majority must be willing to assist and accept their efforts.

2.12   URBANIZATION AND COMPETITION FOR JOBS

Most ethnic groups banned together in distinguishable communities during early American urbanization. They were distinguished by physical appearance (Blacks, Puerto Ricans, Mexicans), language (Italians, Germans, French), religious practices (Jews, Irish), or some combination of these. Those that were English-speaking and of Anglo-European descent were less conspicuous in terms of color and culture as a group, and were therefore more socially mobile within and among many cultural groups. In describing ethnic conditions in Greenwich Village during the 1920's, Caroline Ware cites one of the fundamental sociological conditions, namely, fear of diluting cultural beliefs that has perpetuated and reinforced ethnic prejudice.

> In their first impact, the clash between Irish and Italians resulted from fundamental economic competition. When the Italians began to invade the Village, they were a direct menace to the homogeneity and the residential quality of the area. Some of the better-class Irish met the invasion by moving to other parts of the city, while the rest retreated gradually westward, slowly abandoning block after block to the newcomers.

> In this situation, it was not surprising that active conflict between Italians and Irish should arise. In the first stages, the fight came mostly from the Irish side, in resistance to the invasion of foreigners. Gangs of Irish boys did their best to prevent Italian children from using the public library by lying in wait for them and destroying the books. Interblock fights with bricks and stones were not uncommon. The Italian boy knew which streets it was good for him to walk on and he also knew the consequence of walking on the side of the park which the Irish had set apart for themselves. One street was, for many years, the no man's land where the major fights

between the "Wops" and the "Micks" were waged—fights not always confined to youngsters.[3]

Indeed, there is little doubt that members of each ethnic and cultural minority can identify with this scenario, and even under considerably more appalling conditions of fear, anger, and brutality. It has been passed on to each succeeding generation by families who have begun to see their traditional, time honored, threads of cultural homogeneity fading, and it has been heavily reinforced by film makers through their portrayal of gang honor, non-Anglo inferiority, ethnic subservience, and intercultural violence.

It has often been said that labor unions had as the basis of their original formation a sort of collective white protectionism against the four million freed slaves who might threaten the holding of jobs by northern whites. Not so coincidentally, it was in 1866 when the National Labor Union, and in 1869 the Knights of Labor, were founded and became the forerunners of the present American Federation of Labor/Central Industrial Organization (AFL-CIO). Neither of these early unions were recognized by the federal government as lawfully protected interests until adoption of the National Labor Relations (Wagner) Act in 1935. Those northern blacks who held trade occupations for many years were allowed to join these early unions, but they were concentrated as a representative group in specific local chapters. Hence, Title VI of the 1964 Civil Rights Act placed emphasis on the prohibition of discrimination in union membership, representation, and entrance into union sponsored apprenticeship programs. Additionally, many court decisions have closely scrutinized seniority systems used in layoff decisions to determine if they were being used as a method of protecting the jobs of longer employed whites—as a deliberate past practice of excluding blacks and other minority members.

From the turn of the century through the early 1940's, it became common practice for white employers to use blacks as strike breakers in northern industries including aluminum, steel, coal mining, meat packing, railroad, and longshore. It was this very struggle for jobs that became the underlying cause of race riots in Springfield, Illinois (1904 and 1908) in East St. Louis (1917), Chicago (1919), Detroit (1943), Philadelphia (1944) where the Army was called in to maintain peace while black bus drivers reported to work, and unemployment among blacks became a contributing factor in the eruption of racial rioting in Watts, California (1964). As more jobs became available during the early years of industrial growth, blacks eventually replaced whites in the aluminum ore, meat packing, and coal industries.

As early as the 1930's, the movement toward nondiscrimination in employment and workplace equality began to take political prominence, initially in various states

---

[3] Ware, Caroline F. *Greenwich Village, 1920-1930: A Comment On American Civilization in the Post War Years.* Boston: Houghton Mifflin, 1935.

and later nationally. In the late 1930's, hearings were held in New York that ultimately lead to the passage of the first fair employment practices law. As Paul Burnstein notes on this period:

> Attention soon shifted to the federal level. However, blacks in particular realized that a federal law would be necessary because most of them lived in the south where no state government would pass an antidiscrimination law. In addition, residents of the more liberal states worried that the passage of EEO laws in their states would simply encourage business to move elsewhere; a federal law would remove the incentive to do this.
>
> As the depression ended and employment levels rose, blacks came to see federal action as especially urgent and appropriate because many of the new jobs were created by the government itself in defense industries. Not wanting blacks to be kept out of the new jobs and believing that President Roosevelt could influence the hiring patterns of defense contractors, A. Philip Randolph and other black leaders urged the President to sign an executive order banning discrimination in defense industries. Unless such an order was signed, they threatened, 10,000 people would march on Washington to protest employment discrimination. President Roosevelt responded in June 1941 by signing Executive Order 8802 which declared that, "There shall be no discrimination in the employment of workers in defense industries or government because of race, creed, color, or national origin," and required that all defense contracts have a nondiscrimination clause.[4]

The order was in many respects modest and of little consequence; it provided no specific sanctions against violations, its legal power was uncertain, and it applied only to federal defense contractors. It was, however, the first federal move explicitly aimed at reducing employment discrimination in the private sector since Reconstruction.

It was about this same time when economists began to take an interest in the struggle and competition for jobs in urbanized America. Their theories, like those of social and political scientists, attempted to rationalize the existence, causes, and prospective outcomes of this notable event. One of the more popular economic theories of the time was that of Classical versus Contemporary Marxism.

Classical Marxism postulates that an advanced capitalist economy would remove racial and sexual barriers to economic achievement in order to maximize the number of potential workers for each job, thereby enhancing competition among workers and keeping wage rates low. This tactic would simultaneously keep the working class heterogeneous and prevent the formation of a strong class consciousness. This perspective would have blacks and women increasingly integrated into white male occupations, and differences in wages should also decline.

Contemporary Marxism, on the other hand, holds that capitalists are the creators of racial and sexual antagonisms, and that by keeping blacks (or any significant minority group) and women in marginal occupations and paying them menial wages, the

---

[4] Burnstein, Paul; *Discrimination, Jobs, And Politics.* Chicago: University of Chicago Press, 1985, p.7.

capitalist class is capable of realizing huge profits. By a continuation of such oppression, the theory goes, white males would be able to demand servile behavior and retain a class of underlings upon whom they can vent hostilities. This perspective would, of course, support a continuation rather than diminishing of racial and sexual barriers to full workforce equality.

In his 1940-1970 study of occupational integration and wage differentials among assorted U.S. industries, the economic theorist Alber Szymanski tested these Marxist theories. In terms of general trends, Szymanski found that blacks were most closely subject to the classical model, and women to the contemporary model. His reasoning was that white males found it easier to keep women subservient in work roles since they were already trained or possessed culturally patterned behavior as such.

Almquist presents a slightly different, less deliberately conspiratory point of view on ethnic economics concerning at least labor intensive industries which comprised most American industry until technology errupted in the 1900's. She states:

> Employers are basically indifferent toward the race or ethnicity of employees. However, they do take advantage of split labor markets, that is, if situations in which one group has fewer resources and is motivated to offer its services for a lower wage than another. Employers quite willingly hire the lower-priced group, if they believe the workers are no less efficient or productive than the higher-priced workers. The higher-priced workers (usually the white majority) who are displaced retaliate against any members of the group who have been substituted for them. Examples include vigilante raids against Filipinos who had begun work in the asparagus and lettuce fields in California. Hostility against Asian immigrants developed rather promptly after the arrival of each new group.[5]

Taking this condition from a sociological perspective, it can be expected that people individually (and especially as a group) who offer themselves up for a particular set of conditions such as abnormally lower wages are likely to elicit similar forms of substandard, subservient treatment. If they then accept that treatment, they become stigmatized and eventually characterized for those traits as resultant conditions—a self-fulfilling prophecy of sorts.

As a perhaps little known fact, in 1948 Harry S. Truman's name did not appear on the Democratic ballot because he was politically seen as being too liberal on the issue of race, yet in 1949 several congressional representatives testified before both houses that equal employment opportunity legislation that would end discrimination in the workplace would be their top priorities. However, political posturing remained unsettled as evidenced by similar treatment given to Lyndon B. Johnson fourteen years later during his renewed efforts to end racial barriers to employment by having Title VII added to President Kennedy's 1963 version of a civil rights act. Even then, it wasn't until 200,000 blacks and minority rights supporters gathered at the nation's

---

[5] Almquist, ibid., p. 20.

capital to demonstrate their interest in passage of the 1964 bill that Congress decided there was sufficient national inclination to do so. We should not overlook though, that passage of this comprehensive and controversial bill was the ultimate culmination of years of racial, separatist, sexist, antisemitic conduct, and sometimes brutality across the country. More contemporary highlights were the National Guards being called upon to assist in the desegregation of American communities during the late 1950's following the U.S. Supreme Court's decision in *Brown v. Board of Education,* and those nationally televised events in connection with the attempted march from Selma to Birmingham, Alabama by various black coalitions lead by Martin Luther King, Jr. in March 1964 to encourage Governor George Wallace to abide by federal anti-discrimination and desegregation orders.

From passage of the Civil Rights Act in 1964, its various amendments including the Equal Employment Opportunity Act of 1972, and proceeding into the 1980's with the adoption of the Immigration Control and Reform Act of 1986, most civil demonstrations and protests over discriminatory and inequitable conditions moved into the courts. Case by case of systemic employment practices and employer decisions, the courts began the interpretive process of untangling a complex mixture of statutory law, administrative regulation, legislative intent, evidentiary fact finding, evaluation of legal precedence, and often such illusive issues as the reasonableness of the employer's actions.

A plethora of individual and class action suits ensued pitting job applicant, employees, and former employees against employers much like the consequence of collective bargaining and other employment rights laws had created in earlier years. Finally, in 1971 stemming from a 1968 lower court decision, the U.S. Supreme Court rendered its first major employment discrimination decision in *Griggs v. Duke Power Co.* where a black man was denied employment for an unskilled maintenance job due to failing a general aptitude written test; the decision of which made it unlawful for employers to administer any type of preemployment test that was not directly and adequately corresponding to the nature, level, or scope of actual duties performed in particular jobs.

Since the *Griggs* case, employers have been learning—sometimes the hard way as case-by-case decisions continue to establish precedential trends—how to modify their policies, practices, decisions, and actions in a vast array of human resource management matters. Topping the list has been hiring, firing, and layoffs, with secondary prominence given to such "during employment" conditions as training, promotion, evaluation, pay, promotion, and discipline. In most business organizations it is mostly line and departmental managers who make these types of decisions and who assist in the formulation of policy, while it is the work unit supervisor who affects each employee's treatment through daily interaction. Because it is here, with unit supervisors and departmental managers, that most problems occur pertaining to illegal discrimination, it becomes imperative that upper management take decisive measures to ensure that lower level managers and supervisors become familiar with employment laws, what they mean, how to identify and solve problems, and concisely what is expected of them in their decision making role.

2.20 THE LAWS AND WHAT MANAGERS SHOULD KNOW

Much like the history of social order and change in the United States, the laws, regulations, and legal decisions concerning various types of employment discrimination can be very confusing. It becomes particularly burdensome to various managers, from operations to the executive level, who are necessarily preoccupied with keeping the enterprise headed in one direction. These specialist managers are often found to characterize equal opportunity employment compliance a nuisance and a constraint to free choice. In these circumstances, the role that becomes cast for the human resource manager is to make the best possible attempt at meeting both the letter and spirit of compliance standards, while remaining persistent in the education of those superiors who view the human resource function with tolerant contempt. In such cases, the effort to establish legal practices, unbiased policies, and a thorough records system becomes patch work (often after the fact) and is done under conditions of protest from upper management who would prefer that human resource managers would just do what they're told.

Let's be honest and admit it. Nobody, especially human resource managers, likes to be controlled. Given the latitude to freely exercise the principles of the discipline, human resource managers would delight at being able to focus attention on positive—service oriented—activities that develop enhancements to the organization. However, a major conflict in the organizational role to be played by human resource managers arose in the early 1960's, and has been escalating sharply since then. The escalation legal, control-oriented compliance has been due to the emergence of an unprecedented number and variety of employment laws—most concentrating on the adversity of employment discrimination. In order to protect their organization's time, resource, and monetary interests, human resource professionals have had to turn their attention toward internal control measures, thereby lessening the time available to service activities.

The conflict between the role of service and control for the human resource functions is no less agonizing for the operations or executive manager than it is for the human resource manager. Each manager in the organization, regardless of responsibility or specialty, must eventually come to the realization that their jobs are at least fundamentally the same—to serve the best interests of the organization even if it means doing some things we would prefer not to. Knowingly disobeying the laws or violating professional principles does not serve the best interests of the organization.

The portrayal of the human resources function operating under tolerance conditions by other managers including executive officers is not intended to be impetuous, but it is the rule concerning those measures that human resource managers are obliged by law and other compelling standards to take when it affects discrimination in the workplace. While there are admittedly other signs within corporate America suggesting that dinosaur management styles are giving way to a more important human resource role and its effect upon the bottom line, there remain many dinosaurs in the swamp that keep the waters murky with discrimination claims, legal actions, outright non-compliance, and other adverse conditions controlled by non-conformist attitudes and overbearing management styles.

For those managers who wish to get out of the bog and move beyond, part of this maneuver lies in gaining a better understanding of discrimination laws—based on race, color, and national origin in the case of this chapter—and their effect on employment practices which your employees have the right to expect from you and your organization. In the same way we read the motor vehicle operators manual before taking our driver's test, it is now incumbent upon every manager to learn about the employment law rules of the road. What follows, then, is a thorough but general treatment of those laws concerning discrimination on the basis of race, color, and national origin. Managers are equally encouraged to read the other chapters in Part I for a more complete understanding of these and other laws relating to the remaining types of discrimination that frequently give rise to problems within and for the organization.

2.21 CONSTITUTIONAL PROTECTIONS AGAINST DISCRIMINATION

First Amendment, Due Process

The due process clause states that "No person...be deprived of life, liberty, or property without due process of law..." Although conceptually abstract as it might relate to employment conditions, it has been used in some court cases to demonstrate that an employee or job applicant was further denied rights by not being allowed to represent their case or claim to the employer. Because some courts have made findings in behalf of claimants due to the absence or denial of using an employer's due process (internal complaint) mechanism, many employers have implemented a grievance, complaint, or conflict resolution procedures within the organization in an attempt to establish "administrative remedies" to such issues as discrimination complaints, and to thereby avoid costly and time consuming litigation.

Fourteenth Amendment, Equal Protection

The equal protection clause prohibits certain actions against citizens by state governments.

> All persons born or naturalized in the United States and subject to the jurisdiction thereof, are citizens of the United States and of the State wherein they reside. No state shall make or enforce any law which shall abridge the privileges and immunities

of citizens of the United States; nor shall any state deprive any person of life, liberty, or property, without due process of law; nor deny to any person within its protection the equal protection of the laws.

As it relates to employment, the equal protection clause means that all citizens are to be afforded equality with regard to access, opportunity, privileges, and responsibilities, and that each citizen will be protected by applicable laws evenhandedly. It additionally means that no state, or its political subdivisions, may treat one group of citizens in any way differently than any other group similarly situated (i.e., preferential or detrimental treatment of a class of people).

2.22 FEDERAL STATUTORY PROTECTIONS

Application of the various federal antidiscrimination statutes and regulations cover public and private employers, unions, apprenticeship programs, and employment agencies. Contractors and subcontractors of the federal government, as well as organizations who are recipients of federal funds or participate in federal programs, are required to comply with federal executive orders. Further, most employers must additionally comply with corresponding state employment statutes which in many cases can be more restrictive than federal law. Since most states frame their laws around the principles of federal law, it is useful for the manager to become familiar with these uniform, guiding doctrines of federal antidiscrimination compliance.

Civil Rights Act of 1866 (42 U.S. Code ss:1981), Equal Rights Under Law

> All persons within the jurisdiction of the United States shall have the same right in every state and territory to make and enforce contracts, to sue, be parties, give evidence, and to the full and equal benefit of all laws and proceedings for the security of persons and property as is enjoyed by white citizens, and shall be subject to like punishment, pains, penalties, taxes, licenses, and exactions of every kind, and to no other.

This Act is enforced by federal and state courts. The question as to whether this section applies to national origin discrimination has been resolved by a federal district court in 1986 and the Supreme Court in 1987. In *Malik v. Combustion Engineering* (1986), a district court in Connecticut rejected earlier views that Section 1981 allows only claims for race discrimination, and held that claims may be based on ethnic origin. Likewise, the U.S. Supreme Court held in *Saint Francis Hospital v. Al-Khaziaji* (1987) that Section 1981 is applicable to (Caucasian appearance) persons subjected to job bias because of ethnic characteristics.

Concerning race discrimination, the courts have held that proof of the employer's intent to discriminate is required, and that "disparate impact" is inapplicable (*Johnson v. Railway Express Agency,* 1975). However, in cases where race discrimination can be demonstrated to be intentional, Section 1981 of this Act suggests that the claimant can obtain a substantial (federal) tort remedy consisting of compensatory and punitive damages, and legal fees, whereas awards under Title VII of the 1964 Civil Rights Act is limited to up to two years back pay.

Civil Rights Act of 1871 (42 U.S. Code ss:1983), Deprivation of Rights

> Every person who, under color of any statute, ordinance, regulation, custom or usage, of any state or territory of the District of Columbia, subjects, or causes to be subjected, any citizen of the United States or other person within the jurisdiction thereof to the deprivation of any rights, privileges or immunities secured by the Constitution and laws, shall be liable to the party injured in an action at law, suit in equity, or other proper proceeding for redress.

This section is usually cited in conjunction with Section 1981 in many types of discrimination cases, but race in particular, because it allows violations of U.S. Constitutional and federal law to be resolved by trial. This has a potentially greater monetary award benefit if the claimant prevails than if the case were reviewed by an administrative compliance agency in a Title VII action.

Civil Rights Act of 1964 (42 U.S. Code s:2000 e et seq.)

The act contains several titles which deal with differing circumstances of discriminatory prohibitions. For employment purposes, it is Title VII, Section 703(a) of the Act that makes it an unlawful practice for an employer:

1. To fail or refuse to hire or to discharge any individual, or otherwise to discriminate against any individual with respect to his compensation, terms, conditions or privileges of employment, because of such individual's race, color, religion, sex including sexual harassment, or national origin; or

2. To limit, segregate or classify his employees or applicants for employment in any way which would deprive or tend to deprive any individual of employment opportunities or otherwise adversely affect his status as an employee, because of such individual's race, color, religion, sex, or national origin.

Title VII therefore deals with most forms of discrimination excluding age and handicap discrimination. In 1972, the Equal Employment Opportunity Act modified applicability of Title VII to public and private employers with 15 or more employees, excluding elected officials and their appointees. Title VII is more pervasive than other titles in the act inasmuch as it affects virtually all employment practices, policies, and procedural decisions.

Title VII is enforced by the Equal Employment Opportunity Commission (EEOC) through its 59 regional and district offices. Complaints may be resolved by the EEOC; it may find insufficient grounds to proceed but issue a "right to sue" letter to the complainant; or it may proceed against the employer on its own through federal district courts—usually in cases where there is a controversial or significant issue it wants judicially tested, or if it ascertains a pattern or practice of obvious discrimination on the employer's part. The complainant has 180 days from the date of the alleged discriminatory act to file with the EEOC in those states not having their own antidiscrimination laws or compliance agencies. Where states have equivalent laws and enforcement agencies, the time for a complainant to file with the EEOC is extended to either 240 or 300 days.

The few exceptions to Title VII are:

☐ It does not prohibit an employer from giving Veterans' preference to qualified job seekers.

☐ It does not prohibit discrimination when deemed necessary to protect the interests of national security.

☐ It does not prohibit employers from using "bona fide occupational qualifications" (BFOQ) that are reasonably necessary to the operation of the business, such as black actors or Mexican food servers, but the employer bears the burden of proof of the operational necessity and the courts have viewed these conditions narrowly. Mere preference to hire people with particular personal characteristics is irrelevant in the eyes of this law.

☐ It does not prohibit seniority systems or intend to interfere with lawful collective bargaining agreements. Seniority and merit pay systems are lawful so long as they are not the result of an intention to discriminate. Therefore, seniority that accrues within a job or department may be seen as perpetuating past practices of (unintentional) discrimination, while company-wide seniority would be less vulnerable to such allegations.

NATIONAL ORIGIN DISCRIMINATION DEFINED

It is important for managers to understand not only the laws, but the definitions and practical meaning of antidiscrimination statutes in order to prevent even their unintentional occurrence. Too often it has been discovered after the fact—usually in a courtroom or through administrative hearings—that managers did not fully understand the meaning of a particular type of prohibited discrimination. Since these laws, nor the courts that hear them, allow ignorance of the law as a suitable defense, it becomes imperative that every employer of 15 or more employees take action to thoroughly train and acquaint managers with their meaning in terms of workplace conduct.

As it applies to national origin discrimination, the EEOC has defined it to include, but not limited to the denial of equal employment opportunity because of an individual's, or their ancestors', place of origin or because such person possesses the physical, cultural, or linguistic characteristics of a national origin group. Examples of such national origin associations include:

☐ Marriage to, or association with, persons of a national origin group;
☐ Membership or association with an organization seeking to promote the interests of a national origin group;
☐ Attendance or participation in schools, churches, temples or mosques, generally used by persons of a national origin group; and
☐ The name of an individual, or spouse's name, that is associated with a national origin group.

NATIONAL ORIGIN HARASSMENT

In accordance with EEOC guidelines concerning prohibitions against discrimination based on national origin, managers should be aware that the guidelines expressly forbid acts of a harassing nature occurring in the workplace whether such conduct is created by employees, supervisors, or other persons in the course of work (e.g., vendors, contractors, customers). In particular:

☐ Ethnic slurs and verbal or physical conduct pertaining to a person's national origin constitute harassment when the conduct:

• has the purpose or effect of creating an intimidating, hostile, or offensive work environment;

• has the purpose or effect of unreasonably interfering with an individual's work performance; or

• otherwise adversely affects an individual's employment opportunities.

☐ An employer is responsible for its acts and those of its agents and supervisory employees with respect to harassment on the basis of national origin regardless of whether the specific acts complained of were authorized or even forbidden by the employer and regardless of whether the employer knew *or should have known* of their occurrence.

☐ With respect to conduct between co-workers, an employer is responsible for acts of harassment in the workplace on the basis of national origin, where the employer, its agents or supervisory employees, knows or should have known of the conduct, unless the employer can show that it took immediate and appropriate corrective action.

☐ An employer may also be responsible for the acts of non-employees with respect to harassment of employees on the basis of national origin, where the employer, its agents or supervisory employees, know or should have known of the conduct and fails to take immediate and appropriate corrective action. In reviewing these cases, the Commission will consider the extent of the employer's control and any other legal responsibility which the employer may have with respect to the conduct of such non-employees.

RETALIATORY CONDUCT

Managers should be particularly aware that it is prohibited under Section 704(a) of the Act to take retaliatory actions against employees who file Title VII claims. This section provides that:

> It shall be an unlawful employment practice for an employer to discriminate against any of his employees or applicants for employment, for an employment agency to discriminate against any individual, or for a labor organization to discriminate against any member thereof or applicant for membership because he has opposed any practice made an unlawful employment practice by this title, or because he has made a charge, testified, assisted, or participated in any manner in an investigation, proceeding, or hearing under this title.

The courts have established a considerable amount of precedence on employee retaliation,[6] and have consistently taken a harsh view of any form of retaliatory measures against employees who exercise their lawful right to file discrimination claims, whether or not the employer has and encourages use of an internal complaint mechanism. Examples of retaliation, or retaliatory actions by an employer, consist of such things as telling employees they will sacrifice future promotional consideration, or they can (or will) get fired; suggesting that they're trouble-makers; and any other threatening, harassing, or coercive acts to impede employees' unprejudiced freedom to file a complaint.

Immigration Reform and Control Act of 1986 (P.L. 99-603)

On November 6, 1986, President Reagan signed this Act into law placing regulatory authority with the Attorney General. The purpose of the Act is twofold: 1) to curb the economic incentive for illegal aliens to enter the country to secure employment by making it unlawful to employ such persons; and 2) to provide a one-time opportunity

---

[6] Pettway v. American Cast Iron Pipe Co., 411 F. 2d 998, 1 FEP Cases 752 (5th Cir., 1969).
Tidwell v. American Oil Co., 332 F. Supp. 424, 3 FEP 1007 (D. Utah 1971).
Francis v. American Tel. & Tel. Co., 55 F.R.D. 202, 4 FEP Cases 777 (D., DC, 1972).
Barela v. United Nuclear Corp., 462 F.2d 149, 4 FEP 831 (CA, 10th Cir., 1972).
McDonnell-Douglas Corp. v. Green, 411 U.S. 792, 5 FEP 965 (1973).
EEOC v. United Assoc. of Journeymen, 311 F. Supp. 464 (DC Ohio 1974).
Brown v. Rollins, Inc., 397 F. Supp. 571 (W.D., N.C. 1974).
OC v. C & D Sportswear Corp., 398 F. Supp. 300, 10 FEP 1131 (M.D. Ga. 1975).
Hochstadt v. Worchester Foundation, 545 F.2d 222, 13 FEP Cases 804 (1st Cir., 1976).
Garrett v. Mobil Oil Corp., 531 F.2d 892, 12 FEP Cases 397 (8th Cir., 1976).

for those unauthorized aliens working for American employer's prior to enactment of the law to obtain legal employment status.

Sanctions or penalties include civil fines for each illegal alien hired, but does not include simple, unintentional mistakes in the hiring process. However, blatant disregard of the law, or repeated violations may result in criminal penalties including jail terms of up to six months.

This law dramatically strengthens the prohibition against national origin discrimination under Title VII, while at the same time exposes employers to the requirement to obtain pre-employment information concerning their citizenship (if they have the legal right to remain in the country and whether that right includes employment). Under this Act, employers with four to fourteen employees are prohibited from engaging in *national origin discrimination* (to conform to the 15 employee coverage of Title VII), while employers with three or more employees are prohibited from discriminating on the basis of *citizenship*, with one exception: a U.S. citizen may be preferably hired over an alien if their qualifications are equal.

PROHIBITIONS

It is unlawful for an employer to knowingly hire, recruit, or refer for a fee any alien not authorized to work in the United States, or to continue employing an alien once the employer knows that the alien is not authorized to work in the United States.

Employers may not discharge or refuse to hire an individual because of his or her national origin, or because of the individual's status as "citizen" or "intending citizen." "Citizen" is defined as a citizen or national of the United States. An "intending citizen" is one who is a permanent resident alien, a newly legalized alien, a refugee, or an alien who has been granted asylum, and who has completed a Declaration of Intention to Become A Citizen. However, the Act provides that notwithstanding any other provision, it is not an unfair immigration-related employment practice for an employer to prefer to hire, recruit, or refer a citizen or national of the United States over an alien if the two individuals are equally qualified.

EMPLOYMENT VERIFICATIONS

The Act requires employers to verify the legal right of new hires to be employed in the United States by examining any of the following illustrative documents.

- U.S. birth certificate

- Social Security card and driver's license or similar document

- U.S. passport

- Certificate of U.S. citizenship

- Certificate of naturalization

- Unexpired foreign passport, if endorsed by the Attorney General authorizing employment

- Resident alien card, or other alien registration card, containing the individual's photograph with authorization of U.S. employment.

Further, an employer representative must attest under penalty of perjury on a form to be provided by the Attorney General (I-9 Form), that one or more of these documents have been examined and verified that the applicant is not an unauthorized alien. The job applicant must do likewise, however a federal district court in Texas determined that terminating illegal aliens for falsifying their Social Security cards would also be a discriminatory act under this 1986 law since doing so would contravene the Congressional intent to allow illegal aliens a window period to become legalization candidates. Here, in *League of United Latin American Citizens v. Pasadena Independent School District* (1987), also stated that generally an employer's policy to terminate employees who falsify documents would be valid and upheld by the court, this particular situation raised a paradox of exception to the rule.

REMEDIES

The Act provides new remedies to individuals who believe they have been discriminated against on the basis of their national origin or citizenship status by creating the Office of Special Counsel in the Justice Department to investigate discrimination claims. If the Office of Special Counsel files a complaint against the employer, a hearing will be held before an administrative law judge. However, if the Special Counsel does not file a complaint within 120 days after receiving a charge of discrimination, the individual making the charge may file a complaint directly before the administrative law judge. Upon a finding of unfair immigration related employment practices, the administrative law judge has authority to order reinstatement, back pay, attorneys' fees and a civil penalty of up to $2,000.

2.23 FEDERAL EXECUTIVE ORDER REQUIREMENTS

As pointed out earlier, only contractors and subcontractors of the federal government, as well as the federal government and organizations receiving federal grants, are required to comply with Executive Orders relating to employment discrimination. The three applicable orders are 11246, 11375, and 11478.

Executive Order 11246

As early as 1941, President Roosevelt issued Executive Order 8802 in which it became unlawful to discriminate in defense-related industry employment on the basis of race, creed, color, or national origin. Since then, nearly every president has issued similar orders, but the most impacting on applicable employers came in September

1965 when President Johnson signed Executive Order 11246. The central purpose of this measure was to advance the employment opportunities of minority group members. This was to be accomplished by requiring that employers take affirmative action to ensure that minorities were given equal opportunity to apply and compete for jobs within the federal government and its contracting or grant agent employers. For employers with grants or contracts of more than $10,000 per year, the employer merely has to demonstrate that it was taking "affirmative" measures to provide employment to minority members. Contractors receiving $50,000 or more per year are additionally required to prepare and follow a written affirmative action plan in accordance with federal guidelines (41 CFR, Part 60-2). Employers covered by Executive Order 11246 must:

☐ Refrain from discriminating against any employee or job applicant because of race, color, religion, or national origin;

☐ Take affirmative action to ensure that applicants are employed and employees are treated without regard to race, color, religion, or national origin (the obligation extends to working conditions and facilities such as restrooms, as well as hiring, firing, promotions, and compensations);

☐ State in all solicitations or advertisements that all qualified applicants will receive consideration without regard to race, color, religion, or national origin;

☐ Advise each labor union with which they deal of their commitments under the order;

☐ Include the obligations under the order in every subcontract or purchase order, unless specifically exempted;

☐ Comply with all provisions of the order and the rules and regulations issued; furnish all information and reports required; permit access to books, records and accounts for the purpose of investigation to ascertain compliance; and

☐ File regular compliance reports describing hiring and employment practices.

The mandatory starting point for affirmative action programs is analysis of areas in which the employer may be underutilizing "protected" persons. The employer must consider at least the following factors:

☐ Minority population of the labor area surrounding the facility;

☐ Size of the minority unemployment force in the labor area;

☐ Percentage of minority work force as compared with the total work-force in the immediate area;

☐ General availability of minorities having requisite skills in the immediate labor area;

☐ Availability of minorities having requisite skills in an area in which the employer can reasonably recruit;

☐ Availability of promotable minority employees within the employer's organization;

☐ Anticipated expansion, contraction, and turnover in the labor force;

☐ Existence of training institutions capable of training minorities in the requisite skills; and

☐ Degree of training the employer is reasonably able to undertake to make all job classes available to minorities.

Unlike Title VII, executive orders relating to employment are the administrative responsibility of the Department of Labor, Office of Federal Contract Compliance Programs (OFCCP). In addition to enforcement of Executive Order 11246, the OFCCP also requires covered employers to prepare affirmative action plans for veterans, disabled veterans, and handicapped persons under authority of Section 503 of the Rehabilitation Act of 1973 and the Viet Nam Era Veterans Readjustment Act of 1974. Since the legal standards of these two laws are different than the protected groups under Executive Order 11246 (e.g., requires good faith recruitment, selection, and accommodation efforts, but not goals and timetables), many covered employers prepare a separate affirmative action plan for veterans and handicapped persons.

Executive Order 11375

In 1967, Executive Order 11375 was issued having the singular effect of adding sex-based discrimination to the list of protected characteristics covered by Executive Order 11246. Therefore, in addition to making it unlawful to discriminate on the basis of an applicant's or employee's sex, the OFCCP also requires in its guidelines that covered employers take affirmative action to recruit women for jobs in which they had previously or traditionally been excluded. The guidelines also prohibit employers from:

☐ Making any distinction based on sex in employment opportunities, wages, hours, and other conditions;

☐ Advertising for workers in newspaper columns headed "male" and "female" unless sex is a bona fide occupational qualification for the job;

☐ Relying on state protective laws to justify denying a female employee the right to any job that she is qualified to perform; and

☐ Denying employment to women with young children or making a distinction between married and unmarried persons, unless the distinctions are applied to both sexes.

Executive Order 11478

This order was issued in 1969 by President Nixon. It had the effect of amending Part I of Executive Order 11246 thereby establishing that federal employment shall be based upon conditions of merit and fitness. Other than setting employment standards guidelines for federal department heads to establish, the order also requires that companies who advertise job openings specify that they are an equal employment opportunity employer and to post antidiscrimination notices on company bulletin boards.

2.24 FEDERAL REGULATORY REQUIREMENT

The EEOC and other agencies have issued regulations supplementing the various statutes they are required to enforce. The principal sets of regulations, all of which are found in the Code of Federal Regulations, are enumerated below. Each represents the technical standards for compliance with the statutes, and are too comprehensive for the purpose of this chapter.

1. EEOC Guidelines on Affirmative Action, 29 CFR, Part 1608.

2. Office of Federal Contract Compliance Programs, Guidelines for Affirmative Action programs, 41 CFR, Part 60-2 (Implementation of Executive Order 11246).

3. Department of Labor, 29 CFR, Part 32.4 (handicap discrimination).

4. EEOC Interpretations of the Age Discrimination in Employment Act, 29 CFR, Part 1625.

5. EEOC Sex Discrimination and Pregnancy Guidelines, 29 CFR, Part 1604. Note: The EEOC has guidelines on sexual harassment, found at 29 CFR, Part 1604, Section 1604.11.

6. EEOC National Origin Discrimination Guidelines, 29 CFR, Part 1606.

7. EEOC Testing Guidelines, 29 CFR, Part 1607.

8. EEOC Regulations on the Age Discrimination Act of 1975, 29 CFR, Part 1616.

2.30 PERSONNEL POLICY AND PRACTICE ISSUES ANSWERED BY THE COURTS

In the following discussion, a number of insightful court cases are examined in summary detail to illustrate current thinking on matters related to race, color, and national origin discrimination. While these examples touch on only a few different circumstances of ethnic discrimination related to an employer's personnel practices or operating methods, many more examples are presented in other chapters dealing with programmatic problems within the human resources function. The intent here, then, is to capture the philosophical flavor of Title VII violations as seen by the courts pertaining to employer actions and other conditions that constitute discriminatory policy or practices regarding one's race, color, or national origin. Topics selected are:

- Interracial Marriage
- Accents
- English Only Rules
- Promotions

- Reverse Discrimination
- Harassment
- Layoffs
- Predecessor Liability

Human resource and other managers would do well to read these illustrative problems in light of their current policy language, training of supervisors, and known styles of leadership within the organization to determine the need for change or other measures that might help prevent these kinds of occurrences. We should bear in mind that problem solving has two separate components: preventing its occurrence, and handling it the best way available to us if they occur. Emphasis should always be placed upon its prevention, but the true skills lie in its proper handling.

Can An Employer Refuse To Hire Someone On The Basis Of Their Interracial Marriage?

According to *Parr vs. Woodmen of the World Life Insurance Co.* (1986), the answer is unequivocally no. The case arose when a white male was refused employment as an insurance salesman due to his interracial marriage. Here, the basis of action is not so much the applicant's race itself that resulted in direct race discrimination, as it is that a race relationship existed in association with the applicant, and he therefore became subject to indirect discrimination. To be successful in defending this employer, it would have been minimally necessary for the employer to establish that this applicant was not hired for factors other than his interracial association through marriage; i.e., another applicant was better qualified with respect to skills, experience, training, product knowledge, and the like.

It is also reasonable to assume that the courts would hold a similar opinion concerning an applicant or employee's casual association with another racial or ethnic group such as an organization whose goal is to promote the interests of the group (NAACP), and so long as their activities are not illegal (Klu Klux Klan). It is equally important to guard against creating pretextual reasons for refusing to hire or otherwise adversely affecting one's employment condition where the underlying cause is racially or ethnically motivated. For this reason, managers ought to closely examine and document specic factual, job related reasons and conditions associated with *all* personnel actions.

What Can An Employer Do If An Applicant Or Employee Has A Heavy Accent?

Accents and "manner of speaking" can constitute a form of either racial or national origin discrimination due to the accent itself or the use of idioms and culturally based slang. This policy was announced by the EEOC in 1986 to its field offices, and warns against some important distinctions in examining such cases based on recent litigation. Two suits in particular illustrate basic conditions: one in which a Filipino was denied a job in a dental lab because of his accent; another where a school refused to hire a classroom teacher whose accent was "too heavy" to be reasonably understood by students.

In the first case, national origin discrimination was found due to the determination that the accent did not interfere with the job, and the applicant could be understood for the normal course of communications related to job conditions. In the second case, the heavy accent was determined to be a condition sufficiently interfering with the ability of the applicant to carry out primary job duties. Obviously, in cases involving different kinds of jobs and the nature of verbal communications within a job, there is a very fine line between a light, moderate, or heavy accent, and to what extent an accent begins to affect the person's ability to perform in a reasonably acceptable manner. It is a determination of how heavy is too heavy, what are the associated job conditions that set the standard, and what effect will occur that will cause the accent to become detrimental to the employer?

The EEOC has also cautioned its field offices to be watchful for cases in which heavily accented people were given other reasons for their denial of employment, as such reasons may be a mere pretext for denial of employment on the basis of "accentuated" national origin discrimination. In cases of clearly apparent pretext of any kind, there is a strong prospect that the EEOC will want to pursue legal action on behalf of the claimant. If the EEOC prevails, sizable punitive damages can be deducted from the employer's profit and loss statement since these costs are not covered by customary business insurance policies.

Can An Employer Establish Rules And Enforce English-Only Speaking At Work?

Conditionally yes, if there is a reasonable business necessity to do so, says the EEOC as a matter of policy in investigating job conditions that have as an effect discrimination based on national origin. However, the EEOC points out that:

- Unnecessary prohibition of employees speaking their primary language at *all times* in the workplace may have the effect to disadvantage their employment opportunities and conditions on the basis of their national origin.

- Where unnecessary (lacking business necessity or requiring English at all times) policies are found to exist, it will be *presumed* that it creates a working condition atmosphere of inferiority, isolation, and intimidation to those who more comfortably speak another language.

- Employers having conditional (business necessary under specified kinds of conditions) policies for English-Only speaking must inform all employees of its policy and allow for occasional, unintentional error. In the absence of an employer's notification of the policy to their employees, and where an adverse action has been taken against an employee for violation of the policy, the employer will be found in violation of national origin discrimination. This is the EEOC's way of saying if such a legitimate policy isn't communicated to employees, they will not be held liable for its violation.

A good example of a court's application of these standards was in *Jurado v. 11-50 Corporation* (1987) where the Ninth Circuit Court of Appeals rejected plaintiff's claim of race and national origin discrimination. Jurado was a disc jockey who began using "street" Spanish to attract Hispanic listeners, but when ratings declined he was told to discontinue bilingual broadcasts and revert to English only. After refusing to comply Jurado was fired. The court found the employer's reasoning for English Only to be based on valid business reasons and absent racial motivation. Further, no disparate impact occurred since Jurado could have easily reverted to the English Only broadcast format.

Employers should thus carefully evaluate those conditions of its business in which employees are required to verbally communicate with each other, customers, clients, vendors, or others to determine the times and circumstances under which English is the only language to be spoken. In particular, those employers in regions or business types that tend to attract people who speak English as a secondary language may be in a better position by establishing a (preventative) policy rather than continue to operate by unwritten custom. Such a policy should initially be evaluated in light of its business necessity; next in terms of the times, conditions, and business transactions where it is to apply giving general illustrations; it should require progressive discipline for violations; and it must be thoroughly circulated with explanatory notification to employees— preferably in their primary language to assure understanding. This last step should be documented in detail with periodic follow-up and incorporation into the orientation process for all new hires.

What Should An Employer Do When Considering The Promotion Of Applicants, Some Of Whom Are Minorities?

This is one of the more common and difficult problems for employers today, and in particular those employers who have taken affirmative steps to integrate their workforce. It represents a natural consequence that more recently hired employees will at some time seek promotional opportunities, and the competition for one such opportunity will be sought by employees representing various races and possessing other protected characteristics. The screening and selection process thus becomes a damned-if-you-do, damned-if-you-don't proposition for employers. The person(s) not selected may well feel or believe they were passed over because of their protected characteristic, and seek relief under that supposition. The employer, and each manager involved in the process, should be aware of this ever present prospect and proceed accordingly. One method to avert some of the personal hostility that often accompanies those rejected (a deeply rooted psychological effect in each of us), is to inform each rejected candidate of the specific reasons—job related mind you—that the other person was selected. Use this as a learning and development opportunity for the unsuccessful candidate, rather than a form of rejection, then focus on what the candidate can or should do to place themself in a more competitive position for future promotional considerations.

A couple of illustrative cases may help clarify these situations, as well as point out some of the legal standards that apply in such matters.

In the case of *Bibbs v. Block* (1985), seven applicants were competing for a supervisor's job. Bibbs, a black man, was known by the selection committee composed of three white individuals to have a history of disciplinary problems, was difficult to work with, and caused irritation among coworkers. Under normal circumstances, this would have been sufficient grounds to deny him the promotion. However, during the screening process one of the committee members referred to Bibbs as a "black militant", a "boy", and "nigger". This is a classic set of conditions for the legal "but for" rule. That is, had it not been "but for" the racially derogatory remarks, the employer's decision in the promotional selection would have been free of racially oriented evidence.

While the court reasoned that giving Bibbs back pay and the supervisory job was not an appropriate remedy due to his work record, the fact was established that racial discrimination polluted the process. The court points out that Title VII speaks equally to conditions that "tend to deprive...an employment opportunity," regardless of whether the employee suffers a loss of some employment entitlement. The court concluded by establishing a rather liberal standard for an employee to establish cases of this type: that being the prepondence of evidence that a "discernable and determining factor" played a part of any personnel decision, regardless of the outcome of the decision.

Here, it was the racial remarks that created discernable evidence that race became an aspect of the process resulting in discriminatory conduct on the part of the employer, despite the fact that the plaintiff would not have gotten the job anyway. This case is a clear signal to employers to ensure that every step in employment processes is discrimination-free, and that managers involved in such processes must avoid remarks and other types of bias that tend to pollute these processes. It is not enough for employers to conduct sound preliminary screening of applicants only to learn later that a final interview by an untrained departmental manager or unit supervisor did something having a discriminatory effect. Train them, then hold them accountable for their actions!

Two other similar cases involving promotional consideration where the employer prevailed may be of contrasting interest. In *Warren v. Halstead Industries* (1985), two black employees brought suit after being passed over for three white employees who were promoted to leadman positions. The company's stated policy was to promote on the basis of those most qualified having departmental seniority, yet one of the promoted white employees had six weeks less seniority than plaintiffs, but who worked as a temporary leadman for two weeks in the absence of his supervisor. The company was able to show that it had, in fact, a history of using departmental seniority as a primary consideration, and that other blacks had been promoted under such a policy. The court concluded no case of prima facie evidence of discrimination had been made; that there was no evidence of the employer's use of its policy as a pretext for discrimination; and that the white employee's temporary leadman assignment was sufficiently isolated as to give no cause for evidence of racial discrimination.

In *Toliver v. Community Action Conn'n to Help the Economy* (1985), plaintiff was a black male who alleged his denial of promotion to executive director of a nonprofit corporation was racially discriminatory. The board of directors, composed of three black men and three black women of the eleven members, appointed a black female to the executive director position after plaintiff was rejected and additional recruitment took place. Plaintiff was subsequently terminated based on disputes and personality clashes between he and the board which rendered him difficult to work with. In dismissing the case on grounds of failing to establish a prima facie case by plaintiff, the court concluded that the board demonstrated good faith business justification for his termination and that such a decision was not a pretext for discrimination.

There are a couple of important lessons to be learned from these latter two cases. One is to ensure that policies concerning selection, promotion, transfers, and the like, do not have discriminatory effect or implication. Also, make sure that policies do not serve or are allowed to be used as any type of a pretext to cover up an act of discrimination, and that each and every application of the policy is followed to the letter. If you find a legitimate, unanticipated condition where the policy language is counterproductive to the justifiable interests of the organization, change the policy to fit your needs and make sure the change is communicated before acting.

The second lesson is to assure that those persons involved in the personnel decision making process use legitimate criteria in their decisions and actions (e.g., recruitment standards, qualifications screening, interview questions, and reasoning behind final decisions), and that these are documented in some way that can be relied upon as evidence of the employer's good faith, non-pretextual acts. In the absence of objective, nondiscriminatory decisions or their documented recounts, the employer may have nothing more for a defense some time later than speculative and vague testimony.

If An Employer Hires Or Promotes A Minority Applicant, Does That Imply Reverse Discrimination Against White Applicants?

No, not in and of itself. It depends to a considerable extent on the employer's reasoning for its actions, such as a well known attempt to overcome disparities of minorities in the workforce, and to what degree a blatant disregard is shown toward an applicant's race. Here are two opposing examples.

In *Lilly v. City of Beckley* (1986), a white applicant for a police officer position to this small West Virginia community passed a lengthy examination and was offered a position which he refused in favor of another job. Thereafter, the town was told to improve its minority hiring or federal funds would be in jeopardy. Having reconsidered his decision two years later, plaintiff again applied for a police officer position, but this time the test had been changed to encourage a higher minority pass rate. Further, during plaintiff's interview, he was all but told that he would not be selected in spite of being highly qualified because he was white. There being little to say in their defense, the city was found guilty of reverse discrimination. The courts rarely set aside such blatant disregard of the letter or spirit of antidiscrimination law; and that race means any race, not merely black but white, yellow, red, and brown as well.

In *Parker v. The Baltimore and Ohio Railroad Co.* (1986), an opposite decision was rendered by the court concerning the employer's effort to establish improved minority representation in their workforce. The company, in its attempt to remedy past underutilization of minorities and females took two formal measures: first, they adopted an affirmative action plan setting a 20 percent hiring goal for blacks, but no fixed percentage for females; and, second, they established a "seniority modification agreement" with the union in which qualified black and female employees would be promoted without regard to strict seniority as a priority consideration.

Here, the white brakeman plaintiff alleges reverse discrimination after being denied promotion to fireman twice. The first round of promotions went to two each white and black males, and one each white and black females. Five months later, additional fireman positions were filled by nine white males. In this second testing, the plaintiff was rejected for failing a reading test, and did not request retesting. The court found that the employer's affirmative action plan was legal because it did not impair, conceptually or in practice, the employment opportunities of whites any more than to offset past disparities of minority representation in the workforce—at least pertaining to the promotion of existing employees (see also the U.S. Supreme Court's decision in *Johnson v. Transportation Agency* in Chapter I: 3). However, as it relates to layoffs, the U.S. Supreme Court seems to take a slightly different position as demonstrated later in this section.

What Is The Distinction Between Harassment And Giving Necessary Direction To Minority Employees?

There has been no published legal decision where the court has ever admonished a supervisor or manager for carrying out unbiased, necessary, and well mannered responsibilities related to counseling, evaluation, instructions, or discipline. In fact, in *EEOC v. Union Camp Corp.* (1982), the court specifically held that a Mexican-American worker was not harassed by his foreman when his performance was criticized, he was disciplined for not following safety rules, and was subsequently terminated for insubordination. The employer was able to show that the employee had a history of inadequate performance and intemperate behavior. This is also to say that supervisors should not underreact or become unduly tolerant of minority employees any more than non-minorities. Since employers are legally obliged to control and safeguard the workplace, the courts have generally supported the rights of supervisors and managers to carry out their customary responsibilities (hiring, directing, controlling, and firing) and attendant decisions—so long as such decisions are not predicated on discriminatory intent or other unlawful purpose.

Nevertheless, since enactment of Title VII, there have surfaced a number of situations in which particularly contemptuous, racially or ethnically oriented harassment has occurred in which the courts have found them to be in violation of Title VII. These cases have also served to establish certain elements that should be incorporated into personnel policy as well as supervisory and management training to avoid these occurrences. For example, in *Croker v. Boeing* (1982), the court determined that employers will generally be held liable for racial and national origin harassment when it has notice of the condition and fails to take reasonable measure to correct the situation. Conversely, according to *Howard v. National Cash Register* (1975), where such harassment has been repetitive and conspicuously overt, then the employer will be held liable under the "should have known" doctrine for inaction or failure to correct regardless of whether or not a complaint was filed. Some of the most common types of racially and ethnically-oriented forms of harassment are:

1. Derogatory cartoons placed on bulletin boards, employee's work stations, or other obvious places for the effected employee or co-workers to see.

2. Jokes, jesting, slang or derrogatory terms used in reference to racial or ethnic groups, such as "wetback", "chink", "darkie", and the like, whether directed toward a particular person or in the general course of conversation.

3. Bullying and physical intimidations that are regarded as threatening the working conditions based on one's race or national origin (try to prove that a verbal or physical altercation between employees of different races was *not* the product of racial consciousness resulting in a hostile work environment— for either one!). Employers should bear in mind that while race or national origin harassment may well result in a Title VII violation, physical violence related to employment may create a greater civil liability by charges of negligent hiring.

4. The condoning, encouraging, or acquiescence toward any form of racial or national origin harassment in general, or targeted against a particular employee beyond a singular and isolated incident (as determined in *EEOC v. Murphy Motor Freight Lines, Inc.* 1980).

Are There Penalties Or Other Sanctions Imposed Against Employers Found To Be Guilty Of Tolerating Harassment?

Yes, depending on 1) the severity or blatancy of the circumstances connected to the harassment, 2) the circumstances of the victim versus the offender, and 3) measures taken or not taken to correct it by the employer, both compensatory and punitive damages can be awarded to a victim. To illustrate different court approaches based on these factors, there were two 1985 cases and one 1986 case in which the court found the existence of both racial and national origin harassment, and insufficient correction by the employer.

In *Snell v. Suffolk County* (1985), white correctional officers were found to have continuously harassed their black and Hispanic coworkers through jokes, jests, and slurs, and that these acts were ignored by the warden who also failed to take reasonable steps to correct the situation. The court ordered three measures to be taken: 1) that racial, ethnic, and religious slurs be henceforth prohibited; 2) that the warden make it known that future offenders will be severely disciplined; and 3) that improved methods for the filing of discrimination complaints be established. Overall, the result was mild, but remedial in intent, and demonstrative of moderately unacceptable behavior on the part of offenders and the employer (warden).

However, in *Erebia v. Chrysler Plastics Products Corp.* (1985), a Mexican-American supervisor was awarded $10,000 compensatory and $30,000 punitive damages as a result of upper management's *intentional* discrimination due to their failure to act when the supervisor reported various situations in which subordinates repeatedly referred to him as a "wetback" and made other ethnic slurs toward him. When the supervisor reported these incidents to upper management, he was told to ignore the remarks and regard them as mere "shop talk". The court chose not to take such a passive approach to the situation, and levied a punitive damage award to express their disdain for such an unreasonable solution by the employer.

Third, in *Hunter v. Allis-Chalmers Corp.* (1986), a federal appeals court found the employer guilty of "a vicious campaign of racial harassment" for failing to take desist measures against employees working with a black male employed as an engine tester, and therefore liable for the prolonged "barrage of racist acts, epithets, and threats" toward the black worker. In 1979, after six years of employment and notice to supervisors of these harassing incidents such as writing "the KKK is not dead, nigger" on bulletin boards and restroom walls, some of which were due to his outperforming white employees, he filed a complaint with the Illinois Fair Employment Practices Commission.

Shortly thereafter, he began to receive disciplinary actions by supervisors and was eventually fined for allegedly falsifying test records. Evidence later established that such record irregularities were common and that it was not the normal practice to discipline testers for these errors. The court found the firing to therefore be a pretextual cause for his release, and held the employer further liable for knowingly subjecting the employee to racial slurs that was "so egregious, numerous, and concentrated as to add up to a campaign of harassment." The court held the employer liable for $25,000 punitive damages, $25,000 for emotional distress to the plaintiff, and three years back wages. If these damages aren't enough to get your attention, then consider such additional issues as the employers collective attorney fees, administrative time dedicated to the complaint process, what happened to the employee's supervisor, the reaction of employees, and the negative publicity received by the employer that impacts their business. See also *Robinson v. Hewlett-Packard Corp.* (1986).

In addition to the obvious need for employers to establish personnel policies prohibiting racial and ethnic harassment of any kind between all employees, and periodic training of supervisors to handle these situations (both of which are required of government contractors subject to Executive Order 11246), it is equally crucial for employers to establish and publicize the existence of a complaint system that easily accommodates the filing of such matters. The complaint system should include timely and vigorous investigation of the complaint, documentation of findings, and specific action taken or conclusions reached. If appropriate to serious offenses based on the types of conditions and elements previously described, disciplinary action including termination should be considered.

Should Employers Use An Affirmative Action Plan Or Other Agreements In Layoffs To Maintain Racial Balance?

Employers are cautioned that there remains considerable legal debate among various court jurisdictions about the manner in which affirmative action plans (AAP) or similar agreements (e.g., collective bargaining) can or should be used to make hiring, promotion, or layoff decisions. It is advisable for employers to review earlier precedent decisions in this area to gain more insightful context of this issue in conjunction with the case that follows; particular review should be given to:

Bakke v. Regents of the University of California, Davis (1978)
Weber v. Steelworkers (1981)
Stotts v. Fire Fighters Local 1984 (1984)[7]

The collective effect of these cases seem to suggest that the application and resultant decisions of affirmative action plans hinge on:

1. That voluntary affirmative action developments are aimed at remedying present minority and other inbalances in the employer's workforce.

2. That employment decisions made in light of the affirmative action plan goals do not infringe upon, or otherwise displace, non-minority employees.

3. That fixing of hiring quotas without an official determination (court or administrative agency) of present inbalance due to past discrimination under voluntary affirmative action plans being unwarranted and therefore unlawful.

4. That seniority systems used to determine layoffs be viewed as an inherently color-blind device to protect employee rights, however that in itself will not necessarily be an impediment to the courts granting prior seniority to individual minority group members who show they have been specific victims of discrimination.

The relationship between affirmative action and its discriminatory effects during layoffs—whether toward specific minorities or whites generally as reverse discrimination—continues to be inextricably intertwined. This can be no more clearly demonstrated than in the *Wygant* case where the U.S. Supreme Court addresses a public sector dilemma between affirmative action and layoffs. In *Wygant v. Jackson Board of Education* (1986), the Supreme Court held that a collective bargaining agreement provision requiring a proportional number of minorities to whites be released in the event of a layoff, regardless of seniority, was unconstitutional based on the Equal Protection Clause of the U.S. Constitution. The fact that, so far, only public employers are subject to that constitutional provision and therefore, the court's decision becomes applicable only to public employers, it suggests that the same rationale will likely be applied to a factually similar situation emanating from the private sector. Private sector employers should thusly heed the circumstance of this case, and take preventative measures to avoid becoming the private sector test case. Here are the circumstances associated with this case, presented in the classic pattern of sequential, if not frustrating, justice.

---

[7] A synopsis of these cases can be found in Levesque, *Manual Of Personnel Policies, Procedures, And Operations*. New Jersey, Prentice-Hall, 1986, pp. 322-325.

Some Background:

During the mid-1970's, the school board became mindful of its affirmative action goals and decided to establish a contract provision with the teacher's union that would extend some additional protection to more recently hired minorities by requiring that, during any layoff, minority teachers would be laid off in their proportion to white teachers even though white teachers held a disproportionate amount of seniority. The stage was set. During the ensuing years, there was some concern by white teachers but no changes to the contract provision were effectuated—people tend not to get too excited about things that don't affect them, until it does! When the school district announced its plans to commence teacher layoffs, suddenly the reality of the contractual mechanism became more vivid. Through vigorous protests, the white teachers convinced the school board to set aside the union contract and use strict seniority as the layoff mechanism. The union and two minority teachers brought suit.

Round 1: Federal District Court

Case dismissed based on the union's inability to establish that the school district had engaged in discriminatory hiring *prior* to, or as a condition of, negotiating the contract provision.

Minority teachers remain laid off.

Round 2: State Court

The union seeks enforcement of the collective bargaining agreement as a matter of contract law. Even though the state court came to the same conclusion as the district court, it determined that the contract, and not seniority, should be used for layoffs because of their contractual attempt to arrive at a legitimate remedy to the effects of "societal" discrimination.

White teachers are laid off and minority teachers with less seniority are reinstated.

Round 3: Back to the Federal District Court

Laid off white teachers request relief from the contract provision based on their allegation that it violates their constitutional rights under the Equal Protection Clause. The court ruled in favor of the contract provision (the employer) based on a determination that racial preferences do not have to be based on a prior finding of discriminatory hiring practices, but can be used to merely ameliorate the effects of societal discrimination and such is not violative of the Equal Protection Clause.

White teachers remain laid off.

Round 4: Sixth Circuit Court of Appeals

The court reaffirms the trial court's conclusion.

Round 5: U.S. Supreme Court

Laid off white teachers make their final appeal. The court concludes that societal discrimination alone is not a sufficiently compelling purpose (there must be convincing official evidence of past discrimination by the employer) to justify the use of racial preferences in an affirmative action plan that has as part of its use the layoff of employees. The court further notes that there was less intrusive means available to the school district to effectuate increased representation of minority teachers, principally through hiring goals. In other words, the court makes the distinction between the lesser consequence of not being hired as an effect of discrimination, to that of loosing the entitlements afforded by employment through the discriminatory lose of employment.

Conclusion:

Unless the employer is under a compelling court or other official order to remedy the effects of established past discrimination, race should not enter into layoff mechanisms. While the courts have generally not infringed upon bona fide seniority systems used as a determinant in layoffs, seniority is not required by law to be used in layoff decisions.

Moreover, the court's decision makes a rather indirect assertion that hiring goals, and perhaps even preferences, are legal as a remedy so long as past discrimination has been officially determined to be caused by inadequate hiring practices. Layoffs, however, are another matter and the high court now tells us that race (or ethnic classification) should not be a part of that mechanism.

Solution:

This and other U.S. Supreme Court decisions suggest that employers should give consideration to the following actions:

1. Those employers not required to adopt affirmative action plans (i.e., those that are not public employers, governmental contractors, and those under a consent court order) may be well advised to avoid creating one, or abolish voluntarily adopted plans.

2. Employers required to have affirmative action plans should consider deletion of any application to layoffs and focus on the manner in which minority representation can achieve parity through changes in hiring and other personnel practices.

Can Companies Who Merge Or Acquire Another Company Be Liable For Predecessor Discrimination?

Yes, according to the Seventh Circuit Court of Appeals in *Musikiwamba v. ESSI, Inc.* (1985) wherein the court held that the doctrine of successorship is applicable to employment discrimination under Section 1981 of the 1866 Act. The successorship doctrine was established under the National Labor Relations Act (29 USC 151 et seq.)

and requires that, under certain conditions, a successor employer assumes the obligations and liabilities of the predecessor. Three conditions must be present:

1. The successor must have had notice of the charge, or pending legal action, prior to acquisition of the predecessor's business;

2. The predecessor must be unable to provide relief; *and*

3. There must be considerable continuity of business operations by the successor employer through use of the same facility, equipment, and workforce.

As a result of this decision, companies considering the purchase or merger with another business ought to give careful attention to any type of known or pending litigation, and require that the predecessor attest in writing to their knowledge of these liabilities.

2.40 SUMMARIZING THE ORGANIZATIONAL IMPACT OF DISCRIMINATION TOWARD MINORITIES: WHAT CAN BE DONE TO SOLVE THE PROBLEM?

History, or historical events, can be viewed in two ways: one is the factual recounting of what took place for no other purpose than to know about events; the other leads us to a better understanding of the present, and may, in turn, lead us to conjecture about future probabilities. The former is merely *knowing about* the past, the latter uses this information as *learning* for present and future application. If we can at least agree that racial and ethnic history in the United States has been seriously less than that deserving of the most affluent and educated society in the world, then perhaps we ought to question whether we merely know about our social history or if anything has been learned at all. If learning has occurred, how are we applying this information to our present advantage, and why do racial and ethnic distinctions persist by manifest discriminatory conduct in the workplace? Perhaps the answer is that some have learned while there remains others who merely know, but choose not to yield. Clearly, those who cannot or will not learn from the past are destined to become a part of its repetition.

In the 25 years prior to enactment of the Civil Rights Act of 1964, this country ironically became engaged in a worldwide war whose initial threat was political racism. Yet during the same period, American social history is repleat with incidents of internment, racial violence, and widespread civil disobedience in cities small and large spanning the continent.

Some would have us believe that the mere existence of a democratically governed society, with its egalitarian promises, can produce revolutionary results from the parched pages of congressional law or supreme court rulings concerning the manner in which an altogether heterogenious society thinks and behaves. History, being the actual rather than intended events, on the other hand, suggests that we have grossly underestimated the more influential, if not pervasive elements of power, control, socio-economics, cultural variation in values, and the willingness to seek independence from constraints by fighting for one's principles. Absent true equality, there remains only true persecution. Whether it takes the form of racism, antisemitism, white superiority, or ethnic prejudices, or whether it manifests itself in employment, housing, education, or public accommodations, the end result remains the same—a refusal to accept the differences between people.

History has shown that reducing social values to a state of unlawfulness does not correct the problem. Only the changing of social values and the end to prejudicial treatment can solve the problem. Like other human traits conditioned over time, the response to change has, and will continue to take time, but it will change. It will, that is, so long as the nation as a whole remains relentless toward its 200 year old goal to achieve equality among its people. While laws and their interpretive court decisions may not, in and of themselves, eliminate such problems as those associated with discrimination, they have done one very important thing: they create a national public awareness of the types of discrimination that will not be tolerated, and the (adjudicary) mechanism to deal with it. So, while the Civil Rights Act of 1964 and its amendments has not put an end to the societal ferment over discriminatory, prejudicial conduct, it did shift emotional public attention from politicians back to those effected by such inequities.

Since then, the "demonstrations" have taken place, person by person and situation by situation, in the courts and by compliance agencies. Stated another way, when the emergence of a problem is accommodated by a remedial mechanism, the problem will have the appearance of being solved—sometimes because its novelty or notoriety fades, and sometimes because we believe that it is truly a more effective way of isolating particular problems. Perhaps one day we will reach a state of one mindedness where the discussion of racial and other forms of equality will be as fruitless as past debates over heredity and environment—after awhile we must question what point is to be made!

That question should have been posed to the many residents of Cumming, Georgia in January 1987 when blacks and other civil rights activists were jeered and hit with rocks as they proceeded through the town that has not had a black resident since they were run out in 1912 after an 18 year old white farm girl died from an alleged beating by three black youths. Change is not easy when exaggerated by emotional attachments, but change must remain certain in its direction toward the improvement of conditions, lest we have learned nothing and will prosper similarly.

Having examined the problem of racial and ethnic discrimination from a historical, political, socio-economic, and legal context, it is fitting to conclude this chapter with a brief yet insightful view of how minorities are affected by organizational values and behaviors once they are brought into the structure. The impact can be as dramatic as visiting a foreign land since, for many minorities, that is precisely what the experience represents. It is for this reason that all managers should be more in tune with the attendant psychological conditions in order to improve their effectiveness in preventing or handling problems that so often accompany the introduction of minority employees into a predominantly non-minority workplace. It is also fitting to draw this illustration from those who have personal, more qualified experience than I.

The first example is that of a black manager recalling his initial employment with a corporation following graduation. What started out to be youthful excitement about an aspiring career, quickly turned into rather vivid experiences of his difference, and the struggle to adjust and achieve acceptance.

> My tension increased as I was repeatedly called on to be the in-house expert on anything pertaining to civil rights. I was proud to be black and had many opinions about civil rights, but I did not feel qualified to give "the" black opinion. I developed the feeling that I was considered a black first and an individual second by many of the people I came into contact with. This feeling was exacerbated by the curious executive visitors to the training class who had to be introduced to everyone except me. Everyone knew my name and I constantly had the feeling of being on stage.[8]

In recalling his early years with the company and his difficulty concerning performance comments by several white superiors, he notes:

> I was not knowingly insensitive to other people or intent on antagonizing them. What this man and others failed to realize was that being a black man in a unique position in a white company, I was extremely tense and ill at ease. Levels of sensitivity, polish, and tact, which were foreign to me, were now necessities of life. The world of white business presented me with an elaborate socio-political organizaiton that required unfamiliar codes of behavior...it is critical that companies understand this point, for it indicates the need for increased guidance to help blacks adjust to an alien set of norms and behavioral requirements...One of the phenomena that develops in every corporation is a set of behavioral and personal norms that facilitates communication and aids cohesiveness, moreover because this "informal organization" is built on white norms, they can reinforce the black-white differences just mentioned and thus reject or destroy all but the most persistant blacks.

> The informal organization operates at all levels in a corporation and the norms become more rigid the higher one goes in the hierarchy. While this phenomena promotes efficiency and unity, it is also restrictive and very selective. It can preclude promotion or lead to failure on the basis of "fit" rather than competence.

It is presently speculated that three-fourths of the growth in the U.S. labor market during the late 1980's and through the 1990's will be attributable to women and minori-

---

[8] Jones, Edward W., Jr.; "What It's Like To Be A Black Manager" in *The Executive Dilemma*, Harvard Business Review, N.Y.: John Wiley & Sons, 1985, p. 212-219.

ties. Simply stated, if companies hope to remain competitive, they will have to put more effort into creating a conducive, supportive environment for minority workforce members to feel there is at least open minded opportunities for inclusion, promotion, and success.

Those of you who are aware of the existence of workplace discrimination based on prejudicial conduct or bias against minorities, it is time to come forward by letting those that can do something about it know about the circumstances. To assure the utmost confidentiality and discretion, this kind of information ought to be conveyed jointly to the human resource manager and company president. In addition to sharing the details of your observations, you should be prepared to offer your insight into how the situation might be best approached, including the traits of those involved. As a former personnel director and current consultant called upon in numerous situations of this type, I can assure you that the solution to these problems lies in confronting and dealing with them from the same objective evaluation as given to any business problem. One of the greatest problems many organizations have is acquiring information early enough to resolve it internally. Left unattended, any problem will worsen and you can count on it pertaining to situations involving the perception and interaction of people with different values, cultures, languages, and appearances. Upper management must, of necessity, rely on those who have access to troublesome situations to bring them forward for early correction—without regard to territorial responsibility.

From the view of those effected by discrimination in the workplace, their entire world becomes threatened and it should not be surprising that corresponding defensive behavior will ensue. Whether the effect is unwarranted employment rejection, promotional pass-over, intentional harassment, or conspicuous employment separation, the cause will almost always seem to be the minority employee's race, color, national origin, or a similar distinguishing personal characteristic. This is not to imply that minorities should be given preferential treatment in these employment conditions— merely equal opportunity and to be treated based on individual ability. On the other hand, those employers who recognize that their workforce is far from an appropriate representation of the available minority labor force would do well to commence more affirmative measures in their recruitment of job vacancies at all levels to begin achieving a more unbiased balance of what should have occurred naturally in an objective recruitment and selection process.

The same holds true in cases of layoffs, yet the dichotomy exists for many companies who will work vigorously toward hiring more minorities while at the same time holding their time honored seniority system reverent, which later becomes the Achilles' Heel for more recently hired minorities. Let's face it, good employees don't need to hide behind the kind of artificial protection afforded by a seniority system. Seniority systems have outlived their purpose, and they stand as one of the sorest contradictions to employment based on ability and continuing fitness. If American business is to succeed as an economic way of life and a morally-conscious segment of society, it must hire, promote, and otherwise deal with all people based on their individual abilities, and upon their performance outcomes. Here are a few specific ways in which this can be achieved, and race-related problems either prevented or solved without undue repercussions.

1. Make your organization color and racially blind by adopting firm philosophies that communicates the organization's commitment to employing any individual who demonstrates desired abilities.

2. Hire and promote into supervision and management jobs only those people whose inclinations toward others is positive and without strong proclivity toward adverse forms of discrimination.

3. Provide thorough and regular training of supervisors and managers on human relations, legal issues associated with employment discrimination, organizational policies, and how to handle discrimination problems.

4. Make it clear to supervisors and managers that it is their job to ensure a discrimination free workplace, and that they are to confront and promptly resolve acts of discrimination including jokes, harassment (however mild), and investigate rumors and complaints.

5. Ensure that job descriptions, recruiting standards and selection examinations, and all job conditions do not arbitrarily create artificial barriers for minority employment.

6. Rather than develop a voluntary affirmative action plan (AAP), prepare an annual audit report reflecting the workforce composition compared to the available labor market composition; where improvements in workforce parity could be made and by what measures; and identify other efforts that ought to be taken to achieve the goal of meaningful equal employment opportunity.

7. Review personnel policies and operating standards periodically in light of the potential for a discriminatory effect, particularly with regard to hiring, pay, promotions, benefits, layoffs, and other practices that often give rise to discrimination events, however unintentional they may be.

8. Determine if English Only rules serve a legitimate business interest. Establish them only where they are valid and can be defended from a business necessity point of view, then communicate the policy to all employees but allow some forgiveness for minor infractions.

9. Require that all personnel actions are centrally reviewed and approved by a human resource professional or other knowledgeable person to ensure objectivity and consistency of decisions, particularly as they relate to new hires, pay setting and increases, performance appraisals, promotions, disciplinary actions, layoffs, and terminations/resignations.

10. Use the human resource department as an internal consulting service, or external sources when qualified staff is not available, to obtain advice and assistance on vulnerable personnel actions *prior* to deciding or acting on them. Most human resource professionals prefer the service role over the control role, and they are trained in ways to make organizations run smoothly.

11. Establish an "administrative review" procedure that encourages employees to take complaints to higher management; requires them to bring forth any condition related to discrimination including harassment; and you may want to add the required reporting of such conditions as malfeasance, dishonesty, theft, and the like.

12. Ensure that both federal and state antidiscrimination posters are displayed on bulletin boards at each work location in a prominent place.

13. Where seniority is a matter of policy or practice for the purpose of any employment decision, expert legal counsel should be consulted before drafting or using such a policy, including the construction of seniority clauses in collective bargaining agreements. Although some courts have intimated that organization-wide seniority is less likely to be discriminatory than job or departmental seniority, the inverse would be more accurate since employees with longer total service are more likely to be the beneficiaries of past practice discrimination.

14. Do not use race, color, national origin, or any other protected characteristic of employees as a determining factor in layoff plans for the purpose of maintaining parity in the remaining workforce. When such factors are used they become the basis of liability for reverse discrimination, unless of course there exists a substantial inbalance in the workforce and such factors are used to overcome this effect, or where the organization is under authoritative order to maintain parity. In the absence of these two exceptions, organizations confronting a layoff (or downsizing as some prefer to call it) would be better off using performance and other job factors to determine who among any group of employees is to be laid off.

CHAPTER I: 3.0
PROBLEMS ASSOCIATED WITH GENDER DISCRIMINATION, SEXUAL HARASSMENT, AND ROMANCE IN THE WORKPLACE

In furtherance of society's goal to eliminate all arbitrary forms of discrimination from employment decisions and workplace events, there has evolved a substantial number of laws and court decisions that prohibit employers from acting adversely against employees due to their gender related discrimination, and in many states sexual orientation (homosexuality) and marital status. Other associated problems being encountered by most employers include workplace romances and accommodating the child care needs of a workforce creating this demand in order to participate in the labor market.

Conversely, organizational managers are struggling to find answers that will resolve these kinds of problems. Some of these measures include recruiting females into nontraditional jobs, validating preemployment tests, adopting strict nonharassment policies and complaint procedures, establishing antinepotism rules, adopting flex schedules and liberalizing maternity/paternity leaves, and generally attempting to discourage workplace paramours.

These are difficult but very real issues for every manager in today's workplace, and Chapters I: 3 and 4 will provide the reader with the necessary background, diagnostic insight, and problem solving approaches to deal more effectively with these delicate matters.

There exists a strong parallel between female and racial discrimination, both generally and in particular to employment conditions, since both women and racial groups represent a type-specific class of people that has been historically a minority member of an otherwise predominantly white male workforce. Quite similar to ethnic minorities, we are faced with the very real issue that women as a group have been subjected to various forms of inequitable employment treatment for decades. There have been countless arguments for and against this conclusion but, today, it serves little purpose to be argumentative about this fact in light of the evidence brought forth in successive studies, scientific literature, through judicial reviews, and publicity that now unequivocally supports such a conclusion. This chapter examines how such problems have evolved, occur in employment decision making, and can be solved if managed properly.

3.10 THE UNDERLYING ISSUES AND CONDITIONS OF GENDER RELATED DISCRIMINATION

Much of the discrimination that has disadvantaged those women seeking employment opportunities, whether out of desire or economic need, has taken the form of exclusion from predominantly male jobs or being cast into subordinate jobs based on what has been regarded as traditional life-pattern expectations of women. Like so many other aspects of the human condition, and more specially our contemporary society, we as human resource and other kinds of managers are quickly coming to realize that what may have once been traditional can so very rapidly become obsolete, and before we notice turn into myth. No doubt, one of the strongest, most stigmatizing myths about women in general today is their presumed life-pattern which suggests that the real social role of women is that of housewife, mother, and only supplemental wage earner with few skills, little ambition toward business world interests, and marginal education. As psychologist Jane Torrey puts it:

> Like other elements of prejudice, this pattern is attributed to every woman regardless of her individual situation and regardless of the fact that increasing numbers of women do not follow this pattern. If a woman is, in reality, single, it is still assumed that she will marry and quit. If childless, she is expected to become a mother and quit. If she is already a mother, it is decided for her that she will soon [or inevitably] leave employment to become a housewife. Her salary and her credit standing are decided on this basis, even if her husband is unemployable and she is the sole support of her family. Women are expected to quit their paid jobs because of some irresistible, instinctual lure of motherhood, even though statistics show that the better the job (the higher the status and pay), the less likely it is that a young mother will quit to become a housewife. If a valued male employee quits, his employer asks himself what could have been done to keep him. If a valued woman quits, it is assumed that nothing could have been done, that she is merely following the typical life-pattern of women. It is assumed that her commitment to the work was low because she was a woman, never because it was a low-pay, low-status, no-future job.[1]

---

[1] Torrey, Jane W.; "A Psychologist's Look At Women" in Beach, Dale S.; *People And Productivity*, p. 147.

EMERGE CONDITION #1: Women tend to be collectively grouped by many men holding employment decision making authority into the presumed life-pattern of transient workforce member whose true interest, if not instinctive lot in life, is the role of housewife, mother, and social centerpiece. While this prescription for happiness and fulfillment may be true for some women, it is clearly not accurate for many others as will be elaborated on in the next section.

We should also recognize that, at times, there arises the condition to separate ourselves as managers from what we are, and how we think and act as individuals based on our own set of values, beliefs, customs, and methods. Indeed, one of our own problems and those within our organizations may be the belief that the role of individual and the role of manager are separable. They are not. We ought to come to grips with the fact that what our managers are as people, they will be like as managers, including their fundamental beliefs, behaviors, decision making processes, and communications styles.

One such characteristic of managers that tends to provoke bias actions and thinking is emotional response (attitudinal maturity) toward situations in which they hold some type of vested belief that is outside the range of open-mindedness. It is typically these individuals who are identifiable by their particularly noticable reaction to such emotionally tainted terms as racism, sexism, and feminism. With some managers, you might just as well call them (or imply they are) communists instead of chauvinists or antifeminists. Terms and labels such as these may be worn proudly by proponents, but they attack the very self-image shield many opponents carry around them to protect their own sense of righteousness. Arousing their emotions in a way that triggers a self-protection retaliation serves no positive purpose, but it will continue to reinforce and perpetuate negative behavior!

EMERGE CONDITION #2: The beliefs and conditioning that makes us (men and women) what we are as individuals is part of what we are as managers and business decision makers. Some have biases about certain things, others have biases about different things. Biases are passive, prejudices are not. Prejudices evoke emotional responses, whether conscious or unconscious. When the emotional response unjustifiably disfavors someone, discrimination results and our thinking as to what decision best favors the organization is dampened by the obscuring of our objectivity. It certainly should be no surprise to recognize that we all have human frailties; that one of them can tend to be a judgment and decision making blindspot; and that recognizing it should be followed by a reexamination of our view toward the issue, gaining more experience with it, or by compensating for it through monitoring our own actions (retraining our behavior).

Just as men have tended to see women in light of the traditional life-pattern, women have tended to see men as uniformly tunnel visioned and stigmatizing. What may come as something of a surprise to many women is that men have been acting on long standing biases about other men in matters of hiring and moreso promotion. Men have tended to exclude other men (even of the same race) due to height (taller is better), voice (deeper and commanding is best for upper management potentials, while confident but humble for lower management positions), hair and dress (meeting the desired corporate image), and school attended (Yale and Stanford are on their way out, Harvard and USC are in—particularly if you worked your way through!).

These, too, are traditional values held by now obsolete corporate Americans who have failed to keep abreast of social, economic, and demographic conditions that have reshaped the American workforce during the 1960's period. Regardless of the culprit or the victim, discrimination will result any time a person is evaluated on personal characteristics rather than individual talent, preparation, ability, and adaptation to the conditions of any given job.

We must also give recognition to the fact that not all women have ascribed nor otherwise endorsed the women's liberation principles, goals, or actions. Clearly, women as a group (if such a thing exists any more than men as a group) are heavily divided in their attitudes toward those feminists who advocate that Domestic Woman is as passive as Neanderthal Man, and that such women are oppressed victims of male domination—this is about as close to childlike name calling as one can get for the purpose of eliciting a favorable response based on guilt or the presumed inability by one for another to think and decide on their own behalf.

Feminists are no more representative or demagogical of all women than is Archie Bunker for all men. This is to say that there will always be the likelihood that many women will continue to make the free and well thought out choice of a family career, others will elect a business career, while yet others may wish to pursue concurrent or successive family-business careers. The point to be made is that whichever choice is made, or changes pursued, the business world should evaluate and treat women on the basis of ability and results, not on intent, motives, life-pattern, or potential for exploitation of any kind.

EMERGE CONDITION #3: Men have long held many biases toward other men in employment situations, and women likewise continue to hold many biases toward other women about career, economic and social position, and how change should occur. Neither is more correct than the other; both positions are inherently unfair, without factual and realistic basis of true conditions, and certainly not appropriate any longer to an altogether different society. In fact, it would be more fitting to conclude that there exists so much diversity among men and women's attitudes and desires for family, career, and other options that it would be difficult to find a male or female doctrine that thoroughly represents either. The "women's liberation movement" launched by feminists during the 1970's served the same useful purpose as did the civil rights demonstrations in the 1960's—it forced people to look at the need for changes in values, attitudes, and aspirations; it served as the catalyst for changes in laws and discriminatory employment practices; and it began the process of opening opportunities for those who elected to pursue them. Yet these changes are recent, they have been slow, and proponents impatient to overcome ingrained patterns of decision making.

Gender discrimination can be subtle or perhaps even undetected by those not closely examining the behaviors and practices within an organization, or it can be overt based on accepted norms by those in authority positions. In the former case, the absence of complaints or other equally visible signs that communicate gender discrimination problems (or their potential) can be easily taken as a content, non-victimized workforce. Quite the contrary may in fact be the real case simply because of such temporary conditions as:

- Present female workers may not see themselves as victims. It is not uncommon in some types of businesses for entry level and supervisory positions to be occupied by passive women who are grateful for the opportunity to work, and overlook other kinds of sexual discrimination going on around them.

- Some employees are still unaware of how to recognize sexual and other forms of discrimination. Sexist job requirements, male dominated jobs, differential leave and benefit policies, innuendo remarks of a sexual nature, and questions relating to personal status may seem harmless to some employees.

- Reactionary management is likely to make the mistake of taking the position that nothing is wrong until a problem is raised (by an employee), then we'll tackle it (i.e., fire the complainer or defend the law suit). Proactive management will initiate a diagnostic process even in the absence of symptoms and design a treatment plan that prevents such problems, thereby alleviating the prospect that employees become victims or effected by unjust operations.

Blatant and overt gender discrimination has in some organizations become a coveted way of business life. Some employees can handle it, some can't, most don't want to, and all usually know it's wrong. But it does exist, and more often than not because of the perpetrator's lack of training, the strength of their values and prejudice, their purposeful use of power to feed an otherwise weak ego, and a significant lack of maturity that would otherwise control such behavior or decision making. Blatant and overt discrimination is indicative of intent, and that normally requires a certain amount of conscious, deliberate action. Yet there are other types of coveted discrimination and they are most often found within the accepted (but not so maliciously intended) personnel decisions, practices, policies, and interaction customs that have been in existence for many years by companies. Examples include:

1. Type-casting women into traditionally female jobs such as clerk, teller, flight attendant, nurse, and similar occupations where the nature of the job is one of subordinancy and requires maternal diplomacy.

2. Pay, leave, and employment benefit policies that take into account or result in a particular advantage to one sex differently than the other. The singular exception might be pregnancy leave since it is a physical disability confined to women while other forms of physical disability can occur fairly equally between the sexes. In situations such as this, we might ask ourselves if there is any reason we could not set the same standards for the male employee recovering from prostrate surgery as the women who gives birth or undergoes a hysterectomy? If these are key employees, couldn't either handle a little work during their recovery?

   With regard to pay practices, employers should give careful and thoughtful scrutiny to the pattern of hiring rates among men and women, as well as the development of salaries based on the compensable factors of each job regardless of the sex of incumbents who customarily fill such positions. Similar analysis should be given to insurance and other benefit plans to eliminate such subtle forms of sex discrimination as differing premium or benefit rates due to sex-based actuarials.

3. Promotion decisions based on a presumptive conclusion that a woman (or man) would not be able to handle the situation as well as the man (or woman). Many an appointive decision maker willing to venture beyond traditional assumptions has been pleasantly surprised to find that some women are well suited to higher level and unusual types of jobs previously regarded as an exclusive male occupation or set of conditions (pilot, doctor, lawyer, chief executive officer, and head of state).

4. Routine interpersonal behavior that condones sex stereotyping, yet disrespectful behavior that would not otherwise be tolerated in a different (social) setting. Included here are such activities as referring to women as "girls" or a particular woman as "dear", "sweetheart", "honey", or similar subordinancy terms; referring or commenting on another person's anatomy in a sexual nature; patting a person's buttox or similar touching; making sexually suggestive or explicit remarks; and requesting or requiring sexual encounters with another person are a few illustrations of the behavior between men and women that

undermines effective working relationships. These behaviors may be acceptable by some people in certain other settings, but they have no place in the business environment; and that's an important distinction between workplace versus personal time conduct.

EMERGE CONDITION #4: While many changes have been made to remove and alter sex-based discrimination, there remains many other forms that are institutional in nature: they are ingrained in the behavior of decision makers and their subordinate employees; they have become a part of operating policy and practice, and many employees are either unaware or unconcerned about the prospect of being (or becoming) victimized by its effect. Some employers will proactively change as they discover problems of these types, some will change under protest conditions, while others would rather fight than alter the sanctimony of dominant control in every aspect of their role as employer. As regrettable as many managers and employees find it, behavioral and systemic problems still exist within many organizations and it has the effect of perpetuating inequitable conditions and disrespectful treatment of women. If not addressed and altered, the organization will indeed remain in a productivity dark age that will seriously impede its efficient use of human resources due to deteriorated working relationships as evidenced by high turnover, absenteeism, low morale, and a poor community reputation.

Psychologically, humans are social animals that require particular kinds of treatment and activities to feel nourished. In that process, our behavior tends to be shaped by our personality traits, experiences, and how we perceive things. Biologically, humans differ by sex and gender make-up characteristics. The combination of psychological and biological conditions that exist within each person makes them uniquely different from any other person, and it is this difference that translates to sometimes very complex interactions between people, decisions made by individuals, and reactions to varying situations.

On occasion, the result will look like discrimination but it isn't; it may look like it but it wasn't the intent or purpose to do so; it may be unavoidable discrimination; or it may be the vestiges of coveted bias and unconcerned prejudice. We would all find ourselves in a more equitable work atmosphere if we would merely support and utilize those positive differences rather than wasting time criticizing what each views as negative differences about the other. It's a condition to be reckoned with rather than avoided as if it will not affect operations or that it will be one of those things that, given time, will resolve itself.

Women have come into their own as a very real, worthy, needed, and permanent contributor to the workforce. As managers of our organization's human resources, it is time to begin the inclusion process by more thorough use and development of this source of labor supply, to identify and alter those barriers to the equitable employment condition of both sexes, and to create an organizational model in which both sexes can identify comfortable patterns of behavior, opportunity, and ultimately equality to the extent that is possible, not improbable.

3.11 WOMEN AS PERMANENT WORKFORCE MEMBERS

At the turn of the century, and prior to adoption of the Eighteenth Amendment by which our previously proclaimed egalitarian government granted women the right to vote, some 20 percent of the workforce were women. Jobs and prevalent life styles were very different in those years; in fact, during that period clerical jobs were some of the highest paid salary positions but reserved for men because they had families to support and job tasks required mathematic, writing, and thinking skills not common to women (education beyond the eighth grade, where available, was often frowned on for women since it was their duty to marry and bear children, whereas men needed work skills). Life was often described as simply meaning that values were clear, roles narrow but well defined, expectations and rewards few, and hope reigned eternal so to speak. Simple did not mean easy. The period required hard work—predominantly physical—and long hours for men and women alike whether the work was farming, manufacturing or merchantile. Work was equally hard and prolonged for women occupied by arduous domestic tasks.

By 1940, technology began to take root through consumerism by providing a number of modernized household appliances, and high school education was the desired conclusion for women's premarital lives. Post high school educations by women were few and generally regarded as mavericks, rebellious, and in other ways out of social character. Workforce representation by women grew to only 29 percent of which 15 percent were married, thereby providing second full-time incomes to the family unit. In the succeeding years, a well known employment anomaly occurred as the result of several hundred thousand men being called into wartime military service leaving women to work in war effort factories, gas stations, banks, stores, and virtually all types of enterprise. These were, of course, essentially worker level positions since wartime service only calls upon young men leaving the older, well established men to continue operating and managing the nation's businesses.

When World War II ended and servicemen returned home to resume their civilian lives, there was an national effort to create the social and patriotic expectation for women to leave their jobs to make room for returning veterans. Politically, it was an expedient campaign to transition from the massive wartime mobilization of men to military service and women to assume the jobs of absent men, back to a peacetime society. Women obliged by returning to domestic roles, and the country turned its attention to the development of happier days, almost miraculously forgetting that women of all walks successfully performed predominately male jobs for the better part of six years. How quickly we forget, and how easy it is to fall back into role expectations. By 1950, women's participation in the workforce had fallen to a mere 14 percent and most of them were heads of households, widows, and singles.

The 1960's and 1970's were marked as a two decade period of social change, and the women's liberation movement—sometimes considered equally liberating for men— was quick to follow the national awareness of social issues initiated by civil rights activitists. Feminists denounced male dominance in general, along with the inequities suffered by women in employment, education, housing, credit, and the like. They advocated the need for women to pursue education before marriage, for men to share in domestic responsibilities, for equality in employment opportunities and conditions, and in other ways for women to shed those ideals, lifestyles, and patterns of behavior that were simply reinforcing their acceptance of being treated as second class people.

Betty Friedan, the patriarchial mother of modern feminism, author (*The Feminine Mystique*, 1963 and *The Second Stage*, 1981), and one of the founders of the National Organization of Women (NOW), who is presently in her late 60's and a grandmother, says that her generation possessed a rather uniform proclivity to want the family sup- port role. That is, it was simply the natural order of things for women to identify their purpose as marrying, childrearing, and attending to domestic chores; sort of a Step- ford Wife was the reinforced value for women of the time. Friedan reflects back on the generation that followed (1960's), identifying this group of women as those who evolved into a new version of the support role by working to help put their husbands through college or get established in a new career, and thereby willing to delay child- birth and related acquisition plans in hopes that this early preparation would lead to a brighter, more secure future in which their later domestic role would be secure if not picturesque. Those born after World War II and into the 1950's became the real bene- ficiaries of the 1960's-1970's women's liberation movement. They came into a world aware that there were choices and options to be examined and exercised by women.

Not suddenly but at least progressively, more young women began to see via the "male model" that getting a college education would lead to better competition for employment opportunities, and that family decisions could always be pursued later— if at all. They began to see and accept that social value need not be attached solely to the family support role, and personal achievement, fulfillment, and economic security could be realized by individual effort. The need for the latter—economic security— became concurrently vivid for women who predominantly occupied lower paid jobs but had to suffer the effects of a rapid inflationary economy during the 1970's through the early 1980's (gas shortages, interest rates, housing and transportation costs, etc.). This major economic shift, coupled with the underlying principles of women's libera- tion, was to thereafter become a significant ingredient in the education-career-lifestyle decision making process for generations to come.

In her book *The Second Stage*, Friedan depicts contemporary women in the aftermath of changes in the economy, technology, and strides made in employment equality and opportunity (examples of which were brought about voluntarily by some employers, and through litigation such as that illustrated throughout the remainder of this chapter with recalcitrant employers). She sees these women as deferring marriage into their mid 20's to early 30's and childbirth into their mid to late 30's when it becomes perilously risky to the health of both mother and child. These are the women said to have acquired the Superwoman Syndrome; i.e., wanting simultaneous professional career, soul mate (husband or other significant partner), and children in a more pronounced style of the new American dream consisting of two professional incomes, a custom home, distinguished cars, fashionable clothes, vogue furniture, electronic everything, and one or two bright children both parents can spoil rotten.

Also, she notes that fewer women are electing marriage and/or motherhood as a lifestyle, and that through divorce and other consequences more women are assuming the single parent head of household responsibility; and thus rounding out the diversity of needs, motives, and aspirations of a new breed of woman seeking employment not as an alternative or supplement to lifestyle incomes, but as a very real necessity of their own. So, by 1975 women in varying economic, educational, vocational, and lifestyle situations rose to an unanticipated 46 percent of the workforce. Of those working women, 30 percent were heads of households and another 44 percent were married.

By 1985, women's participation in the workforce surpassed the 50 percent mark and thereby exceeded the labor force representation held prominently by men for two centuries. Men rather suddenly have found themselves in the unusual position of being the minority workforce sex by a slight and probably stabilized margin reflective of the approximate proportion of the male/female population. The fact that women now participate equally or greater in the workforce than men is somewhat deceiving since women have been clustered in certain occupational strata:

> With respect to white collar jobs, women hold 78 percent of all clerical positions, 91 percent of all bank teller slots, and 87 percent of all bookkeeper jobs. Furthermore, those who hold administrative positions tend to occupy staff jobs...With respect to management jobs, Business Week reports that women comprise only 15 percent of entry level positions, 5 percent of middle level positions and barely one percent of the top level jobs.[2]

While the full ingress of women into a broader range of occupations is a yet incomplete process due to the fact that women are relative newcomers—even moreso than most ethnic minorities—it is fair to say that classical feminism has accomplished its initial goal of providing more economic choice, opportunities, acceptance as non-threatening equals, and the preliminary dismantling of paternal forms of discrimina-

---

[2] Woodworth; "The Female Takeover: Threat Or Opportunity", in Beach, Dale S., Managing People At Work. N.Y.: Macmillan, 1980, p. 76.

tion. Once again, we as managers have yet a different decision making choice: we can approach the issue of equality among the sexes as threats to cherished assumptions and stereotypic myth to be defended righteously; or we can approach the issue as an opportunity to share resources, decisions, skills and talents, and—if you will—the load of perplexing, strenuous, and stressful work. The one thing that remains certain is that we need all sorts of competent people, and those lacking should not be allowed to acquire ill-suited opportunities at the expense of any other more capable person.

In my own experience dealing with male and female professionals, managers, and executives over the last 15 years, I can earnestly conclude that there is no less competence among women than exists among men. Each must guard against impatience, expecting advantage without taking self development initiatives, taking on premature or ill-suited responsibilities, and trying to force outcomes to match their perceptions of how things ought to be. In this regard, it has become my considered belief that employers ought to engage in a thorough and widespread program of mentorship—placing new employees with the best performers to work closely and serve as a model, trainer, and advisor until the desired skill, knowledge, and behavior are assimilated.

In other words, as managers of our organizational resources, we need to start paying more attention to the installation of methods that contribute to desired results rather than assume they will occur merely by hiring followed by attempts to stay in control. We need to recognize and begin to accommodate the bulk of our employees, no less for men than women, who have many differing personal interests that they very much want to pursue outside of their employment be it a softball league, family events, educational classes, or civic affairs. What has been staring us in the face for some time now is the fact that today's employee is also more dedicated to their job than they are to the particular employer, and will change employers instead of occupations when the employer is insensitive, overbearing, unfair, inflexible, or absent new opportunities.

It should be clear to all managers and other types of decision makers involved in the economic future of our society that the American workforce is unlike that of past decades and is ever-changing. Today's mobile, multi-interested workforce places more demand for innovative employment practices and conditions on employers if they are to gather a labor pool that will put forth the effort, remain interested and motivated to apply themselves, and to feel a sense of loyalty and pride in their work. It will require the mutual recognition of new lifestyles of employees, productive work result needs of employers, the sharing of ideas to resolve problems and improve efficiency, and ultimately the equalizing of relationships as defined by the "organizational model". It is an undeniable fact, and consequence of a long social evolution process, that women have become a permanent, prominent member of the American workforce.

3.20 LEGAL PROHIBITIONS AGAINST
GENDER RELATED DISCRIMINATION

It is sometimes very difficult for human resource professionals and line managers to untangle what at times seems to be a complex array of federal and state laws prohibiting discrimination due to sex (gender). Most states have by now adopted their own version of federal antidiscrimination laws that equal or exceed federal statutes, and they are typically contained in comprehensive, singular legislation with periodic amendments. States also tend to enforce these "fair employment practice" laws by a singular enforcement agency. Not so at the federal level.

Essentially, there are three legal bases of gender-related discrimination at the federal level, and they consist of:

1. Federal Law
   1963   Equal Pay Act
   1964   Civil Rights Act, Title VII

2. Equal Employment Opportunity Commission Guidelines
   1966   On Discrimination Because of Sex
   1972   Revision on Discrimination Because of Sex
   1980   On Sexual Harassment Discrimination

3. Federal Court Decisions

The result of these legal authorities during the last 25 years has had a significant impact on the decision making policies and practices of countless employers, as well as presenting a rather vast number of routine operational problems for managers and human resource professionals alike. Generally, the most vulnerable and effected areas of the employment relationship are:

- Recruitment, screening, testing (particularly interviewing and medical exams), and selection.

- Promotion, demotion, transfer (including relocation), and layoff.

- Pay, insurance benefits, pension plans, and leaves.

- Performance appraisal, discipline, and termination.

- Behavioral conduct by others toward employees that creates an offensive work environment.

As you can see, this leaves very few of the day-to-day operations of any business immune from the potential for a complaint, claim, or legal suit by an employee who feels or perceives that an action by their employer (manager) has rendered them a victim of gender-related discrimination.

3.21 CHRONOLOGY OF FEDERAL LAWS AND REGULATIONS

The information contained in the discussion throughout the remainder of this section is intended to acquaint managers with the laws, legal principles, and ways in which to avoid or solve these kinds of problems. First, let's start with a basic overview of the chronology of guiding legal bases upon which gender-related discrimination becomes a prohibited activity in the workplace, and to establish a historically understandable order of events leading up to present conditions.

1963 – EQUAL PAY ACT: Although there were federal laws passed during World War II and earlier which formulated the current law under the EPA, they were generally regarded as weakly defined and difficult to enforce. As a result of growing social issues of equity, wage claims filed with the Department of Labor, and increased participation of women in the workforce during the late 1950's to early 1960's, the EPA was adopted as an amendment to the Fair Labor Standards Act. In the period of 1969-1972, the Department of Labor reported that claims filed (mostly women) nearly tripled, and awards likewise rose from $4.6 million to $14 million paid to some 29,022 individuals.

In 1972, positions classified as exempt under the FLSA (executive, administrative, professional, and outside sales) were held not to be excluded from the provisions of the EPA, and, in July 1979, enforcement of EPA violations was placed upon the EEOC. The EPA itself essentially requires "equal pay for equal work" for men and women doing the same or substantially similar work requiring equivalent skill, effort, and responsibility. The few exceptions allowed under the Act are:

> . . . where such payment is made pursuant to (i) a seniority system; (ii) a merit system; (iii) a system which measures earnings by quantity of production; or (iv) a differential based on any other factor other than sex: Provided, that an employer who is paying a wage rate differential in violation of this subsection shall not, in order to comply with the provision of this subsection, reduce the wage rate of any employee.

1964 – CIVIL RIGHTS ACT, TITLE VII: Once again, Title VII becomes the comprehensive basis for the prohibition and elimination of all types of discrimination in employment matters, including that based on gender-related discrimination (Section 7.3). As the result of subsequent amendments and court decisions, Title VII has evolved to cover gender induced decisions including those based on a person's homosexuality, pregnancy and related condition, and sexual harassment. Only state laws address issues related to marital status at the present time, but it should not be surprising to see a future amendment of this area to Title VII.

1966 – EEOC ISSUES GUIDELINES ON DISCRIMINATION BECAUSE OF SEX: Following adoption of the 1964 Civil Rights Act there naturally arose many substantive concerns and questions by employers. In response to such legislation the EEOC customarily issues guidelines printed in the Federal Register which is the enforcement agency's way of communicating definitions, explanations of prohibitions, compliance requirements, and procedural matters.

1971 – U.S. SUPREME COURT DECIDES *PHILLIPS V. MARTIN MARIETTA CORP.* **CASE:** In this early landmark decision, the Supreme Court held that a woman with pre-school age children had been subjected to unlawful sex discrimination, and that this condition did not constitute a "bona fide occupation qualification" (BFOQ) employer defense reasonably related to the performance of the position in question, nor exclusion therefrom. This was the case that quickly moved employers to alter interviewing questions (existence of children responsibilities, availability of child care, etc.), and to reexamine prior assumptions about absenteeism, sick leave use, and turnover of women with children.

OFFICE OF FEDERAL CONTRACT COMPLIANCE PROGRAM: Late in the same year, the OFCCP revised its Order No. 4 covering employers with government contracts to amend their affirmative action goals and timetables on increasing the number of women who were underrepresented or underutilized in their employ.

1972 – AMERICAN TELEPHONE & TELEGRAPH CO. enters into a $30 million dollar consent agreement to raise the initial pay of women promoted to managerial positions similarly to that received by men previously promoted, and to change pay setting policies to prevent a continuation of sex-based pay differentials.

1972 – EEOC AMENDS GUIDELINES ON DISCRIMINATION BECAUSE OF SEX: In reaction to a large number of Title VII and EPA claims filed and court decisions rendered since issuance of the 1966 Guidelines, the EEOC determined that there were a number of substantive issues to be redressed, elaborated upon, presented anew, and otherwise clarified. Included in this amendment was the EEOC's narrowing interpretation of the BFOQ reasoning or defense used to make adverse employment decisions because of one's sex, and thus making it nearly impossible for employers to contend that there was reasonable job or business conditions requiring one sex or the other.

1980 – EEOC ISSUES GUIDELINES ON SEXUAL HARASSMENT:[3] Sexual harassment in the the workplace has become a prominent issue for employers since the Equal Employment Opportunity Commission issued its November 1980 guidelines (Section

---

[3] Supplemented discussion taken from Levesque, Joseph D.; *Manual Of Personnel Policies, Procedures, And Operations*. N.J.: Prentice-Hall, 1986, pp. 299-300.

1604.11). This form of workplace conduct was brought within the meaning of sex discrimination under Title VII of the 1964 Civil Rights Act in at least two 1978 precedent court decisions. This is not to say that the issue of uninvited sexual conduct was less than prominent prior to regulatory involvement. Quite the contrary, for it is a well researched and longstanding fact that the workplace provides a diverse range of opportunities for men and women to develop an affinity, but it also provides unique problems that would not exist in situations other than the workplace.

The issuance of the 1980 EEOC guidelines on sexual harassment was in response to an alarming number of complaints by female employees that they were being sexually harassed and threatened with termination or other retaliatory measures by male supervisors. The intent of the guidelines was to establish the definitions, standards, and conditions of sexual harassment so that employers would understand how to initiate remedial measures, and to establish methods of processing complaints. Yet the definition of sexual harassment remains something of a problem for employers because of the seemingly subjective aspect of a person's perception, and the fact that some courts recognize the right of the alleging person to define harassment. However, the general trend in legal thinking is that sexual harassment is more often the insensitivity of the initiating person than it is the sensitivity of the recipient, but even the courts acknowledge that perceptions of such abusive treatment as sexual harassment vary widely among individuals. More precisely, the guidelines define sexual harassment as follows:

> Unwelcome sexual advances, requests for sexual favors, and other verbal or physical conduct of a sexual nature constitute sexual harassment when (1) submission to such conduct is made either explicitly or implicitly a term or condition of an individual's employment; (2) submission to or rejection of such conduct by an individual is used as the basis for employment decisions affecting such individual; or (3) such conduct has the purpose or effect of unreasonably interfering with an individual's work performance or creating an intimidating, hostile, or offensive working environment.

To offer some reassurance to employer and employees alike that claims will be viewed within the context of guideline intent on the facts and merit of individual cases, the guidelines go on to state:

> In determining whether alleged conduct constitutes sexual harassment, the Commission will look at the record as a whole and at the totality of the circumstances, such as the nature of the sexual advances and the context in which the alleged incidents occurred. The determination of the legality of a particular action will be made from the facts, on a case-by-case basis.

Additionally, the guidelines hold employers liable for the acts of their "agents," regardless of whether the conduct was forbidden by the employer, or whether the employer "knew or should have known" of the occurrence of sexual harassment.

Employers are again reminded that the burden of proof in any type of discrimination case rests with them after the employee's showing of prima facie evidence. In defending a claim of sexual harassment, it is advisable to be able to demonstrate an awareness of applicable law, taking preventive measures such as distributing policies and training supervisors in sexual harassment prohibitions, and demonstrating a willingness to take immediate corrective action when these conditions surface. In addition to awards of back pay and injunctive relief (restraining further harassment), plaintiff attorneys frequently pursue damages under state tort law for assault, battery, and (intentional) infliction of emotional distress in order to gain access to the payment of attorney's fees, and compensatory and punitive damages. Doing so obviously makes litigation a lucrative prospect for attorney and client.

3.30 SOLVING GENDER DISCRIMINATION PROBLEMS

There are two ways to solve the various forms of gender related discrimination in our workplaces: by legal reaction or managerial proaction. The former approach is one in which the organization and its managers either transform only those practices deemed unlawful by statute or some relevant case decision, or they are postured to carry out known illegal employment decisions until caught, then defend it the best way they can with little future regard for the spirit and intent of such laws. Both are reactionary and treat only the effect and not the cause of such problems. The managerial approach, on the other hand, acts proactively to first prevent problems from arising, but when they do to then have ready an effective resolution that eliminates its continuance or exaggeration into formal, counterproductive recourse such as arbitration, litigation, or other outsider involvements.

Although the problem solving approaches of reactionary versus proactive measures differ considerably in their result and long term effect organizational credibility (and therefore productivity of employees), both approaches can find diagnostic value in examining some of the decisional trends in case law. The rationale applied by various courts can be very insightful in terms of what kinds of factors managers need to pay more attention to when rendering workplace decisions.

3.31 CASE LAW SOLUTIONS: THE LEGAL REACTION APPROACH

Beginning in the late 1960's, the various states and federal courts began handing down numerous decisions reinforcing the underlying principle of Title VII—that employers simply cannot make adverse decisions affecting the employment circumstances based on one's gender, whether male or female, absent a defensibly necessary reason for doing so. Few employers have successfully defended their case based on the BFOQ necessity. Despite having two decades of well publicized court cases barring discrimination where a person's sex was at least a considerable factor in adversely affecting an applicant or employee, managers reponsible for their decisions continue to err. So, to illustrate how issues become problems, and to learn more about handling them, let's examine some common situations already addressed by the courts. These illustrated cases include the following issues:

- Affirmative recruitment of female applicants
- Preferential promotions
- Antinepotism rules
- Differential benefits
- Domestic tasks for secretaries
- Repeated violations

What Should Be Done If We Don't Get Enough Female Applicants For A Predominantly Male Job?

This, of course, has been one of the more agonizing problems for companies who have wisely taken an aggressive stance on seriously trying to remedy gender inbalances within their workforce. Typically, the best way to ensure the equitable distribution of female applicants is through a systems approach consisting minimally of:

1. A thorough and aggressive recruitment effort that publicizes (sells) the job in detail to sources of your targeted group (females in this case) in addition to general advertisements. Post job announcements on company bulletin boards with a note encouraging employees to refer applicants, or ask some of your best performers for referrals.

2. Document each phase of your remedial efforts including the job analysis, recruiting methods, applicant intake characteristics, and testing and selection results (applicant flow).[4]

3. If you receive an insufficient number of total applications, notify applicants of this situation and continue your recruitment effort until you have a sufficient number to begin the selection process (or announce at the beginning that recruitment will remain open until a sufficient number of applications have been received).

4. If you still have too few female applicants, or you can demonstrate that further delay in filling the job would cause visible operational problems, then proceed with your selection process. Should you be challenged because you eventually hired a male irrespective of the number of female applicants, you are now at least in a much better position to provide convincing evidence of your dilemma in acquiring a reasonable or proportional number of female applicants who've demonstrated an interest in the particular job.

---

[4] Forms used for this purpose can be found in Levesque, Joseph D.; *Manual Of Personnel Policies, Procedures, And Operations*, N.J.: Prentice-Hall, 1986.

This example is fairly well illustrated in the case of *EEOC v. Sears, Roebuck and Co.* (1986) wherein a federal district court found that the EEOC's use of mere statistics was insufficient proof of sex discrimination in the filling of commission sales jobs in the automotive, plumbing, and home siding departments within 900 stores during the 1973-1980 period (imagine the defense costs of a seven year law suit and the record-keeping costs of 900 stores over a seven year period—large in itself but small compared to potential settlement costs!). In support of its allegation, the EEOC showed that women occupied only 27 percent of the commissioned jobs, but women represented 60 percent of Sears' applicants. The court concluded that the EEOC's inability to produce a particular victim, together with Sears' ability to adequately explain the greater interest of men in these jobs and that Sears had in other respects pursued a "sincere dedication and commitment to affirmative action," resulted in dismissal of the sex discrimination charges.

Conversely, rather than continuing its defense in *Brockman v. Lucky Stores, Inc.* (1985), the company decided to enter into a $3.1 million out-of-court settlement over a 10 year period to remedy sex discriminatory hiring at its San Leandro, California distribution center. The settlement, believed to affect some 4,000 women either deterred or denied past employment, also requires the company to set specific hiring goals for women in various jobs predominantly occupied by men.

Moral to the story: do it right (objectively) the first time; have a superb defense; or pay up!

What About Promotions? Do We Have To Give Preferential Treatment To Women As A Cure To Occupational Imbalances?

Preferential treatment is only lawful under a consent degree (court order) or upon instruction of a compliance agency who has determined the existence of past discrimination and therefore establishes a compelling public interest to order preferential action of some type. Generally, however, employers are within their rights to carry out affirmative action consciousness to remedy imbalances by hiring or promoting a female over a male applicant where they are both equally qualified. The thinking of many courts on this issue has been, all things being equal and assuming the selection process was not inherently discriminatory, the final selection determinant has to be something, and gender balancing can be regarded as that valid something. A good example of this was decided by the U.S. Supreme Court in *Johnson v. Transportation Agency* (1987) where the court determined that a female applicant for the promotional position of dispatcher scored only two points less in the interview exam than the plaintiff male who was bypassed in favor of the female.

The ruling of the high court has some noteworthy key elements to an employer's use of affirmative action plans as a determinant in hiring and promotion decisions. They are:

- Title VII does not prohibit the use of sexual or racial preferences when used to eliminate *clear* imbalances in jobs traditionally segregated, as long as the rights of men and non-minorities are not "unnecessarily trammeled."

- The voluntary affirmative action plan should specify long term numerical goals for the employment of women and minorities where imbalances are found, yet be temporary in nature to achieve parity—as opposed to maintaining it.

- Meeting these conditions, and since test scores were reasonably equal, the court held that the employer acted properly in its decision to promote the female as a means of bringing about greater job integration.

What this case demonstrates is not only the apparent validity of promoting a female into a predominantly male job where test scores are nearly the same (substantially equal qualifications), and where there exists a historical pattern of occupational gender imbalance or even underrepresentation, but also it demonstrates the different position held by the U.S. Supreme Court concerning (the illegality of) preferential treatment in layoff situations compared to the apparent legality when the decision involves hiring or promotions. Once again, the high court would seem to be conveying to us that there is less detrimental impact on the person not hired or promoted than to the victim of preferential layoff who might have more job investment.

In a second example involving a company's policies on promotions from factory to salaried positions, the better qualified female applicant challenged the policy as preferential toward males due to the company's promotion of a male forklift operator to the position of international order correspondent. In *Henry v. Lennox Industries, Inc.* (1985), the Sixth Circuit Court of Appeals found that the plaintiff was better qualified on the basis of:

- performing the job in question for three and one-half years.
- a seven year record of good performance.
- being asked to train the promoted male (who had no experience) who would then supervise her.

Further, the promoted male was placed five pay grades higher than that of plaintiff currently doing the job, and the company violated yet another policy by later demoting plaintiff instead of making any attempt to relocate displaced salaried employees as called for by policy. The court concluded that Lennox used its policy on promotions from factory to salaried jobs as a pretext to sex discrimination (courts are typically unsympathetic to companies to try to solve internal problems at the discriminatory expense of an other employee), and the company's failure to follow its own policy on relocation of displaced salaried employees in this instance merely reinforced the pretextual conclusion.

Applying similar thinking (i.e., judgment based on demonstrable fact and valid job performance issues) to a slightly different situation, the Ninth Circuit Court of Appeals held that the hiring of a better qualified male over the female plaintiff was not sex discrimination in *Schuler v. Chronicle Broadcasting Co.,Inc.* (1986). Here, the issue is both racial and sex discrimination since a white male was hired instead of a part-time temporary black female. Plaintiff was one of five temporary technicians and she was hired to operate studio cameras, but was inefficient in the added tasks of operating video tape and other equipment, so she was returned to former duties. Her assignment was extended due to the maternity leave of a regular employee who later decided to resign. All five temporary employees applied for the position, and when filled by one of them, she was terminated. The court concluded that plaintiff failed to show sufficient facts to be convincing that the employer's action was a mere pretext of discrimination (e.g., her comments that she "felt" competent and was "confident of her skills" was subjective personal judgments), whereas the employer demonstrated more factual and convincing evidence of the male being better qualified.

As a rule-of-thumb, the courts have no initial predisposition favoring or weighted toward employees who allege discrimination as opposed to employers defending such allegations; but such predisposition is often the case with the EEOC and state enforcement agencies who frequently feel compelled to advocate for claimants sometimes even when the facts point to the contrary.

Do Antinepotism Rules Constitute Sex Discrimination?

They have an inherent tendency to do so which is why many companies have either abandoned them or, if regarded as operationally desirable, have made them more flexible about their application to assure that the hiring of a spouse or close relative presents no *particular employment* problem. This is to say that blanket no-spouse or broader antinepotism rules that do not obviously guard against specific kinds of operational problems are frequently struck down by the courts for being discriminatory; particularly where it can be shown that the *effect* has been to terminate or refuse to hire a particular group of protected persons such as females and minorities (disparate impact & theory).

However, the courts usually do not have a problem with antinepotism rules where the employer decides each case by its circumstantial merits using the objective factors (reasons for refusing to hire) of supervision, safety, security, or morale as illustrated in the following policy.

EMPLOYMENT OF RELATIVES

A.   Employment Of Spouse

It is the policy of the Company not to discriminate in its employment and personnel actions with respect to its employees, prospective employees, and applicants on the basis of marital status. No employee, prospective employee, or applicant will be denied employment or benefits of employment solely on the basis of marital status. This policy also applies to the selection of persons for a training program leading to employment or promotion.

Notwithstanding the above provisions, the Company retains the right

1. To refuse to place one spouse under the direct supervision of the other spouse where such has the potential for creating an adverse effect on supervision, safety, security, or morale.

2. To refuse to place both spouses in the same department, division, or facility where such has the potential for creating an adverse effect on supervision, safety, security, or morale, or involves potential conflicts of interest.

B. Employment Of Other Relatives

1. Relatives within the third degree of kinship by blood or marriage of the Company's senior management/administrative employees, or any person exercising hiring, promotion, and termination authority, may not be hired into the Company service without written approval of the President/General Manager.

2. Relatives within the third degree of kinship by blood or marriage of any Company employee, regardless of status, will not be hired in the same department, division, or facility where such has the potential for creating an adverse effect on supervision, safety, security, or morale, or involves potential conflicts of interest, without the written approval of the President/General Manager.[5]

Just so you're convinced that antinepotism rules can absolutely serve as the basis for sex discrimination, the U.S. Supreme Court decided on a rather obvious situation in *Roth Packing Co. Creditors' Trust v. EEOC* (1986) where the high court refused to overturn a $1 million judgment against this bankrupt company. It seems that the company had a policy whose intent was to protect women from the "distasteful cut-and-kill aspects of its hog-slaughtering plant" and had a rule prohibiting spouses of employees from working in the same plant. Statistical evidence showed that:

1. a mere seven women out of 554 applicants were hired over a five year period;
2. 26 out of 95 female applicants were eliminated due to the no-spouse rule; and
3. about one-half of the plant's 250 employees were, in fact, related to another employee.

---

[5] Levesque, Joseph D.; *Manual Of Personnel Policies, Procedures, And Operations.* N.J.: Prentice-Hall, 1986, p. 11.

The court(s) easily concluded that this was a clear and apparent act of sex discrimination, and that there was no evidence that the rule served as anything other than intentional, selective discrimination.

Historically antinepotism, and in particular no-spouse, rules have been weighed by the courts on the basis of its justification and business necessity as opposed to the result of a discriminatory effect due to disparate impact on females refused hiring or terminated under such rules.[6] The best defense for employers seems to be that of showing, preferably by statistical application of the rule, that the rule has been used equally for both sexes, and that each separate application was weighed by the employer on the basis of the business necessity.

Other elements of antinepotism rules also should be included in the employer's policy. For example, where two employees marry, they should be given an opportunity (30 days) to decide which will resign their position if the employer has notified them of the inimicability between the relationship and jobs. Such other actions as transfer, demotion, or reassignment should also be explored with *both* partners. Where the employees fail to decide, the employer should reserve the right to make its decision on the basis of such non-gender factors as value to company operations, performance, and seniority. Finally, the policy should include an appeal mechanism whereby employees adversely affected by application of the rule can have the decision reviewed by higher management.

Could It Be Construed As Sex Discrimination To Pay The Benefits Of Some Employees But Not Others?

Be careful, you're treading on very thin and highly suspect ice when dealing in the benefits arena. It's prudent to bear in mind that employee benefits are not only subject to such issues as sex and pregnancy discrimination, but they are also regulated by state laws, Internal Revenue Service codes, and the Employment Retirement Income Security Act (ERISA).

Neverthless, there are certain circumstances in which an employer can avoid sexual discrimination damages where a policy of paying for the benefits of one group of employees and not another group is implemented. As you might suspect by now, these preconditions should be examined closely in light of the business necessity, reasonableness, and non-discriminatory intent (objectively applied to positions not individuals).

The illustration of these conditional elements is drawn from the summary judgment dismissing the case of *Seville v. Martin Marietta Corp.* (1986) in which a group of women in predominantly female clerical positions alleged sex discrimination because the company's policy precluded the payment of benefits for clerical jobs, but it did pay

---

[6] See such case summaries as *Thomas v. Metroflight, Inc.* (1987), *Domingo v. New England Fish Co.* (1984), *Yuhas v. Libbey-Owens Ford Co.* (1977), *EEOC v. Rath Packaging Co.* (1986), *Harper v. Trans World Airlines, Inc.* (1975), and *Tuck v. McGraw-Hill, Inc.* (1976).

the ("overseas") benefits of predominantly male technical employees. The elements found by the court in favor of the company were:

1. Technical and clerical job classifications were distinctively different clusters of the nature and scope of various jobs, and the company had attempted to recruit and hire men and women for both occupational categories.

2. Under the disparate treatment argument, there was no evidence that the company intended to discriminate since female technicians received benefits, and male clericals would be (if they had any) denied benefits.

3. The company was able to establish a reasonable business necessity for the policy due to the difficulty of getting and keeping technicians in their West Germany operations, whereas there was a sufficient labor supply of clerical workers thereby creating no reason to provide the 15 percent (of base pay per diem) incentive benefit (cost of living allowance, housing and moving expenses, and dependent education allowance).

4. The company had consistently applied their policy since 1960 (imagine the cost of loosing this case on retroactive costs alone!)

5. The policy was considered reasonable since the U.S. Government, who paid these benefits through its contract with the employer, never objected to these payments.

6. The company was following what it perceived to be a legitimate business necessity and was under no legal obligation to conduct a market study prior to or after implementation to justify it as was the contention of plaintiffs.

7. There was insufficient and insubstantial evidence to show, as plaintiffs asserted, that all technicians needed or received allowable benefits. The fact that these benefits were available to any and all technicians was enough to prove the policy was administered equally to all technicians.

Can An Employer Be Held Liable For Sex Discrimination By Attempting To Correct An Employee's Provocative Dress Or Behavior?

Generally, employers will not be liable for sex discrimination as a result of establishing and enforcing reasonable rules about the appearance and sexual-oriented behavior of employees. To be reasonable such rules ought to have a pertinent relationship to the nature of work being performed, the work setting, the nature of employee contacts, and any other business reason supporting the employer's legitimate interests in controlling workplace appearances and conduct (morale, avoidance of potential sexual harassment inducements, professional image, and so forth).

There are, however, a number of conditions that employers overlook and thereby create several forms of liability for acts against employees. The case of *Atlantic Rich-field Co. v. District of Columbia Commission on Human Rights* (1986) clearly illustrates some of these conditions. First, the employer had no policy on dress or appearance of employees and, second, company officials demonstrated an inappropriate pattern of dealing with an otherwise legitimate concern.

The employee in question was a clerical worker who appeared for work on a number of occasions wearing provocative clothes (tight and revealing) and whose behavior was objectionable to her supervisor (too friendly to visitors, sat with legs open, noisy and flirtatious at a company party). Instead of counseling, confronting, disciplining, or otherwise correcting these problems, the supervisor waited for the next evaluation period wherein she noted that another company official regarded her behavior to be likened to a prostitute (with speculation that she could not afford such clothing on her salary). When the employee filed a formal complaint, her supervisors let her know that her job and future employment opportunities were in jeopardy. The employee resigned and filed suit. The court found in her favor on the basis of personal appearance (sex) discrimination, illegal retaliation, and constructive discharge.

In another personal appearance case, the employer (supervisor) was charged with sex discrimination when a pregnant front desk clerk was fired for refusing to comply with a new policy requiring the wearing of make-up. In *Tamimi v. Howard Johnson Co.* (1987), an appellate court concluded that the supervisor's adoption of a policy requiring only employees under his supervision to wear make-up—which was adopted after plaintiff informed him of her pregnancy and his subsequent complaint of her "pale looking" appearance—amounted to a Title VII violation. It was clear to the court that the policy was promulgated in a work unit predominately composed of female employees and was implemented with the principle purpose to regulate one employee who was fired for disobeying the rule. Such arbitrary and reactionary management practices rarely favor the employer, and they do little for employee confidence in the objectivity of those that supervise them.

And For Those Department Managers Wondering If You Can Require Your Secretary To Keep Your Ice Water Fresh Without Commiting Sex Discrimination...

The EEOC, in its Decision No. 86-5, determined that a company's policy of requiring departmental secretaries to fill water pitchers and place them on the desk of their departmental managers was less a factor of sex as asserted by the complainant, than it was a support function of those secretaries irrespective of the incumbent's gender as asserted by the employer. Despite there being no male departmental secretaries in this instance, and therefore no proof that male secretaries were treated any differently (disparate treatment), the EEOC concluded that there was no particular cause to believe the policy was based on sex discrimination.

Additionally, there have been a few isolated court cases in which female secretaries have brought suit against their employer for sex discrimination due to being asked or required to perform such similar "domestic" activities as preparing and delivering coffee to their manager, watering office plants, cleaning desks and dusting office furniture surfaces, and the like (this does not include performing personal tasks such as the buying of gifts or similar forms of personal servitude). It is not enough to use the customary caveat in the job description of "and other duties as required." If you're going to use such an all-inclusive short phrase, it ought to be "and other *related* duties as required." Then make sure that all tasks assigned to an employee are reasonably within the realm of being related to the nature of the job. You may also wish to use a more explanatory disclaimer in bold type at the end of each job description given to employees that says:

> This job description should not be construed to imply that these requirements are the exclusive standards or duties of the position. Incumbents will be expected to follow any other instructions, and perform any other related duties as may be required by their supervisor.

Is There Any Cumulative Effect Of An Employer's Repeated Discrimination Violations?

Yes, not only because repeated violations related to the same or even separate forms of discrimination annoys the courts' efforts to educate employers, but also because it can demonstrate the employers' clear intent to continue violating public interest law. It's sort of like judicial insubordination, and the courts, the EEOC, and state enforcement agencies are quite likely to apply their own version of progressive discipline by successively more thorough scrutiny of employment practices and more costly remedies.

An example of this was demonstrated in *Kilgo v. Bowman Transportation, Inc.* (1986) where this trucking firm had an established record of serious discrimination complaints that lead to the meticulous evaluation of this case. Here, a woman brought a complaint of sex discrimination involving the company's policy of requiring applicants to have a minimum of one year over-the-road experience (driving a truck more than 75 miles from the point of dispatch). The Eleventh Circuit Court of Appeals found such a rule to be lacking merit on the basis of any apparent business necessity, and that it has a disparate impact on women in that it eliminated a significant number of them from qualifying. The court ordered the company to not only establish a corrective hiring plan to increase its representation of female drivers, but also required the company to make periodic compliance reports to a court-appointed agent. Care to guess what the next overt violation will bring? The counterpart of judicial discipline for contemptuous violations of tort law is punitive damages, and they tend to be both outrageously high and inversely proportional to the amount of substantive defense of the employer's intent or negligence.

3.32 HUMAN RESOURCE SOLUTIONS: THE MANAGERIAL PROACTION APPROACH

There is one very distinctive difference between this approach and the legal reactionary one: this approach operates at all times under the presumption that human resources are the single most important asset to the organization, they should be managed accordingly, and problems dealt with in an equitable, common sense fashion. There is an underlying philosophy that human resource assets are an investment in the continued success of the organization, and that assets of any kind should be managed with an investment mentality. Emphasis in dealing with human resource issues is therefore placed on prevention of problems, support measures such as training and monitoring, and thorough problem solving rather than fault-finding. Examples of proactive human resource management solution to gender discrimination problems include such measures as:

1. **Reviewing Policies** and decision making practices on a routine basis to assure proper understanding, coverage, and application by all managers and employees alike concerning matters of employment; ensuring that the organization has a clearly defined policy and upper management support of nondiscrimination on the basis of gender, marital status, pregnancy, and sexual harassment; and adoption of both informal and formal complaint procedurals that encourage employees to bring such matters to the attention of higher management for resolution.

2. **Conducting Job Analysis** on all separate classes of employment to remove any artificial barriers for female and minority applicants (sexist job titles, height and weight requirements, physical requirements, and an evaluation of alterative means of job redesign to accommodate females, minorities, or the physically handicapped without compromising the nature of the job); refining pay systems to ensure that employees are compensated on the basis of job and performance rather than personal or gender characteristics; and limiting any differentiation of job groups (for fringe benefit or other considerations) to work content similarities rather than their dominance by one gender or another.

3. **Provide Regular Training** for managers and supervisors in topics related to discrimination avoidance, human relations, organizational policies, areas needing special (watchful) attention, and why their role is important to organizations' goal of a harmonious workplace. Provide training opportunities for

all employees that enable them to develop new skills, prepare for promotional opportunities, and gain confidence in the organization as an equal opportunity employer.

4. **Be Proud** of being an "open door" equal opportunity employer by advertising that fact: in job advertisements, posted notices of job vacancies, EEO posters on bulletin boards, on application forms, and in vendor contracts. Contact those community organizations who have access to both male and female job seekers to let them know of your interest in considering them for employment. Publicize special achievements or personal interest stories of employees; women working in an unusually non-traditional job and men being the sole parent of their children are popular themes.

5. **Monitor Results** of these and other efforts to measure progress, effectiveness, recognition of those who are making a difference or special efforts, and to refine goals achievement. Such measures might involve doing semi-annual data collection and analysis on the composition of your workforce by such factors as departmental and occupational gender representation, gender distribution of recent hires or separations, and promotions by gender.

Monitoring can also consist of such things as discussing gender related employment matters in management meetings, or when conferring with another manager on a particular employment decision about to be made. It can also entail reviewing performance appraisals, pay increase recommendations, and simply talking to employees informally once in awhile to see how they are doing.

It should be apparent by now that there is a vivid difference between reactive and proactive problem solving in employment matters such as gender related discrimination. Reactive solutions are better than blatant disregard, but proactive approaches result in fewer problems, more effective solutions, and more enduring confidence among about the motives of their employer—and its managers. What we sow we too shall reap, and the choice is ours to make as a conscious decision about how we want to manage our organization and its most vital resource.

3.40 SEXUAL HARASSMENT DISCRIMINATION: CONDITIONS, LEGAL EVOLUTION, AND WORKPLACE IMPLICATIONS

When we think of employment or the daily routine of carrying out one's career, we are normally prone to consider those activities associated with performing tasks, making decisions, interacting with various people, and the like. For many, it is a social experience and one that offers personal growth and self-esteem rewards for assuming new responsibilities, getting a promotion, or the satisfaction that accompanies doing a job well. Periodically, however, what can dampen this otherwise emotionally gratifying opportunity are those extraneous situations where the result is a personal conflict with another individual. The worst kind is where one person, the victim, feels powerless in being able to resolve the conflict, or underlying problem creating the conflict.

So it is with sexual harassment in the workplace. What sets it apart from other kinds of problems is the enormously complicated and ill-fated emotional price to be paid by virtually everyone concerned. Not only do the victims of sexual harassment suffer emotionally from this type of personal afront (mental anguish, fear, anger, grief, depression, frustration, and disillusionment) but, once the problem is finally known, others become a part of the emotional difficulty in clearing the problem up. Administrators must get involved, the perpetrator must come to terms with events, and quite often other employees and family members are affected by the situation.

3.41 THE PERSONAL AND ORGANIZATIONAL PRICE

The longer sexually harassing events go on, or the more serious singular incidents progress, the less possible it becomes to create a harmonious recuperation. The economic price for violations of this legal prohibition quite simply does not begin to compare to the internal and personal damage done to valuable employees. As managers, we have an obligation to protect the conditions under which our employees work, and to create necessary controls that guide the type of behavior we want or don't want from those who represent our organization. Good management implies planning for events, averting problems, and maximizing opportunities. Here are just a few incidents in which companies failed at taking adequate prevent-planning measures, and they suffered the consequences:

1. A woman is frequently told by her department manager of his sexual fantasies about her and he creates opportunities to feel her breasts while pressing her into a corner in the privacy of his office.

2. A woman is raped by her male supervisor on a business trip.

3. A buxom woman is harassed by another employee who makes frequent jokes about her body in front of co-workers.

4. A secretary receives regular salacious remarks from a mid-level executive she does some work for, but he never behaves this way in front of others.

5. A waitress in a men's club is threatened with the loss of her job after refusing offers of sex by members, one of whom pulled her top down to expose her breasts in front of others.

6. A female sales representative is terminated after being sexually assaulted by her manager in the hallway of their district office.

7. A woman complains that her supervisor habitually embraces her touching various parts of her body. When she protests, she is accused of being a poor sport.

And the examples go on and on, ranging from suggestive comments to physical assults including abusive battery. Those who believe that their organizations are free of this affliction are being naive. It can happen anywhere, at any time, and by some of the most unsuspecting people. Unlike most other forms of conflict where it takes two people to create a problem, sexual harassment only takes one person who decides to seize power over another person. While there is more opportunity for sexual harassment to occur by co-workers and by supervisors merely because that is the level where most employees are in the organization, it is a situation certainly not immune from propogation by highly placed officials. In fact, it would almost seem that the higher the rank of the propogator, the higher the price of settlement and publicity. For example:

- In 1985, an out-of-court settlement of $15 million was reached between Cecily Coleman and the American Broadcasting Corporation (ABC). She brought harassment charges after being fired from her $60,000 a year job, alleging that *former* vice president James D. Abernathy conditioned her career in conjunction with repeated and unwanted sexual advances.

- Also in 1985, a female executive of a CBS-owned radio station, Elisa Dorfman, received a settlement of $250,000 against the network for the sexually harassing and humiliating remarks made to her by a CBS executive in front of 30 people at a 1982 company sales dinner.

- Eight female employees of William Mitchell College of Law settled for $300,000 for being inappropriately touched and subjected to suggestive remarks by the *former* dean, the controller, and a professor.

- A well established independent bank settled for $1.5 million with the secretary of the *former* president for conditioning her sexual favors, after the bank discovered that four other secretaries had transferred or quit for the same reason.

These are not, I repeat not, isolated incidents. Like other forms of abuse, the problem tends to be ubiquitous and serious enough to generate concern by every manager responsible for the workplace conduct of employees. Those who require more factual evidence may wish to consider the following:

1976; Redbook Magazine polls 9,000 women and learns that 92 percent of the respondents have found sexual harassment on the job to be a problem.

1980; A survey of 694,000 women and 1,168,000 men in federal jobs concluded that 42 percent of the women and 15 percent of the men had experienced some form of harassment.

1981; A Merit System Protections Board survey found that most sexual harassment comes from co-workers.

1985; The EEOC receives a record 7,273 sexual harassment complaints. During the latter half of the year, one state's (California) Department of Fair Employment & Housing received 884 sexual harassment complaints representing a 60 percent increase in sexual harassment complaints since 1980, and a ratio of one in every ten complaints filed.

Similarly, 42 percent of the 216 complaints filed with another state's (Hawaii) Department of Labor & Industrial Relations were based on sex, exceeding the combined complaints for race and physical handicap discrimination.

Other studies include:

- A finding by Cornell University that 70 percent of the respondent employees had personally experienced sexual harassment on the job.

- A law professor in Southern California who has conducted numerous sexual harassment studies estimates that up to one-third of the working women in Los Angeles have at one time quit or lost their jobs due to sexual pressures.

- A study of women working at the United Nations found that 49 percent had experienced sexual pressures on the job.

- A study found that most of the five to eight million working women in Western Europe were required to quit their jobs or say nothing about sexual pressures related to employment.

And these are only those examples of employees, predominantly women, willing to respond to their experiences on the job either by survey or through formal complaint methods. Considering the greater anonymity of surveys, those results are likely to be more representative of the actual prevalence of the problem than the few risk-takers who are moved to file formal complaints.

3.42 WHY SOME VICTIMS DON'T COMPLAIN

There now seems to be little doubt that our organizations are beseiged by the problem of sexual harassment in its various forms, and that we probably have more than a few employees who may feel impeded from coming forward to make their situation known to us so that it can be addressed. Some of the reasons that have been discovered concerning employee reluctance to disclose sexually harassing conditions are:

1. **They Don't Feel They'll Be Believed.** Many of these situations are propogated by supervisors or managers having more inherent authority, believability, and interaction with higher management.

2. **They Fear Punishment.** Most lower level employees develop a serious concern for being fired, denied a pay or position increase, getting lousy assignments or performance evaluations, and other retaliatory measures that they fear will and can happen.

3. **They Don't Trust the Objectivity of Higher Management.** Because most harassment is toward women by men, and most upper-management jobs are held by men, there may be the perception that the men in higher management positions will condone or "soft peddle" the issue. If not handled thoroughly and decisively, the complainant is left in a very vulnerable position in the closed confines of the work unit with the perpetrator.

4. **They Don't Want to Cause Problems.** Despite being a victim themselves, many do not want to affect the employment, reputation, or life of the person harassing them; nor do they want their co-workers to think less of them for making an issue of the problem. Ironically, some investigations have discovered that other employees have also been victims of the same perpetrator or were sympathetic to the victim.

5. **They May Be Accused of Inviting the Harassment.** This may be caused by uncertainty, partial responsibility, or even guilt about what might be construed as contributing to the interaction by smiling when remarks were made, being too friendly, laughing at sexual jokes, or perhaps wearing suggestive clothing.

6. **They Cannot Provide a Detailed Accounting of Incidents.** Most employees are aware that facts speak for themselves and they objectify situations where credibility is at stake. Since it is difficult to capture the essence of what is often casual interaction, and to distinguish between informal and offensive interaction, victims frequently do not begin recording (mentally or in writing) incidents until the situation reaches blatant conditions.

Also, because it is a situation with an emotional effect on the victim, the accounting of specific details can tend to become obscured. I recall one investigation I conducted for a client in which one of the perpetrator's early victims had also experienced the death of a close family member. A thorough investigation disclosed that he seized the opportunity provided by her depressed condition to comfort her by various forms of fondling. During this investigation of a second complaint some two years later, this initial victim became confused, disoriented, and vague about the incident; and said that he has pretty much left her alone since he discovered that she started psychiatric treatment over a year ago.

If sexual harassment does nothing else, it absolutely destroys working relationships. Moreover, when it occurs between people in authority and an employee they oversee, it destroys trust and respect which are fundamental ingredients of a desirable employer-employee relationship. Employees are generally accustomed to being told what to do by their workplace superiors, but to be told something that violates the employee's sense of dignity is a breech of the authority entrusted to supervisors and managers when they become perpetrators of sexual harassment. The exemplary conduct that is supposed to be the model for subordinate employees is shattered, and it must be dealt with affirmatively and rapidly. This is no less true for sexual harassment occuring between co-workers, or outsiders toward employees, even though it tends to be easier to stop in these situations once it's known or observed.

3.43 LEGAL EVOLUTION OF THE ISSUE

Sexual harassment has been with us no doubt since the dawn of mankind. It is a social disorder whose explanations are supplemental to the purpose of any discussion here, but suffice it to say that it has been a problem for its victims wherever employment offered the opportunity and circumstances for men and women to work together, and thereby develop a particular affinity even if it was one-sided, unwelcomed, and subdued.

As an issue in the American workplace, sexual harassment did not take on legal definition until the mid-1970's, and even then its initial appearance was of a secondary nature to sex discrimination where the courts were spending much of their attention due to the EEOC's 1972 revision of its Guidelines On Discrimination Because Of Sex.

In 1975, the first reported law suit on sexual harassment emerged from Arizona where two female employees resigned due to the repeated verbal and physical advances of their supervisor. The District Court's finding in *Corne v. Bausch & Lomb, Inc.* was no liability for the employer, and holding that the supervisor's actions served no policy, did not benefit the employer, and was merely his own proclivity.

Other courts followed the rationale in Corne until 1977 when the District of Columbia Circuit Court of Appeals decided *Barnes v. Costle* in which it held that when sexual harassment affects job conditions (evidence of such economic harm as loss of job, denial of promotion or pay increase, etc.), it is an act of sex discrimination under Title VII. Similarly, in *Tomkins v. Public Service Electric and Gas Co.* (1977), the Third Circuit Court of Appeals ruled that Title VII was violated because the employer did not take "prompt and appropriate action" when advised of a supervisor's dismissal of a female employee who would not submit to his demands for sexual favors. Also, in *Miller v. Bank of America* (1979), the Ninth Circuit Court held the employer responsible for the sexual harassment of a discharged female employee by a bank supervisor because she refused to submit, even though the bank had adopted a policy of prohibitng such harassment activity.

In 1980, the EEOC released its Guidelines on Sexual Harassment Discrimination making harassment on the basis of sex a violation of Title VII, subsection 703.

In 1981, the District of Columbia Circuit Court of Appeals again established precedent law by creating the principle of relationship between sexual harassment and conditions of employment in *Bundy v. Jackson.* Here, the Court held that sexual insults and demeaning propositions were detrimental to the psychological and emotional terms, conditions, and privileges of employment whether or not there resulted tangible loss of employment benefit.

In 1982, the *Quid-Pro-Quo* (something given or received for something else) theory of sexual harassment was established in the case of *Hensen v. City of Dundee* where the Eleventh Circuit Court crystalized the effect of sexual harassment having a discriminatory effect not only on the victim, but other employees who might otherwise have their employment effected if the object employee of harassment were to acquiesce to the pressure of sexual favors and thereby gain greater benefit of employment because of such sex discrimination (see also *Toscarro v. Mimmo,* 1983). So the quid-pro-quo theory is one in which yielding to the sexual favors of a superior becomes conditional directly upon employment benefits such as keeping one's job, receiving specialized training, being promoted, getting the earned pay raise, and the like. Here, the employer was found liable for the sexual harassment of a female dispatcher by the police chief who denied her access to attend the police academy. In such situations, the courts have consistently found employers liable for the actions of their supervisor's regardless of whether or not the employer knew of the supervisor's actions. The courts feel that it is the responsibility of each employer that they know or should know what supervisors do since it is the employer who delegates broad authority for the hiring, pay, promotion, discipline and termination decisions to supervisory personnel.

And finally in June 1986, the first sexual harassment case reached the U.S. Supreme Court in *Meritor Savings Bank v. Vinson* where the hostile work environment theory was articulated, much to the consternation of many employers who held firmly to the belief that: 1) employers should *not* be held liable for sexual harassment where the complainant fails to inform management of the situation through an established complaint procedure; 2) the employer should not be liable where the complainant has submitted to repeated sexual involvements; and 3) the employer should not be held liable when there is no economic loss that results from sexual harassment. The high court disagreed.

POINT 1: While the bank had a complaint procedure to handle problems such as sexual harassment, plaintiff's position was that it required lodging the initial complaint with her manager who was the perpetrator of repeated demands for sex over a four year period in which she submitted to intercourse some 40-50 times. Most appellate courts have held that employers are strictly liable for knowing about the acts of supervisors (or should have known), others have disagreed, and the Supreme Court failed to issue a ruling on this matter. Interestingly enough, the EEOC itself submitted its position to the court indicating that employers should not be held liable, provided the employer has a complaint policy and the employee does not use it. A majority of the court noted that such a position would be stronger when a) the employer has a policy of nondiscrimination wherein it encourages employees to come forward, and b) the complaint procedure allows bypassing the supervisor or other perpetrator of sexual harassment.

POINT 2: Here, the court split circumstantial evidence between the parties. The court agreed with the employer to the extent that plaintiff's provocative dress and sexually-oriented conversations are admissable evidence since it contributes to the totality of events. (See *Gan v. Kepro Circuit Systems,* 1982) However, the court disagreed with the employer's contention that plaintiff's actions constituted voluntary participation, holding that the greater issue is whether or not the supervisor's conduct was unwelcomed.

POINT 3: Of all issues decided in this case, the high court at least resolved the question of whether or not sexual harassment ought to be confined to only quid-pro-quo (economic loss) results of sexually harassing conduct. Here, the court concluded, relying in part on the EEOC Guidelines, that where unwelcome sexual harassment has the effect of interfering with performance or creating a hostile work environment, it is a Title VII violation.

In reporting the Supreme Court's decision, the *Wall Street Journal* and *New York Times* regarded the decision as a necessary step toward workplace quality, but the *Times* also added that, "Social behavior at work is a murky area, and it is often hard to distinguish between friendly interaction and sexual harassment." Similarly, the *Los Angeles Times* reported that "Employers fear that court trends and the liberal legal standards are setting them up to police if not intervene in even the most innocent office romance. By setting up harsh policies and insisting on such formal business behavior, the workplace is quickly becoming a very unfriendly place to be." While it is undeniably true that the plethora of new laws and liberally interpreted court decisions are defining a new social character to matters of employment conduct, it does not necessarily follow that the workplace has to be coldly formal. Rather, management merely has to be more precise about how it affects the lives of its human resources who have rights too. As for the innocence of office romance, we ought to consider its workplace effects and potential outcomes as discussed in Section 3.50-3.56 before concluding that they are always heart-warming events.

Two other sexual harassment cases emerging in 1986 and 1987 have set similarly important precedence for the handling of this problem by managers. In *Schroeder v. Schock* (1986), a district court in Kansas held that the off-duty harassment by a supervisor of one of his employees, and the employer's absence of knowledge about this conduct, did not relieve the company of their liability. In upholding the plaintiff's charges against both the company and the harassing supervisor, the court rejected the employer's defense that it could not be liable for unknown acts, and those that occur outside work hours and off employer premises. The court considered these arguments irrelevant inasmuch as employers are considered liable for any act at any time when such acts are an extension of their employment authority; in this case to extort sexual favors.

This case provides good justification for employers to establish strict policies on the outside employment activities of all employees, but supervisors and managers in particular, where such conduct may have a detrimental effect on 1) their employment, 2) company liability, 3) company welfare and reputation, and/or 4) their own credibility in performing their assigned job responsibilities.

The issue of timely action and resultant intentional infliction of emotional distress by an employer failing to properly act on the sexual harassment complaints of an employee concerning her supervisor was addressed by the Arizona Supreme Court in *Ford v. Revlon* (1987). Here, the plaintiff was subjected to the sexual harassment of her supervisor for about two years, and during this period brought it to the attention of management several times. Management either ignored her or would stall in their action. Plaintiff developed high blood pressure, chest pains, rapid breathing, and other symptoms of physical anxiety related to emotional stress. The employer's defense of emotional distress being a workers' compensation exclusive remedy was rejected by the high state court who determined that the injury suffered was intentional rather than accidental, unexpected, or extraordinary.

3.44 SUMMARY OF ITS ELEMENTS BASED ON COLLECTIVE LAW

With little more than a decade of experience in watching the legal prohibitions unfold case-by-case, we can now at least stand back and examine the larger picture based on those elements of both developed legal opinion and fundamental trends. It is essential that all management personnel understand these elements in order to begin consideration of how to proceed in evaluating, handling, and resolving this problem should its prevention fail.

Sexual harassment law is equally applicable to males and females, and to hetero-

sexuals and homosexuals alike. It applies primarily to superior-subordinate relationships, but also includes harassment occurring between peer employees, and between
nonemployee and an employee. Historically, and based on sociocultural conditioning
of role behavior, women have been the predominant victims of sexual harassment. To
them, the issue is ever-present, while many men have difficulty believing the issue is a
serious one (or that it exists in their organizations) simply because they don't behave in
those ways and don't see those traits in other men. Denial that sexual harassment is
taking or might take place, whether a conscious or unconscious attitude, will undoubtedly complicate the matter for employees, or impede the resolution of a situation that
emerges. The fact that a complaint hasn't emerged doesn't mean that sexual harassment isn't going on.

It should also be pointed out that the guideline prohibitions on sexual harassment
do not include friendship or even romance among employees. The key here, and the
likely reason for its exclusion, is that friendship and romance are assumed to be conditions mutually entered into and fostered by both persons, unless it turns one-sided and
becomes harassing in nature.

By being unwelcome activities and thereby offensive, as determined largely by the
recipient, the result becomes an intimidating, hostile, and coercive environment that
affects the employee's terms and conditions of employment. When the harassment is
conditioned on job benefits, it amounts to a form of physical extortion that is no less
violative of an employee's rights than condoning physical or psychological assults on
them.

Consequently, the three most common elements in determining sexual harassment
are:[7]

1. **Unwelcome/Offensive Behavior** (Hostile Work Environment)
   Exchanges of sexually suggestive conversations, jokes, and the like among
   employees is not, in itself, considered unwelcome or offensive behavior if everyone participates, but even these situations can lead to offensiveness for by-
   standers and should therefore be discouraged. In the stricter sense of unwelcome and offensive behavior, the perpetrator has used bad judgment by advancing explicit sexual remarks, gestures, invitations, or some act that the
   recipient did not invite and does not want continued. Often, the recipient
   won't say anything for fear of reprisal from the perpetrator (termination,
   poor evaluations, denial of pay increases or promotion). However, studies
   have shown that in the case of a male perpetrator and female recipient, most
   men would have discontinued their behavior if they were told by the woman
   that their interest was not mutual or pleasing. The point to be made here is

---

[8] The remainder of this discussion is taken from Levesque, Joseph D.; *Manual Of Personnel Policies, Procedures, And Operations*; N.J.: Prentice-Hall, 1986, pp. 300-301.

that the law does not require the recipient to confront the perpetrator—only to bring it to the employer's attention, then it is up to the employer to take corrective action quickly (and in a discreet manner).

2. **One-Sided vs. Mutual Interest** (Participation By Recipient)
   If one's behavior is unwelcome or offensive, the situation is also one-sided. If it is, the employer should act to correct the condition. If, on the other hand, the situation started as a mutual one, then later became one-sided, both parties should be held responsible to some degree in the employer's resolution. Additionally, while (implied) mutual consent between employees who are engaging in sexually oriented behavior (touching, inuendos, etc.) is not considered harassment within the legal meaning, employers should consider eliminating this behavior early, as it can, and often does, become offensive or interfere with the work of other employees, or it becomes a one-sided attraction that creates other problems.

3. **Authority** (Quid-Pro-Quo)
   Sexually harassing conduct can be initiated by a subordinate, a co-worker, a superior, or an outsider. The most serious case is that in which the harassment is initiated by a superior toward a subordinate, because of decision-making authority held, directly or indirectly, by the superior, providing a more intimidating work condition for the subordinate. The existence of authority over another person's job and related work conditions presents a particularly threatening situation for subordinates, and for this reason it is imperative that employers adopt an internal complaint mechanism that provides discreet handling of these situations, without fear of reprisal, and which allows bypassing the immediate supervisor.

In summation then, sexually harassing behavior (1) is unwelcome or offensive, (2) is one-sided and repetitive (except in cases of sexual assault), (3) involves authority that produces an intimidating environment, and (4) makes the recipient feel powerless to stop the behavior. The existence of a sexually harassing situation is dependent on the recipient's perception of these conditions, not the initiator's intent or perception. Here are some specific examples of conduct that should be communicated to all employees as unacceptable by the employer.

☐ Verbal: sexually oriented compliments, remarks, inquiries, or manner of referring to another person; personal or telephone pressuring for dates (dinner, drinks, etc.) or sexual encounter, and jokes of a sexual nature.

☐ Referring to another as honey, sweetheart, doll, girl/boy, dear, and the like.

☐ Comments like, "You turn me on"..."Don't be afraid to show your merchandise"..."You seem tense—aren't you getting enough?"..."You'd have a better chance for promotion if we got to know each other better"..."I enjoy watching you when you wear[[tight clothes, low-cut blouses]"

..."Did you hear the one about the lesbian that..."

☐ Nonverbal: flirting; leering (visually undressing); protruding tongue in a sexual expression; leaving notes of a sexual nature on a desk or in a mailbox; allowing the display of nude or sexually suggestive photos, centerfolds, or cartoons; touching—particularly on the waist, hips, leg, and buttocks—or restricting the movement of another (blocking passage or physically restraining); pinching; and unsolicited neck or back rubs.

Given the diversity of the workforce, their differences in life styles, preferences, and perceptions, and the nature of workplace interaction between men and women that can set the stage and provide the countless opportunities for a sexually harassing situation, employers can no longer rely on unwritten or implied standards of sexual conduct. Nor should employers take a passive position merely because they recognize that most of their employees behave in a responsible manner. The time has come for employers to address this problem of workplace conduct openly by stressing its unacceptability, the complaint and investigative methods, and types of corrective action including possible termination, in written policies, communications with employees, and training for those in positions of authority. Failure to do so will only perpetuate the problem, leaving the employer with a greater potential for unproductive employees; loss of credibility, respect, and trust in those with authority; and the persistent threat of litigation. Prevention has always been the best solution.

3.45 STEPS TO TAKE IN SOLVING THE PROBLEM

There is simply no accurate, reliable way of determining where and by whom sexual harassment will emerge in the organization; and to approach any one person on that basis could produce secondary problems of mistrust and being singled out for no substantive reason. Nevertheless, just as the small aircraft pilot must be always conscious of the need for an emergency landing in the event of engine failure, so too must all managers be cognizant of the potential for sexual harassment by being aware of his or her employees' behavior and the nature of their interaction. It requires frequent contact as well as observation, even if the manager has to create reasons to maintain this type of contact when he or she is not located in the vicinity of subordinate personnel.

Remember, you are obligated to know what's going on with your employees which is only good business sense anyway. Human resource professionals also ought to make it a regular practice of getting out among employees, supervisors, and managers to stay abreast of events and situations in the organization. Many problems have been resolved early by just such a method. Kenneth Blanchard, in his book *The One Minute Manager,* refers to this as "management by walking around."

Diagnostically, there are a few situations and behavioral characteristics that you should stay alert to that tend to set the stage for sexual harassment, or make someone vulnerable to it. Watch for those that are:

1. Going through separation or divorce (or the death of someone close).

2. Single or without a significant relationship.

3. Unhappily married or experiencing family problems.

4. Preoccupied with sexually-oriented comments, jokes, or innuendos.

5. Enjoy exerting their authority over others (i.e., prone toward demonstrative power over people).

6. Flirtatious, playful, jokester, sexually liberal, provocative in dress or conversation, or hold a low opinion of women.

7. Working in a sexually integrated setting, especially where two people work frequently and closely together, and have access to privacy conditions.

This is not to imply that you or any other manager should or need to become an organizational sleuth. Rather, these are general conditions that tend to contribute to the motive and opportunity for sexual harassment to occur. When you become aware of these conditions in the normal course of workplace events, you should pay closer attention to these individuals—even if one of them is another manager, regardless of their level.

Other common conditions in sexual harassment situations has to do with a pattern of development. In many cases, the type of human behavior that accompanies the aforementioned personal conditions is predictable and often develops in sequential order—assuming the perpetrator is the least bit rational of course.

- *First,* some sort of sexual affinity is sparked. It can occur by any number of preconditions (intoxication, proclivity toward certain physical characteristics, personality attraction, or being very friendly), but the result becomes attraction and fantasizing. Fantasy can create the desire to experience what has been mentally conjured. Also, the attraction need not be in the customary sense of physical qualities. In cases of sexual harassment, desire is in the mind of the person wanting to be the beholder!

- *Second,* the person in pursuit of the other wants to "test the water," but doesn't want to draw unnecessary attention to themselves or get in trouble (this is the principle of hedonism which is to seek out pleasure and avoid those things that cause pain). So, the person initiates some form of mild verbal communication to elicit a response upon which the initiator can determine how to proceed. If the recipient is seen as friendly, open, and perhaps naive, the communication will often take the form of a joke, humorous inquiry, flirtation, or friendly inuendo. The more intelligent or sophisticated recipient is usually tested by sexual inference, a compassionate remark, flattery, or by direct suggestion. Both types of initial testing are usually done in privacy or with no one else close enough to overhear, and they foretell the type of perception the initiator has of the recipient.

- *Third,* if the comment, gesture, or other initial attempt has not met with a clear, concise, yet diplomatically face-saving rebuff (it can be important to leave the initiator with their self-esteem or a way out to avoid reprisal behavior since both fantasy and ego are being put asunder), the initiator may see a green light indicating safety to proceed. This next and sometimes obsessive level of behavior often leads to such conduct as repetition of sexual jokes, increasingly more lurid comments or suggestions, sharing details of the fantasy with the recipient, sexual touching, open invitation or threats to engage in sexual activity, or sexual assult.

The net meaning of this sequential pattern of behavior is that employers should address the initial rebuff in a complaint procedure as being the first step of notice, followed by lodging notice of further activity to the next higher level of management or one singular and highly placed person designated to receive and investigate such complaints. Managers and the employer should not set themselves up to second-guess what employees perceive as unwelcome, offensive, or intimidating sexual harassment beyond stating the more commonplace type of prohibitions in company policy.

With regard to the complaint mechanism, the company might be better off letting individual employees take responsibility for what is uncomfortable to them by asking that they make their discomfort known to the initiator first, as they would with any other type of interpersonal difficulty, unless they feel a genuine fear of reprisal (and if so, this factor ought to be examined as well). The more formal, structured steps that should be taken are either preventative in nature or require handling situations "by the numbers". Again, the underlying intent is to establish and maintain a workplace free of any type of harassment, counterproductive behavior, and inappropriate treatment. The structured steps are:

1. Develop a strict and complete policy that *explains*, provides *examples*, and *prohibits* sexual harassment. The policy should also include a *complaint mechanism*, preferably with direct access to a highly placed neutral manager such as the Human Resources Director; a requirement to *investigate* and reach

a finding on each matter; and that offenders will be dealt with through the *disciplinary process* based on the evidence of each circumstance. Finally, the policy should provide assurance to employees that reported incidents will be treated with the greatest possible degree of discretion and *confidentiality*, and that any form of apparent *reprisal* will be dealt with under the same policy and procedures.

2. Disseminate the policy to every employee, requiring that each unit manager discuss it thoroughly at least annually in a group meeting with their employees, and individually with each new hire during their initial orientation period.

3. Provide *thorough* training to all supervisors and managers so that they completely understand all the factors, consequences, basic diagnostic elements, methods of handling, and to discuss among themselves their concerns and problems in this area. A comprehensive training on this and other sources of workplace discrimination ought to be done every two to three years, with facilitated problem-solving sessions on a range of similar human resource matters conducted semi-annually.

It is also very important to have the company CEO either sit in on these opportunities to hear what's going on in the organization, to show support, or at least to open the session. Depending on the nature of the organization and managerial relationships, it is frequently more productive to use consultants or outside subject experts to conduct these training and problem-solving sessions. The total cost of any preventative measure will always be less than one error.

4. Train the person who will be responsible for conducting internal evaluations (investigations) of sexual harassment complaints to be knowledgeable about legal infringement on employee rights, techniques of interviewing including the construction of open-ended and other non-judgmental factfinding questions, the order and development of evidence, separating facts from speculation, and the factors to consider in reaching a concluding course of action. What must be remembered in this very delicate phase of problem solving is that all employees have rights, and one of them is to not be falsely accused. If taken at too great of face value, a complaint of sexual harassment can predispose the evaluator into a bias belief (verdict) before all concerned have an equally objective opportunity to provide information.

By having the appearance, or posing a question that implies guilt early on, you can easily lead the alleged perpetrator to believe that an accusation is being made resulting in a defensive reaction, or that the victim is lying and therefore discredited. These conclusions should be avoided until all of the facts are in. Moreover, making or implying an accusation without substantial fact where blatant sexual misconduct is involved may well turn into a defamation lawsuit. If it is based on provable fact, the perpetrator's actions may constitute a moral turpitude or felonous conduct violation that might have legal implications.

It is for these collective reasons that the evaluator of sexual harassment complaints be trained in matters of employment law, evidence gathering, and defensible methods of complaint processing. While the use of such experienced investigators to conduct internal evaluations is likely to arouse suspicious, distorted, or defensive attention to the circumstance (even if it is internal counsel well known throughout the organization), they absolutely ought to be consulted at the onset of a complaint, at the point of decision-making conclusion, or if any party to the complaint expresses any kind of legal reservation about proceeding. We must respect and preserve the rights of each employee to receive fair treatment, including a reasonable opportunity to be represented, even if the courts become the forum for judgment.

CHAPTER I: 4.0
PROBLEMS IN A MIXED WORKFORCE:
ROMANCE BETWEEN EMPLOYEES,
PREGNANCY DISCRIMINATION AND
ACCOMMODATING CHILD CARE NEEDS

The three topics of this chapter are not intended to infer a particularly usual or even customary sequence of events between employees in the same workplace. Rather, it is more normal that they are mutually exclusive events but representative of the individual, isolated, yet frequently encountered life pattern of nearly every employee. While romance is both a natural and hopeful event in one's personal life, it tends to take on less desirable connotations when it occurs between employees. Similarly, childbirth and pregnancy related conditions of our employees is normally considered a personally rewarding event, but it has presented some difficult problems for managers in the employment context. There has also evolved a resurgent interest by employees in family life while maintaining careers. This and the growth of single working parents has created a monumental demand for employers to begin examining the need to accommodate child care in order to maintain valued human resources.

4.10 DEALING WITH ROMANCE BETWEEN EMPLOYEES

On a somewhat different aspect of sexual involvement in the workplace—yet more related than we might care to consider—is the romantic liaison that can and frequently occurs between co-workers. There are a number of explanations of how and why it occurs, the effects created by it, and the obvious difficulties of dealing with these situations. Some of these issues will be examined here, but at the onset it is interesting to note a few common characteristics of workplace romance, and they are:

- More often than not it becomes a problem to the organization, co-workers and subordinate employees, and ultimately the romantic partners.

- The nature of the problem(s) produced by romantic liaisons are often not diagnosed until the situation has become irreparable.

- The romantic partners think they are being discreet and are usually the last ones to realize the effect they're having on others.

- Management typically feels inept or inappropriate in stepping in, and consequently avoids addressing the issue until complications occur—and then it's usually handled by a termination or forced resignation.

4.11 PREVALENCE OF THE PROBLEM

There are few subjects pertaining to human behavior at work more commonly known than various types of romantic involvement between men and women. The subject has been thoroughly addressed in professional literature, the media, and in the corridors of probably every business organization throughout the developed world. It is a global issue confronting each manager who must deal with conduct in the workplace, particularly when the conduct begins to create some type of detrimental effect.

We all know it has occurred in our business environments, and it continues to exist. We probably know of at least one or two situations going on right now—either involving someone we know, heard about, supervise, or you yourself may have had the experience—and it is a condition that by its very nature will continue to exist from time to time. For these reasons, and because it represents one of the more thorny interpersonal problems for management, it needs to be better understood, then squarely addressed by both the organization and each manager responsible for the productivity and harmony of employees.

Although the subject of romance in the workplace is one of the most commonly known phenomenons in business life, the number of empirical studies on the topic is surprisingly small—fewer than a dozen—and most have been anecdotal accounts or case studies. Some of these stories have received national attention because of the prominence of those involved, not the least of which were the highly publicized relationships that occurred between well-placed corporate officers such as Mary Cunninham and Bill Agee of the Bendix Corporation, and Cecil Parkinson and Sara Keays in England.

In nearly every one of the studies conducted on this subject, virtually every person who was questioned either personally knew about or had a personal experience of a workplace romance—including one study of various people at an airport! In most cases, those questioned could account for several cases they had personally witnessed and the manner in which they evolved and concluded. Nearly all respondents in these studies felt that management handled the situation properly, if at all, and many felt the problems were known but ignored until unavoidable. Other insightful results were that three-fourths of the romantic involvements were those in which the male held a direct superior position with the female partner: in one-half of these cases the female was the male's secretary; one-fourth were other direct subordinate females; and the other one-fourth were females two or more levels below the male's position.

Conversely, only one out of four situations involving romantic liaisons involved either a female superior and male subordinate, or between men and women of equal position stature in the organization. However, with the rapidly increasing number of women acquiring professional and managerial jobs, recent literature is now demonstrating that one of the most frequent kinds of romantic or sexual relations occurring in the workplace are those involving male-female mentorship, referred to as developmental relationships.

The most difficult problems that tend to result from workplace romance—that is, those liaisons where there evolves the most pronounced kinds of adverse effects—are the romantic involvements between those in the management ranks and those between managers and subordinate employees. Why? Simply because they inherently have the capacity to do more damage to the structural integrity of the organization, their own credibility as objective decision-makers, and those that rely on their judgment and guidance. These conditions and their effect rarely develop to a level of significant impact on the organization when romance takes shape between non-management co-workers. In these cases, the worst effect is typically minor productivity problems within their work unit, and these problems are easily correctable through keen supervisorial monitoring of employee work activities and diplomatic early discussion of the situation.

Human resource managers and executives questioned on how their companies view and address the issue of workplace romance (or sexual liaison) is also interesting, and is perhaps further testimony as to why these situations so frequently become organizational problems having painful conclusions. American human resource managers seem to be the most fearful of romantic liaison due to the sometimes narrow distinctions between mutual attraction and the employer's liability for condoning unwelcome harassment (one-sided attraction) that has been profusely litigated in the United States. Yet, whether American, Canadian, British, French, Swiss, German, or other capitalist economy, human resource managers rather universally admit that;

1) it's a problem,

2) their companies shy away from interceding in the personal lives of employees,

3) it's rarely addressed as a policy issue, and even then such policies may have little deterent effect,

4) that these situations are given a blind eye until it becomes of notable damage, and

5) the underlying (unspoken) management philosophy is that the common sense of those involved in the relationship should prevail—which is grossly naive at best, and clearly a form of avoidance of the kinds of effects these relationships have in the workplace.

4.12 THREE KINDS OF WORKPLACE ROMANCE

Not all romantic or sexual affinities between employees are the same, and it is important to be able to distinguish which kind of relationship is occurring in order to understand its emotional significance, evolutionary conditions, behavioral dynamics, effects, probable risks, and proper handling. Like any other business problem-solving matter, it is of some significance to the outcome of a course of action to first be able to identify as many accurate elements and conditions of the particular problem before pondering its possible resolution, or at least the initial approach to address it. Failure to properly diagnose the situation usually complicates the matter and often tends to fall short of alleviating the real problem(s). With this thought in mind, let's take a brief look at the three most common kinds of romantic relationships that occur between people at work.

1. *THE FLING*

   Whether we call this relationship a fling, affair, or flirtatious experience, the situation has a rather consistent pattern. They may occur as the result of a long term association or a given set of conditions that rapidly draw two people toward mutual attraction. This relationship tends to spark quickly; it usually has a heightened sense of passion; it centers on mutual sexual attraction; one or both participants are usually married; and their alliance fades or ends entirely after a few months.

   Merely because the fling is normally a short-lived event is no reason for mangement to look the other way or avoid the signals (or intuition) that it is going on. These can be the most painful to the participants and their family members, the most disrupting to their own productivity and credibility, and ultimately lead to impossible work relations between them when it ends. Socially and organizationally it has long been held as a taboo, and there is almost always at least one who loses more than they imagined possible.

2. *LOVING COMMITMENT*

   This relationship is, of course, the one everyone admires and hopes it will flourish into a permanent, meaningful bond. It is rarely held as a company secret for any length of time by the participants (as if their behavior doesn't give them away sooner than they think) since they often want their intent to be known by others as a source of pride. As the relationship progresses, a deeper sense of commitment begins to replace those charmlike flirtations that brought the situation about in the beginning.

Assuming there are no unusual obstacles between them, or damaging effect upon others that causes them to part, this relationship frequently evolves to marriage—which, in some instances can present a new problem for companies having antinepotism policies. At least in its premarriage stages, this romantic relationship is considered to be morally acceptable, therefore untouched, than the other two kinds of relationships that violate moral and ethical taboos.

3. *THE MENTORSHIP*

Mentorship involves the close working relationship between one superior and their subordinate. It can be two professional employees, a senior manager and new or junior manager, or even between an executive and a secretary. In fact, mentor relationships are inherently of an intimate nature because of the concentrated amount of time and work activity spent together whether or not there develops a romantic or sexual bonding.

Perhaps one of the more prevalent features of a mentorship liaison is the element of "power attraction" between the two that progressively become more attracted to each other on a personal level. The power to attract the opposite sex, whether based on culturally or biologically imprinted stimuli, can become so strong that it disregards taboos and social norms of behavior. It diminishes reasoning and it develops blind disregard of others. Here are a few sources of power attraction characteristic of the sexes who become involved in a mentorship romance.

Male Power Attraction	Female Power Attraction
Job Status	Admiration
Position Power (authority)	Helplessness/Helpfulness
Prestige	Learning/Inexperienced
Intelligence	Complimentary
Sensitive	Sympathy And Compassion
Confident And Decisive	Sincerety And Interest
Dresses Well	Physical Attractiveness
Physically Fit	Vitality

These same type of power attractors can, and usually are, influences in the development of Fling and Loving Commitment romances, but to a much lessor degree. For example, the fling may start with one or two subtle types of power attraction—which are merely sources of stimuli—such as the female being attracted to the male's prestigious or authorative position, or the male being attracted to the female's compassion and compliments. However, in the mentorship romance more of these power attractions come into play, intimacy becomes more expansive, there is a deeper sense of infatuation that is seen as (or can develop into) love, and there is usually a struggle within both persons to deal with the ethics and other risks of verifying that the other person feels the same romantic inclination.

4.13 CONTRIBUTING CONDITIONS AND BEHAVORIAL DYNAMICS

Social scientists and human resource professionals have long recognized that the workplace is probably the most social, active, challenging, energetic and, yes, even sexy places that people gather; and they do so under unique, varying, and unassuming conditions all of which make romantic attraction not only normal, but sometimes even fostered. Many employment environments, especially the formal office setting, establish fashionable dress standards or expectations. Even if this is inadvertent, it sets up a certain type of sexuality by encouraging employees to look their best—to look professionally attractive.

Workplace activities by the very nature of interaction between people contributes to the presence of intimacy and therefore the opportunity to become attracted and, if not self-managed, personally involved. Work related interaction gives people the rather unsuspecting opportunity to get acquainted with another's ideas, feelings, ambitions, interests, mannerisms, values, preferences, and personal habits—the very things we examine on a more conscious level when engaged in such mating rituals as dating. When people's work bring them together in close association with each other, the stage can easily become set for unconscious development of attraction whether it becomes the product of a lengthy and involved project, a singular business trip, or sporadic but intense contact with each other.

Once the attraction becomes known as mutual, the die is cast so to speak. What follows is very predictable patterns of behavior in spite of the fact that they think they're being discreet enough to avoid being ostracized in the case of Loving Commitment liaisons, caught and punished in the case of a Fling, and embarassed by the loss of credibility in the case of Mentorship romances. The fact of the matter is that powerful emotions take over, and otherwise rational judgment is nowhere to be found. Those that become personally attracted and reach out to each other for romantic and sexual intimacy seldom realize that others know exactly what's going on. Those engaged in workplace intimacy fear the effect it can have on their jobs, and eventually it will anger others because of the participants' irresponsible attention to their work and other work relationships.

So, the workplace conditions and behavorial dynamics that tend to contribute to the development of romantic liaisons are:

1. A socially stimulating environment to interact with others.
2. An unsuspecting setting for attraction to develop.
3. Close and frequent contact creating an opportunity for familiarity.
4. The intensity of some work relationships that fosters mutual affinity.
5. The matching or exchange of power attractions.
6. The willingness to become romantically involved despite risks.
7. The (sometimes blatant) disregard of the effect on others, the company, and their own welfare.

The very conditions and interactions that contribute to a romantic liaison create a tough paradox for management since it is equally well known that people are usually most productive when these very same conditions are present. In fact, many companies work hard to deliberately achieve these conditions—not to foster romantic ties and their attendant complications, but to create such positive types of productivity stimulation as congeniality, informality, friendship, trust, respect, and enthusiasm. These are conditions that make work relationships harmonious, cooperative, energetic, and therefore more productive. The dilemma exists with regard to where and how to draw the line between desirable productivity conditions and undesirable romantic entanglements. The line needs to be drawn between numbers 4 and 5 above.

4.14 THE RISKS AND COMPLICATIONS: WHAT PRICE FOR ROMANCE?

When two people in the same organization find themselves romantically involved, there immediately develops the conflict between personal role and organizational role. It is this very conflict that makes the relationship difficult to manage between themselves, it precipitates negative emotional feelings (guilt, fear, anguish, etc.), and these in turn lead them to conduct their clandestine liaison as discreetly as possible and thereby avoid detection or exposure of the relationship to others. Often, situations will arise in the course of business that require the couple to choose between their loyalty to the relationship or the organization, such as the need to avoid each other at meetings and social functions. In other words, the power of various emotions battle it out within each person, and, with some frequency, desire for the other person prevails over guilt associated with violating organizational norms. Rarely does the couple fully consider the extent of the risks they take, or the problems such liaisons cause others.

Here are a few of the more direct types of risks and problems generated by romantic affiliations at work, and they become increasingly more serious in their impact the higher each is positioned in the organization and/or if one or both are already marrried.

FOR SELF:

While there may be a small percentage of workplace romance liaisons that have pleasant and fulfilling culminations (usually marriage), these situations are typically infrequent compared to those that become painful and end that way. This is particularly true for management employees as well as those who have spouses and family. Nearly all of these situations (Fling and Mentorship relationships) produce feelings of guilt, potential embarassment and sometimes shame, anger, annoyance, and fear. These feelings produce the desire to "go public" to relieve the social pressure, and consequently, their behavior toward each other becomes more apparent much like the thief who unconsciously wants to get caught. Most of what they risk by their getting involved or having the liaison revealed is the loss of everything most of us work so hard to achieve. They consist of the loss of:

- professional credibility
- self-confidence and esteem
- reputation in the organization
- sense of objectivity and ethical codes of conduct

- spouse and family
- former social ties
- promotions and advancements
- career and income
- employment references

At the extreme, there can also be the risk of litigation resulting from a discrimination suit where one of the participants engages in favoritism decision making, or where one of the participants decides to drop out of the liaison that's forming, but the other persists resulting in one-sided sexual harassment.

FOR OTHERS:

Other people quicly become affected by romantic liaisons whether their relationship to the participants is that of being a superior manager, peer, subordinate employee, or family member. Whether intentional or not, the behavior that typically accompanies romantic liaison has a disturbing impact on others. Subordinates are subjected to poor decisions, forgetfulness, moodiness, impatience, lack of concentration and objectivity, imbalances in the distribution and flow of work, and less open communications from the involved manager who may also be late or absent more frequently.

For peer co-workers and superiors, the involved person becomes less reliable in their decisions, judgments, and getting work done in a timely, thorough fashion. Quality drops that affect the work of colleagues, business transactions suffer, and bosses develop concern, frustration, then anger. Co-workers become disappointed, less trusting, and sometimes resentful when the decline in performance begins to reflect on them, or they have to pick up the slack (or feel initially obligated to cover for their involved colleague).

For the spouse(s) and family members that learn, usually in the worst way (indirectly), about the involvement of their husband, wife, or parent in a morally unacceptable relation, the effect is just plain ugly. Everyone becomes a painful loser including the new liaison. Imagine how complicated this situation becomes when the spouse of one of the involved persons comes to the company to ask why you or some other official did nothing to stop it from happening when you knew it was going on. What do you suppose you might say to the spouse?

For the organization there is loss too. Inevitably there is a decline in performance, be it productivity, decisions, objectivity, or morale. There also evolves the disruption of working relationships, the emergence of rivalries, inappropriate disclosure of organizational information, damage to the company reputation, and all too frequently having to release an otherwise valued- employee. By then, the damage within the organizational structure, including other established managerial and work unit relationships, is done and it will likely take some time for those that remain to recover from its consequences.

Two different yet interesting legal cases in 1986 demonstrate not only potential discrimination issues that can become a by-product of romance in the workplace, but also take the organization public. In *DeCintio vs. Westchester County Medical Center,* the Second Circuit Court found that a boss' promotion of a woman with which he was romantically involved was not discrimination on the basis of sex because in addition to five male therapists, the boss also refused to promote another female at this New York medical facility. A similar finding was reached in *Miller v. Aluminum Company of America* (1988). In other words, sex discrimination does not (presently) include one's biased actions that are predicated on romantic or sexual liaison. However, it would be a monumental mistake to take this case as the definitive judgment of such a circumstance based on broader interpretations by other courts who seem to hold that any form of preference due to sex (in general) that adversely affects others equally qualified is discrimination, and therefore unlawful.

With regard to an organization's policy prohibition against romantic associations between employees where one or both were married, the court ruled in *Federated Rural Electric Ins. Co. v. Kessler* that such a policy did not violate a law prohibiting marital status discrimination. Here, the court concluded that, "The employer's work rule was consistent with the public policy of discouraging extra-marital affairs."

Although both employers prevailed in court, it is doubtful either enjoyed having their laundry aired in view for the world to see their organizations in quite this light.

4.15 DETECTING ROMANTIC INVOLVEMENTS

Those who have worked together for any length of time are quick to recognize even the smallest change of behavior, work routine, or moods. It should not be surprising then to find that co-workers of those becoming involved in a workplace romance can easily detect that something has created a change. By merely observing them it can be figured out rather quickly. Not so for the supervisor or manager of a romantically involved subordinate because their personal familiarity and observation opportunities are less frequent than among co-workers. The unsuspecting superior may at best feel that the pair have become a "good team" and seem to enjoy working together. What are the signs a superior should watch for that usually signals the existence or development of a romantic liaison? Pay close attention to these changes in behavior, moods, and work routines.

- Increasing frequency of having lunch or taking breaks together.
- Being seen together away from work.
- Longer or more frequent talking to each other.
- Both persons being late, leaving early, or absent on the same day.
- Exchanges of flirtations or admiring facial expressions.
- Touching and holding hands.
- Creating unnecessary reasons to be together.
- Showing favoritism toward the other, or defending the other.
- Learning that one has information provided to the other.
- Clock watching.
- Decline in concentration and becoming easily distracted, yet otherwise emotionally stable.

Above all, there is an irresistable need for the pair to have contact as frequently as possible, and contact of any type becomes better than no contact. In thinking it would be more shrewd and less observed, they will often use various methods of contact such as telephoning each other, bumping into each other, passing by the other's work station, leaving little notes, and the like even though they may work within eyesight of each other.

4.16 SOLVING PROBLEMS THROUGH INTERVENTION: POLICY POSITION AND MANAGEMENT HANDLING

Each situation of romantic or sexual involvement between co-workers should be evaluated on the basis of each case and set of circumstances. However, to avoid arbitrary, inconsistent, or sex-based discrimination, a company would do well to establish at least general parameters or perhaps even explicit prohibitions contained in company policy. An example of such policy, prepared in conjunction with the company's policy on sexual harassment or nepotism, might be along the following lines.

SAMPLE POLICY

Although the company generally confines its involvement in the private lives of employees, there may be some circumstances in which it becomes necessary for the company to intervene. Romantic or sexual liaisons that develop in the workplace are instances that the company sees as potentially disruptive to performing one's job, affecting the working conditions of others, damaging to business relationships, and adverse to careers and the company's reputation as a harmonious workplace.

Those employees that become involved in this regard should be aware that serious risks and consequences can develop as a result of its effect on business matters, at which time the company may intervene by discussing the issue with effected employees, or taking remedial measures when, in the company's opinion, it is necessary to do so to maintain the integrity of work relationships.

Further, it is expressly prohibited for management employees to date or become similarly involved privately with any other employee of the company, or for any married employee to establish a romantic or sexual relationship with any other employee. Should these kinds of relationships become known to company officers, the company will determine an appropriate course of action on a case-by-case basis. Such action may include counseling, transfer, demotion, or termination.

The company would rather avoid these situations altogether, and we therefore encourage employees to use common sense judgment in managing their work relationships so that this type of awkwardness does not develop.

The fact that you have a policy prohibiting at least certain kinds of romantic liaisons will, of course, not stop them completely. At best, it gets the issue in the open, serves as a deterent, specifies the company's position, acts as a source of reference for others to come forward to disclose the existence and effect of a liaison, and may even get a couple or two to work it out themselves. Therefore, it would probably be worthwhile to include such a preventative measure in company policy.

But, does such a policy infringe on, or conflict with, the company's stance on antinepotism? Not normally, because most antinepotism policies deal with the issue of married couples working together, particularly where one has direct or even indirect authority over the other. However, because romantic relationships almost always occur within a work unit, an innocent romance may occur followed by their marriage. As the romance developed, others may have thought it was delightful to observe the couple's joy and positive changes, but now that their marriage is pending, this will likely present a whole new problem in terms of the reasons the company developed its policy on nepotism. In a legal context, the courts have generally upheld an employer's antinepotism policy when applied to conditions that would clearly affect business conduct, lines of authority, harmony of the work unit, and other reasons of business necessity. In other words, the antinepotism policy should focus on the employer taking action to remove one or the other married employees (by transfer, reassignment, termination, etc.) when their relationship has the likely potential to affect morale, security, safety, or supervision.

When a romantic or sexual liaison develops, management should intervene as diplomatically as possible at the earliest stage, even if such a development is only suspected. If you suspect it, it's probably true and careful informal conversation at the early stage is considerably easier than dealing with damage done at a later stage. If the people involved require you to handle preliminary intervention, here are some pointers in deciding your approach.

1. First and foremost, express your concern for both persons involved and use non-judgmental statements in letting them know that you (and perhaps others) feel that a liaison may be developing on a private level. Don't ask for confirmation, just discuss the issues.

2. Focus on the need for everyone to work closely and in a respectful, trustworthy fashion to achieve best performance; but be precise about the potential adversity of private liaisons on one's own work, business judgments, the effect on co-workers or subordinates, families, careers, and morale. Try to get them to see clearly and as objectively as possible what could be at risk and what could be lost.

3. Point out the company's policy on workplace liaisons and antinepotism, if applicable, and let them know in advance that even if they were to marry, one or both of their jobs could be jeopardized.

4. Talk to them separately and privately (away from the workplace is best), but encourage them to talk it over together. If they volunteer acknowledgment of their involvement, tell them you'd like to hear about their decision after talking it over. Let them know you want to help resolve the conflict in roles.

If only one of the involved employees is in your span of control, talk the situation over with your human resources manager, the other employee's department head, or both before initiating informal intervention. This allows the most immediate level of responsible management to compare their observations, determine an appropriately mutual course of action, and establish a monitoring or decision making mechanism should informal methods fail.

If the liaison persists, higher management must begin to document the performance or other types of adverse effects the relationship is having. If the liaison violates company policy outright, and the company has solid proof, immediate formal action should be considered even if it is only to have a high ranking official discreetly tell them to cease and desist or face consequences.

Once documented effect of a liaison that does not violate policy per se has been gathered, and the participants have been given (documented) forewarning, the next step should be to present the evidence to the human resource manager and/or company president, and request that one or both of them call the participants to order a cease and desist or face consequences. By bringing the entire set of circumstances to a neutral top manager (human resources) and the one ultimately responsible for workplace matters (president), it will be much easier to determine the proper course of action beyond formal warning to disengage the liaison. Even then the relationship may have progressed to a point where disengaging will have a residual effect on their ability to work (now differently and more emotionally sensitive) together, which should equally be assessed and corrected.

Generally then, the best approach is an early one that encourages open communications, honesty, and problem solving rather than leaving impressions of deviant behavior and intimidation which will only provoke defensive reactions from the couple.

The real issue that must be addressed by management is the conflict of interests that are occurring between the couple's personal role and their organizational role. Management needs to stick to the issues of how this role conflict manifests itself in specific ways that are detrimental to company expectations, performance, judgment, working relationships, the effect on others, and similar business interests of a clear and legitimate nature.

While it is no longer appropriate for employers to take a paternalistic stance by trying to overcontrol the behavior, thoughts, and motives of employees, the line must be drawn somewhere so that all employees—including higher management employees—develop a clear understanding of what standards of conduct are desired as well as prohibited. Such standards ought to be thoroughly communicated, periodically reinforced in meetings, and promptly acted upon when these situations occur.

Failure to maintain the conviction of policy intent by not acting on a known workplace romance that's having an adverse effect will render any communicated standards on the subject rather shallow. As managers, we might not be able to alter the course of the very powerful emotions connected to romantic or sexual liaisons, but as awkward as we may feel about stepping in, we are obliged to maintain control and order over many workplace situations. Many others in the organization may well be relying heavily (if not hopefully) on our ability to intervene and resolve these problems. It need not always result in termination. Remember, the goal is always to resolve the problem, keep damage to a minimum, and utilize our human resources in the most efficacious manner possible.

4.20 PROBLEMS OF PREGNANCY DISCRIMINATION AND RELATED CONDITIONS

The pregnancy of female employees and its sometimes related conditions (medical complications, abortions, miscarriages, and post-pregnancy child care including nursing), have presented numerous thorny problems for employers. The problems typically relate to operational, administrative, economic, legal, and moral issues. Bearing in mind that one of the fundamental needs of any employer is to maximize productivity—and that can only be achieved when employees are available for work—any form of reduction in work hours harms the employer's bottom line profits and other organizational goals. It is twice as damaging to the employer's interests when an employee's absence and benefit continuation costs become an additional expense to the employer on top of the loss of productive work.

With women now representing more than half of the active workforce—a doubling since pre-World War II participation—and their utilization in a wider array of jobs diffusing them more thoroughly as a permanent member of the workforce, the problem becomes much more acute; particularly when we consider that over 70 percent of the female workforce is of childbearing age. Generally though, many companies are now finding that most of these problems, and in particular the work-disrupting absences, can be resolved through advanced planning measures.

It also seems reasonable for us to conclude that, as managers of our organization's human resources, we ought to begin a more sensitive reexamination of our approaches and practices governing the periodic absence or turnover of employees. It is a given fact in today's diverse society that people will encounter a variety of events that will influence their direction or alter their lifestyle; some are by choice, some by circumstance, and others by uncertain motive. Whether our employees choose marriage, to remain single, to divorce, have children, adopt, or whatever is of no business concern to us. The manner in which their personal situations affect their job attendance and performance does. True, many employers having very tight (unforgiving) controls over attendance and performance have been able to prevail in court on refusal-to-hire and termination actions against pregnant and child caring women, but these employers usually pay a greater price within the organization for their insensitivity and inflexibility. Morale is likely to be affected by other employees who see this form of unfair treatment, and those female workers who become pregnant are likely to feel they would be unwelcome by their employer after childbirth.

When we examine a more global perspective of how pregnancy is dealt with by employers in other countries, we might begin to see that the U.S. is not always the leader in the liberalization of benefits that might encourage well trained and loyal employees to return to work after such events. For example, consider how these developed countries provide for pregnant workers.

COUNTRY	LENGTH OF LEAVE	TO WHOM GRANTED	BENEFITS
Austria	16 weeks; extended leave until the child is a year old	Mother	100% of earnings for 16-20 weeks; monthly allowance until the child is a year old
Canada	16-18 weeks, 37 weeks in the public sector	Mother	60% of insured earnings for 15 weeks
Czechoslovakia	26 weeks; extended leave until the child is 2 years old	Mother	90% of earnings for 26-35 weeks; monthly allowance until the child is 2 years old
Italy	5 months, plus 1 month if the woman's work is arduous; extended leave during the child's first year	Mother	80% of earnings for 5-6 months; 30% of earnings for 6 month during the child's first year
Norway	108 working days	Mother; father may care for child up to 72 days	100% of earnings for 108 days
Sweden	360 days	Either parent qualifies for post-natal leave	90% of earnings for 270 days; flat-rate allowance for next 90 days
Soviet Union	16 weeks; extended leave until the child is a year old	Unspecified	100% of earnings for 16-18 weeks; monthly allowance until the child is a year old
West Germany	14 weeks; extended leave until the child is 6 months old	Mother	100% of earnings for 14-18 weeks; monthly allowance until the child is 6 months old

Source: Congressional Research Congress, Maternity's Parental Leave Policies: A Competitive Analysis

In total, some 117 developed countries provide similar benefits to employees as a matter of public policy (law), and the average paid leave in Europe is six months with most countries paying 100 percent of salary. Given the estimation that two-thirds of those entering the United States workforce through the 1990's will be women, employers ought to begin recognition, acceptance, and planning for the fact that these are inevitable lifestyle events for these employees, and that they represent a resource worth keeping. The way you keep good people is to treat them well and provide for their needs.

A company's policies and practices, then, are a reflection of the overall philosophy about employees—how the organization and management views the employer-employee relationship; whether you intend to treat employees as responsible adults or paternalistically; whether there is open or closed problem-solving or shared thinking; and the level and manner in which they are to be rewarded for their contributions. It's not difficult to scan a company's personnel policy manual or employee handbook to get a reading of the underlying philosophy of top management. Those companies that tend to evoke organizational pride among their employees don't give up control, or necessarily exceed legal (minimum compliance) requirements; they share control at each level of the organization; they collectively confront new problems; and they create (policy) approaches and solutions with human compassion toward the issue knowing that fair treatment of employees is a long term investment that pays off at a more consistent rate than the stock market. And probably nowhere else is this more true than with the more recent and controversial issue of how to deal with employee pregnancy, or any other type of personal disability, and its attendant business operation problems.

Once again, many of the solutions to these problems are found in particular compliance cases addressed by the courts concerning leave policies, benefits, interviewing and hiring, and terminations to name a few of the more common concerns that occur with regularity. The issue is worth at least a brief examination of applicable law, followed by illustrative court cases and their impact on human resource operations. These discussions will also include some advisory points from the human resource management perspective.

4.21 LEGAL PROHIBITIONS AGAINST PREGNANCY DISCRIMINATION

The Pregnancy Discrimination In Employment Act was signed by President Carter in 1978, and has since been embodied as an amendment to Title VII (ss: 701(k)). The basis for this Congressional law was in response to the displeasing U.S. Supreme Court's 1976 decision in *Gilbert v. General Electric Co.* wherein the high court determined that the company's policy of excluding pregnancy-related medical expenses from insurance benefit plans was not a form of sex discrimination. Consequently, the PDA amended Title VII to make pregnancy-related discrimination part and parcel of sex discrimination by providing that:

> The terms "because of sex" or "on the basis of sex" include, but are not limited to, because of or on the basis of pregnancy, childbirth, or related medical conditions; and women affected by pregnancy, childbirth, or related medical conditions shall be treated the same for all employment-related purposes, including receipt of benefits under fringe benefit programs, as other persons not so affected but similar in their ability or inability to work...

Guidelines subsequently issued by the EEOC, as well as court decisions, provide that

1. Employers with 15 or more employees cannot refuse to hire a woman because she is or may become pregnant, or because of pregnancy related conditions and medical needs. Here, preferences of other workers is not considered a reasonable purpose for exclusion. However, a more legitimate reason (BFOQ) for refusing to hire, or needing to transfer, a pregnant or fertile woman would be in cases of unavoidable exposure to substances creating a reproductive hazard.

2. Employers having medical plans that provide pregnancy benefits must see that the costs for and benefits of the pregnancy benefits are dealt with the same as any other type of disability, except where excluded because of the pre-existing pregnancy condition, or in cases of abortion where the life of the mother would not be threatened. Thus, medical plan premiums, deductibles, co-insurance payments, and other expenses cannot be on the basis of pregnancy-related benefits in more or less than for other disabilities.

3. Employers may not maintain leave policies that treat pregnant or related condition female employees differently than for any other type of personal, temporary disability; except that, female employees disabled for this reason must be allowed to return to the same or substantially similar job with the employer upon her physical ability to do so unless she declines. Therefore, employers can require medical certification to insure the pregnant employee is physically able to continue or resume employment so long as other disabled employees are likewise required to substantiate their medical suitability. Employers may not require pregnant employees to leave or return to their employment by a prescribed number of days.

   Similarly, if an employer's leave policy allows use of accrued vacation or leave of absence to attend to such "external purposes" as education, death in family, travel, and the like, employers ought to recognize that the same rationale would be applied, if tested, to the granting of such leave for child care. Also, while on leave for pregnancy-related conditions, employers should extend the same benefit maintenance privileges to these employees as it does with other types of physical disability.

Some states have likewise enacated even more liberal leave benefit laws. For example, California's law requires employers to grant leave up to four months with a guarantee to return to the same or similar job. Connecticut, Montana, Minnesota, Tennessee, Oregon and Massachusetts have equivalent laws while comparable regulation of leave benefits is a matter of discrimination law in Illinois, Ohio, New Hampshire, Washington, Kansas, and Hawaii. Given this developing pattern of mixed legal standards on the issue of sex-related discrimination due to the pregnancy, childbirth, or adoption of infants, employers in all states would be well advised to alter their practices to provide for gender-neutral, and disability condition neutral, treatment.

4.22 CASE LAW SOLUTIONS: HOW THE COURTS VIEW REFORM

Are There Any Limitations On Interviewing Questions; And Suppose I Can See A Female Applicant Is Pregnant?

As with all other forms of discrimination, there are limitations on questions pertaining to personal, non-job related characteristics of job applicants. For this reason, it is prudent to: 1) ask the same basic questions of all applicants; 2) ask only questions that are directly related to the applicant's qualifications to perform what is required of actual job conditions; and 3) keep a record of the questions you ask. With respect to unlawful sex, marital status, or pregnancy related questions, you should not ask:

- Are you married?
- Do you have children?
- Do you intend to have children?
- Would you like to have children?
- Do you require child care services?
- Have you ever had an abortion?
- If you had a child, would you return to work...how long would you be off work...etc.?

Questions that even indirectly infer sex-related discrimination should be avoided, such as "Do you have plans or would you like to get married someday?" The inference here, even if marital status is not covered by state antidiscrimination law, is that the female applicant who says yes will "probably" get pregnant shortly thereafter. People who still make these kinds of overgeneralizing assumptions are likely to conclude a negative answer means the female applicant is either lying or doesn't know her own mind. There's virtually no winning for this applicant in these kinds of unlawful interviews!

Take, for example, the case of *King v. Trans World Airlines, Inc.* (1984) in which a female kitchen helper applicant was asked during her interview questions pertaining to her relationship with an employee, how many children she had and were they legitimate, her child care arrangements, and future child-bearing plans. The Eighth Circuit Court of Appeals provided injunctive relief on the basis of clearly apparent evidence of sex discrimination. For similar cases involving unlawful interview questions and applicant screening, see *Thorne v. City of El Segundo* (1984), *Delaney v. Tanzler* (1984), *Altschuler v. Walters* (1983), and *Haskins v. Secretary of Health and Human Services* (1984).[1]

On the issue of interviewing a currently pregnant female, or learning of her pregnancy prior to a job offer, the situation should be treated no differently than if any applicant informed you of an impending medical condition they had that would render them temporarily disabled during a particular period in their initial employment year. Unforseen temporary medical disabilities can and do occur among male and female employees during their first year of employment so, in a sense, one can take the position that a pregnancy-related temporary disability is at least more predictable for replacement planning purposes than are unforeseen disabilities. However, refusals to hire currently pregnant applicants that might be held as lawful would be on the basis of either a bona fide occupational qualification (BFOQ), such as job exposure to fetal-harmful substances, or reasons of business necessity related to the job. An example of the business necessity reasoning was applied in *Marafino v. St. Louis County Circuit Court* (1983) where the employer (should this be surprising since the employer was a court!) was upheld as lawfully withdrawing a job offer after learning of plaintiff's pregnancy on the basis of its disruptive and harmful effect during her training program.

A word to the wise in your deliberations about refusing to hire a pregnant applicant. First, ask yourself if the company would endorse a similar position on, say, a male applicant known to be contemplating knee surgery. In other words, would you refuse to hire *any* applicant where it is known in advance that their absence due to a temporary disability would (or could) have a detrimental effect during their initial employment training? Second, how lucky do you feel about your state court upholding the rationale that a known pregnancy disability is any more or less disruptive to initial training than unforeseen disabilities? After all, is it not true that virtually all new hires are "in training" during some period of initial employment? Finally, is the "training program" for the position in question formal (classroom, at a special location, or structured), or is it really on-the-job informal training? Clearly, the former has an arguably better chance of prevailing as a defensible business necessity.

Another example of an employer who won their case (but shouldn't have) involving their refusal to interview a pregnant applicant was in *Tranquilli v. Irshad* (1983). The position was that of secretary and, says this appellate court, because only women applied and a woman was selected, the employer was not found guilty of sex discrimination. While the employer may not have been guilty of sex discrimination per se based on the facts, it seems that the court rather blatantly errored by overlooking the

---

[1] Norbach, Craig T. ed.; *The Human Resources Yearbook, 1986 Ed.* New Jersey: Prentice-Hall, 1986, pp. 8.41-8.42.

questionable PDA violation. Refusing to interview a pregnant applicant is about as obvious of intent to discriminate as you can get!

Do We Have To Allow The Use Of Accumulated
Sick Leave For Pregnancy Related Absence?

First, you should know that there is no law that requires a company to make paid sick leave available to employees, though most employers do to remain competitive in the labor market. If you provide such paid absence for any form of temporary physical disability, routine medical visits, surgery, or any other reason common to a pregnancy condition, then you have to allow it for pregnant employees. Modification of policies, including collective bargaining agreements, should be thought out carefully to avoid making the impact any less favorable to either the sex or pregnancy of employees; see *Zichy v. City of Philadelphia* (1979), *Nickels v. Brown City Community Schools* (1981), *Northville Public Schools v. Michigan Civil Rights Comm.* (1982), and *United States v. Buffalo Board of Education* (1984).

Sick leave policies should also require the employee to return to work once recovery is substantiated sufficient to resume normal duties; unless, of course, you wish to allow them the opportunity to return early to perform "light" duty. For example, one of my clients had an employee on leave due to childbirth. The employee was allowed use of accumulated vacation and sick leave in accordance with policy. About three to four weeks after her delivery, the employer requested that she provide a doctor's certification as to her current state of disability and expected date of return to work. After two more weeks of excuses by the employee who had exhausted all forms of paid leave by then, she brought in the doctor's notice saying she was physically able to resume work the next day, and was so instructed by the supervisor. Rather than appearing for work the next day, she submitted a written request for a 60-day leave of absence to care for her newborn, and verbally threatened the supervisor with a pregnancy discrimination lawsuit if it was denied. Seeking the advice of legal counsel, the employer was told to avoid the potential of a suit even though the employer had done everything else correctly; no employee had yet requested a leave of absence (no precedence in the reasons for its use); and basically to disregard this employee's refusal to return to work. My consultation with the employer disclosed that:

1. The employee told another employee she had no intent on returning to work, and that she simply wanted her benefits continued since they were better than her husband's.

2. The employer had well documented evidence of compliance with its own policies and state law (more liberal than federal).

3. That the supervisor did in fact instruct her to return to work, and documented that instruction to her in a letter while her leave request was being considered.

4. The employer was concerned about the effect on other employees knowing she violated a return-to-work order and made it known she only wanted to take advantage of the employer.

Had it not been for all four conditions, it would have been appropriate to concur with the employer's legal counsel. However, given these circumstances and its net (or greater) effect internally on policy and setting the standards by which employees are to be guided, the employer was advised to risk litigation in support of its operating principles. Further, instead of terminating the employee for insubordination and, by policy, create a grievable condition as well as unemployment eligibility, the employer was advised to notify her that her action constituted job abandonment in accordance with policy, and that as such was being construed as a voluntary resignation which the employer was accepting. The employee was not heard from again.

You should not interpret this case illustration as a patterned treatment. Each case of handling any new situation or deviation from the norm should be carefully examined for its facts, conditions, effects, evidence, precedence of the same or similar nature (consistency of rationale), and legal implications. The illustration does, however, point out that not all of the solutions are necessarily the most litigation preventative. We have other, sometimes more influential, principles that need to be applied in the work setting than merely jumping through every legally liberal hoop placed in front of us.

I Know Pregnancy Leave Has To Be Treated Like Any Other Disability, But Should We Grant Leave For Child Care?

Generally, it's a matter of policy discretion on the part of each employer—at least so far, but Congress has expressed an interest in requiring employers with five or more employees to grant this type of leave for both male and female employees requesting it. Until such a federal law is adopted, first see if this type of a leave provision is required by state law. If not, you're on your own. You may next wish to examine past applications of your leave of absence or similar policies in which employees have been granted paid or unpaid leave to attend to family matters, educational pursuits, travel, care of someone else—things not related to their own personal disability. If you have granted such leaves, you've set a precedence that will serve as prima facie evidence of pregnancy-related discrimination. If you don't want to grant leave for child care, then don't allow these other forms of non-personal disability. If you do want to offer it, then it must be available to both male and female employees alike.

In deciding on your policy, you may also want to consider the potential usage. It may well be an issue like bereavement leave—not everyone is going to need it every year, and most employees today cannot maintain their lifestyle without income for very long. Nor is it unreasonable for an employer to set limits beyond which operations are affected. You can limit the length of such leaves, exclude certain key positions (watch for disparate impact) or allow for home-work arrangements on a case-by-case basis. If the employee feels compelled to take a brief child care leave with a clear intent to return to work, they might feel forced to quit in the absence of such leave being available. So, we should consider whether it is better to lose a few employees for a brief period, or a few (and perhaps good ones) forever.

Should We Comply With A Federal Court Decision
Pertaining To The Law Of Another State?

You do not have to comply unless your state has an identical law in which case the federal court precedence is fair warning that you should voluntarily comply. This is equally true for state law cases heard by the U.S. Supreme Court. Take, for example, the California case of *California Savings and Loan Association v. Guerra* (1987)—also known as the Garland Case—where the high court held that California's more liberal treatment of pregnancy leave (up to four months) and guaranteed reinstatement to the same or similar job (unless impossible due to economic necessity) does not give preferential treatment to women in contravention to the PDA, even though the same provisions do not have to be extended to employees having other kinds of disabilities. There was no majority opinion of the court, but they voted 6-3 in favor of letting the California law stand; and noted that the states of Connecticut, Hawaii, Illinois, Massachusetts, Montana, New Hampshire, Ohio, and Washington have similar laws. Those states will want to examine the California decision carefully, whereas other states are not yet affected.

Yet another example on the issue of state law extending greater leave benefits for pregnant employees—particularly with respect to reinstatement rights—was in *Kansas Gas & Electric Co. v. Kansas Commission on Civil Rights* (1988). Here, the state supreme court ruled that the state's pregnancy discrimination law properly favored female employees and was justified by the court as a necessary means of affirmative action. Consequently, the male employee brought this action by filing a (reverse) sex discrimination claim because he was not given similar reinstatement guarantees when he requested a leave of absence for shoulder surgery. This decision seems to deny the fact that federal law encourages employers to treat pregnancy no differently than any other physical disability, but it does point out that employers should proceed with caution when dealing with state laws and state courts who may be looking for any excuse to justify what they want to accomplish—even in light of more superior legal theory!

If Employees Vote To Exclude Pregnancy Benefits From
A Disability Plan Of Their Choosing, Can The Employer Be
Held Liable For Pregnancy Discrimination?

Yes; as you probably know from the U.S. Supreme Court's decision in *EEOC v.*

Newport News Shipbuilding & Dry Dock Co. (1983), employers who provide pregnancy benefits in their medical plans must see that the same benefits are provided to female employees and the spouses of male employees. Applying similar reasoning in *Schiffman v. Cimmaron Aircraft Corp.* (1985), the court held that a 1979 (the year after the PDA became effective and the Newport News Case was held to be retroactive to) disability plan adopted by the company's employees based on a 50-50 cost split was discriminatory and therefore violative of the PDA irrespective of employee choice or collective bargaining agreement. The employer was held liable for the pregnancy-related benefits of plaintiff's wife.

Are There Any Circumstances In Which It's Lawful And Appropriate To Fire An Employee Concerning Pregnancy?

Technically yes, you can terminate a pregnant employee for good cause or any other normal reason you would terminate an employee. However, realize that your action may be perceived as being a pretext for pregnancy discrimination. Be certain your course of action is based on sound policy (cause), that documentation is thorough, that you can show alternative remedies attempted (perhaps progressive discipline), and, preferably, can show that the company has taken a similar course with other employees under the same circumstance.

For example, the employer prevailed in its termination of a pregnant employee who exceeded its absenteeism policy in *Eblin v. Whirlpool Corp.* (1985). Here, the employee was unable to establish that the policy which treated all disabilities equally had a disparate treatment of her based on similar absenteeism of four male employees. The court accepted the different factual situations of the male employees, and held her discharge valid as to unreliable attendance (see also *Mason v. Continental Insurance Co.* (1983), and with regard to documented performance deficiencies see *Mazzella v. RCA Global Communications, Inc.* (1986)).

Conversely, the employer was held liable for constructive discharge in violation of sex and pregnancy discrimination in *Goss v. Exxon Office Systems Co.* (1984). After two pregnancies and two miscarriages, this female sales representative was given the option of transferring to a less rewarding territory or resigning. The court regarded the employer's action as setting up intolerable working conditions forcing her resignation. In light of the impropriety of reinstating her, the court awarded both back and front pay.

Similarly, in *Garner v. Wal-Mart Stores* (1987), the Eleventh Circuit Court found the employer guilty of sex discrimination but not constructive discharge of a female department manager after her return from pregnancy leave. The plaintiff asserted that a male employee with less experience had been given her job during her leave, and that the company refused to transfer him elsewhere in the store upon her return. She was given a "floater" position with less authority but no reduction in pay or benefits. She quit after her first day back to work. While the employer was found to be guilty of sex discrimination on the basis of seemingly permanent replacement of her with a less experienced male manager, the court concluded that the woman did not give the employer a realistic opportunity to work her back into a departmental position, nor did the employer create such unpleasant conditions as to compel her to quit.

Are Pregnant Employees Automatically Entitled To Unemployment Insurance During Or After Their Maternity Leave?

This will depend on the laws in each state, however such state laws cannot be in contravention to the Federal Unemployment Tax Act (FUTA). While states vary in the liberalness with which eligibility for unemployment benefits are established, most states will deny benefits to those who leave their employment voluntarily and without good cause attributable to their work or employer. Under these circumstances the question becomes, is leaving employment for pregnancy related conditions attributable to their work or employer; and, if not, is it otherwise discriminatory?

According to the U.S. Supreme Court's decision in *Wimberly v. Labor and Industrial Relations Commission of Missouri* (1987), it was neither a violation of FUTA or discrimination law for the state to deny plaintiff unemployment insurance benefits when she was refused reinstatement after childbirth because no position was available by her employer. The high court noted that, although FUTA requires that there shall be no denial of unemployment benefits "solely on the basis of pregnancy or termination of pregnancy," the law was intended only to prohibit states from treating pregnancy unfavorably rather than mandating preferential treatment.

In other words, it would seem that the high court's position on employees who leave work for pregnancy related conditions is that they are neither eligible during their physical disability (which prevents them from seeking work), nor particularly eligible thereafter where the sole reason for their unemployment was due to their pregnancy (meaning eligibility might constitute preferential treatment). *However*, the court's opinion in this case does not bar a state from creating statutory eligibility for pregnant workers who leave employment for this reason, and who are so disabled or otherwise remain unemployed thereafter. Therefore, employers facing a particular situation in which a pregnant employee has filed for unemployment benefits should contact a labor attorney or other professionals familiar with state statutes and eligibility criteria.

And so, as it has been with all the other forms of employment discrimination, pregnancy-related discrimination will no doubt be with us for a considerable time, and the law suits will continue to modify corporate policy and practice. Indeed, the presence of pregnant employees is beginning to become more apparent, more accepted, and less the difficult adjustment thought to be needed by companies. Hopefully, as time passes, this form of discrimination will fade with others, litigation will become very isolated, companies will have adjusted to our more diverse and demanding workforce, and morale will remain high because treatment is equitable.

Meanwhile, for those companies who choose to continue operating on policies based on assumptions, myth, and other counterproductive beliefs attached to what may have been characteristic of the workforce two to four decades ago, be prepared to see the battle-lines drawn between an "us-and-them" relationship with your employees. Perhaps ironically, those employers resisting the opening of doors to accommodation of pregnancy and child care have overlooked the very creation of our future workforce. Accommodating a future workforce is like education; no one seems to want to pay for it, but we want it there when its needed. In other words, there's a sort of hypocracy in pregnancy and child care discrimination. Think about it. One of them may supervise you at some future time!

4.30 ACCOMMODATING THE CHILD CARE NEEDS OF EMPLOYEES: A NOT-SO-NEW HUMAN RESOURCE PROBLEM

In the early 1970's, women's participation in the workforce increased sharply. It not only ushered in those baby-boomers of the late 1940's and early 1950's who wanted to benefit from new opportunities and choices created by the feminist movement, many of whom developed the Superwoman Syndrome ("I want it all") during the 1980's, but it was also a period of economic recession that caused a permanent surge in the number of female reentrants back into the workforce forming the two-income family arrangement that has now become a predominant feature of the American middle class. Both groups of female workers either had, or would soon encounter, a major obstacle to focusing their attention on employment and careers unlike their male co-workers—how to obtain reliable and nurturing child care.

For single parents, it also represented a substantial expense consisting of one-fourth to one-third of their gross earnings compared to only moderate expense for the two-income family or no expense for childless workers. Thus, it is not uncommon to find that the incentive to pursue full-time employment is absent for many single parents, particularly those who would only qualify for lower paying jobs. People in such a position having more than one child often see welfare as a more realistic option. Child care gets paid for one way or the other; it just depends on which pocket of the economy it comes out of.

Historically, employer involvement in some form of child care accommodation has been around for some time, but only in moderation and then for an isolated purpose. During the Civil War, female workers in uniform factories could use the factory's day nursery. World War II factory and shipyard workers were likewise provided with day care for the children of working mothers, and other 24-hour businesses such as hospitals where female workers are employed in large numbers have provided child care facilities since the 1940's. Banking, insurance, and other female-intense industries began various forms of involvement in the 1970's.

The existence of a permanent workforce comprised of both male and female employees in need of child care accommodation is clear, but yet to be fully recognized. Presently, one-half to two-thirds of all mothers with school age children are employed. They number over eight million of our employees, and the Bureau of Labor Statistics estimates that nearly 200,000 more will join the workforce every year. Over 40 percent of the working mothers have children under three years of age, and it is estimated that there are about seven million children under the age of 13 who are left unsupervised at home for some part of the workday (latchkey children).

Quite simply, we have not come to terms with the fact that the traditional family (working father, domestic mother, and home-cared children) is now only 10 percent of our population, and even that small group is predicted to have 80 percent of both parents working by the end of the century. And, with increasing equalization of sex roles in the American society, more and more men are finding themselves cast into either single parent roles or sharing more of the responsibility for attending to child care needs. Given present circumstances, the issue of giving birth and attending to the child care needs of our future generations has become an issue of national prominence that touches on the lives of the majority of our workforce, men and women alike, and at all career levels—not just the younger, lower-paying and therefore insignificant positions in our organizations.

How is child care a human resources problem, and why should employers and managers take an interest? Why should employers have to shoulder yet another cost or employment accommodation when benefits already exceed 40 percent of payroll? One answer to these questions is because you're already paying for most of it through the loss of productivity (e.g., absenteeism, late arrivals and early departures, turnover, lack of concentration, personal problems, administrative control time), payment of taxes instead of tax credits, and lacking competition to access a considerable segment of the available labor supply which is expected to lessen by the end of the century.

As further testimony, in 1986 Fortune Magazine surveyed working men and women with children under age 12 and found that 1) child care has as much impact on productivity as the employees' relationship with their supervisor, and 2) 41 percent said they had taken at least one day off in the previous three months for child care reasons. If you need more reasons, then you may be interested to know that there are several different approaches to accommodating child care needs, not all of them will cost you any bottom-line expenses, but each of them have proven effective in terms of cost, productivity, competitiveness, and a boost to morale.

Of the approximately 6.6 million employers in the United States, only about 44,000 of them employ more than 100 people. Yet, by the late 1980's only 2,500-3,000 companies will be involved in some form of an employer-sponsored child care program, and many of these companies participate in consortium arrangements making the number of actual facilities very small. The two most active states have been Massachusetts and California. In California, for example, only 157 companies participate in some kind of child care assistance program out of an employment base of 100,000 companies, and only 47 companies have child care centers; a few of which are:

- American Savings & Loan
- Syntex Corporation
- University of California
  (San Diego, Los Angeles, and
  San Francisco)

- U.S. Government Naval Weapons Center
- NASA Aimes Research Center
- Paramount Studios
- Numerous hospitals

Even with the small number of employer-involved child care centers now present throughout the United States, it represents a growth of an astounding 600 percent just in the four year period of 1982-1986 that is suggestive of some very rapidly awakening, opportunistic-seeking, trend-setting employers. Trend-setting, that is, except for many western European countries such as France where 95 percent of children ages 3-6 are enrolled in free public preschools, while less than 10 percent of similar American children are enrolled in fee-paying licensed day care centers.

The American society and business community is changing rapidly in many respects, including its attitudes and approaches toward child care accommodation. In the first of its kind by any major U.S. city, San Francisco adopted an ordinance in 1985 that requires office building developers to include child care facilities in their plans, or make substantial contributions to a city-administered child care fund. 1985 saw the introduction of over 20 bills on child care into Congress. In 1986, the Parental and Medical Leave Act (HR 4300) was introduced into the U.S. Congress to provide for up to 18 weeks of leave for the birth, adoption, and serious illness of a child in each 24 month period with required reinstatement. The issue is being addressed not only by politicians, but by business magazines, professional journals, trade newspapers and conferences, and in the corridors of nearly every employer. Says economist Sylvia Hewlett, "The lack of any kind of mandated benefit around childbirth is the biggest single reason why women are doing so badly in the workplace...Unless you support women in their role as mothers, you will never get equality of opportunity."

How then can employers approach the issue of accommodating child care, and can it be done without considerable expense or damaging to work unit operations? Can it be done without creating a preferential, sex-based benefit that will only cause more potential for discrimination liability? These answers lie in the discussion that follows. The options available to an employer's accommodation of employee child care needs consist of several approaches such as:

- Personal Disability and Parental Leave Policy (with job reinstatement)
- Flexible Benefit Plans (IRS section 125)
- Flexible Work Scheduling Arrangements
- Part-Time and Job Sharing Opportunities
- Home Work Assignments (particularly in conjunction with leaves)
- Information and Referral Service (ocenters)
- Subsidized Child Care Centers (on-site or near employment location)
- Employer Sponsored Child Care Consortium

4.31 EXAMPLES OF SUCCESSFUL EMPLOYER INVOLVEMENTS

As early as 1971, *Stride Rite Corporation,* a children's shoe manufacturer, became a model for many employers by establishing a child care center in its Boston factory. According to company chairman Arnold Hiatt, "It's made a difference in the lives of the children in the community...and it's given Stride Rite an advantage in the selection and morale of its people." Half of the Stride Rite child care center is caring for the children of company employees, with another one-half enrolled by other working parents in the community.

Hoffman-La Roche in New Jersey began sponsoring subsidized child care services for employees in 1977. According to Leonard Silverman, Vice President of Human Resources, "The impetus for child care assistance is based on very real business terms... There's no question that our child care program has helped us compete very effectively for talented people...We consider support for child care to be an investment—one that has already paid us handsome dividends." One such talented person in the La Roche organization is Dr. Alvin Stern, a senior scientist and single parent of three children since his wife died in 1983. Dr. Stern testifies that, "The center saved my peace of mind...I see child care as an essential benefit like medical and life insurance... Because of the center, I wouldn't even consider leaving (despite having had lucrative offers)."

Wang Laboratories in Massachusetts has operated its program since 1980. Of the 217 Wang parents representing all levels in the organization, 84 of them are fathers that use the center for the care of their children. The center, located a few miles from corporate headquarters in a former elementary school being leased by Wang, accommodates 206 children ages six months to six years. The center charges $150 per week for infants and $100 per week for pre-schoolers, with Wang contributing one-fourth to one-third of the fee. One product manager says of the center, "I'd think seriously before moving to another company...Now it's not only my career at stake, it would mean having to put my kids in a new situation."

In 1982, *Group 243 Inc.,* a 150 employee advertising agency in Ann Arbor, Michigan, started its own day care center. Likewise, at the Polaroid Corporation in Cambridge, Massachusetts, those parents earning under $30,000 per year receive subsidies to pay for child care, while the Shawmut Bank of Boston allows working parents to work three-fourths time so they can leave early to be with their children.

Levi Strauss Company in San Francisco took yet a different approach. They found that employees did not prefer on-site child care due to commuting and environmental concerns from their suburban homes, but they did have considerable interest in temporary leave opportunities. So, the company instituted a disability and child care policy that allows up to five months absence for men and women to take after childbirth or adoption of an infant, as well as flextime and job sharing provisions.

Yet another arrangement is the child care center in Burbank, California, sponsored by a consortium of local businesses, and it has been filled to capacity since opening in October 1984. The businesses pooling their resources to create the center consist of:

- City of Burbank
- Lockheed
- Walt Disney Productions
- NBC
- Columbia Pictures
- Warner Bros.
- St. Joseph's Hospital
- The Burbank Studios

Located only three and one-half miles from the Disney Studios, many participating parents often visit their children on occasion during their lunch hour.

4.32 EXAMINING THE PROS AND CONS OF EMPLOYER INVOLVEMENT

Whether or not the idea of employer involvement in various forms of child care accommodation for employees appeals to us personally or as business managers, we need to recognize the fact that whatever affects our employees, affects our business. Ask any employer, manager, or human resource professional about their experience with even one employee who had child care difficulties of some type. With the number of people in the workforce having this need, firing the employee doesn't eliminate the problem—just the employee who then has an even greater problem with only two immediate sources of income, unemployment insurance and welfare—and guess who pays! In essence then, the problem of our parenting employees becomes at least partly ours, where the nature of the problem becomes secondary to the need for its solution.

Employees today are quite simply unimpressed with the insensitivity of older, well paid, and childless top management who take a position of, "Too bad, it's not our problem and we don't want any part of it." While it may not, in fact, be the employer's problem per se, employers have always been, and will remain, subject to the consequences of employee problems so long as the underlying cause remains unsolved.

The advantages that tend to accompany employer involvement in child care accommodations can be one or more benefits, and they ought to be weighed against the short and long term effect on the organization's goals in the areas of profit, operations, and expenditures on human resources. The advantages derived by many companies have included:

1. **Recruitment and Retention:** A study of the Methodist Hospital in Southern California found that 41 percent of their working parents said the child care center was the deciding factor in taking the job.

2. **Payroll Cost Reduction:** Employers who have adopted flexible benefit plans wherein an IRS, Section 125 Benefit Expense Account is used to let employees contribute pretax earnings have gained considerable payroll savings (lower FICA contributions).

3. **Tax Credits:** It is estimated that tax credits for child care amount to about $3 billion annually.

4. **Increase Productivity:** Child care assistance and accommodation has been proven several times to reduce costly absenteeism, disruptive departures and turnover, and the down time a position remains vacant.

The disadvantages, depending on the nature of employer involvement or accommodation, can include:

1. **Center Start Up Costs:** Initially, this may require considerable administrative time, and several hundred thousand dollars in facilities, equipment, supplies, and staff (the use of working parents has not been found to be very effective in lieu of paid center staff).

2. **Administrative Oversight:** This burden is eased significantly in the case of consortia centers and those developed in business parks. For policy (leaves, benefit plans, and schedules) accommodation, there will be an increase in the number of transactions that will need to be processed, but with the aid of a computer, time should be nominal once institutionalized.

3. **Increased Liability:** This becomes part of the start up and operations cost of an employer-sponsored center, and it can be partly offset by charging employees a fee for use through payroll deduction. If the center falls below a needed enrollment level, take in the children of other working parents and watch your waiting list grow.

4. **Potential Sex Discrimination:** As long as the program, policy, plan, or other nature of an employer's participation in child care accommodation is openly available for male and female employees alike, you can regard it as a lawful employment practice. Consultation with professional advisors concerning specific provisions is highly recommended though, just to make sure that no inadvertent bias is present, and that the intent is well established.

5. **Inferior Program:** The inferior quality of employer-involved child care facili-

ties, staff, meals, and other provisions may lead to the working parents' concern over long-range detriment to their child's development.

The disadvantages noted above are easily correctable through intelligent planning and administrative oversight by qualified professionals. Absent thorough planning and administration, these disadvantages will quickly become serious and counterproductive problems that will destine almost any program approach for failure. The following, then, are some suggested approaches where employer involvement can occur at different levels of participation, and with successful results.

4.33 ACCOMMODATION APPROACHES FOR THE EMPLOYER

There are any number of approaches that empyers can take to strengthen its commitment to more equalized and innovative human resources management. Listed below are just a few ideas, and you need not feel confined to just one, nor should you avoid exploring any other method that better fits the nature of your business, operations, or mix of employees. Because of these varying conditions among employers, it may serve the best interests of all to conduct a preliminary study as presented in the discussion that follows these approaches.

1. **Personnel Policies:** The greatest interest typically lies in the areas of:

   - Sick leave use for pregnancy and sick child care.

   - Personal leave from three to six months for initial care of newborn or adopted infant, or at other times when warranted by unusual need.

   - Flexible schedules to allow for such arrangements as late arrival or early departure, and half or three-fourth time hours (even if on a temporary, time limited basis).

   - Job sharing provisions where two employees might agree to share the same job for a period of time.

In most cases of leave, employees want some assurance that they can get their job back without a lot of aggravation, or at least one very comparable to it. Again, be careful in designing policies to not exclude the eligibility of male employees.

Yet another policy that has been successful with professional and managerial positions, on a case-by-case basis, has been allowing homework during periods of disability or child care leave, and we are likely to hear a lot more about its use in the coming years.

In some of these policies, it would be advisable to develop some general guidelines under which employees may request its use, but leave yourself the discretion to evaluate the impact and possible alternatives on a case-by-case basis. You want to avoid setting up policies you can't abide by.

2. **Flexible Benefit Plans:** In essence, this can become a form of financial assistance by allowing employees to shift existing employer contributions into payments for child care rather than, say, a medical plan which they may already have through their spouse's employment. Additionally, employees can put pretax earnings into an employer adopted Benefit Expense Account (under Section 125 of the IRS codes) to pay the balance of their child care expenses created by their employment. The annual cost of child care amounts to about $3,000 for the average family. About 1,000 employers use the Benefit Expense Account approach, while some 300 other employers pay their employees parenting preschoolers an additional subsidy. No doubt some are based on years of service with the company.

Another benefit approach used by a few employers has been to negotiate a discounted fee for employee use of a nearby center.

3. **Information and Referral Services:** Included in this approach are such services as sponsoring seminars on dealing with work and family, how to parent when you have to work, selecting a child care facility, and the like. They can be during or after-hours, brown-bag lunches, or offered on Saturdays through hospitals and community service organizations.

Of even greater assistance are the referral services that can be handled in-house, by contract, or through specialized consulting services. Referral services typically track all available child care services in the company's sphere of (commuting or nearby) influence, and refers employees to those facilities by request. Some local government agencies and non-profit organizations are also equipped to provide this service. Presently, there are about 500 companies offering this type of service to employees.

4. **CHILD CARE CENTERS:** There are three options here. The first is to develop your own on-site or near-site center for parenting employees, and supplement enrollment from other parents if and when needed. Typically, due to start-up expenses, this option is confined to larger employers with 250 or more employees at one location, and even these centers require fee-paying parents to cover at least the bulk of operating expenses. There are presently about 600 such centers offering the children supervision, care, games, educational experiences such as field trips, healthy exercise, and nourishing meals.

The second option for an employer is to contract with an existing, experienced, and reputable day care provider. Parents who enroll their children also authorize a payroll deduction, so the contractor merely bills the company, and the company pays it from the payroll deduction child care fund.

The third option would seem to have the greatest potential for the largest number of all employers; that being the consortium approach. The reason; small and medium size employers can share in its development and administration without undue burden on capital outlay. The consortium can be created by two or more businesses of the same operational type such as the Broadcasters Child Development Center in Washington, D.C.; it can be a mixed group of employers occupying the same industrial business park like the Hohokam Child Development Center in Tempe, Arizona; or it can be a limited number of sizeable employers in near proximity of each other, and who want to maintain specific control over operations. Local governments, school districts, chambers of commerce, and non-profit organizations can be very helpful in the development of these efforts since they tend to get a good deal of public notoriety in the community from those that will be inspired by the effort.

4.34 FINDING A SOLUTION: EVALUATING THE PROSPECTS

As with any business matter having economic and/or operational impact on the organization, the issue of child care accommodation ought to be evaluated on the basis of actual employee needs and what approaches are likely to serve the best mutual interests of the company and effected employees. One of the better ways of accomplishing this task is to develop a survey questionnaire and ask that all employees take it home, give their answers careful thought, answer questions honestly in light of their own present or probable future circumstance, and deposit the questionnaire in a designated box (or mail it to a specific person). The survey should be conducted with anonymity for responding employees. Why; because many employees would not want their employer to know that they're having any sort of child care problems, or that they desire and would use alternative employment terms if they were available, for fear of resulting in greater than usual scrutiny of their attendance or performance. Others may fear being labeled a complainer or troublemaker.

The survey form itself should include a cover memo explaining the purpose of the survey, and pointing out that it's merely the company's present interest to get a clear indication of various types of child care accommodation needs and interests. The company will want to examine results of the survey carefully to determine the area(s) in which there may be a possible match between employee needs and company abilities. You do not want to raise false hopes or expectations prematurely since inaction following employee surveys tends to lower morale. It is better to advise employees that right now you want to collect information to get a clearer picture of their needs and interests in this area, and that once compiled, further evaluation will be necessary to determine if the company can take accommodating measures. As a matter of keeping employees appraised of how the evaluation is progressing, you may want to use the company newsletter or other communications device to let them know about the survey results in summary fashion. Here are just a few questions that might be considered for such a questionnaire:

---

1. Respondent Sex: ☐ female ☐ male
2. Marital Status: ☐ married ☐ head of household ☐ single
3. Age Category: ☐ 18-25 ☐ 26-35 ☐ 36-45 ☐ over 45
4. Number of Dependent Children Living With You:
   ____Newborn to 3 yrs.   ____3-6 yrs.   ____6-12 yrs.   ____13 yrs.
5. Who Attends To Your Child Care During Work Hours?
   ☐ Spouse   ☐ Sitter's Home   ☐ Other Relative   ☐ Child Care Center
   ☐ In Home Sitter   ☐ Other (specify)_____
6. How Far Do You Travel To Child Care Location?
   ☐ 0 miles   ☐ 1-3 miles   ☐ 3-5 miles   ☐ 5-10 miles   ☐ over 10 miles
7. How Far Do You Live From Your Work Location?
   ☐ 1-3 miles   ☐ 3-5 miles   ☐ 5-10 miles   ☐ 10-20 miles   ☐ 20+ miles
8. If Child Care Facilities Were Close To Your Work Location, Would You...
   ☐ not use it   ☐ prefer to use it
9. How Frequently Have You Had Trouble Obtaining Child Care Services?
   ☐ no problem   once every few years☐ once a year   ☐ several times a year
10. Would A Child Care Information And Referral Service Be Helpful To You?
    ☐ Yes   ☐ No
11. What Would You Estimate To Be The Number Of Work Hours Of Your Absence Over A Six Month Period Due To Child Care Matters?
    ☐ 0-4 hrs.   ☐ 4-8 hrs.   ☐ 8-16 hrs.   ☐ 16-24 hrs.
    ☐ 24-32 hrs.   ☐ over 32 hrs.
12. Which, If Any, Of The Following Work Hour Programs Would Help You Overcome Any Child Care Problems?
    ☐ Flexible Scheduling Of Work Hours
    ☐ Reduced Work Week Hours For Specified Period Of Time
    ☐ Job Sharing With Another Employee
    ☐ Change Full-Time Status To Permanent Part-Time
    ☐ Be Allowed To Do Some Work At Home During Temporary Disability
13. If The Company Set Up A Program Allowing You To Put Pretax Earnings Into Your Own Benefit Expense Account, Would You...
    A. Use it for
       ☐ Child Care expenses
       ☐ My share of premium payments for benefit insurance plans

☐ Payment of insurance co-payments and deductibles
☐ Payment of uninsured medical expenses
B. Would not use it

14. If You Were Temporarily Disabled From Work Due To Pregnancy, Would You...
☐ Definitely want/need to return to work once physically able
☐ Probably would return to work once physically able
☐ Would not return to work for _____ months once physically able

15. If The Company Had An Unpaid Parental Leave For Male And Female Employees Following Childbirth Or Infant Adoption, Would You...
A. ☐ Likely use it if the situation occurs
☐ Not likely use it if the situation occurs
B. ☐ Like to have it for 1-3 months after it occurs
☐ Like to have it 3-6 months after it occurs
☐ Not interested
☐ Don't think it should be offered

16. Please provide any other comments you have on the subject of the company's accommodation of your child care needs:

_____

_____

_____

Once this information is compiled, you should be able to draw some specific conclusions about the extent and nature of child care problems in your organization, as well as where company emphasis should be placed, or at least given further consideration of accommodation. Depending on your results as to whether the need or interest is in policies, benefit plans, information and referral services, or the development of a child care program, you may now want to establish a small committee or task force to give the identified approach further evaluation of feasibility and development. The committee can be composed of a cross-section of employees or designated company officers such as those representing human resources, finance, operations, and public relations. Outside consultants can also be very helpful in these kinds of developmental processes since they can add their expertise and objectivity.

If the selected approach involves personnel policies, benefit programs like the Benefit Expense Account, or information and referral service, your committee might want to check out other companies to see they've had in developing it, problems encountered, degree of measured success, and what they wished they would have done differently. Then proceed with a draft proposal, have it reviewed by legal counsel, followed by an evaluation and problem-solving discussion of all top management prior to implementation.

If, however, the selected approach is to consider the development of a child care program, it would be prudent to assemble a top-notch task force to conduct a more formal feasibility evaluation that examines the options of:

1. An internal, company sponsored child care facility
2. An off-site consortium child care facility sponsored by specific companies
3. Contracting for child care services of company parents at a nearby contractors location
4. Some combination of the above

The issues that should be studied at a minimum are:

5. Administrative oversight costs
6. Number of children to be accommodated
7. Operating hours and expenses
8. Methods of subsidized operation expenses

Indeed, tackling problems associated with the child care needs of our employees is no easy task. It's been that way for *them* for a long time, and chances are they would deeply appreciate any assistance their company would give to help them solve these *mutual* problems. To do so would create more reliable and productive employees who would have greater peace of mind that all is well both with their employment and family. How many employers can boast of creating that state of mind among their employees? It's an opportunity that should not remain unexplored even if the initial effort is to provide some type of assistance, support, or available services in the community where preschool children with minor illnesses can receive care comparable to home care so that your working parents can report to work confident of their child's health and welfare. Clearly it's a human resource issue worthy of more attention.

CHAPTER I: 5.0 PROBLEMS WHERE THE WORKER IS PHYSICALLY HANDICAPPED OR A RELIGIOUS OBSERVER

The last two major categories of unlawful employment discrimination relate to those in our society that have some form of physical impairment rendering them handicapped, and those who adhere to various religious practices. What makes these two forms of discrimination similar in both an employment context and management problems, is the employer requirement of accommodation. Though accommodation of handicapped persons usually means very different kinds of actions and decisions than does the accommodation of an employee's religious beliefs, they equally bring to each manager's attention the need to change irrelevant biases, employment practices, and workplace treatment that tends to disfavor or otherwise adversely affect individuals because of these characteristics. Yet, discrimination due to physical handicap and religious belief are different subjects involving wholly different circumstances, and for these reasons will be treated as separate discussions in this chapter.

For those having read the first four chapters, some redundancy in the "theme" of this final chapter dealing with problems relating to type-specific kinds of discrimination will be found—and with good reason. That reason is that Congress, state legislatures, the courts, and society as a whole have been trying to send a loud and clear message to the employment community that artificial barriers and prejudicial treatment in employment decisions are no longer acceptable. While the social revolution that brought about contemporary laws prohibiting these various forms of discrimination have occurred only during the last few decades, it represents the culmination of centuries of exclusion, deprivation, humiliation, and dispair. Who wouldn't eventually fight for their rights under such prolonged circumstances when the flag of a democratic society and its constitutional guarantees waves over their heads?

The heritage of American society provided these rights and the political mechanism to be recognized. Those who realized that legal protection was the only meaningful way to achieve national fair-share rights finally gained stature in the employment arena by obtaining Congressional support for making discrimination illegal. Using the model of civil rights activism of the early 1960's, an otherwise passive and fragmented collection of handicap groups, individuals, and their supporters finally developed political attention in the early 1970's to achieve more than mere custodial care. And rightfully so, since previously they had generally been cast aside as unable, unsuitable, and undesirable for employment; and with little more thought given to ways in which employment barriers could be removed to allow a more just appraisal of individual ability to perform.

5.10 THE EVOLUTION OF RIGHTS AND WORKFORCE PARTICIPATION OF THE PHYSICALLY HANDICAPPED

Unbeknown to most managers who perhaps gave little attention to the social issue of physically handicapped and disabled people before 1973 when prohibitions against employment discrimination were federally mandated, there exists considerable history in terms of the evolution of care, treatment, benefits, and eventually the acquisition of rights for this segment of our society. Some of the best illustrations of their treatment, and regard by society that created present stigmas, are depicted in early motion pictures of the 1930's and 40's where the emotionally disturbed were placed in asylums, those with degenerative diseases were portrayed as freaks to be isolated until death, and their physically handicap to be pitied. Regrettably, the novel and motion picture accounts of people with impairments have been accurate and sometimes even underdramatized portrayals of the isolation, mistreatment, apathy, humiliation, and often despicable conditions to which these people have been subjected. Equally unfortunate for many of them has been the stigma that continues to be carried by those nonhandicapped who do not bear its burden, but who have been influenced by media that sensationalizes the adversity of their differences from "normal" people.

Institutional services for the handicapped and disabled population have been with us for centuries. Initially, they provided care and later in the twentieth century added services and benefits. Providing for such people was regarded as a moral issue of how best to isolate and gain custodial control over their "afflictions" rather than the development of a system that would aid the greatest number back into the mainstream of productive living. They were visibly different from others, they often required considerable assistance from others, and medical technology was lacking adequate cure, treatment, or adaptive means to compensate for their condition. For example, in 1260 an asylum was established in Paris to attend to soldiers blinded by combat, and several attempts were made in Western Europe during the sixteenth century to establish institutions for the care and training of handicapped children. As with most social issues, America lagged behind European countries in their provisions and treatment of the physically handicapped until the turn of the eighteenth century, and it was to take another 150 years before American medical technology would surpass Europe, yet only begin to address social needs. The following, then, is a brief chronology of the events in America that characterizes the evolution from a custodial society of the handicapped to the beginning of one that provides rights and opportunity for this group of human resources.

1812	School for the blind opened in Baltimore; others in Boston in 1823.
1817	School for the deaf founded in Hartford.
1829	Louis Braille developed printing system for the blind.
1879	Salvation Army, founded in England, came to America
1881	American Red Cross was established.
1902	Goodwill Industries founded.
1913	National Vocational Guidance Association founded.
1918	Smith-Sears Veteran's Rehabilitation Act; first law mandating rehabilitation for disabled veterans and providing vocational training.
1920-1965	Smith-Fees Act; provided services for the physically handicapped, vocational training, placement, and counseling. The program grew from a federal allocation of one million dollars in 1920 to $300 million in 1965, and progressively expanded services into vocational education, sheltered workshops, treatment for the severely disabled and mentally retarded. Programs were eventually placed under the Department of Health, Education and Welfare.
1921	American Foundation For The Blind formed.
1932	Disabled American Veterans were chartered by Congress; currently has about 700,000 members.
1960's	Social attitudes and national awareness began to transform from a parochial treatment of the handicapped and disabled (services and benefits) to that of providing rights and advocacy. Also, medical advances surged in the areas of treatment methods, drugs, therapy, and prosthetic devices creating more opportunity to participate in society. Some of the organizations formed during this period and led the way toward national recognition of the contemporary needs of the handicapped and disabled were the:

> Paralyzed Veterans of America (PVA)
> National Association of the Deaf (NAD)
> American Council of the Blind (ACB)
> National Association for Retarded Citizens (NARC)
> United Cerebral Palsy Association (UCPA)

1968   Architectural Barriers Act; transportation and building design requirements to accommodate the physically handicapped.

1970's   National Rehabilitation Association (NRA); the first organization made up of rehabilitation professionals who became activists for social and political reforms.

1972   Title XVI of the Social Security Act; added disability benefits for disabled workers.

1973   Vocational Rehabilitation Act; continuation funding of the original Smith-Fees Act, but with precedent changes aimed at affirmative measures to end discrimination in employment and federally financed programs.

1974   Eighteen states had adopted handicapped non-discrimination in employment laws applicable to private sector employers.

1978   Executive Order 12106; establishing the EEOC as the monitoring agency to insure that the hiring, placement, and promotion of the handicapped in federal service met non-discriminatory standards. Aggressive promotion of the effort was intended to serve as a model for private sector employers not required to do so under the 1973 Act.

Developmental Disabilities Act; provided for at least partial funding of advocacy services in each state for persons with developmental disabilities requiring the assistance of trained professionals to help them deal with pursuing legal and administrative remedies for the protection of their rights and benefits.

1982   Forty-five states had adopted physical handicapped laws; of those, only public employees were covered by laws in Alabama, Arkansas, Idaho, Mississippi, and South Dakota. The five remaining states without handicap non-discrimination laws were Arizona, Delaware, North Dakota, South Carolina and Wyoming.

So, historically, the physically handicapped and other disabled people have been a highly fragmented group, separated into small clusters of people with similar impairments and geographically dispersed, unlike the other groups of civil rights seekers who were more homogeneous in their representation and ability to amass recognition. As a segregated group of people until the 1960's, they simply lacked cohesive clout to enter the political arena to effectuate mandated change in their access to facilities and jobs, and to gain rights by which they and professionals could advocate in their behalf.

While no one seems certain as to the exact reasons such sweeping reforms for the handicapped and disabled became legislatively successful in Congress and various states, it would appear that a series of social movement events fostered the opportunity to transform American ideals about past transgression disfavoring this group. The 1960's and 1970's became an era of social reform, and the following events no doubt played a major part in legislative, judicial, and general attitudinal changes that began to take place.

- The social period inspired thousands of college students to study social sciences and move into various social careers such as advocacy with the idea of making a difference in the lives of those they were to represent.

- Different segments of the handicapped community had begun to form national organizations and join forces to create lobbying coalitions.

- Much of the guilt attached to American involvement in Viet Nam became the backdrop of publicity given to the plight of disabled veterans returning home to eventually become spokesmen, activitists, and public awareness models for the needs and abilities of those with impairments.

- Other civil rights movements came before them to show how successful public awareness of social issues can be p resented to an otherwise preoccupied legislative regime.

- The groups representing the interests of handicapped and disabled people had well established credibility as self-initiating achievers who merely wanted more opportunity, not handouts of special privileges.

Quite simply, non-handicapped people had not given much thought to ways in which those with physical, sensory, or mental limitation could be accommodated in the workplace. They felt there was little reason to give it much thought or attention since there always seemed to be more than a sufficient supply of workers without these shortcomings. Not understanding how to evaluate the limitations of handicapped applicants, job requirements, and workplace conditions, most managers have felt inadequately equipped to accommodate the handicapped in an accepting, comfortable way either socially or in terms of workplace productivity. As social psychologist Jennifer Macleod points out:

> . . . the true locus of the problem is not the handicapped people themselves; it is the society and institutions that treat handicapped people as less-than-whole human

beings who deserve sympathy, protection, and special care but are something of an uncomfortable nuisance when they seek full participation in the mainstream of life and work.[1]

Certainly, not all people who are handicapped or severely disabled are capable of participation in the workforce. Yet studies have shown that as much as 60 percent of the handicapped population can easily adapt to normal working conditions, and are capable of being productive employees given the opportunity and, in some cases, only nominal cost accommodation by employers. Like other forms of visible bias, the key to overcoming attitudinal barriers to employment of the handicapped is looking at the person's skills, abilities, and motives rather than impersonal appearances. Those with severe limitations will simply have to await advances in their care and treatment.

With the aid of medicine, physical therapy, prosthetic devices, adaptive equipment, and sheer determination, many handicapped people have become testimonial tributes to their kind by employers willing to give them a try and happily surprised by their results. As with any other employment decision, what leads to the success of handicapped workers (and any other person for that matter) is the proper assessment, skills-to-job matching, placement, and workforce integration with a supportive environment.

From an administrative point of view, it is also interesting to note that handicapped workers in general have fewer industrial accidents, less turnover, better attitudes, create no effect on the cost of medical plan or workers' compensation premium rates, and that the majority of workplace accommodations cost less than $500.00. Altogether, it would appear that business has been overlooking this potentially effective group of human resources. We will come back to the human resouce aspect of utilizing handicapped workers in later sections, but first, managers ought to develop some awareness of fundamental legal issues connected to handicapped discrimination such as applicable laws and guiding court decisions.

5.20 LEGAL ISSUES GOVERNING WORKPLACE ACCOMMODATION FOR THE PHYSICALLY HANDICAPPED

As with other types of civil rights legislation, the laws and regulations prohibiting employment discrimination on the basis of physical handicap and requiring affirmative action stem from both federal and state statutes with regulations issued by the enforcement arm of the government. The difference between prohibitions against discrimination on the basis of physical handicap and other groups covered by the Civil Rights Act of 1964, is that federal law does not require compliance by the general private sector community of employers under the Vocational Rehabilitation Act of

---

[1] op. cit., p. 165.

1973. Interestingly enough, several efforts were made by disability activists in the early 1970's to get Congress to amend the Civil Rights Act to include the physically handicapped. But, fearful that such an addition would dilute the vigor with which employers were expected to comply with already covered groups (e.g., females and minorities), these efforts failed. However, when refunding of established vocational and rehabilitative programs came to Congressional attention in 1973, the opportunity arose to add new requirements for those recipients of program and contractor/subcontractor funds. Those additions became sections 502, 503, and 504 of the Vocational Rehabilitation Act of 1973.

The exclusion of private sector employers and others not receiving federal financial assistance did not necessarily relieve them from compliance with non—discrimination requirements concerning handicapped persons. As it has been pointed out, by 1982 some 45 states had adopted labor laws fashioned after the intent of federal law, and most states have made non-discrimination in the employment of the handicapped applicable to most all private employers. Although these state laws vary in detail of covered employers, definitions of handicapped people, and conditions under which compliance and accommodation are required, they generally follow the federal model. In summary form, the federal law is as follows:

Vocational Rehabilitation Act of 1973

Section 502: Created the Architectural and Transportation Barriers Compliance Board (ATBCB) to insure compliance with the Architectural Barriers Act of 1968 requiring that all new federal buildings be accessible to disabled people, and that all renovations provided for their accessibility. State laws have required similar requirements of county building departments where building plans are checked and construction licenses issued.

Section 503: Requires the development and pursuit of affirmative action hiring plans for contractors or subcontractors receiving federal funds in excess of $2,500 per year; it compels employer consideration of hiring and promoting "qualified handicapped individuals"; and such requirements are enforcable by the Office of Federal Contract Compliance (OFCC) within the Department of Labor. The courts have determined that legal suits cannot be brought against violative employers, however the courts have upheld the right of DOL to discontinue funding if any part of a recipient employer's action violates this section even if the employment has no bearing on the program or project being funded.

Federal regulations further require that *any* federal contractor or subcontractor with a contract of $50,000 or more, and having 50 or more employees, must prepare and maintain an affirmative action plan (AAP) for the employment of handicapped persons at each of its establishments. However, unlike AAP requirements under Executive Order 11246, employers are not required to establish goals and timetables for hiring handicapped workers, but rather to periodically review personnel procedures, examine the validity of physical and mental requirements of jobs, and to provide reasonable accommodation and accessibility.

Section 504: Applies to recipients of federal financial assistance (grant, loan, contract, services, or property) and prohibits discrimination against qualified handicapped individuals in programs or activities supported by federal assistance. The major objective is to insure program accessibility for *qualified* handicapped persons, rather than all forms of handicaps or disabilities. This section is administered by the Department of Health, Education, and Welfare, and violations are enforceable in court.

There are a few noteworthy definitions under Section 504 that help clarify the meaning of discrimination against handicapped persons.

Handicapped Person: Any person who:

- Has a physical or mental impairment that substantially limits one or more major life activities (e.g., caring for oneself, performing manual tasks, walking, seeing, hearing, speaking, breathing, learning, and working);

- Has a record of such an impairment (has a history of, or has been misclassified as having, a mental or physical impairment that substantially limits one or more major life activities); or

- Is regarded as having such an impairment. "Regarded as having such an impairment" may mean:

  - having a physical or mental impairment that does not substantially limit major life activities but is treated by a recipient as constituting such a limitation;

  - having a physical or mental impairment that substantially limits major life activities only as a result of the attitudes of others toward such impairment; or

  - having no physical or mental impairment but is treated by a recipient as having such an impairment.

Additionally, the particular types of prohibited discrimination as this section relates to employment pertains to:

- Recruitment, advertising, and the processing of applications for employment;

- Hiring, upgrading, promotion, award of tenure, demotion, transfer, layoff, termination, right of return from layoff, and rehiring;

- Rates of pay or any other form of compensation and changes in compensation;

- Job assignments, job classifications, organizational structures, position descriptions, lines of progression, and seniority lists;

- Leaves of absence, sick leave, or any other leave;

- Have the effect of subjecting qualified handicapped persons to discrimination based on handicap.

A couple of key areas in which most employers find particularly difficult to refrain from discrimination, or fail to even initially accommodate, is adapting selection examinations to those with sensory, manual, or perhaps speaking impairments; or conducting normal preemployment medical examinations. In these situations, employers would do well to:

1. Make sure that the Personnel Office or location of making application is accessible to the handicapped.

2. Be prepared to provide a reader to assist the sight impaired applicant with written examinations, or the physically impaired (writing) with an assistant.

3. Refrain from interview questions about the severity of an applicant's handicap, but rather focus on their ability and needs to perform essential job functions.

4. Make offers of employment conditional on medical exam results provided:

   - all similar employees are given such an exam.
   - results are not used in a discriminatory fashion.
   - records are kept confidential.

Physical or Mental Impairment: a condition that weakens, diminishes, restricts, or otherwise damages the individual's physical or mental ability; impairment need not affect the individual's general employability—only that it serves as a bar to employment—nor does it have to be a current condition (e.g., epilepsy, prior history of drug addition, etc.). Federal regulations define impairment as:

- Any physiological disorder or condition, cosmetic disfiguration or anatomical loss affecting a body system.

- A mental or psychological disorder, including mental retardation and specific learning disabilities.

- Various disabling and debilitating diseases and conditions, and [current] drug addition and alcoholism.

Qualified Handicapped Individual: this is the primary person for which legal protection was sought, and therefore of greatest interest to employers. This definition refers to a defined handicapped person who can perform the essential functions of a job with reasonable accommodation. In this regard, employers are not expected to abandon legitimate job requirements or create burdensome sacrifices to normal working conditions. Rather, employers are expected to make reasonable changes in order to accommodate the otherwise qualified handicapped person. Consequently, there is a three-part analysis employers should go through when considering handicapped persons for employment or promotion.

1. Whether the applicant is capable of performing the job (possesses requisite skill, training, experience, etc.).

2. If not, whether the applicant would be able to perform the job if the employer makes reasonable accommodations.

3. Whether these circumstances would impose an undue economic hardship, unsafe working conditions for applicant or others, or any other reason to reject the applicant on the basis of a sound bona fide occupational qualification (e.g., a blind person applying for position of bus driver!).

Reasonable Accommodation: there are no specific definitions per se of the kinds or costs of accommodations required by those applicants or employees having physical or mental limitations. However, examples are provided in federal guidelines, and they include such actions as making facilities accessible to and usable by handicapped persons, restructuring jobs, instituting part-time or modified work schedules, acquiring or modifying equipment or devices to be used by handicapped persons in the course of work, and providing readers or interpreters. Accommodation need not be provided if the employer can establish that doing so would result in an "undue hardship." Factors for the employer to consider in determining whether an undue hardship would result may include:

• Overall size of the employer's organization relative to number of employees, jobs, type of facilities, and budget.

• Type of funded program and composition of the workforce.

• Nature and cost of accommodation needed.

Given these definitions, the language contained in federal and state laws and regulations should become more understandable. They are also helpful concerning the interpretation of defenses to the employer (i.e., those legitimate reasons not to hire a particular handicapped applicant), as well as developing a clearer picture of the courts' rationale in deciding Section 504 cases. The four basic defenses for an employer's refusal to hire or promote a handicapped individual are:

1. The handicap is such that the individual is *unable to perform essential functions of the job*. Here, the first question that can be examined is whether the individual is a "qualified handicapped." If clearly not, rejection may be automatic. Additionally, if accommodation were made and it is subsequently found that the individual cannot perform essential functions of the job at a reasonable level of performance required of the position, then inability to perform becomes a reasonable defense for termination—but such an evaluation and decision should be made during the initial training (probationary) period so long as the individual has had an opportunity for adequate instruction, supervision, and time to demonstrate proficiency.

2. The handicap would likely prove threatening or dangerous to the *health or safety* of the individual and/or other employees. In these cases, the employer ought to be able to demonstrate the health and safety nature of the job in question (e.g., work environment, work activities, equipment used, hazardous materials, required emergency procedures, and the like), and the specific way(s) in which the particular handicap would prove dangerous.

   For example, the height of fire extinguishers would not be a good reason to reject a wheelchair applicant because the reasonable accommodation rule implies that it is no major obstacle for the employer to lower them in the assigned work unit. However, refusal to hire the same wheelchair applicant having impaired mobility in a warehouse where objects can fall from high shelves (and they have on occasion) can jeopardize the safety of the handicapped person as well as provide an obstruction for other employees to run clear or obtain shelter from falling objects.

3. The handicapped applicant's accommodation would prove to create an *undue hardship* on the employer. Typically, this is a consideration of cost, time, and efficiency. Larger size employers have had difficulty escaping the burden of cost as a legitimate hardship, but smaller employers who can show narrow profit margins seem to gain greater sympathy from the courts.

   Generally, the courts do not expect any employer to provide highly elaborate or expensive accommodations, or those that would prove disruptive to the workplace. The exception might be architectural accommodations that provide obstacles not only for the handicapped applicant, but for many handicapped people. Also, if the time to acquire adaptive equipment or make workplace modification for the handicapped applicant would prove severely inefficient or disruptive, or the accommodation would seriously reduce the efficiency of the position, an undue hardship defense can be advanced.

4. The necessary *scope and nature of the job* itself creates a bona fide occupational qualification (BFOQ). Once again, employers are not expected to abandon legitimate job requirements, and if non-handicapped persons are more qualified with respect to such necessary physical, sensory, or mental characteristics of the job, then the employer might be able to establish a BFOQ defense. However, employers are cautioned not to give mere cursory analysis or hold traditional ideals about those elements of a job that absolutely necessitate prohibitions for handicapped people. Each job should be carefully examined for various types of physical, sensory, or mental demands. Also, employers would be well advised to avoid blanket exclusions of handicapped people from certain jobs. Bear in mind that not all handicaps are the same, and those that are the same have varying degrees of severity (limitation in work function).

It is imperative for managers who make hiring and promotion decisions to examine each job and each individual handicapped person on a case-by-case basis. The results of the evaluation of both the job and applicant ought to be documented with sufficient detail given to explicit circumstances of the manner in which they are incompatible; presuming, of course, accommodation is impractical or merely cannot be achieved.

5.30 WHAT IS AND ISN'T HANDICAP DISCRIMINATION: QUESTIONS, CASES, AND PROBLEM SOLVING ANALYSIS

One of the most common problems that confront employers with regard to handicapped applicants or employees is the question of whether a particular physical, biological, or emotional condition constitutes a handicap within the meaning of either Section 504 of the Rehabilitation Act or applicable state law. As you might presume, state laws have tended to be far more liberal concerning what conditions are covered, and it is advisable for human resource managers to acquaint other management staff with such variances in state law precedence.

Since adoption of the Vocational Rehabilitation Act in 1973, and similar state legislation through 1982, there has been a limited yet divergent amount of litigation history over the issue of what is and isn't handicap discrimination. However, by blending decisions of both federal and state courts, we can get a much clearer picture of legal trends, definitive answers, and a clearer understanding of how the underlying principles of handicap discrimination are applied in differing circumstances.

For purpose of organizing the cases that touch on handicap discrimination, they are discussed under the categories of communicable diseases, addictions, and physiological disorders and they include the topics of:

1. Communicable Diseases

   • Tuberculosis (TB)
   • Acquired Immune Disorder Syndrom (AIDS)

2. Addictions

   • Alcoholism   • Drug Abuse   • Smoking

3. Physiological Impairments

   • Amputation And Paralysis   • Left Handed
   • Sight Limitation Or Blindness • Weight (Obesity)
   • Back Condition (Scoliosis)   • Heart Condition And High Blood Pressure
   • Epilepsy And Nerve Deterioration
   • Cancer   • Height (too short)
   • Neurosis   • Transvestitism

The more classic forms of handicap discrimination were no doubt those for which federal law had intended to eliminate, and they included predominantly the physically handicapped such as the amputee, wheelchair bound, persons adaptable by prosthetic devices, the sight and hearing impaired, and similar persons encountering artificial barriers to employment; barriers of not only an architectural nature but also barred by stereotyped prejudice and biases against their social adequacy. Given the continuing national sensitivity to broad social issues, as well as the very general language in handicap discrimination law opening the doors to liberal interpretation by the courts, the definition of what conditions constitute a physical handicap for purposes of employment discrimination have rapidly expanded well beyond the realm envisioned possible by most employers. Nor is it likely that qualified handicap conditions will narrow in the future. For these reasons, managers would do well to become better acquainted with at least present conditions and the circumstances under which various courts have addressed the problem encountered by other employers.

5.31 COMMUNICABLE DISEASES

In nearly back-to-back decisions, the U.S. Supreme Court and a host of state courts have made at least two forms of communicable diseases the newest category of physical handicap: Acquired Immune Deficiency Syndrome (AIDS) and tuberculosis (TB). While the cases do not have universal application because of their circumstantial nature, they strongly suggest a consistent legal inclination to allow these (and perhaps other) communicable diseases to be protected to some degree in an employment context. They will also become highly influential precedence in the hearing of many future state court cases on the same conditions or legal testing of other types of communicable diseases. The consequence creates an interesting dilemma for the employer—which is the higher risk to avoid; litigation over intentional discrimination, or exposure of the workforce to possible transmission of a serious disease?

Tuberculosis

In *School Board of Nassau County, Florida v. Arline* (1987), a classroom teacher who had been hospitalized for treatment of tuberculosis was terminated from her job. In reviewing this case, the U.S. Supreme Court concluded that persons with a contagious disease may fall within the protection of Section 504 of the Rehabilitation Act based on medical evidence and other circumstance of the employment situation, rather than an employer's fear, stereotyping, or speculation of future consequences of the disease.

The court noted that the law covers any person with a physical or mental impairment which substantially limits one or more major life activities, as well as anyone who has a record of the impairment or is regarded as having an impairment, even though they may not be presently incapacitated. However, in order to obtain relief, the individual must be both handicapped and "otherwise qualified" or subject to accommodation by the employer.

The court's position in Arline was that Congress intended that a handicap on the basis of a contagious disease be for either of two reasons: 1) because the employee has been left physically impaired by the disease; or, 2) because the disease is contagious, fear of the disease becomes the reason of an employer's (termination or other adverse) action. The court rejected the employer's defense of fear that the contagious disease would be spread to others, noting that such assessments ought to be based on reasonable medical judgment concerning the nature, duration, and severity of risk of the disease to others rather than mere speculation. While the court determined that the medical condition of tuberculosis was a covered handicap within the meaning of Section 504, it remanded the case back to the District Court for an evidenciary determination of whether the plaintiff was "otherwise qualified."

The question to be examined in such cases is, can employees with a communicable disease be reasonably accommodated without undue risk to others, and can they perform essential functions of their job given the accommodation? In the example of Arline, the answer is probably yes; she can be given reasonable time off for medical treatment without undue instructional disruption, she can be accommodated with a reasonable means of preventing transmission of the disease to others (i.e., facial mask), and as long as her health condition permits her to function, she can carry out her teaching assignments. If, on the other hand, a medical evaluation were to conclude that her condition is presently a high risk to others even with reasonable (protective) accommodation, the employer might then have to evaluate the existence of other types of accommodation such as a more isolated job assignment—if she is qualified and such a job is available. If the risk to others is medically determined to be too high, the employee thus becomes otherwise unqualified. In Arline, the employer failed to examine or attempt accommodation of any type, and they failed to evaluate whether she was otherwise qualified.

In a similar case, although not involving a communicable disease, a school board was held within its right to terminate a classroom teacher who had epilepsy. In *Father Flanagan's Boys Home v. Goerke* (1987), the Nebraska Supreme Court found that the employer demonstrated appropriate findings of fact that the employee could not perform all of the essential duties which included driving students in a school bus, and that elimination of that portion of his job would be unreasonable accommodation in this case (other cases of epilepsy conditions are contained in Section 5.33).

Acquired Immune Deficiency Syndrome (AIDS)

Out of all the conditions that employees can bring to the workplace, this disease and its related disabling, eventually fatal effect has created monumental concern for all employers and their managers who must now learn how to deal with it. It is a justifiable concern moreso from the standpoint of potential business risks where opportunity exists for transmission of the disease, however narrow it might be, and from the employer's economic liabilities than it is for the issue of employment discrimination.

Information and research concerning this disease began to emerge only since the early 1980's, yet it has already been classified as an epidemic which may well account for the level of alarm by employers, community leaders, and even the medical community. The problem is one of nearly global proportions, not merely a condition indigenous to the United States. For example, in 1987 it was estimated that between 5-10 million people worldwide have been infected with HIV (Human Immuno-Deficiency Virus). In the United States, the Centers For Disease Control estimated a total of 1.5 million HIV infected persons consisting of about 41,000 cases of AIDS with the balance being cases of ARC (AIDS Related Complex) which is believed to have a 5-10 times greater incidence than AIDS. Further, there is no existing system in the United States for reporting ARC cases, nor is the condition covered by Medicare, Social Security, or most other private disability plans.

Statistically, AIDS can be substantiated as an epidemic because the total national case count is doubling about every 13 years. As of August 1987, the Centers for Disease Control report the following numbers of confirmed AIDS cases in each state. It is further estimated by the United States Public Health Service that there will be about 270,000 cases of AIDS diagnosed by 1991, and of those, 179,000 will have already died and these calculations do not include the higher incidence of persons with ARC.

AIDS Cases By State Of Residence, August 1987
(Cumulative total since June 1981)

New York	11,656	Oklahoma	146
California	9,419	Wisconsin	138
Florida	2,754	Tennessee	126
Texas	2,714	Nevada	99
New Jersey	2,352	Rhode Island	91
Illinois	1,103	Kansas	84
Pennsylvania	990	Kentucky	84
Massachusetts	865	Utah	70
Georgia	841	New Mexico	4
District of Columbia	755	Arkansas	63
Maryland	606	Delaware	55
Washington	496	Mississippi	55
Louisiana	481	Iowa	54
Virginia	464	Maine	46
Connecticut	461	Nebraska	35
Ohio	441	New Hampshire	35
Colorado	424	West Virginia	35
Puerto Rico	394	Alaska	34
Michigan	379	Vermont	13
Missouri	275	Idaho	10
North Carolina	272	Montana	8
Arizona	260	Wyoming	8
Minnesota	221	Virgin Islands	7
Oregon	197	North Dakota	5
Indiana	189	South Dakota	5
Hawaii	162	Guam	1
South Carolina	154	Trust Territory	1
Alabama	148	**TOTAL**	**40,845**

Source: Centers For Disease Control

    Perhaps the most significant difference between the person with AIDS versus ARC is that the former is fully symptomatic with the infection. People with ARC, on the other hand, may or may not evolve to a fully symptomatic level of the disease, but both are fatal conditions at present. Even though the incubation period between the presence of HIV antibodies in the blood and the occurrence of death can take an estimated 3 months–5 + years to evolve, once the person becomes fully symptomatic, their physical deterioration and death progresses rapidly. Consequently, it is the person with AIDS who begins a fully symptomatic evolution that presents the most obvious problem for employers in terms of workplace accommodation until the person can no longer perform or physically endure their duties.

    Yet, there remains the even greater employment as well as societal problem of the growing number of male and female employees (present United States ratio is 15:1) who possess HIV, and thereby present a risk to others under those conditions where it is commonly known to be transmitted. These include:

Method Of Transmission	High Risk Group
1. Sexual contact such as by infectious semen to vaginal or anal canal (absorbed into bloodstream)	Homosexuals
	Intravenous Drug Users
2. Direct blood receipt of infected blood	Females having sex with the above, and/or with hemophiliacs
3. Fetal infection of a newborn by infections prior to or during pregnancy	Prostitutes & those having sex with them
	Sexually active, non-monogamous heterosexuals

For purposes of managers knowing a bit more about confirming the existence of an HIV infected employee, or being told by such an employee of their condition, before you start rendering a "what to do" evaluation or decisions, there are a couple of things you should know about AIDS (or more properly HIV) testing. First, there is no existing singular test that diagnoses AIDS with complete accuracy. The most reliable test currently available is called ELISA which simply measures the presence or absence of HIV antibodies in the blood supply.

However, a positive result does not necessarily mean the *presence* of AIDS, only that there is a high probability for the person to develop AIDS or ARC over the 5-10 year period from the time of infection mentioned earlier. A person who presently has (or has evolved to) an AIDS condition should test "true positive" which requires a test sequence consisting of a second ELISA test when the first one was positive. If the second ELISA test is also positive, then these results should be confirmed by one or both of these tests: the Western blot or the Immunofluorescence tests. If either or both of these secondary tests confirm the ELISA results, then the person is regarded as being true positive for having AIDS.

Naturally, any information related to this type of testing is to be regarded by managers with the strictest form of privacy. Aside from the matter of attending to the medical needs and employment accommodation of the employee with AIDS or ARC, managers will also want to anticipate how best to deal with the justifiably emotional concerns of other employees if the word gets out or speculation begins. With respect to employment accommodation, you should be aware that by 1987 six states had rendered either court decisions or legal opinions that AIDS and ARC is considered a handicap under state discrimination law; and they include California, Florida, Oregon, Massachusetts, New York, and Wisconsin. Further, there is some attention given in these laws to the prohibition of employers and co-workers engaging in the harassing or threatening of persons who have AIDS or ARC should their condition become known.

In reaction to the U.S. Supreme Court's 1984 ruling in the *Grove City College* case, Congress brought AIDS within the meaning of a physical handicap under Sections 503 and 504 of the Rehabilitation Act for government contractors and recipients of government assistance by adoption of the Civil Rights Restoration Act of 1988. Clearly, this Congressional action marks the legislative intent to see that AIDS is treated as a physical handicap on a national level even though it only affects contractors and recipients of federal assistance under the 1988 Act. In a related move, the U.S. Office of Personnel Management issued a March 1988 policy that prohibits discrimination against federal workers who have AIDS.

In the first case in which a federal court has ruled that AIDS is a physical handicap under federal law—using the die already cast by the Arline case—the Ninth Circuit Court of Appeals ruled that a classroom teacher having AIDS was a qualified handicapped and discriminated against by removal from his job for being infected with the virus. In *Chalk v. U.S. District Court* (1988), the court held that plaintiff's condition was likened to that in the Arline case, and that he was discriminated against because he was physically able to perform classroom duties without risk of infection to his students.

Again, employers are reminded that their obligation is to accommodate physical handicaps so long as the employee is able to perform essential portions of their job, unless doing so would present a clear risk to others or an unreasonable hardship on the employer.

What is more influential on most private sector employers is state laws prohibiting discrimination on the basis of physical handicap, and their respective legal treatment of whether AIDS and ARC are protected conditions. The six states that had AIDS related cases brought before administrative or judicial hearing determined that AIDS is a protected condition within the meaning of state handicap discrimination laws, and have thus established considerable precedence for fait accompli decisions by other states. The cases in California, Massachusetts, and Florida serve as good illustrations of what now appears to be common legal application of the same principles used by the U.S. Supreme Court in Arline.

In *DFEH v. Raytheon Company* (1987), the California Department of Fair Employment and Housing Commission brought this action in behalf of the estate of John Chadbourne, a deceased AIDS victim who was a quality control analyst with Raytheon. In December 1983, Chadbourne took a medical leave due to complications of his AIDS condition, and the next month his physician released him to resume full employment duties. Despite the employer's effort to learn more about the control and transmission of AIDS, it was ultimately decided to terminate him due to concern over the reaction of other employees. By August 1984, Chadbourne had become physically unable to work and died in January 1985. The Commission, in rejecting the employer's argument of fearing risk to others, noted that the employer had no particular evidence of medical authority that would suggest the presence of a real, substantial, and immediate danger to other employees.

In the seemingly clear-cut case of AIDS related discrimination in *Cronan v. New England Telephone Co.* (1986), a Massachusetts court ruling found AIDS to be not only a protected handicap, but charged the employer with both job discrimination and invasion of privacy. Following top management's conducting of group meetings with employees to inform them of Cronan's contagious condition, Cronan received threats from co-workers and chose not to return to work out of fear for his well-being. The court held that a person with AIDS may qualify as a handicapped individual based "solely on an employer's erroneous perception of him as someone who is contagious to co-workers. If an employee is not in fact likely to spread AIDS, but is erroneously perceived to be contagious by an employer, then the employee may be someone regarded as having such impairment."

One of the earliest decisions on AIDS as a protected employment handicap by a rule-making body was handed down by the Florida Commission on Human Relations in *Shuttleworth v. Broward County Office of Budget and Management Policy* (1985). Here again, the claimant was terminated after the employer learned of his AIDS condition and was unable to substantiate its decision on the basis of medical risk to others or the existence of a legitimate BFOQ. The Commission thus held that the employer's adverse action based only on its perception, rather than substantive fact, of the effect of AIDS on his job, ability to perform duties, or risk to others makes AIDS a handicap within the meaning of the Florida statute.

What these cases point out is that there remains much for employers to learn about AIDS. This includes its various medical aspects and implications, distinctions between persons with AIDS (symptomatic) and ARC (asymptomatic), means of transmission, more accurate testing for the presence of the condition, what the legal threshold of tolerance will be in terms of an employer's reasonable accommodation, and what evidence is necessary to establish the existence of a sufficient health risk to others.

For purposes of employment discrimination, these cases would seem to imply that an AIDS infected employee does not have an absolute right to continued employment or accommodation. Rather, they suggest that the burden of proof rests with the employer to demonstrate by substantive evidence a reasonable cause for any adverse employment action such as:

- a qualified medical determination that others would be at risk (creating a vicarious liability for the employer if others contract the disease);

- the employee's condition is such that they cannot perform some essential function of their job (no longer a qualified handicap);

- that reasonable accommodation cannot be made without creating an undue hardship or, if accommodation were available, the employee's condition is medically determined to be deteriorating rapidly enough to make it a mere temporary benefit;

- that some other equally legitimate BFOQ exists.

Shielding co-workers from information that an employee has AIDS is a difficult problem even when management takes care measures to maintain confidentiality. Each of the aforementioned cases dealt with this issue, and it is a considerable, very real concern for management in terms of the possible consequence of reactions from the entire workforce, not merely co-workers. For this reason, it is advisable for all organizations to sponsor educational programs concerning known facts rather than myth about the virus, its carriers, and the limited circumstances in which it can be transmitted. Other approaches to dealing with the issue of AIDS in the workplace have been cited by Stuart Bompey, a senior partner with a New York law firm, at a seminar on AIDS sponsored by the District of Columbia Bar Association. His "Ten Commandments" are:

I   Treat AIDS like any other disability.

II   Educate the workforce about AIDS before an actual case presents itself.

III Do not formulate a special policy on AIDS.

IV   Institute good cost containment programs to keep down the medical costs of treating an AIDS patient under the group health policy.

V   Maintain the confidentiality of all medical records.

VI   Do not discriminate against someone with AIDS: Be able to document any discipline.

VII Do not automatically exclude AIDS patients from training or consideration for promotion.

VIII If it becomes common knowledge in the workplace that an employee has AIDS, be willing to discuss the situation with other employees; have a medical person on hand.

IX   Accommodate an AIDS patient by, for example, offering the employee a comparable or similar job at the same pay.

X   Don't test for AIDS: whether in the context of job applicants or current employees.

5.32 ADDICTIVE HANDICAPS

Thus far, the three types of physical addictions that have come to equate as a physical handicap are alcohol abuse, drug abuse, and smoking. The latter, although no less a problem than the other two, has received little attention as a litigated matter since workplace smoking is typically controlled by ordinance at the local government level or by individual employers, and it is a thorny issue for most employers who recognize that to satify one group is to deny another group of their civil liberties.

With respect to alcohol and drug abuse, the question of whether or not the condition constitutes a protected handicap tends to focus on the distinction of past versus present addiction. However, in cases of employee substance abuse once it becomes known to the employer, accommodation means that the employee ought to be granted reasonable time off to voluntarily undergo treatment (rehabilitation). By policy, most employers will allow the employee to use available vacation and sick leave in order to continue pay and benefits during such absence, particularly if other personal disabilities would be treated in that manner. Recognizing the importance of the full recovery of valuable human resources, many employers now pay the cost of the rehabilitation program. Conversely, should the employee refuse or not follow a treatment program after being offered the opportunity by the employer, the employer may generally regard the employee as not being "otherwise qualified" and terminate their employment.

Alcohol Abuse

In *Northwest Airlines Inc. v. Gomerz-Bethke* (1984), a federal district court enjoined the Minnesota Human Rights Commission from denying plaintiff's sick leave use for the treatment of alcoholism on the basis that employment benefits are preempted by federal statute (ERISA).

In *Walker v. Weinberger* (1985), plaintiff was terminated unlawfully under protection of the Rehibilitation Act due to excessive absenteeism, part of which occurred due to pre-treatment of alcoholism. Here, the court distinguishes between pre-versus post-treatment violations of an employer's policy that carries disciplinary consequences, and the court notes that there ought to be some degree of forgiveness for pre-treatment violations if the employee succeeds at voluntary treatment of the condition that was the underlying cause of the policy violation.

In *Robinson v. Devine* (1985), plaintiff's drinking was affecting his performance and safety in operating machinery thereby rendering him to not be a "qualified handicap" under Section 504. The employer offered reasonable accommodation by allowing him leave to pursue treatment and any other assistance they could to combat his alcoholism, but that if his performance was not corrected upon his return, he would be terminated. Plaintiff took time off, returned to his same job, continued to demonstrate related performance problems, and was terminated. The court, in recognizing the employer's good faith accommodation and warning, sustained the termination.

Drug Abuse

In *Davis v. Bucher* (1978), a district court held that persons with histories of drug use were handicapped individuals within the meaning of the Rehabilitation Act and therefore, employers could not absolutely refuse to hire persons because of their former drug abuse.

In *Heron v. McGuire* (1986), the Second Circuit Court of Appeals determined that present drug addiction rendering an employee unfit for duties is not protected by handicap discrimination law. In this case, a police officer had become addicted to heroin creating not only a dependence on an illegal substance for which the officer was entrusted to enforce, but physically compromised his ability to perform life-threatening and emergency activities. The employer's termination was sustained.

Smoking

In *Vickers v. Veterans Administration* (1982), the plaintiff alleges a health hazard due to hypersensitivity to tobacco smoke produced by co-workers in the work unit. The court determined that the employer showed evidence of trying to reasonably accommodate the plaintiff but, in the absence of a law requiring the ban of smoking in the workplace, such an accommodation would be an undue hardship on smokers.

This case is by no means a definitive answer to the problem of health risks to non-smokers where smoking is allowed in the workplace. Even in the absence of a local ordinance banning smoking in public facilities and encouraging private employers to do likewise in the workplace, employers are free to establish either no-smoking areas (public corridors, elevators, congested work areas, offices, etc.) or even a completely smoke-free workplace. That may also create what appears to be the circular dilemma for employers, and that is, by banning smoking entirely a smoking employee may then allege their need for accommodation as a "qualified handicap."

Many employers have tried to stay out of the battle of rights between smoking and non-smoking employees by asking that they work it out on their own. Even if they do, or management handles on a case-by-case basis, it only serves as a temporary if not evasive solution to a larger problem that will need to (and should) be addressed by company policy. In what may be a compromise measure, the best policy for management to take as a means of ameliorating the double-edged problem might be to allow smoking only in private offices when occupied by the smoker who must provide an air detoxifying system, and in designated smoking areas. With the present level of awareness of the health risks associated with smoking and growing interest in physical fitness, it has been speculated that the number of smokers will diminish markedly during the next two decades. Meanwhile, employers ought to be confronting and dealing with the issue before it reaches problematic proportions.

5.33 PHYSIOLOGICAL IMPAIRMENTS

There has been a rather wide assortment of physiological impairments that have been brought before various courts and administrative agencies. Not all such impairments have been held to be handicaps within the meaning of state or federal law. Interestingly enough, in the relatively short amount of time legal remedies have become available to those with different types of impairments, there remains nearly an absence of cases involving either mental, emotional (particularly stress related), or hearing impaired handicaps. With increased advocacy services representing the interest of those with mental and hearing limitations who have been adversely effected in some employment context, and the increased sensitivity some employees have toward workplace stress, these two kinds of impairments are strong prospects for more legal attention than in the past, and there is a very high probability they will be classified as a protected handicap. Other examples of physiological impairments that have already been addressed are as follows.

Amputation And Paralysis

This category would also include anyone with the loss, restriction, or limited use of any extremity including those aided by wheelchair or prosthetic devise.

The first case involves an amputee who lost a leg while working for a railroad, and the employer was able to skirt any further accommodation because of the obligation railroads have for passenger safety. In *OFCCP v. Missouri Pacific Railroad* (1983), an engineer learned to walk with a prosthesis and was felt to be capable of resuming his job by two orthopedic surgeons. The physician to which the employee was referred by the railroad disagreed. Although the court found the employee to be 95 percent able to perform engineer duties, the remainder of activity (walking on rough trackside—often in poor weather) was viewed by the court as an influential factor in the safety of a train's operation, other train crew, cargo, and passengers. The employee was thus held not to be "otherwise qualified." In less extreme employment circumstances, it is not likely the court would make a similar finding.

A Missouri case involved a police officer paralyzed by being gunshot. In *Simon v. St. Louis County* (1981), the employer terminated plaintiff for being unable to resume normal police officer duties. The district court agreed with the employer, holding that any accommodation would have to be substantial and, as such, he was therefore not "otherwise qualified." The Eighth Circuit Court of Appeals disagreed and believed there must be an examination as to whether the requirements of St. Louis County were reasonable and necessary for the job. These requirements consisted of being able to effect a forcible arrest and render emergency aid in addition to having the capacity to be transferred to any position within the police department. The Court of Appeals believed that substantial evidence existed to demonstrate that the physical requirements "were not in fact necessary and were not required of all officers." The court also stated that consideration should be given to the plaintiff's actual physical condition in addition to his police experience and a determination should be made as to which functions within the department the plaintiff had the physical capacity to perform.

Overall, this conclusion reached by the Appellate Court is more representative of what employers should expect to consider, and be prepared to prove, in the way of available accommodation before terminating a handicapped employee. In other words, accommodation means looking beyond the employee's job and into other positions where the handicap would not preclude essential duties. The courts can also be expected to be especially sensitive to handicaps incurred in connection to employment (i.e., current employees as opposed to preexisting conditions of job applicants).

Sight Limitation Or Blindness

In one of several discrimination charges brought against the EEOC in what might be thought of as "the hunter becomes the hunted," the EEOC was successful in its defense for refusing to hire a blind law clerk in *Coleman v. Darden* (1979). The Tenth Circuit Court of Appeals upheld the EEOC's rejection on the basis that the EEOC did not automatically exclude the applicant from consideration, but rather made an individual determination that he was not qualified for the requirements of the position.

However, had the blind applicant been qualified for the job, the court may well have found that hiring an additional sighted reader was within the EEOC's reasonable realm of accommodation.

In *Quinn v. Southern Pacific Transportation Co.* (1985), a trial court awarded plaintiff $60,000 in back pay and the Oregon Court of Appeals affirmed the lower court's findings involving a railroad employee who was rejected for a Fireman's training program (leading to the position of Engineer) due to twice failing the "Ishihara" color-blind test. However, plaintiff did pass a bright red-green color chart test whereby the testing physician recommended acceptance to the training program, but the employer's chief medical officer disagreed.

Both the trial and Appellate courts determined that plaintiff's Ishihara color-blindness would not affect his ability to perform the job since he could distinguish brighter colors that was more akin to rail traffic signals. Further, the court of appeals found a persuasive list of evidence in the fact that at least two other employees with similar vision deficiencies were employed as either firemen or engineers. The case obviously points out the need for employers to use selection tests that accurately simulate and replicate performance aspects for a job.

Back And Spinal Conditions

Most cases of this type involve an employer's rejection of a job applicant on the basis of a preemployment x-ray revealing some type of deformity, irregularity, or disc compression of the spinal column which employers have been led to fear as a probable future (workers' compensable) injury. Yet one of the most prevalent conditions of our human species since the evolution of Homo Erectus is a condition called scoliosis, or a slight lateral displacement of the lower spine. Little scientific evidence exists to show this condition as more probably disabling in the future to employees even with physically-oriented jobs than those without the condition. Even if such evidence did exist, the law prohibits discrimination that is generally based on uncertain future probabilities. Employees and applicants must be evaluated in light of present physical conditions, and present ability or inability to perform the job in question.

For example, in *E.E. Black, Ltd. v. Marshall* (1980), an apprentice carpenter who had accumulated 3600 hours of on-the-job training was denied employment by this construction contractor on the basis of a preemployment medical exam that disclosed the presence of a congenital back problem. The physician advised the employer that the applicant would be a poor risk in terms of heavy labor. The court, having found that the disorder was a handicap, determined that the applicant was capable of performing the job at the time of application and was therefore an "otherwise qualified" handicap. Barring any immediate risk of injury, the court regarded the employer's reliance on possible future injury as ill-founded and having the effect of discrimination.

Likewise, under Maine's handicap discrimination law, employers may not use potentially disabling back conditions that are conjectured from preemployment x-rays. So says the Maine Supreme Judicial Court in deciding the case of *Rozanski v. A-P-A Transport, Inc.* (1986) where the trucking company terminated two drivers (after probationary employment by the way) due to the discovery of spinal defects revealed in back x-rays even though the employees were asymptomatic of back problems. In their examination of this evidence, the court concluded that the employees were young, in good physical condition, and that their back defects were unlikely to result in injury from truck driving duties. Each employee was awarded over $80,000 in back pay (no pun intended) and benefits.

In contrast, the Michigan Supreme Court upheld General Motors refusal to transfer an employee with a back condition to a job involving heavy lifting in *Carr v. General Motors Corp.* (1986). This case points out that it makes no difference whether the employment decisions involves hiring, promotion, transfers, or any other employment transaction, the employer's decision ought to be made on available evidence and characteristics of the job's essential functions. In this case, the employee had undergone ruptured disc surgery and was given a weight lifting limitation by both his personal physician and the company physician. As a result, the court found that disabilities so directly related to an employee's capacity to perform a job are not protected handicaps.

Epilepsy And Nerve Deterioration

Probably nowhere else than with epilepsy does the issue of case-by-case examination of individual circumstances come to light because of the condition's varying degrees of effect and measures taken for its control. Further, should seizure occur, the victim may well lose bodily control thereby creating an imminent hazard to self and others depending on job circumstances. Epilepsy has clearly been held as a protected handicap, and its condition or history of such should not serve as an automatic exclusion unless other laws protecting public health or safety compel it. An example of a more compelling interest was decided in *Costner v. United States* (1983) where a truck driver was terminated once the employer learned of his epilepsy history. Despite being seizure-free for 15 years and under medical control, plaintiff was fired due to a Transportation Department regulation prohibiting persons with medical histories, or diagnosis of epilepsy, from driving interstate commerce. The Eighth Circuit Court of Appeals determined the regulation to be a legitimate state interest and upheld the employer's action.

Another employer was upheld in their termination of an employee working as a butcher who suffered a seizure at work in *Jansen v. Food Circus Supermarkets, Inc.* (1987). Here, the court noted that blanket termination policies concerning epileptic employees would not be lawful, but under the circumstances of evidence presented by the employer, the court held their action justified. The employer was able to demonstrate:

- the seizure occurred at work with a knife in his hand;
- the employee's physician could only certify that he was under fair control while on medication;
- the employer offered a transfer prior to the termination; and
- the employer had two other epileptic employees, one a baker and the other a clerk.

In a somewhat unusual case involving an applicant who, like the Carr case, would have no doubt incurred further personal suffering had the employer granted the plaintiff's bid for the job, a Missouri district court upheld the employer's rejection. In *Carmi v. St. Louis Water District* (1979), the complainant's charges of discrimination were dismissed because his rare hereditary disease caused muscle and nerve deterioration, weakness of grip, uneven gait, and inability to lift over forty pounds and thus he could not show that he could perform on a daily and continued basis the requisite job-related skills of a storeroom keeper. In addition to meeting the definition of handicapped to qualify as an "otherwise qualified applicant," such individual must be able to prove that he is capable of performing the particular job with reasonable accommodation to his handicap.

Despite these cases where a few employers were upheld by the courts in their action, the more usual circumstance is where an employer fires or takes other adverse action against an employee with epilepsy out of the employer's fear or apathy. A good case in point is *Reynolds vs. Brock* (1987) in which plaintiff's requests for additional training and accommodation in her job with DOL (even the feds error on occasion) were denied by her supervisor following her first seizure at work; a condition unknown to DOL. Thereafter, she was given low performance ratings then terminated after refusing the offer of a receptionist position. Summary judgment for the employer was denied by the court on the basis of Reynolds being a qualified handicapped person and denied accommodation consideration, and the suspect nature of the employer's motive for termination.

Heart Condition And High Blood Pressure

Theoretically, any bodily organ having a deficient function such as the heart, lungs, kidney, and the like would be considered a handicap where there is the presence or history of such a disorder. As with most handicap conditions, employers must rely on the advice of applicable medical specialists to help them evaluate all relevant factors before making a good faith decision or weighing the prospects and consequences of any feasible form of accommodation. When contradictory medical evaluation is present, the employer ought to seek out a third specialized medical opinion since liability will ultimately rest with the employer for erroneous decisions.

This situation is exemplified in *Montgomery Ward and Co., Inc. v. Bureau of Labor* (1977) where the Oregon Supreme Court found the evidence of an applicant's own cardiologist more convincing as to his ability to perform the job given his heart condition than was the company's (preemployment) examining physician who felt that the applicant would be at serious risk of another heart attack if hired.

Since heart conditions and strokes are often the product of high blood pressure, it is reasonable to assume that state courts holding heart conditions to be a protected handicap would regard adverse employment decisions based on a person's high blood pressure to be subject to the same legal tests as any other handicap. Such was the case in *American National Insurance Co. v. FEHC* (1982) where an insurance company that had terminated a sales and debit agent on account of his elevated blood pressure sought judicial review of an administrative decision that the company had violated the California Fair Employment and Housing Act which prohibits employment discrimination against one with a physical handicap. Although the agent's high blood pressure did not impair his ability to work, the employer believed, on medical advice, that it would expose him to a greater than normal risk of disability or death. Concluding that high blood pressure was a protected physical handicap under the Act, and that the findings of the Fair Employment and Housing Commission were supported by the evidence, the trial court denied the company's petition for administrative mandamus.

The Supreme Court affirmed. The court held that high blood pressure may be a "physical handicap" under the FEHA, as the statutory definition of such term is not restrictive, thus permitting consideration of all handicaps that are physical, and as the state legislature did not intend to cover only those health problems that are presently disabling.

Cancer

Not all forms of cancer are alike, nor do they develop within the body in the same way. Some forms can be treated with medication, some removed by surgery, and others by radiation therapy. Some afflictions turn out benign, while others become malignant with varying consequences from some physical impairment to death. In just about any case of cancer, an employee is going to require some time off from work for at least medical examinations and treatment, or possibly time off for surgery and recovery. Like most physical handicap conditions, cancer-related disability or impairment ought to be viewed in the context of individual circumstances of the medical condition, the employee's job requirements, applicable forms of accommodation, existing policy, and operational impact of the position.

Presently, cancer is not one of the handicaps that has been brought within the definition of federal law or regulations, nor by federal court ruling. However, some states such as California have expressly included cancer as a protected condition. It is also likely that those states having broadly defined language of what constitutes a handicap will bring cancer in as a condition as these cases find their way to court since the same fundamental principles apply to cancer as it now does to heart conditions, back problems, and epilepsy.

Accommodation with regard to cancer victims typically is of two types: 1) work schedule accommodation to allow time off for necessary medical treatment; and 2) job restructuring to accommodate any physical limitations that result. For the job applicant, this means that the employer will need to determine if the applicant is cured, rehabilitating, or has a deteriorating condition. If cured, are there any residual limitations and what are the frequencies of medical check-ups? If rehabilitating, what frequency and durations will be required? If the condition is active and either of unknown or deteriorating, what prognosis would expert medical advisors give concerning the individual's likelihood for recovery, absence needed, and prospective physical limitations during or after treatment? Presuming that the applicant or employee is determined to be "otherwise qualified" with their cancer condition, an employer who simply cannot operate with the degree of time off flexibility necessary to accommodate a cancer victim may need to develop specific effects of such an instance to use as an "undue hardship" defense on the basis of operational impact.

Left Handed

There is a limit to everything and, according to the Fifth Circuit Court of Appeals in *Torres v. Bolger* (1986), being left-handed is not a physical handicap under the federal Rehabilitation Act. The case involved a left-handed postal carrier who was fired for being too slow. Since the characteristic of being left-handed could not be shown as "limiting one or more of the individual's major life activities," even though it apparently had some effect of slowing his work, the court concluded that this personal characteristic does not qualify as a handicap.

Height (Too Short)

Height has been found not to be a handicap per se under at least one state law in *American Motors Corp. v. Labor and Industry Review Commission* (1984). As height relates to a physical handicap condition, the Wisconsin Supreme Court ruled in favor of the employer's rejection of a 4 foot, 10 inch woman due to the employer's determination, and support of a medical test that her short stature would preclude her ability to properly perform the job in question. Ultimately, the court's conclusion was that height was not a protected handicap within the meaning of state law.

However, there is another component of discrimination on the basis of one's height, and that is national origin and sex discrimination where it has frequently been legally argued with success that certain nationalities (Asians, Filipinos, and some Hispanic groups) and women in general are shorter than the average Caucasian or the average male. Therefore, the only legitimate height requirement that can be associated with a job is that part of the job that absolutely requires given height standards without the ability to use alternative methods to accomplish the task (e.g., short flight attendants can step on a seat to reach overhead compartments, step ladders can be used to reach high shelves, etc.).

Weight (Obesity)

Once again, this physical condition has not yet fallen into the definition of federal handicap law by court test, but it is something of a foregone conclusion that it will given the fact that some state courts have at least shown an inclination to include obesity under certain circumstances. Too, with approximately 14 percent of the male and 24 percent of the female population in the age 20-74 range categorized at least 20 percent overweight, it again becomes an issue that time will classify. There are two prominent state court cases that have dealt with obesity as a form of physical handicap discrimination: rejected in the 1982 Pennsylvania case, and accepted in the 1984 New York case.

In *Philadelphia Electric Co. v. Pennsylvania Human Relations Commission* (1982), the Commonwealth Court overturned the Commission finding of handicap discrimination and award of $20,000 to Joyce English, a 5 foot 8 inch, 341 pound applicant for a clerical position with the utility company. Despite passing a series of preemployment tests, company physicians considered her unsuitable due to abnormal weight for the position. The court, however, determined that morbid obesity does not, in itself, constitute a handicap, and that no evidence was shown to indicate that the applicant was handicapped at the time she applied for the job. The court concluded that an employer "has the inherent right to discriminate among applicants for employment and to eliminate those who have a high potential for absenteeism and low productivity."

Not so in the state of New York, says the Appellate Division of the New York Supreme Court in *State Division of Human Rights v. Xerox Corp.* (1984). Here, the company had extended an employment offer to a female applicant after which the company physician recommended rejection due to excessive weight and advising that obese employees tend to have higher absenteeism, disability and medical benefit utilization, and life insurance costs. Having found the applicant qualified, the company requested that the doctor reconsider, but to no avail. The company thus acted on the doctor's recommendation and rejected her. In an unanimous decision, the court ruled that obesity is a handicap within the meaning of their state human rights law, and Xerox violated that law by refusing to hire her solely on the basis of her weight without showing particular ways in which her obesity would impair job performance. In other words, she was in all respects an "otherwise qualified" individual.

In order for employers to defend a discrimination claim due to the obesity of an applicant or employee, much more homework will be necessary to stand up in court as a well constructed, job and business related defense. One example is the use of medical and industry studies that will substantiate that this condition does cause greater absenteeism, use of sick leave, lower productivity, medical complications resulting in disability, and the like. Another element is the job itself with regard to the pressure of physical stress and endurance such as considerable walking, climbing, bending, stooping, or getting up and sitting down repeatedly. Whatever the physical requirements of the job are, they should be replicated in the preemployment medical evaluation to determine both ability and any decline in endurance. Yet a third measure is to obtain the individuals authorization to access their former employment records concerning absenteeism and performance evaluations.

Transvestitism/Homosexuality

According to the Diagnostic and Statistical Manual of Mental Disorders of the American Psychiatric Association, transvestites are "generally male heterosexuals who cross-dress, i.e., dress as females, for sexual arousal rather than social comfort..." As such, it is classified officially as a mental disorder. The federal Rehabilitation Act defines a "handicapped individual" as one who *has* a physical or mental impairment, or as one who is *perceived* to have such an impairment.

Relying to some degree on the earlier case of *Ulane v. Eastern Airlines, Inc.* (1984), a federal district court in the District of Columbia ruled that transvestites are protected under the federal statute in a case involving the application for reemployment of a former Treasury Department employee, released after eight years of service by a reduction-in-force, and who cross-dressed during his former employment as well as for the reemployment interview. In *Blackwell v. United States Department of the Treasury* (1986), the plaintiff successfully contended that the position he sought was eliminated after his interview because he was perceived as mentally ill and handicapped. He further alleged that the interviewer conspired with the personnel officer and director to take this action, but plaintiff's private suits against these individuals were dismissed.

However, upon appeal and review by the U.S. District Court of Appeals for the District of Columbia, the lower court's decision was reversed. The basis of the district court's opinion was that plaintiff was rejected for perceived homosexuality rather than transvestitism, and that homosexuality is not a qualified handicap under the Rehabilitation Act. Although the appellate decision led to an apparent convolution of law and the factual evidence in this case, it points to two conclusions—which may well be temporary in nature. First, transvestitism will probably continue to be regarded as a qualified handicap on the mental disorder theory; and, second, homosexuality (sexual orientation) is a protected form of sex (not handicap) discrimination only in those states who have incorporated it into their non-discrimination statutes, but for now no federal law treats it as such.

Moreover, what this case points to as a problem for employers is twofold: first, other approaches to dealing with the issue of transvestites in the workplace; and second, the personal liability carried by personnel professionals when dispensing advice, direction to other managers, or decision making where the action is known to be illegal.

In the first instance, eliminating a job after interviewing would arouse suspicion in anyone who examined for the position, and who would see the action as pretextual for a refusal to hire. In the case of Blackwell, it was apparently not that difficult to get inside information as to why the job was really eliminated. When a transvestite (or any handicapped individual) applies for a job and is qualified in other respects, process the applicant as you would any other. If you find a more qualified person, you are free to hire them knowing you can demonstrate the particular ways they were more qualified than others. If you hire someone and later find they practice transvestitism, you may examine company policy and state laws concerning the enforcement of apparel and personal appearance standards. Also, should the job involve public or customer contact in person, and you can provide business necessity evidence of the offensive nature of an employee's transvestitism, a defense might be established should the employee refuse to comply and is thus terminated. Should the act of cross-dress become offensive to employees, the employer may also have a legal course of action by applying its sexual harassment policy against the transvestite.

With respect to the second instance, many management officers carry the burden of rather constant liability of one type or another concerning business decisions and actions of authority. The Blackwell case reminds us of the exposures human resource managers can bring to themselves and their organization if they give or are involved in decisions or actions known by the manager to be illegal. Obviously, this can be a major concern to those human resource managers who are required to give advice, counsel other managers, and independently transact personnel decisions.

Some human resource managers who report to the CEO or President of a company sometimes find themselves in the precarious position of being told by higher authority to make some particular personnel decision or carry out an action known to be absolutely illegal and improper. This situation is precisely what has created the legal modification of at-will employment principles and the major basis of wrongful discharge litigation when an employee is fired for refusing to perform some illegal act. For one's own protection in circumstances where the human resource manager is told to act illegally, the following measures ought to be considered:

1. Be sure the higher authority is clear about the illegality of the action, and liability consequences for the organization as well as their own personal liability for the intentional decision.

2. Request that the organization's legal counsel be consulted as a means of getting another professional to persuade the higher authority to take some other approach.

3. Make it clear to the higher authority that they are exposing you personally to legal action if you comply, and ask if that is the intent.

4. Clarify, at least in your own mind, if you are being ordered to carry out the illegal action, whether there is threat by inference, or it is merely a strong suggestion.

5. Document events and conversation thoroughly, and seek the advice of a criminal trial attorney.

It should be understood that the above is not intended to include those infrequently encountered situations where the human resources manager and other executives involved in an employment situation confer with the result of taking some action that has a high probability of litigation and an equal probability of losing the case. These are normal business decisions where judgment and risk are inherent factors of business operations and, in some cases or peculiar circumstances, it may be more meaningful for the organization to risk litigation than to bend too far creating a more consequential impact on operations, the integrity of policy standards, or the morale and respect of employees. These decisions, as opposed to the subversive type suggested, are more openly collaborative and have other business reasons as their intent—sort of a "we're willing to take it on the chin if we have to" approach when strict or proposed legal compliance is operationally unacceptable.

Neurosis

Having just created some discomfort for decision making human resource managers, it becomes apropos to conclude this section with the condition of whether one's neurosis can be considered a handicap protected by federal or state law. The condition has not yet been postulated as the basis of a dejected worker's handicap in federal court. It therefore remains fertile ground with regard to the manner in which it becomes a manifest handicap limiting, or being perceived as limiting, one or more of the individual's major life activities. However, for your enjoyment and relief, you'll be pleased to know that the Pennsylvania Commonwealth Court rejected the claim of an otherwise competent computer programmer who asserted that his persistent lateness to work was the result of a "neurotic compulsion for lateness," whereby the court staunchly held such a propensity to be outside the meaning of a handicap under state law in Philadelphia School District v. Friedman (1986).

5.40 HIRING HANDICAPPED EMPLOYEES: ADVANTAGES AND PROSPECTIVE PROBLEMS TO BE OVERCOME

Often referred to as the "last minority" (sorry, I'm skeptical), there are an estimated 28-36 million handicapped and disabled Americans. Estimates vary depending on the criteria used to determine a handicap and the number of workers disabled by injury at any point in time. Of these, there are an estimated 60 percent who possess job skills and the desire to obtain gainful employment; to become less reliant on disability benefits; and to acquire the same self-esteem that accompanies the use of employment skills enjoyed by the balance of society. There are, indeed, advantages to hiring the handicapped worker. Many present little to no problem in terms of the decision-making or accommodation process, but some handicapped people require more detailed analysis of work characteristics that non-handicapped people take for granted, or would otherwise give little thought—and to that extent it represents something of a problem for human resource and other managers. Whether or not you have experienced the decision-making job competition difficulty between handicapped and non-handicapped applicants, it would be prudent for every manager to consider the following issues, then proceed to effect necessary changes as a proactive measure in advance of the need. It's just plain good management to do so; that is, unless your organization prefers resolving business issues by intuition or after-the-fact decisions.

5.41 ADVANTAGES OF HANDICAPPED UTILIZATION

One of the most ubiquitous problems facing employers for decades has been turnover and absenteeism. It is also a common myth that by the very nature of handicapped employees, they have less job stability and require frequent absence for therapy or medical treatment. Quite the opposite is true for the majority of handicapped people currently working. Surveys and studies conducted on this subject have consistently demonstrated that—properly matched to a job—handicapped workers are less inclined to change jobs and have better absenteeism records than their non-handicapped co-workers.

First, in those cases where a person's handicap prevents full-time work, here is an opportunity to match an able worker to a part-time job that typically is difficult to keep filled (remember: it takes nearly as much time, effort, and cost to fill a part-time vacancy as a full-time position). Should it evolve or even be planned to enlarge from a part-time position to a full-time schedule, you may want to experiment with job sharing of the position in which you get two different talents for the price of one. One of my smaller organization clients did this to successfully meet their needs in data processing. During the morning hours, the wheelchair-bound systems programmer did his work, followed in the afternoon by an applications programmer. Both were exceedingly skilled from prior career pursuits, but their needs and priorities changed favoring part-time employment. The employer is ecstatic with the arrangement and their combined talents.

Yet another human resource that remains insufficiently used are the many useful and worthy people who are mentally handicapped only to the extent that their intelligence level has been impaired (educably handicapped). For employers having low-skilled, repetitive, if not monotonous jobs where turnover becomes a constant source of aggravation, this type of a handicapped person can be a significant improvement in the reliability of employees performing such jobs.

Second, there are two sources of tax advantages for employers who hire handicapped workers. Under the Tax Reform Act of 1976, and the Tax Equity and Fiscal Responsibility Act of 1982, employers can save up to $4,500 per year for the first two years of a handicapped employee's wages. Additionally, the federal government provides tax incentives for the removal of architectural barriers that provide greater access to the handicapped, and for providing accommodation devices to handicapped workers.

Third, the hiring of handicapped people increases the employer's workforce diversity, and thereby provides more visible evidence of its commitment to the principles of equal employment opportunity. In this same vein, once a handicapped employee becomes integrated into a particular work unit, the productivity and morale of the general work unit often increases. Psychologists correlate this phenomenon to such factors as admiration for the handicapped person (productivity inspiration), unconscious performance competition (non-handicapped workers would not want to be "shown up" by one who is impaired), and improvement in employee (attitudinal) relationships felt to be associated with the positive demeanor of one in their midst who is less fortunate in some visible respect.

5.42 SOLVING THE PROBLEM OF RECRUITING THE HANDICAPPED

The recruitment for any position in an organization should not be taken lightly with respect to time, effort, and imagination since many human resource problems stem from the improper collection and selection of job applicants. When it comes to the recruitment of protected groups in an effort to enhance the effectiveness of EEO selection decisions, special effort must be made to routinely communicate and encourage interested, available, and qualified job seekers to apply for job openings by those previously overlooked or underrepresented in the workforce. This is particularly true concerning the physically handicapped since, unlike other protected groups, their mobility, access, and means of normal communications are in some respect limited. Simply stated, you won't be able to find handicapped applicants by merely searching the files of those who came in to submit an application; you will need to take active measures to recruit them from local sources.

Written announcements of the job opening should contain not only a description of the duties and qualifications required, but also statements relating to particular physical requirements that absolutely are necessary for performance of essential functions of the position. For example, a Communications Installer "must be able to drive a service vehicle, walk and climb to overcome obstructions, climb ladders, bend and kneel to attach wiring, have color vision, work in inclement weather, etc." Such identification of physical and other necessary conditions of a job allows the employer to analyze each job in terms of: 1) what are essential requirements; 2) what requirements could be accommodated and in what ways; and 3) what customary requirements are not as absolutely necessary as perhaps those traditionally held. I, myself, am aware of a few amputees and another person with one eye who have been performing the above job successfully for years with the aid of prosthetic devices.

The job announcement should then be mailed to those organizations and services where qualified handicapped people can be reached. A follow-up telephone call reinforces your interest in reaching this pool of human resources, and it serves to spark additional effort for referrals on the part of the organization's staff. It's a good idea to establish a personal contact with at least one person from each organization contacted. Here are just a few of the organizations that deal with handicapped people where job referrals can be obtained, and they can be found in nearly every metropolitan area.

- State Employment Office
- State Department of Social Service
- State Department of Vocational Rehabilitation

- State Department of Health, Education, and Welfare
- Protection and Advocacy Service
- School District Vocational Education Office
- Disabled American Veterans Association
- United Way, Goodwill Industries, and American Red Cross Offices

From these sources, you should have no problem developing your own "labor market area" list of organizations, services they provide, contact person, and type of job referral service they offer. Put this information on your word processor to other affirmative action organizations so that repetitive mailings of job announcements can be performed as a matter of routine ease. And, don't be surprised if occasionally you're asked to be a speaker at one of these organization's meetings to give their members or staff the employer's view of hiring the handicapped. Seize the opportunity to tout your company's efforts in this area—and ask that the media be invited if you have a proud story to tell.

5.43 SOLVING THE PROBLEM OF PREEMPLOYMENT INTERVIEWS AND PHYSICALS

It is difficult to glean from an employment application or resume if an applicant will require any sort of accommodation (access, sighted guide, or sign language interpreter). If you have done the type of recruitment that has been suggested, you should at least anticipate the possibility of being called upon or notified that these provisions need to (or will be) made. At a minimum, the interview location should always be set up in a place that is wheelchair accessible. Whether or not you are required to provide guides and interpreters as a matter of law is essentially aside from the fact that you should be prepared to demonstrate such good faith equal employment opportunity efforts when called upon to do so by advanced notification of applicant needs.

There is a natural tendency for those interviewing handicapped applicants to ask questions related to the individual's particular handicap or their ability to do the job. The former is an illegal question and will give rise to the disparate treatment theory of discrimination law since it is not likely you're going to ask the same question of other applicants. The latter question, on the other hand, can be a legitimate question provided that: 1) the same question is asked of other applicants; and 2) the job clearly contains elements of essential physical, sensory, or mental performance. Learning to avoid questions based on "protected", distinguishing characteristics of an applicant can be a difficult habit to break, but preparing basic interview questions in advance will help avert this problem. It will also provide you with an important written record should you be called upon to defend the interview process.

An effective way to deal with ascertaining interview information concerning the physical requirements of the job in question is to:

1. Qualify the question by illustrating a few customary tasks that require particular physical traits.

2. Then ask *each* applicant; "Do you possess any present limitation, restriction, or inability to effectively perform such tasks?" If the answer is yes (or possibly), you should ask; "Do you know what type of accommodation you would need in order to effectively perform such tasks?", and note the applicant's response.

The courts have concluded—and reasonably so—that questions pertaining to the physical condition and health of applicants should be very limited and carefully constructed so as not to create a disparate treatment impurity in the interview process. Their reasoning is quite simple; interviewers are simply not qualified to make these kinds of determinations, which is why it is still lawful to refer those applicants being given serious consideration to a qualified physician. Qualified physician means one who specializes in industrial medicine or otherwise has noteworthy credentials qualifying them as an expert on matters of industrial health, physical and other medically related conditions of employment, and the practical nature of workplace activities.

You may not always choose to follow the advice of your company physician concerning the results of an applicant's medical evaluation, and when you don't, you should bear a couple of things in mind. First, the ultimate burden of a hire or rejection decision rests with the employer to defend and, second, you may feel considerably more comfortable about your ability to prevail in a defense of the decision if you have a highly reputable medical source to call upon to give testimony in your company's behalf—even if it is to do nothing more than to demonstrate your good faith effort to make sound decisions based on legitimate (physical) interests of the job.

Qualified physicians and other medically-related sources, such as industrial psychologists and vocational rehabilitation professionals, can be of immense value long before a finalist applicant becomes subject to selection evaluation. For example, as a proactive measure and once thorough job descriptions have been prepared, these experts could be asked to delineate relatively precise standards of medical, physical, mental, and emotional (stress) conditions that exist within each job, or those jobs where these conditions are predominant. Then preliminary guidelines can be established by which these jobs should be evaluated with respect to new hires, industrial injury rehabilitation, employee wellness programs, and employee assistance programs (EAPs).

Concerning new hire decisions, this approach has the unique advantage of pre-established types of medical tests that will be performed on each of these jobs relative to conditions within the job; i.e., the medical exam would then be job related, or valid with regard to particular requisite demands of the job in question. The fact that the company can additionally demonstrate that it has undertaken such expert assistance and analysis will enhance its defense of a physical handicap discrimination claim should one arise, but you should know that after-the-fact analysis is looked upon with immense skepticism by compliance agencies and the courts!

When you find yourself prepared to hire a handicapped worker, medical and professional experts can be instrumental in the successful adaptation and integration to their assigned job and work unit. If accommodation of the handicap is involved, the physician and vocational rehabilitation professional can assist you in determining what is needed and how to acquire or accomplish it, and what alternatives, if any, are available to you. Often the accommodation can require little more than a telephone amplifier for the receiver, raising the leg clearance of a work counter a few inches for wheelchair access, or placing an extendable magnifying glass next to a computer terminal.

If all of this sounds cumbersome or terribly time consuming, it isn't. Frequently, with good planning and organization, the time required to interview, get medical exam results, and arrange for typical kinds of workplace accommodations (if any) is about two weeks. If a project is undertaken to have outside professionals evaluate the medical, physical, mental and emotional conditions of all or a particular group of jobs, these assessments will normally not take more than two or three months depending, of course, on the number of jobs and the ability of the assigned company representative to monitor progress of the project.

5.44 DEALING WITH WORK UNIT INTEGRATION PROBLEMS

Integrating the handicapped worker into the work unit can raise some problems for both the work unit supervisor and the handicapped new hire. Generally, there is a time lapse between the offer/acceptance of employment and the start date. Whether or not problems are anticipated in the work unit once the job has been accepted by the handicapped worker, the time lapse presents a good opportunity for the department manager to inform work unit employees of the hiring decision and starting date of the new employee. In fact, as a matter of customary practice, it is a good idea to begin the orientation process of every new employee in this way. It is also helpful and adds something of a personal touch to give other employees some general background about the employee, but be careful not to divulge too personal information, or what may be regarded as confidential information that the new employee might find as a deprivation of their privacy rights.

Rather than letting it be an awkward surprise or allowing unnecessary speculation about the new employee based on rumors, tell other employees that this individual has a handicap. Tell them what the general handicap is (e.g., wheelchair bound, speech impediment, prosthetic left arm, hook on right hand, etc.), and discuss with them any necessary forms of accommodation, needs the employee may have, and your desire to see them help this employee adapt and succeed in their job. What you will want to instill in work unit employees by this early information is their desire to help rather than judge the new employee (personalized interest versus indifferent or biased behavior) who has the same needs as any other new hire, but those needs tend to be more acute with the handicapped. The two most important needs of a handicapped new hire is a sense of belonging and their acceptance by other, non-handicapped employees who are already familiar with each other and comfortable with their ability to do their jobs; and, second, to gain the feeling that they are involved as an equal, integral part of the work done within the work unit.

The first issue is one of acceptance and a sort of social inclusion. This process can be aided and enhanced by the aforementioned discussion with employees prior to the start date of the new hire. Additionally, employees should be encouraged to openly discuss their views, feelings, and ideas during this discussion so that you can deal with potential problems before they turn into serious interpersonal problems or rivalries. You may also be surprised to find a high level of acceptance among existing employees, one or two of which might state their desire to help. Take advantage of such offers by suggesting to the supervisor that one of these employees be assigned to train or act as the new employee's "sponsor" (new employee sponsorship programs, like mentorship, are gaining popularity among employers). It can be helpful to point out something as obvious, but sometimes forgotten, as the new hire's probable personal discomfort or sense of inadequacy in light of new surroundings and challenges. You should also stress that employees should not overcompensate for the new hire's handicap by doting over them or becoming patronizing; just be friendly, show sincere interest, and be helpful.

The second issue has to do with involvement. Here, the type of inclusion that is needed pertains to work tasks, work flow, coordination and cooperation over work matters, productivity, and becoming a part of work decisions. Once again, the hiring of any new employee presents a useful opportunity for the department manager to discuss with the supervisor and employees the need for all employees to work in the most positive, productive fashion possible, and that means cooperatively and with equal involvement from everyone. Naturally, it takes new hires some time to adjust; to learn their tasks, the way things work, as well as what others do in their work unit; and to develop a sense of their own competence. But rather than leaving this learning and adjustment process entirely on the supervisor, other employees should be asked if they would be willing to participate in such things as providing the new hire information, answering questions, taking the initiative for "show and tell" guidance, and the like.

After a short period of indoctrination when the new employee begins to show some confidence and comfort with their tasks, they should then be made more aware of the jobs of other employees, the functions of the department, and goals of the organization thereby progressively expanding their level of understanding of the relationship between their job and its role in the organization. Additionally, at about this same time it is appropriate to further enhance the handicapped worker's sense of contribution to the work unit by asking for their input. This can pertain to a variety of involvement topics such as:

- Does he/she see any areas or aspects of their own job that could be done better, or more efficiently?

- Does he/she see ways of improving the performance of, or processes used within the work unit?

- How he/she feels about taking on more, new, or different job responsibilities?

- Involvement in work unit meetings where work problems, employment issues, and other work-related topics are discussed for the purpose of general information or decision making solutions.

Deliberate and thorough steps taken to integrate new employees into an unfamiliar environment and group of work unit employees consistently prove worth the time and effort. Because of the special needs and circumstances of handicapped workers, this becomes particularly apparent and influential in their speed and ability to adjust. Consequently, work unit integration becomes instrumental in each employee's individual competency and productivity, as well as the harmony of relationships within the work unit.

5.45 SOLUTIONS TO INHERENT TRAINING AND EVALUATION PROBLEMS

Rather than self doubt, which is what most non-handicapped people feel is influential upon most handicapped people (re)entering the workforce during their initial year, the greater inner struggle among handicapped new hires is uncertainty. This uncertainity can produce a weak or vulnerable level of confidence in either the person's ability to do a given job to the same or better extent as a non-handicapped worker, or in terms of their acceptance by co-workers. Yet another manifestation of uncertainty is anxiety which, when positively controlled, results in an overachiever pattern of behavior (determined, keeps trying until success is achieved or surpassed, while the negative extreme is acute obsessiveness). While it is true that these same characteristics exist in varying degrees among most all new hires, regardless of position or level in the organizational structure, they tend to be more pronounced with handicapped workers who have good reason to feel they have something extra to prove—sometimes to themselves and sometimes for acceptance by peers. All eyes are upon them; they know it, and they know that they symbolize the struggle for other handicapped people like them to establish their rightful place as a productive, equal contributor among the employer's non-handicapped workforce.

During the initial training period of the handicapped worker, which may be little more than a thorough orientation for the already skilled worker, the supervisor ought to be cognizant of the possibility that these psychological characteristics may be present. Despite all other conditions favoring successful adaptation, these characteristics can cause unsuspected failure if not taken into consideration and dealt with effectively when observed. Here are some approaches to training the new handicapped worker that the supervisor should consider, and periodically review, to prevent false start and other performance problems during initial employment.

1. Treat the employee on a personal level like you would any other employee—open, friendly, interested in them, but not patronizing. Look beyond their handicap and focus on both their ability and difficulties.

2. If the employee's learning or skill difficulties are related to the handicap, try to show or explain the task in another way that may be easier for them to understand or perform. Don't be afraid to discuss the effect their handicap might be having on performing some part of the job, nor should you avoid asking them how they think it can be improved (what is it they need—time to practice, shown a few more times, being left alone to practice, etc.). The approach should be an observation-instruction-problem solving one rather than pointing out deficiencies.

3. The supervisor as trainer is a teacher. The way you teach adults is to relate to them on their level and, in the case of handicapped workers, in their condition. The supervisor should try to put themself in the role of the handicapped worker. If wheelchair bound, the supervisor should demonstrate each task seated; if the handicap is a prosthetic arm, then the task should be demonstrated slowly so the employee can fully observe arm, hand, and digital (finger) motion, then ask the employee to try it slowly. Once the routine of a task is absorbed and manipulative accuracy accomplished, the employee should be left alone to practice for increased precision and speed.

4. Make it a point to check back with the employee periodically for a "let's see how you're doing" check. If they have the task mastered, acknowledge it by compliment and move on to the next task or more advanced phase of the same task. If, on the other hand, some improvement is observed but still short of what is needed, go over the demonstration a few more times with emphasis on helping the employee conquer that part with which they're having difficulty.

5. In those cases where the nature of the handicap is such that task instruction may be outside the normal realm of ability of many supervisors to deal with, it is often extremely useful to call upon the skills and specialized background of a vocational rehabilitation professional to come in and work with the training

and adaptive needs of *both* the employer and handicapped worker. Too, these professionals are better equipped to diagnose and correct difficulties if they occur. Such developmental assistance is usually made available to employers without cost through state vocational rehabilitation services. However, the presence of a specialized professional to conduct the employee's training should by no means relieve the supervisor of their involvement. The supervisor should be deeply involved in pointing out essential functions to the training specialist, observing and participating in the bulk of instruction, learning the specialist's methods, and consulting with the specialist on key issues. Employer utilization of such specialists has been a grossly overlooked resource that should be more frequently tapped by the business commmuity, including the following organizations and their services.

Job Accommodation Network
P.O. Box 468
Morgantown, WV 26505
1-800-526-7234

• Provides information to businesses on how to accommodate handicapped workers to particular jobs or conditions

Mainstream
1200 15th St. N.W.
Washington, D.C. 20005
(202) 833-1136

• Provides job referrals and employment information services to the handicapped.

National Organization
   on Disability
2100 Pennsylvania Ave. N.W.
Suite 234
Washington, D.C. 20037
(202) 293-5960

• Promotes full participation of persons with mental and physical disabilities. Among its goals are improving accessibility to buildings and broadening employment opportunities. It also serves as a clearinghouse.

National Rehabilitation
Association
633 S. Washington Street
Alexandria, VA 22314
(703) 836-0850

• Various efforts and services to advance the rehabilitation of all handicapped persons.

When the time arrives to formally evaluate the handicapped worker, the rating supervisor should remember a cardinal rule—no surprises! Through routine and frequent discussion, instruction, and coaching the new employee, they should already be aware of their areas of progress and where further development is needed.

What becomes more of a problem issue concerning the evaluation of a handicap worker's performance is the rating against normal standards. Managers should be clear about the fact that performance standards are not expected to be abandoned, or even overly compromised when they pertain to handicapped workers. The job has to get done, and at an acceptable level, in a reasonable amount of time. The judgment call comes in the way of determining what is an acceptable level of performance and what is a reasonable amount of time to accomplish it. In other words, what are the expectations of a handicapped worker against which outcomes can or should be measured? It should be apparent that most handicapped workers are going to have unusual obstacles to overcome, and the speed or precision of their initial skills development may be impaired in some respect—at least during the developmental stage. Given these circumstances, what the supervisor should be looking for, and rating against, is an acceptable level of job interest, responsibility (for errors and self-initiative to improve), effort, and job progress such as increased learning, skills-building, and environmental conditions adaptation.

If and when it becomes apparent that the handicapped worker has shown that they are in some significant and unchangeable way ill-suited for the job, the employee's supervisor and department manager should confer with their human resource manager as to the decision to reassign to a more suitable job based on demonstrated abilities, redesign the present job without sacrificing operational needs, or terminate the employment relationship which should always be a last choice as a means of resolving human resource problems.

5.50 DISCRIMINATION DUE TO RELIGIOUS BELIEFS, OBSERVANCES, AND PRACTICES

Employer prohibitions against discrimination based on an individual's religious beliefs, observances, and practices is by no means new law. It has, however, been one of the lessor litigated areas of discrimination law under Title VII of the 1964 Civil Rights Act. The reasons for its relative inattention are fairly straightforward. First, the law's primary focus is upon employer accommodation of religious observances, meaning the ability to work out job assignments and schedules to allow for Sabbath and other religious observances. Since the majority of the American population is either without religious commitment or observe Sunday as the Sabbath, this issue is not a major problem for the conventional Monday through Friday workweek employer. For many other employers who operate their business on shifts, weekend days, or seven days a week, their vulnerability to the issue is ever-present and they're playing the odds so to speak in terms of eventually being confronted with religious accommodation. Much of their danger of violating religious discrimination lies in refusing to hire someone who declares their need for religious accommodation during the hiring process, or failing to at least demonstrate a good faith effort at attempting to accommodate an employee's sincere request.

Another reason religious discrimination violations have not been heavily litigated, and therefore not well publicized, is because the basic employer requirement to comply is merely one of two actions: 1) don't refuse to hire solely because of the applicant's religious pursuits unless there is a very good reason to do so (a lawful *exemption* for religious organizations, or doing so would create an *undue hardship*); or 2) allow the employee a reasonable amount of time off or other modest arrangements so they can observe their religious practices. Under most employment circumstances, neither of these actions create major obstacles for management. Indeed, those cases that have been litigated serve as good case examples of employment circumstances and particular conditions of employment where one or the other of these actions did prove to be a problem for the employer.

In all but a few litigated cases, the nature of the religious discrimination was unintentional, or perceived by the employer to be unavoidable and thereby not construed as negligent or willful by the courts. Absent willful or intentional violation of discrimination law, both the courts and enforcement agencies have used back pay and reinstatement for plaintiff awards as the penalty for employer wrongdoing, with the greater cost being the litigation itself. That fact alone should serve as advice to employers that when such a problem surfaces, particularly if a claim of an alleged violation is being handled by an enforcement agency, it will be considerably less costly to conciliate a settlement based on factual circumstances, or even pursue arbitration, than to litigate the matter. This is especially true if it becomes apparent you were wrong in your handling of the situation that gave rise to the complaint!

During the 10 year period after religious discrimination was embodied into the 1964 Civil Rights Act, litigation was sporadic and confined to the federal appellate courts or state courts. Neither the courts nor EEOC had provided very clear guidelines for employers concerning any defined meaning or circumstances of religion, its preferred means of accommodation, or definitions of undue hardship accommodation for the employer. The definition of religion was addressed, even if rather obscurely, by both the U.S. Supreme Court and the EEOC in 1970, and again by the U.S. Supreme Court in 1974. In 1970, the high court defined religion as "a sincere and meaningful belief which occupies in the life of its possessor a place parallel to that filled by [the] God..."[2]; and the EEOC took the position that employee beliefs are protected by discrimination law if they are as "deeply and sincerely held as more conventional religious convictions,"[3] including individuals who are not members of an established church (atheists). The sincerity of one's beliefs are of course a vague area of judgment at best for managers trying to deal with these, sometimes impromptu, situations, and

---

[2] Welch v. United States, 1970

[3] EEOC Decision No. 671-779, 1970

even the courts have generally been skeptical of employees' sincerity in cases where:

1. The employee knew what work schedule was required for the job;

2. The employee worked the schedule without notice or objection to the employer for some length of time; and

3. The evidence suggests that the employee's belief is more "circumstantial convenience" than sincere since the employee's notice has been in conjunction with such employment conditions as shift changes, reassignments, or unpleasant work assignments.

In 1974, the U.S. Supreme Court added to the definition of religion, for purposes of discrimination, that it "includes all aspects of religious observance and practice as well as belief,"[4] unless an employer demonstrate the inability to reasonably accommodate the employee.

In the absence of clearer guidelines, it was not surprising to find that most arbitrated cases of alleged religious discrimination up to 1974 were decided in favor of employees. What arbitrators and the courts were quick to learn about religious discrimination cases, unlike other forms of discrimination, is that they involved the employee's observances (Sabbath and holy days) more than the employee's beliefs thereby creating a focus on the employer's practices and operational flexibility. This need for operational flexibility soon came to mean that it need be only of a limited nature since to do more would likely sacrifice rights of other employees unnecessarily.

At least some of the confusion surrounding religious discrimination was finally resolved by the U.S. Supreme Court in their 1974 decision favoring the employer in *Trans World Airlines v. Hardison.* Here, the plaintiff alleged that TWA did not satisfactorily accommodate his need to observe a Saturday Sabbath, and he could not work on this day because of the religious observance. Evidence showed that TWA made several attempts to accommodate the employee's request for getting Saturdays off including possible job reassignments and schedule trades, but none of these worked out to the employee's liking. The court concluded that TWA had made reasonable efforts to accommodate the employee, and went on to set forth four guiding principles of the meaning of accommodation, and they are:

1. The rights of other workers need not be sacrificed to provide for one employee's request for religious accommodation.

2. Employers may not breech the (seniority) provisions of a collective bargaining agreement to provide more benefit to the special needs of one that would not be equally enjoyed by others.

---

[4] Trans World Airlines v. Hardison, 1974

3. Accommodation need be no more than "de minimus" action (need not require the paying of overtime for another worker or the replacement of a productive worker).

4. Accommodation having the result of losing the work unit efficiency shall also be considered an undue hardship for the employer.

Similar to other protected groups under Title VII, it is prohibited for employers to refuse to hire, promote, train, equally compensate, or to discipline, lay off, or terminate on the basis of an individual's religious beliefs, observances, or practices.

Exemptions are provided for in the law, as follows, but they have been increasingly given more narrow interpretations by the courts as evidenced by a couple of the cases presented in the section that follows. Nevertheless, the exemptions consist of... "religious corporations, associations, educational institutions, or society with respect to the employment of individuals of a particular religion to perform work connected to the carrying on of such corporation, association, educational institution, or society of its activities" (USC § 2000 e-1, 1976). Despite the seeming intent of this exemption, several court cases in the late 1970's through early 1980's held that at least some faculty and support positions in such organizations were not exempt merely because the employer was of a particular religious persuasion.

However, in 1987 the U.S. Supreme Court decided in the case of *Corp. of the Presiding Bishop of the Church of Jesus Christ of Latter-Day Saints v. Amos* that secular employment decisions by *non-profit* organizations was not a violation of the First Amendment nor equal protection Constitutional guarantees. Thus, the high court held, the employer's termination of an employee who failed to qualify as a member of the church, and who worked in a Morman- operated gymnasium, was legally terminated on the basis of the employer's religious interests exemption. But, perhaps as a warning, four justices noted that such an exemption might not be sustained in similar circumstances where the religious organization operates on a profit basis.

5.51 RELIGIOUS ACCOMMODATION: PROBLEM CASES, PRACTICES, AND THEIR SOLUTIONS

**Can An Employee Suddenly Claim A Religious Objection
To Working On Their Sabbath Eve
Though They've Been Working It In The Past?**

They can and sometimes do, but it's typically because they no longer want to work that day and want a more favorable schedule, or an employee who chooses this as a device (or excuse) to force their supervisor to make a schedule change under the pretense of religious accommodation. Normally, someone holding a strong (sincere) religious conviction would make their commitments known early—or it would become apparent through informal means of acquaintance—especially if they were assigned a work schedule that conflicted with their days of religious observance. However, the suspiciousness of the employee's motives should not be a reason to dismiss their request for accommodation as less than serious; the matter should be given further examination with respect to why the request is being made now, what religion is ascribed to and what are their observances, and how long has the employee participated in these religious practices?

A good example of an employee's alleged lifelong religious observance was struck down by one court and holding it as a convenience belief was in *Hanard v. Johns-Manville Products Corp.* (1973). It seems that the plaintiff accepted a job knowing his work schedule, had worked that schedule which included Sundays for some time, then made a claim that working Sundays violated his religious beliefs. Where these situations may become more arguably favorable to employees is where the employee might be able to demonstrate that their past silence on notification to their employer was based on a legitimate fear of reprisal or harassment by their supervisor. This possibility should serve as fair warning to managers to insure that supervisors and employees alike refrain from even casual comments, jokes, or any other references to various religions or religious practices.

Is Accommodation Required Where The Religious Objection Is Payment Of Union Dues?

This issue was addressed by the Seventh Circuit Court of Appeals in *Nottleson v. Smith Steel Workers* (1981) where the employer was willing to accommodate the employee's offer to pay an equivalent amount to a non-religious charity, but the union held that doing so would violate the contract's security clause and that the entire matter was preempted by the NLRA. The court, in upholding the constitutionality of ss 701 (j) of the Civil Rights Act of 1964, held that the union security provisions of the NLRA do not relieve an employer or union of the duty to accommodate individual religious needs of employees, and that so doing does not confer any special benefit on those so accommodated since it does not take anything away or abridge the benefits of others.

Do Employees Share In The Responsibility To Reach Accommodation Of Their Religion?

Courts have taken different positions on this point, but more often than not the answer is yes. Several courts have held that employees should carry two parts of the burden to resolve conflicts between work and their religious pursuits. First, employees should notify their employer when a conflict arises between either their work schedule or nature of their work to the dictates of their religious belief, practice, or observance in order to establish the need for accommodation. The employees notice should be timely to the extent that the employer has sufficient opportunity to make accommodating arrangements which need not be more than de minimus action, but it may require some inquiries about schedule changes, contacting others, conferring with other managers, and the like.

Second, at least some courts have held that employees are obliged to help the employer arrive at a reasonable accommodation by offering suggestions, giving the employer adequate time and opportunity to find a solution, or perhaps agreeing to some compromise solution where the employee's desired action is totally workable for the employer.

Even though courts vary in these two forms of employee cooperation, it would nevertheless be worthwhile for employers to document whether they were given adequate notice by the employee; whether the employee offered more than one solution to the accommodation when asked; and to what degree the employee was willing to compromise based on the employer's limitations.

For example, an employee requesting religious accommodation will normally be required to cooperate with the employer's good faith and reasonable attempt as determined by the Ninth Circuit Court of Appeals in *APWU v. Postmaster General* (1986). Here, two post office window clerks lodged religious-based protests in 1980 when their jobs began to require the processing of military draft registration applications. To accommodate employees with religious objections, the postal service issued a regulation instructing those individuals to apply for transfers to other positions. Plaintiff claimed that this was not a reasonable form of accommodation, but the court held that the allowing of transfers effectively removed the religious conflict and the employer thereby met its accommodation obligation. Further, the court held that affected employees have a corresponding duty to resolve such conflicts by holding that, "(a)lthough the statutory burden to accommodate rests with the employer, the employee has a correlative duty to make a good faith attempt to satisfy its needs through means offered by the employer."

Do We Have To Accept The Employee's Preferred Accommodation, Or A "Negotiated" One?

No, says one of the latest U.S. Supreme Court decisions where they further defined limits of what constitutes reasonable accommodation by employers. While an employee's preferred or suggested form of accommodation should not be merely cast aside, it does not have to be accepted by the employer if more than de minimus effect would result even if the employer cannot demonstrate undue hardship. In *Ansonia Board of Education v. Philbrook* (1986), plaintiff was a teacher and member of the World Wide Church of God who observes six holy days a year. The collective bargaining agreement allows employees to take three days paid leave for religious observances and three days for personal business (expressly excluding religious observances). Plaintiff was denied use of personal leave for religious day observance; he offered to pay for a substitute if his employer would allow him such paid leave; but the employer would only authorize unpaid absence as their preferred accommodation over his. In reversing the Second Circuit Court of Appeals who held that an employer must comply an employee's preferred accommodation unless it can prove an undue hardship, the Supreme Court made two noteworthy observations.

1. That an employer does not have to accept an employee's preferred accommodation, but satisfies such a requirement any time an offer is made that removes the conflict between the employee's religious beliefs and employment.

2. That the policy of allowing employees to take unpaid leave for holy day observances is generally a reasonable form of accommodation (although payment of overtime for a replacement may be grounds for undue hardship denial).

However, on the second point in this case, the Supreme Court noted the presence of apparent bias in the labor contract concerning exclusion of personal leave use for religious occasions, and remanded the case back to the lower court for finding. Clearly, the religious use exclusion was a red flag to the court, and for this reason the parties to the collective bargaining agreement would have been better off with a combined six day "all purpose" leave provision.

Can You Fire Employees Who Take It Upon Themselves To Carry Out Their Preferred Accommodation?

Yes, but you'll probably have to pay unemployment insurance to the fired employee even if their behavior was misconduct, says the U.S. Supreme Court in *Hoffie v. Unemployment Appeals Committee of Florida et al* (1987). Plaintiff informed her supervisor of her conversion to a religion prohibiting Saturday work. She arranged with her supervisor to work his Sundays if he would work her Saturdays. Their manager found out and ordered the plaintiff to resume her normal Saturday work. She refused and was then fired. The high court found plaintiff to be responsible for her own action (misconduct) thereby relieving the employer of liability for religious discrimination. However, the court also found that it is unlawful for states to deny such statutory benefits as unemployment insurance where disqualification is based upon adherence to one's religious convictions.

Can Employers Restrict The Wearing Of Religious Apparel By Employees?

Once again, the courts have treaded lightly on the wearing of religious apparel since it can be construed as a constitutional right of free expression. In the few cases on this issue, the courts have acted narrowly on the circumstances of the case thereby avoiding the establishment of any sort of general guidelines for employers. For example, in *Cooper v. Eugene School District* (1985), the Oregon Court of Appeals held that revoking a teacher's license because she wore a turban was too severe of an action. The employer's position was that wearing such apparel violated the school's obligation to keep religion out of the schools, while the employee claimed she was merely exercising right to religious freedom (First Amendment). The court elected not to address the constitutional issue. However, in *Goldman v. Weinberger* (1986), the U.S. Supreme Court determined that no First Amendment violation of rights occurred when a Jewish Air Force officer was prohibited from wearing a Yarmulke (skull cap) while on duty, and found the restriction to be reasonable with respect to creating uniformity for the vital purpose of necessary military unity and discipline.

While both of these cases are very different in nature and perhaps even representative of extremes, their common point is that both employers had very good business reasons for wanting to restrict religious attire. A more common occurrence for most employers is likely to be the wearing of religious jewelry, button slogans, and clothing. In this respect, employers do have the right to set reasonable and job related dress (and grooming) standards, and the right to protect the personal interests of other employees as well as controlling most anything that would prove offensive to customers.

So while the wearing of small personal, religiously symbolic jewelry would likely be held as a religious freedom right, more demonstrative apparel, slogans, and personal vestments could be regarded as an infringement upon the religious beliefs of other employees, or not in keeping with the necessary business image the employer is attempting to create, and therefore within the realm of legitimate restriction by the employer. When policies are framed to address this issue, care must be given to attach any restrictions to the employer's business rationale for establishing the restriction and deferring their First Amendment rights to their own personal time.

Can Employees Be Hired Or Excluded Based Upon Their Religious Beliefs?

Only where there exists a legitimate, religiously based interest in the occupation under consideration or the religious purpose of the business such as those defined in the law as exemptions. One of the illustrative court cases on this question also touches on the U.S. Supreme Court's position with regard to infringement on employees' First Amendment rights. Here, the high court refused to hear the employer's appeal and thereby upheld the position taken by the Minnesota Supreme Court in *Sports and Health Club, Inc. v. Minnesota* (1986) which was that discrimination will not be allowed in the name of religious freedom. This case disclosed the common practice of the personnel officer for this born-again Christian chain of health stores who asked job applicants such religious-oriented questions as:

- did they attend church, read the Bible, or pray.
- were they married or divorced.
- had they engaged in premarital or extramarital sex.
- did they believe in God, heaven, and hell.

Hiring decisions were found to be made on the basis of answers to these and similar questions. Further, the employer had policies wherein employees could be promoted or terminated due to their religious practice. In reaction to these outright violations of religious discrimination, the Minnesota Supreme Court affirmed the state agency's order for the employer to abolish these practices based on the state's interest in creating a discriminatory-free work environment having superior standing in such cases to that of religious freedom rights.

Can Employees Be Prohibited From Using Their Religious Beliefs In Conjunction With Their Job?

According to the federal district court in Michigan, yes but...the nature of the employee's religious beliefs, preaching, or application of such beliefs ought to be demonstrated as having some reasonably damaging or detrimental job effect. For example, in the case of *Spratt v. County of Kent* (1985), a social worker refused to comply with his employer's request that he stop using "spiritual means" such as the casting of demons when counseling prison inmates. The court upheld the termination of the employee, and found such action to be devoid of both religious discrimination since his worship was not being denied, and not a violation of the employee's First Amendment rights since the employer was merely trying to stop the damaging effect on others of his beliefs.

Using this same rationale, an employer would probably be within their rights to restrict employees imposing their religious beliefs on other employees, customers, or other business related people, particularly if these others express their objection to management.

What Is Considered To Be Insufficient Accommodation Of An Employee's Religious Beliefs, And Do We Have To Accommodate With Every Job Change?

There were two enlightening cases in 1986 on the issue of insufficient accommodation by employers: one had to do with the simple insufficiency of accommodation action which cost the employer $74,000 in back pay damages; the second had to do with the employer's accommodation in a lower position but refusal to continue accommodation after promotion to a new position.

In *Protos v. Volkswagen of America* (1986), the plaintiff was an assembly line worker originally hired for a Monday through Friday work schedule. As a member of the World Wide Church of God whose Sabbath is observed from sunset Friday to sunset Saturday during which work is prohibited under penalty of excommunication, the assigned shift presented no problem until, in 1979, the employer announced its need to initiate mandatory overtime work on Saturdays. Protos then informed her supervisor of her need for accommodation; the supervisor said she would try to accommodate Protos; but she was scheduled and refused to report for three consecutive Saturdays. When Protos was given a written warning that future refusal to work on Saturdays would be dealt with by disciplinary means, she filed a Title VII violation complaint with the EEOC. It wasn't until then that the employer sought a seniority waiver from the union to assign Protos to a new shift but the union, with 200 more senior workers on a waiting list, refused. The Third Circuit Court of Appeals learned that the company regularly maintained a crew to cover absentee operators and demonstrated an inadequate defense of its undue hardship claim.

In *Proctor v. Consolidated Freightways* (1986), the Ninth Circuit Court of Appeals came to a similar conclusion regarding the employer's failure to follow through with reasonable accommodation, but in this case it had to do with successive promotion and position changes of the employee who was a declared Seventh Day Adventist (also observing a sundown Friday to sundown Saturday Sabbath). Plaintiff's positions were:

    1968 Payroll Clerk
    1974 Data Input Clerk
    1981 Balancing Clerk

In 1977 Proctor became a member of the Seventh Day Adventist church and the employer used other employees when Saturday work was required. However, upon promotion in 1981, the employer scheduled her for Saturday work and subsequently suspended then terminated her for refusal to work on Saturdays. The court determined that the employer failed to make a good faith effort to reasonably accommodate Proctor in her new position and could not otherwise demonstrate a significant undue hardship.

The central issue here, then, is that merely warning an employee that a new job or assignment may conflict with their religious practice or observance will not serve as a defense for the employer. Also, each position occupied by an employee requesting religious accommodation ought to be examined carefully in light of compelling work requirements as opposed to alternatives in scheduling that might be available without creating more visible undue hardship. As a practical matter, employers who know that a particular employee requires religious accommodation ought to explore and work out schedule and other potential conflict situations with the employee in advance of a job reassignment or promotion to determine if accommodation is both feasible and mutually acceptable. If not, then at least the employer can demonstrate its good faith effort to attempt accommodation.

Do We Have To Make Any Special Effort To
Allow Paid Time Off For Religious Observance?

No—at least not in terms of creating a benefit that would not be equally enjoyed by other employees. Employers need not pay the employee for a day off to observe a religious day if such is not extended by policy or collective bargaining agreement to all such employees, nor does the employer have to allow an employee to work overtime in order to accrue "compensatory (comp) time" off to receive pay for religious observances as was the finding of the Third Circuit Court of Appeals in *Getz v. Commonwealth of Pennsylvania Department of Public Welfare* (1986).

However, this case did clarify that if an employer, such as defendant, has a policy of providing "personal" leave (which may include floating holidays, vacation, and the like within one general category of paid absence), it must permit the employee to use any accrued time for paid absence to observe religious days. Plaintiff in this case was an Orthodox Jew who wished to observe 13 religious days per year, and the employer's policy allowed for 20 days of personal leave. Plaintiff requested and was denied working some overtime each week in order to accrue enough paid time to take the 13 religious days off without diminishing available personal leave. Because of denying her request, she brought suit for an alleged failure by her employer to reasonably accommodate her religious needs. The court, in noting that employers need not accommodate where an unnecessary cost is involved, found that the availability of adequate personal leave served as sufficient accommodation. Additionally, there is nothing in federal statutes that require an employer to otherwise pay for an employee's time off for religious observances when the employer accommodates by permitting the employee's absence.

5.52 MEASURES MANAGERS CAN TAKE TO SOLVE
RELIGIOUS DISCRIMINATION PROBLEMS

Based on existing federal law and the various circumstances involving employment practices addressed by the courts during their most active decade from 1978-1988 during which religious discrimination became a more clearly defined body of law, the following are a few suggestions that highlight areas of the principal problems that can be solved by managers exercising these forms of problem prevention.

1. Do not refuse or otherwise avoid hiring an applicant merely because of his or her religious beliefs, practices, or observances. Also, be careful about framing interview questions so that they do not elicit information about the applicant's religious beliefs. If rejection of an applicant is on grounds of a religious conflict with the nature or schedule of work, you should be certain that the reason you cannot make an accommodation is because doing so would create an undue hardship (e.g., require overtime payment, be operationally disruptive,

conflict with the legitimate interests of a collective bargaining agreement, etc.).

2. Take employee requests for religious accommodation seriously. Ask that they give you a written statement as to the specifics of their religion, what in particular is the conflict, and what is their requested or preferred accommodation. Before making a decision, consult with the human resources manager to ascertain the organization's (policy) position and other effects such as a collective bargaining agreement. Try to find one or more ways of easily and reasonably accommodating the employee's religious conflict—presuming of course you have found the employee to be sincere in their religious conviction.

3. Document each discussion you have with concerned individuals on the matter, including your own position concerning the employee's sincerity, extent and type of conflict, and methods of possible accommodation. If you can arrive at a de minimus accommodation, discuss it with the employee to see if the employee is willing to agree, then confirm the details in a memo to the employee with a copy placed in their personnel file. If, on the other hand, the employee is reluctant or fails to agree, you should make a deliberate effort in writing to get the employee to agree, perhaps by reexplaining your reasoning for the selected method of accommodation and request that the employee reconsider their position.

4. If the employee continues to disagree, or a form of reasonable accommodation simply cannot be found, then the employee should be notified in writing that they are to either do their job as instructed, resign, or be terminated if their performance becomes effected.

5. Handle religious accommodation requests in a thorough and expeditious manner, and deal with each case on an individual basis (avoid blanket policies and practices).

5.60 CONCLUSIONS AND FUTURE PROSPECTS ABOUT DISCRIMINATION

For those professionals responsible for human resource planning, policy and program development, decision-making, and overall administration, the period since the early 1960's has created an environment of constant change—if not turmoil—due to the unending regularity with which new laws have generated greater complexity of human resource decisions, operations, and controls. To a large extent, the laws and legal decisions in the areas of employment discrimination at both the state and federal level have occurred so closely on the heels of each other that employers, their managers, and their business practices have had insufficient time to adjust. If and when the flow of legal requirements in employment matters end, or even recede which is more likely, it will probably take years for employers to catch up with necessary attitudinal and institutional changes that will, in turn, begin to reduce the need for political or legal intervention into matters of employment discrimination. Regrettably, however, there is no evidence that discrimination will ever be eliminated. It is therefore appropriate to expect the courts to continue into the foreseeable future as the guardian of individual and group rights.

Given the history of employment-related discrimination in America, it would not be prudent for the student or seasoned manager to conclude that this chapter, and those that precede it, represent the only forms of discrimination with which we must concern ourselves. Such a view would be naive and shortsighted. Indeed, there are many more realms of social prejudice that are beginning to manifest themselves as barriers to employment or result in adverse employment actions. Some states have begun to recognize and deal with them, and it is probably only a matter of time before they become embodied in federal law or legal principle that mandates compliance and correction by all employers. Now that the foundation of non-discrimination in employment has been constructed for those *general* groups of people traditionally affected by biases, we are likely to witness a more *specific* deepening into those groups and the emergence of new groups where injustice exists as such groups become more visible during the next several decades. They will consist of those with medical and mental limitations, prior criminal histories, homosexual lifestyles, those under the age of 40, marital and dependent status, and those employees who by circumstance require leaves of absence for personal, parental, guardianship, and rehabilitative reasons.

We have only just begun to deal with ways in which to neutralize the effects of adverse employment discrimination. There remains much to do, much to change, much to learn, and much more to come. For now, we need a little time to adjust and internalize what has already been brought to our attention. Taking the time and effort to do so will produce the desired results, and will make our places of employment a more productive and fruitful experience for us and others that rely on our managerial integrity.

PART II. SOLVING PROBLEMS RELATED TO EMPLOYMENT RIGHTS

The evolution of employee rights within the American workforce is a condition that has developed through a complex arrangement of historical changes in our social, economic, political, and legal systems over the last two centuries, and in some respects even before then. These rights, and the resultant problems they have created for American business managers, are best described and most easily understood in terms of those historical events that accompanied the American labor movement, its antecedents, and the present posture of an altogether new breed of society. For some, it has been and remains a particularly painful and certainly frustrating series of events because, to those that manage the resources of enterprise, the acquisition of any employee right is viewed as a distraction or threat to the fundamental goals of enterprise; that being the freedom to make choices and maximize profits.

Looking back into American history, we note that the singular and underlying principle to the formation of our democratic society has been the economic force of commerce. This force shaped and guided national decisions on foreign and domestic policy, the economy, trade, constitutional rights, labor, technology, social welfare, and the rights of individual citizens. Coupled with a strong Puritan ethic dictating the moral ideology that people should work hard, save, and remain loyal to God, employer, and family, our capitalistic society became deeply attached to the notion that foresaking one's employer in even the most remote way was a heinous crime. In this regard, we might say that the first historical departure from this commerce (employer) dominant society was the controversial *Hunt v. Commonwealth* decision in 1842 where the court determined that it was not an act of treason against the country (economy) for employees to discuss collective representation.

Despite this landmark court case, it took another 70 years before labor unions became a visible source of representation for the advocacy of employee rights, and another 23 years before such activities were proclaimed by the government as a legal right when the National Labor Relations Act was adopted in 1935. As unions organized and began to flourish, a new wage of employee rights emerged through more favorable laws, legal decisions, and collective bargaining agreements.

If they did little else, unions brought to the American labor movement a needed form of representation and advocacy — a national voice in those matters that affected the health, safety, and welfare of the working society. While much can also be said about the extremes of abuse in the powers exercised by unions, and their disrupting effects upon a free enterprise system of business, it is time we as managers admit that absent their influence upon employment laws, working conditions, and a greater balance in employment rights, we might still be running the kinds of abusive, autocratic organizations that were associated with the turn-of-the-century sweatshops. Sadly, some still exist and yet other employers are making decisions using a sweatshop mentality only to find that neither employees nor the courts support abusive management.

Concurrent with the growth of unions and other forms of national attention being given to the lawful rights of America's working society, there began to emerge a major legal contradiction that was to challenge the very fabric of the nation's democratic principles. This contradiction had to do with the balance of rights between the economic interests of commerce, the regulatory interests of government, the opportunity interests of individual citizens, and the justice interests of our legal system. Central to the controversy was the question of whose interest should prevail when tested against such doctrines as the Constitution and similar guiding laws of the sovereign states. With respect to the contradiction of national interests, legal controversy began to focus on the differences of rights between individuals (discrimination); the rights between individuals and entities (government, business, etc.); and the rights of individuals in their role as citizen versus the subject of an entity (employer).

Given the strain of these legal questions and challenges between opposing forces as to whose interest should prevail under certain conditions, the pillars of a long standing democratic doctrine that heretofore leaned toward the interests of entities began to give way to a more firm recognition and advancement of individual rights. This trend in the laws and associated court decisions during the last three decades is most apparent. The pendulum of history has swung toward the rights of individuals, and it has brought new meaning to the rights of our employees — and we should not forget ourselves, because even we managers are employees even though our employers might like to think different!

So, while the growth and expansion of employee rights has been slow in a historical sense, it has been the progressive outgrowth of successive changes in our political leadership, national policy, the sovereign government of each state, advances in education and technological automation, a society characterized by its own diversity, and the demand for a more skilled workforce. Ultimately, what has now emerged as the legal rights of our employees represents more of a challenge than a threat to managers. Those managers and business leaders who see it as a threat are likely to resist and be defeated. They will miss the point that employee rights do not necessarily equate to the taking away or even diminishment of employer (management) rights.

If viewed in a more objective light, employers are more likely to see that they still retain the fundamental and important rights to operate their enterprise and make business decisions. The manager who sees the challenge will be the one who finds a solution when problems arise. This manager knows that both employee and organizational rights must be protected for the mutual benefit of both; that objectivity in the actions and decisions of managers is tantamount to judicious problem solving; and that managers must practice humane and precise methods of dealing with a more complex, informed, and idealistic workforce.

To give you more specific insight into some of the areas in which employees have legally protected rights, the following is a brief summary.

1. To collective representation of their employment interests by affiliation with, and membership in a recognized labor union or employee organization; or to represent their own interests before their employer.

2. To file claims (discrimination, wage and hour, workers' compensation, safety) with administrative compliance agencies to have a complaint or alleged employer wrongdoing adjusted without coercion, harassment, retaliation, or recrimination by the employer.

3. To have their employer treat personal information about them with the utmost confidentiality.

4. To not be the victim of arbitrary or capricious decisions that affect their employment or life in an adverse fashion.

5. To receive fair and reasonable treatment in their employment relationship with their employer.

6. To not be required to violate laws, public policy, or perform any illegal, unethical, or otherwise harmful employment obligations in their employer's interest.

7. To be treated with the same dignity and respect that would reasonably be afforded to any human being.

Granted, this list is rather vague, but then so are the laws and legal principles used to interpret them during the court's circumstantial findings. For those of you who have already read any of the chapters in Part I, some of these generally stated employee rights are no doubt much more meaningful. For those of you going on to read any of the chapters in Part II, these rights will become dramatically more clear with very specific illustrations of each. For purposes of focus, I have selected the issues of privacy rights and wrongful discharge since these two areas of rights have presented managers with some of the greatest, most costly, and difficult problems. And, in keeping with the theme of this book, emphasis has been placed upon giving you diagnostic insight into the nature of each problem issue so that you are better able to see them in your own organization, and to discuss each issue in light of the proper approach to their solutions.

CHAPTER II: 1.0
PROBLEMS CONCERNING WORKPLACE PRIVACY: LEGAL OVERVIEW, DRUGS/ALCOHOL CONTROL, AND HEALTH RIGHTS OF EMPLOYEE

For quite some time now, employers, managers, and yes even human resource professionals have been perplexed about employee privacy rights. The reason? Because very little has been written on the topic in a collective yet understandable form. So most managers responsible for carrying out even routine decisions and actions with their employees have become aware of some basic principles of employee privacy, usually by bits and pieces when they want to do something (or already did it) and are told about limitations as a result of some law or court decision.

To fill this void and provide managers with essential problem solving background, Chapters II: 1 and 2 are dedicated to the delicate matters surrounding workplace privacy rights. Chapter 1 presents the basics of laws and legal elements that create both an obligation and liability for employers, then addresses the difficult issues of drug/alcohol problems, the use of polygraphs (lie detectors), and health-related privacy problems.

Chapter 2 provides a thorough discussion of the questions and problems commonly associated with the privacy of employee information—especially those relating to employee documents and personnel files—with specific solutions to resolve these concerns. Because every manager has direct involvement with the personnel transaction and records process of employees, this chapter should not be dismissed as only applying to human resource professionals.

Indeed, the line between the practical business needs and authorities of employers, and the privacy rights of employees is oftentimes a fuzzy one. In these situations, we must examine the totality of the circumstances through the principles of law and, in essence, try to second guess what a court might say about our actions. Sometimes the issue is not so much whether the employer can or cannot do something, rather it is more an issue of how to do it with regard to the approach and common sense limitations. Creating and enforcing nepotism, no smoking, off duty employment, and derogatory conversation (about the company) policies are good examples of this. These kinds of issues within the workplace suggest several types of problems.

- That the issue of privacy exists and has become a widespread concern.

- That problems related to privacy have either surfaced or is anticipated as a high probability that should be predisposed to policy.

- That employee privacy carries with it some meaningful impact on business operations.

- That there is the need to deal with privacy rights based on uniform guidelines, procedures, and resultant actions.

Some of the more prevalent privacy rights questions in the minds of employers and managers fall into two categories: routine and special condition. Here are some examples of topics that might fall into these categories.

Routine	**Special Condition**
Written and Verbal Reprimands	Unionizing Activities
Disciplinary Conversations and Notices	Exposure to Toxic Substances
Personnel Files and Records	Acquired Immune Deficiency Syndrome
Safety On The Job	(AIDS)
Discrimination	Workers' Compensation Claims
Employee's Health	Polygraphs
Nepotism	
Off Duty Activities	
Verifying Sick Leaves	
Drug/Alcohol Abuse	
Employment References	

It would be impractical to attempt a comprehensive discussion of each one of these issues. Some have been treated in other chapters and point out limitations and approaches to take to ensure privacy safeguards. Whether in this or other chapters, each of these issues is addressed to some extent as they pertain to employee privacy rights.

In this chapter the emphasis is entirely upon employee rights, the problems they pose for employers, and how best to deal with them. Therefore, on a selective basis, and to some extent as a reinforcement of topics in other chapters, this chapter will deal with both routine and special condition issues of employee privacy. What will begin to unfold in this growing but somewhat obscure area of law is the sometimes delicate balance between the needs of business and the rights of individual employees. Only careful judgment will keep these two factors—often opposing forces—in proper balance. The goal here then is to bring greater clarity and definition to the boundaries of employee privacy rights, in some cases illustrated by vulnerable human resource practices, and thereby resolving many of these problems by avoiding their occurrance or replication.

1.10 THE LEGAL BASIS OF EMPLOYMENT PRIVACY RIGHTS

There are three legal areas in which individual privacy rights have evolved in the employment context since the turn of the century. They are: federal and state constitutional law, state statutory law, and various forms of related tort law. Much of the present condition of privacy rights law has been developed through the courts' application of general legal principle attached to such terms as "intrusion", "invasion", "surveillance", "defamation", and the like, in cases involving a variety of unique factual circumstances. In these cases, the courts have observed the apparent need to begin formulating some guiding principles that would create the foundation of at least adjudicary public policy.

One of the first attempts to establish a legal basis for individual privacy in the U.S. was asserted by two Boston attorneys, Charles Warren and Louis Brandeis, whose 1890 article on the press coverage of Warren's family appeared in the Harvard Law Review. Brandeis, by the way, went on later in his career to become a Supreme Court Justice. Later, in 1903, New York adopted a law prohibiting the commerical use of a person's name or likeness without written permission, and in 1905 a Georgia court made a similar ruling using the Warren-Brandeis theory of violating one's personality.

It wasn't until 1965 when the U.S. Supreme Court, in *Griswold v. Connecticut,* gave recognition to a "penumbra" (a lesser issue in the shadow of major provisions) of Constitutional rights of privacy; in this case the invasion of privacy involving married couples' decisions over birth control. Again in 1973, the high court rendered its still controversial abortion decision in *Roe v. Wade* as an inherent right to privacy through Constitutional shadow provisions. In these and other cases where the constitutional issue of privacy has been postulated in the absence of more concrete statutory provisions, the more commonly cited penumbra, or shadow provisions, are those embodied in the First, Third, Fourth, Fifth, Ninth, and Fourteenth Amendments.

Autonomy And Confidentiality

Most courts applying provisions of the U.S. Constitution have focused on two primary issues: autonomy and confidentiality. Autonomy has been normally limited to matters of free choice involving such personal and sensitive issues as marriage, sexual affiliations and practices, and contraception. More recently it has touched on such employer policy issues as nepotism and extramarital relations. For example, in *Thorne v. City of Segundo* (1983) the Ninth Circuit Court of Appeals determined that plaintiff, a clerical employee, had her constitutional privacy rights violated when she was rejected from admission to the police academy due to prior off-duty sexual activities.

Confidentiality has usually been a more straightforward issue involving the disclosure of information known or believed to be of a confidential nature. Yet even the U.S. Supreme Court has vasilated on the boundaries of confidentiality relating to personnel records in two decisions: one before and one after the 1974 Privacy Act. In *Donaldson v. U.S.* (1971), the high court ruled that plaintiff employee had no basis upon which to object to a subpeona served on his employer for a copy of his personnel file. However, in *Whalen v. Roe* (1977), the court found that employees do have a legitimate interest in the "disclosure of personal information", and in another case involving a privacy interest the court denied a union access to an employee's psychological testing information (*Detroit Edison Co. v. NLRB,* 1979). The Third Circuit Court of Appeals passed down a similar decision in *New Jersey Bell Telephone Co. v. NLRB* (1983) when three union employees sought to challenge the company's Employee Privacy Protection Plan that required employee written authorization to release information. The union, in attempting to press an attendance grievance on behalf of the employees, was denied their attendance records by the company because it had no authorization to do so from the employees. The court upheld the company's interest in privacy among its employees.

1.11 FEDERAL STATUTES

Privacy Protection Act

In response to this growing area of public concern, and prompted by two recent and highly publicized Supreme Court decisions, Congress passed the Privacy Protection Act of 1974 which set forth strict controls for the collection, control, and disclosure of employment-related information on individual employees. For probable reasons of political expediency, the Act did not require compliance by private sector employers per se (except those doing business with the federal government). Instead, the Act took an indirect approach to overcoming private sector resistence to the Act by setting up a Privacy Protection Study Commission to determine if private employers should be covered by the Act. Not surprisingly, the Commission's 1977 conclusion was that private employers should not be covered, but made several recommendations on the handling of employment privacy matters that were encouraged to be followed by private employers on a voluntary basis such as:

- Review personnel information practices to determine how and for what purpose information is collected.

- Limit information collected only to what would be relevant to employment decision making.

- Inform employees about the type of information kept on file and how used.

- Allow employees to inspect their file and, if necessary and appropriate, correct inaccurate information.

- Keep sensitive material such as medical records and investigations apart from the primary personnel file.

- Limit the internal use and exposure of personal information to only those that have a need to know.

- Limit external disclosure of employee information in the absence of the employee's written authorization.

- Keep records current to ensure their accuracy.

Two other federal statutes that have come into play, with much less frequency and applicability but nonetheless relevance, with employee privacy rights are the Federal Omibus Crime Control and Safe Streets Act of 1968, and the Federal Fair Credit Reporting Act.

Crime Control Act

This federal law essentially prohibits the deliberate interception of private telephone (wiretapping) and oral communications, and carries with it civil and criminal penalties for violations that depend on circumstances. As it applies to employment matters, it serves as a bar to supervisors from listening in on employee telephone conversations without their permission or knowledge that is in conjunction with some business purpose (e.g., coaching on sales calls), the "bugging" of someone's office, or even intentional eavesdropping on the conversation between two people—excepting perhaps the breakroom or other non-private place where people congregate. A good example was heard by the Eleventh Circuit Court of Appeals in *Watkins v. L. M. Berry & Co.* (1983) where the company had a policy allowing supervisors to routinely listen in on sales calls from extension phones. In this case, the supervisor overheard plaintiff reveal her intention to take another job during a personal call to another person. The court noted that while surreptitious interception is not violative of the Act so long as the listener hangs up once the call is determined personal (and what was overheard is not used against the employee), in this case the supervisor went beyond these bounds and in so doing violated her privacy rights.

The most obvious way for employers to avoid this type of a privacy violation is to adopt a policy limiting or even prohibiting (except for emergencies) the making or receiving of personal telephone calls during business hours, then discipline employees for policy violations (rather than for the content of their personal calls) once the personal nature of a call is made.

Fair Credit Act

This law is a little abstract from the normal course in which employers obtain personal information about employees or prospective new hires. The Act and its notice requirements apply only when information is obtained by the employer through direct third-party (external) interviews such as credit bureaus, law enforcement agencies, or even employment agencies and executive search firms. Notice and disclosure requirements by the user of such information necessitates:

1. Delivery or mailing of a written notice to the concerned individual that an investigative report "possibly concerning an employee's character, general reputation, personal characteristics and mode of living" will be made.

2. Providing a complete disclosure of the nature and scope of the investigation to the individual upon request.

The most frequent relevance of the Act, though not known to be the subject of federal litigation, pertains to many employers who seek credit rating information through credit bureaus and other sources, and general character information through employment agencies and executive search firms. The former is usually immune from the Act since information is not gathered by personal interview, however the latter sources may derive direct information by interviews or (psychological) tests and make reports to the employer making this vulnerable source of information that may require disclosure to the (prospective) employee.

Employee Polygraph Protection Act

In June 1988, President Reagan signed this law that would take effect in December 1988, and thus ended an 18 year stretch of unsuccessful attempts by Congress to reach a suitable compromise bill covering private sector employers. In fact, this law specifically excludes federal, state, and other public employers—who are covered by existing federal and state laws—nor does this law apply to those involved in national security.

This federal law will henceforth prohibit private sector employers requiring or requesting an applicant or employee to submit to a lie detector test; or from discharging, discriminating against, or denying employment or promotion to an applicant or employee who refuses to submit to testing. As defined in the Act, "lie detector" consists of such devices as a polygraph, deceptograph, or any other methods of rendering diagnostic opinions of an individual's honesty or dishonesty. Theoretically then, attaching such devices to an individual without their consent could be legally construed as assault, while the questioning of individuals under these circumstances could also be considered an unlawful invasion of privacy.

There are, however, a few conditions under which private employers can test applicants and employees, but there are strict limitations on the administration of these tests. Lawful testing conditions consist of:

- The test is part of an ongoing investigation of losses suffered by the employer.
- The tested employee had access to the property in question.
- The employer had reasonable suspicion of the employee's involvement.
- The employer provides a statement of the bases of the above conditions.

Job applicants may likewise be lawfully tested when applying for jobs with:

- Certain types of security firms.
- Manufacturers or distributors of controlled substances where the employee would have direct access to these substances.

1.12 STATE CONSTITUTIONS AND STATUTES

As you can easily see from the following chart that depicts the various states where privacy has been adopted by constitutional and/or statutory law, there is considerable home rule philosophy that still shrouds the employment privacy rights issues. While only twelve states have incorporated what might seem to be a fundamental democratic right into their state constitutions, as many as twenty-seven states have laws imposing some type of restriction on the use of polygraph (lie detector) tests.

With increasing liberal attitudes by state legislators toward employment and other privacy rights of individuals, along with well-funded lobbying by labor unions, progressively more states are taking the position that employees possess a personal right to the restriction of information that is private by one means or another. This is particularly true with regard to personnel files. As you will see in the next section, most state statutes apply to the file access of employees and former employees ranging from six months to three years from separation, including supervisory files and informal notes. In these states, employers are typically encouraged or required, to establish procedures for employee access. Generally, these state laws allow the exclusion of sensitive records such as medical records, reference letters, and investigative reports, meaning they may be kept in a separate, confidential file. States like California employers may not release an employee's medical records without the employee's written authorization, unless by compelling court order.

Much of what has been written in the way of state statutes has been modeled from federal law, but remoulded to state interests in regulating this rather delicate if not

	State Constitution Privacy Rights	Fair Credit Reporting	Polygraph Restrictions	Fingerprinting & Surveillance	Arrest Records w/o Conviction	Employee Access to Personnel File
Alabama						
Alaska	X		XX			
Arizona	X	X	XXXX			
Arkansas						
California	X	X	XXX	F,M,S	X	X
Colorado						X public employees
Connecticut		X	XXX		X	XX
Delaware			XX			X
Dist. of Columbia						X public employees
Florida	X	X				
Georgia					X	
Hawaii	X		XXX			
Idaho			XXX			
Illinois	X		XXX			X
Indiana						
Iowa						
Kansas		X				
Kentucky		X				
Louisiana	X					
Maine		X	XX			X
Maryland		X	XXX		X + psychol. records	
Massachusetts	X	X	X		X	
Michigan			XXX		X	XX
Minnesota			XX			
Mississippi						
Missouri						
Montana	X	X	XXX			
Nebraska			XXX			
Nevada			XXX	S		X
New Hampshire		X				X
New Jersey			X			
New Mexico		X	XXXX			
New York		X	X	F		X staff employees
North Carolina						
North Dakota						

	State Constitution Privacy Rights	Fair Credit Reporting	Polygraph Restrictions	Fingerprinting & Surveillance	Arrest Records w/o Conviction	Employee Access to Personnel File
Ohio					X	X
Oklahoma		X				
Oregon			XXX		X	X
Pennsylvania			XXX		X	X
Rhode Island	X		XXX		X	X
South Carolina	X					X public employees
South Dakota						X public employees
Tennessee						X public employees
Texas		X				
Utah						X public employees
Vermont			XXXX			X public employees
Virginia		X	XXXX		X	
Washington	X		XXX			X
West Virginia						
Wisconsin			XX		X	XX
Wyoming						

Polygraph Restrictions: X—absolutely prohibited use on employees
          XX—prohibits "request, require, or suggest" to take
          XXX—prohibits requiring as condition of employment
          XXXX—restricts operator questions

Fingerprinting & Surveillance: F—prohibits fingerprinting requirements
          M—prohibits 2-way mirrors in rest area
          S—prohibits "spotter" shoppers

Employee Access to Personnel File: XX—requires employer to establish procedure for employee to challenge accuracy.

Source: Craig T. Norback (ed.), *The Human Resources Yearbook,* 1986 edition. Reprinted with permission, Prentice-Hall Information Services. All rights reserved.

controversial form of employer-employee activities. Certainly both sides have to be weighed, but ultimately the issue revolves around who can access what kinds of personal information, and how it is used in employment decisions and treatment. Generally, then, legislators tend to focus on the employer's information collection practices, while the courts tend to scrutinize both employer practices and the type of information obtained as well as how it was used—the degree to which it adversely affected the employee's customary benefits of employment.

1.13 DEFINITION AND ELEMENTS OF UNLAWFUL ACTIONS

When constitutional and statutory laws are violated, the victim can recover compensatory and punitive damages which can be substantial in a number of situations where the employee was terminated, denied promotion, or became "stigmatized" by wrongful publicity of an alleged act. In this regard, the most common causes of legal action posed by employees is defamation, invasion of privacy, false imprisonment, and assault and battery. Here are some basic elements of these causes of action:

Defamation

Occurs when one communicates false, injurious information about another. The most common occurrence of this act has been well publicized accounts of providing prospective new employers information about a former employee during a reference check that is damaging enough for the employer's rejection of the employee. Somehow, the employee learns about the information provided by the former employer and sues for defamation. The majority of these cases where the employee has prevailed were well deserved by the employee because often unsubstantiated, biased, or just plain untruthful information was given to another employer who based his rejection decision on this information. In fear of defamation suits, and as an overreaction to controlling such a liability, most employers have made it a practice to provide only the former employee's title(s) and dates of employment. However, in more recent cases, courts have found no problem with former employers providing additional performance-related information about the employee, upon request, that is both factual and objective. In any case, employers would be well advised not to release information until a signed release is received from the employee. Some employers ask departing employees if they'd care to sign such releases when they leave the organization.

Yet another common way defamation can arise is during and after the conduct of internal investigations of employees such as for misconduct, sexual harassment, drug abuse, and AIDS. Special effort must be made in these situations to handle the investigation and related documents in a highly discreet, confidential manner involving only those that legitimately need to be involved. Questioning should be framed in such a way as to avoid the implication of an accusation until all facts are gathered.

One noteworthy exception to information handling that may be defamatory in nature is the doctrine of "privilege". Privileged information and situations can, under guarded circumstances, set aside the liability that might normally otherwise occur because the information is sufficiently valuable, factual, obtained by good authority, and communicated discreetly—even if it somehow leaks out. Situations in which one can expect the information to be privileged are:

1. To protect a legitimate personal interest.
2. Providing it to someone who has the right to know.
3. Providing it to one who shares a common interest.
4. Providing it to a public official in conjunction with their duty.

Additionally, derogatory information that is shared between selective, usually internal, individuals can be protected from liability. This type of communication is referred to as a "qualified privilege", providing, of course, the information being shared is true. This is the type of communication that commonly occurs between supervisors, managers, human resource professionals, and the company's agents or perhaps even the union concerning particularly delicate employee matters. However, privileged communications can be rejected for abuse where the information is knowingly false, a reckless disregard of truth, spiteful, or excessively shared (*Dillard Department Stores v. Felton,* 1982).

Invasion of Privacy

There are four different forms of personal invasion that can create a cause of action.

- Appropriation of another's name or likeness.
- Placing another in false light in the public eye.
- Public disclosure of private acts.
- Unreasonable intrusion upon the seclusion of another.

While it is generally not a misappropriation of an employee's likeness to photograph employees for personnel file records, it would be to use their name or photo in company publicity without their consent. Placing another in public false light refers to a deliberate form of deceit using mass media such as lying about an employee in a newspaper, radio, or television coverage of their act (or why they were terminated).

Intrusion, on the other hand, is more individualized and typically is physical in nature although some cases have been decided on the basis of psychological intrusion such as through repetitive personal questioning (*Phillips v. Smalley Maintenance Service,* 1983). It is also commonly cited in cases of sexual harassment and personal conduct investigations.

Intrusion is also associated with entering a place held or entitled to be private such as someone's office, desk drawers, their file cabinet, personal mail (*Vernors v. Young,*

1976), and the acquisition of personnel information by those who do not have the right to know. For example, in *Kobeck v. Nabisco* (1983), a man who believed his wife was having an affair asked her supervisor about her attendance record. Upon learning that she had recently missed several of her night shifts the man committed suicide. Although an extreme and tragic conclusion, the same intrusion of employment privacy rights rationale could be applied by employees where their employer mails disciplinary, termination, absenteeism, and other private information notices to them at their home address where it could be opened by another. If mailing is necessary, send it by certified mail where the employee must sign to receive it.

False Imprisonment

To be a libelous cause of action, false imprisonment requires proof that the person was deprived of the reasonable ability to move, and not necessarily by physical restraint. Most often, the elements of false imprisonment go well beyond the normal functioning of the employee's duties (say sitting for long periods of time) such as confining them against their will in a room where they are being interviewed, interrogated, or otherwise held for a long period, and where there is the refusal to let them leave or take a break.

False imprisonment does not mean that you cannot order employees to work overtime, but if they express more than mild objection, you're better off to find someone else to work it. Most employees will not object too adamantly because they know they can be fired for insubordination. As it relates to confinement, false imprisonment could be such acts as:

- Requiring overtime work in one location without a meal or rest break in which the employee is free to move about somewhat.

- Refusing to allow an employee to leave their work location after they have expressed a legitimate need to do so.

- Not allowing an employee to leave their work location for meal or bodily function reasons.

Assault And Battery

This occurs when a person has been deprived of their bodily privacy. Most of us tend to think of assault and/or battery as a brutal act, yet it need not be so for one's privacy to be violated. In fact, there are many people who emotionally and psychologically react adversely to merely being touched or the subject of starring. By legal definition, battery is the nonconsenual touching, hitting, pushing, and offensive bodily contact by another; while assault is the creation of placing one in fear of battery such as by voice (yelling), language (provoking terminology), and body gestures (clenched fist, finger shaking, standing within arm's distance).

It is well and good for us to say that these actions are simply unacceptable in the workplace, and that they are most common among line employees. The fact of the matter is that the former position would be terribly naive, and the latter position is pure bunk. It is far more common for ego-centered, power-oriented supervisors and line managers to become guilty of both assault and battery actions toward employees than it is for employees among themselves. Many supervisors feel employees are powerless to act against their authority, so the supervisor exercises these actions more freely than do employees who know there are controls in place to regulate their behavior. If supervisors and higher-ups were not the culprits of assault and battery behavior, it is doubtful that sexual harassment would have received the widespread notoriety that it has.

Assault and battery is just one more reason employers should take extra caution in the selection, evaluation, and training of its supervisory and managerial staff. The element of an assault and/or battery can create precisely the kind of employee intrepedation that could transform an otherwise mild misunderstanding or claim of wrong-doing (grievance) to a major law suit. By then, it's too late for the company to correct the misbegotten behavior of its agent, and the best the company can expect is an out-of-court settlement.

1.20 DRUG/ALCOHOL TESTING AND INVESTIGATIONS

Employer testing of employees and job applicants for drug, alcohol, or other controlled substance use has been one of the more controversial privacy issues of the 1980's that will continue well into the 1990's. However, unlike many other sensitive employment issues that have risen in the past where employers must persist in opposing someone to defend their business need to act, drug and alcohol testing is rapidly becoming a more workable debate between the opposing forces employee privacy and reasonable employment interests.

Due largely to the public notoriety of extensive drug and alcohol use by American workers during the 1980's, employers developed a growing concern about the workplace effect of its use and abuse. In 1980, a government study estimated that drug use by employees alone cost American business $25.7 billion related to illness, absences, health care premiums, reduced work quality, decreased productivity, and theft. By the mid 1980's, other studies estimated the actual cost to employers to be closer to $75 billion per year. Other common concerns of employers that has prompted a reaction to this situation are the liabilities created by employees working under diminished capacity (judgment and safety hazards), loss or damage to the company's reputation and image, and credibility of the company to its customers.

For example, a company can be held vicariously liable for the acts of an employee, including managerial personnel, if the company had knowledge (or should have known) that the employee's condition, propensity, or history created a risk and safeguards were not put in place. In other words, an employer's liability can arise with action that is too hasty (e.g., discrimination, deprivation of privacy rights, or wrongful discharge), or with action that is too slow (undercautiously executed where damage to another results). The issue of effectively dealing with drug and alcohol problems for the employer, then, becomes one of the proverbial "rock and hard place" condition for employers.

Opposition, on the other hand, has been voiced by employees, labor unions, and civil rights groups. Although not strictly opposed to the need of employers to control substance abuse in the workplace, these individuals are mostly concerned with protection of the employee's privacy rights that are unilaterally sacrificed by such employer approaches to the problem as random, arbitrary, and/or all-inclusive testing of entire work groups. Their position is one of there being no justifiable need to intrude into the privacy of a larger number of employees to find only a few offenders. Moreover, they say, requiring mandatory testing without reasonable cause is a form of illegal search and seizure in violation of their constitutional rights under the Fourth Amendment.

By 1987, it was estimated that over one-half of all employers with more than 100 employees were either currently testing for drug and alcohol use or were considering plans to do so. The study was conducted by Business & Legal Reports among 2,000 small (up to 100 employees), medium (100-500 employees), and large (over 500 employees) companies nationwide. Results of the survey indicated that 17 percent of the large companies currently test employees for drug use while 23 percent test job applicants as part of the routine pre-employment physical examination. Smaller employers, having fewer resources and ability to keep abreast of these kinds of issues, have tended to overlook the need for testing programs and therefore opting to operate more at risk with fewer employees than their larger competitors. However, for those non-testing smaller employers, their risk may become even more than proportionately higher since they may become the potential recipients of applicants who have been rejected by those employers who do test.

Chart 1. Testing Practices and Plans

	Now Testing	Definite Plans	Considering Testing
Small	3%	2%	28%
Medium	7%	4%	42%
Large	17%	10%	47%
Overall Average	9%	5%	39%

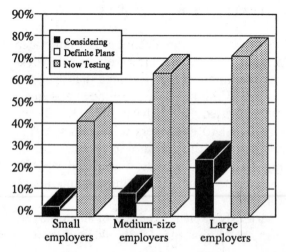

As it can be easily seen by comparing Charts 2 and 3, depicting those employers currently testing, about twice as many employers are testing job applicants as opposed to existing employees. This result is due to the greater sensitivity of privacy rights being invaded by testing employees in any large-scale approach—and the employer's vulnerability to having employees litigating their privacy rights—compared to job applicants. According to many courts, applicants have less of a vested right to protection and are less effected by potential discrimination if such tests are performed on all applicants whose jobs would normally be subject to a pre-employment physical exam.

Other responses from the survey indicated that three-fourths of the companies regard alcohol use and abuse to be a greater problem than drugs, but over one-third felt that drug-related problems have been on the increase since the early 1980's and one-fourth regarded the drug problem sufficient to warrant the commencement of testing. Of those employers who take a more adamant approach to abating the workplace introduction of drugs, 70 percent search lockers and personal effects on an individual basis where there is reasonable suspicion, 24 percent perform unannounced random inspections, and 12 percent have done announced inspections.

Chart 2. Percent of Employers Testing Employees

	All Employers	Manufac- turing	Finance/ Services	Civil Service	Communi- cations/ Electronics	Transpor- tation	Health/ Education
Small	3%	5%					5%
Medium	7%	10%	2%	8%		29%	
Large	17%	17%	8%	18%	6%	47%	11%
Overall average	9%	11%	3%	10%	2%	38%	5%

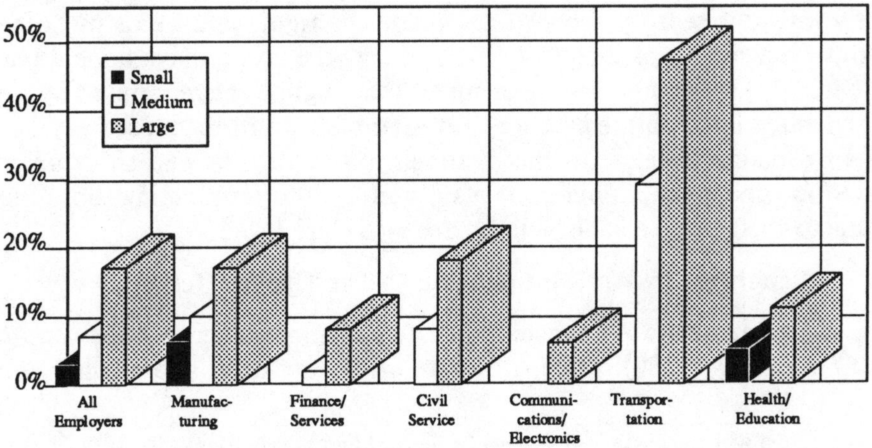

Chart 3. Percent of Employers Testing Job Applicants

	All Employers	Manufac- turing	Finance/ Services	Civil Service	Communi- cations/ Electronics	Transpor- tation	Health/ Education
Small	9%	13%	5%			33%	7%
Medium	14%	22%	4%		4%	43%	4%
Large	23%	34%	11%	18%	6%	47%	5%
Overall average	15%	23%	6%	7%	3%	45%	5%

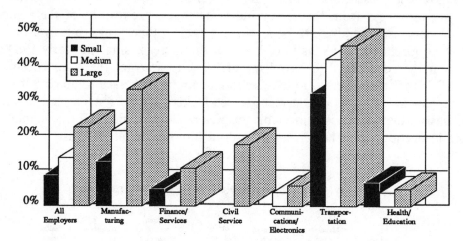

1.21 CASE LAW ILLUSTRATIONS

Prevailing case law is an insightful source of information about the nature and circumstances concerning privacy rights. With regard to drug/alcohol testing, and the information and decisions that result, the courts have only recently begun to deal frequently with this sensitive area of balancing the rights and needs of both parties. Yet, in this brief period of case law development, the courts have done a reasonably adequate job of clarifying important elements that ought to be recognized by employers and incorporated into routine practice. For example, two of the most frequently asked questions by managers relate to the treatment of employees who show up for work intoxicated (or under the influence of a substance), and terminating those excessively absent due to their drug/alcohol habits. See also Part I: 5.32.

Reporting To Work Intoxicated: Is The Offense Terminable?

Yes, according to the Wisconsin appellate court in *Squires v. Labor and Industry Review Commission* (1980). Here, the state law treats drug and alcohol abuse as a

Charts 1-3 reprinted with permission of Business & Legal Reports, Madison, CT., 1987.

handicap similar to that of the federal Act. The court determined in this case that the employee was not fired for being an alcoholic, but for showing up to work in an intoxicated condition such that he was unable to do his job. Similar rationale was imposed on an employee who was fired after his third conviction for driving under the influence of alcohol, after which he sought protection of the Rehabilitation Act in Huff v. Israel (1983). The judge likewise found the termination to be based on legitimate job related conditions.

Excessive Absenteeism Due To Drug/Alcohol Use: Can We Fire The Employee?

Yes, but this should be a last resort measure and you should be able to establish a specific effect the absence has had on the functioning of the work unit. The courts prefer to see that an employer has taken a tolerant and compassionate approach to resolving the problem, such as offering a rehabilitation absence even if it's conditioned on proof of completion and recovery before termination.

Even though some courts hold public employers slightly more accountable for good faith compliance with laws and practices, the case of *Walker v. Weinberger* (1985) serves as a good illustration. Here, an employee of a federal agency was fired for excessive absenteeism related to his alcoholism. Absence records were initially related to the drinking problem, and later to rehabilitation participation. The court rejected the employer's action since it was based in part on pre-treatment absences which demonstrated the employer's lack of accommodation. Similarly, in *Whitlock v. Donovan* (1984), the employer fired an employee for failing to complete an offered rehabilitation program. Since the employer did not follow its own policy procedure by first insisting the employee return to complete the program or face disciplinary action before initiating a termination.

This and other cases like it point out the need for human resource professionals to take two important programmatic measures; 1) train supervisors and managers on the identification and effects of drug and alcohol use, and (2) ensure that liberal rehabilitation benefits are included in the company's medical plan(s).

Drug/Alcohol Testing: When And How Can We Do It Legally?

There have been a substantial number of Appeals and District Court cases decided on this question during the 1980's. The result of these legal holdings has been based almost solely on the basis of the circumstances in each case, but frequently focus on such issues as:

- the nature of an employee's job.
- the legitimacy of interest being protected by the employer.
- the existence of "reasonable suspicion."
- testing methods used to confirm results.
- the existence of notice to employees through publicized policy or advance warning.

1.22 DRUG/ALCOHOL CONTROL PROGRAM APPROACHES

Many of the early law suits by employees who were fired, or applicants who were rejected for employment, due to drug and alcohol tests were brought by public employees because of their direct protection under the federal Privacy Act. Since the early 1980's, however, many states have adopted constitutional and/or statutory laws modelled after the federal law, and many of these states included compliance by private sector employers. Thus, as the states adopted new laws convering private employers, litigation since the mid-1980's has been on the rise by private sector employees and these cases were typically in response to the actions of an employer once the employer inaugurated a new testing program.

Some of these employers, looking to quickly thwart the problem and see where they stood with current employees, initiated a program consisting of a drug and/or alcohol test for all employees, or random unannounced testing of entire work groups. Much more often than not, such random or blanket testing has been regarded as an unnecessary deprivation of employee privacy rights by the courts. In response to this general limitation, many employers have developed programs that take the following kinds of approaches.

Policy Development And Notice

The most logical and practical starting point is to develop a policy on how the company is going to treat and deal with the presence or effects of drug and alcohol use. The policy is then disseminated to all employees with a cover memo explaining the company's reasoning for the policy, while at the same time accounting for employee privacy rights.

Reasonable Cause

All current employees will be subject to testing where the company obtains evidence, including suspicion, that would create a reasonable cause to require search, surveillance, and testing of individual employees. With regard to an employer's violation of the Fourth Amendment rights prohibiting "unreasonable search and seizure" (with due process of law), applies exclusively to government or state action according to *Monroe v. Consolidated Freightways, Inc.* (1987). Once again though, such an exemption for private employers may not relieve them from a similar cause of action by employees under state constitutional or statutory law.

Sensitive Or Hazardous Jobs

Many employers having particularly sensitive or hazardous jobs in the organization where poor judgment, safety practices, or similar types of diminished capacities can have a profound effect have generally prevailed in court even where the testing of these employees has been a matter of routine. Two of the more notable examples are

National Treasury Employees Union v. Von Raab (1987), and *McDonnell v. Hunter* (1987). In the Von Raab Case, a district court held that the random urine sampling by the U.S. Customs Service of employees applying for promotional positions was unconstitutional as a violation of their Fourth Amendment rights. However, the Fifth Circuit court held that there existed a stronger governmental interest by ensuring that those responsible for drug enforcement were not themselves drug users. The court pointed out that the Custom Service drug testing program was only limited intrusiveness since 1) employees were not watched during urine sampling, 2) testing was scheduled in advance, and 3) testing did not occur until they met all other qualifications.

In the Hunter case, the Eighth Circuit Court of Appeals determined that it was appropriate for the Iowa prison system to conduct random drug tests on prison guards based on the more compelling need to assure security interests and prevent drug interaction between guards and prisoners. While these cases do not have much application to private employers, they do suggest that the courts are willing to be somewhat responsive to the more practical considerations of sensitive jobs.

Regrettably though, the courts find public service jobs *more* sensitive to the public interest than the business sensitivity that private employers might try to argue as a justification. The objective for private employers thus becomes to be able to articulate definitive and profound impact a particular position (or group of positions) has on the safety of others, product liability, the economic health of the company, the effect on the company's well-being, and other issues that distinguish some jobs from others by dramatic impact that is detainmental to critical business interests.

Testing Job Applicants

A majority of employers doing drug and/or alcohol testing apply it to all new hires who would otherwise be subject to pre-employment physical exams. A few conservative employers are also requiring tests of all promotional employees, theoretically on the basis of their added job responsibility, but this is a weak position when applied to all promotional positions since many would not meet sensitive or hazardous standards of interpretation.

Also, while it's worthy to note that studies have revealed a 10 to 40 percent rejection rate by employers using drug and alcohol testing in pre-employment physicals, it is likely to be regarded by the more liberal courts as an arbitrary and unnecessary intrusion that can have (minimally) discriminatory effects. Consider, for example, the case of *Davis v. Bucher* (1978) where the City of Philadelphia rejected three job applicants who passed all qualifying tests except their pre-employment physical. The rejection of these applicants was based on the city's rule prohibiting the hiring of anyone with a history of drug use. You'll recall from Part 1, Chapter 5, that mere history of drug use can be a protected physical handicap under the 1973 Rehabilitation Act which was precisely the cause of action filed by the rejected applicants.

The judge in this case noted that the city's policy was not only violative of the Rehabilitation Act, but was also unconstitutional since it deprived the applicants of due process and equal protection of the law. The point raised in this case was that the rejected applicants were not *current* drug users and thus the city merely jumped to the conclusion that their past history was synomymous with probable use. While employers have the right to be wary of drug or alcohol abuse in any case, they ought not make hiring decisions on presumptions. Rather, employers should base rejection decisions on greater evidence related to the individual applicant and the job in question.

Refusal To Be Tested

This element of employer programs most often provides that such employee refusals will be dealt with by termination of employment. What is sometimes overlooked though is the situation where an employee's response to mandatory testing is covert such as making excuses to miss an appointed time or place to be tested, particularly if they're seeking a sufficient delay to clear their blood or urine of revealing substances. Naturally, those employees terminated for refusing are the most likely to sue, so employers wanting to use termination as a sanction against employee refusals ought to base its demand for testing on reasonable suspicion. For example, in *Luck v. Southern Pacific Transportation Company*, 1986, a computer programmer was awarded $500,000 in a wrongful discharge suit involving the employee's refusal to submit to drug testing and was not under suspicion, but was fired for refusal.

Search And Surveillance

The last thing employers and employees alike want is what George Orwell depicted as "Big Brother" where everyone becomes subject to suspicion under the watchful eye of cameras and super sleuths probing into designated work spaces. Unfortunately, there are more than just a couple of employees in any business setting that would take advantage of a democratic employer by storing drugs and alcohol in well-concealed places at work where they can inauciously consume it during work periods. It is for this reason that many employer programs have reserved the right to conduct searches of employee lockers, desks, packages, and personal effects on company property, and to conduct some sort of surveillance. Here again the employer is vulnerable to a legal action alleging deprivation of an employee's right to privacy unless, of course, the employer has very sound evidence of reasonable cause for its actions.

Camera surveillance is only lawful under the 1968 Crime Control Act if it is done in the open such as that used by banks and retail stores for security reasons. Searches of employee's personal property, on the other hand, should generally be with their permission but need not be as long as the company has reserved the right to conduct searches of anything in or brought to company premises. Care should be exercised and sound advice obtained before conducting searches of personal property, and employees should never be strip-searched. In fact, where a situation involves drugs or criminal conditions, an employer may be better off requesting the assistance of law enforcement personnel.

A common interest for many employers is the ability to search employee lockers. One such case was decided by the Texas Supreme Court in *Trotti v. K-Mart* (1985) where a store manager cut an employee's padlock on her assigned company locker and rummaged through her purse. He ordered the search of a few other lockers in response to an alleged stolen watch. In court, the manager said employees were told upon hire that their personal effects were subject to search, but testimony from other company executives was contrary.

Further, the company had allowed this employee to use her own lock thereby creating a rightful *expectation* to privacy, and the employer lacked justifiable suspicion of this employee. The trial court awarded plaintiff $8,000 compensatory and $100,000 punitive damages; the Supreme Court affirmed these damages. Similarly, the U.S. Supreme Court has determined that a public employer need not obtain a search warrant in order to search an employee's office or desk where there is reason to suspect some wrongdoing by the employee in *O'Connor v. Ortego* (1987). The court noted that an employee's expectation of such (office) privacy "may be reduced by virtue of actual office practices and procedures, or by legitimate regulation."

Confirming Test Results

Most all employer programs condition any employment action on confirming their suspicion or other reasonable cause through laboratory tests. For sake of objectivity, it is advisable to use independent labs, and in some of the more serious or doubtful cases to order either a second or alternate test if available. Additionally, caution should be exercised when ordering an employee to be tested immediately where your suspicion or reasonable cause is based on physical signs of their being under the influence of any substance. In such cases, you're better off ordering that they *be taken* by someone else to where the test is to be conducted and forbidding them to drive until test results are known; or sufficient time passes to eliminate risks connected to their condition.

1.23 POLICY DEVELOPMENT CONSIDERATIONS

In developing any policy on issues that have become subject to the kind of balance associated with protection of the company's business interests and that of employee privacy rights, it is important to give considerable thought to any unique conditions of the company's operations, nature of business, basis for control, and types of jobs. From the previous discussion it should be clear that employees do have privacy rights related to drug and alcohol testing, and the courts are only supportive of random or group testing when there exists a very strong public interest to protect.

Careful and thorough consideration needs to be given by private sector employers before developing their drug/alcohol policy to what jobs would most likely meet a strict definition test of being hazardous, responsible for critical judgments and decisions, or highly influential upon the welfare of the company should they become impaired by substance abuse. Other consideration ought to be given to program support such as how discipline will be used as a behavior modifier, the availability of quality counseling and detoxification (rehabilitation) services, leave programs, and the readiness of professional surveillance and investigatory techniques.

Basic policies on drug and alcohol use/testing should minimally address the following elements, supplemented by any appropriate conditions that are unique to the company's legitimate *need* to create control measures.

Prohibited Employee Activities

It should be prohibited for any employee who is not specifically authorized by upper management to possess or use any form of drug or alcohol, and that possession, concealment, or distribution on company premises is absolutely forbidden, and thereby a terminable offense. Likewise, it should be prohibited for any employee to report to work unfit, under the influence, or become under the influence of unauthorized drugs or alcohol. Employees who become impaired to adequately perform their job due to such use or influence should be dealt with on a case-by-case basis, and subject to termination.

Searches And Surveillance

For many employers this policy element may become highly instrumental in their legal ability to thwart drug, alcohol, or theft problems as long as the employer doesn't go too far in the role of supersleuth. The policy should generally express the fact that a good employment relationship is built on honesty and trust, but there may arise occasions in which it becomes necessary for the company to conduct investigations based on an incident.

Therefore, the company needs to reserve and communicate their right to search personal and any other property on company premises, and when this is done at the company's request, the employee must comply or be subject to disciplinary measures including possible termination. In cases of desks, lockers, and the like, the policy should indicate that only company locks and keys are to be used by employees. Failure to comply with a request to the employee by an authorized company representative to search their personal property, assuming there is reasonable cause to suspicion this employee, can be conditioned on termination.

Should you also conduct a personal interview to acquire information from an employee, and the employee is a union member who requests the presence of a representative of their choice, you should allow them reasonable time to have such a representative present to comply with the "Weingarten Decision" first decided by the NLRB and confirmed by various courts.

Testing

Job applicants should be notified that they may be subjected to drug/alcohol testing prior to employment, and at periodic (unannounced) intervals but not more than twice per year thereafter if they occupy a designated "sensitive" position. In terms of current employees, the company ought to develop a listing of those positions it considers sensitive, and the rationale applied, by virtue of the position's inherent hazards, physical demands, criticality of decisions, or customer or public contacts.

Other than the above scheduled testing, the company should reserve the right to test virtually *any* employee whenever there exists strong evidence to support a reasonable cause to suspect that use or abuse is occurring. The suspicion should be based on such factors as the employee's performance, behavior, or physical signs of substance influence. Remember, the company may develop exposure to vicarious liability if it had sufficient reason to suspect substance influence and failed to act with resultant harm brought by the employee to another person (e.g., physical altercation, auto accident, rape, negligent death).

Like any other form of unacceptable performance or behavior, the incident should be precisely documented including what conditions, signs, or other evidence has given rise to the employer's reasonable cause. Then the employee should be *ordered* to undergo *immediate* testing, and the employee should understand that it is an order and your reasons for the order. The employee should be transported to the test site, and/or taken home—whichever is most appropriate to the situation. In some cases of affirmative test results, you may want to confirm those results by having a second or alternative method of testing performed to verify the reliability of the first test. In doing so, you thereby obtain more defensible evidence of the employee's condition (and what may be needed for detoxification, diet, and related medical information helpful to a rehabilitation program prognosis).

Finally, the employer should assure employees in the policy that information obtained about drug and/or alcohol tests will be treated in a confidential manner—such as placing records in a nonaccessible file—including any resultant action taken by the employer.

Actions

Most policies on the subject of drug and/or alcohol use are discipline oriented, or at best will allude to the possible availability of either counseling or rehabilitation, usually through the company's Employee Assistance Program. In developing a good policy, remember that the first priority is to eliminate the problem and retain the employee if possible. While eliminating troubled employees may eliminate the immediate problem for you, it also creates new problems (e.g., cost and time of replacement) and will probably only intensify the employee's problem which may remain unresolved. Therefore, the policy emphasis should be on problem solving such as medical and perhaps even psychological diagnosis, treatment, and reorientation counseling, and using disciplinary measures including termination as a serious offense or last resort action. In fact, in some cases the potential threat of loosing one's job may be the needed form of motivation for an employee to enter and complete rehabilitation.

So, while the policy should address both rehabilitation and disciplinary action that can occur in connection with a case-by-case assessment of circumstances, other preventative actions may lessen the need to rely on your policy to handle problem situations. In this regard, there is a desparate need for managers and human resource professionals to begin a more analytic examination of workplace and job conditions that might be contributing factors to employee attraction and dependency on drugs or alcohol. Such an analysis should give careful attention to the factors of workloads, work hours, intensity or boredom of job tasks, stress elements, and types of conflict to name a few.

Additionally, supervisors who are the ones most likely to become knowledgeable about the personal characteristics of their employees—regardless of level—should learn to watch for early signs of depression, problems occurring in the employee's personal life, lowered moral, an employee who rather suddenly experiences a negative shift in their attitudes, an employee's unusual increase in single day (Monday/Friday) absences, and similar behavioral changes that may well be embryo factors leading to substance use, then abuse. This is a much better stage for the employer to act in a supportive problem solving manner, than later in a punitive or embarassing manner. Bear in mind that most other employees will quickly figure out why this person has decided to take a one or two month leave, particularly if they work with him/her.

1.30 POLYGRAPH EXAMINATIONS

Polygraphs, or lie detector tests as they're commonly called, have been considered an infringement of employee privacy rights for a number of years, usually on the basis of unreasonable (information) search in the context of questions asked and information obtained that often has little relevance to job performance ability. Also, the reliability of polygraph tests has been suspect for several decades, with studies revealing a frequent error rate of over 50 percent which has led the courts to regard polygraphs as inadmissable evidence in legal proceedings.

As it was pointed out earlier, Congress has considered at least one bill each year for over the last decade that would prohibit polygraph testing of job applicants and employees. This failure of Congress to adopt a national policy on polygraph use in employment matters has led many states to enact legislation setting limitations on its use. By 1987 as many as 32 states had adopted such laws with the following restrictions:

	Cannot require as condition of employment	Cannot ask for voluntary test	Restriction on questions asked
1. Alaska		X	
2. Arizona			X
3. California	X		
4. Connecticut		X	
5. Delaware			X
6. District of Columbia			X
7. Georgia			X
8. Hawaii	X		
9. Idaho	X		
10. Illinois			X
11. Indiana			X
12. Iowa			X
13. Maine			X
14. Maryland	X		
15. Massachusetts		X	
16. Michigan		X	
17. Minnesota		X	
18. Montana	X		
19. Nebraska	X		
20. Nevada			X
21. New Jersey		X	
22. New Mexico			X
23. Oregon		X	
24. Pennsylvania	X		
25. Rhode Island	X		
26. Texas			X
27. Utah			X
28. Vermont		X	
29. Virginia	X		
30. Washington	X		
31. West Virginia		X	
32. Wisconsin	X		

The essence of polygraph utilization in employment decisions is that its reliability has been overly glorified by the motion picture and television industry depicting confessions by the bad guy while connected to the machine. The first polygraph machine was introduced by the Italian psychologist Cesare Lombroso who felt that lies could be detected by changes in a person's blood pressure when responding to questions. In the 1930's, an American psychologist by the name of William Moulton Marston introduced a polygraph machine said to be more reliable simply because it measured changes in a person's breathing (respiration), perspiration, and blood pressure which, it was presumed, would occur if the subject gave false responses.

Since polygraphs are unusable as a form of defensive evidence, the information obtained through their use is of little value when it becomes the basis of rejecting an applicant or terminating an employee. At best, polygraphs should be confined in employment matters to no more than a voluntary secondary source of verifying information already known by other more reliable means. Ultimately, employers are far better off taking the time to personally check out a new hire's references and past employment, or conducting thorough and professional investigations of any employee wrongdoing.

1.40 MEDICAL, HEALTH, AND SAFETY RELATED PRIVACY RIGHTS

It has been mentioned a number of times throughout previous chapters that both state and federal courts have developed many new legal principles that become binding on employers. These principles occur less from interpretation of existing statutory law—which may be either vague or absent in some employment matters—but moreso from the court's view of how some disputed matter ought to be handled. Application of mere principles is often the case in the lingering fuzzy area of employee privacy rights as they relate to a myriad of events that tend to occur less frequently than other types of employment problems. For example, only in the last few years has professional literature begun to appear on the privacy related issues of computerized personnel data security and access, smokers versus non-smokers rights, identification and reporting of those employees exposed to toxic or hazardous substances, and an assortment of labor relations activities that can give rise to privacy concerns. Legal decisions in these areas of privacy are sparse and not yet clearly developed. Of perhaps more frequent concern to employers as a privacy problem are those concerning medical evaluations, health conditions, and job safety.

1.41 MEDICAL EVALUATIONS

As mentioned earlier, employee medical records are the confidential property of the employer and, excepting those states that require an employer to allow employee examination of their medical records, they can be withheld from review. There is one general exception to this withholding rule, and that pertains to notifying the employee that a health problem has been discovered and they should consult with their own physician who may want or need to see the employer's medical evaluation report.

The most common situations in which employers are likely to obtain medical information that an unanticipated problem exists is during:

- Pre-employment medical exams
- Workers' compensation medical tests and evaluations
- Return-to-work physicals following layoff, leave of absence, or a questionable sick leave (e.g., contagious condition).

Employers should thoroughly review these medical reports and, if needed, consult with the hired physician to clarify terminology, the nature and effect of a particular medical condition, methods of treatment and prognosis. This information makes the employer better informed to discuss it with the employee; to give preliminary thought to the effect on the employee's job; to consider whether the condition might be work related; and to help the employee work through a needed course of action such as disability leave, medical coverage, and salary continuation.

Most physicians retained by an employer to conduct these kinds of medical evaluation will not divulge any medical problems discovered during the course of an examination or tests to the employee. It is therefore the employers responsibility to inform the employee of any unusual medical problem, which may be unknown to the employee. Rather than turning over the medical examination document to the employee or their personal physician, most employers prefer to simply advise the employee of the *possible* condition and suggest the employee be examined by their own physician. Should the employee's physician desire the employer's medical record(s), it is advisable to obtain the employee's written authorization and release.

1.42 HEALTH: SMOKING AND AIDS

Two of the most controversial and emotional workplace health issues that began in the 1980's are the effects of smokers on non-smokers and working with those afflicted with AIDS or ARC. Both issues are sensitive as they affect individual privacy rights as well as general employee rights no matter which side of the issue one takes. Once again, the employer's duty is to strike a workable balance between the opposing forces of employees' rights and the need to establish workplace controls.

Despite a few futile attempts, there is no constitutional basis for non-smoking employees to state a right to a smoke-free work environment. However, such rights do exist under OSHA (General Duty Clause) and many state labor laws. In fact, by the late 1980's numerous counties and cities initiated strict ordinances on smoking in public places such as office buildings, stores, public transportation, and restaurants. These ordinances have either prohibited or restricted smoking to designated areas. The fact that employees have smoking or non-smoking rights over their own health is a self-asserted one, including a degree of privacy with respect to their immediate workplace surrounding and the ventilation system that provides needed air to each employee. As one superior court judge stated in the case of Shimp v. New Jersey Bell (1976), "The right of the individual to risk his or her own health does not include the right to jeopardize the health of those who must remain around him or her in order to properly perform the duties of their job."

The right of non-smokers can be, and has been, put forth in a number of legal ways where there is little room for rebuttal by smoking employees. These legal causes of action include workers' compensation claims due to an employee's development of allergies, respiratory problems, or even cancer from secondary smoke exposure; employer negligence in providing a healthy work environment under OSHA; wrongful discharge where the employer fired rather than accommodated a complaining employee; or under handicap discrimination where one worker is physically affected by the smoke of others.

In other words, both smokers and non-smokers have a form of privacy rights, but ultimately it is non-smokers who can assert the greater right since they can demonstrate more victim-oriented cause for their rights to be protected. From a more purely practical point, both require accommodation, and most employers are finding that the best solution lies in establishing designated smoking areas and confining their use to rest and meal periods.

Employees afflicted with AIDS and ARC can raise a very serious privacy issue for employers. Typically, the employer learns that an employee is afflicted with AIDS/ARC through either medical examinations in which laboratory tests were performed, or directly from the employee whose health is declining and requires the use of sick and/or disability leave. The privacy aspect of an AIDS/ARC employee is twofold: first, the employer may not divulge the results of employment-related medical exams or an employee's medical condition to those who do not have the need or right to know; and, second, an employer's use of such information to make an adverse employment decision can violate state and/or federal handicap discrimination laws where AIDS has been included as a protected form of physical handicap that should be accommodated.

On the other side of the controversy are other employees whose health must also be protected from contagious diseases. The legal obligation of an employer to protect, take precautions, and disclose to other employees that an employee is afflicted with AIDS is just beginning to become a strong counter-privacy matter. It is also becoming increasingly more apparent through national media that AIDS may be more easily transmitted than initially publicized in an effort to abate undue fear. Until more information is brought forward by medical sources dealing with the problem, employers should continue to protect the privacy rights of those with AIDS/ARC, yet take precautionary measures to guard against the prospects of transmission to other employees (exposure to the afflicted person's bodily fluids), and provide good faith attempts to accommodate the absence needs of the employee as you would with an employee dealing with cancer or tuberculosis.

1.43 JOB SAFETY AND WORKER COMPENSATION INJURIES

There are two primary concerns for employers as they relate to employee rights, yet neither are privacy rights in the strictest sense of the term. Rather, they require the employer to either withhold and treat as confidential certain worker compensable job injury information, or to ensure that employees are aware that they are working with or exposed to toxic/hazardous substances (e.g., they possess a legal right-to-know under federal law).

However, with regard to some situations of an employee's job injury claim, you may have good reason to withhold certain documents related to the claim from access by the employee and others. Technically, the Supervisor's Report of Work Injury itself is a safety record of little importance other than to log lost workday accidents for OSHA compliance. It also serves as the initial document of a needed "paper trail" should it be, or later become, a worker compensable injury (i.e., singular incidents of minor back injuries may not require lost workdays or medical treatment, but they may evolve to a "cumulative" injury, or the aggravated injury resulting from preexisting conditions).

So, while this initial injury report—usually completed by the supervisor based on the employee's explanation—is almost routinely placed in the employee's primary personnel file, there are some situations in which this document should also be placed for a more confidential file in anticipation of probable medical reports by company paid doctors, investigative reports, workers' compensation hearing orders and judgments, and in extreme cases legal documents relating to court appeal of the claim. These documents are clearly the property of the employer and should be treated with the strictest confidence and security. The use of separate personnel files for such sensitive and confidential documents is discussed in detail in Chapter II: 2.

The more common situations that tend to create a need for worker compensable injuries to be set up a restricted access file are as follows:

1. You have reason to believe the employee has filed a false claim involving no witnesses, no evidence of injury, the employee is a malinger, or the employee found out they were about to be fired or laid off and you intend to conduct an internal investigation.

2. You believe the employee to be overstating the severity of their injury (in other words lying) in order to delay their return to work and enjoy the benefits (tax free in some states) for as long as possible. The typical injuries susceptible to this type of abuse are back injuries, stress (particularly emotional and psychological symptomology, and referred to as "cumulative trauma" in alleged advanced conditions), and an assortment of pains or restricted body movement. The reason attending physicians are reluctant to return employees to work who claim any of these conditions is that their actual condition is difficult if not medically impossible to substantiate, and the physician wants to avoid already abused malpractice suits. In other words, in conditions such as these, doctors merely have to rely on their patient telling the truth about their pain, limitation, or disorder.

At this point it becomes a selective judgment call for the employer. In cases where the employer is suspicious or develops reason to believe the disability is not as serious as being claimed by the injured employee, the employer may elect to call upon the worker compensation insurance carrier to have a "sub-rosa" investigation conducted. Alternatively, the employer may wish to have the carrier take depositions from the employee and any witnesses including the treating physician. These depositions, investigative evaluations, medical reports, and in some cases motion pictures of the employee engaged in physical activities they claim they can't do become instrumental defenses for the employer's rebuttal of potentially very costly claims—consider the cost of six months of benefits, lost workdays, payment of $35,000 to $50,000 for back surgery, and vocational rehabilitation expenses.

3. You may want to "subrogate" or share the employee's legitimate injury costs to another insurer. The other insurer can be either a former employer's workers' compensation carrier in the event the employee's injury can be medically established as the aggravated result of a preexisting injury with the former employer, or the other insurer can be your own former workers' compensation carrier who could be held responsible for sharing the cost of a present claim as a reinjury of the same condition under which a claim had been filed with your former carrier.

Generally, in order to subrogate a workers' compensation claim, you will need to conduct an investigation into the employee's former employment work injury records, or determine if the same injury occurred (for which a claim was filed) while the company was covered by another workers' compensation carrier—particularly if your company is now self-insured! In either case, you will also need a highly reputable physician (specialists are best) to provide you with a medical report that reasonably connects the cause or complicated condition of the current injury to a preexisting worker compensable injury during employment with a former employer or under your previous carrier.

In cases such as these, your goal may not be to argue the legitimacy of the claim, but moreso to defer at least some of the present and possible future costs connected to the injury, medical needs, and perhaps later (if not presently) the vocational rehabilitation of the injured employee. These records then are not only medical and investigatory documents, but they often lead to intricate litigation proceedings and they can be very personal records depending on the type and extent of the employee's injury. There are numerous anecdotal horror stories of complicated, extraordinarily expensive, and very personally sensitive worker compensable (job related) "injuries" such as rape, suicide, murder, homosexuality, and alcoholism. As these and other incidents develop or occur, and their related documentation, must be treated with the utmost confidentiality and extremely limited need-to-know access.

1.44 WORKPLACE PHOTOGRAPHY

One last area of privacy that may be of interest to many employers, particularly those in manufacturing or other security-oriented process operations, is the matter of photographing the work setting by outsiders. Most employers in the situation of wanting to protect trade secrets, processing methods, materials used, and the like, are understandably sensitive to any form of breach in security about product development. Under most circumstances, the company can put almost any type of control(s) or security measures in place to protect its commerce interest, excluding applicable branches of the federal government or judicial system who possess lawful access to the premises, employees, and records during authorized audits and investigations.

As a rule, these infrequent appearances by external authorities do not involve photographing the work setting, and results they produce are treated confidentially. However, a federal court in New York has determined that OSHA investigators may photograph plants and other facilities, even where trade secrets may be revealed in the photographs, so long as doing so is germane to the necessary analysis of the investigation. In Brock v. Nabisco Brands, Inc. (1986), the judge also indicated that while such photographs are permissable under these conditions, OSHA is obliged to treat the photographs as confidential documents.

By now, it is no doubt very apparent that a great deal of an employer's liability over mishandling privacy rights has to do with the treatment of sensitive employment documents. For this reason, I have dedicated the next chapter exclusively to the problems and solutions to proper records handling, and you are urged to continue your reading of Chapter II: 2 before taking any action that may infringe upon employee privacy rights.

CHAPTER II: 2.0
PROBLEMS WITH THE PRIVACY OF PERSONNEL
FILES AND EMPLOYMENT RECORDS

There are a number of different federal and state laws that require employers to acquire and maintain personal information on employees. These laws relate to wages, hours, fringe benefits, safety, discrimination, and the like. This information is not only legally mandated, but is also required to be retained for various periods of time after employment separation. Other, more discretionary information is collected by many employers as a matter of initial selection of employees and ongoing collection of information needed by the organization for the effective administration of its human resource program. While legally compelling information is essential, great care must be exercised in terms of the collection of discretionary information. The latter must be able to stand the test of pertinence to 1) the individual's job related activities, and 2) the organization's necessary use of the information in the administration of its human resource program (e.g., attendance records to evaluate sick leave usage).

2.10 OFFICIAL PERSONNEL FILES AND RECORDS

Most of the state laws adopted concerning personnel files and records address two types of privacy interests: 1) preventing release of information to third parties without the employee's consent (unless the third party is a contractual agent of the company); and 2) allowing employee inspection of their file—some states allow the employee to challenge the accuracy of its contents which has become a major concern of the courts. Other recently developed interests of the courts is a fairer handling of information in the II.2.47 file that is used in adverse decisions affecting the employee. These court interests include:

- Improper disclosure of information.

- Reckless maintenance of information.

- Not taking voluntary measures to periodically purge files of outdated or irrelevant derogatory material.

- Not applying the "fairness" principle in discharge cases by informing the employee about the presence of adverse information in their file and, prior to initiating the discharge, giving the employee a chance to correct inaccuracies or provide mitigating evidence (if the employee has it, you'll find out about it in court anyway!).

The compilation, maintenance, use, access, and disclosure of personnel records—whether by written or verbal means—is perhaps one of the most troublesome areas of employee privacy today. For that reason, special attention ought to be given to this aspect of the human resource program by professionals, and diligent care by all managers.

2.11 COMPILATION AND CONTENTS OF FILES

Initial compilation of employee personnel files typically starts with hire-in documents such as the employee's application form and/or resume, reference letters, and sometimes various reports related to medical, credit, bonding, citizenship, driving, and educational verification information in support of the selection decision. This and other personal information can only be obtained legally once the employer has expressed a *tentative* offer of employment to the individual.

Once the employee is hired and reports to work, other sensitive records are developed such as the orientation checklist and several forms upon which the employee divulges a great deal of personal information as it relates to payroll deductions for taxes and benefits, beneficiaries, emergency notifications, and the like. Thereafter, other documents emminating from either the human resources office, the employee's superiors, the employee, or interested third parties (unions, insurance and pension plan representatives, etc.) will begin to collect in the employee's file—each of which should receive close review by one person designated as the company's personnel records custodian. To name only a partial collection of the types of documents that are placed in personnel files or become a source of personnel data collection, are the following:

- Performance appraisals

- Changes in position, position title, pay rates, and benefits

- Work injury and medical/insurance reports

- Attendance Records

- Changes in personal information

- Requests for training and conferences

- Wage garnishment orders

- Investigative reports pertaining to safety, discrimination, or civil/ criminal violations

- Disciplinary warnings and notices

- Union registration

- Grievances and arbitration hearing reports

The two issues that are very important for employers to bear in mind is that: 1) employee personnel files are the property of the employer—not that of the employee— despite the fact that all information relates to the employee; and 2) each and every document in the file is confidential even though they may have varying degrees of sensitivity. The documents having the greatest sensitivity, and which employers may generally exclude from even the employee's knowledge (access), include:

- Medical reports including those related to workers' compensation.
- Employment references.
- Security, credit, and bonding reports.
- Investigative reports related to the employee's industrial injury, civil or crimi- nal activities, discrimination complaint, and similarly sensitive investigations.

2.12 SETTING UP PERSONNEL FILES

Most employers have established one official personnel file for their employees, but wonder what to do with a highly sensitive document once it emerges and recogni- tion is given to the issues of both privacy protection and restricted confidentiality. There are a couple of ways of overcoming this problem, the second of which is probably more effective and prudent than the first.

1. Place senitive documents in a sealed envelope with the notation, "Confidential Document—To Be Opened Only By (title of officer(s))". The inherent problem here is that these documents can create awkward bulk to the file, and creates curiosity or suspicion for the employee upon their review of the file.

2. Establish a second official file on all employees in which these sensitive and highly confidential documents are placed. There is no law prohibiting employ- ers from creating two official files, but they should be located in the same location under the official guardianship of one person—a records custodian so to speak—which is usually the Human Resource Director. They can be designated as File A for routine and ongoing personnel transaction records, and File B for sensitive and limited access records. This also reduces the prob-

lem of security for employers using computers to record employee information since only certain parts of File A data would be subject to computer input, and even that data should be coded for limited access security.

Even when personnel file information and data is stored in computer systems, many documents are required to be on file as "hard copy". The more common methods of maintaining hard copy documents is by either file size individual envelopes or file folders. Envelopes are hard to handle and easily become disorganized since nobody likes to file and they require removal of all documents in order to find the proper location of a new document. The preferred method is a heavy-duty legal size folder with two-hole fasteners at the top. The left side can be used for wage, benefit, promotion, attendance, and employment history data documents; and the right side for all other ongoing documents in reverse chronology (most recent on top).

Files can be established in simple alphabetic order, or in alphabetic order by the employee's department, geographic location, or some other designation by which the company finds useful for distinction. Files should also be stored in a secured area, and in file drawers with locks where only a few designated persons have the key. Fireproof file cabinets are a little more expensive, but are prudent investments in the case of personnel and other sensitive company records.

2.20 CONTROLLING ACCESS OF PERSONNEL RECORDS TO PROTECT PRIVACY INTERESTS

Other than determining what information is to be collected on employees and how to store it, access and use of file contents is the core of the file privacy issue. Employee privacy rights cannot be violated as long as no one knows what information the employer has in its possession and is never used. So the problem begins when someone—be it the employee, a supervisor or II.2.51 manager, or third person—sees or learns of the presence of private information, then uses it in some way that violates established law, legal position or principle, of the employee's due privacy.

2.21 GENERAL ACCESS AND USE OF FILE DOCUMENTS

In addition to those situations and causes of action already mentioned, there are a couple of other legal conditions that bear more directly upon personnel files and records, and they are:

1. NEGLIGENT MAINTENANCE/FAILURE TO USE DUE CARE

This relates broadly to the mishandling of file records such as in:

• Providing employment reference information.

- Determining what constitutes relevant information in a file in conjunction with a disclosure process (i.e., giving only pertinent and applicable information in relation to the needed source of disclosure).

- Placing, or allowing the placement of, false information in a file.

- Providing others false information about the employee even if the information is not particularly damaging to the employee.

- Failure to keep records accurate and current; failure to keep consistent records among employees.

- Providing information to any person who does not have a legitimate right to know.

Because the issue concerning due care of records is one of their handling, the liability is slightly different than a cause of action for libel which requires the element of publication such as revealing private information to some other person(s) who do not have the right to know. However, both libel and negligent maintenance are tortious actions.

A good example of a tortious due care violation was in *Bulkin v. Western Kraft East* (1976), where a paper box manufacturer laid off salesmen due to a paper shortage. Plaintiff was one of those salesmen who thought he left the company under favorable conditions since the company gave him both a letter of recommendation and a letter of introduction to help in his job search. The salesman subsequently learned that his former employer had damaged his credit rating by filing a report with the credit bureau asserting the employee's departure by "mutual agreement" over his poor sales record. The salesman alleged that he was the subject of a false report as the result of negligent maintenance of his records, and the court agreed. You may ask, "If the information filed by the employer was damaging, why didn't the salesman file a defamation suit?" The answer may well be that the information was not false; rather, it was different than what he was told and he suffered from its disclosure in terms of its effect upon new employment. (See also *Quinones v. U.S.*, 1974, and *Moessmer v. U.S.*, 1983)

2. FALSE IMPRESSION

This relates to the selection of words—written or spoken and intentional or unintentional—that puts the employee in false light concerning their employment, past employment, or other private circumstance. Examples of false impression can be such things as a generic use of the word "terminated" or "termination" to mean any type of employment separation. The word clearly infers that the employer was the moving party (*Patton v. Royal Industries,* 1968). Specific terms should be used in reference to former employees such as resigned, laid off, retired, mutually separated, or discharged. Other references, too, can create false impressions by inference such as:

- The former employer indicating the employee is not subject to rehire (there can be any number of harmless policy reasons for this position, but the inference is the employee did something inexcusable).

- A supervisor telling other employees, "I think we've solved the theft problem" following the transfer, demotion, reassignment, or discharge of one of the employees in the work unit.

There are an endless number of examples to demonstrate false impression, but the point is the same—it is the transmitting of information that tends to create an impression or conclusion by inference about an employee that results in an inaccurate portrayal of them.

2.22 INTERNAL ACCESS TO FILES

From a purely legal perspective, only employers in those states that mandate employee access to their own personnel file, and federal government agencies, are required to let the employee review their file. But let's back away from this technical point for a moment to look at the more practical aspects of why the file exists in the first place, and how it is used operationally.

First, as it has been mentioned, the file is confidential and the property of the employer. That requires certain security measures but not an armed guard. There are particular individuals in any organization that may have legitimate need-to-know rights to access, review, and modify (add, delete, correct) file documents during the normal course of transacting a variety of employment matters. These internal company representatives, aside from the employee, consist of:

- The Human Resources Director who has ultimate internal responsibility for establishing and maintaining personnel files.

- Human Resource staff whose job requires access to files for analysis or records processing purposes.

- Senior, companywide officers who have some stated and relevant purpose for access (Controller, General Manager, Executive Director, President, etc.).

Each of these individuals must have a legitimate company or employee interest in order to establish their right-to-know, and they ought to have a special purpose in seeing or doing anything with the file. Under most circumstances, the file should never leave the area in which it is kept. To accommodate internal access then, there should be a desk or other review station within eyeshot of the person who is responsible for monitoring those allowed access.

There are a few rather grand mistakes employers should avoid concerning internal access by company representatives. One is never allow supervisors to use the file as a depository for assorted hand written notes, however informal and harmless they may seem at the time. Supervisors should be instructed to keep ongoing logs of job related performance, conduct, attendance and other employment related information for purposes of preparing performance appraisals or disciplinary notices which, then and only then, become official file records.

Second, never allow co-workers or indirect managers access to an employee's file even if the co-worker is a union steward trying to represent the employee's (grievance) interest, or the manager is a high ranking official but lacks a direct relationship to the employee and has no relevant purpose. Such was the case with a Marketing Director who gained access to an attractive secretary's file (in another department) to ascertain if she was married and, if not, to get her home telephone number since he couldn't find it in the telephone directory. He called, she questioned then objected, and she now probably owns a few shares in the company with the proceeds from her suit.

With regard to co-workers being provided confidential information about an employee, the general rule is *never,* but the California case of *Duffy v. City of Oceanside* (1986) provides an unusual exception concerning an employer's duty to warn a particular (interested) employee about another employee's criminal record. In 1978, Duffy informed her supervisor that she was being sexually harassed by a co-worker, Larroquette. Duffy was not then nor thereafter made aware of the fact that Larroquette was on parole for kidnapping, rape, and sexual assult. During the ensuing four and one-half years, Duffy and Larroquette developed a friendly working relationship, but in May 1983, Larroquette kidnapped and murdered Duffy. The Court of Appeal, in finding for Duffy's children, determined that releasing information to all female employees would have been improper but, under the circumstances that Larroquette focused his obvious attention on Duffy, the employer owed a duty to warn Duffy.

Employee access to their own personnel file is a persistently debated topic even in those states where such is mandated to some extent. Beyond meeting any prevailing statutory requirements, the issue becomes one of the organization's (upper management) philosophy. Parameters concerning access for employees are used to frame this philosophy. Decisions must be made concerning:

- Whether or not to allow employee access if not required by law; and if so, where, when, and how often it can be reviewed;

- Should the employee be allowed to copy, challenge, or supplement its contents;

- What documents should be excluded from review;

• Who will observe to ensure nothing is removed; and

• Can the employee authorize someone else to review the file?

There are doubtless other questions that will come up when deliberating this matter, but beyond statutory requirements it is a matter of management discretion. So long as care and reasonable caution is exercised by the custodian of personnel files, most employers' experience has shown that an open policy of employee access contributes to a higher level of employee trust, confidence, morale, and general employee relations; while a non- or overly limited access position breeds suspicion, paranoia, and mistrust.

In a joint survey by Prentice-Hall and the American Society for Personnel Administration (ASPA) on the employee access policies of 600 ASPA members, the following results were reported:[1]

	Mfrs.	Offices	Banks	Ins. Firms	Hosp.	Wholesale/ Retail	Educ. Inst.	Utilities
Written request required	37%	30%	60%	49%	60%	40%	100%	44%
Personnel staffer present	95	80	93	88	95	92	90	100
Employee can photocopy	37	48	68	30	53	43	70	15
Employer will photocopy	44	35	34	47	65	71	50	47
Access limit: once a year	10	8	9	7	17	12	10	5
twice a year	15	4	11	7	13	4	5	34
unlimited	66	88	80	86	70	84	85	61
other	9	-	-	-	-	-	-	-
Employee can attach statement	85	84	99	97	78	84	90	94

Those employers responding consisted of 225 manufacturers, 93 offices, 69 insurance companies, 65 financial institutions, 63 hospitals, 50 wholesale and retail companies, 20 private education institutions, and 18 utilities. In terms of employer size, 90 respondents were small (under 500 employees), 75 were medium (500-1999), 46 large (2,000-10,000), and 14 the largest (over 10,000).

The results of the survey seems to support the notion that employers are taking a more liberal, open stance on employee access to their own file information, even to the extent of an extraordinarily high number of employers allowing unlimited (frequency) access. It is also true that denying employees access and rebuttal to the basic contents of their file can be damaging evidence against an employer attempting to defend an employee's privacy claim. Take the case of *Stoller v. Marsh* (1982, cert. denied 1983) where an employee successfully held that position where unfavorable performance appraisals dating back several years should not have been considered in his denial of

[1] Reprinted with permission from Personnel Management – Policies & Practices @ Prentice-Hall Information Services, Paramus, NJ.

promotion since 1) he was never allowed to see or challenge these evaluations, and 2) an investigation of each negative evaluation was never conducted, (see also *Bigelow v. Village Board, New York,* 1984).

2.23 ACCESS BY THIRD PARTIES

Most external third parties who may desire or have a need to examine otherwise confidential personnel files can be placed in three categories:

1. Those who represent the employee's interests.
   * Union business agent
   * Private attorney

2. Those representing the employer's interests.
   * Company legal counsel or retainer attorney
   * Human resource consultants
   * Company insurance representatives
   * Special investigators (security and bonding personnel)

3. Those representing compliance activities.
   * OSHA and NIOSH investigators
   * EEOC and state fair employment representatives
   * FBI and Department of Justice agents
   * Courts (subpeona)

Not all of these representatives have an automatic right to access any personnel record they wish, and not all records in any particular file are pertinent to their purpose which is the first thing that needs to be established. Once the purpose for access is established, the company's "records custodian" needs to determine: 1) is the purpose proper and necessary; 2) should access be allowed, do we want access, or do we have to allow access; 3) which individual files are involved, and of those, what records and documents are pertinent to examination; and, 4) should copies of any documents be copied and allowed to be given to the external representatives. If the company determines there is a legitimate purpose and allows an external access to certain files and documents, the company's records custodian should participate in the actual examination process. In some cases, it may be worthwhile for the records custodian to privately go through each designated file to see if there are any highly sensitive documents that ought to be excluded from external examination. The general principles that apply to access by external representatives are:

* That a balance must be striken between the employee's privacy rights and the legitimate interests of the company's disclosure.

* That some attention ought to be given to isolating disclosure to only documents and files relevant to the purpose.

• That the employee's written consent to disclose or release information should be sought beforehand when it is appropriate to the access or disclosure.

Access By Employee Representatives

As a general rule of thumb, it is *not* a given requirement for an employer to allow access by a union business agent (and in particular to not allow another employee who is a union steward) to an employee's personnel file. This is true even if the union is advancing the employee's grievance which might relate in some way to contents of the file (absence records, disciplinary notices, etc.). This is, of course, contrary to what the union's business agent will tell you since denying access opposes their view of reasonably representing their member's interest. However, employers should automatically deny the union's request since the decision can vary by a number of differing circumstances.

Union complaints filed with the National Labor Relations Board (NLRB) have usually been decided in favor of the union (does that surprise you?), but not all such decisions have been upheld by the courts. For example, in the 1983 New Jersey Bell case mentioned earlier, the Michigan Supreme Court overturned an NLRB decision and thereby supported the employer's refusal to allow the union access to psychological test scores that were in the respective employee files. However, in *Salt River Valley Water Users Association v. NLRB* (1984), a federal appeals court held that the employer should not deny union access to the file of two employees. The employee, represented by the union in this case, was suspended for sleeping on the job, while another employee had a concurrent arbitration case pending where he was fired for the same offense. Yet another NLRB decision that was not appealed involved the union's desire to examine the personnel files of several employees in preparation of an arbitration case involving an employee discharged for refusing to submit to a sobriety test. In *Washington Gas Light Co. v. NLRB* (1984), the union wanted to establish how the company handled other similar cases and its consistency in discharge decisions. The NLRB determined the union should have access to particular personnel files, but not medical records in those files.

In other words, it is not appropriate to summarily reject a union's request to examine personnel files. If their purpose is legitimate and does not infringe upon the company's interest in protecting employee privacy rights (or other confidential/sensitive information involving company security), then it may be entirely reasonable under some circumstances to allow union inspection of the file(s) or parts thereof. The same holds true where the employee has retained private legal counsel. In these situations the attorney will normally obtain a subpeona to access (copy or inspect) the file. In either case the employer ought to do two things; 1) consult with an experienced labor attorney, and 2) notify the employee of the request for access (don't assume they've thought through all the contents of their file) and see if the employee is willing to provide a written consent.

Further, there are two important things for the employer to avoid; 1) never allow access or release of personnel documents when "demanded" by letters from attorneys or insurance representatives until you've resolved their legitimate purpose and other aspects of propriety to release information, and 2) never "sanitize" (purge documents) a particular employee's personnel file for the purpose of eliminating evidence that may be detrimental to the company's interests.

Concerning the issue of "sanitizing" personnel files, I learned of an (ex)client company who did just that. The situation involved two Senior Vice Presidents; one a male, the other a female, and both with about four years service and several differences in their personality that periodically resulted in cold war clashes. Unbeknown to the female, the male had politically gained the favor of the company president who was being fed misleading accounts of the female's behavior and decisions. Finally, the president told the male to go downstairs, stop by the personnel office and remove all of her performance evaluations from her personnel file, then go tell her that she's fired and give her 30 minutes to clear out her personal effects and wait in her office to make sure no company property was removed. Having been treated this abruptly and without any idea or notice of what reasonable case the company might have for such action, she sued. During her attorney's depositions it was discovered that the president ordered the Senior Vice President to sanitize her personnel file (of positive performance appraisals), and the company quickly reached an out-of-court settlement of a sizeable amount.

The issue of attorney demands, or even subpeonas, for "any and all" personnel records of an employee—irrespective of whether or not the employee(s) is represented by the attorney—is simply not appropriate in most instances given the more dominant interest of privacy rights. This issue was made clear in *El Dorado Savings and Loan v. Superior Court* (1987) where, once again, an appellate court overturned a trial court's decision compelling the employer to turn over personnel records of a male employee. In this case, a group of former female employees retained an attorney to sue the employer on grounds of sex and age discrimination, alleging the male employee was receiving better pay and benefits while occupying the same job. The employer rightfully denied the attorney access to the male employee's file.

The California Court of Appeal, in overturning the lower court's decision made special note of the male employee's right to privacy as provided in the state constitution. The court went on to say that the trial court ought to first examine whether there is a less intrusive means of obtaining relevant information, such as deposing the male employee, and that by no means was the entire personnel file relevant to the discrimination claim in question. The court ultimately ordered the trial court to inspect the male employee's file in private and then order a disclosure of only that information relevant to the discrimination claim.

Access By Employer Representatives

Under most circumstances where there exists a legitimate company interest related to the access or disclosure of personnel file information to an external agent of the company, such disclosure is considered qualified privilege information. That is, it is confined to a particular company agent who has a specific purpose that serves a reasonable business interest of the company where only pertinent files and documents are examined, and the agent maintains confidentiality over the contents of what is disclosed. Additionally, the information provided by the agent to the company (e.g., situational discussion of confidential information and recommended course(s) of action), whether presented verbally or in writing, is generally protected as privileged information that does not need to be disclosed to others nor subject to liability so long as the information exchange is maintained as confidential.

Access By Compliance Representatives

Generally, any representative of a state or federal government compliance agency has a regulatory right to inspect personnel files and other records of the company relating to their official charge and the nature of their investigation. In fact, in many cases of compliance representative it is compulsory for the employer to cooperate fully and promptly upon their presentation of proper identification and a reasonable statement of the purpose of their investigation; both of which the records custodian should require.

The third consideration for the records custodian before allowing access is to determine if the compliance representative is from an agency having proper jurisdiction over the matter of inquiry as well as the employer. For example, employers with fewer than 25 employees are considered exempt from many federal non-discrimination laws, and therefore may not have to open their personnel files or otherwise be answerable to an investigation by the Equal Employment Opportunity Commission. If, however, the same employer were not exempt from similar state non-discrimination laws, the employer would have to respond to state compliance agency representatives investigating the same or a different claim.

One employer who was not exempt from the EEOC's jurisdiction discovered that the agency does in fact have the right to inspect confidential personnel records if such inspection is germane to the claim in *EEOC v. Franklin and Marshall College* (1985). Here, the Third Circuit Court of Appeal upheld the EEOC's right to inspect performance evaluations of a foreign professor completed by other faculty even though the documents were understood to be confidential. The court essentially said that the mission of the EEOC was a greater interest than maintaining absolute confidentiality of such records.

The two most common circumstances that can bring compliance representatives to the workplace are routine inspections and response to complaints filed by employees or other effected persons. Routine inspections are usually scheduled with the employer, but they can also be unscheduled drop-ins where their primary objective is to see something under actual, unprepared conditions—general safety and job hazards is an example of routine drop-ins by OSHA inspectors. The most prevalent reason for compliance representative appearances is, of course, in response to a claim of some wrongdoing by the employer that has been filed by a single or group of employees. Claims can involve discrimination, wage and hour, health and safety, alien hiring, and other kinds of legally controlled practices of which the employer might be guilty of violation, and employees have a legal right to report alleged violations *without reprisal or recrimination* from their employer.

This situation is well illustrated by a vast array of cases over the last several decades, but as it relates to the privacy of personnel files, the case of *U.S. v. Westinghouse* (1980) decided by the Third Circuit Court of Appeal stands out. This case involved a 1978 inspection of a plant in which employees claimed an allergic reaction to a chemical used in epoxy molding. A team from the National Institute for Occupational Safety and Health (NIOSH) appeared to investigate the claim.

NIOSH is the research and development component of federal OSHA, and is responsible for making recommendations on standards to alleviate problems rather than having enforcement capabilities. The NIOSH team found the original problem had been corrected, but another chemical being used could have the same effect. As part of their evaluation, they requested and were denied access to employee medical records knowing that the company voluntarily conducted annual medical examinations. The company's denial was based on their interest in protecting employee privacy, even after NIOSH obtained a subpeona and later a favorable decision from the trial court.

On appeal by the company, the court concluded that there is a genuine interest for employers and employees alike to protect the privacy rights of individuals from government intrusion into those matters of confidence that are not relevant. Therefore, only that information that is relevant to the nature of the investigation is accessible to such government representatives, and even then it may be subject to each effected employee's consent to permit examination of those particular documents (medical records in this case).

In many instances such as the Westinghouse case, it is fairly common for the compliance agency representative to want to inspect certain records in other employee files who may not even know an investigation is being conducted. The reason for examining other employee records is for some type of comparative evaluation. So, when an investigation extends beyond access to relevant documents in the claimant's personnel file, the company is within its right to be concerned about protecting the privacy interests of other employees that may become a part of the investigation. In protecting that right, the company may either challenge the agency's right in toto or in part (confining inspection only to relevant information). If the latter approach is taken, the company should either inform effected employees that an agency inspection of (specifically named) information within their file is being made in conjunction with a lawfully filed claim, or the company may seek employee written consent.

Company records other than those contained in employee personnel files may also be requested for inspection by compliance agency representatives, but those records are generally not protected by employee related privacy laws. Examples might include such general records as payroll reports, affirmative action data, and lost workday injury records. In this regard, employers ought to keep in mind that, while you have a legitimate right and an obligation to protect employee privacy, undue withholding or caution about obvious records needed to be seen in a particular investigation will likely provoke suspiciousness on the part of the investigator. In many cases, these public official investigators have rather broad authority of how detailed their investigations can be. A knowledgeable, non-obstructive employer is much more likely to be seen as having nothing to fear from an investigator who simply wants to get on with their job since they have better things to do than get entangled with what may appear to be a concealing employer. Make life easier for yourself by cooperating politely and to the fullest extent that circumstances will permit.

2.30 ESTABLISHING AN ACCESS POLICY

For those employers who truly desire a forthright and open approach to matters of employee privacy rather than leaving the issue subject to quizical and suspicious minds, it can prove very worthwhile to publish and disseminate a company policy. Prior to adoption and release of such a policy, the company should enlist the help of qualified legal and human resource advisors, as well as internal key managers, to identify various components and conditions of such a policy as thoroughly as possible. It is important to think through various scenarios based on the collective experience of these individuals; to obtain a current and clear understanding about state laws and legal decisions; and to realize that written policies do not apply only to those in which the company wants a particular outcome.

Each employer's development of a policy on access to personnel files and related information may well be different because of unique conditions of the business, state laws, or management philosophy. As a means of at least starting the process of deliberating what components and conditions might be included in an access policy, the following are some preliminary items to consider.

1. Identifying the kind(s) of information obtained and maintained by the company on employees. You may wish to mention specific information about the contents of File A (routine and ongoing personnel documents) and only gener-

ally about the contents of File B (sensitive and highly confidential documents).

2. What information the employee can access (File A), or review and how often.

3. The employee's right to have copies of what kinds of documents.

4. Where, when, and under what circumstances the employee can review their file (or any other limiwill be monitored).

5. Whether employees have the right to rebut or challenge certain document statements; if so, by when and how.

6. What othe internal or third parties might have access to personnel file (need-to-know principle). You may want to distinguish access by others to Files A or B, or both.

7. What information will be disclosed to a verified prospective future employer upon a reference inquiry; with, or without, the employee's signed authorization to do so.

8. How long after employment separation the employee has to request (in writing) a review of their file.

2.40 DEALING WITH EMPLOYMENT REFERENCES

As it was alluded to earlier, the disclosure of information on former employees to prospective employers has become a highly guarded process by nearly all employers. Employer restraint is due to the vulnerability of defamation suits filed by these former employees who did not get the job because information given the prospective employer was in some respect adverse, and was found to be defaming. The problem becomes more pronounced since it has two opposing effects on employers. First and foremost, employers want to protect their liability for making unintentional defamatory statements about former employees, and second, employers find it difficult to obtain information about prospective new hires from their former employers that would aid in the selection decision among finalist job applicants. So it has become a two-dimensional process; if you don't give, you can't expect to receive.

Defamation Liability

Defamation itself, as previously defined, generally has the components of libel and slander. Libel is written while slander is verbal. The majority of (past) employment-related defamation suits have been based on slander or verbally casting false light on the former employee. This means that the reference was given verbally—usually over the phone—where the former employer representative either said something slanderously false ("he's a thief"), or something was said that inherently created a false impression ("I wouldn't expect him to always tell the truth").

The common thread in most defamation suits is that whatever was said about the former employee was not truthful or based on evidenciary fact. Even when the former employer does possess factual evidence of a serious nature such as related to theft, fraud, falsification, incompetence, and the like, employers must still respond to reference inquiries with considerable caution. This is particularly true if the employer's evidence has not been tested for its strength in a court of law, arbitration hearing, or similar ajudicary process with formal rules and tests of evidence (e.g., *Harrison v. Arrow Metal Products,* 1970).

While many courts differ widely on their view of reference defamation based on those cases brought before them, it is worth noting the following conditions that can give rise to a defamation suit.

1. A defaming statement is made by one employer to another about a particular former employee.

2. The result or effect of the statement was damaging to the former employee (s/he did not get the job solely because of the reference statement).

3. The former employer giving the reference is guilty of creating the defamatory statement.

These considerations, then, would lead one to conclude that so long as truthful and factual statements are made, the former employer (you) has little to worry about. In most courts that's true, but there are still other courts who adhere to a much more conservative test of defamation. Those courts would likely hold that most any evidence possessed by a former employer would not necessarily be relevant in a situation of new employment where conditions were going to be different in some respect; unless of course the employee's past transgression was of a criminal nature and the former employer could prove it!

Providing Nondefamatory Reference Information

Each circumstance of an employment reference is different depending on the employee's history with the former employer and conditions surrounding the separation. Giving other employers the time-honored "name, rank, and serial number" information about former employees is absolutely useless for the intended purpose, and we all know it. It is an overreaction to legal vulnerability that has finally begun to run its course with more rational thinking taking the place of heretofore blanket prohibitions. The courts are indeed becoming more sophisticated in their evaluations of employment matters over the last few decades, and more cases are now being decided on individual merit rather than cursory application of general if not vague principles. What this more balanced legal approach to defamation means to the former employer is that more reference information can be safely and appropriately given so long as it is within reasonable parameters and the context of employment.

Therefore, to begin overcoming the dual problem of defamation liability and the inability to obtain worthy information from other employers, it is time for all employers to consider taking the following approach to reference inquiries.

1. Ask the caller for their name, title, company, and phone number. Tell the caller you'll have to check the former employee's file and talk to their supervisor before you can answer any questions. By calling them back, you can verify the caller is who they say they are. Also, ask the caller if they've obtained a written authorization from the former employee to acquire past employment information specifically from your company (you can insist on receiving a copy of the employee's release if you wish).

2. Centralize the task of responding to past employment inquiries to one person who is knowledgeable and well trained in employee privacy issues including state laws and court decisions. This should be the only person to receive and respond to such inquiries.

3. A thorough review of the former employee's personnel file and any other employment-related records should be made along with a brief discussion with the former employee's supervisor to obtain any overall, updated, reflective, or "unpublished" information.

4. Keep notes for placement in the former employee's personnel file reflecting the date, caller, nature of the inquiry, position applied for, questions asked by the caller, and information given.

5. Give consideration to providing the following information:
   • Dates of employment and positions held.
   • Training received.
   • Employee's stated reason for leaving (if applicable).
   • Strengths, accomplishments, weaknesses, or problem areas of their skill, knowledge, or abilities as determined by objective and unbiased evaluations and other performance related reports.

As a rule, all information that is provided to a reference caller should be known by the former employee either by being told during employment or by their knowledge of personnel file contents. Just about all other information that might be requested should be regarded as confidential to the former employer and not necessarily relevant to new employment. If the employee was fired or allowed to resign under derogatory conditions, you're better off asking the caller what reason did the former employee give and, if it corresponds, then simply acknowledge it without elaboration. If, however, the reason given is different than actual circumstances, or is seriously misleading, tell the caller you will only clarify that issue if they will give you a letter guaranteeing that their company will treat the disclosure as a qualified privilege.

This was the finding of a federal judge with agreement by the Third Circuit Court of Appeal in *Zuschek v. Whitmoyer Laboratories* (1987). Here, the former employer responded to an employment inquiry by stating the former manager was "intelligent and hard-working", but he was also "very dictatorial, quite devious, and often demoralizing". The reference further observed that the manager could be very effective if placed under close supervision. Generally, to be considered a qualified privilege, the information given must be true, and it must be a good faith response to someone who has a legitimate interest and will treat the information as confidential. The privilege can be lost if the former employer goes beyond those two conditions, as in the case of *Costas v. Olson* (1976) where the former employer volunteered that the employee might not be trustworthy, or it can be lost if the receiver of the information publishes or broadcasts the information to any other person(s) not having a proper interest.

Self Publication Liability

Yet another periodic occurrence related to references where employers could experience liability for defamation is an area referred to as self publication. This involves the former employee's own disclosure of the reason they were separated from employment—because it was the reason given to them and they're simply being truthful by disclosing the reason to a prospective employer—but the reason itself is defamatory. In other words, the reasons and conditions connected to their discharge forces or otherwise obliges them to defame themselves.

While most courts will not hold an employer liable for defamation in the case of self disclosure by the former employee, the issue takes on an entirely different complexion when the employer is responsible for creating a self defamation disclosure to prospective employers. Such was the decision of the Minnesota appellate court in *Lewis v. Equitable Life Assurance Society* (1985) where a supervisor fired four employees and compelled them to tell future employers they were fired for "gross insubordination". The situation involved these employees returning from a business trip and submiting vouchers for their actual expenses. Their supervisor ordered them to submit new vouchers claiming lower expenses which they refused to do, and were subsequently fired. The court held the company responsible for libel under the exception that libel can occur when one person compels another to disclose defaming information to someone else, and that the person compelling self disclosure could reasonably foresee the damaging effect.

In a somewhat similar situation, the U.S. Supreme Court allowed a lower court's award of over $2.7 million in damages to a Houston insurance salesman by his former brokerage firm. The case of *Frank B. Hall & Co. v. Buck* (1985) proved that it can be very costly to slander a former employee, particularly to a "prospective employer". Here, the prospective employer was a detective hired by the terminated salesman to ascertain what kind of reference his former employer was offering. The managers of the brokerage firm characterized the salesman as a "classical sociopath", "a zero", and "lacking in scruples". Those statements cost the company $1.9 million for libel and slander, $479,000 for breach of contract, and $335,00 attorney's fees (see also *Austin v. The Torrington Company,* 1985).

On that rather costly note, it would be worth your while to now delve into another frequently and costly area of employment litigation pertaining to a different type of infringement upon employee rights: that being the wrongful actions of employers in handling employee discharges. Chapters 8 and 9 are dedicated to these problems associated with employee rights, and the particular steps managers should take to prevent or solve these formidable legal repercussions.

CHAPTER II: 3.0
PROBLEMS OF WRONGFUL DISCHARGE, PART I:
WHY EMPLOYEES SUE, LEGAL BACKGROUND, AND
FIRING FOR GOOD CAUSE

Chapters II: 3 and 4 are divided into two parts and they address one of the newest forms of employee rights. These rights are perhaps best expressed as a sort of law-abiding, evenhanded and honest relationship with the employer. Like other kinds of employee rights, the issue of wrongful discharge as an illegal deprivation of rights focuses on the type of treatment received by the employee from the employer—including such representatives as supervisors, managers, executives, and human resource professionals who are advisors in matters relating to working conditions and terminations.

The rights due employees under wrongful discharge theory, then, consist of the employer's abidance by its own policies and rules; fair and reasonable treatment; good faith decision making (where the intent is to serve legitimate business rather than personal interests); abiding to the terms of an employment contract; and not making continue employment contingent upon the illegal actions of employees. Chapter 3 will give the reader important background insight into these issues, while Chapter 4 provides a more detailed discussion of particular legal problems, the employment situation that created the unlawful employer action, and how to solve these kinds of problems.

FIRE ME AND I'LL SUE seems to have become the battle cry of employees beginning in the early 1980's. In some states, suing former employers has become quite profitable for both employees and their attorneys. The legal cause of action is referred to as wrongful discharge and it is based on relatively new legal theories aimed at creating a greater balance of power in the heretofore employer-dominated, at-will employment relationship. The term at-will refers to any employee who works for their employer without a written employment contract covering a fixed term of employment. At-will employment, in essence, allows an employer or employee the mutual right to terminate the employment relationship at any time, for any reason, and with or without advance notice to the other, is the product of state labor law.

There is no federal law per se that addresses this aspect of the employer-employee relationship. Unlike discrimination and other types of employment law that provide such "make whole" monetary remedies as reinstatement and back pay, wrongful discharge is a tort claim and represents a considerable monetary liability for all employers whether suits are won or lost. For example, in California—which, by the way, is one of the most active and liberal states along with Michigan struggling with these suits— 70 percent of the 51 cases that went to court between October 1979 through January 1984 were won by employees. The average jury award was $178,184, while the 19 largest awards averaged $553,318. Even if wrongful discharge suits are won by employers, the average cost for legal fees alone approximates $100,000, which is why even more cases are settled out of court, but at sizeable settlement costs.

3.10 WHY SOME EMPLOYEES SUE AND WHO ARE THEY?

As managers of our organization's human resources, we might well ask ourselves "why do seemingly conscientious, dedicated, and hard-working employees become disloyal and sue their employer when terminated from their jobs?" While many of you may seriously question whether these former employees were ever conscientious, dedicated, and hard-working, we should first separate terminated employees into four groups:

1. Those justifiably fired who were poor employees.

2. Those justifiably fired who were good employees but declined.

3. Those poor employees fired for reasons other than their performance or conduct (e.g., pretextual or discriminatory reasons).

4. Those good employees fired for unjust cause.

Generally speaking, those in the first category don't pursue legal remedies nearly as frequently as the others because litigation is risky for both parties, poor workers usually know it, and they usually recognize that their former employer can demonstrate their deficiencies. Similarly, those in the second category might have once possessed a dedicated, work-ethic orientation toward their job and employer, but they recognize the futility of defending their own performance or behavioral decline— presuming, of course, management did a proper job of pointing it out—and chose not to sue.

Those in the third category make up probably the largest group of troublesome employees for most employers. These are the employees who bend and test personnel policies, who are behavioral thorns in the side of supervisors, who disrupt and/or antagonize others, and who frequently demonstrate the "I'm in this world for what I can get out of it" behavior often referred to as an *instrumental* work orientation—but they never seem to create a good or sufficient reason, or condition, under which they can be terminated for solid cause. Therefore, managers often become so frustrated with this type of employee, and their own inability to do anything about it based on necessary standards of termination, that they will get fed up and fabricate some other secondary reason to justify a firing. There is a better way to deal with these employees which will be discussed not only later in this chapter, but by more specific examples in Part II, Chapter 4, and Part III, Chapter 3. The point here is that these employees will seek external redress of their termination if there is adequate reason for them to believe their termination to be one of pretext, deceit, or conspiracy. Surprisingly enough, many workers in this category can be bright and efficient performers but other aspects of their work render them poor employees.

Employees in the fourth category, and some in the third category, tend to be those conscientious, dedicated, hard-working employees during employment, but most prone to file formal complaints or sue their employer when terminated for pretextual reasons, without warning or stated good cause, and/or when the notice is handled poorly such as being insensitive, brutally blunt, second hand, or impersonal. So why do they sue? Consider these preexisting conditions.

Unrepresented Professionals

It has been estimated that between 70-80 percent of the approximately two million employees terminated each year are from the managerial, professional, and technical ranks of organizations and do not have their interests represented by collective bargaining agreements which usually provide grievance and arbitration mechanisms for their members. These "unrepresented" employees choose to sue for the same reasons other employees unionize—to obtain protective review of real or perceived mistreatment by management representatives who oversee their work, and who possess considerable inherent authority to influence their employee's economic, social, and emotional well being. For this group of exempt and unclassified employees, few employers offer so much as an internal complaint mechanism but may, at best, have such termination decisions reviewed for justification or alternative correction by an impartial manager.

But, you say, these are particularly at-will employees so why create an impediment to spontaneous terminations. To this, I would remind you that they are human beings first, paycheck-cashing employees second, and third a workforce group that rises high above all others in loyalty, decision making, and cognitive skills *so long as they maintain a vested interest in their employment.* When that interest is abused or taken away—

especially in a malicious manner—they'll retaliate or fight back in the only way available, and they'll do it with vigor!

Emotional Pride

Together with death of a close family member and divorce, being fired is right up there with the most painful and disorienting emotional events in life. It is well recognized that managers and supervisors tend to avoid dealing with employee conflicts, disciplinary actions, performance reviews, and terminations because of the nature of this type of interaction. These are almost always difficult, feared, and frequently botched forms of workplace interaction. If mishandled, both the employee and supervisor know the relationship can deteriorate to even more uncomfortable interaction.

Emotionally, most employees within the management, professional, and technical ranks possess and operate under the force of their pride—in their abilities, accomplishments, occupation, and industry. Emotional pride can be positively reinforced by recognition (thereby motivating the employee), or it can be negatively reinforced by mistreatment (thereby lowering morale or worse). Employees with a strong sense of emotional pride often have very firm principles of right and wrong, good and not so good, and fair versus unfair. They may not agree among themselves about such principles on any given topic, but their convictions are strong as you have probably witnessed in meetings and routine interaction with them. These principles can also have the strength of being blinding to its possessor, and when it happens they can become tunnel-visioned and/or risk everything to prove their point (win—or at least put up a good fight).

Being fired is damaging to one's ego, self-esteem, and sense of balance. That's painful enough, but when it's done without obvious reason, good cause, dignity, or some element of justice, the human psyche will sometimes look to the strength of one's principles to determine whether they should feel immobilized, move on to another endeavor, or fight back by suing. The length, time, or cost of the fight becomes secondary to the pursuit of their principles and sense of justice.

So, there are at least two types of the FIRE ME AND I'LL SUE employees: the one who uses it (or its implication) during employment as a threatening, manipulative device to keep superiors at-bay; and the one who acts on their principles after being terminated in a truly or perceived unjustified way or reason. Having reviewed more court cases and dealing with professional accounts of discipline and termination actions over the years than I care to think about, I hasten to add that there remains just as many managers and employers as there are employees who are guilty of contemptuous behavior toward others, to say nothing of poor performance and decisions. It is hoped that this and other chapters will begin making a difference with both parties. Clearly, we as managers of human resources need to seek new and better methods of dealing with workplace problems—especially if the problem is sometimes us. As it pertains to discipline and termination actions, a good place to start is at the beginning and proceed to a fuller discussion of the issues, conditions, and illustrations, then examine prevention and problem-solving methods.

3.20 THE HISTORICAL BASIS OF AT-WILL EMPLOYMENT

The progressive erosion of at-will employment has been viewed by many employers as a rather devastating blow to their fundamental right to eliminate unwanted and undesirable employees whenever it was deemed appropriate by the employer. As it has been pointed out in earlier chapters, legal history in employment matters suggests that whenever some obvious, blatant, and widespread form of manifest injustice arises, legislators and/or judges are likely to create new safeguards intended to protect individual rights. Had it not been that some employers were abusing the at-will employment privilege by terminating employees who refused to violate laws, not following their own policies, or by harassing and coercing employees, we probably wouldn't be confronted with the additional liability for wrongful discharges.

Viewed in the context of diminishing employer rights through statutory regulation and judicial trends (or, conversely, increasing employer liability for violating laws), wrongful discipline and discharge is the third major phase in a sequence of regulatory employment limitations. The first phase of major legislation set limitations on wages, hours, and conditions of employment in the mid-1930's to early 1940's through enactment of the National Labor Relations Act and Fair Labor Standards Act. Suddenly, organized labor was legally at the doorstep of employers wanting to intervene in the employment relationship by representing employees in such matters as pay, benefits, hours, schedules, job security, and arbitration of grievances. It was a harsh period in employment history, and a major adjustment for employers to accept "outsiders" having a hand in what has long been the accepted paternalistic practice of employers deciding their own destiny and that of their employees—but abuses of employees had reached national attention.

The second major phase came in conjunction with a significant shift in societal attitudes toward social issues including employment. The 1960's brought forth a transformation in the ideals, values, methods, and composition of our workforce that was to unfold remarkable changes in the employment relationship for the next several decades. These social changes in attitudes and lifestyles placed new emphasis on individual rights as evidenced by the frequent reference to the concept of "fair and reasonable" expressed in many summaries of cases that came before federal and state courts across the land.

New or expanded limitations were beset upon employers by the establishment of legal prohibitions against discrimination, required health and safety practices, and standards to be followed in the administration of employee compensation and benefits.

With such sweeping federal and state regulatory oversight of employment decision making, it seemed by most employers that virtually little remained as sacred ground reserved for the employer's autonomy of action, and discretionary judgments to serve the best interests of their business.

The third and most recent major phase of limitation on employer discretionary decision making strikes at the heart, and last remaining vestiges, of an employer's prerogative—to employ people at-will of the organization's needs, inclinations, desire, and changes that occur over time. While the legal liability over wrongful discharge is quite new, the doctrine of at-will employment goes back several centuries where its origin is found in English common law. The common law dealt with an array of circumstances bearing on the master-servant relationship in which it became commonly held that servants were the rightful property of their masters who could buy, sell, or use them in whatever fashion served their commercial interests with little restriction. By 1877, the at-will doctrine had begun to gain acceptance as a legal definition of an appropriate employment relationship, and by the turn of the century, it became codified in most state labor laws. Although worded differently in some states, and with varying limitations in a few other states, most at-will employment statutes merely state that, absent a written contract binding the employer to some term or condition of employment, the employer was free to terminate the relationship for any reason at any time.

Inconspicuously, what began to modify this at-will freedom to terminate employees was the onslaught of unionism and collective bargaining. For purposes of designating groups of employees to be represented by one or more unions (or bargaining groups within the same union), labor relations laws provided for the exclusion of certain employees such as management and confidential employees from representation. Through the collective bargaining process, unions gained contractual protections that were embodied in the collective bargaining agreement; the provisions of which have been rarely disturbed by the courts since these documents are viewed as not only contractual, but mutually agreed upon as well. One such provision now contained in nearly all collective bargaining agreements (or at least every union's objective to acquire it) is the formal grievance mechanism that ends by binding arbitration over such employment matters as promotion, transfer, reassignment, demotion, discipline, termination, and other employment decisions of management. With considerable consistency, the courts have held that individual employees subject to collective bargaining agreements are subject to its terms, and that their remedy for disputes over unjust termination lies within the provisions of the labor contract and the union as their representative.

In the eyes of the courts such an appeal and review mechanism (grievance procedures) satisfies the essence of due process guarantees under the U.S. and state constitutions. Due process of law is, of course, that protection afforded individuals that they cannot be divested of their rights (e.g., they possess the right to a speedy trial, review evidence, face accusor, testify on own behalf, etc.). Rights can also include one's property and some courts consider employment as a form of property due to one's length of continuous service. Formal grievance and arbitration mechanisms provide the elements of due process, so the courts have tended not to become involved in wrongful discharge cases concerning employees covered by collective bargaining agreements. Therefore, those cases finding their way into the courtroom, usually pertains to those approximately 60 million employees not protected by labor contracts, written employment contracts, or other state laws that set conditions for their employment, termination, or right to an (internal) administrative due process review of adverse employment decisions.

3.30 THE LEGAL BASIS OF WRONGFUL DISCHARGE

One of the first court cases to suggest that at-will employment may have its limitations, and may have set the stage for the debut surge in the number and variety of wrongful discharge cases during the 1980's was the matter of *Petermann v. International Brotherhood of Teamsters* (1959). With eighteen years of service and an otherwise unblemished performance record, the plaintiff was fired for refusing to lie in connection with his job. In recognition of the injustice of terminating a long term employee for refusing to violate public policy (lie, falsify records, and the like), the court concluded that the employee had obtained a property right in his employment due to the implied contract inherent in long-term employment, and could therefore only be terminated for just cause.

Since the Petermann case, nearly all states have heard and adopted various legal causes of action that set limits on at-will employment in an effort to protect employees from abusive terminations, or alleged inequities resulting from their employer's application of some unusual employment condition. By and large, the wrongful discharge cases won by employees most frequently are those in which the termination can be shown as having arbitrary, pretextual, or retaliatory motives of the employer. The three most common causes of action are based on the following legal theories.

"Public Policy" Violations

Evidence supplied to the court proving that an employer—or any representative, officer, or agent of the employer—was moved to terminate an employee because of the employee's refusal to lie, steal, falsify records or information, or perform any other act that violates common laws will frequently serve to create a tort liability for employers. This is also one of those rare areas of law where a supervisor or line manager can lose personal immunity as a company representative, and therefore be held individually liable for misconduct (including criminal prosecution) if he or she is found responsible for initiating the order to lie, steal, or otherwise violate laws. By late 1988, about 35 states had adopted the public policy exception to at-will employment.

One of the earliest and well publicized cases involving a public policy violation was in *Tameny v. Atlantic Richfield Co.* (1980). Here, the employee refused to be involved in a price-fixing scheme. The court held that because of "malicious conduct" by the employer, the employee could bring a tort suit. That is, the employee was not limited to breach of contract (employment) damages, and could therefore recover compensatory and *punitive damages* (designed to punish the offender based on the net worth of a particular form of malicious conduct).

A second notable case in the early development of public policy theory was *Palmater v. International Harvester* (1981). In this case an employee who was discharged after sixteen years of service alleged he was fired for supplying information to the police regarding another employee who was possibly involved in criminal conduct, and for agreeing to cooperate in the police investigation. The court reversed a dismissal of the employee's claim and held that a valid cause of action for retaliatory discharge was presented. The court cited *Tameny* as its justification for holding the employer's termination as illegal.

Usually, to be a public policy violation most courts require that the public policy be expressed as a statute, yet some state courts have accepted cases and rendered decisions on implied or generally accepted standards of conduct and custom. A few other examples of terminations that have been regarded by some state courts as a contravention to public policy are firing an employee for:

- Informing a customer that the employer has stolen property from the customer.
- Attending jury duty service.
- "Whistle blowing" or reporting illegal conduct by the employer.
- Filing a worker's compensation claim.
- Refusing to take a polygraph examination.
- Refusing to lobby for a law or political candidate favored by the employer.
- Refusing to commit perjury in a court trial or before a legislative committee on the employer's behalf.

Breach of Implied or Expressed Contract

The courts will examine both expressed and implied covenants made by the employer that create, or could reasonably be construed by the employee as creating, a belief in the assurance of long term employment, and termination only *for* just cause. The most common document used and cited by the courts for this assessment is the employer's personnel policies and rules, or employee handbooks. Employment letters, contracts, and even verbal comments such as, "As long as you keep doing the same fine work, you'll never have to worry about being terminated," can extend a contractual obligation to the employee.

For example in *Pugh v. See's Candies Inc.* (1981), an employee with 31 years of service was terminated for an undisclosed reason. Not being able to defend its reasoning for the firing by the employer, the court determined that service length itself created an implied contract for termination by just cause only, and in this case where the employee had received commendations and been told (oral representation) that she would have a job as long as she wants it so long as her fine performance continued.

Later, in *Pine River State Bank v. Mettille* (1983), the Minnesota Supreme Court held that procedural restraints on termination of employees that were contained in an employee handbook were contractually binding on the employer. The court followed *Pugh v. Sees Candies* in their reasoning. Similarly, the Wisconsin Supreme Court cited the *Pugh* case in *Ferraro v. Koelsch* (1985) where the court held that an employment handbook may convert an employment at-will relationship into one where termination can occur only by adherence to the terms contained in the handbook. In this case yet another employer had failed to follow the terms in their own handbook (see also *Southwest Gas Corp. v. Ahmad*, Nevada Supreme Court, 1983).

By 1988, some 37 states had determined that breach of an implied contract related to personnel manuals, employee handbooks, and other written or verbal representations of job security, and that such contracts created an exception to at-will employment. They are:

☐ Alabama	☐ Illinois	☐ Montana	☐ Oregon
☐ Alaska	☐ Kansas	☐ Nebraska	☐ South Carolina
☐ Arizona	☐ Kentucky	☐ Nevada	☐ South Dakota
☐ California	☐ Maine	☐ New Jersey	☐ Texas
☐ Colorado	☐ Maryland	☐ New Mexico	☐ Vermont
☐ Connecticut	☐ Massachusetts	☐ New York	☐ Virginia
☐ Dist. of Columbia	☐ Michigan	☐ North Dakota	☐ Washington
☐ Hawaii	☐ Minnesota	☐ Ohio	☐ West Virginia
☐ Idaho	☐ Missouri	☐ Oklahoma	☐ Wisconsin
			☐ Wyoming

In an interesting, singular case in Washington, the state adopted both the public policy and breach of implied contract theories limiting at-will employment, and the illustration is noteworthy. The case was Thompson v. St. Regis Paper Co. (1983), where the employee alleged that he had been fired for instituting an accurate accounting program in compliance with the Foreign Corrupt Practices Act of 1977, which prohibits employers from offering a bribe to foreign officials in order to obtain business, and requires employers subject to the Securities Exchange Act of 1934 to devise and maintain a system of accounting that insures compliance with the antibribery provisions of the law. The court found that these laws represented a clear expression of public policy regarding bribery of foreign officials. The court noted that the at-will employment doctrine is a court-developed legal principle taken from a nineteenth-century treatise on the subject of master and servant, and went on to note statutory and judicial developments that serve as exceptions.

First, the court noted that a (employment) contract is terminable by the employer only for cause if:

1. there is an express or implied agreement to that effect; or
2. the employee does something different and beyond the intended (contractual) scope of the job.

The court noted, however, that "independent consideration" did not exist where an employee merely signed an employment agreement assigning any inventions or patents during his employment to his employer. Moreover, the court cited an earlier decision that properly held that a nonnegotiated unilateral grievance process did no more than implement a company policy to treat employees fairly, and that such provisions, as well as a provision establishing a probationary policy, merely implemented company policies to treat employees in a fair and consistent manner; it did not provide evidence of an implied contract that the employee can be discharged only for cause.

Second, the court concluded that policy or practice statements made in an employer's personnel handbook may, in certain situations, obligate the employer to act in accordance with those promises. Furthermore, "once an employer announces a specific policy or practice, especially in light of the fact that he expects employees to abide by the same, the employer may not treat its promises as illusory." However, the court identified several potential means by which employers can attempt to confine their obligations in employee manuals. For example, they "can specifically state in a conspicuous manner that nothing contained therein is intended to be part of the employment relationship and are simply general statements of company policy. Additionally, policy statements as written may not amount to promises of specific treatment and can merely be general statements of company policy, and thus, not binding. Moreover, the employer may specifically reserve the right to modify those policies or write them in a manner that retains discretion to the employer."

Third, the court determined that employers can be held liable in the discharge of an employee for reasons of violating a public policy mandate where the employer's conduct clearly imposes on the letter or purpose of a constitutional, statutory, or regulatory provision.

Some states have begun to take a different approach to the wrongful discharge problem. Rather than leaving these legal theories subject to court testing, a few states such as Montana's adoption of House Bill 241 in 1987 redefined at-will employment by prohibiting certain kinds of wrongful terminations. The statute therefore reinforces that both employer and employee are free to end the relationship so long as it had no fixed term, and provided the employer's action:

1. Is not in retaliation for the employee's refusal to violate public policy, or for reporting a violation of public policy (whistle-blowing);

2. Is based on "good cause" where the employee has completed a probationary period; or

3. Does not violate the express provisions of its own written personnel policies.

Further, the law defines "good cause" to mean a reasonable, job related purpose for termination that is based on a failure to satisfactorily perform job duties, a disruption of an employer's business, or other legitimate business reasons. While the last item is no doubt intentionally vague in order to assess a vast array of circumstantial reasons for an employer's action, at least one state has attempted this proactive measure to unclog the courts from this abused form of employee retaliation, while at the same time setting down standards for employers.

Good Faith And Fair Dealing Obligation

This theory proports to obligate employers to set and abide by reasonable standards of conduct in dealing with employees and employment matters. As you might guess, the principle of an employer's good faith and fair dealing with employees is difficult, if not obscure, to establish. It requires looking into the employer's intent and motives. Therefore, this cause of action tends to have a very broad range of interpretation which is perhaps why only less than a dozen states have accepted it by late 1988. But, don't allow its present acceptance by so few states to serve as a reason to discount the underlying principles, because these principles represent some very questionable management actions that could easily be adopted by many other states. Management activity that can create an action based on the good faith and fair dealing exception include:

- Distorting, falsifying, altering, or destroying performance appraisal records.

- Malicious supervision including harassment, abusive behavior, and inadequate training.

- Arbitrary and capricious demotion or creation of excessive assignments in attempt to provoke resignation (referred to as "constructive discharge"—see Section 3.60).

- Retaliatory termination for such employee activities as joining a union, filing a complaint, filing a workers' compensation claim, or the exercise of any other right (see Section 3.50).

- Any other malicious conduct on the part of the employer that tends to unnecessarily create an adverse effect upon the worker's right to reasonable employment conditions.

In addition to stating a claim of action for one or more of these three new legal theories as exceptions to at-will employment in termination cases, it has become rather common practice for the plaintiff employee to add other tortious claims to raise the prospects of a larger award of damages. Among such add-on claims are defamation, invasion of privacy, (intentional) infliction of emotional distress, and fraud and misrepresentation. Clearly, the ability of the plaintiff's attorney to establish such claims, or even establish their likelihood, will often create an emotional reaction of sympathy on the part of award-deciding juries—and most juries are composed of rank-and-file employees, not corporate officers!

If a law suit alleging the wrongful discharge of an employee seems imminent, one of the first things an employer should do is consult with their business attorney to determine if any active insurance policies will cover the cost of attorney fees and compensatory damages—if awarded. Most general liability policies will cover these costs, but not punitive damage awards. However, the insurance company may wish to have their legal staff represent your interests in court by handling the case. Concede to this arrangement *only* if you have the highest confidence in their background defending wrongful discharge cases, otherwise retain independent legal experts and so advise the insurance company who will usually be held liable for the independent attorney's fees. Examples of the type of insurance coverage that may cover these costs are:

- Comprehensive General Liability
- Errors And Omissions Liability
- Directors And Officers Liability
- Workers' Compensation/Employers' Liability
- Auto And Personal Liability
- Excess/Umbrella Coverage

3.40 WHAT CONSTITUTES JUST CAUSE DISCIPLINE, DISCHARGE, AND OTHER EMPLOYER ACTIONS

Unless you're an attorney, it may come as an immense surprise to learn that in the hundreds of court cases decided in matters of dispute over discipline and wrongful discharge, the courts have failed to articulate any sort of clear standards to guide employers in making determinations of just cause. The courts have tended to convey what isn't acceptable reasoning or conduct by employers to take these actions through frequent reference to such vague terms as unreasonable, not in good faith, intolerable, arbitrary, malicious, reckless, without adequate cause, and negligent. But, the courts have only implied what just cause means by application of the reciprocal to what they construe as wrongful cause.

At some risk of having it tested somewhere in court or other adjudicary process, you may wish to consider the following conditions under which an employer would be most likely held as having just cause to initiate discipline or termination proceedings. These conditions have been constructed from actual court cases, my own theories as the product of observing legal trends, and my professional experience in applying them to a substantial number and variety of actual situations.

1. **Express Policies**
   An employee's violation of express policies, rules, standards, and procedures that are contained in personnel policy manuals, employee handbooks, standard operating procedure manuals, written directives including instructive memos, and verbal information or instructions given by a person of authority serve as justifiable cause. Such rules, standards, and the like should be reasonable, clear, communicated, followed by everyone, and enforced when applicable. The underlying principle here is that the employer should have a reasonable and justifiable purpose for taking something away from the employee (demotion, pay reduction, privileges, or the job).

2. **Express Standards Of Conduct And Performance**
   General standards of conduct that have been conveyed to employees, preferably in writing, such as being honest, efficient, polite, wearing appropriate attire, avoiding offensive mannerisms, telling dirty jokes, using profane language, being disrespectful, and the like are also considered a justifiable cause for employers to act against employee violations. Again, so long as there is good business reason to adopt such standards, they are clearly expressed so as not to be overly vague, and you can show that they have been or are enforceable, then you're on legitimate ground for exercising your rights to control these kinds of workplace conditions.

3. **Enforcement Of Societal Standards**
   Expressing to employees that the organization will invoke societal standards of conduct which, under some circumstances, may even include certain conduct during off-duty hours will generally be considered justifiable cause. Such societal standards consist of violations of criminal offenses, civil laws, acts of discrimination, offensive profanity, sexual misconduct, inappropriate exposure or the wearing of suggestive clothing, physically threatening a co-worker, bringing dangerous objects onto company property, and the unauthorized consumption of alcohol or drugs.

   Obviously there are many forms of off-duty conduct that are not enforceable by an employer, but might be if done during work hours. There are also many types of personal conduct that are none of the employer's business or concern when done during off-duty hours. So, while wearing revealing clothing at a company social event might be regarded as being in poor taste, it is only enforceable if it is done during business hours. The same holds true with the use of alcohol, drugs, (unless incarcerated!), profanity, or even the violation of many laws.

The distinction as to when an employer can act on an employee's off-duty conduct is when that conduct renders them unavailable for work, damages or destroys their job credibility, or adversely reflects upon the welfare or reputation of the organization (e.g., their employer was named in a news item). In other words, a job nexus (relatedness) should exist between their conduct and the performance of their job or damage to the organization.

4. Behavioral Obstruction Of Business Interests

Other areas of an employer's justification for taking action against an employee relate to various kinds of behavioral obstruction. These include conduct that has the effect of adversely affecting the performance of other employees (be it chronic tardiness, horseplay, or excessive visiting), obstruction of the orderly management of operations (instigating a clique against the supervisor or not following chain-of-command procedures), and disrupting the maintenance of normal business operations (intentional causation of damage or destruction to property, knowingly fouling equipment so that it won't work, hiding keys, and the like).

For decades, employers have been perplexed as to the best method of writing personnel policies that will adequately serve two important functions: one is to let employees know in advance that events can result in disciplinary and termination action so they won't do them (the no-no's); and the second reason is to have written rules to use as a defensible citation for initiating action against violators. The trend has been to be either very explicit—resulting in a very long list of possible infractions and fearing that something has been overlooked (it has, you know), then adding it *after* it has occurred—or to be brief and grossly vague such as stating "any conduct considered unbecoming..." All too frequently, courts have thrown out causes for discipline and termination that are too abstract, vague, and global on the basis that there is no apparent job nexus between the rule and circumstances of events that might fall within the rule.

In addressing those causes or events that might give rise to discipline or termination, employers should consider using a policy clause reserving management's right to initiate similar action for other just cause reasons (such as those given above) even if not itemized in the policy illustrations. An example of such a policy might use a preamble statement followed by illustrative examples such as:

The illustrations of unacceptable conduct cited below are to provide specific and exemplary reasons for initiating disciplinary action, and to alert employees to the more commonplace types of employment conduct violations. However, because conditions of human behavior are unpredictable, no attempt has been made here to establish a complete list. Should there arise instances of unacceptable conduct not included in the following list, the (Company) may therefore find it necessary and appropriate to initiate disciplinary action in accordance with these policies and procedures.

A. Attendance

1. Improper or unauthorized use or abuse of paid leave.

2. Excessive absenteeism, regardless of reason, the effect of which disrupts or diminishes operational effectiveness.

3. Being absent without authorized leave, or repeated unauthorized late arrival or early departure from work.

B. Behavior

1. Willful or negligent violation of the Personnel Policies and Procedures, unit operating rules, or related directives.

2. Failure to carry out an order from a superior, except where the employee's safety may reasonably be jeopardized by the order.

3. Engaging in a conflict of interest activity.

4. Conduct that discredits the employee or the (Company), or willful misrepresentation of the (Company).

5. Conviction of a crime, including convictions based on a plea of nolo contendere or of a misdemeanor involving moral turpitude, the nature of which reflects the possibility of serious consequences related to the continued assignment or employment of the employee.

6. Knowingly falsifying, removing, or destroying information related to employment, payroll, or work-related records or reports.

7. Soliciting outside work for personal gain during business hours; engaging in off-duty employment for any business under contract with (XYZ, Inc.); participating in any off-duty employment that adversely affects the employee's performance of work for the (Company); and engaging in unauthorized off-duty employment.

8. Discourteous treatment of the public or other employees, including harassing, coercing, threatening, or intimidating others.

9. Conduct that interferes with the management of the (Company) operations.

10. Violation or neglect of safety rules, or contributing to hazardous conditions.

11. Unauthorized removal or use of any (Company) property, or that of its (clients, customers, agents, etc.).

12. Physical altercations.

13. Any act or conduct that is discriminatory in nature toward another person's race, color, national origin, sex (including sexual harassment), age, religious beliefs or political affiliations.

C. Performance

1. Inefficiency, incompetence, or negligence in the performance of duties, including failure to perform assigned tasks or training, or failure to discharge duties in a prompt, competent, and reasonable manner.

2. Refusal or inability to improve job performance in accordance with written or verbal direction after a reasonable trial period.

3. Refusal to accept reasonable and proper assignments from an authorized supervisor.

4. Intoxication or incapacity on duty due to the use of alcohol or drugs; possession and/or sale of illegal substances on (Company) property.

5. Driving under the influence of alcohol or drugs while on duty.

6. Suspension of driver's license where job duties require driving.

7. Careless, negligent, or improper use of (Company) property, equipment or funds, including unauthorized removal, or use for private purpose, or use involving damage or unreasonable risk of damage to property.

8. Unauthorized release of confidential information or official records.[1]

To reinforce and further illustrate the application of just cause to discharge actions based on the judicial view by some state courts, the following cases may be illuminating with respect to legal thought concerning legitimate reasons for terminating employees. These cases address circumstances involving personnel policy violations, off-duty conduct, incompetency, philosophical differences with management, use of profanity, preemption of union employees, and the employer's strongly held belief that it was acting in good faith.

For those of you who may be inclined to dismiss the importance of having rather firm just cause reasons for terminating an employee merely because of your high confidence over being an at-will employer, or because your state courts have not conceded to some wrongful discharge theories, I can only urge you to heed the warning that legal thinking and attitudes about employer rights are changing rapidly. I can also refer you to several employers who made just such a mistake in their approach to terminations. On the other hand, managers should not be overly deterred from initiating a necessary termination; the point is you should have sound (non-discriminatory, objective, non-malicious, and legal) reasons for the action—it's more defensive if the cause is justified—and good documentation of the circumstances that brought about

---

[1] Levesque, Joseph D.; *Manual Of Personnel Policies, Procedures, And Operations.* Prentice-Hall, 1986. pp. 69-70.

the necessity to terminate. To clarify, and perhaps raise your confidence over just cause, let's look at a few court interpretations.

3.50 HOW THE COURTS VIEW JUST CAUSE DISCHARGE

Personnel Policy: Discrediting The Employer

In *Martinez v. County of Tulare, California* (1987), plaintiff was a full-time welfare service aide and had an extra part-time job in a fastfood restaurant to wit she did not report income for purposes of her welfare entitlement. Even though she didn't work directly with recipient benefit determinations, she was fired under a personnel rule that was both protracted and vaguely stated, but included the phrase..."employee conduct which reflects discredit upon public service..." The appellate court determined that, despite the rule's vagueness, the facts of the case clearly constitute a defrauding of her employer and such action brings discredit to the services intended to be legitimately provided to recipients.

Public employers are, of course, more susceptible to public ridicule than are other employers. Nevertheless, there is no reason any other employer cannot apply the same rationale and approach in matters involving such employee actions as theft, speaking in disdain about the company to one of its customers, lying, and the like. In other words, acts like these may not be terminable reasons in and of themself, but their discrediting effect upon the employer or company may create a legitimate reason to consider a discharge. To be a terminable action, there should exist a strong correlation between the employer's policy and the seriousness of the offense.

Personnel Policy: Immediate Discharge Only For Misconduct?

In *Enis v. Continental Illinois National Bank* (1986), the Seventh Circuit Court of Appeals (federally chartered bank) rendered a decision I have been watching for some years now. The case involved a bank employee fired for misconduct due to locking and delaying several important customer papers in her desk drawer. The employee filed a claim for wrongful discharge under the theory that the employee handbook created a contract of employment, thereby limiting the at-will relationship to the terms of the handbook, and the employer did not follow prescribed disciplinary procedures. The court found that it was unnecessary to determine if the handbook created a contract, since the handbook itself cited such things as extreme insubordination and various security violations as being subject to immediate discharge. Moreover, the court contended that it would be irrational for an employer to be limited only to those stated causes for immediate discharge in its handbook. The court stated:

> The language could not sensibly be limited to the instances given. That would imply that if an employee murdered a co-worker he could not be immediately dismissed because he was not being insubordinate, or stealing, or drug dealing. The words

"include" and "such as" show that the specific instances [listed in the handbook] are illustrative, not exhaustive.

Personnel Policy: Safety Risk (Drug Use)

In *Watts v. Union Pacific Railroad Company* (1986), the Tenth Circuit Court of Appeals (employer subject to Railway Labor Act) determined that the employer's use of its personnel policies and collective bargaining reasons for discharge as "unbecoming conduct" would be upheld in this case involving the employee's off-duty use of cocaine for which he was convicted and given six months probation. With respect to the plaintiff's employment termination, the court concluded that this incident, together with a previous termination for on-duty use of alcohol, created a risk to the safety of the public and co-workers.

Had the employee not had a history (prior termination) of using poor judgment concerning such substance use as alcohol—and while on-duty—the court might not have been so tolerant as to stretching the employer's use of "unbecoming conduct" reasons for the termination since the incident occurred off-duty and therefore absent any risk to the public or co-workers. That's a legal argument, not a moral one!

Off-Duty Crime: Dishonesty

In *Kissinger v. U.S. Postal Service* (1986), the First Circuit Court of Appeals upheld the termination of a mail handler (federal employee) for his acts of dishonesty in connection with his off-duty role as a union treasurer. In his union capacity, plaintiff previously pled guilty to extorting some $31,000. In his termination suit, he alleged that the off-duty act was not just cause, but the court concluded that such acts, whenever and wherever they occur, "cast a sufficient shadow over a person's trustworthiness to justify the conclusion that he is unqualified for a position implicating the public trust." Here, then, the court clearly linked the job nexus of his act to the role and responsibility inherent in his employment as the basis for termination in conjunction with off-duty dishonesty. Similar reasoning can be applied to employees required to handle money or financial transactions or similar kinds of job entrusting.

Performance: Incompetence

In *Michelson v. Exxon Research and Engineering Company* (1987), plaintiff had been a materials inspector for seven years before becoming one of seven inspectors out of 22 subjected to a reduction-in-force in 1983. One month prior to being laid off, plaintiff stated he planned on filing a workers' compensation claim once he heard he might be laid off due to poor performance and was, in fact, offered to participate in the company's voluntary resignation severance program. He declined and brought suit as a retaliatory motive for his employer's wrongful termination.

The court found three reasons to set aside the employer's liability for wrongful discharge:

1. The company had documented evidence that, one year earlier, another company representative who was working on a joint project reported that the employee demonstrated inadequate performance in the inspection of locomotives (preexisting performance deficiencies);

2. The company was able to demonstrate that other laid off employees had a history of deficient performance; and

3. That plaintiff knew about the layoffs prior to his stated intention to file a workers' compensation claim.

Professional Differences With Management Philosophies

In *Newman v. Legal Services Corp.* (1986), plaintiff brought suit under the public policy violation theory of wrongful discharge claiming that the termination violated First Amendment (free speech) rights. Here, two employees were fired due to their disagreements with superiors over the delivery of legal assistance to the poor. The court ruled that an employer's discharge of employees who would not adhere to management's legitimate interest in maintaining harmony among employees, and its own idealogical positions concerning its business, is a reasonable application of the at-will relationship.

Obviously, there exists a fine line of judgment in cases involving differences in opinion on work-related matters including those having some bearing on overriding philosophical positions between people engaged in work. Differences in opinion are frequently very healthy in business matters, and they can often point to weaknesses in a prevailing or long endured approach to something. So, the degree to which an employer finds such differences of opinion disagreeable to the extent of terminating an oppositional employee should focus on two effects of this behavior:

1. The extent to which it creates a manifest disharmony with others that has not been corrected through warnings; and,

2. The extent to which the behavior contravenes the employee's own ability to carry out their job responsibilities in the manner directed or desired by management.

If an employee disagrees, or even seems to see things differently—and regularly—but carries out their job well, you probably have a weak case of just cause as it relates to disruptive differences in opinion.

Use Of Profanity In The Workplace

In *Martin v. Parrish* (1986), plaintiff was a teacher at Midland College in Texas and brought suit for deprivation of his First Amendment rights after being fired for repeated use of offensive profanity in the classroom based on student complaints. Since plaintiff was making remarks toward students rather than merely expressing views on matters of public concern, the court found no violation of free speech rights, but regarded the use of profanity as inconsistent with his position as a college teacher.

The common practices and range of acceptability of profanity in the workplace varies considerably among employers, the work setting, and type of employees hired. Given the increased sensitivity of the courts to offensive (sexual) conditions in existence within many workplaces, as evidenced by a growing number of cases involving discrimination related to harassment and disparate treatment, managers would be well advised to rid their workplace setting of all but the most mild forms of profanity—even if the setting is one of those "macho" places characterized by traditional identity with such expressive, if not limited vocabulary. You might also consider the fact that profanity is usually directed toward someone and, if received as offensive or more, may feel that the remark is sufficient provocation to respond in kind, escalate the interaction, or end in an altercation.

However, a somewhat different conclusion was drawn by an Oregon court in *Frasier v. Minnesota Mining and Manufacturing* (1986) where an eight year service employee of 3M was held to be wrongfully discharged for insubordination and use of profanity. Here, the court concluded that the employee handbook was contractual in nature since it stated that discharge would occur for "proper cause". Testimony revealed that profanity was common among male workers in the plant suggesting that the female plaintiff was the subject of discriminatory discharge. It should be understood that the court was not condoning the prolific use of profanity; merely that it cannot be discriminatorily controlled at the convenience of the employer.

Preemption: Collective Bargaining Agreement

There were two cases, California and Washington, in 1986 that reinforced the principle that employees covered by a collective bargaining agreement have gained rights under enabling federal labor relations laws not otherwise enjoyed by non-union employees. The courts have therefore been fairly consistent in their holdings that collective bargaining agreements are contracts, express various agreed-to terms and conditions of employment, preempt state laws related to at-will employment, and that conditions (reasons) related to performance, conduct, discipline, termination, and grievance rights are limited to the collective bargaining agreement. Consequently, employers with a "mixed house" should strive for the same type of language flexibility in their discipline policy between the labor agreement and company policy such as the illustration provided earlier.

In *Friday v. Hughes Aircraft Company*, a 28 year service chemical storekeeper was terminated after several reprimands and suspensions. The collective bargaining agreement allowed the filing of a grievance that would go as far as arbitration in such cases. The employee failed to file a grievance under the terms of the agreement, but brought suit against his employer for wrongful discharge. The California Court of Appeal held that his state claim was barred by preemption of Section 301 of the Labor Management Relations Act.

In *Trumbauer v. Group Health Cooperative of Puget Sound,* the employer discovered that a probationary employee had a prior sexual relationship with his supervisor who had hired him. The company indicated that unless he could find another position for which he was qualified in the company, he would be released under their antinepotism rule. He could not find another position, was fired, and brought suit alleging that the antinepotism rule didn't apply to his circumstance, and was therefore an unjust discharge. The court concluded that the plaintiff was covered by a collective bargaining agreement which, itself, allowed probationary employees to be terminated without use of a grievance right therefore waiving such right and preempting a state claim for wrongful discharge.

Employer's Strong Belief In Good Faith

I wouldn't stake my life on this argument for just cause terminations, but it may be worthwhile for you to know that at least one state court accepted an employer's erroneous termination because the employer demonstrated a strong belief that there was good reason and was acting in good faith when they initiated the termination. It represents a little different slant than merely telling the court, "Okay, you say we were wrong so how much do we owe?" A defense based on good faith intent would say, "Okay, you say we were wrong in the justification for a termination, but we intended no maliciousness, and we firmly believed that it was necessary given information and circumstances at the time—what more could a reasonable employer do?"

The circumstances in *Ketchu v. Sears, Roebuck & Co.* (1987) involve a salesman with 23 years service who engaged in a physical altercation concerning credit for a particular sale. Conflicting evidence over details of the altercation resulted in both employees being suspended, but plaintiff subsequently stated he would not work with the other employee and would do the same thing (fight) if the incident was ever repeated. He was then fired. The court, in giving instructions to the jury, noted:

> An employer who acts in good faith on an honest but mistaken belief that discharge of an employee was warranted by a legitimate business reason has not breached a covenant of good faith and fair dealing. If you find that defendant honestly believed that the termination of plaintiff was for a legitimate business reason, you must find for defendant even if you find that defendant was mistaken in that belief.

In other words, the employer should not be held liable for a mistake in the facts upon which its termination decision is based, but should only be held liable when there is more culpable wrongdoing by the employer. Both the California Court of Appeal and Supreme Court, on review, noted two significant elements of the employer's rights in this case:

1. The employee's application form bore a notice that termination can occur without reason or notice; and

2. The company did conduct an investigation into the matter in an attempt to gather enough information to act in a good faith manner, and that something had to be done in the instance.

Ultimately, it was held by the courts, that the company's erroneous information was of less pertinence than their motivation for legitimate business reasons to terminate the employee. Also, in *Reid v. Sears, Roebuck & Co.* (1986), the Sixth Circuit Court of Appeals determined that the at-will disclaimer on Sears' application form was not overriden by any implied contract resulting from specific causes for discipline stated in the employee handbook.

In conclusion, employers should be aware that there is no federal law that obligates them to provide employees with the reason for termination. Some state laws may require stated (just cause) reasons, and this is often the case for public employees who pass their probationary period, or it may be required by the terms of a collective bargaining agreement. If an employer is not required by state law, collective bargaining agreement, employment contract, or company rules to specify the reason in termination situations, you might be better off to avoid a statement of the reason altogether since employees can use the reason provided them as a cause of action for discrimination or wrongful discharge suits.

If you wish to state the reason(s), or are required to do so, be absolutely certain that any reason given is well documented. As a matter of prudence, virtually any termination should have well documented support be it supervisory notes, performance appraisals, written warnings or notices of disciplinary action, in the event you're ever called upon to provide evidence of your actions leading to termination.

Such a holding that employers need not state a reason for termination was made by a Maryland court in *Castiglione v. John Hopkins Hospital* (1986). In this case, a respiratory therapist was fired after attending an evaluation hearing. The employer took no action on her grievance provided by personnel policy since, by that time she was an ex-employee, but offered her reinstatement without back pay a few months later. Upon filing a claim for wrongful termination due to breach of contract, the court found that the particular handbook language did not contractually obligate the employer, nor was the employer required to give an at-will employee reasons for its decision to terminate.

Armed with the background in this chapter, it becomes highly advisable for managers to continue into Chapter 4 where further detail is presented concerning how employers have violated the legal theories of wrongful employment actions. Solutions to these problems, as well as the means to prevent their occurrence, are included throughout these discussions and in the concluding sections.

CHAPTER II: 4.0
PROBLEMS OF WRONGFUL DISCHARGE, PART 2:
DIAGNOSING MANAGEMENT'S VIOLATION OF
EMPLOYEE RIGHTS AND FINDING SOLUTIONS

In Chapter 3, the three principal legal theories used by terminated employees to make a showing of wrongful discharge are:

1. *That the employer violated a public policy (law) or retaliated against an employee for exercising their lawful rights;*

2. *That the employer breached an implied or expressed (written) contract such as an employment agreement on their own personnel policies; or*

3. *That the employer's action was not in keeping with good faith and fair dealing with the employee, and this usually means that the termination was forced, conspired, pretextual, arbitrary, or capricious.*

This chapter will examine these three theories in more detail with respect to the more commonly encountered circumstances that arise for employers, and thereby illustrate for managers the important factors that are considered by the courts in deciding what is and is not proper action for employers. In order to avoid exposing your organization to this costly and counterproductive form of litigation, or legal error, it is imperative for every manager to become better informed about these risky decision making problems, their avoidance, and how to solve them if they occur.

4.10 DIAGNOSING PUBLIC POLICY VIOLATION PROBLEMS

Terminating employees for their refusal to lie, cover up or remain silent, falsify documents, or in other ways to violate laws is what more and more states are recognizing as public policy violations, and they are being regarded as the most common exception to a purely at-will employment relationship. Some state courts have even gone so far as to interpret public policy as not only law in statutory form, but additionally can mean any regulation, rule, directive, or commonly known practice. While such interpretation is the extreme, it does point out the intention of some courts to impress upon employers the need to stop using employees, under the threat of termination, to carry out improper acts solely to benefit the employer's interests, and that arbitrary or malicious retaliatory terminations for employee refusals will not be tolerated—except perhaps in Ohio or a handful of other ultra-conservative states where they still defy any limitations to at-will employment no matter what the employer's action is!

For example, in *Phung v. Waste Management, Inc.* (1986), a chemist for this Ohio hazardous materials disposer company was fired for exercising his "whistle-blowing" rights concerning certain irregularities in the company's practices. Whether or not the employee's complaints were valid within the context of legal standards of waste disposal methods or practices is beside the point of being fired over the exercise of such complaints, even to the extent of being annoying to the employer. In cases such as this where there is a vital public interest, the employer would normally be justified in the termination if an employee becomes overly disruptive to operations and can be proved to be incorrect in their belief that the employer is violating legally prescribed standards. Nevertheless, the Ohio Supreme Court upheld the employer's termination of plaintiff.

This case probably represents the exception, not the rule, in cases involving terminated employees over their whistle-blowing due to some form of legal violation by their employer. The issue has been heavily and successfully litigated by a number of employees, so at the outset employers should remember even winning law suits is extremely expensive and time consuming, so these circumstances should be approached with considerable thought and facts; or better yet avoided where feasible. The following, then, are perhaps better examples of those employment circumstances where employers have been found liable for public policy violations, and to have wrongfully discharged employees.

Whistle Blowing: Improper Incarceration

In *Wagner v. City of Globe* (1986), the Arizona Supreme Court ruled that it was inappropriate for the police chief to fire a police officer who reported to the magistrate that a man had served 21 days in jail for vagrancy, but the vagrancy law was repealed a year earlier. The man was then released but the magistrate reported the officer's "meddlesome and insubordinate behavior" to the chief who fired the officer. The court pointed out, in ruling in behalf of the plaintiff, the societal seriousness that would otherwise accompany the legality of firing employees who bring forth information on injustice, or the violations of law that are necessary for and intertwined with societal order.

Whistle Blowing: Preempted By Federal Activity Employer

In *Snow v. Bechtel Construction, Inc.* (1986), plaintiff was a union employee of the defendent company at the San Ofre (California) Nuclear Generating Station. He was fired one month after he made a whistle-blowing accusation that the plant was not following emergency evacuation procedures, and brought suit for wrongful discharge. The case was thrown out of state court on two points: 1) the employer's business activity was preempted by federal law, in this case the Energy Reorganization Act of 1974 which provides a remedy for employees fired over the making of safety complaints; and, 2) the fact that the employee was represented by a collective bargaining agreement which provided a grievance procedure concerning terminations. The employee did, in fact, file a concurrent grievance and may pursue litigation in federal court, but may not prevail with the colossal awards associated with state jury trials since most remedies under federal statutes of this type are reinstatement and back pay.

With regard to the preemption of a state wrongful discharge claim based on federal regulation of the employer's business activity, another case was thrown out of state court in *Berry v. American Federal Savings* (1986). Here, because the employer was regulated by the Federal Home Loan Bank Board which requires that employment contracts be in writing if they are entered into for particular employees, the employer was able to avert a state suit alleging breach of contract in that the employer allegedly failed to follow its employee handbook concerning the firing of a regional manager.

Violating Subpeona From Unemployment Hearing

In *Ludwick v. This Minute of Carolina, Inc.* (1985), the South Carolina Supreme Court ruled that it was a violation of public policy for the employer to threaten termination of an employee if the employee responded to a subpoena concerning testimony in an unemployment benefits hearing. The employee was awarded compensatory as well as punitive damages for the employer's obstruction in answering a lawful order and giving testimony. The same principles would apply where an employer required an employee to give false testimony (i.e., require that the employee commit perjury), or any other form of falsification that is in some respect linked to laws and by such act would violate them—including the alteration of employment records with deceitful intent.

Refusal To Fix Raffle Ticket

In *Beasley v. Affiliated Hospital Products, Inc.* (1986), the Missouri Court of Appeals upheld the employee's claim of wrongful discharge under the theory of a public policy violation. The employee, an executive of a hospital products company was asked to fix a raffle in which the company was to donate products. He refused and was fired. The court concluded that it was a prime example of the public policy exception to at-will employment inasmuch as the employee was fired for refusing to commit a criminal act.

Refusal To Violate Law: Grievance Procedure Inapplicable

In a 1986 Los Angeles arbitration case involving The Boys Market, Inc., a clerk was fired for refusing to sell lottery tickets to a young girl under the statutory age (18) for such sales. The employer argued that the union employee should have used the grievance procedure within the collective bargaining agreement despite the law rather than pursuing direct arbitration. The arbitrator's finding is noteworthy with respect to a possible new twist to the public policy exception for employers who have grievance mechanisms. The arbitrator concluded that discharging an employee for refusing to violate a law, notwithstanding the collective bargaining agreement, provides the employee a right of action above all other principles of remedy. That is, employees have an inherent right to refuse an illegal order (or one which jeopardizes their health and safety) without punitive results.

The implication of this decision is that employees—theoretically union or non-union—do not have to use an established grievance procedure when the termination involves a public policy violation. Although union employees have been routinely preempted from filing state wrongful discharge claims, the rationale applied in this case by the arbitrator is strong, could easily be used by a court concerning non-union employees, and may even alter the notion of preempting union employees who were fired over refusal to violate a state law!

Public Policy More Than Statute Violation

Not all states are in agreement with how broadly or narrowly public policy exceptions to at-will employment should be interpreted. In fact, most state courts accepting the public policy theory have also expressed their intent to apply the exception narrowly, thus suggesting that it will only be used in cases of alleged violation of statutory law as opposed to more liberal and broadly held interpretations by a small number of state courts. These broader intepretations may remain the product of isolated states such as California, Michigan, and Illinois, or they may gradually become hard to avoid precedence as other states confront a broader variety of circumstances surrounding the expanded view of public policy terminations. The following case illustrating an expanded interpretation of public policy violations is, hopefully, the extreme but then again the underlying legal principle may well find its way into other states. By being aware of the illustration, you might be able to avoid it.

In *Dobbs v. Cardiopulminary Management Services* (1987), the California Court of Appeal reversed a trial court ruling that dismissed the plaintiff's claim for wrongful termination due to an alleged public policy violation. The plaintiff was a respiratory therapist working the night shift at San Clemente General Hospital. She was fired after refusing to work with only one other therapist who was said to be underqualified when the general practice was to have three therapists on duty to insure the safety and welfare of patients—a standard healthcare practice rather than statutory requirement compelling the employer to comply.

On review, the court examined the kinds of conditions that can create public policy. The most widely accepted are requiring an employee to violate a statutory law (retaliatory discharge for refusing to engage in an unlawful act), or asserting their rights by statute or governmental regulation. However, in this case the court noted that it is not a necessary requirement for a plaintiff to demonstrate that their employer is in violation of a statutory law, and fired them for refusal to disregard or disobey the law, but may in fact make a claim on the basis of judicial law (court interpretations), or even professional practices where the intent is to safeguard some public interest such as patient care. Specifically, the court asserted:

> We do not believe the existing case law requires such a narrow interpretation (that an employer's action violates statutory law)...fundamental public policy may be expressed either by the Legislature in a statute or by the courts in decisional law. Insofar as affording remedies to an employee discharged in contravention of a fundamental public policy is concerned, it is immaterial whether public policy is proclaimed by statute or delineated in a judicial decision...California has a public policy favoring qualified care for its ill and infirm.

What more could the court have said to tell us of their intent to reach out—through its judicial powers—and touch someone!

Reporting Harassment Of Another Employee

Sexual and other forms of harassment of employees violates federal laws protecting employees from discrimination, and most states have similar laws. In *Jenkins v. Orkin Exterminating Company, Inc.* (1986), a female employee confided in a well regarded salesman for the company that she was being sexually harassed by the branch manager. The salesman urged the district manager to investigate, who did, and the branch manager was warned to desist or face termination. The female resigned shortly thereafter when told she would be fired by the branch manager, and the salesman was fired one month later. In court, the employer was unable to demonstrate a reasonable cause for the termination that would override plaintiff's allegation that the discharge was in retaliation for his aiding the harassed employee. The employer was therefore held liable for a public policy violation with regard to the discriminatory and retaliatory firing of an employee merely trying to protect another employee from being subjected to an act of illegal discrimination by a representative of the company.

4.20 DIAGNOSING BREACH OF CONTRACT PROBLEMS

The breach of contract basis of a wrongful discharge suit can stem from several sources of deviation between what is expressed by the employer in writing to employees, or what has been implied to employees either verbally or in writing. Most sources of the contract theory in those states accepting it come from personnel policy manuals, employee handbooks, employment letters, and yes, even simple statements made to an employee by a company representative having decisional authority—usually in some context other than intending to impart an expectation of everlasting employment!

Yet another frequently cited factor that can serve as a source of creating a contractual relationship in employment, at least in terms of discharging only for just cause, is the implied contract some courts feel are inherent in an employee's length of service with a company. Thus far, there have been no specific years of service that creates such a "property interest" in one's continuous employment whereby an employer can only be terminated for just cause reasons. However, from the court's point of view, the longer the relationship continues in a mutually satisfactory way, the more an employee can reasonably conclude that they will be subject to termination for only substanitive reasons (*e.g., Pugh v. Sees Candies,* 1981 et al.).

Obviously, dedicating only a portion of a chapter to the many complex and varying conditions under which employment contracts can arise does not do thorough justice to this increasingly sensitive area of managing human resources. Given this limitation and what is a more probable interest for most managers, the goal here is to take a broad-brush approach to examining the essence of the contract theory, then illustrate trends and common situations that have arisen through court review. The sources of employment contracts presented here include personnel policy manuals and employee handbooks, written employment agreements, verbal agreements, performance agreements, non-competition agreements, and "forum selection" clauses.

4.21 PERSONNEL POLICY MANUALS AND EMPLOYEE HANDBOOKS

"To write or not write" in some states is rapidly becoming synonymous with "To risk liability or keep them in the dark" concerning the manner in which policy manuals and handbooks have backfired on employers. The purpose in having such documents remains unchanged over the years, but the manner in which they have been interpreted, scrutinized, and legalized has changed markedly since the early days of discrimination law, and more heavily and frequently since the emergence of wrongful discharge litigation. Clearly, the courts have begun anew to place more emphasis on conceptual employer-employee relationships by their regularity of references to the notion of the employer's "good faith and fair dealing" when executing numerous kinds of employment decisions; particularly discharge decisions because of the seriousness of the effect upon the lives of employees. the courts view it as a sort of corporate capital punishment.

Decidedly, in many states the courts have created a greater liability on an employer's adoption of written policies, rules, and procedures. In reaction, employers have either turned over the writing of these documents to attorneys who understand law better than operational problems, to consultants who may not have a sufficient grasp of law, to internal staff who can't keep up with changes affecting all aspects of personnel operations, or they may burn all copies in existence and see how it goes without it—and thus throw the baby out with the water so to speak!

The point is that policy manuals and handbooks serve a very important operational function, and any function which serves a majority of our employees well shouldn't be abandoned merely because a few employees might succeed periodically at finding some unintended weakness. What we as managers ought to be doing in our search for a proper solution is first diagnose the particular weaknesses being identified by the courts and others, then periodically revise these documents to correct vulnerable language and operational situations needing clarification.

Policy manuals and handbooks still serve as an important decision-making, rules-setting, and procedures-guide that creates structure, order, efficiency, and needed consistency of operations affecting our human resources. We just need to be more precise and thoughtful in their development, and committed to following it when the need arises. A few illustrations may help to point out some vulnerabilities that you might want to examine with regard to your existing situation, or avoid in the future. You may also wish to read applicable portions in Part III, Chapter 2.

Breach Of Good Faith/Infliction Of Emotional Distress

In *Read v. City of Lynwood, California* (1985), plaintiff was promoted to a higher level position, but was not successful in completing her probationary period so sought retreat to her former position provided for under the employer's personnel code. Concurrently, the city council decided to eliminate (abolish) her former position and she was thus terminated. The appellate court agreed with plaintiff's allegation that the employer violated its covenant of good faith when it eliminated the position solely to avoid retention of the employee (and avoid compliance with the code provision), thereby constituting a wrongful discharge that additionally inflicted unnecessary emotional distress.

Failure To Comply With Own Handbook

This is a common problem for many state courts where the employer creates rules and procedures but doesn't follow them—probably because their rule or procedure didn't coincide with what they wanted to accomplish. No excuse, say many courts, who are also quick to add that employers are free to establish whatever legal and reasonable policies they want but, once established, the rule should apply to all those classes of employees to which it was directed—not just those held in the employer's favor.

Too, the degree to which various courts find policy manuals and handbooks to be contractual in nature varies considerably, and the determination usually rests with case-by-case evaluations of specific policy language and factual conditions associated with its application.

For example, in *Mobil Coal Producing, Inc. v. Parks* (1985), the Wyoming Supreme Court held that the employer's handbook on "Standards of Conduct" and "Policy of Progress Discipline" used a "tenor" and created an implication that the at-will relationship was set aside in lieu of a for-cause only termination process, and awarded defendent-employee damages. Although the court held that manuals and handbooks may not always give rise to an alteration of at-will employment, in this case it did because the employer apparently overcommitted itself to follow progressive discipline procedures, and failed to do so with defendent when he violated safety rules and was terminated.

A related situation was found in *Sloan v. Taylor Machinery Company* (1987) where a Mississippi appellate court came to a different conclusion. Here, plaintiff was given an employee handbook four months after being hired, and the handbook contained conditions for termination and hearings. He was fired four years later and brought suit alleging the employer's failure to comply with the contractually binding handbook. The court disagreed that the handbook created a contractual obligation inasmuch as there was no employment agreement at the time plaintiff was hired.

The events and implication of the court's ruling in this case is that employers should not provide new hires with handbooks until after they have reported to work, which is an expression of the employee's willingness to work under whatever conditions have been stated up to that date (see also *Garcia v. Aetna Financial Co.,* 10th Circuit, 1984). To better insure that the subsequent giving of handbooks does not imply a modification by the employer of its at-will intent, employers may want to provide new hires with letters which, among other statements, says the employee will eternally remain an at-will employee unless expressly modified by individual agreement.

On the issue of progressive discipline policies, the Sixth Circuit Court of Appeal reached the conclusion that they do not create an enforceable contract merely because an employee has a subjective expectation that termination is for-cause only or that due process must be carried out in every termination. In *Dell v. Montgomery Ward & Company* (1987), plaintiff was terminated after 12 years of service for deceptively covering up the inappropriate conduct of his subordinate. He brought suit alleging breach of contract based on his belief that the progressive discipline and due process guidelines given to supervisory personnel created an expectation in just cause termination only, despite specific language that indicated the procedure did not form an employment contract, and that employees could be terminated any time, without notice, and with or without cause. Evidence indicated that he was afforded due process by virtue of being advised of charges, having charges investigated, and an opportunity to respond in writing. Having noted the employer's policy and procedure disclaimers in the guide, the court concludes:

> It is difficult to imagine what more defendent might have done to make it crystal clear to Dell, and all Montgomery Ward employees, that, unless some other arrangements were made [individual employment contract]...Montgomery Ward employees were employees at will who may be discharged with or without cause.

Also, a Colorado court in *Continental Air Lines v. Keenan* (1987) determined that an employee handbook does not, in and of itself, become an employment contract nor limit the employer to terminate only for reasons specified in the handbook, including subsequent revisions to the handbook. In other words, unless handbook language, or revised language, creates an expressed or strongly implied statement that would lead one to expect definitive treatment or terms, it probably will not alter the employer's flexible handling of unique situations. This is precisely why employers need to state some policies generally and others in some detail, but with a caveat or two such as liberal use of phrases like "at the company's discretion", or "in the best interests of the company".

Conversely, there are still many other states who may not regard personnel manuals or employee handbooks as inherently binding with respect to its contractual nature, but these documents will be evaluated individually to determine whether or not their language created a particular expectation. For example, the Illinois Supreme Court has stated that not all provisions in an employer's handbook give rise to an enforceable contract, they ruled that the employer's discipline and termination policy did create a clear promise of particular treatment that employees could reasonably expect as an offer in *Duldulae v. Mary of Nazareth Hospital Center* (1987). Similar to other court findings, the employer's handbook stated that permanent (should use the word "regular") employees would only be terminated after investigation and proper notice, and warnings were required prior to discharge except in serious offenses. Both serious and non-serious violations were itemized. Plaintiff, who was terminated for "unsatisfactory service" and without notice, was awarded damages for breach of contract.

Even more opposed to the implication of policy manuals as an employment contract was the Fourth Circuit Court of Appeals in *Bailey v. Merrill Lynch, Pierce, Fenner & Smith, Inc.* (1986) under North Carolina law. Here, the court ruled that employers may promulgate and change their policies, or even attach them to individual employment contracts and they will not necessarily be held exclusively binding with respect to the reasons an employee may be fired (I wouldn't recommend testing this in many other states!). Similarly, but on a more moderate stance, the Fifth Circuit Court of Appeals reviewing the Texas case of *Joachim v. AT&T Information Systems* (1986) ruled that absent a (individual) written agreement as to what procedures would be followed in the event of discharge, employee handbooks create no contractual rights with regard to the terms and conditions of employment. Pennsylvania has drawn much the same conclusion in *Martin v. Capital Cities Media, Inc.* (1986), where the appellate court went so far as to question whether the judiciary ought to be involved in prospective alterations of the time-honored at-will employment standard.

Once again, great care must be exercised by employers in their preparation of personnel policies, by supervisors and managers in their statements to employees, and by all company representatives to insure that no promises are made to employees—or even inferences of promises—unless you're absolutely certain such promises can and will be met. Consequently, the writing of manuals and handbooks has become something of an art-form in terms of how to best satisfy opposing forces that can arise in many and varied circumstances. For this reason, you are encouraged to read the suggestions contained in Part III, Chapter 2.

Breach Of Good Faith: Firing Probationer

On the surface it may seem rather extreme to hear that a court has ruled on the wrongful termination of a probationer, but the situation in *Steward v. Mercy Hospital* (1987) points to a major error in the employer's use of handbook language, and how some courts regard it as contractual. Here, the California Court of Appeal found that plaintiff had been employed for 14 years, took a medical leave of absence from 1979 to 1982. She was rehired as a phlebotomist and terminated four months later during her probationary period for allegedly switching or mislabeling viles of blood. She filed suit claiming these were pretextual reasons, and that the handbook provided: 1) an expressed assurance that termination would only be for good cause and not in an arbitrary or unreasonable manner; and, 2) a requirement to discuss and use progressive discipline before the occurrence of a suspension or termination. The court, in articulating those contractually-implied factors for good cause termination, said:

> The duration of [the employee's] employment, the commendations and promotions she received, the apparent lack of any direct criticism of her work, the assurances she was given that if she was loyal and did a good job her future would be secure, and the employer's practice of not terminating personnel except for good cause. An agreement to terminate only for good cause may be shown by the acts and the conduct of the parties, interpreted in light of the foregoing factors and surrounding circumstances.

In other words, what the employer said they would do by policy was not congruent with how they treated this employee, who in all other respects was a satisfactory performer, and the court could not support the idea of saying one thing and doing another.

On the issue of the employee's probationary status, which most of us know is the highest order of at-will termination, the court went so far as to even limit this status to termination only for good cause in certain circumstances by saying:

...the employment contract can be such that even probationary employees may be dismissed for cause only...In fact, there may be an assurance that if the probationary period is completed in a satisfactory manner, i.e., the employee establishes his or her suitability and competence, the probationary employee will be promoted to permanent employee status...Thus the term probationary employee does not always translate into an employee who may be terminated without cause.

The court's rationale escapes me, but it is a published decision and you should probably be aware of the extremes in legal opinions (see also *Crenshaw v. Bozeman Deaconess Hospital,* Montana, 1984).

Similarly, whether or not an employer clearly retains and maintains its at-will relationship with employees was the subject decided by the jury when they awarded plaintiff damages in the Maine case of *Kerrny v. Port Huron Hospital* (1986). On appeal, it was determined that since the employer did not expressly retain the right to terminate employees at-will, the jury acted properly to decide that the employee handbook did create a contractual type of expectation to be terminated only for just cause.

Breach Of Contract And Good Faith: Layoff

In *Kerr v. Gibson's Product Company of Bozeman* (1987), plaintiff was one of twelve employees laid off due to the employer's alleged poor financial condition. The employer's personnel manual stated that employees laid off for lack of work would be terminated without prejudice and eligible for recall. Shortly after the layoff, the employer hired eleven new employees at substantially lower wages and, upon request refused to give plaintiff a letter of recommendation; in fact her discharge letter stated she was not eligible for rehire. Upon appeal, the Montana court sustained the lower court's (jury) findings of the employer's breach of an express contract and breach of the covenant of good faith and fair dealing. Plaintiff was awarded $50,000 in compensatory damages.

Voluntary Resignation Bars Claim

In what might have otherwise amounted to a breach of both an expressed and implied (verbal) contract, the California Court of Appeal has ruled that an employee's voluntary resignation may act as a bar to any claim of wrongful termination. In *Duerksen v. Transamerica Title Insurance Co.* (1987), plaintiff was a long term claims adjuster. When the company took over plaintiff's former employer 20 years earlier, he was told his job would be secure "as long as he didn't screw up or steal." The employer's handbook gave similar assurances of job security unless employees violated ethical standards or failed to perform in a reasonable manner.

More recently, plaintiff was told to either double his productivity or be assigned the work of two or three experienced employees. After deciding to retire instead, he filed state and federal age discrimination claims, and brought suit for wrongful discharge under multiple claims. In a rather surprising decision (for California courts who have been very liberal in these matters), the Appellate court held there can be no wrongful termination when an employee voluntarily quits, nor constructive discharge in the absence of a pattern of discriminatory treatment (this view is contrary to many other interpretations of constructive discharge conditions). The court found that:

> ...there has been no attempt by plaintiff to rescind his retirement or to show that grounds exist to do so. On the contrary, he stands on his supposed right to terminate his employment and then utilize his own act as the predicate for recovering damages. We emphatically reject the idea that whenever an employee is faced with "impossible" job demands he or she may retire or resign and then challenge the employer's policies and practices through the singularly inappropriate medium of a tort suit.

4.22 SERVICE LENGTH AS AN IMPLIED CONTRACT

Some courts have held that mere service length of an employee creates a property interest and implies that they can only be terminated for just cause. Many such cases decided in favor of employees have also been riddled with poor judgment on the part of the employer's treatment and conditions under which the employee was released; often for pretextual, discriminatory, or reasons other than job related performance and conduct. The courts frequently turn to the employer's policy manual, handbook, and employee performance records in these cases, and weigh them against testimony of the factual circumstances. Absent the appearance or presence of such arbitrary and malicious reasons for terminating long term employees, the courts will likely support the employer's at-will rights.

The general trend has been for those liberal state courts to use the implied contract due to an employee's longevity as a reason to decide in favor of employees where their release is for no apparent good reason and was handled poorly by the employer. In essence, these courts are saying that employees who provide long-term and dedicated service deserve better (e.g., advance notice, reasonable cause, and perhaps even severance pay and other independent consideration such as help in finding new employment).

In more conservative states, it is not uncommon for these courts to reject the notion that an employee's length of service creates an implied contract for just-cause only termination.

For example, in *Harris v. Arkansas Book Co.* (1985), the Arkansas Supreme Court rejected plaintiff's claim of intentional infliction of emotional distress when she was discharged without severance pay or pension benefits after 49 years of service. The court held that an act would have to be "so extreme and outrageous as to go beyond all possible bounds of decency and be regarded as atrocious and utterly intolerable in a civilized community" to qualify as an intentional infliction that would result in one's emotional distress. Also, a California federal district court held in *Cox v.*

Resilient Flooring Division of Congoleum Corp. (1986) that the termination of a 27 year service regional sales manager, without notice but with severance pay as part of a reduction-in-force, was completely within the employer's discretionary power of at-will employment to do so. This court rather vehemently expressed the opinion that there is no contractual obligation that becomes an inherent entitlement with the length of one's employment (contrary to some earlier opinions).

4.23 WRITTEN EMPLOYMENT CONTRACTS

With greater frequency, state and federal courts are giving contractual meaning to both written and oral employment agreements made by the employer through managerial representations. The most common agreement is, of course, the written employment agreement—usually reserved for management employees—entered into at the time of hire. Some courts have additionally held that the language in simple "welcome aboard" letters to new hires can become contractual if its contents express or imply such promises as "as long as you perform your job in a satisfactory manner, you should enjoy a long career with us", or "you will be given an employee handbook which contains all of the terms and conditions of your employment."

Termination Notice

One of the most common types of employment contract violations is the breach of a termination provision. Such was the case in *Curacare, Inc. v. Pollock* (1986) where the employer continued to maintain that the one year written agreement was invalid and sought a reversal by an appellate court of the jury award for $8,500 in damages. This agreement, however, contained a two-week notice termination provision, but the employee was terminated only four months into his employment and with only verbal notice and no severance pay. The Alabama Court of Appeal upheld the breach of contract in behalf of the employee, but remanded the case back to the lower court to adjust the award to a recovery of two weeks pay.

Guarantee Based On Salary Review Promise

In what might appear to be a novel decision by the U.S. Court of Appeals, this court reversed a district court's holding that the promise of a salary review at the end of one year as provided in an employment agreement did not create a guarantee that the contract was therefore (impliedly) intended to be one year in duration. In *Hartman v. C.W. Travel Inc.* (1986), the Court of Appeals held that promising a salary review at a predetermined time created an implied guarantee to be employed for that term due to ambiguous language in the employment agreement, and plaintiff who was terminated after five months was wrongfully discharged.

Again, this case points to the need for employers to be very careful about wording employment agreements. This employer probably could have avoided this liability had the language been more clearly constructed such as, "During your term of employ-ment which will remain at-will, you may be eligible for salary reviews at intervals and by standards established by the company at its discretion."

"Mutually Agreeable" Term Means At-Will

In a further illustration of the importance of terms used in employment agree-ments, the California Court of Appeal in *Mahnstrom v. Kaiser Aluminum & Chemical Corp.* (1986) held that the employment agreement's reference to a length of employ-ment that was "mutually agreeable" to the parties was sufficient to establish an at-will relationship even though plaintiff's interviewers assured him that he wouldn't be fired without just cause. The agreement also stated that it superceded all previous agree-ments, and he signed it after the interviews.

After working four years in California, his job was being transferred to Florida which he accepted as an alternative to layoff and based on alleged promises of another three years employment until his retirement. Nine months later his position was elimi-nated (determined to be for legitimate business reasons therefore just cause). He brought suit on the breach of oral promises made prior to his hire and upon transfer, and a breach of the covenant of good faith and fair dealing resulting from the employ-er's failure to find another position for him. The court summarily rejected these claims.

No Breach Due To Income Offset

In *Feldstein v. Guinan* (1986), plaintiff entered into a one year medical residency contract with the County of Cook, Illinois. Subsequently, he was notified that the position was going to be filled with another person, and he was offered a residency in the following year which he refused. During the year, plaintiff earned a salary of $50,000 whereas he would have earned only $12,800 under his residency contract. Upon appeal from the lower court's dismissal of his claim, the Appellate Court held that a complainant must be able to demonstrate the existence of damages that result from a breach of contract. With evidence to the contrary inasmuch as the salary earned more than offset what would have been earned, there could be no relief through dam-ages. (See also *Reese v. Dow Chemical Company,* Wyoming, 1986) The significance of this case is for employers engaged in wrongful discharge cases to ascertain the termi-nated (or rejected in the case of a potential front pay award) employee's earnings subsequent to leaving to pursue an earnings offset to any award granted by the court in the event the employee prevails.

Jury Awards High For Employer Misconduct

Most wrongful discharge cases are initially tried before juries, and when employer misconduct has been demonstrated to cause the breach of a written employment contract, it is not uncommon for the jury to award exceedingly high compensatory and punitive damages. Take the Illinois case of *Green v. Advance Ross Corp.* (1985) where the defendant company bought a family-owned business in Texas. Later, plaintiff (one of the family members operating the business) expressed interest in starting a competing business, but agreed to enter into a 10-year employment contract with this company instead. The contract required a 180 day termination notice and one year severance pay. Within a few years, plaintiff was ordered by a Chicago representative of the company to fire his father. He did, but with an unauthorized six months severance pay. Plaintiff was fired for insubordination, as was his mother on the same day (consider the emotional appeal to the jury of that act), without requisite notice or severance pay. The jury awarded plaintiff $1.2 million in compensatory damages for lost income through the term of the contract, and $2 million in punitive damages for the employer's willful, wanton, and reckless conduct.

Another example is found in the California case of *Litwak v. The Fed Mart Corp.* (1984) where the jury awarded plaintiff $3.2 million in compensatory damages and $3 million in punitive damages for libel and breach of contract. Here, the 59 year old plaintiff was hired as the company president in May 1980 to head its many store operations throughout the Western U.S. He was given a written contract for three years at an annual salary of $250,000. He was fired five months later and brought suit alleging not only breach of contract, but also asserting that following his termination the company told the press his release was due to business losses and his mismanagement. In trial, plaintiff was able to show that he had turned down other offers at higher salaries before taking this position, but had been unsuccessful in obtaining new employment after the notoriety associated with his termination.

If either of these cases, or many others like them, are appealed and sustained in their awards, neither plaintiff will have to be concerned about job search in the immediate future. Clearly, in both cases the employer erred in a most serious fashion by failing to adhere to the employment contract, and then in making matters dramatically worse by their misconduct in conjunction with the actual termination. It's regrettable that some employers must learn about ethical practices and conduct through litigation where they are publicly judged, than through their own moral attachment to standards of honesty, decency, and commitment to one's word—like it or not based on future changes in conditions! And, because conditions can easily change within short periods of time, employers ought to consider using either shorter term employment contracts, or make sure that the contract contains a precise and short term notification clause in the event either party desires to terminate it.

4.24 VERBAL AGREEMENTS AS EMPLOYMENT CONTRACTS

Even more than written employment contracts, it has been the verbal agreement or promise made to employees that has been litigated with greater frequency and controversy with respect to whether certain verbal statements constitute an implied contractual obligation for the employer. There seems to be no clearly apparent general rule about what the various state courts will do in matters of oral representations to employees, other than the rule-of-thumb that the more damaged the employee has been subjected to, the more sympathetic the jury is likely to be. So, here again, liberal state courts will generally act leniently toward employees damaged in some way by an employer's breach of oral representations, while more conservative courts tend to interpret an employer's verbal statements rather narrowly.

One of the reasons used by some courts for a narrow interpretation of verbal promises is due to the Statute of Frauds found in most states which essentially provide that only written agreements over one year in length can be subject to a tort claim, and thus oral promises are not binding (*Santa Monica Hospital v. Superior Court,* 1985, *Hodge v. Evans Financial Corporation,* 1985, et al.). Such a position used as a defense by employers subjected to breach of oral contract claims may help begin setting some limitations on employees in those states that tend to accept wrongful discharge cases based on the making of oral contracts.

For example, if an employer makes a verbal representation to an employee that is promisory in nature, and the employee not only performs in clear reliance on the promise (e.g., moves to another city) but also that the performance was of an indefinite period (to assume a new job), then it is not likely the statute of frauds defense will work. Let's examine a few cases of the verbal contract theory.

Verbal Offer Of Employment For Life

In *Murphy v. Publicker Industries, Inc.* (1986), plaintiff had been employed by defendent company for 28 years. Three years after his hire, he was offered a promotion if he moved from his newly acquired New York home to Philadelphia. At the time of this offer, he alleges that his supervisor assured him he "would be working for the company forever" if he took the new job. He subsequently moved his family and continued working for the company until 1979 when he was discharged. He brought suit alleging termination without cause and breach of a lifetime employment contract. The jury found for plaintiff on the basis of evidence of an oral contract (statement made by supervisor) for lifetime employment which set aside the employer's at-will termination right.

Absence Of Independent Consideration

In most states, for verbal employment contracts to be enforceable there must be the giving of something more than merely services by the employee—referred to as independent consideration—unless the employee can show they were not paid for their services and did not otherwise breach the contract themself. In the absence of such independent consideration, courts are more likely to conclude that no contract was consummated and, absent other conditions, employees are terminable at-will.

Such was the case in *Romack v. Public Service Company of Indiana, Inc.* (1986), where plaintiff, a Captain having 25 years experience with the Indiana State Police, was hired by this private company in 1979 with the alleged assurance of permanent employment. He was discharged in July 1982 and brought suit for fraud, negligent misrepresentation, and retaliatory discharge. The appellate court affirmed the trial court by concluding employment is at-will unless there is a showing of either a promise of employment for a specific duration, or that the employee had given the employer independent consideration. Since the employment was of an indefinite term and insufficient independent consideration by the employee, his employment remained at-will.

Similarly, in *Ross v. Montour Railroad Company* (1986), a Pennsylvania appellate court found that a 22 year service employee lacked sufficient independent consideration to create an employment contract that would have altered his at-will employment. Here, a productive and competent employee had been successively promoted from mechanic to assistant superintendent, but bumped back to a machinist-welder when business declined in 1983. He walked off the job and failed to return in September 1984, at which time he was fired. In his breach of contract suit, he alleged that the promise of promotion made by the company president created a verbal contract, but the courts found this argument inadequate to alter his at-will employment.

Supervisors' Personal (Vicarious) Liability

Probably more often than not, it is a supervisor or mid-manager that may say something to an employee upon an offer of employment or promotion that gives rise to a verbal contract. Ultimately though, it is the company (President, CEO, owners, or stockholders) who suffer the consequences of the actions of these company representatives which, in itself, should stand as good reason to make sure they are well trained on preventing verbal representation problems of this type.

Periodically, employees filing wrongful discharge suits may try to include the supervisor as a separate defendent on the grounds of personal liability for creating some promise that was not subsequently upheld by the employer. While findings of the courts vary—again based on factual circumstances—the general principle applied by the courts is that supervisors and managers are agents of the employer acting under its corporate authority to carry out business operations. Unless a supervisor or manager commits a willful (knowingly) negligent act, or goes well beyond the authority inherent in their business capacity, courts will tend to find their actions a mere extension of their role as a company representative, but who can create obligations in behalf of the employer. They, too, can be fired by the company when their exercise of authority is erroneous.

In employment situations that can result in a wrongful discharge cause of action, there is always the chance that supervisors can be held personally liable for their acts particularly when an employee can show that the supervisor acted in a negligent, wilfully violative manner in carrying out their authority. Most courts, as evidenced by the following case, are very reluctant to hold supervisors, managers, and other company agents as independently liable, but the possibility of doing so is always present in situations where the actions of these individuals is sufficiently contemptuous to provoke the court's opinion of guilt.

Because the filing of what was considered a completely frivolous wrongful discharge complaint, the Ninth Circuit Court of Appeals levied $2,800 in costs and fees against plaintiff and his attorney in *McCabe v. General Foods Corp.* (1987). Here, the plaintiff was terminated five months after his hire as a production foreman in December 1982. He had previously worked many years for the company, but had resigned on two separate occasions. Upon termination, he brought suit for $100 million claiming wrongful discharge and intentional infliction of emotional distress by the company, the production manager as his supervisor, and the operations manager. The court rebuffed the liability of the supervisor and manager inasmuch as they were carrying out their official duties, and that plaintiff failed to make a reasonable showing on other grounds of wrongful discharge.

4.25 PERFORMANCE APPRAISALS AS EMPLOYMENT AGREEMENTS

Over the last few decades, the courts have progressively scrutinized and reconfigured many technical aspects of the way in which human resource operations are to be administered—from validated selection procedures to fringe benefits and finally to the details that ought to accompany employment separations. Not surprisingly, and perhaps even long overdue, the courts and compliance agencies have begun to take a keener interest in the use and relevance of performance appraisals by employers as one of the sources of documented evidence that helps define the totality of the employment relationship, particularly from an employment history perspective.

Much of the attention given performance appraisals has emerged in conjunction with wrongful discharge litigation beginning in the early 1980's. Why? Because the greatest majority of terminations are for either performance or conduct/behavior reasons. Conduct and behavioral standards are typically defined in personnel policy manuals or handbooks, whereas performance (the skill, knowledge, productivity, accuracy, etc.) is evaluated through the appraisal process whereby specific standards are (ought to be) defined by the appraisal document. This is not to say that conduct and performance are mutually exclusive—quite the contrary in many instances; rather they tend to be dealt with through different processes (policy violations for conduct versus poor ratings or notices for performance problems).

When we terminate an employee for purely performance deficiencies, or for behavioral problems that have performance manifestations, we ought to be prepared to demonstrate the following kinds of managerial efforts to correct and deal with the situation. Whether or not the employee is at-will in the view of the employer has little bearing on the need to follow these types of practices with *all* of our human resources.

☐ Prepare a written "discussion memo" to the employee citing very specific performance deficiencies and illustrate each one with a detailed example. Be sure each problem or deficiency cited is directly related to their particular job. Don't be vague. You can be reassuring about your hopefulness and confidence in their ability to correct the situation, but don't pull punches as an overreaction to avoid hurting their feelings.

☐ Document your discussion with the employee to note the essence of what was covered; whether or not the employee acknowledged the problem(s), and what conclusions were reached.

☐ Closely monitor the employee's efforts without being too obvious. If improvement or correction is too slow or not developing, have another private discussion and document it, but this time let the employee know that unless the identified problems are not corrected by specific dates, and maintained thereafter, they will probably be subject to reassignment, demotion, or termination. At this point, a formal written memo of the issues, discussions, understandings, and potential consequences should be given to the employee with a copy to their personnel file.

☐ If the employee's scheduled performance appraisal occurs during this sequence of events, and your policies state that it is to be done on or about this time, don't delay it. The formal appraisal should accurately reflect both the past (year) and present situation.

☐ Having prepared sufficient documentation of the performance problem(s), discussed it with the employee, and allowed a reasonable period for correction, you are now in a much better position to initiate a termination whether or not you choose to give the employee your reasons (cause). Before preparing your termination notice, be sure to thoroughly check your policy manual/handbook to determine if the employee should be notified of any rights such as the filing of an appeal, grievance, or response before action is taken. You may also wish to read Chapters 10 and 12 which go into more detail about the legal and administrative problems of performance appraisals, and specific ways to solve them.

It should be noted that the above procedure is minimal and general in nature. Every situation leading to or involving immediate termination is different. Some are relatively straightforward and expedient, while others may involve complex if not rather nebulous conditions that should be approached and dealt with very carefully. Various aspects of an employee's job conditions or performance standards that are either discussed or put in writing have the potential of being construed as a performance contract. In its simplest terms, it implies "if you do this (e.g., meet performance goals, standards, and the like), we'll do this other (e.g., keep you, increase your salary, promote you)". In other words, it can be an expressed or implied promise to exchange mutually rewarding benefits from the relationship, therefore having at most some elements of a contract and at least elements of good faith and fair dealing within the relationship.

One of the most plaguing and perplexing problems associated with performance is that of the long term employee who has a thick file full of complimentary notices and glowing written appraisals. Their deficient performance comes to someone's attention, and it is discovered that:

1. Their performance has declined gradually; or

2. Their performance dropped suddenly; or

3. Their performance never was up to a desirable level, but no one was honest enough to address it and create accountability; or

4. They have not been able to adapt to technical or other changes in the job, supervision, company direction, or related kinds of employment conditions.

Without following the aforementioned procedures, or even more detailed efforts to bring light to all the issues that would enable you to either correct the performance problem or succeed in a termination, you stand a good chance of being on the losing end of a wrongful discharge suit involving allegations of breach of implied contract (longevity of service), breach of good faith and fair dealing, discrimination, infliction of emotional distress, defamation, and perhaps constructive negligence (previous satisfactory evaluations or recent ones which are found to be lacking the rater's honesty).

A case in point is that of *Chamberlain v. Bissell* (1982). This case involves an employee with 22 years of adequate service who was discharged for performance-related deficiencies. Although this Michigan court found in behalf of the employer due to plaintiff's contributory negligence in his job performance, the court made special note of the employer's duty to use "reasonable care" in carrying out its performance evaluation process.

The conclusion of the court was that the employer had a contractual duty to review the employee's performance, and a duty to use ordinary and reasonable care in conducting the performance review. The court set the standard of care as being that of a reasonable person performing a review, and then the court questioned whether the reviewer conformed to the standard. The court concluded that a reasonable employer under the circumstances would have informed the employee that his discharge was being considered, or was possible, unless a rapid and drastic change in job performance came about before the time of subsequent evaluation. **A failure to warn the employee was equivalent to negligence on the part of the employer.**

This case raises the potential liability of an employer for wrongful discharge where the employee is terminated based on a formal performance evaluation instrument that is less than objective or insufficiently related to the employee's job standards of performance, and where the employee is not warned that failure to correct performance deficiencies may result in termination. (See also, *Flanigan v. Prudential Federal Savings & Loan Association,* Montana 1986, and *Haas v. Montgomery Ward & Co.,* 6th Circuit, 1987.)

Some employers may be inclined to regard the concept of constructive negligence as rather far fetched, but it would be a mistake to do so. While the Chamberlain case may be an isolated incident in the State of Michigan, the same was thought to be true of the Cleary case in California that subsequently served as a catalyst for the spread of wrongful discharge suits across the country and into federal courts. In fact, with some consistency there has been an increasing number of cases focusing on the legal implications of performance appraisals during the 1980's, some of which are illustrated in Part III, Chapter 3.

Another example—again from the Appellate Court in Michigan—deals with sales productivity as a measure of performance where a six year sales representative was terminated for failing to meet new minimum requirements for sales. In *Farrell v. Automobile Club of Michigan* (1986), plaintiff brought suit for breach of contract despite the fact he was given warnings and offered a salaried position before being terminated. He rejected the salaried job as a demotion since it paid less. He was also told by his supervisor not to be concerned about the union contract in which the new sales production requirements were being negotiated. This statement, coupled with the absence of past sales requirements led the jury to enter a judgment for plaintiff and the Appellate Court to affirm their findings.

Clearly, performance appraisals and related documentation are rapidly becoming synonymous with good defense in support of initiating termination actions. Managers would be well advised to heed the warnings contained in this mounting legal trend to connect appraisal systems, written standards, and communicated expectations to various causes of legal action. Appraisal systems should be more precisely related to the duties and standards of differing jobs (correlated to job descriptions and other job conditions), thoroughly communicated to employees, and raters trained in the process and legal implications. Now that the American Bar Association has publicly endorsed such an approach, you can be certain that it has become a prominent national issue.

4.26 NON COMPETITION AGREEMENTS

As a matter of employment contracts, it is not unusual for an employer to want to protect the company's market interest—mostly in terms of its product and market territory—or trade secrets. Such an issue is frequently incorporated into the employment contract upon hire, and requires that the employee not engage in, or be affiliated with, a competitive business during and following employment for a specified period and/or a specified region. Disputes almost always arise following employment when the employee feels prepared to venture out on their own to apply what they have learned from their previous employer. It's a risk each employer takes when we hire and train employees.

Although not generally an issue associated with wrongful discharge suits, it is a matter of employment contract and is periodically litigated on that basis, so I believe it to have relevance here. Additionally, unlike wrongful discharge cases, it is the employer that tends to bring suit for breach of a non-competition clause.

Take for example the case of *Satellite Industries, Inc. v. Keeling* (1986). Here, the plaintiff company designs, builds, and sells portable restrooms throughout the United States. All employees are required to sign an employment contract containing a non-competition clause that prohibits them from working for a competitive business during or within two years after employment in any state where the company does business, or to reveal any of its inventions, improvements, or discoveries.

Defendant was hired as a salesman in 1974 and rose to the position of Vice President of Sales over the years where he gained access to trade secrets and the larger customer accounts. Just prior to his leaving the company, he established a relationship with a competitor that had improvements similar to those of plaintiff. Plaintiff sought a temporary injunction and enforcement of the non-competition clause. The trail court found the clause only partially enforceable because it was unreasonable to include the entire United States. On appeal, the court not only found the clause reasonable and fully enforceable (because of doing business in each state), but that the company was entitled to damages by remand to the trial court.

Another example was in *Allan J. Richardson & Associates v. Andrews* (1986) where plaintiff's business was structuring settlements in personal injury cases, and brought suit to enforce the non-competition clause contained in the employment contract of several employees who pooled their resources in a competitive fashion. The nature of the business is highly competitive for clients who can be dealt with nationwide since most work is done by telephone. The trial court granted an injunction that restrained employees from competing not nationwide, but in a five state area. Effected employees and the employer appealed. The lower court's decision was affirmed on the basis of granting a nationwide injunction would in this case be an unreasonable restraint of trade, yet the clause is enforceable to the extent of necessary protection of the business and good will of the employer.

4.27 "FORUM SELECTION" CLAUSES

For those employers who use employment contracts, especially those with employees in different states or multinational employers, it may be in your best interest to consult legal counsel about including a "forum selection" clause in these and other agreements. Forum selection is essentially the designation of what state and/or legal authority will be used to resolve any dispute that might arise in carrying out the terms of the contract. With regard to wrongful discharge or enforcement of non-competition clauses, it allows the employer to predetermine which state and accompanying laws it will be litigated (the employer's home state or where the employee is located). Having to travel to some other state and acquire local legal counsel may serve as a worthwhile deterrant to some employees filing wrongful discharge cases.

Forum selection clauses, while not automatically valid, will generally be held enforceable if:

☐ the provisions are reasonable and understood;
☐ there was no fraud in its construction or application;
☐ it was not in contravention of a strong public policy; and
☐ not seriously inconvenient for trail action (foreign location).

A model forum selection clause is provided below but, again, employers should consult legal counsel to take into full account the circumstances of its use and to examine the elements of its reasonableness.

> All parties to this contract agree and acknowledge that this contract will be governed, interpreted, and construed in accordance with the sustentive and procedural laws of the State of _____. All parties to this contract further agree and acknowledge that the court of competent jurisdiction for any dispute arising out of or related to this contract is the _____ (identify court by exact name).

4.30 DISCRIMINATORY AND RETALIATORY TERMINATIONS: SPECIAL PROBLEMS OF ILLEGAL DISCHARGE

Increasingly, many terminated and laid off employees who might otherwise file claims of discrimination seeking back pay and reinstatement because they felt strongly about the discriminatory intent of their release, are filing their cases as wrongful discharge in order to pursue tort damages under the statute of frauds. Another way in which mere discrimination cases can quickly take on some elements of civil or even criminal law is that during the investigatory, discovery, or hearing phase of an alleged discrimination case it becomes apparent that the disparate treatment is not only factual, but also bear strong evidence of malicious intent, defies good faith and fair dealing, was of a retaliatory motive, required deception to execute, or breached other covenants of the expressed or implied employment relationship.

In this case three executive employees, each of whom was over age 40 and had 17, 18, and 25 years service with I. Magnin, were discharged in 1979 alleging that their release was the result of a deliberate corporate policy to create a new appeal of a more youthful retail market, and that the company therefore wanted to replace them with younger executives. They brought their case under the Age Discrimination In Employment Act (ADEA). Moreover, because of their service length and the malicious nature of their terminations, they also stated a cause of action for breaching the covenant of good faith and fair dealing, and intentional infliction of emotional distress. Damages were awarded to plaintiffs in the amounts of $1.9 million compensatory damages, $640,000 punitive damages, and $400,000 attorney's fees.

While the court never implied that I. Magnin was not free to change its corporate policy concerning the new appeal to a more youthful market, the court did make it clear that the termination of executives, merely because of their age, bore no reasonable relationship to such a marketing change. What is also important for employers to recognize is that by creating a cause of action under federal statutes, suits for wrongful discharge can be filed in federal courts who may well take a very different position on the issues and evidence than might be taken by the jurisdictional state courts!

Yet another important area of caution for managers are terminations predicated on retaliatory motives. Such underlying reasons, if surfaced (and they usually will be), can be violative of other laws—such as labor relations, wage and hour, workers' compensation, and discrimination—or they can support a finding of breach of the covenant of good faith and fair dealing.

Admittedly, it can become very difficult for the manager to cope with strong feelings against an employee who demonstrates such behavior as being manipulative, threatening (to sue or file a claim of some sort), is a chronic complainer, abuses privileges, or avoids doing productive work. In circumstances such as these, it is tempting for the manager to become the stereotyped cop following the red sports car, or hidding behind a barrier, waiting to catch them doing something—anything—wrong that might justify a ticket. That something they did wrong, when examined in conjunction with another action on their part that may have caused the manager to take offense, can easily take on the appearance of a retaliatory discharge.

Take, for example, the case of *Herrtzel v. The Singer Co.* (1982). The plaintiff had been employed as a senior patent attorney for five years when she was terminated. Coincidentally, her termination closely followed her complaints about other employees smoking in and around her work area. She filed suit alleging that the discharge was retaliatory, that there was intentional infliction of emotional distress, and that the company had implied that she would not be discharged so long as her services were satisfactory (implied contract). Evidence revealed that her performance had been rated superior. (See also *Gates v. Life Of Montana Ins. Co.* 1983, where punitive damages were awarded to plaintiff because her supervisor forced her to write a letter of resignation after firing her without notice—breach of good faith and fair dealing).

Another, perhaps more explicit, example of a retaliatory discharge was that of *Roussequ v. Teledyne Movable Offshore, Inc.* (1986). Here, the company employed 63 people to work on its offshore oil derrick barges. Employees were required to spend seven days on the barge before getting time off to leave, and were only paid for hours worked. With declining demand for oil, the employees worked fewer hours and brought a claim under the FLSA alleging they should be paid for all hours on the barge excluding meal and sleep time. When 37 employees were then laid off, they conceded on the hours worked claim due to findings, but brought suit alleging retaliatory discharge. Evidence was introduced that supported the claim of retaliation: 1) a supervisor posted a copy of the wage claim suit on a bulletin board and gave a speech threatening those who were party to it; and 2) even though it would have saved the company money, it rejected a plan to allow laid off workers to work part-time. Evidence of the supervisor's action would have probably been enough to make a showing of retaliation, but the rejection by the company of a cost saving measure affecting those laid off no doubt provided reinforcement to the notion that the employer had a retaliatory motive for the lay offs.

It is because of the implications of discriminatory and/or retaliatory reasons on wrongful discharge that managers and human resource professionals should give careful attention, and close (self) examination, to both the underlying motives behind each disciplinary and termination action, and to any preexisting event on the part of the effected employee that may be viewed as precipitating such a secondary motive. These motives demonstrate fraudulent and malicious intent, and thereby bring them within one or more of the three causes of wrongful discharge actions through either state or federal courts!

So how do you solve the problem of the employee who becomes a persistent source of aggravation? In answering this question, perhaps the first thing that ought to be done is to determine *who* the problem is: the employee or supervisor. I have found too often that, as managers, we tend to assume that all other managers and supervisors are competent, fair, and objective when it comes to dealing with problem employees. We tend to avoid questioning their judgments, behavioral interaction with employees, and the basis of their decisions affecting "their" employees. Too, we tend to shield, overprotect, try to smooth over or cover-up, and often unduly forgive their errors and manner of dealing with employees.

When upper management finds it is taking such a posture with line managers and unit supervisors, the organization is very likely standing on the threshold of fostering an "us-and-them" workforce. It is simply not appropriate any longer for upper management to *assume* that a particular personnel problem brought forth by a supervisor equates to a problem employee. It may be more factual that the real problem is the supervisor; that this particular employee is not as tolerant of a poor or untrained supervisor as are other employees in the unit (who might have become passive out of fear for their jobs); or some combination of the supervisor's loss of objectivity in relation to the personality characteristics of a particular employee. Quite frankly, many intelligent employees tend to be highly resistant to a less intellectual or ego-oriented supervisor.

The point then is for upper management in general, and human resource managers in particular, to conduct very thorough and objective fact-finding, such as those steps contained in Section 3.0, before formal discipline or prospective termination of a "problem employee" is developed with respect to intended action. Minimally, such fact-finding ought to include the nature of the circumstances and on-going relationship between the supervisor and employee, the supervisor and other supervisors, and the employee and other employees. The fact-finding process should be undertaken in every case of a supervisor with less than two years experience, or where it is either common knowledge or suspected that the supervisor is lacking in these kinds of skill, knowledge, behavior, and objectivity. A key sign is when they demonstrate undue emotionalism.

If managerial fact-finding reveals that the problem is the subordinate employee, and that the supervisor is not a contributory or provocation factor to circumstances surrounding the problem, then focus must be given to the employee's performance—not his or her personal conditions. The "I just don't like him," or "His work just isn't very good", or "He's a constant source of aggravation" just aren't solid business reasons in and of themselves. We must look deeper and carefully examine precisely what the person is doing or not doing in the context of performing their job.

In other words, what should be identified are those behaviors and activities of the employee that have negative effect upon the productive performance of their job, or that of others. Once these are properly identified in terms of job performance or organizational effects, it is time to begin thorough documentation and counseling (also documented). Records of this type should exist to demonstrate that the employee was made aware of their job responsibilities, expected levels and types of performance, and company rules and standards of conduct. They should be told exactly what is to be corrected, how to correct, and by when.

If the employee doesn't comply, then follow the principles of progressive discipline until you have sufficient reason to terminate their employment. Contrary to prevalent belief, it doesn't take long to reach termination in many cases, but it does require more thorough thought and process on the part of management to develop convincing evidence that no other alternative was reasonably available, and that no other motive provoked the decision to terminate.

More importantly from the human resources perspective, a surprising number of turnaround employees have been successfully managed when using this type of an approach to employee problem solving. Likewise, when the problem turns out to be the supervisor, they should be dealt with using the same process and with equal precision. Lest we forget, supervisors are also employees in the eyes of law, and they have been known to sue their employers with growing regularity. That should serve as no reason to avoid their correction, discipline, and if necessary their termination (or demotion to a non-supervisory position).

4.40 CONSTRUCTIVE DISCHARGE: POTENTIAL PROBLEMS WITH INVOLUNTARY DEMOTION, TRANSFER, REASSIGNMENT, AND PERFORMANCE EXPECTATION CHANGES

Just as the issue of wrongful discharge has evolved as a legal doctrine since the early 1980's, so too has the doctrine of constructive discharge which had its inception by the National Labor Relations Board (NLRB) in its review of cases under federal labor law. The doctrine and its underlying principles have been progressively adopted by various courts in its application to civil rights and tort claims. It tends to be a highly circumstantial doctrine to the extent that the facts of each case must make a showing of working conditions so intolerable as to force a reasonable person to resign to free themself of the condition in order to prevail in the claim.

What is at the root of the constructive discharge doctrine is that there may exist some unjust reason (pretextual, discriminatory, or retaliatory) the employer wants to get rid of an employee, so initiates some action short of termination that is hoped will prompt the employee to resign or retire. The most common actions used by employers that can give rise to constructive discharge litigation are demotions (position status and/or pay), reassignments such as requiring unfamiliar job tasks, assigning unrealistic production levels, and transfers to an intentionally inconvenient or unreasonable location.

In most but certainly not all constructive discharge cases, it is the employee who is generally held responsible for showing evidence of the employer's intent to provoke a resignation. However, often because the courts are the only forum for at-will employees to obtain redress of an employer's alleged wrongdoing, some courts have accepted the mere perspective and alleged effect of the employee as sufficient evidence to state a cause of action rather than hard evidence proving the employer's intent. Additionally, the present pattern of cases where judgments favor employees, there has usually been some evidence of a discriminatory *atmosphere* involving race, age, sex, and sexual harassment.

A (liberal) case in point is that of *EEOC v. Hay Associates* (1982) where a female financial analyst was found to be subjected to a sexually discriminatory environment. Her male supervisor treated her in a paternalistic, condescending manner, then replaced her with a higher paid male employee when she resigned. The court found the manager's treatment of her to be intolerable and the employer liable for violation of the Equal Pay Act.

Yet another anomaly among the usual trend in constructive discharge cases—this representing a conservative finding of the court—was in *Duerkson v. Transamerica Title Insurance Co.* (1987). This case was decided by the California Court of Appeal as perhaps part of their belt-tightening to begin neutralizing the proliferation of wrongful and constructive discharge cases that have clogged the courts in that state since the early 1980's. In this case, plaintiff was a long term employee who had received raises, promotions, and bonuses with the company over the years, and there were no adverse performance criticisms in his personnel file. Then, in October 1983, he was told to either double his productivity (under surveillance conditions), transfer to another job (having unreasonable requirements), or the company would "fire your ass". He was given until the next morning to make his decision. After remaining in his position another three weeks, he quit and filed suit under various wrongful discharge theories including infliction of emotional distress. The court rejected each of his successive claims based on:

- No claim could be made for wrongful discharge where the employee resigned.

- Conditions were not present to support a claim of discriminatory constructive discharge (abhorrent to public policy or violative of specific statute), nor sufficiently aggravating.

- The employer's conduct was not sufficiently outrageous to support a claim of emotional distress.

The court also concluded its findings by noting that part of its decision in this case was that any different holding might create a flood of litigation!

The conclusions reached in the two previous cases are not necessarily reflective of the norm in constructive discharge case law—at least during the last decade. Generally, there are four elements that have evolved to embody the principles of a cause of action under the constructive discharge doctrine. Some employees have prevailed when only one of the elements was sufficiently present, but the more elements that can be demonstrated, the better the chances are for employees to gain court (jury) sympathy and handsome awards. The four elements are:

1. Humiliating behavior directed at the employee in person by one of their superiors on a regular if not daily basis.

2. Being given new responsibilities or assignments that are unreasonably inferior to the job previously held and their demonstrated ability.

3. Subjected to aggravated discrimination such as racial slurs, insults, physical abuse, and the like.

4. Any evidence of the employer's deliberate or intentional creation of intolerable working conditions so severe that a reasonable person would have no alternative but to resign under protest.

Here are a few, perhaps more classic, cases to illustrate how erroneous demotions, reassignments, and transfers take shape as constructive discharge and thereby open the door to wrongful discharge suits. It should be noted that in many of these cases the action was an erroneous judgment or handling by management rather than an employee who did not deserve to be dealt with for operational reasons. This is simply to say that there are any number of approaches to resolving human resource problems, but creating elements of constructive discharge is not one of them.

Focusing on elements 2 and 3 above, the U.S. Court of Appeal for the Sixth Circuit found that a benefits clerk of five years had been constructively discharged when demoted eight pay grades to a mail clerk in *Williams v. Caterpillar Tractor Company* (1985). Plaintiff, a 52 year old female with an above average performance record, got a new supervisor who came to the opinion that she was not right for the job based on the belief she: 1) was divulging confidential information to nearby employees about other employees; 2) did not understand procedures; and, 3) made errors—none of which was adequately documented nor discussed with her. Rather than bother with any attempt to correct these alleged deficiencies, the supervisor merely demoted her to a job she could not perform (lift and carry 50-80 pounds of mail over a 28 acre plant area), so she quit and filed suit.

In court, her contention was that being demoted eight pay grades and to a job she couldn't possibly perform was more than mere discipline. On the issue of revealing confidential information, she countered that her desk was close enough to other employees to be overheard while on the telephone, and she easily rebutted other alleged deficiencies since the supervisor had no precise records. Ultimately, the court used the "reasonable person" test and concluded that under these circumstances she was justified in quitting and may sue for wrongful discharge.

On elements 3 and 4, a court in Wisconsin remanded the case of *EEOC v. Miller Brewing Company* (1986) to a jury trial for a finding of fact (summary judgment denied for employer), and held that discriminatory practices of a company do not have to be deliberate to the extent of showing the employer's intent to force a resignation. Here, the employee was a black male who was employed for four years. He had average performance appraisals, but had been criticized for his written and verbal communication skills even though his job was that of a bottle washer. After being allegedly harassed physically, insulted racially, and denied educational and vacation benefits received by employees with less seniority, he resigned and filed a claim of discrimination with the EEOC. In his behalf, the EEOC filed a constructive discharge suit.

Concerning element 2 above in connection with a breach of employment contract, an employer may not make significant alterations in an employee's job during the term of the contract unless mutually agreed to in writing as a superceding amendment of the original contract. Such was the equivalent ruling in *Weisman v. Connors* (1987) where an appellate court affirmed the trial court's judgment in favor of defendent employee on grounds of negligent misrepresentation and breach of contract which amounted to constructive discharge under the circumstances. Defendent had been a Ford Motor Company executive and entered into a three year employment contract with the owner of Frederick Weisman Company. When plaintiff complained to defendent that he was not performing well, defendent quit. Plaintiff filed suit to enforce the contract but evidence backfired. The court found that plaintiff employer had reduced defendent's duties and assigned them to another person. The court noted:

> When an employee contracts to fulfill a particular position, any material change in duties or significant reduction in rank will constitute a constructive discharge which, if unjustified, is a breach of contract.

From these and numerous other cases like them, the message is clear from the legal, ethical, and human resource management point of view—do it right or don't do it. This is not to say that employers should discontinue terminating those that no longer "fit", become disappointing performers, or lack the necessary ability to adapt to changing conditions. Rather, it means that employees have acquired legal rights to fair, honest, and dignified treatment, and employers merely need to honor those rights. If employees don't work well in some respect, by all means do them and the organization a favor through corrective action or termination, but do it in accordance with sound human resource principles. When termination becomes necessary, make sure your action is well documented, fair, and timely.

4.50 SOLVING WRONGFUL DISCHARGE PROBLEMS THROUGH FACT FINDING REVIEWS AND SEPARATION AGREEMENTS

Separation agreements can be a very useful means for the employer and employee to reach mutual and somewhat more positive accord on the terms and conditions of a termination. It is most often used with the employer's termination of supervisory and management personnel because of the higher probability of a wrongful discharge suit by these employees. However, separation agreements are not, in and of themselves, absolute insulation from litigation. If not drafted carefully, or if carried out improperly, they can and have been set aside by some courts hearing post-employment claims of coercion, fraud, negligent misrepresentation, breach of good faith, and/or breach of contract (see *Valenti v. International Mill Services,* 1985; *Van Heest v. McNeilab,* 1985; *McNasby v. Crown, Cork & Seal Co.,* 1987; and *Oglesby v. Coca-Cola Bottling Co. of Chicago/Wisconsin,* 1985) Conversely, if the agreement is thoroughly relevant to all issues concerning the employee's situation, benefits, limitations, and special conditions, and the separation process executed properly, courts have generally tended to hold both parties to its terms.

Separation agreements are not boilerplate, fill-in-the-blanks documents. Given that their primary aim is to avert wrongful discharge, discrimination, and other types of employment related litigation, and as a demonstration of the employer's good faith effort to minimize harmful effects to the employee, each separation agreement should be drafted only after a very thorough review of all issues that might come into play concerning its legal interpretation. For purposes of added objectivity and good faith effort, many employers are now using outside consultants and labor attorneys (or both working in conjunction) to conduct such reviews *at the time the employer concludes that termination action is necessary with an employee.* Here are just a few of the kinds of documents and details that ought to be scrutinized:

1. **Fact Finding:** A detailed discussion with those supervisory or management employees who are in a direct line of oversight of the employee to ascertain a chronology and factual basis of the present situation and what has lead up to it. Issues of importance should be the nature of the problem, its effect, supporting documentation, communications with the employee, degree of employee's acknowledgement, warning(s) of advanced discipline or termination, and the prospect or reasonableness of alternative problem-solving measures.

2. **Employee's Personnel File:** Establishment of just cause if it becomes a necessary issue such as might be contained in warnings, disciplinary notices or actions, ratings and statements made on performance appraisal forms as opposed to positive records of promotions, pay raises, commendations, or written statements suggesting an implied contract or lifetime employment. Special attention should be given to the presence of a written employment contract and any modifications thereof.

3. **Personnel Policy Manual or Employee Handbook:** Language that implies or expresses the employer's commitment to providing employees certain rights, benefits, and procedural assurances such as the presence of at-will employment statements, termination only for cause, progressive discipline assurances, grievance and appeal rights, non-discrimination policies, severance pay policy, and the employer's past practice applications.

4. **Benefit Documents:** Ascertain the type, cost, effective dates, and rights accumulated by the employee concerning payoff of any accrued leaves, investments, or other forms of due compensation; vesting or conversion rights in pension program; continuation of healthcare plans; and the existence of an active workers' compensation claim.

Remember, each termination has its own individual set of circumstances; they vary on issues of fact surrounding the situation and how it developed or was handled, position(s) held, job responsibilities and performance versus conduct, length of employment, and a vast array of conditions that make up the total picture of the employment relationship that make it unique from other employees. Consequently, separation agreements need to be customized to fit all pertinent factors of the employee, employer, and their mutually acceptable agreements.

In its basic form, a separation agreement is an exchange of benefits expressed as terms and conditions provisions—"I'll give you this if you go away and don't sue me for that (even though we're not guilty)." It constitutes the employee's waiver of rights to sue or file employment related claims in exchange for "independent consideration" by the employer, usually meaning monetary compensation in some form such as:

1. **Severance Pay:** Income that is additional to any other monetary entitlements and which may be construed as a means of replacing the employee's lost income for a temporary period while they find other employment. To be independent consideration, this amount or duration of severance pay should be additional to severance pay made available to employees by policy. The most prevalent severance pay provision in separation agreements is 90 calendar days to six months at full pay processed with the normal payroll and deductions as if they were still on the payroll, but mailed to their home address.

   It may be worthwhile for the employer to add to this clause something to the effect of, "Should employee obtain other employment prior to the end of the severance pay period, employee is to notify employer promptly at which time severance payments shall be discontinued by employer effective on the date of employee's new employment."

2. **Fringe Benefits:** Similar to severance pay, this provision extends the employer's commitment to continue payment of the company's normal contribution toward the employee's existing participation in health-care and income protection plans such as major medical, dental, vision, life insurance, and disability plans. Normally, the employer will not continue any contribution toward the employee's pension plan or allow any continuation of related rights that might otherwise accrue. Fringe benefits agreed to be paid by the employer should also discontinue at the conclusion of either the severance pay term or upon new employment. Also, don't overlook your (COBRA) notification obligation so the employee knows their rights to convert their health policy to a private plan.

3. **Accrued Entitlements:** Income that has already been earned, excluding perhaps pension rights payable through plan-specific criteria and by application to the

plan administrator, should be fully paid on the termination date. Such items would include salary payoff for hours worked to the last date of employment, accrued vacation and any other compensable leave, as well as any other entitlements of monetary value accrued in connection with their employment.

4. **Other Independent Consideration:** Most forms of truly independent consideration are those things of monetary value above and beyond normal entitlements. However, the employer is in a much better position to demonstrate its good faith toward the employee if the company can show that it additionally took into account other concerns of the employee. So it may be worthwhile for employers to separate themselves somewhat from the process by having an independent consultant or attorney meet with the employee in a pre-termination meeting to: 1) try to smooth any ruffled feathers; 2) get an impression of how the employee sees the situation; and, 3) find out if there are any special concerns the employee has that should be contained in the agreement (and to make them feel more comfortable about having a part in its development and signing it without a claim of duress!).

A few examples of issues raised by employees where their company retained me to serve as an independent facilitator in termination actions were 1) future employment references (a delicate area of defamation law), 2) the employer paying the cost for executive out-placement counseling and job search (highly recommended), and 3) the employer's agreement not to bring suit against the employee or in any other way breach the confidentiality of the employee's action that prompted a termination decision.

Employer interests, too, are covered by various provisions of the separation agreement with the most paramount one being the employee's waiver of any past, present, or future rights to file claims or legal actions against the employer under an array of stated laws, regulations, and legal precedence relating to employment. Other employer interests that are often addressed in the separation agreement are:

1. **Understanding:** That the employee clearly understands their release of all legal rights for actions against the employer, but also their understanding of all other terms and conditions of the agreement.

2. **Confidentiality:** That the employee will not divulge the contents of the agreement to any other person except, at his or her option, immediate family members and private legal counsel. This is a means of discouraging the "me too" syndrome among other employees who learn of the settlement and later become subject to termination.

3. **Entered Voluntarily:** That the employee is signing the agreement voluntarily and without pressure from the employer to do so (to eliminate the challenge of there being duress or coersion).

In support of these and other provisions of the agreement, there are a few items that employers ought to take into account in carrying out this separation transaction. They are:

1. Prepare two original drafts of the agreement to give to the employee, and keep a copy. Ask the employee to sign both originals, compare them to the copy (to verify no alterations) and verify the employee's signature, and return one original to the employee when signed by the company.

2. Let the employee know (by cover letter) when you want the signed drafts returned. Allow the employee three or so business days to look over the agreement and to have ample time to consult with their own legal counsel. The Eighth Circuit Court of Appeals, in *Lancaster v. Buerkle Buick Honda Co.* (1987), has determined that review by the employee's legal counsel is not necessary to be held binding, but by stating to the employee that they are encouraged to consult with their own attorney becomes more reassuring to the employee that the contents are fair—presuming they are!

3. Avoid the use of such terms as "termination" and "resignation" since these words imply that one or the other is the moving party rather than the decision and attendant agreement being a mutually neutral one; use the term separation of employment. Also, in any communications with the employee, be cordial but remain businesslike.

Whether or not there exists the possibility of litigation or filing of claims by employees, the termination process does not have to be frought with anxiety, pain, reckless abandon, or resentment. If handled properly by recognizing the delicate nature of these situations, and special need for humanity, it can be a much less emotion-driven transition from one life phase to another. There is a desperate need for employers to help reduce the fear and consequences of an employee's job loss no matter how much it may have been deserved.

PART III. SOLVING PROBLEMS INVOLVING DIFFICULT EMPLOYEES AND WORKPLACE CONTROL MECHANISMS

There is little else more disruptive to managers and the productivity of organizations than having to deal with a problematic employee. Whether the issue is their attendance, attitude, declining performance, self-serving behavior, or any other problem among a myriad of dysfunctions that affect productivity, the focal point is dealing with people in the organization's setting. Indeed, the net effect of damage caused by difficult employees can be dramatic in terms of direct and indirect costs of productivity. Too, people problems are often the toughest to prevent, observe developing, or diagnose with much accuracy for problem solving purposes. Consequently, most managers don't begin to recognize problem employees until the result of the employee's causal source of a problem takes on a visible effect in their work relationships, performance, or responsiveness to working conditions.

When situations in the workplace involve problem employees, or difficult people problems, a manager's attention quickly turns from carrying out routine tasks to spending many trying hours to resolve the inherent complexities of dealing with someone who is out of stride in some respect. If the manager becomes intolerant or inadequately skilled in handling these matters, the situation will only worsen. It will also probably be handled poorly in which case the problem will only magnify, the manager-employee relationship will deteriorate (or escalate adversely), and sooner or later a termination will result—usually because the problem was never properly addressed, nor was it skillfully handled.

Quite simply, we as managers can no longer afford to neglect our responsibility to deal with employees in ways that are thorough, sensible, and fair to the extent that is reasonable in organizational life. To continue doing otherwise has already been proven too costly as evidenced by increased employee litigation, the cost of lowered morale on productivity, unnecessary absenteeism, and adversarial turnover to name only a few. When management mis-handles an employee situation it brings attorneys, courts, compliance agencies, and unions to our doorstep. It's a sign of bad business practices, and the inability (or unwillingness) of managers to cope with and intelligently resolve people problems in organizations is breaking the back of American business.

So, you ask, how should we be solving the vast assortment of people problems in our organizations? The answer is that there are three absent or terribly weak features within our business organizations that are paralyzing truly effective solutions to our people problems, and they are not mutually exclusive of each other. First, the decision makers in our organizations are all levels of managers such as yourself. Managers come from a diverse range of backgrounds, training, and education that has prepared them (and you) to perform business *functions* with little attention given to development of the knowledge or skills necessary to deal with *people* situations. Similar to giving birth to and raising children, there is no particularly intense developmental training or prerequisites that accompany what we have been lead to believe is a completely natural process. Our attitude seems to be; "since we are people, and we feel we understand ourselves, then it follows that we can inherently understand and deal effectively with others." If that were true, then why do we continue to have high rates of divorce, employment terminations, suicides, wars, and interpersonal conflicts in organizations—daily?

So the first area that must be addressed by business organizations to begin dealing more effectively with people problems is to learn more about, and applying the skills related to, human behavior in the workplace. We must begin by recognizing that people are instrumental to the success of our organizational operations, but we are behaviorally very different from each other. These differences demand managers who are insightful of human conditions, and who possess a broad range of skills in dealing with the diversity and complexities of human behavior in the workplace setting.

Second, many of our organizational control systems and mechanisms that are theoretically intended to *prevent* problems and guide our people toward productive work results are either absent or so weak that they lack relevant meaning to those for which they were aimed. Control is a necessary part of any business if it is to achieve order, consistency in the effectiveness of its operations, and the acquisition of desired results. While many organizations and their managers establish concise quality control programs, there remains a grave deficiency among organizations in their human resource control systems and related mechanisms. Simply stated, a control system is the integration or linking of independent but related operational functions in a way that then gives it (synergistic) meaning and relevance.

One such example is a performance control system that ties goals, objectives, work plans, policies, and appraisals together to assure their relevance to each other, and meaningfulness to each person in the organization. A control mechanism is merely a component of the system—personnel policies concerning the performance appraisal program for example—and if these mechanisms are a weak link in some respects, then the chain of the control system can break, thereby making their relevance to organizational standards obscure. The thoughtful, thorough, well-organized development of control systems and mechanisms is an essential ingredient to effective operations that involve the performance of work by people. We can no longer avoid that inescapable fact.

Third, people in organizations require the reliance of those that manage them, the systems that guide them, and the employment and operational programs that support them. In this regard, managers need to become more focused on developing greater consistency of the leadership styles and methods that reinforce both employee and organizational needs. Too, all managers need to become more active participants in the creation, development, and implementation of programs and other organizational efforts aimed at positive forms of reinforcing the retention of valuable employees, the reform of those having difficulty, and the removal of those whose presence poisons what all others are trying so hard to achieve. Only by the full participation of all levels and functions of managers are our organizations—and those that derive benefit from being in them—likely to achieve the kind of operational excellence that is now required in an economic atmosphere of global competition for resources.

The chapters that follow, then, will help you as an organizational and human resource manager to solve many tough problems related to the people in your organization; to deal more effectively with human behavior in the workplace, and to become more successful in your personal role as one of perhaps several managers trying to deal with creating new systems, mechanisms, and operating methods to deal with difficult people problems. Use the information contained in these chapters to develop your own skills and spark interest within your organization to undertake new, fresh, and sensible approaches to solving operational problems that have lingered far too long, and have impeded your organization's potential success.

CHAPTER III: 1.0
PROBLEMS OF WORKPLACE BEHAVIOR:
UNDERSTANDING THE NATURE OF
HUMAN BEHAVIOR BEFORE ATTEMPTING
ITS RESOLUTION

Our ability to more effectively handle—to successfully resolve—problems in the workplace that stem from troublesome behavior can only be strengthened by progressive development of those supervisors and managers responsible for guiding operations. This requires a deeper understanding of the sometimes complex nature of human behavior, more analytical thought about the actions of our employees, patience, and practice. While success always moves faster when the entire organization operates in unison and with commitment toward such goals, the absence of those conditions should not serve as a reason or excuse for individual managers to delay their own development in this vital area of human resource problem solving.

It is therefore the objective of this chapter to provide you with basic, yet absolutely necessary, background in the nature of human behavior as it applies to the workplace. Such background not only puts real world situations into perspective, but also provides us with more reliable insight into underlying causes of behavioral situations. It also leads us to ascertain the best possible approaches to treating the condition—not merely its effect. Using this chapter as a backdrop for a clearer view of human behavior in the organizational setting, Chapter 2 goes on to define and diagnose specific behavioral and performance problems with suggested approaches to the most effective resolution.

1.10 THE NATURE OF OUR WORKFORCE AND ORGANIZATIONAL BEHAVIOR

There are probably very few supervisors and managers who would argue that the singular most trying responsibility they have is dealing with problem employees, be they subordinates, peers, or the higher ups. Dealing with troublesome people in the workplace is something we all have to do, but we do it with varying degrees of effectiveness. Since most people rather instinctively resist many of the negative implications that are commonly associated with handling problem employee situations, it can quickly create an emotional and physical effect on the supervisor who knows well that things aren't right but struggles within themself to find an answer.

Invariably supervisors and managers wait too long, become emotionally connected to the problem or its effect, misread the underlying cause, and/or use the wrong approach or method to deal with the immediate situation rather than resolving the problem. The consequences are all too often reoccurrences of the same problem, damaged work unit morale, diminished respect and credibility for the supervisor, and at least one employee whose negative behavioral patterns may be more reinforced through mishandling in some way than controlled or corrected by effective means.

In my experience over the years being involved in a myriad of simple to complex situations within organizations, and in working with psychologists, organizational behavioralists, and evaluating the applied research in the area of organizational behavior, I have found that there is almost always a common thread that separates those companies that are successful at effective problem employee solving and those that aren't. That thread is a well developed understanding of human behavior in the workplace by all levels of management and an organizational commitment to apply a full range of problem solving skills, techniques, mechanisms, and support systems to insure precision at every stage of problem handling. The effective company recognizes the value of its human resources, develops its supervisors and managers around those resources, understands the complexity of human resource and behavioral problem solving, and makes effective problem solving a primary mission through support systems. Those companies that continue to struggle with behavioral problems in their organizations are quite simply focused elsewhere, their supervisors are underdeveloped in human behavior skills, their approach is hit-and-miss, and employees are seen as a transient and sometimes nuisance resource.

1.11 THE NATURE OF BEHAVIORAL PROBLEMS

The problem of difficult employees is that they behave in ways that are counterproductive to the goals and setting of business operations. To complicate matters, not all employees misbehave in a similar manner nor for the same reason. In fact, in some instances of misbehavior the employee doesn't even know why they did it, but clearly something drove or compelled them to be demonstrative; the act had a negative effect;

others saw it or were subjected to it, and now you recognize the need to address it. If experience has taught us anything it is that when we avoid addressing a deteriorating situation, it is sure to worsen.

One of the more obvious conditions in the workplace is that people, in their roles as employees, are distinguished by their vast differences. They come to us in all forms, divergent experiences and backgrounds, and in remarkably unique psychological makeup. Some are quite stable in their values, lifestyles, reasoning, actions, and direction. Others may be self-serving, deceptive, rebellious, or in many other ways problematic. When we hire employees, we typically view them (using our intuitive sense of their reaction to our interview) as a stable person who is motivated to have the job—I don't know of too many employers who have hired people to the contrary! Thereafter, and almost always with at least a few employees, things change. They begin to show up for work late or leave early, they violate conduct rules, they begin to lie or steal, their performance declines in some way, or they take on other manifestations of a nuisance employee. Invariably, when managers compare the behavior of a problem employee to the person they saw during the interview or initial employment period, they wonder what happened to create such a change.

What is certain about the lives of people is change, and all people will change in a number of ways and at different times. This change process is no less active during employment. In fact, for most of our employment is an essential life experience that aids our growth, provides opportunities for personal growth and development of our identity and worth, and enhances our orientation toward social, economic, and political matters. So, both the stable and not-so-stable person will undergo personal changes in the course of their employment years—if for no other reason than the fact that change is a very natural condition of human behavior and development. But, not all change is positive nor what most of us as managers would consider to be developmental.

We would also do well to recognize that organizations change in a number of ways over time, and these changes too become influential conditions that can, and often do, trigger reactional behavior from those subject to it. Consider, for example, both the plight of the newly appointed supervisor with stronger work values than their predecessor (organizational change), and the attendant resistence of some employees to accept or comply with new conditions (behavioral change). Too often, we tend to jump right in and treat things that happen in the work setting as an instant or isolated condition rather than as a symptom of perhaps something much broader, multi-faceted, and developed over time. In other words, we tend to react only to what we see which is the effect of some condition at that moment without realizing (i.e., stopping to think and diagnose) the cause. The result is often a mishandling of the situation, glossed over by rationalizations about being too busy, the employee being a pain in the ass anyway, or "it's not my job to be their parent." When it comes to the value of work and the nature of behavioral change, perhaps Eli Ginzberg said it best when he remarked:

> Human beings require an opportunity for self-expression through work, which is the best tie
> between themselves and reality. We have failed to use work properly as an instrument of
> therapy and rehabilitation.[1]

If we managers are to become more successful at dealing with behavioral conditions and changes in the workplace, we must learn to distinguish those ingredients of human behavior in order to make more accurate determinations of a course of action in line with organizational needs. We must learn which situations should be decided with speed, allowed room for change under controlled conditions, or be accommodated with intentional flexibility. Also, we need to recognize when some behavioral conditions are justified, in which case it might be the organization that ought to change. When we stop looking at the organization as the possible culprit of behavioral problems, we're in deep trouble as managers of our organization's welfare, let alone its resources.

1.12   CHANGES AND TRENDS IN INDUSTRY AND OUR WORKFORCE

The unquestionable fact that contemporary workers are uniquely different than their counterparts of 30 or more years ago has been referred to frequently in other chapters, and heavily documented in research publications. Indeed, there has been a massive restructuring of the American society in most aspects of life, social conditions, and orientation toward values and beliefs. Our industrial and economic base has likewise undergone rather dramatic transformation during this same period resulting in a shift toward services as the leading industry, a consumption economy, technology as our salvation, and global competition for markets and resources as our impetus to retool business practices.

When we look at this bigger picture it becomes more apparent that these two sources of economic development—the workforce and industry—have not changed in unison based on mutual goals, in the same direction based on creating shared benefits, nor in the same time sequence that might otherwise complement mutual needs during the last three decades. These changes have been out of sync, often with cross-purposes, and with disjointed lag time between change in one area (employer or workforce need) and adjustment to it (workforce or employer response) some years later. It may sound like a physics theory, but whenever two sources become opposing forces they will repel, not complement, each other and remain at cross-purpose until one yields enough to draw closer to neutralize their respective positions.

Looking closer at societal (and consequently workforce) changes, it is somewhat insightful to make note of some features about our present workforce and, with continued reading, why many of our traditional approaches to resolving workforce problems are ineffective. Here are some issues to ponder, but as you read them, begin to

---

[1] Ginzberg, Eli; "Man And His Work"; in Dale S. Beach, *Managing People at Work.* p.5.

formulate in your own mind what implications go with each one in terms of how they are likely to influence workplace behavior or work orientation.

1. Only 10 percent of the American population live in a family structure where the head of household is a male and sole wage earner—"traditional" American family. Additionally, over 70 percent of the workforce brings in more than one source of income.

2. By the mid 1990's, 80 percent of American women in the 25-44 age group will be in the workforce.

3. American youth are making such life decisions as marriage, career, education, and child-raising at later ages (mid 20's to mid 30's).

4. Maternity and parental leave, child care, and health care are national issues as a reflection of the increased difficulty in balancing family-work needs.

5. The largest working population, meaning now a majority, is living in what used to be referred to as an alternate lifestyle—single or divorced, living alone, single parent with one or more children, or sharing a residence with a roommate or a "significant other."

6. Despite a high number of reading illiterate, the workforce as a whole is remarkably well educated; and in many cases overeducated in proportion to the availability of jobs that make proper use of it.

7. Both jobs and employment conditions are much more complex with respect to technology, skills, processes, and relationships; there are more things to cope with, adjust to, and deal with.

8. Over 95 percent of American businesses (six million) are classified as small (having fewer than 100 employees), and there is an unprecedented increase in the number of entreprenuerial or employee-owned businesses along with a continuation of acquisitions and mergers among larger employers.

9. One in every ten employees are drug or alcohol abusers, and most employees want more attention given to workplace health (smoking, asbestos, toxic substances, work space, etc.).

10. Flex time, Employee Assistance Programs, employee training programs ($13 billion per year), Cafeteria Benefit Programs, and other efforts toward responding to workforce needs have increased but lag behind demographic changes and workforce demand.

11. Although labor union membership is on the decline from a 1980 peak at 22.4 million members, they can be expected to shift their representation emphasis more toward policy and social issues—both having large price tags.

12. Despite movement of employers toward better pay, benefits, leave and work schedule options, and less autocratic management styles and practices, studies have identified the paradoxical condition of the highest rate ever of job dissatisfaction among workers. Workers' expression of their job dissatisfaction is evidenced with a high continuation of:

    - Turnover
    - Absenteeism
    - Poor Morale
    - Sick Leave Abuse
    - Alcoholism/Drug Abuse
    - Union Affiliations
    - Strikes
    - Law Suits
    - Theft/Sabbotage
    - Workers' Compensation Claims

    While job dissatisfaction is not the only explanation for these workplace maladies, it is a major contributor to behavioral reactions.

From the above and other sources of worker characteristics, we can profile our present workforce in contrast to years past by saying they are more diverse in lifestyle, values and beliefs, age, and personal development; they are more educated, skilled, affluent, and resistent to authority and control; they are more open in their pursuit of equality, fair treatment, being involved, being properly utilized and challenged, and other forms of shared power; and they are more individualistic in their needs and approaches to work. Many sociologists and organizational behaviorists have begun to see a slow yet gradual shift from the intense emphasis of diversity and individualism over the next 20 years as the somewhat rebellious social theme of the 1960's and 1970's becomes the older, more conservative and establishment worker, and the more "synthesizing" youth of the 1980's take their place in the workforce. The synthesizing generation is said to have greater maturity and less idealism; to possess values about work and family reminiscent of the 1950's era, and more rational views of business, the economy, and world events. Let's hope so!

American business can likewise be characterized. We seem to be moving rapidly toward a two-tier industry base; the greatest majority is very small size businesses and then there are a very few large and mega-large (conglomerate) businesses with the middle size company disappearing through failure or absorbtion by larger corporations. Global economics and the competition for exchange of goods has made business move more intensely toward innovation and effective use of its resources. Jobs have become more skilled and specialized, emphasis is on getting more done with less, and middle management positions have become victim of the movement toward efficiency downsizing. Payroll, production, marketing, and research and development costs are being stretched compared to their return, yet the demand for more of everything persists. Vast improvements have been made in pay, incentives, benefits, working conditions, leadership styles, and worker treatment, however the need for further and more ubiquitous workplace reforms still outrun response by the business community at large. In short, conditions within organizations are better, but externally things are worse. As it has been in the past, it will be those external forces on business that determine its relative ability to shape and respond to internal needs be they pay raises; benefit programs; the number, content, and structure of jobs; or the ability to cope with workforce conditions.

1.13 WHAT EMPLOYEES WANT

When we compare our present workforce to that of a few decades ago—many of whom are now in key decision making positions—we see some very interesting differences. First, conditions were very different in the past with respect to demographic characteristics of the workforce. The predominant worker was a white male and sole wage earner of a family unit; divorce meant social rejection; authority was not to be questioned; national patriotism and company loyalty was expected; and those that worked hard and stayed out of trouble got promoted—the basis for promoting "good workers" to supervisory positions. So what workers wanted most then was good pay, opportunities for overtime, job security, a chance for promotion and more responsible work, and better benefits. In other words, conditions at that time prompted worker interest in lower threshold, personal needs and wants—money, security, and position esteem.

In contrast, the present workforce has moved up beyond those lower thresholds of needs and wants, partly due to improvements made in earlier years and partly due to the new breed diversity and sophistication of an evolving workforce. Accordingly, studies performed during the 1980's have consistently shown that employees occupying clerical, technical, professional, and administrative jobs have the greatest needs and wants for:

- interesting and challenging work
- the right help and equipment to do the job
- enough information and authority to get the job done right
- opportunities to develop special skills
- seeing and being recognized for the results of their job
- being asked for their participation in things that affect them
- promotional opportunities

The central theme to these needs and wants is the job itself as a means to self-actualize the individual through responsibility and opportunity, but there are two separate dimensions to this theme.

1. **Work Unit Dimension:**
   This involves those direct work conditions and the nature of the job itself; other jobs and peers in the work unit; the quality of supervision; relationships with other work units; environmental pleasantness; and the power base of the unit to acquire resources, information, and opportunities.

2. **Organizational Dimension:**
   This involves such conditions as managerial cohesiveness and philosophy toward its human resources; the degree to which policies and practices reinforce employee needs; the effectiveness of operational methods; information sharing (communications thoroughness and style); job structuring (promotional paths); and soundness of pay, benefits, and training programs.

The issues of worker wants and needs, and its two-dimensional framework, are critical elements of job satisfaction. What is important about job satisfaction is that studies have determined a strong positive correlation between low satisfaction (an absence of the needs and wants) and turnover, absenteeism, declines in productivity, and in a few studies poor physical and mental health. It is therefore reasonable to conclude that employees subjected to an absence of their needs and wants will become progressively more effected psychologically, physiologically, and attitudinally with resultant changes in their behavior at work and toward their job and employer.

For those of you that like lists, here are two concerning job satisfaction that I've compiled as a result of my client work and teaching over the years. As you read them, consider your own behavior as a manager or supervisor, that of others who supervise, and in what ways your organization supports or creates job satisfaction conditions.

SUPERVISORY ACTIVITIES THAT GENERATE COMPLAINTS AND JOB DISSATISFACTION

1. Does not communicate openly
2. Criticizes in front of others
3. Does not listen
4. Does not do performance reviews on time; does but inadequately
5. Does not plan the work of the unit
6. Does not go to bat for subordinates
7. Does not keep promises
8. Cannot be trusted
9. Throws jobs at people without explanations, reasons, or assistance
10. Does not help people learn and grow toward higher jobs
11. Not receptive to new ideas, suggestions, or other forms of employee participation
12. Violates rules others must obey (does not set a good example)
13. Never asks subordinates for their suggestions (makes all changes and decisions unilaterally)

14. Does not provide sufficient training

15. Shows favoritism toward some

16. Passes the buck

17. Does not handle complaints properly

18. Does not give up detail work

19. Does not treat subordinates with dignity

20. Makes unreasonable demands on subordinates

21. Oversupervises (hovers over subordinates); does not allow subordinates to make decisions in their own jobs

22. Does not face up to and handle discipline problems within the unit

23. Holds back good people for selfish reasons

24. Brings up problems on the annual review that have never before been mentioned

25. Discusses one subordinate with another subordinate

26. Uses fear, threats, intimidation

27. Is a perfectionist

28. Only gives negative feedback

29. Has people drop everything to do a project, then the project sits untouched on the supervisor's desk for weeks

30. Does not share information openly nor stand up for subordinates

FACTORS INFLUENCING JOB SATISFACTION

Supervision: technically knowledgable, *considerate,* personable, clear communication and direction, personal interest, consistent, ethical and objective, responsible, *participative* (consider and use employee input, and help with work).

Job Challenge: variety of tasks; opportunity for creativity, responsibility, and progressive difficulty; and use of personal skills or traits. The opposite of challenge is boredom which breeds absenteeism, declining productivity, grievances, disciplinary actions, and turnover.

Job Clarity: *role clarity* with others and in own job (job description in clear, unambiguous terms), and *feedback clarity* (how one is doing).

Job Content: standardization and specialization have increased productivity industrially, but they can be highly detrimental humanly if not designed with a proper balance of job challenge.

Promotion and Compensation: existence and understanding of career paths and customary efforts to achieve; clear ties between training, supervision, evaluation, and employee promotion plan; being paid wages at or above the average for similar work; receiving employment benefits that communicate a "we want you" employer attitude.

Informal Group Processes and Social Identification: supporting positive and useful informal group interaction among employees; encouraging their ideas for improved work situations; and creating the opportunity and means to identify with the organization on a social level (e.g., company picnics, softball teams, interdepartmental competitions, etc.).

1.14 WHAT EMPLOYERS NEED

As managers and social creatures, we sometimes overlook one undeniable fact about the organizations we operate within; that being that they are an economic entity with very explicit needs if they are to survive, grow, and prosper—in that order. Forgetfulness about this fact is perhaps easier among the public and non-profit sectors who provide fixed services and, merely because their services are needed, there evolves a false sense of the organization's economic welfare. What each and every one of us need to remind ourselves is that our employer is paying a sizeable amount for our existence in the organization. Paying this price means that every employee ought to be contributing some form of an economic return that exceeds their cost in the total scheme of revenue production versus expenditures. It is generally referred to as "value-added" resource management. It's a very simple aconcept held near and dear to upper management, and who become quite annoyed at its disregard by those below.

By using this economic orientation to the needs of business—be it profit motive of the private sector or service motive of public and non-profits—it is perhaps easier and more meaningful for us to understand the organization's (employer) human resource needs, and they are:

1. **Productivity;** well skilled, good attendance, few errors or repetition, good work quantity and quality, positive contributor, and works well with others.

2. **Efficiency;** self-motivated, requires minimal supervision, uses time and other resources effectively, helps others, follows instructions and procedures, and is thorough.

3. **Innovation;** seeks new opportunities and growth challenges, contributes ideas, helps resolve problems, looks for and develops cost saving measures, and develops new procedures, methods, or products.

4. **Honesty;** being truthful and trustworthy, not stealing or falsifying, doing what needs to be done and what is right, being fair and objective, admitting error and being earnest about self-correction, having personal integrity, and treating others in a mature, responsible manner.

5. **Loyalty;** having commitment toward the goals of the organization, the nature of the business, the supervisor and work unit, and peers. Avoiding any form

of damage to the organization and respecting its efforts, taking pride in the work and organization—defending its good name, giving the job the best effort and sincerity, and not abandoning the organization when the least thing goes wrong.

Sound simple? Maybe not, but it's really not asking too much of employees to provide these types of straightforward economic returns in exchange for their list of needs and satisfiers. Moreover, each of these five employer needs are positive revenue generators and/or contribute toward their industry success. On the other side of the same coin are the disruptors and resource wasters that slowly and incidiously undermine the economic welfare of employers, and they are:

- Turnover
- Absenteeism
- Disharmony
- Low Morale
- Grievances
- Law Suits
- Poor Communications
- Disjointed Leadership
- Biasness

Take a look around. See which organizations you're familiar with that are getting their five needs, as opposed to those having the kinds of disruptors mentioned above. Ask yourself who's getting ahead and enjoying it, and who's on the verge of collaspe? Now evaluate your own organization and your role in determining its course. **If you're not contributing to each of its five needs, then you're probably creating one or more forms of disruptions. If those you supervise or manage are disruptors rather than satisfiers, you ought to be considering some prompt action—after you read this entire book!**

Beyond those personal quality needs of employers for their human resources, there is yet another rather universal need organizations have, and that is control. Much like the family unit—another evaporating condition in our society—the organizational unit must establish, follow, and enforce various types of control measures to assure consistency and determine the parameters of how it is to function. With regard to the control of behavior we have rules, and for performance we have standards. While no one particularly likes rules or standards because they are often inflexible and can become an obstacle to our individualism, we must recognize and accept them as practical instruments of productivity control. That is, so long as the controls are clear and reasonably associated with guiding the organization toward the achievement of its goals. If so, then it becomes our responsibility to make the controls (rules and standards) clearly known, observed, and if necessary enforced through sanctions. If the controls are not adequately aligned (i.e., they are too harsh, unreasonable, vague, or lax) with organizational goals, then our responsibility is to change those controls.

More often than not, when organizational conflict and disruption occurs from within its structure, it is likely due to opposing forces using their available sources of power to satisfy cross-purpose needs. Opposing forces—such as upper management with their policy and control needs, middle management and supervisors with their implementation needs, and employees with their fulfillment needs—periodically collide under certain circumstances, interactions, and behavioral conditions much like the resultant mixing of air masses. We may get a little rain or staggered showers; it can snow at higher elevations (ever hear of a high-level manager being cold?) or we can get a blizzard; or we might get some rumbling thunder, a flashy lightning show, or both. The axiom is simple; the more conflict you get, the more serious are the contributing conditions, and the faster you need to find relief.

1.15 THE NEEDED FOCUS OF MANAGEMENT

It should be clear by now that American business has reshaped its industry base to the point where human resources have become the most essential ingredient of our economic development. To make the most effective use of any resource we must employ the proper techniques. Only in recent years have the executive and other managerial ranks given much credence or attention to the importance of its human resources, and the adjustments have been slow in coming and narrow in scope.

Indeed, we have learned much about the human condition and behavioral aspects of our kind only during this century. There remains much more to learn about human behavior and perhaps this realization of the economic significance of our human resources will serve as the impetus to open new doors to further research and deepen understandings. Only by such increased attention to the underlying conditions of human behavior can we begin to effectively redesign our work processes and relationships, create meaningful and compatable employment opportunities, and become accurate and confident problem solvers.

Perhaps more presently apparent with respect to human behavior in the workplace is that the work consciousness (ethic) of our workforce (our society) depends largely on how each individual's wants and goals are shaped. It also depends on the ability of business organizations to frame compatable opportunities. We need to work toward creating more neutral ground where both employee and organizational needs can be satisfied. To do so, we need to begin developing a higher consciousness among employees about the business world and our organization's place in it (including being clear about the organization's expectations and needs). Conversely, we need to help our organizations develop a more focused consciousness about managing the needs of its human resources.

To be an effective manager of people, we can no longer afford to attach ourselves to one way of thinking based on our own values and experiences, nor should we adhere too strictly to one or another style of leadership. The reality of most work unit operations is that there will exist a very diverse array of personalities, backgrounds, values, and perceptions among your employees. This condition requires "situational management" where the manager must be skilled in a wide range of leadership techniques and possess a sound understanding of human behavior. Where there is limited diversity in the work unit, the manager can use a more narrow, uniform style suitable to the nature of those being supervised. For example, autocratic managers will have little success supervising a unit of say scientists, engineers, or social workers since these occupations tend to inherently attract intelligent, responsible, and self-motivated people. However, this same manager who finds a particular management style suitable to the work unit may experience some difficulty when interacting with other components of the organization. **So, one of the needed focuses of management is to adopt our styles of leadership and interaction to individuals by situations, and to embrace rather than resist changing conditions.**

Another focus of management ought to be the clarity and structural development of the organization. Precise and understandable goals need to be developed with operational meaningfulness. Those goals should transcend by clear linkages from the top of the organization to each work unit. There needs to exist a stronger association between what the organization is trying to achieve—and how—to the role of every job in the organization. Too, management at all levels must be pulled together so that it functions as a syncronized, goal-oriented *group* of individuals. It requires maturity, responsibility, compromise, commitment (willingness), team players, and sound leadership. Both responsibility, information, and decision making must be reinforced at all levels, including employees. If people are expected to be a serious part of something, they must have a share in it and understand it. Rules, procedures, performance evaluations, pay plans, interview questions, and all other aspects of human resource operations should be linked to the nature of organizational goals. We've moved away from this, and it's time to refocus.

In dealing with particular employees, we have misdirected our attention on the absoluteness of rules and procedures, the compelling need for consistency, and the effect rather than cause of problems. We should to begin a reexamination of our ingrained premises about these approaches to dealing with human problem solving situations. While those approaches may have served our organization's need for control to one degree or another with success in years gone by, workforce and other conditions are different now and our own experiences in trying to resolve people problems should suggest to us that we need new approaches. Let's face it, most of the old ones aren't working very well!

First, there is nothing absolute about such controls as rules, procedures, practices, and standards. In most cases these are meant to be guidelines to follow under normal circumstances. So when things become other than normal, we need to exercise our judgment, open mindedness, objectivity, and flexibility. We need to adopt to new and changing circumstances, not use mindless adherence to what then becomes rigid controls for treatment of each situation. We also need to become clearer about our own authority and less fearful about exercising it in decision making.

Second, when it pertains to human behavior, we might solve more problems by dealing with inconsistency rather than our preoccupation with consistency control. Consistency is an *effect* but inconsistency can be a *cause*. Take the act of theft as an example. Theft itself is not a consistent condition because it is not a consistent behavioral trait—nor is it normal or desirable behavior. Rather than focusing on whether or not stealing is a consistent trait and which employees are potential culprits, we might be better off trying to ascertain under what circumstances (inconsistency) is the behavior most likely to exist and under what conditions (e.g., frequency, value, and method). I didn't say these new approaches were going to be easy, but there is an absolute need for managers and supervisors to think more deeply about the nature of human behavior before acting to resolve resultant problems.

Third, observing and addressing the effect (usually meaning impact) of any given behavioral problem does little to solve the problem, unless of course the effect is itself serious enough to disregard causal conditions and take prompt action to remove the culprit, ostensibly for reasons of safety or welfare. The effect may be the only thing we see and it is certainly easier to deal with since it is normally tangible—we see the employee arrive late, we hear about someone's missed deadline, and we investigate complaints about customer treatment. If our approach and method of dealing with these sorts of behavioral problems are determined by the effect of the act, we have solved nothing more than communicating to the employee our lack of ability to understand, cope, or willingness to help correct the real situation.

In most situations of negative behavior, its effect by appearance is merely symptomatic of a not-so-visible cause, or set of preexisting conditions, that underlies a given behavior. The cause or preexisting conditions may or may not even bear a corresponding relationship to the behavior. For example, a person's sudden short tempered behavior will have a clear effect on others at work, but the underlying cause of the behavior will not always be associated with anger or frustration. We will not be effective at changing the behavior by pointing out its effect or what will happen if the person doesn't self- correct—at best we may get momentary control of the behavior by the person, but its cause still exists. We will not solve the problem until we can get to and deal with the cause. As Snyder points out:

> ...solutions are too often based on false assumptions about the *underlying* causes. In such cases, symptons typically reappear soon after the intended remedy has been implemented...
> By trading assumptions for more objective, diagnostic methods, managers can accurately identify the actual cause of most human resource problems in their departments and implement effective, long-term solutions.[2]

Fourth, management needs to renew its focus upon the role of their position as decision maker as it effects the lives and conditions of the organization's human re-

---

[2] Peg Snyder; "The First Steps In Solving People Problems." Management Solutions, November 1987, p. 18.

sources, and less toward individual biases, vulnerabilities, and idiocyncracies. Many of the mistakes made in workplace interactions between managers and employees are the result of personality differences. One personality—that of the manager—usually prevails if for no other reason than their position power over the employee. So, the employee must yield at some point or face consequences (meaning personal reprisal). In a different situation, an employee's behavior starts getting out of control, but the overly sensitive vuln erability of the manager results in their avoidance of taking measures to control the employee. Inaction is accompanied by further deterioration of work relationships within the unit until the manager's credibility is severely damaged or destroyed. The same result can occur when the manager interacts with employees based on personal affinities (liking or disliking certain personality types). As Sheppard comments:

> When a supervisor likes an employee, there will be more contact between them and more spontaneous reinforcement of the behaviors that lead to a good job being done. The supervisor is more apt to compliment some activity that was being done well. He or she will smile more in the presence of the employee...It is a basic law of human behavior that actions that are rewarded tend to be repeated with inceasing frequency.[3]

What these situations, and their resultant errors in management handling, point out is the loss of role focus. While the personalities and other characteristics of people, including managers, cannot and should not be completely set aside as a factor to achieving interactive success, it does need to be held in proper perspective of the manager's *decision making* role. Business can ill-afford decision makers and leaders who manage by favor, temperment, subjective values, domineering strengths, or passive shortcomings. **The focus of management needs to be on the acquisition, development, and use of those decision making and action skills reflective of the organization's, not personal, goals.**

1.20 SOME INFLUENTIAL PRINCIPLES OF WORKPLACE BEHAVIOR

It would be impossible to introduce the reader to the many elaborate principles that allow us to better understand the nature of human behavior within the scope of this chapter. There are many excellent books that go into great detail on this subject, and the reader is encouraged to delve deeper into this subject area. However, the intent here is to introduce at least some of the fundamental, yet influential, principles as the basis of workplace behavior, and thereby begin creating new insights into underlying causal conditions. To provide a succinct format, these principles will be provided in the form of seven theorems. You are encouraged to give some interpretive thought to the applications of each one since discussion is necessarily limited.

1.21 BEHAVIORAL DIFFERENCES

It is easy enough to see that we are all physically different, so it should not be a surprise to know that we are equally different with respect to our mental, psychological, and emotional makeup. However, when a group of people are placed in a given situation, it is considered controlled behavior, and this pattern of behavior is learned early in life through the socialization process. These patterns of behavior become the norm and participants are expected to act accordingly. When one behaves contrary to established norms, which is often, the person's behavioral difference becomes more obvious to the group. While we all can't and shouldn't be alike in our behavior toward work situations, some behaviors fall outside the realm of being constructive. These are the behaviors with which managers must be most observant.

Theorem 1. To carry out its mission with any sense of order, organizations require controls and conformity. To some employees this structuring of behavior provides a needed sense of stability, while others may see the environment as rigid and confining. Quite simply, people react differently to any single set of conditions.

Theorem 2. Humans have limitations as well as particular attributes that differentiate us as people and employees. Limitations are considered negative and attributes are regarded as positive. Behavior is produced by both our limitations and attributes, but undesirable behavior is usually the product of our limitations. Consider judgement, processing information, completing assignments, responsibilities, skills, and maturity as limitations.

Theorem 3. Some people are more personally developed than others. They are in touch with reality, mature in their approach, able to cope with changing conditions, keep events in perspective, remain confident and thoughtful, and stay on purpose. The others are struggling with or resisting their own development by oppositional behavior which damages the organization, but hurts only themselves. Consider your own example of the behavioral differences between a well respected/admired person and one that is a known obstructionist.

1.22 PERSONALITY

Personality is essentially our genetic blueprint. It is the composite of our behavioral and emotional tendencies that distinguishes us as unique individuals by the development and use of our values, beliefs, habits, and social orientation. It is also the manner in which these various developmental characteristics produce an enduring pattern of behavior in response to situations and choices. Personality is one of the most common measures we intuitively use to evaluate others socially, for job selection, in the performance of duties, the assignment of particular responsibilities, promotion, and a host of other decisions that may or may not have positive results since personality can express behavior in a variety of ways.

Consistency theory, developed by socio-psychologists, holds that humans strive for balance in our attitudes, beliefs, and surrounding experiences, and we use this balance to reinforce our sense of purpose and righteousness. When contradictions occur, they say, we feel compelled to reduce or eliminate the contradiction. This means that one's behavior in these situations becomes supported and justified by the interrelationship between our beliefs, attitudes, and personality.

Theorem 4. A person's personality type is often expressed through their work behavior and the choices they make concerning occupations, working conditions, and work relationships. Those who seek personal challenge, solitary work situations, and a focus on their own objectives are self-motivated whereas other personalities require external sources of motivation such as group involvement, persistent supervision, and coercive incentives.

Decision making personalities *are those that use either thinking or feeling as the basis of their judgments. Thinking people analyze, organize, formulate, rationalize, develop methods, and require consistency. Feeling people rely on intuition, past experience, appearances, emotional reaction, and flexibility in execution.*

Methods personalities *are guided by result or process. Result people cut through red tape, people, or anything else in the way to reach the goal—they are the bottom-liners. Process people take a systems orientation viewing the process equally important as the goal; they see life as a journey rather than a destination.*

Work in itself, along with organizational life, often produces something of a natural selection process. Those who are ambitious, outgoing, and eager are more likely to acquire the necessary skills and seek out only fruitful opportunities in which they perceive the achievement of their personal goals. Those that work out of pure necessity or circumstance will expect an employer to train them (a paradox since they don't currently possess good skills), they will be inclined toward "feeling" decisions because they lack intellectual ambitiousness, and their methods will be short-cut results— meaning they really don't want to be there. And there are many other work personalities between these two types. Evaluate your own work personality type and how it affects others.

1.23 BEHAVIORIAL INTERACTION, MANIPULATION, AND CONTROL

Each of us have three ego states and various types of drives that often control our behavior with respect to how we act out our needs, values, beliefs, and perceptions. Our three ego states represent those characteristics associated with the three developmental roles by which behavior is modeled; adult, parent, and child. Their respective role characteristics are:

Adult: objective, rational, thinking, decisive, in control, confident, and un-
emotional.

Parent: nurturing, telling, judging, controlling, demanding, biased, and manipulative.

Child: emotional, irrational, feeling, spontaneous, self-centered, rebellious,
wanting, and playful.

Each of us is said to possess one of these roles, or ego states, in greater proportion
to the other two; or we may have two strong states and one weak; or we may have one
predominant state, a moderate state, and a weak state. For example, people who are
described as boring (low social orientation) workaholics are held as having a strong
adult and weak child state. When interacting with others at work, they may stay in
their adult state, but they may also move into a parent state when interacting with less
intelligent or skilled people under them, or the child state (defending themself) when
interacting with those above—particularly if the above person is in a strong parent
state.

The proper state for people at work is the adult, but it is also one of the rarest
because constant interaction among people engaged in work under trying conditions is
a natural trigger for our emotions; hence parent and child states. Also, because of the
inherent closeness or intimacy of work relationships and the nature of job responsibilities, the supervisor's and line manager's job is most akin to that of a parent (showing,
telling, judging, etc.), and the instinctive response to those behaviors is for subordinates to react in the child state (emotional, irrational, feeling, rebellious, etc.). People
who have jobs more distant to the intensity of group interaction, including upper
management, usually do not have as many, or as frequent, of these emotional triggers,
so they are more likely to be seen as adult state people. That may be one explanation as
to why employee complaints should be appealable to higher (impliedly more objective)
levels in the organization.

Drives, or those inner-emotional conditions, are another source of our behavior.
Usually it is these inner-emotions that move us toward certain actions, and tend to be
one or another of a set of opposite emotions such as fear and challenge, pleasure and
pain, achievement and failure, or dominance and submission.

To illustrate how ego states and inner-emotional drives can work together, let us
take the case of an ambitious parenting supervisor driven (action oriented) by fear of
failure and dominance, and who works under an adult state superior driven by challenge and dominance. The superior is likely to reinforce the supervisor's parent state
by being a dominant (in control and decisive) adult who creates pressure situations
from challenges that are seen as demands and expectations by the supervisor. Being
ambitious, the supervisor accepts these demands without question, but due to an under-

lying fear of failure, the supervisor worries about their ability to accomplish it. Using their parenting role and dominance (controlling) drive, the supervisor interacts with employees on the assignment in a way that triggers their child state (rebellion). Seeing the reaction of employees, the supervisor's parenting behavior becomes even more exaggerated by obsessive control, or the supervisor takes over the assignment completely (child state). The supervisor's fear of failure becomes a self-fulfilling prophecy, and if not corrected, this supervisor can become paranoid and illusional.

Theorem 5. People's ego state and inner-emotional drives work together to form a strong influence of their interactive behavior. The most positive results in the workplace are achieved when people are in their adult state using constructive drives such as challenge, pleasure, achievement, and moderations of dominance and submission. The parent and child interactive ego states result in behavior that is counter-productive to the organizational setting since these states, in themselves, do not breed the requisite characteristics of responsibility, maturity, and objectivity. Thus, the parent and child states become even more damaging to workplace interactions when they are driven by such destructive inner-emotions as fear, pain, failure, and extremes of dominance and submission.

Consider two different people you work with in terms of their various interactive behavior. See if you can describe them based on their apparent ego state(s) and inner-emotional drives. What is your own predominant ego state(s), what drives do you use, and how does this influence your work behavior?

Theorem 6. When people's ego states and inner-emotional drives become threatened, they will seek out other states and drives, or escalate to achieve balance, control, defensiveness, or adaptation to the situation. This is to say that humans have an intrinsic need to be or become adaptive in order to acquire and maintain a sense of security and well-being in any given situation. If the environment is not compatable with this need, people will instinctively try to control the environment in ways that will facilitate adaptation through manipulative behavior. People who seek to control others have a strong dominance drive resulting from their attachment to the possession of power, and associated with exaggerated, aggressive, self-righteous, and territorial behavior.

Consider the ways in which you, and others close to you, manipulate your behavior to become adaptive or gain control.

1.24 BEHAVIORAL CHANGE

By the time humans have reached the stage of adolescence, the genetic blueprint of behavior is deeply imprinted, and not subject to change easily nor by most operative devices that shape it in the development years. It follows that, as we grow older, our attitudes, perceptions, values, and personality traits become more well defined. Our behavior in response to new conditions thus more fixed—predictable and consistent. With normal behavioral growth and healthy development of our psychological self, we are supposed to mature through our experiences to a level of self-guided responsibility, control, and decisiveness.

Age alone is not a factor of behavioral development. It is easy enough to see those among us of all age groups, occupations, intelligence levels, and socio-economic status who mature behaviorally faster than those who are older, smarter, richer, and so forth. Some may never fully mature and some may never mature period—they are too preoccupied fighting off the external dragons that seemingly threaten their sense of righteousness.

Behavioral change creates somewhat of an emotional contradiction for many people. On the one hand, humans are capable of absorbing, processing, and integrating considerable amounts of change. We do this to various extents daily and as a matter of routine. On the other hand, we become resistant and less *willing* to make behavioral changes as we gain more experiences that solidify our beliefs and behavioral patterns. As this occurs it becomes more difficult to impose radical changes in behavior. This may have all of the appearances of the proverbial "hard head" who won't give an inch, but those individuals are more prone to be behaviorally immature, not behaviorally developed into comfortable and constructive patterns of behavior that solidify. When people begin to solidify their behavioral patterns, and these become secure and satisfying experiences for them, they can become rather self-righteous—what's good for them must be good for you! There also becomes a natural tendency for them to selectively attach themselves to other people and situations perceived to be conducive to supporting their values, beliefs, preferences, and the like. By seeking out only those conditions that reinforce existing behavior, the person self-denies other experiences and opportunities that are more likely to induce reexaminations of their options and stimulation of consequent change. In short, when we cut ourselves off from new experiences, we become isolated and stagnant.

> ***Theorem 7.*** *Behavioral change is the product of people's ability to allow new experiences throughout life, to be open-minded enough to examine the results of each experience, and to be willing to select and learn from that which proves beneficial to our development. Those that allow behavioral change to occur from learning experiences are the most likely to mature. The rate of maturity will be dependent on the strength of preconceived ideas, and the person's willingness to adopt new behaviors that eminate from the benefit of their personal experiences.*

Consider those behavioral changes you have willingly initiated over the years. What caused you to change? Do you insulate yourself from change; if so how? What opportunities have you missed as a result?

1.30 WHAT DETERMINES AND ALTERS HUMAN BEHAVIOR

Through many years of research and study, human behavior is becoming a much more understandable condition in our society and therefore increasingly more helpful as a decision making, problem solving body of instructive knowledge for managers. By better understanding what determines behavior we gain useful insight into the nature of individuals for such purposes as selection, job assignments, compatability, and their likely response to varying situations. We also are more likely to succeed at problem solving through the application of more individually tailored approaches of behavioral change in any given situation.

Some of the determinants of fundamental human behavior have been previously touched; namely one's personality, environment, and instincts. The other determinants of workplace behavior are genetics, culture, perception, and attitudes. Following a brief discussion of these determinants, we will examine the ways in which behavior is altered.

It is most commonly held that human behavior is learned. That statement is true to the extent an individual becomes cognitive of those conditions that shape or influence behavior, but not true about precognitive development such as the influences of genetics, culture, and environment. Learning is a process by which the sources of our behavior (personality, attitudes, perceptions, etc.) is both determined and later solidified or altered in accordance with new learning. So learning is conditional on a cognitive state of being, and selective by what we accept or reject in our experiences. Let's take a closer look at the remainder of the source and pre-cognitive determinants of behavior.

1.31 GENETIC DEVELOPMENT

Genetics is a relatively new science but it has been learned that much of what we are has its origin in the genetic reproduction process. It would be difficult for most of us to deny the likeness of ourselves to one or another of our parents or perhaps grandparents. The likeness can be anatomical, physiological, behavioral, or some combination. We may have very similar body structure, voice tones, and mannerisms. We may also become "genetic heir" to certain dysfunctions which is why medical doctors will ask their patient questions concerning the family's medical history as a matter of prevention or treatment of disorders including mental illness. If genetic reproduction can pattern or replicate these human features, then there is no reason for us not to surmise that other characteristics of ourselves are not equally the result of genetic development. This includes our particular talents, thought processes (brain development), habits, interests, and behavioral traits.

Clearly, many of the origins of our human behavior lie in the complex and peculiar composition of our genetic heritage. While its arrangement produces many "new person" features, there is likely to be some degree of direct lineage of genetic behavior passed from parents or even grandparents to each of us. At present, we do not know exactly how it all works, or how to measure it, but we do know of its anthropological existence.

1.32 CULTURAL DEVELOPMENT

Culture, as used here, is intended to mean those external elements to which each of us is introduced to or exist during some part of our life. As collective exposures, these form the culture of the individual starting from birth. We are given sex identification and we become one part of a very large but distinguishable society with prescribed ways of doing things. We know and care little about those things in the beginning because our world of external influences is much more limited to basic needs. We are quick to learn a language or two, the identification of our own kind, auditory impulse (screaming and crying) and associated response (food, diapers, holding)—early behavioral manipulation and attention-getting devices. At this stage, our cultural development is very limited.

With growth one gains more awareness to their economic, social, and geographic environment. We become acquainted with others who look and behave differently than we do, but they have the same language accent, socio-economic status, music preferences, education system, and so forth. Even though we begin to see differences in behavior among this group of early associations, behavior is still within a distinct set of values determined by the group as cultural antecedents of their mores. Such groups are subcultures and they are as distinct as the ghettos of New York and barrios of Los Angeles to the affluent in Beverly Hills and southern comforts of Kentucky.

During late adolescence and early adulthood our cultural base may have an opportunity to expand through travel, education, relocation, or socio-economic changes in the family unit. We are introduced to other subcultures, more knowledge, new sights, and we acquire some skills. Our individual culture becomes redefined in proportion to our exposure as does our values, ways of thinking, and patterns of behavior. These cultural inducements continue to influence our behavior throughout life, but the rate of inducement to, and changes in, behavior slow down in later years when we tend to limit the amount and type of inducements.

1.33 PERCEPTION DEVELOPMENT

Perception is the internal mechanism by which we process and handle sensory information. Sensory information are those inputs that shape and produce our experiences (feelings, mannerisms, language terminology, personal style, etc.). Information is received, screened, then evaluated by our feelings, experiences, values, and instinctive impulses. As we process information or interactional situations, we generate a response based on the collective results of the perception process. **Perception, then, is the foundation of our judgment and decision making.**

Humans tend to be remarkably consistent about the evaluation of others, but inconsistent about evaluating ourselves. We tend to make judgments based on internal or external determinants of causation for other people's behavior (e.g., the person is overworked, having family problems, is feeling trapped). We like to figure things out as part of our inherent reasoning, ability, and on an analytical level we know that we need to verify our perception or other information sources of a given situation. We rationalize, and properly so, that if we can determine the cause of a problem we will become more insightful as to its cure. However, where one's perception often errors in the evaluation stage is when the perceiver has stereotyped another's behavior and thus views them in a particular way; extends their own values and vulnerabilities to the other (projection); or sees and processes only certain things (selective perception). Perception, then, plays a large part in our evaluation of other people and situations, and behavioral responses to them. Just about any one-on-one interaction in the workplace serves as a good example of how perception induces behavioral response and judgments, but may be most exemplified during employment interviews, performance reviews, and employee counseling sessions.

1.34 ATTITUDE DEVELOPMENT

Attitudes serve to reinforce perception and they are used as a screening and evaluative device when receiving and translating input, be it information or situation. Attitudes are those predispositions of thought and feelings toward people, objects, and a variety of other things, thus attitude is multi-dimensional. Attitude is also directly linked to behavior insofar as the emotional level of an attitude becoming the catalyst for an action or response to stimuli. Behavior, unlike attitude, is observable and measureable to the extent that the person exhibiting the behavior can be held accountable. For this reason it is important for managers taking actions to control or correct an employee's attitude (or making reference to attitude) to focus on behavior rather than attitude, since attitudes are a mental state and not a behavior until acted on. One's attitude may be the root of a particular problem and helpful to know when talking things over with the employee about their behavior.

Throughout life we learn to develop attitudes about virtually everything. It is these learned, developed, and ever-evolving attitudes that provide us with particular meaning and a sense of orientation toward our interpersonal, physical, and emotional environment. **Attitudes can be altered but only voluntarily, and usually only by new experiences where there is a significant enough impact on the person to alter the attitude and thereby change related behavior.** The renowned sociologist, Dr. Morris Massey, refers to such an experience as "a significant emotional event." Sometimes, to reach a level of significance in order to stimulate learning, we have to discipline or fire employees. People vary in their thresholds of learning significance which is why it's important for an organization to train and offer managers a variety of learning and experience tools to use with employees—and among themselves.

The relationship between attitude and behavior is a good example of cause and effect. In dealing with a particularly difficult employee, we might be forced to deal more directly with the effect (behavior) since we are not experts in dealing with their mental state (attitude), nor is it reasonably measureable in performance outcomes, but as I stated earlier we are not likely to truly resolve this type of behavioral problem until the attendant attitude is altered by the employee. It has been found that supervisors and managers most likely to succeed in inducing attitudinal change in others are characterized as:

- Believable (trustworthy)
- Pleasant in their presentation
- Allow free expression
- Able to read reactions
- Respected
- Objective (non-judgmental)
- Evoke positive feelings
- Organized in thought
- Persuasive
- Use proper setting

What these characteristics represent is that the manager is a good teacher, counselor, and coach rather than judge, jury, and executioner.

1.35 ROLE CAST BEHAVIOR

When we combine all of the determinants of behavior we have a "body" of knowledge and understanding, but the body is a shell—somewhat inanimate—until we cast it in a role in which it can apply all of these behaviors to actual events. The role one plays in organizational life is different than other roles we experience given personal choice which may often have considerable bearing on organizational behavior since we individually have less influence over the environment, conditions, and people than in personal roles.

To people, organizations are a social and cultural institution. Rules are set, procedures established, and people selected to participate on their apparent ability to carry out the functions of a designated position. Each position is defined in some relation to the organization by its duties, responsibilities, qualifications, accountabilities, methods, and expected patterns of behavior. The combination of position and behavioral expectations is what we call one's organizational role. The role itself is impersonal since it supposes predetermined activities and attendant kinds of behavior thereby disregarding individual idiocyncrocies. The task then becomes one of pairing role conditions to such personal conditions as an employee's job skills and abilities, experience, manner, presentation, and other characteristics we use to determine their "fit".

For purposes of learning and adaptation to one's role in an organizational setting, there is an axiom that states the clearer the role and various expectations that can be developed for employees, the better and faster success will be achieved. Explicit, understandable, and agreeable roles and expectations are best, while ambiguity and inconsistency will lengthen and/or confuse adaptive learning. Structuring of the adaptation process for employees is important since most of our employees come to us from other organizational learning experiences where they may have developed some characteristics we're soon to find contrary to our organization's culture.

This is precisely the reason I have been so adamant over the years trying to impress upon organizations the critical need to strengthen those aspects of human resource operations that bear directly on the initial adaptation period. It includes thorough job descriptions, accurate (valid) performance appraisals, well trained supervisors, and strong orientation/integration programs. With regard to the latter, it makes no sense to me to turn over a new and very impressionable employee to a marginally skilled supervisor, or to a random coworker—who may be a productive worker but a behavioral thorn in the side of supervisors! A few of the more insightful organizations have benefitted remarkably by establishing "sponsorship" orientation programs whereby new employees are assigned to work with selected model employees during some initial period of time until skills, job, and environmental adaptation becomes apparent. The profoundness with which role models influence learning is certainly not a new idea, but its application to employment adaptation has somehow escaped human resource and other managers.

1.36 BEHAVIORAL LEARNING IN THE WORKPLACE

Learning is both a major determinant of behavior through cognitive development of the sources of behavior, and an agent of behavioral change. Learning, in fact, involves change through the acquisition of new information, insights, and values resulting from personal experience. Yet not all learning involves behaviorial change. For instance, we can learn about the famine in Ethiopia and its devastating effect on the mortality of their people, but during the next television commercial we go to the refrigerator for a snack rather than mail a check to the Ethiopian Food Foundation. We learned of the event but it did not change our values, habits, or behavior. If, on the other hand, we were dispatched to the scene as a news correspondent where we gained personal experience, it is more likely that we would return with wholly new values and behavior toward those less fortunate. **And so, for behavioral change to occur on any permanent or enduring level, it must involve personal experience either by observation or participation.**

The learning process as an instructional device is intended to be developmental; to provide new knowledge, skills, and abilities. To have sustaining value it requires practice, feedback, and reinforcement. Reinforcement can occur by negative means such as through criticism or punishment, or it can be achieved by such positive means as training, showing, helping, and rewarding. Here again, people are different in their learning abilities but most respond best to positive reinforcement. Where people differ greater is in the source of their interest to learn. Some will respond to the value derived from the job itself—referred to as intrinsic factors—such as responsibility, challenge, achievement, and recognition. Others may find more value from organizational or external sources—referred to as extrinsic factors—such as pay increases, making the job easier, doing something different for the day, or to be entertained. These kinds of developmental learning processes have little value in altering behavior; unless the process is changed to apply to behavior! So stop sending employees to training sessions with the hopeful intent of changing their behavior!!

Now, let's take a look at learning as it applies to organizational behavior. We know that learning occurs at a behavioral level when people are given the opportunity of personal experience. The result is voluntary behavioral change. However, in organizational life we cannot afford to wait or rely on voluntary change that may or may not occur when employees are given an experiential opportunity. In many cases of behavioral problems we need immediate or at least rapid change, so we create an arsenal of stimuli—some positive, some negative because people respond differently.

Behavioral modification theorists would have us believe that we should only reinforce positive behavior (use positive stimuli exclusively) and ignore undesirable behavior (discard application of negative stimuli). As a practitioner and not a pure theorist, to this I say bunk. The workforce and workplace conditions are far too diverse to allow such a narrow, if not naive, concept to work other than among a few of the more intelligent, responsible, and mature employees who would be willing to modify their behavior if someone merely told them its effect (mirroring). But for all others we need to have available discretionary use of a wide range of stimuli to create the proper impact on the individual that is most likely to induce change; and now, not later, unless a developmental approach is appropriate to the situation. Sources of stimuli available to organizational settings are, to name a few:

Positive (bilateral)	Negative (unilateral)
Responsibility	Reprimand
Autonomy	Demotion
Job Enhancement	Suspension (rarely works)
Counseling	Transfer (almost never works)
Assignments	Termination (capital punishment)
Evaluation	
Recognition	
Supervision	

As harsh as it may sound at first, one of the best learning experiences an employer can give to some employees is to fire them. In these few extreme cases of behavioral maladjustment it takes the loss of a job—income, social, and esteem value—to create a "sufficient emotional event" for the individual to either modify their own behavior, or find some other place where it will be accepted. In yet other cases, I have seen and been party to terminations where it came as a relief to the employee who knew things were not right for some time but felt helpless in their ability to conform. Both the organization and these employees have become more content for the decision. Learning goes both ways but, once again, it requires personal experience in handling these delicate situations.

1.40 ORGANIZATIONAL CONFORMITY AND COMMON BEHAVIORAL DYSFUNCTIONS

The core of behavioral problems in most organizational situations is that the behavior of a particular employee does not conform to the organization's (management's) needs as expressed through its rules, standards, operating practices, and expectations. This includes not only behaviorally related job performance but relationships as well—with other employees, customers, and subordinates and superiors. Supervisors and managers too can fall prey to developing behavioral patterns that are inconsistent with appropriate work relationships, but in their case damage can be even more severe because they retain decision making power over others.

Therefore, human resource professionals and upper management ought to keep close tabs on events and signs of potential behavioral problems throughout the organization in order to detect and correct them quickly, easily, and without complications. One means might be to frequently monitor various indices of job dissatisfaction such as by surveys, casual interviews, turnover and absenteeism rates in the various work units, and similar measures. When preestablished indexes exceed a certain rate, the work unit should be given a comprehensive audit to determine the source of the problem, followed by a corrective plan of action. Be prepared to take whatever action is necessary because nothing is worse than management conducting studies then doing nothing about the results—or having the appearance of doing nothing.

1.41 ORGANIZATIONAL CONFORMITY: NEEDS AND ASSOCIATED PROBLEMS

Organizations have people cast in established roles, and these roles require them to interact with other people in particular ways. This results in a unique mix of personalities and relationships, and the dynamics of human behavior begins. It is precisely these elements and their blending that gives organizations the characteristics of a social system, yet it is intentionally more formally structured than other social systems. The smaller the organization, the less formal is its social structure. But, whatever structure is developed, its intent is to control, correct, or maintain conformity. The efficiency and accuracy of business operations necessitate particular kinds of conformity. So, the degree to which such control measures are developed should correspond to both the size of the organization (number of interactions and work transactions) and its mission. Conformity controls can be excessive or insufficient if not attended to regularly, and this task is properly one of the functions of human resource professionals working in conjunction with upper and lower management.

Many organizations, and most employees, view conformity controls as a negative; something confining, stifling, and an impediment to creativity and self-expression. Frederick Herzberg, the noted motivation theorist, calls such control measures "hygiene factors" which are said to contribute to job dissatisfaction. His belief is probably an accurate one in those organizations where there exists excessive and/or harsh controls (strict conformity), and where management exercises dogmatic interpretation and application of their controls. This is precisely why autocratic organizations experience greater turnover among self-motivated employees.

Conformity in a social context such as that within a work unit is very different than conformance to the more intangible requirements of organization. The work unit is usually small, interactive and therefore somewhat intimate, informal to a degree, understandable, and emotionally managable. The larger the sphere of the organization, the less understandable and meaningful these elements become to the individual employee. Employees who are social by nature may have good work unit relationships but insufficient productivity or concentration skills. Other social employees may deal effectively with one group of people (customers) but poorly with other groups (co-workers, management, vendors). They are often seen as poor team players but upper-management may resist taking formal conformity action because the employee is so good with customers. Nonsense; the employee may well be causing serious aggravation among many co-workers who are doing a good job and we ought to start evaluating employee behavior on the basis of the totality of the job and not be swayed by the halo effect of one attribute.

Conversely, people who aren't terribly social may have the inverse problem. They may be introverted in group settings, or their preference lies in autonomous work habits. They are private people by nature but the strength of their individualism may offend others who will see this person as aloof, distant, cold, and not a part of the team (more perception than reality).

Consequently, the way an organization positions itself through its controls (policies, rules, standards, philosophies, leadership styles, job relationships, and people hired) will very largely determine the degree of internal, inherent conflict that can arise over conformity issues. To make matters more confusing, what organizations typically want is constructive conformity with respect to conduct and performance, and not conformity controls that stifle ambition, creativity, independent thinking, or self-initiative, yet these are precisely the characteristics of people who will resist structural conformity measures. There can be a fine line between constructive and stifling conformity controls. The secret to separating the two is determining specifically what you want and don't want, then proceed to define conformity controls exactly in that vein.

To do this we need to undertake careful examination—if necessary through commissioned studies—of the legitimacy of our organizational rules, operating styles and methods, job scopes, and working relationships to find ways of minimizing the structural creation of conformity conflict.

1.42 SELFISH AIM EMPLOYEES

Selfish aim employees are those whose major behavior dysfunction lies within their motivational goals, sources of weakness, and their maturity. They are a particular breed because of their need for attention and conscious, skilled supervision. Left to their own devices they can become a destructive force by undermining others and dominating the organization's time and attention. Matejka refers to them as follows:[4]

Type/Behaviors	Character/Solution
1. Attention Seekers Exhibits an overabundance of attention-getting behavior to obtain recognition and acceptance; will interrupt, take credit, always agree; ask persistent questions, and constantly ask questions or want approval.	Emotionally and socially this is an insecure person who needs slow but gradual opportunity to build their personal confidence. Start autonomous assignments then work them into small group settings. Counsel regularly on wants and dislikes.
2. Power Players Seeks power over others, is argumentative, displays anger or rejection, sometimes discourteous or disrespectful, and in other ways behaviorally demonstrative in an effort to manipulate and rule others.	This person possesses a dangerous manipulative personality—a back stabber. Here, the need is for a strong, confident, and firm leader who will exercise narrow control, watch closely, and follow through.
3. Concealers Blames others and makes excuses by having an explanation for everything; will avoid accepting fault; conceals by using only partial or distorted facts; and will bend rules as needed.	Has personal inadequacies not the least of which is paranoia. Make them confront their concealments (face the truth) as they occur, but give them a sense of safety about truth and its greater value to the organization.

[4] J. Kenneth Matejka et al.; "Managing Difficult Employees: Challenge Or Curse?" Personnel, July 1986, pp. 44-45.

4. Creative Malcontents

Demonstrate behavioral resistance to their job tasks, supervision, co-workers, and the organization; negatively vocal about change; will use their creativity and intelligence in counterproductive ways; will continuously test supervisors; and will be quick to judge and point out problems but not be a part of solutions—often seen as the "poor attitude" employee.

Frustration is the central problem here—personally or intellectually. Compare past behavior to present and examine this person's test scores. Something may have happened to demotivate them or they may be trapped in an underutilized job. Investigate and counsel thoroughly. If they are not agreeable to working it out, start documenting for a termination action.

5. Retaliators

These individuals seek out various means to exercise their own sense of justice, equity, or balance of power due to their perception and feeling of being used, manipulated, violated, or punished; may attempt some form of sabotage ranging from work slowdown to criminal conduct but most common behavior is planned resistance. These are the most likely people to pursue legal action if fired.

These employees operate from being hurt or mistreated and have an acute sense of pride and fair play with strong principles. Counseling by a neutral should occur to uncover the employee's perception, then investigate facts. If the employee is wrong they should be set straight and warned about their actions. If the employee is justified, the wrongdoing should be corrected immediately and retroactively.

1.43 REBELLIOUS AND DEFIANT EMPLOYEES

Employees whose behavior is rebellious and defiant have their purpose in creating change, usually in some aspect of the organization or working conditions. The behavior is an expression of their rejection of something, and it turns to rebellious behavior out of resentment. On a positive note, the employee at least hasn't given up since the opposite side of the same conditions that cause this behavior can be absolute indifference. It is most characteristic of the rebellious and defiant employee to become triggered by ill-conceived conditions in the organization or their work unit. They may choose to dislike heirarchies, dress codes, forms, antiquated this, and stupid that. They are not good at managing their own emotional reactions to workplace conditions, but instead store things up until feelings of being smothered or frustrated become unbearable. The ensuing behavior can take several forms: overtly or covertly disruptive, antagonistic, oppositional, bending rules and cutting corners, or indifference and productivity decline with an increase in errors.

Standing alone against the Goliath organization, these are the only means available to this individual to condemn it and its ways. We may recognize that the mature thing to do is for this person to realize they don't fit in the work setting, and should leave. This is clue 1: the employee who elects to stay and take on rebellious behavior is not in a mature state. The behavioral defiance toward the organization is equivalent to the parent-child relationship with respect to power and control over personal matters. The parent has all of the controls (paycheck, rules, resources) and the child feels powerless and so, uses devious means to punish the parent for exercising control. The issue becomes one of psychological (emotional) immaturity of the employee to satisfy individual needs, but whose needs are incongruent with that of the organization. In his classic 1957 work Personality and Organization, Chris Argyris stated:

> An analysis of the basic properties of relatively mature human beings and formal organization leads to the conclusion that there is an inherent incongruency between the selfactualization of the two. The basic incongruency creates a situation of conflict, frustration, and the failure of the participants... [5]

The organization's response to rebellious, defiant behavior often reinforces the employee's perception of medieval servitude. Company officers (supervisor, department manager, and personnel officer) join forces, put on their armor, strategize the counter-attack, and deploy the first line of offense (supervision) with battle instructions. While in some cases of non-compliant employee behavior it may be true that the best defense is a strong offense, it is also true that many times a strong (or too strong) offense may simply result in an ugly, complex escalation of the situation. In such cases there is usually no winner, but there are a lot more loosers. This is so because escalation tends to involve more people, including other employees in the work unit, who now hear and see more things going on and thereby become indirectly involved and unintentionally affected by its course. So, at least in some cases where the rebellious employee is unreasonable in their perceptions and willingness to resolve conflicts, a speedy termination may be less painful than the prolonged torture endured by co-workers.

In yet other situations we may find merit underlying the impulsiveness of defiant behavior. Rebelliousness itself is a rather subjective term used by many supervisors to characterize the least insolent behavior which could be nothing more than an employee's courageousness in standing up to the supervisor (who may be an overcontrolling type) and speaking frankly. So, before we take any action against rebellious and defiant employees, we ought to first take an open-minded approach by: 1) getting all the facts; 2) ascertaining the underlying issues causing the behavior; 3) investigate and/or evaluate those issues; 4) objectify conclusions; and 5) initiate corrective measures.

---

[5] Chris Argyris, Personality And Organization: The Conflict Between The System And The Individual, N.Y.: Harper & Row, 1957, p. 175.

1.44 ABRASIVE EMPLOYEES

This is the employee who just rubs you the wrong way. At first you thought it was your differences in personality, but as you began to observe their behavior with others you gained the necessary objectivity to see that they're just plain abrasive in their execution and interaction with work situations. Whether their behavior is self-initiated or an emulation of what they believe to be associated with their role, you are likely to witness and perhaps be the victim of this person's self-righteousness, demanding requirements, stubbornness, contempt, impatience, and personal distance. Admittedly, this is hard-to-live-with behavior, but the underlying causes stem from two opposite sets of conditions, and they are:

Negative Source	Positive Source
Anger, isolation, frustration, fear, personal problems, and potential emotional instability. When the behavior is irregular for the person and prolonged, they are likely candidates for an emotinal breakdown, heart attack, or addiction.	Intelligent, strong need and drive for perfection (compulsive), driven in work pursuits, analytical, genial to those they don't supervise, and competitive. Difficulty lies in their uncompromising nature, impatience, difficulty with delegation, and intense self-interest.

Despite viewing themself as extraordinary in their abilities, this person has a vulnerable self-image, a hunger for affection, and eagerness for contact with allies. One of the basic problems is that they do not have an inkling of how they're coming across or affecting others with their offensive if not intimidating behavior. Those who are probably not even aware of their abrasiveness may only need a couple of masterful and informal sessions with an influential manager. Others who may have reached acute behavior causing noticeable stress on operations should be referred to professional help through either the organization's Employee Assistance Program or, at the employee's option, a professional person of their choice and cost. They may also need some time away from work, and if they are an otherwise valuable employee these extra efforts are well worth it.

In determining what prospective sources the behavior stems from (positive or negative) and its workplace effect, ask yourself these questions:

- Is the behavior consistent or irregular? If irregular, under what conditions does it occur?

- Is the behavior a noticeable or progressive change for the person?

- What do I know about changes in the person's work responsibilities or personal life?

- Have others commented on this person's behavior and, if so, what has been said? Can I call upon these people for additional observations and information?

- How receptive would this person be to a discussion with me about their behavior and its cause? What approach would be best, and what can I offer as remedial options?

Most abrasive behavior employees can be influenced to change, but it may take a little time and patience on your part. Here is a suggested approach provided the answers to the questions above lead you to conclude that the situation with the employee is neither acute nor fatal.

1. Initiate frequent discussion with the employee to establish respect and trust.

2. Prepare observational (non-judgmental) notes of specific abrasive behavior and its particular effects.

3. In a comfortable and casual setting, discuss the employee's job with them, but let them do most of the talking so that you can establish a picture of their perceptions. Focus on their perspective of barriers, problems, and feelings toward others. Then give the employee your observations, examples, and effects of their behavior.

4. Be observant of the employee's reactions; do they deny, blame, or acknowledge your observations.

5. If their behavior has angered you or others, let them know it but in a reforming rather than condemning way. If challenged, don't get into a debate, merely restate how you see things and the benefit that can be derived if it's worked out here.

6. After reviewing your examples of their behavioral effect, ask them two things; what they think is the cause of their behavior, and how these events could be done differently.

7. Conclude with specific agreements about how the situation is to change, what actions will be taken by whom, and that you're willing to do what you can to help, but the job has to come first.

8. Thoroughly document the details of your discussion, follow-up by having more opportunity to observe the employee's behavior, and be prepared for a few more "fine tuning" sessions with the employee.

1.45 BEHAVIOR DEPENDENCE EMPLOYEES

It's a frightening thought, but just as the mass of people in Guyana committed suicide to please their leader Jim Jones, there are others in our society and organizations who likewise have a behavior dependency with another person. Behavior dependency can be more difficult to influence or change than self-directed behavior since with dependency the behavior is either controlled or creates reaction by another person(s).

Behavior dependency can be between child and parent, spouses, employee to manager (and vice versa), employee to employee, or manager to manager. The source of origination for behavior dependency is most often the child-parent relationship, but there are two variations. If the child was smothered with a parent's attention, isolated socially from others (as is sometimes the case with a single child), and stripped of all decisions and responsibilities by a fearful or overbearing parent, then the child's dependency is likely to stay with the parent into adulthood. If, on the other hand, the child never established a trusting relationship with a parent, this unfulfilled need may await adulthood when they establish a trusting relationship with another adult.

The person having a behavior dependency typically has a delusion (false beliefs that persist despite facts) about the truth, success, or other outcomes of a situation another person is directing. They tend to lose sight of reality as others see it, and at a minimum they remove themselves from objectifying the situation—"Don't confuse me with facts, my mind is made up" behavior. Kets de Vries characterizes this behavioral state in the following way.

> They inevitably aggravate the situation, make it worse, and become correspondingly more and more reluctant to face external reality. Feeling more comfortable with their own chosen, closed environment, they do not welcome the opinion of outsiders, seeing them as threatening the status quo and disturbing their tunnel vision.[6]

In its exaggerated psychotic form, the French refer to behavior dependency as *folie a deau,* or shared madness, which depicts the Guyana mass suicides or the elite regime of Adolf Hitler. Again, these are extremes but represent a condition of mental and emotional contagion where one person's influence causes another to depart from reality. The vulnerability is said to exist within everyone because of our susceptibility to those who we see as more intelligent, powerful, confident, and skilled than ourselves. However, most people control their own reality despite vulnerable attachments to another by knowing flaws exist in everything, then going about the process of accepting some things and rejecting others.

In organizational life, we may find that at least some employees or even managers that are followers rather than leaders (or those with solid individualism) are prone to behavior dependency. Since active participation in the work world induces a good deal

---

[6] Manfred F.R. Kets de Vries; "Managers Can Drive Their Subordinates Mad"; in *The Executive Dilemma,* Wiley & Sons, 1985, p. 378.

of reality, there is a higher probability that one person's attachment to the influences of another will not develop into a psychotic condition. Rather, what is more likely to occur is a strong alliance between two, or three, or more people. Depending on the aim or goal of the person controlling the influence of others, you can have anything from a clique to a sabotage group. Here are some basic characteristics to watch for:

1. **The Organization;** authoritarian decision culture, strong upper management personalities, unsystematic decision patterns, hiring and promoting "yes" people, erratic information flow, secrecy, and territorialism.

2. **The Initiator;** charming, charismatic, seductive intellect (a cover for conceit, arrogance, rigidity, and self-righteousness); a need to dominate and control; resentence to opposition and authority; suspicious of other's intent, moody, and insensitive toward other's views.

3. **The Recipient;** lacking in basic interpersonal trust in relationships accompanied by anxiety because of humiliating, frustrating, or disappointing experiences; lack of self-cohesiveness; perception of the environment as hostile; and fears betrayal.

If you believe one of your employees to be developing a behavioral dependency—as opposed to a mere personal affinity—toward another employee, spend more time showing a personal and work related interest in the dependent employee (recipient), and show mild but clear disapproving behavior such as slight indifference to the controlling employee (initiator). Try to build a closer working relationship with the dependent employee to connect their trust to you, not others whose goals may be less wholesome than your own.

If you find yourself in the regrettable position of being influenced unduly by another, or realize that your organization has that as its goal, get out! If, however, that goal is held only by your immediate superior, take your concern to your organization's top official. In such circumstances you have little to lose.

1.46 EXCUSE MAKER EMPLOYEES

When the focus of responsibility falls upon these employees, they will predictably begin making excuses, or attempt to create what is called "defensive impression" justifications for their actions or inactions. From a psychological point of view it is an avoidance mechanism based on a fear of consequences and a weakness in their maturity to take responsibility for themselves and others within their charge. With defensive impression behavior the employee will, consciously or unconsciously, attempt to give a scrutinizing superior the impression that all is well, on track, and under control when it is not. This impression is often an excuse just short of a lie with the intent to avoid confronting the real situation which is perceived by the employee as being unpleasant, threatening, and possibly confrontational. The employee might say such things as:

"I couldn't meet our production goals for last month because we had too many people on vacation (excuse; poor planning), but the situation is being corrected (by uncertain means) and won't happen again I assure you (please don't punish me)."

– or –

"It isn't my fault. I had too much work to do before you gave me this assignment (transfer-ance; even though I didn't speak up earlier, it's your fault), and I just didn't have enough time. Besides, no one showed me what procedures to use so I had to figure it out for myself. What we need is more help to get this important stuff done. Would you talk to Personnel about getting another employee?"

Some defensive impression employees attribute problems and failure to external forces such as the supervisor, other employees, mail service, or the copy machine; some use comparisons like, "I'm doing better than so-and-so but you don't get on their case"; and some just shrug their shoulders and indicate they don't know what the problem is (but it's not them) nor why you think there's a problem—they avoid it by refusing to look at it.

One of my clients contacted me about a situation that turned out to be a defensive impression employee. The employee had five years of service with the last three holding a responsible clerical position in the organization's legal department. She also had prior work experience in a legal office. She was in her late 20's, attractive, married with a small child but known to be having some marital problems from time-to-time. She was also known to be somewhat sensitive about any form of criticism and her production was just average.

A year or so earlier, she had been given a new responsibility; to process liens and related legal documents, entering these transactions in a log book, and sending notices to other designated people in the organization. Once she was shown how to perform each phase of the new assignment, the supervisor would check with her to see if all was well, and periodically spot check her work. This was done for the first month or so at which time the supervisor discontinued close monitoring, but would periodically ask how things were going. The employee would respond that things are just fine (even though they were not, but in essence saying "get off my back") and that it was a lot of work.

The supervisor at one point learned second-hand of a major error in the timing and content of one transaction, brought it to the attention of the employee who then responded to the effect that anyone can make one error, it's too much to do in addi-tion to her other responsibilities, and that someone must have moved the document from her prioritized stack of papers (sound familiar?). To lighten the employee's load (eliminate a plausible excuse) the supervisor removed some of her other duties. A few months thereafter the employee took vacation time and during her absence the super-visor received part of her incoming work. In her attempts to process this work, the supervisor discovered missing documents, numerous overlooked log book entries, overdue documents in the employee's in-basket, second and third notices of request for action on some documents, and an assortment of priority documents in the employee's desk drawer.

This is an all-too-frequent scenario in which it took the supervisor literally weeks to untangle and get back on track. The department lost some credibility for awhile, the company lost a sizable sum of money through delays and missed deadlines, and the employee lost her job.

One of the better approaches to handling defensive impression—excuse making—employees is to follow these steps.

1. Deal with this person like you would your spouse or child; i.e., in a consistent style that conveys it's okay to tell the truth. Let them know problems can be corrected once they're known, but if real problems aren't surfaced, they always get worse.

2. Avoid forms of retribution when the truth is told, as opposed to learning it through indirect sources. Deal with the situation using problem solving methods to reveal and dispose of the cause(s) rather than judging the error.

3. Help this person reach a better understanding of what they do, why they do it, and how to approach things better in the future. Treat this as a growth and learning opportunity for them using your role as their mentor.

4. When you recognize you're receiving defensive impression feedback, use open-ended, non-threatenting questions that prompt a deeper, more honest, and responsible examination of the situation. For example, you might say:

   "Let's look at the situation a little more closely. First, let's start at the beginning by going over what you understood to be your assignment, who was to be involved, and how it was to proceed. I'll take notes then we'll talk about what problems came up, overall results, and what might be done to avoid this situation in the future."

   – or –

   "What do you think are some ways in which this (situation) can be done to get better results? Let's outline what could have been done differently so you'll have a better idea on how to get more beneficial results next time."

5. In your discussion avoid comparing employees, supervisors, or work units. People will instinctively react with defensiveness because the implied statement has a diminishing effect upon the person being compared.

6. Realize that the more vulnerable a person is in the organization, the more likely there will be defensive impression feedback to you. This includes the least tenured employees (particularly probationers), the newly promoted (desparate need to prove their worthiness), new supervisors, less confident managers, and most marginal producers.

1.47 PROCRASTINATORS AND PERFECTIONISTS

Not that these two types of employees have anything particularly in common, but it seems that every organization has one or both of them. It is also true that each of us have both procrastinator and perfectionist tendencies to some degree and toward varying aspects of our lives. They become characteristic extensions of our personality, and most people recognize when they're going toward the extreme. When this happens, they will either self-initiate some correction or be fairly responsive when given feedback about its effect; providing, of course, it is handled constructively.

In mild stages these behaviors are not a major problem to other employees or even supervisors, but merely seem as periodically annoying or slightly obstructive. However, when the underlying influences and resultant behavior becomes acute, they can begin to develop serious dysfunctions in their ability to properly carry out job responsibilities whatever their role. A better understanding of their nature may be instructive to deciding a corrective approach, or at least one that minimizes some of their negative effects.

The Procrastinator

Unlike the defensive impression or excuse making employee, this person dysfunctions in their ability to get certain things done on time, in the proper way, or not at all. Their's is a problem brought about by fears of their own inadequacy, uncertainty, disinterest, and/or self-questioning ability. They are likely to fear the effect upon others of their decision, course of action, or even a comment.

The procrastinator can be ultra-sensitive or highly selective, but in either case they usually have weak and vulnerable self-confidence. They often act in a way that shields others from what they perceive may be undue pain, suffering, or just discomfort, and they will use alternate methods to avoid certain situations that are uncomfortable to them. They will give their own version of plausible reasons for their actions, and make excuses; but, unlike the defensive impression person, the procrastinator won't hide their responsibility—they'll feel guilty about it! In fact, guilt plagues this person, so you will only make things worse by using it as a manipulative device to stimulate change.

The first step to managing a procrastinator is to identify what kinds of work, conditions, people, events, and decisional situations they tend to avoid, resist, or handle unproductively. Another way to look at this is to identify what their interests are, and under what conditions they perform productively. You may even want to engage them in an open and frank discussion about these work characteristics since discussion almost always eliminates speculation on your part.

To help the procrastinator overcome at least some of their underlying fears and sense of inadequacy, you must start slowly and proceed at a progressive rate—and have patience. The procrastinator needs time and carefully designed opportunity to begin taking on those responsibilities, particular tasks, and decisional situations that tend to debilitate them in some way. But, they need a clear, supportive structure in which to operate, with close and reassuring supervison. Initial assignments should be short so that results are quickly seen and some confidence can be gained.

Continuous and unchanged resistence or failure after a reasonable period of time (one to two years) for the employee to begin overcoming those areas of procratination under these controlled conditions suggests that the problem is rooted more deeply in a psychological disorder. This condition requires professional attention by those trained to uncover its source(s) and prescribe suitable therapy. In such cases the manager must make the employment decision as to whether the employee's abilities can be used or accommodated productively. If you determine that the employee's level and type of procrastination is so obstructive as to prove unproductive to the work unit, and termination seems to be the necessary course of action, you should check first with your human resource manager and legal counsel. The reason is that if the employee's condition is professionally diagnosed as a form of emotional disorder, the condition may be protected under the federal Vocational Rehabilitation Act (see Chapter 5), and thereby discriminatory to terminate until rehabilitation and accommodation measures have been taken.

The Perfectionist

Perfectionists come in many different forms, and types of people. Perfectionism is generally considered a desirable and sometimes admired characteristic, but acute stages of this and other behavioral conditions can lead to a dysfunction in any person's job. The most prevalent characteristic about the perfectionist is their vivid inclination toward detail: things must be thorough, accurate, on time (unless they get overly caught up in process), and each step precisely—or at least properly—executed. They tend to be process oriented which doesn't mean that they lose sight of goals and results; rather, they enjoy the process on a personal fulfillment level more than the remote gratification from the results produced.

This expectation of detail and process held by the perfectionist can be confined to themselves (suggesting they recognize their personal attachment to it), themselves and others (everyone should be like me perception), or it can be expected even more so from others (a view often held by perfectionist top level managers). Unlike the abrasive personality who also has a compulsion, most perfectionists don't become aggressive in their execution of work or with work relationships. Their emotional focus is with the nature of their work and the process challenge. For this reason they prefer and will try to enlist others to support and join in their process effort. In many cases, this acquisition of support can be a necessary means of achieving solid results, providing the process matches the task and there is adequate time to achieve it.

The most common dysfunction of the perfectionist, then, is their obsessive attachment to detail and process where uncalled for in work situations, the result of which creates a blinding exclusion of productivity objectives. It becomes the proverbial case of becoming so enthralled with the forest that you forget the objective is to merely clear a little land.

Depending on the severity of the dysfunction, the perfectionist can also drive others to frustration with their detail oriented work habits and methods. The effect on other employees, for example, can require that they work harder to pick up the lost productivity, or that their work gets delayed because their work is connected in some way to the results produced by the perfectionist. So, if one employee begins to sound like an excuse-maker in terms of blaming another for causing unnecessary delays, check it out—the excuse may have merit if their work is connected to a perfectionist employee.

Perfectionists need to develop a balance between their enthusiasm for detail and process and their responsibility to be productive. The problem should be presented to them in precisely that light. The best approach then is a direct one, but again constructively aimed. The employee should be admired and reinforced for their fine attention to details but they should also be told the truth about how this work style becomes inappropriate in some work situations, and how it can adversely affect others as well as desired results. Rather than talking abstractly to this employee, give them examples of actual situations you've observed in order to create their visualization and understanding of the issues you're trying to convey. Before you conclude these kinds of discussions with them, ask this employee to give you some feedback on their understanding of the problem (recognition) and their willingness to more consciously strive for the needed balance between process and productivity (self correction).

In managing the perfectionist, use their detail and process talent in those situations where such is vital to achieving the desired results of an assignment or project. When new methods are needed, old procedures need revamping, or procedure manuals need updating, the perfectionist is the one to turn to if their interest can be aroused. If, on the other hand, time is short and results do not have to be precise in every way, the perfectionist will need specific instructions (structuring) on when, how, and what is expected of them with the assignment. This should be followed by regular monitoring of their progress. Don't hover over their shoulder, but do stay on top of their progress and commend them for their adjustment to the assignment—it may be routine work to you, but it's probably a major adjustment to them.

Armed with the behavioral overview provided in this chapter, you are now in a much better position to do at least fundamental diagnosis of possible underlying causes of behavioral problem employees, and then take more suitable corrective measures. Proceed to Chapter 2 where I think you'll now see common workplace problems associated with employee behavior in a different light—which is more solution oriented—than that typically seen by managers having to deal with these potential disciplinary employees.

CHAPTER III: 2.0
PROBLEMS WITH DISCIPLINARY EMPLOYEES: APPROACHES CORRECTING UNDESIRABLE BEHAVIOR AND PERFORMANCE

The previous chapter serves as the natural backdrop to delving into the actions of those employees who are or become disciplinary problems for management. It is management's objective in these situations to first control and then correct discipline problems in the workplace in order to maintain functional order. Because the greatest majority of disciplinary violations that occur are behavioral in nature, it becomes all the more important for those handling disciplinary matters to be fully acquainted with two aspects of it before acting: first is an adequate understanding of human behavior in the workplace which provides important insights into the methods most likely to resolve the underlying cause of undesirable behavior (as discussed in the preceding chapter); and, second, are the legal and management principles that serve as a guidance system in determining a basic approach to these problems (as discussed in Chapters 2-4).

In using this book as a reference source to guide your decisions and actions, there is the natural temptation to go directly to the topic of interest and review it in isolation from other pertinent background information contained in other chapters. To this, I can only remind you that the most common and costly mistakes are made in dealing with human resource problem solving by making hasty, ill-informed decisions. I therefore urge you to read all or part of those chapters that bear on the situation at hand to enhance both your confidence and effectiveness in achieving the most satisfactory resolution to all concerned.

I truly don't know of too many employees who go to work for an organization with the intent, or even a predisposition, to becoming a disciplinary problem—yet we have them. Nor have I found that most employees intend to create a disciplinary outcome as a result of their actions.

If we look around in our organizations though, we are likely to find a small number of employees (5 to 10 percent of the workforce is typical) that comprise our regular disciplinary employees, an even smaller number that are prone to very irregular disciplinary handling or other types of problems, and the vast majority who work hard and conduct themselves in a mature and responsible manner. The lives, work, and behavior of the latter group is self-controlled, and for that reason remains stable. However, the two former groups of employees—regular and periodic disciplinary problems—represent such serious consequences to the harmony within organizations and work relationships that their control and correction become imperative. They are thus the focus of this chapter.

2.10 DISCIPLINARY EMPLOYEES: WHO ARE THEY AND WHAT EFFECT?

Arguably, there are several measures that can be taken by managers to control or correct conduct and performance problems among employees. We can use various motivational or inspirational techniques, we can ignore undesirable behavior, we can endorse the role model method, but when none of these structured behavioral approaches work with some employees we invariably rely on disciplinary measures as the ultimate tool to resolve the problem. Sometimes it works, and happily so when concluded at informal levels, but sometimes it doesn't produce the desired result. When the desired result isn't achieved, both the employee and organization have lost something, but at least the matter reaches conclusions. Regrettably, in many instances of employee conduct and performance the employee will hand you no alternative but to deal with them in a disciplinary fashion.

Organizations seem to have very common and predictable types of disciplinary problems. These problem employees and attendant conditions can be disarming or even go unnoticed by the manager for a time because they can occur among many employees regardless of their occupation, level of responsibility, age, service length, and yes even their sex. However, some violations are more indigenous to one sex than the other, such as physical altercations and profanity being more common among men. The most prevalent types of disciplinary problems can be generally categorized into the following groups:

Poor Attitudes

This one always seems to top the list because of the antagonism that is provoked by the behavior which often accompanies negative attitudes. This type of problem troubles everyone around this person who creates an air of unpleasantness. The person tends to be consistently negative about various things, oppositional to ideas and other people, and contrary to effective working relationships. Their actions quite simply precede their good judgment.

Marginal Performers

These are often mistaken for weakly skilled employees when, in fact, their marginal skills and performance are merely a reflection of their state of ambition, interest, enthusiasm, and basic motivation. They consist of those who work, and see work, solely as a means to an end and to handle—not satisfy—an economic necessity. It can occur among those who are early in their vocational lives (they see it as a job not a career), or it can become a dominant condition among some in their late work life characteristic of at least a few long service employees who hit the doldrums and become minimum performers.

Rule Breakers

These are the company rascals who seem to always be in trouble over one violation or another. Unlike manipulators who cleverly know how to bend rules or test their ambiguity, these individuals seem helpless at staying out of trouble. They tend not to take rules very seriously anyway, so it should be no surprise that they play jokes (prankster), show up late, disobey instructions, abuse privileges (sick leave, extended coffee breaks, etc.), and goof off. They tend to comply with rules only to the extent that to do otherwise would be knowingly and absolutely threatening to their job.

Personal Problems

We all have, and should expect to have, personal problems during the course of our working lives, but then there are those who have (or create) one personal problem after another. They are like hypochondriacs whose survival relies on getting attention from others. Whether real or perceived, these employees seem to be shrouded in personal conflict, pain, tragedy, or unusual circumstance; not by singular occurrance but by an ongoing sequence of events that require special kinds of accommodation, understanding, patience, empathy, absence, irregular attendance, and unreliable behavior to the extent performance is unreliable.

Behavioral Misfits

These are the employees whose actions, styles, and methods are inappropriate to the setting be it the job, co-workers, organizational atmosphere, or the nature of the business. They represent a rather diverse range of behavioral idiocyncrocies but include those who don't dress properly, don't exercise adequate personal hygiene, use profane terminology, have sloppy habits, awkwardly deal with everything, and otherwise behave in what seems to be the most conspicuous manner possible.

For those whose jobs entail the management of any part of their organization's human resources, these five categories of disciplinary problem employees represent some of the toughest situations encountered at work. The reasons they are tough for managers is because of the effect these employees have on the normal order of business and the emotional strife that so often accompanies their handling. In fact, sometimes we can get so caught up in our own emotional reaction to these employees that we have difficulty in objectifying their job related effect. As you encounter these employees, you may wish to consider the following kinds of effects, then be prepared to articulate them based on circumstantial details.

- **Disruptive;** to the flow of work, to the work of others, to established procedures, and to operational standards of productivity. Another term that can be equally suitable is obstructive when applied to an employee's creation of obstacles.

- **Damaging Interpersonal Relationships;** somewhat related to disruptive, this effect carries with it long term consequences that reduce or eliminate the effectiveness and ability for people to work together which just so happens to be one of the most essential requirements of work.

- **Productivity Reduction;** in terms of specific performance measures such as the quantity and quality of work. Other effects on productivity can result from excessive absenteeism, lack of sufficient availability for work, inefficient use of time and resources, and other activities carrying significant and direct effect on the employee's capacity to perform productively.

- **Morale Detriment;** with respect to creating a hostile environment, negative feelings, counterproductive alliances and cliques, instigating rivalries, and otherwise undermining the efforts and goals of others.

2.11 EMOTIONS THAT INDUCE DISCIPLINARY BEHAVIOR

Human behavior is under the constant influence of one or more emotional sources. In our normal, routine conduct, our emotions may appear to be rather subdued because we are preoccupied with the task at hand. At these times our emotions are not dormant, we are simply using those that are positive and rational. However, when people refer to one's emotional state it usually produces an image of demonstrative behavior such as anger. We may sometimes forget that joy can be equally demonstrative and an inducement to positive behavior.

When it pertains to disciplinary behavior, it is more common for the associated emotional sources that induce such conduct and performance to be negative. Negative emotional sources are such thoughts and feelings as frustration, anxiety, fear, guilt, contempt, anger, and failure to name a few. When we're engaged in work and other activities, we're not always in touch with our emotions. Even at those times we are in touch with them—usually when only one or two of them exists with some intensity—we are not always in complete control of them. They can be intensified, reduced, eliminated, or replaced by other emotions as a result of external conditions. For example, an employee can be experiencing contempt for another person for a sustained period of time. If the other person contributes to the emotion held by the employee, the emotion can become anger, and if further provoked to the behavior induced emotion of rage it leads to a fight.

Emotions, then, become progressive in terms of their inducement to behavior; contempt leads to distrust, dislike, and disassociation; anger leads to verbal assaults, insubordination, and disrespectful treatment; and rage to physical assaults. In many instances, the negative emotions that serve as inducements to disciplinary behavior are defense mechanisms that are triggered as a reaction to some event, comment, or situation that was contrary to the employee's perception. This situation is familiar to any manager who, in the course of discussing an employee's performance appraisal, became the surprised target of the employee's defensive behavior being induced by their anxiety over some past assignment, or perhaps due to their dormant negative feelings toward the manager. For purposes of understanding and learning to deal with disciplinary types of problems, it may be useful to examine these negative emotions that so often induce disciplinary behavior.

Emotional Source

Frustration; encountering real or perceived obstacles that act as a barrier to fulfillment, achievement, and a sense of productive worth.

Anxiety; not possessing a sense of being in control of something that affects you, feeling apprehensive about conditions in a given situation, and a sense of uncertainty about an outcome which relies on others.

Fear; a sense of real or perceived danger, people or situations that are believed to be a serious threat, and a state of alarm that something unpleasant is about to occur.

Personal Effect

Causes intense stress, produces aggression or avoidance, and can turn feelings inward. Can result in regression ("who gives a damn anyway") or resignation ("I give up").

Causes nervousness—sometimes acute—and disorientation. Reduces feelings of being in control, confident, and secure. Can cause impulsive reactions to regain control or abandon situation.

Causes preparation for, or provokes, aggression and hostility. Intensifies muscular and nervous system causing nervousness, shaking or unusual strength or weakness.

Guilt; feeling badly or at fault for some wrongdoing, inability to act or perform in a particular way, or intense sense of failure. Being the cause of pain or damage to another person—letting them down in some adverse way.

Causes introversion, withdrawal, and a feeling of remorse and failure. Under cumulative conditions, causes depression and inability to make decisions. Will cause person to use avoidance mechanisms to protect them against those situations to which they are vulnerable.

Contempt; having disdain for another person, lacking respect, or being moved to disobedience out of ill-feelings for a person or situation.

Causes mild to intense hostility and desire to regain sense of power and control by acts of retaliation. Will provoke disrespectful treatment and insubordinate acts.

Anger; being antagonized with a sense of indignation resulting from someone or something considered to be unfair, contemptuous, or aimed at creating harm; a serious inequity.

Causes hostility and the desparate need to regain power or reestablish equity, justice, and righteousness. Can lead to open conflict or even violence when feelings become intense at which time self-control diminishes or disappears.

Failure; sensing the absence of an ability to perform in a particular way; lacking successful execution or completion of some task; falling short of an established goal or desired objective.

Causes a range of feelings about self and others including frustration, guilt, lack of worthiness, absence of esteem and well-being. Can cause serious reluctance to repeat events perceived to be similar, and a breakdown of self-confidence.

Given these emotional inducements to one's behavior, it is perhaps easier to see how some employees can be moved to acts of disciplinary behavior. Sometimes these emotional states accumulate slowly and are not easily observed except for their progressive influence on one's change of behavior. At other times the emotional state can become very sharp, spontaneous, and readily observed, but the behavior may or may not be an accurate reflection of the underlying cause or even the emotion that induced the behavior. For example, an employee may behave in an angry or resentful manner, but the real emotional state may be frustration, anxiety, or failure. For the manager, it is not as important to be able to diagnose these emotional states as it is to be aware of their possible presence as inducements to not so tell-tale behavior.

2.12 COMMON REASONS EMPLOYEES ACQUIRE NEGATIVE FEELINGS

Yet another aspect of some employees lacking a positive behavioral orientation toward work and workplace situations are certain attitudinal conditions that they have learned or otherwise developed. These predispositions of thoughts, feelings, and perceptions—collectively referred to as their attitudes—toward particular life and work situations become another source of those factors contributing to their behavior. As they affect disciplinary kinds of behavior, many of their negative feelings emanate from the following illustrative conditions.

1. They may see work as only the necessary means to a required end; their reason for working is one of having no choice in the matter—their economic survival, and perhaps that of others depends on their income.

2. They may associate work with drudgery, boredom, and even a sort of punishment; they would rather not work or do something entirely different but they lack access, ability, opportunity, or ambition to acquire it.

3. They may feel their work contributes little value and/or that they have little control over their work or conditions that affect them (no one listens, no one asks, so why care?); they lack or lose an orientation toward the value added by the nature of their work or personal participation.

4. They may feel trapped in the work through tedium, or in the job by the absence of promotions knowing that they are capable and interested in doing higher level work; there may be other kinds of barriers to achieving advancement and thereby produce feelings of being trapped.

5. They may realize that there exists one or more forms of an inadequate, unfulfilling match between them and job conditions including pay, poor supervision, overcontrol, management responsiveness, and the like.

6. They may not have some aspect of their personal life in order such as lacking a meaningful relationship, having an unfulfilling marriage, a divorce pending, adjusting to a new lifestyle, problem children, expenses always exceeding income, or the death of a loved one.

Why, we may ask in our terribly rational mind, would people who possess such negative feelings about work even trouble themselves to find it? The answer is more simple than the explanation; they needed work, we offered it, they took it, but they never promised to like it. In cases like this where some employees reveal their predisposed negative feelings about work, managers tend to be rather naively surprised. After all, managers have quite different attitudes than do others in organizational life, and we are allegedly moved by different forces—it is said that we mentally and emotionally own a piece of the rock!

So managers will sometimes feel deceived by an employee whose predisposed attitudes are contrary to our work ethic orientation, and moreso even contrary to the attitude they exhibited when hired. Was the employee deliberately giving us a false impression during the hiring process and initial employment period? You bet—they needed (not wanted) the job and knew what was required to get it. You were deceived and, at least in the case of employees with predisposed negative feelings, it was an intentional act. Nothing personal mind you, but welcome to an imperfect world! In this respect, these kinds of employees become one of your sources of frustration—be aware of it!

2.13 DISTINCTIONS BETWEEN BEHAVIOR AND PERFORMANCE PROBLEMS

Throughout this and the preceding chapter, several references have been made to workplace behavior, employee conduct, and one's job performance. Before proceeding into the reminder of this chapter it would no doubt be helpful to create some distinction to these impressionistic terms for purposes of clarifying their application relative to disciplinary violations.

Generally, the terms "behavior" and "conduct" have been used synonymously to mean how people behave, act or speak in a particular way, or conduct themselves in various situations. The implication is that with behavior and conduct there is a rather complex array of interactions and processes that occur within oneself that determines what kind of resultant behavior will occur from moment to moment in response to ongoing situational changes. Whether the behavior or conduct is carried out at a conscious level or not, it is a conceived and in some cases contrived action.

The term performance, however, has been used to mean what we do and the results produced by carrying out our job functions. Performance is not necessarily devoid of behavior, nor would I propose that much of our performance is influenced if not controlled by behavior. Rather, some aspects of one's job performance does not have an absolute association with behavior or conduct. Take for example the performance issue of job skill. If we assign three carpenters the task of building a furniture-quality bookcase based on blueprint specifications, they will use their skills to produce the product. When their work is completed, we will evaluate it on the basis of certain performance measures such as the work quality, time required, materials use, and so forth.

In these types of performance situations behavior or conduct does not tend to be a significant factor unless the carpenter was sloppy, complained a lot, deliberately made excessive noise, or generally behaved in a notable manner. Even then, the behavior may or may not affect the performance result. Conversely, in many other jobs where the work activities are predominantly behavioral in nature (working with other people) it becomes far more difficult to separate performance and behavior since they then become inextricably comingled.

The point to be made here, then, is that with some jobs there exists greater distinction between one's performance and one's behavior. Where such distinctions can be made, it becomes important in terms of problem solving and, in particular, to disciplinary problems since they represent the more serious type of workplace violations. So, at least for purposes of discussion and perhaps for more insightful evaluation, I have separated the most common and troublesome kinds of disciplinary problems into the three categories that follow, and they are where the problem is a violation of 1) organizational standards, 2) behavioral standards, and 3) performance standards. Arguably, these categorical distinctions of disciplinary problems are subject to challenge, but to do so would be little more than evading the real importance which is to learn more about solving a particular problem.

2.20 CORRECTING VIOLATIONS OF ORGANIZATIONAL STANDARDS

Most organizations will include in their personnel policies regarding causes for disciplinary action at least some of those particularly sensitive situations in which the organization can be damaged or compromised. The usual interest in including certain organizational standards as a disciplinary action is to thwart the probability of their occurrance. The focal points of these organizational standards are typically aimed at protecting trade secrets, private documents, customer relations, the welfare and reputation of the organization, and its economic interests.

2.21 CONFLICT OF INTEREST ACTIVITIES

These policies are designed to alert and prevent employees—especially those whose jobs provide them with access to certain information, skills, and methods—from using their jobs to promote self-interest gains with competitors, or in other ways reduce their credibility in the performance of their job. The following policy statement illustrates these concerns.

> It is expected that all (XYZ, Inc.) employees use the utmost good faith and judgment at all times in their dealings with the (Company) and its customers. Each employee has a fundamental duty to avoid being placed in a position which creates, or which leads or could lead to, a conflict of interest or the appearance of a conflict of interest. No employee who has a real or apparent conflict of interest in a transaction should participate in that transaction or participate in the approval of the transaction. For example, employees shall not conduct business regarding their own (account, credit rating, loan application or appraisal).

> As to (receipt of a loan application from a real estate agent/broker) who is related to the employee, the employee should not be involved in the processing and/or approval of the (loan application). An employee may not bid on (Company security) at a foreclosure sale, nor may an employee acquire (Company-owned real estate) without the written approval of the Chief Executive Officer.

If it could be reasonably foreseen that an action could create a conflict, the employee should avoid it. If the employee has reservations about any action creating such a conflict, the employee should make full disclosure to their immediate Department Head.

Violations of conflict of interest policies tend to be black or white matters. Violations are normally apparent when discovered because there usually exists concrete evidence of some act, or worse yet a series of acts. The offender either carried out their actions willfully and knowingly, or it was an innocent and naive mistake that was done unintentionally. In the latter case, any damage should be corrected as quickly and amicably as possible. The employee should receive a written reprimand stating the policy, how it was violated, what effect the violation had on the organization, and that any type of reoccurrance will result in termination. Once discussed with the employee to assure their understanding of what the policy means, a copy of the reprimand should be placed in their personnel file. Also, if you can see that there is room for misunderstanding within the policy language (ambiguous phrases), rewrite the policy and disseminate the new version.

If, on the other hand, the violation was knowingly willful, the result created a material negative effect on the organization or the employee's job credibility, and you have solid evidence of the employee's action(s), immediate termination may be in order. An exception to immediate termination might be where you know the employee is conducting a serious conflict of interest activity, but you don't have sufficiently solid evidence to support legal scrutiny—when you terminate for this reason you become vulnerable to claims of defamation. In this case, you may wish to have the employee's activities and records formally investigated by professional sources.

In at least some cases of conflict of interest activities, employers have gathered enough evidence to prosecute the employee for criminal conduct, as was the case with one of my clients who monitored an employee for a couple of months after becoming suspicious of some financial transactions. When they gathered needed evidence, the employee was fired and prosecuted, but the web of transactions took two years for the courts to untangle and return some $13 million in awards back to the employer.

2.22 BREACH OF SECURITY/CONFIDENTIALITY

Somewhat similar but not necessarily related to conflict of interest is an organization's policy on security and confidentiality. Depending on the type of business, there are various kinds of interests most organizations want to protect through this policy and thus treat violations as a disciplinary action. Security and confidentiality normally focus on the interests of official records, sensitive documents and correspondence, protection of facilities, accessibility, and use of such things as keys, data, equipment, or whatever else might be regarded as needing defined protection. The following is a general example of such a policy.

It is the policy of (XYZ, Inc.) to maintain strict control over entrance to the premises, access to work locations and records, computer information, and cash or other items of monetary value. Employees who are assigned keys, given special access, or assigned job responsibilities in connection with the safety, security, or confidentiality of such records, material, equipment, or items of monetary or business value will be required to use sound judgment and discretion in carrying out their duties, and will be held accountable for any wrongdoing or acts of indiscretion.

Information about (XYZ, Inc.), its (customers, clients, suppliers), or employees should not be divulged to anyone other than persons who have a right to know, or are authorized to receive such information. When in doubt as to whether certain information is or is not confidential, prudence dictates that no disclosure be provided without first clearly establishing that such disclosure has been authorized by appropriate supervisory or management personnel.

This basic policy of caution and discretion in handling of confidential information extends to both external and internal disclosure. Confidential information obtained as a result of employment with (XYZ, Inc.) is not to be used by an employee for the purpose of furthering any private interest, or as a means of making personal gains. Use or disclosure of such information can result in civil or criminal penalties, both for the individuals involved and for the (Company).[1]

The most frequently encountered violation of this kind of policy are acts of indiscretion—deliberate acts of sabotage are rare perhaps because common knowledge makes it known that such offenders may face criminal prosecution. Breaches of security are typically oversight errors on the part of someone having responsibility for locking things up, leaving something on or in a desk drawer, not putting something away, or exercising due caution when entering or exiting sensitive computer data. There are any number of possible scenarios for what turns out to be neglect by an absence of attentiveness to an organization's security concern. This makes it all the more important for each organization to itemize all of its legitimate sources of security and confidentiality concerns to insure their inclusion in policy form.

Similarly, breaches of confidentiality are usually unintentional. That is, more often than not the employee was not aware (or made aware) that some source or content of information was confidential and not to be discussed or divulged. The consequence of the employee's act may be serious, but the blame may rest with the manager for not making clear what kinds of documents, information, data, or other things are regarded as confidential. Taking the position that the employee should have used common sense may be reasonable to you, but common sense also presumes an understanding of the nature and consequence of misusing things that are confidential.

Where repeated or intentional misuse of confidential information (or breaches of security) occurs, swift action needs to be taken to curtail the activity and remedy its effect. The seriousness of the act will be determined by such factors as the employee's

---

[1] Joseph D. Levesque; *Manual of Personnel Policies, Procedures, And Operations*. N.J.: Prentice-Hall, 1986, pp. 65.

knowing willfulness and intent, the degree to which the act had (or could have had) negative consequences, the involvement of other persons, and if the violation is a repeated incident. Depending on the circumstantial outcome of these factors, the manager's course of action may range from a counseling session with the employee and a written caution, to outright termination. Whatever action is used in any case, the manager should prepare thorough documentation of the event, including any related evidenciary documents, even if the accounting of the incident is retained in the manager's desk files rather than the employee's official personnel file.

2.23 HONEST AND LOYAL SERVICE

Here is where some organizations give the appearance of being a paternalistic employer to many of their employees who might say, "Don't be absurd, of course we're going to be honest and loyal to you, so why demean us by having such a policy." The reason should be obvious even to those who would respond in this way—its intent is to reinforce the idea that people should conduct their work in this manner, and to be able to cite a particular policy provision if they do otherwise in the course of dealing with violations.

Honesty is the more important and less vague of the two. Loyalty to some organizations means undying and relentless allegiance, while more practical definitions might regard it as fairness, diligence, and conscientiousness of effort. In light of these somewhat abstract concepts of loyalty, it is honesty that takes on much greater concern given the fact that most organizations tend to define honesty as the absence of lying, stealing, falsifying, and concealing.

Fearful that such acts can go undetected rather easily, and initiated by virtually any employee, some organizations are combining their policy positions on honesty with a "whistle-blower" mechanism so that any such improprieties will be brought forward and thereby dealt with such as the following illustration.

> An obligation rests with every employee of (XYZ, Inc.) to render honest, efficient, and courteous performance of duties. Employees will therefore be responsible and held accountable for adhering to all (Company) policies, rules, directives, and procedures prescribed by the (Company) through supervisory or management personnel.
>
> A. All employees have a duty to report, verbally or in writing, promptly and confidentially, any evidence of any improper practice of which they are aware. As used here, the term "improper practice" means any illegal, fraudulent, dishonest, negligent, or otherwise unethical action arising in connection with (Company) operations or activities.
>
> B. Reports of improper practice should be submitted through the line of administrative supervision except when the alleged impropriety appears to involve a management employee. In such cases, reports should be referred to the next higher level management employee, who will advise the (President/General Manager) of the situation.[2]

---

[2] Ibid., pp. 64-65.

Those who violate fundamental principles of honesty are generally moved to these acts by fear of reprisal (perceive the need to hide or cover up something, or may have been ordered to do so), and in some cases a weakness in their character such as the compulsive thief or liar. Being dishonest out of fear is a very different type of cause than compulsive behavior weaknesses. There may be other reasons for the cause of these acts, but once the cause becomes known it should be looked at in this distinguishing way.

Fear is more easily correctable by organizational means than are acts resulting from character weaknesses and compulsive behavior. The latter often requires professional psychological treatment and, depending on the nature of their work related honesty problem, the organization may or may not be able or willing to accommodate its correction. I do know of some organizations who in at least a few such cases valued the employee's work enough to simply remove the opportunity to lie or steal from their jobs while undergoing therapy, and it eventually worked out well.

Conduct violations that pertain to lying, stealing, falsifying, and concealing are extremely serious infractions of honesty even if the consequence is small. Where such acts are done out of fear, it can and should be corrected. There are two common scenarios. One is where the employee possesses an internal source of fear over some consequence (often reprisal from superiors) of something they did or didn't do, so the employee falsifies, lies, or conceals their act—by omission, partial facts, or false impression. The best approach to solving this type of an honesty problem, once determined, is to verify whether the nature of the employee's fear is legitimate (that their superior is, in fact, a threatening person). If so, resolve that problem first; if not, or when it is corrected, the employee ought to be counseled in some detail about the need for honesty at all times, and reassured (if it's true) that they are safe and supported by being honest, but not by any further dishonest acts.

The second situation of fear is where the source is clearly external; that is, where the employee is being overtly directed to lie, falsify, or conceal something involving their work by a superior. Such situations have become precisely the basis of large legal damages being awarded by the courts to employees who have been fired for their refusal to comply with directed acts of dishonesty under the tenets of wrongful discharge litigation. Indeed, no employee should be subjected to these kinds of unethical business practices. For this reason, *every* case of dishonest acts that are discovered should be thoroughly evaluated to include a determination of whether or not the employee was being ordered, covertly threatened, or in any other way strongly influenced by a superior to commit such an indiscretion. If so, and your findings are conclusive, the superior should be fired for gross misconduct—perhaps even prosecuted—and a formal apology rendered to the employee.

2.24 DISCOURTEOUS TREATMENT AND PROFANITY

Most business organizations regardless of industry type, but in particular those whose welfare and reputation rely on a strong positive image, are highly sensitive to the discourteous treatment of others by employees. Perhaps against the better wishes of many supervisors who have been told off, had derogatory terms lodged against them, or been the recipient of sarcasm from their subordinates, these are not acts of insubordination in the formal sense of the term. Rather, they are clearly forms of discourteous treatment and are typically dealt with as a disciplinary behavior.

Interestingly, the severity with which discourteous treatment is regarded by many organizations is usually predicated more on who the recipient was than on its provocation, justification, or circumstances. For instance, almost without regard to what specifically was said or done by an employee, if their discourteous conduct was regarded as offensive by either a customer (organizational consumer) or a high level manager, the offense is viewed as serious and the employee dealt with harshly. If, on the other hand, one employee is equally discourteous to another employee, the offense may be regarded as little more than a peer conflict. It may go untreated or, at best, the supervisor asks one to apologize to the other. This same supervisor would likely take a different view of the offending employee's behavior had the conduct been directed at the supervisor.

What we ought to understand about the behavior of discourteous treatment is that its source is most often frustration, humiliation, and anger. It is the emotional form of retaliation from an emotional conflict or irritant that has accumulated within the person. Because the resultant conduct can be sharp, abrupt or even contemptuous, it evokes our emotional response meaning that we want to immediately punish this behavior as we might a young child for their brashness. Knowing the source of the behavior, you can see why a harsh reactionary treatment of its effect on either adult or child only worsens—not remedies—the real reason the conduct took place.

This is not to say that employees who act out some form of discourteous treatment toward another should not be dealt with or have disciplinary implications. Quite the contrary. Such behavior ought to be a warning flag to astute wmanagers that something deeper than the incident itself is awry. The employee should first be removed from the situation, calmed down, and counseled by the manager in such a way as to surface the source of frustration or anger, then warn the employee about the seriousness of their act but concentrate on dealing with its source. Preferably this should be done by allowing the employee to look at its cause, then mutually agreeing on how to resolve both the current effect (an apology to the recipient may do for starters) and any possible future occurrence. After this conclusion of the incident, document it thoroughly for your own files.

Profanity, like discourteous treatment, is an act of behavioral indiscretion when it becomes abusive, insulting, vulgar, or offensive. This behavioral violation of social codes of conduct has been a difficult one for organizations to deal with since nearly everyone swears or uses some profane term at work from time to time. Even the courts have rendered different opinions on the use of profanity in workplace situations—usually where the complaint alleged discriminatory conduct (racially or sexually profane language). Some courts have accepted rather regular use of common profanity terms where the nature of the business and its customary pattern of behavior regarded profanity as more normal than abnormal or particularly violative of anything (e.g., a plant environment). Other courts and certainly other employers would not agree, nor should you.

Profanity in the workplace is not so much a moral issue as it is one of uniformity in behavioral control. It may well have to remain rather subjectively enforced, but clearly its prohibition should be contained in policy form with at least some mention of parameters surrounding the use of any term, phrase, or language that might be regarded by others as abusive, insulting, vulgar, offensive, or discriminatory. When violations occur, they must be dealt with based on circumstances and using the principles of progressive discipline. However, when profanity is intentionally discriminatory, it is appropriate to take more severe disciplinary action. To avoid enforcement of profanity violations is to render its prohibition an empty threat and weak control.

2.25 DISCRIMINATORY CONDUCT

Since the 1960's and 70's when anti-discrimination laws were adopted, then expanded nationally as a means of eliminating artificial barriers to employment, American business has slowly but progressively developed strong opposition to this kind of workplace conduct. During the 1970's and into the 1980's when litigation by employees against their employers was daily news in some part of the country, the issue was looked upon as simply more regulatory control over the manner in which enterprise conducts its business, and an unfair way to rectify a social problem. Despite the posture of, "We don't do those sorts of things here" by many organizations—who may have naively believed it—they began to hear and read about horror story violations within their industry, and how these incidents cost more money in staff time and attorney's fees than the cost of awards. So the reaction of employers in the 1970's was to adopt internal prohibitions against various types of discriminatory conduct, and otherwise comply with state and federal mandates; if for no other reason than to reduce the likelihood of costly violations.

In the 1980's, American business started to become more aware of the "human factor" in determining business success. Such books as The One Minute Manager, In Search Of Excellence, and The 100 Best Companies In America were best sellers for months, and a rash of trendy seminars, training programs, and speeches began to stimulate thought about new approaches to old problems; something that behavioralists such as human resource managers had been advocating for decades but we overlooked the attention-getting device of quantifying profitability of its results. So, the 1980's began to usher in a second, perhaps higher level motivation for business to oppose workplace discrimination; that being its counterproductive effect on morale, employee relations, humanistic sensitivity to the issue, and the credibility of managerial objectivity. The goal then becomes to keep employees happy, free from undue burden, and respectful of management for their humanity. Who is to say it wouldn't have worked 30 years ago?

Whatever the organization's motive, most have developed policies that prohibit discriminatory conduct and regard violations as serious disciplinary infractions of workplace behavior. Literally thousands of policy versions have been written. The following policy illustration conveys not only the organization's position on the subject, but also gives employees examples to clarify prohibited conduct.

Equal Employment Policy

A. It is the (Company's) policy to employ, retain, promote, terminate, and otherwise treat any and all employees and job applicants on the basis of merit, qualifications, and competence. This policy shall be applied without regard to any individual's sex, race, color, national origin, pregnancy, age, marital status, religion, or physical handicap. In establishing this policy, (XYZ, Inc.) recognizes the need to initiate and maintain affirmative personnel measures to ensure the achievement of equal employment opportunities in all aspects of our workplace settings, conditions, and decisions. It shall be the responsibility of all employees to abide by and carry out the letter, spirit, and intent of the (Company's) equal employment commitment.

B. It is prohibited for any employee of the (Company) to refuse to hire, train, promote, or provide equitable employment conditions to any employee or applicant, or to discipline or dismiss an employee solely on the basis of such person's race, color, national origin, age, sex, marital status, religious beliefs, or physical handicap; except where the doctrine of business necessity or a bona fide occupational qualification can reasonably be established. It shall further be prohibited for any employee, contractor, or other agent of the (Company) to engage in the following types of discriminatory conduct:

1. **Race, National Origin, and Religion**
    Making statements or jokes, or committing acts regarding a particular race, ancestry, or religion that are regarded as derogatory, offensive, prejudicial, or harassing.

2. **Sex/Sexual Harassment/Marital Status**
    Intimidating or interfering with an employee's work or work environment, through unwelcome, offensive, or harassing sexual comments, questions, or acts (implicitly or explicitly), including prejudicial statements or acts regarding pregnancy or marital status.

    Any employee who believes they have been harassed by a co-worker, supervisor, or agent of the employer should promptly report the facts of the incident or incidents and the names of the individuals involved to their supervisor or, in the alternative, to the (Human Resource Manager). Supervisors should immediately report any incidents of sexual harassment to the Personnel Department. The (Human Resource Manager) will investigate all such claims and take appropriate corrective action. If you have any questions concerning this policy, please feel free to contact the (Human Resource Manager) at your convenience.

3. **Employment of Relatives**

Nothing in the (Company's) equal employment opportunity policy is intended to be interpreted as preventing the (Company) from reasonably regulating nepotism for reasons of supervision, safety, security, or morale. Generally, employee's relatives will be eligible for employment with the (Company) as long as no conflicts in supervision, safety, security, or morale, or potential conflicts of interest exist. Relatives include an employee's parent, child, spouse, brother, sister, in-laws and step relationships. If two employees marry or become related, and a conflict arises, only one of the employees will be permitted to stay with the (Company) unless reasonable accommodations can be made to eliminate the (potential) problems. The decision as to which relative will remain with the (Company) must be made either by the two employees within _____ calendar days, or by the (Company) on the basis of service value.[3]

Those employees who are most prone to acts of discrimination usually have such behavior imbedded in their early acquired values, beliefs, attitudes, and perception of others. Additionally, there is often a source of some associated emotion such as fear, contempt, hostility, or anxiety that drives or accompanies the behavior. Like other effects of employee behavior, the usual managerial impulse is to get the behavior stopped (to take control) without regard to its source. Once again, managers who deal exclusively with the effect of behavior are guilty of patchwork problem solving. The real problem to be solved is the employee's underlying cause of behavior and associated emotions about the personal characteristics of other people, and until that gets corrected you will only be effective at forced compliance—the employee is told to change their ways or lose their job.

Attitudinal patterns of behavior such as openly discriminating against others is not easily changed. It may take time, patience, new experiences for the employee, and a keen manager. The manager who does not want to lose the employee but wants to resolve a discriminatory attitude problem ought to give thought to these approaches.

1. Talk informally and at some length with the employee to see if you can ascertain any insightful information about their early experiences with the type of discrimination being exhibited. Ask open-ended questions that encourage the employee to delve into these areas and expose any possible values, beliefs, and perceptions. Look for signs of emotional responses and identify them. As the sources and emotions of their behavior surface, begin asking direct, nonjudgmental questions and start discussing them with open candor. This is the counseling and assessment phase.

2. Consider the fact that the employee is more likely to change their own attitudes than you are, and that most attitudes are changed when altered by new experiences. Might your employee gain a new perspective on the issue at hand if you could give them the opportunity for such an experience, and can you find one readily available?

---

[3] Ibid., pp. 7-8.

3. Is the nature of the offense so serious and impacting that the only means of correction is to remove the employee? If so, anything less than termination may aggrevate, not change, their attitudes and emotions, so this approach necessitates thorough and formal documentation with the hope that this experience is sufficient for the employee to change their future attitudes.

2.30 CORRECTING VIOLATIONS OF BEHAVIORAL STANDARDS

True, we have been examining behavioral forms of misconduct in the previous section, and it will come up again as a causal contributor in Section III.2.40. However, there are some forms of disciplinary problems that are sheer behavior and of greatest consequence at the work unit level of operations. The most prevalent effect of these behavioral incidents is some type of disruption to operations be it work relationships, morale, productivity, work assignments, or equipment and materials. Additionally, these violations tend to have direct secondary impact on other employees and the effectiveness of the entire work unit, so they need to be handled promptly to minimize their influence on these inefficiencies.

2.31 PEER CONFLICTS AND ALTERCATIONS

Peer conflicts are typically caused by personality or perception differences, moodiness, impatience, or sensitive emotional states such as jealousy, annoyance, and embarassment. When these rivalries evolve into skirmishes or outbursts, the conflict erupts and people are damaged. Since work relies heavily on the ability of people to interact in a cooperative and harmonious fashion, conflict between employees represents a serious breakdown of those two vital ingredients to effective work relationships. The break must be repaired quickly and completely which means the manager must be capable of *helping them* resolve *all* of the influencing causes to their resultant behavior.

Peer conflicts range from cold wars in which neither employee speaks nor so much as acknowledges the other, to physical altercations where the conflict takes on such emotional intensity that violence is provoked. The highly acclaimed management theorist Peter Drucker once noted that there are three ways to resolve conflicts, which he identifies are the result of differences in perception, and they are:

1. Get the two people to accept and share a new, mutual perception on the subject of their conflict.

2. Support the position of one and reject the other.

3. Force both people to comply with your perception on the subject of their conflict (forced compliance).

What is important for the manager to keep in perspective is that the problem belongs to those in conflict and only they can resolve it, but they will need someone to help—you. The role for the manager in resolving peer conflicts, including physical altercations, is that of third party neutral, objective fact-finder, and dispute mediator. Your aim initially should be to identify all sources of the conflict—that is, the real origin of underlying causal conditions—and this is best accomplished by direct questioning of both parties, individually at first. You should look for:

1. What their perceptual differences are.
2. What is the nature of any personality differences.
3. What approach they have been taking with each other (moodiness, impatience, etc. being used by one toward the other).

After gathering a complete and factual picture of the situation, and having discussed it in some length with each employee separately, the next step is to get them together where you discuss your findings with both of them present. If possible, avoid assigning blame or taking sides. Your job is to present them with the objective picture they haven't seen due to their own emotional blindness. Once you do that, ask them to now discuss it openly. Your role now becomes mediator between the two of them meaning you keep each honest and on track of the issues, keep the discussion under emotional control, and insure that each is given an opportunity to express their views and respond to the other. What you want to achieve at the conclusion of this meeting is the understanding, acceptance, and agreement between these employees of the issues raised. If nothing else, they need to be made aware of the effect of their actions toward each other and that it is unacceptable conduct that should not reoccur. In some instances it is worthwhile to tell them you want them to discuss it between themselves for 20-30 minutes, and when you reenter the room (don't go too far away) you'd like to hear what they worked out.

Where the conflict has resulted in a physical altercation, you almost have to initiate some disciplinary action such as suspension or perhaps demotion where instigated by one whose position dictates better judgment. Bear in mind that touching, shoving, poking, holding, and hitting another person are legally defined acts of assault, and employers can be held liable for not controlling it. Given this seriousness of the act, you are bound to take some measure of discipline even if the employees themselves have resolved their differences. Usually the one who provoked the attack is given the heavier disciplinary hand. If, however, you're considering no disciplinary action, you might wish to contemplate the message you'll be sending to other employees who are aware of the incident and the precedent you're setting. Further, physical harm to an employee in such cases is a worker compensable injury and should be treated as such. Does that change your mind? It ought to, and you may even wish to discuss the situation with your company's legal counsel.

2.32 DAMAGE OR DESTRUCTION TO PROPERTY

Honest accidents that cause damage or destruction to company property do happen, and few would argue that it's an inherent cost of doing business. Most accidents are the result of unintentional carelessness or inattentiveness. Customary handling involves the supervisor's scorn (reprimand), the employee's apology, and the repair or replacement of the object property. Repeated accidents, although unintentional, may have to be dealt with by disciplinary means when transfers, job reassignments and other measures are used to remove the element of risk because these actions are involuntary. Some employees have even been terminated because of their accident prone history when, in fact, they could have been temporarily distracted by some personal crisis, had a causal health disorder, or simply assigned to a job which was ill-suited to skills requiring dexterity and coordination.

Damage or destruction that is done to company property resulting from an employee's carelessness, neglect, or disregard is not an accident whether or not the act was intentional. When you find that such acts were intentional, or done knowing that damage or destruction would occur, you may then describe the act as willful and initiate more serious levels of discipline, including termination for repeated or singular costly incidents. For lesser violations of this disciplinary act, many employers are now using a sort of equity measure whereby the employee's pay is reduced by a small amount over a period of time equal to the cost to repair or replace the item.

Most damage or destruction to property that is not accidental occurs from one of three sources, and they are:

1. **Misuse;** the property is not used in accordance with its function or capability, instructions are not read or followed, or it is handled improperly.

2. **Misjudgment;** the property is used under improper conditions, for the wrong job, overextended, or its user not aware of their own limitations.

3. **Miscare;** the property is improperly serviced, checked before use, maintained, or stored.

Prevention of these kinds of common problems require that procedures be written on the use and care of all equipment, machines, vehicles, and similar kinds of company property, and all employee users trained thoroughly. From the behavioral perspective thereafter, managers should be alert to employee work methods and attitudes that might be suggestive of an employee's lack of concern for the value of property through displays of carelessness, neglect, or disregard. With respect to work productivity, damage is equivalent to destruction inasmuch as the property cannot be used once the act occurs.

2.33 LACK OF COOPERATION/UNWILLINGNESS TO CONFORM

Stated another way, an employee who lacks cooperation is uncooperative and, as such, can present rather complicated impedence to work relations, flow, and progress. Provided the behavior is uncharacteristic of this person, then it should become apparent that something has happened to create this change of behavior or its appearance. The key to solving this kind of problem then is to discover and treat the source of that which obstructs the employee's cooperation. There are three usual scenarios and each produces a slightly different set of behavioral conditions.

When one employee is uncooperative with another, a peer conflict exists or some misunderstanding about their assignments, roles, or expectations of each other has occurred. However, when an employee becomes uncooperative with a number of co-workers, the behavior takes on a much broader attitudinal condition. The employee may be showing disagreement with group norms, or a sort of retaliation for being ostracized in some way by the group such as an overheard remark put forth as the group's opinion about the employee. In response, the employee withdraws from interaction and withholds cooperation.

Emotionally, the employee is hurt, offended, distrusting, and uses rejection as a defense mechanism. Similarly, it is not an uncommon reaction for employees to become uncooperative, edgy, and resistent to conformity when some consequential event has entered into their personal life. In either case, the manager can usually get to the root of the problem by presenting their observations or complaints from co-workers to the employee in light of job needs and work expectations, then asking the employee in a sincerely interested fashion for an explanation. Based on the explanation, proceed with a resolution of its cause accordingly.

When an employee is uncooperative and nonconforming with the immediate supervisor or unit manager, the behavior takes on more serious dimensions and discipline a more likely recourse. There may be some employees who will openly become uncooperative with other employees, but the employee who demonstrates such behavior toward superiors knows, or doesn't care, that they do so at considerable risk. Before you send them packing, give them an earnest opportunity to explain their situation, perceptions, or source of their resistance to your authority. There just may be a reasonable explanation that can be worked out through a better mutual understanding, but if not, then your task is to clarify why they need another employment setting.

The most problematic condition exists when you have one manager who is being uncooperative with another manager. This situation produces a territorial obstruction even if they work in the same division or department. There will often exist strong interpersonal elements of the peer conflict situation such as personality trait differences. But, with lack of cooperation among managers, it is often the case that their position roles have created some source of resistence from one or both of them. For example, feelings of fear, uncertainty, and distrust may emerge within one who senses that their authority, span of control, or decision making power is being threatened by another. To protect these role and position features, they may act through their feelings to withhold their full cooperation and extend only token signs of working together such as talking, but only on a superficial level.

Another possibility is that one has simply become obstinate toward the other which is emotionally equivalent to a child pouting. The very development and existence of managerial lack of cooperation suggests both an unwillingness to self initiate conformity to what is required of the position (mature judgment), and the inability to resolve it among themselves. This situation needs to be taken to a higher authority who can identify the source of discontent, mistrust, or whatever is causing the obstruction, and either help them resolve it or remove the one causing it. There is simply no room among the managerial ranks for lingering malcontents!

2.34 INCAPACITY: SUBSTANCE ABUSE AND OTHER DISORDERS

It is now common knowledge that substance abuse—primarily that of alcohol and uncontrolled drugs—is one of the nation's most prevalent and critical workplace problems. It is a social phenomena of disasterous proportions and our governments, the media, and employers have joined the effort to reduce if not eliminate the problems associated with its abuse. In the work setting, human resource managers in particular have struggled for years on how best to deal with its occurrance. Preventative educational programs have been conducted, managers trained on how to identify symptoms and initiate preliminary counseling, and Employee Assistance Programs (EAPs) established to help rehabilitate troubled employees.

However, the usual dilemma faced by human resource and other managers is balancing the scales of humanity versus business needs. The former approach to solving the problem appeals to our humanitarian and moral qualities that tell us we ought to be compassionate, empathetic, examining of behavioral causation, personally interested in helping, willing to make accommodations, and supportive of their effort to rehabilitate and return to a productive life; presuming their desire to do so exists. Conversely, the latter approach to the problem requires that managers stay in touch with the reality of why we're in business and employed, and that is to be economically productive. Business economics simply does not make room for waste, inefficiency, or unproductive personnel. This side of our managerial obligation dictates that our approach ought to be one of swift and decisive action to correct or remove any obstacle to productive business.

Those organizations large enough to have the resources to take a comprehensive approach to the problem have a distinct advantage over those that don't. They can offer a full array of services and accommodations to the troubled employee for a sustained period of time without appreciable loss of productivity, and they can make their programs available to almost any employee who desires access. Moreover, these organizations then become the recipient of long term dividends from employee productivity and loyalty paybacks when they return from rehabilitation.

For less fortunate, smaller organizations who do not have the ability to make such resources available, they must deal with the dilemma of which approach to take— that of humanitarian or purely business needs. Naturally, the circumstances surrounding each case of substance abuse will play a large role in the determination of which approach will be in the best interests of the organization; quite frankly, that is the bottom line. Some of the factors that tend to be considered in this deliberation are:

1. **The Severity Of Abuse;** whether the employee is seen as a temporary abuser, habitual addict, using and selling drugs, advanced alcoholic, and the like.

2. **The Nature Of Causation;** whether the employee is known to be experiencing some form of personal difficulty or trauma, exposure to bad external influences, loneliness, depression, and similar negative emotions or life events.

3. **Rehabilitation Interest;** does the employee acknowledge their condition, open about the situation, cognizant of its personal and organizational effects, and desirous of change, or is the employee denying, making excuses, and resisting efforts to bring about change.

4. **Criticality Of The Job;** how important or expendable is the employee with respect to their job knowledge, skill, role in the organization, and relationship to others. What impact or influence do they have on the organization's operations or success.

5. **Past Performance;** is the employee otherwise viewed as a productive worker or major contributor to the organization prior to this problem, or are they marginal to average therefore not viewed as worthy of the time, effort, and expense to salvage.

In addition to the manager's dilemma of which approach to take, when factors 4 and 5 become prominent determinants a paradox emerges for the organization. The paradox is the tendency to extend a humanitarian approach to one person but not to others whose jobs and/or performance is not as beneficial to the organization as the other person. While this is perfectly logical from a business perspective that focuses on economic efficiency criteria in its decision making, it produces other problems not the least of which is apparent favoritism, selectivity, and possible discrimination. This paradox of who gets help and who gets ushered out is clearly an inconsistent employment practice, and it may not alter the decision of many organizations when the problem emerges, but a lot of serious thought ought to be given to it before rendering a decision and taking action. If differing approaches are seen by the organization as necessary to its resources and operations, then at least some policy precaution is in order by stating that you reserve discretionary decision making to the best interests of the organization.

Where any form of an employee's incapacity exists, the manager's focal point must rest upon performance results and effects even though the problem itself is best resolved by dealing with its underlying cause. In many cases of an employee's incapacity, the causal condition may not be within the grasp of a manager's ability to effectuate a direct solution to its cause. Also, the employee may not be willing or responsive to help with the problem. In such cases, the solution to the cause may rest with external professionals; or the cause may be of a degenerative nature as in the case of AIDS, cancer, and some mental disorders. Under these kinds of circumstances an employee's incapacity must necessarily be measured against their ability to perform specific, identifiable aspects of their job including the effect of their condition upon others with whom they work.

There are no easy answers to these very difficult situations, only the uniqueness of circumstances and sound guidelines will help us make the best decisions possible. When such serious and complicated situations as these occur, it is time to call for the collaborative assistance of other professionals to diagnose the entire situation, explore approaches, and attempt to achieve a concensus that seems to best serve the conditions at hand and long term implications.

2.35 JOB ABANDONMENT AND UNAVAILABILITY FOR WORK

Not all organizations use these policies but it is a good idea to do so for purposes of having an established procedure to deal with it. Job abandonment takes place when an employee fails to show up for work in accordance with their *normal* work schedule, and fails to notify their supervisor of the reason or extenuating circumstances for their necessary absence. It also occurs when an employee on a leave fails to return and notify by their return date.

Conscientious people do not fail to show up for work unless there exists a very compelling reason. When this occurs, they call in at the earliest opportunity to insure the protection of their job and minimize the disruption caused by their unexpected absence. Short of being held hostage, falsely imprisoned, or similar pecular event, we are left with the conclusion that those who fail to show and notify are not conscientious employees and have therefore intentionally abandoned their job. When it happens, the manager should show a good faith effort by attempting to contact the employee, or their emergency contact person, in the event something serious has occurred rendering them unable to respond. If telephone contact cannot be made, you should then prepare a brief letter indicating they should contact you immediately or they will be terminated for job abandonment. If no response, or a late one, proceed with the termination. If the employee provides you with a plausible (and verifiable) explanation, use your own judgment based on circumstances as to how to deal with the employee.

Along the same lines, some employers have successfully used the reason of "unavailability" or "insufficient availability" for work to terminate those rare occasion employees who become incarcerated due to off-duty conduct, are chronic malingerers, or who are excessively absent from work without approval (unexcused absences). In order to properly use the reason of unavailable or insufficiently available, you ought to be able to demonstrate that the employee's amount of absence (or amount of frivolous time in the case of malingerers) is clearly detrimental to their job and the necessary work of their unit in fairly precise terms. In the absence of such hard evidence, your reason—should you be required to provide it—could have the appearance of being a pretext to simply get rid of the employee for personal reasons.

2.36 INSUBORDINATION

Insubordination is a terminable offense when it is a willful and blatant disregard, refusal, or unnecessary delay in carrying out a superior's reasonable order. The courts have also determined that instructions, requests, and normal means of providing employees with job assignments are sufficient notice to the employee that they are to be carried out. In other words, the superior's command to an employee need not be stated as a direct order to establish an act of insubordination but it's advisable to state your instructions as an order, once the employee refuses, to assure them of your sincerity.

The major exception to an employer's irrefutable right to fire an employee who does not carry out a given assignment is where the employee has reasonable cause to feel that doing so would jeopardize their health or safety (as provided under OSHA General Orders). If there is any question or possibility of a hazard in connection with the job instructions, the employee has the right to refuse performance without retaliatory action by the employer. In such cases, it is advisable to withhold any further order to perform the job until safety officials can render an advisory decision.

In other than exceptional circumstances, insubordination is an act of defiant behavior in which the employee is rebelling against their superior and challenging the superior's authority and decision to give such an order. Unless the employee can offer up a legitimate (even if not entirely agreeable) reason for their refusal, then they are and should be subject to immediate termination. However, managers who encounter this kind of situation should at least ask the employee for their reasons for refusing the order and, if the reason is unacceptable, tell the employee that you are ordering them to comply and if they refuse they will be terminated. Finally, virtually any incident of insubordination, or near insubordination (defiance), should be fully documented promptly while the event is memorable in detail.

2.37 CRIMINAL CONDUCT

Criminal activity by an employee constitutes the ultimate form of behavioral misconduct whether the activity occurs on or off duty. As you would expect, on duty—and particularly job related—criminal conduct carries with it automatically justified disciplinary action including immediate termination and possible prosecution by the employer (e.g., arson, robbery, embezzelment, drug trafficing, etc.). Based on generally held legal principles that allow the employer to protect their property, security, reputation, and welfare interests, the courts have normally preserved the employer's termination of any employee whose criminal conduct jeopardizes those interests or is in other ways clearly compromising to the organization's welfare.

Where the issue of criminal conduct becomes more clouded is where the employee's activity occurred off duty and the offense is unrelated to the employee's job. What must then be examined is whether the offense is reasonably damaging to the organization's reputation (e.g., named in a news item), has a sufficient effect on their property or security (e.g., armed robbery), or has a significant impact on other employees (e.g., moral turpitude). In the absence of these influences on the employer, disciplinary kinds of action are probably not going to be adequately justified. When action is justified by the employer, criminal conduct is one of those offenses where the source of behavioral cause is quite secondary to its effect, and the employer can bypass normal progressive discipline measures and promptly effectuate a termination.

One of the first questions raised by managers once organizational impact has been determined is how much evidence do I need before taking action. You might recall that the legal test for guilt in order to get a conviction in criminal cases is guilt "beyond a reasonable doubt." However, for evidence related to employment decisions, most courts will impose a lesser "preponderence of evidence" requirement meaning that the employer need only establish that a majority of evidence points to guilt. In deliberating the course of action to take in cases of employee criminal conduct, the manager should consider these factors:

- Whether the criminal conduct involved acts constituting a felony or involving moral turpitude;

- Whether the presence of the employee can be considered to present a reasonably serious and immediate risk to the organization;

- Whether the conduct is particularly harmful or detrimental in effect to the organization's mission;

- Whether the conduct will have a harmful effect on other employees;

- Whether reasonable steps have been taken to ascertain whether the risk of continued employment might be mitigated through such techniques as closer supervision or transfer to another position;

- Whether any new facts or circumstances have come to the attention of the organization;

- Whether there exists, or is available, evidence of the offense to conclude that there is a prepondence of evidence in support of the employee's guilt.

2.40 CORRECTING VIOLATIONS OF PERFORMANCE STANDARDS

There is no job performance that can be said to be independent of behavior. It would be more accurate to say that behavior is an ever-present influence upon one's work performance, yet there are some types of performance activities that are routine and rather automatically performed as a conditioned sort of response to our skills, work habits, and understanding we have about work and its requirements.

So, the following discussions of disciplinary conduct employees focuses on specific conditions relating most directly to job performance. This is to say that regardless of the type or intensity of a behavioral influence, the resultant effect on job performance becomes the most vivid characteristic of the employee's contribution to and presence within the organization. The effect of these performance situations are almost always controlled by disciplinary means in the event formal action becomes necessary to correct them.

2.41 INEFFICIENCY OR INCOMPETENCE

These are two of the most frequently used, abused, and vague terms ever applied to an employer's list of disciplinary causes. With some notable consistency, many courts have found these terms, in and of themselves (without definition), too vague and inappropriately applied to the firing of employees relative to their job performance. The first thing employers should do, then, is define these terms in a meaningful and performance related way. Here is a defined example of both terms:

1. Inefficiency in job performance generally means inadequate, poor, or below reasonable expectations of work methods, procedures, processes, and the utilization of time and resources to achieve normal work results.

2. Incompetency in job performance generally means the inability to understand, comply, or carry out particular aspects of assigned work, the result of which renders the employee's overall contribution as inadequate for retention in this job capacity.

Given these definitions, we as managers are in a much better position to not only establish more precise performance related controls, but we are also better able to delineate examples of the employee's performance that more strongly ties into conditions of the term when effectuating correction measures. Once again, the primary job of managers is to control, guide, and when necessary reform the performance and attendant behavior of employees. We also ought to be realistic enough to know that some situations will require the regrettable disciplinary forms of correcting the more extreme cases of performance problems.

There is one very good reason managers should beware of employee problems concerning inefficiency or incompetence. The reason is that it may be equally or even more your fault—or that of the organization's—than it is exclusively that of the employee. Examine this possibility carefully and as objectively as you can, for if you don't now, someone else might do it for you later.

The purpose of pointing this out is because of the outward contradiction between the organization's assessment of the employee's *adequacy* for the job when they were hired or promoted, and the presence of one of these very serious performance deficiencies sometime thereafter. The contradiction causes immediate doubt and question as to how an employee who was evaluated by the employer as presumably the best qualified to do the job is now, or has become, so extremely inadequate. An employee injured by a termination may be moved to seek legal clarity, and thereby require their employer to demonstrate the specific ways in which they were inefficient or incompetent. You can rest assured that the employee will get a chance to tell their story about how they were trained, given instructions, how things changed with their job, what expectations were placed on them, and, of course, how their past performance was evaluated.

In assessing whether the problem is the employee, and perhaps to what degree it may be a shared problem, here are a few questions that you ought to examine carefully.

- Were standards of performance set which were not met by the employee?

- Were standards of performance realistic and made known to the employee?

- Did the employee receive proper instruction as to the nature of their duties and responsibilities?

- Was the employee given a "reasonable opportunity" to demonstrate performance, or correction after notice?

- Was the employee advised of their shortcomings?

- Was the employee offered counselling and/or retraining?

- Was performance assessed objectively, fairly and properly without discrimination against standards which could be reasonably considered "attainable"?

In order to be justified in taking disciplinary action, including termination, against an employee on the basis of their inefficiency or incompetence, you must be able to show that reasonable steps were taken to attempt correction of their particular inadequacy. Such steps might include documented counseling sessions or written evaluation reports in which the deficiency(ies) were pointed out, compared against specific performance requirements, told what was required and expected, and given sufficient time to improve. Other steps can include job simplification measures to eliminate problem responsibilities, additional training, or a job audit to see if they have proper resources, staff, and the like to get the job done.

If none of these preliminary problem solving measures correct the situation successfully, then the next step will likely require that the employee be removed from their position or transferred to one of lesser responsibility. This means either demotion or termination. Experience has shown that demotions are the least harmful of the two for employees in an economic sense, but not so in a social esteem sense. Also, demotions are better for the employer because of retention cost savings and showing a good faith effort to avoid damaging any (long term) employment interests held by the employee. However, experience has additionally shown that the only favorable demotion is one that is agreeable in all respects to both parties. In short, either try to negotiate a positive demotion (retreat to former successfully held position) or graciously terminate them, but never deliver an ultimatum.

2.42 ATTENDANCE AND ABSENTEEISM

Performance standards inherently presuppose that employees be in attendance at work sufficiently to do their job, but because that has not necessarily been the experience of American business, just about all organizations have found the need to establish attendance and absenteeism policies. As a control mechanism, some policies are weak because of their vagueness and lack of usable guidelines for employees and supervisors to follow. Other policies are very explicit in detail on the type, frequency, number, and duration of excused absences. Those organizations with more fully developed attendance control programs tend to use both detailed policy guidelines (including discipline) and various forms of incentives and recognition to reinforce good attendance. Their approach, or culture if you will, is that attendance and absenteeism problems are not an inevitable condition of employment, and that it is the organization's responsibility to do something about it.

Attendance and absenteeism problems are one of those areas of an organization's productivity that is probably more tied to the organization's culture than it is to employee behavior. This means that organizations often get the attendance that they expect, or the absenteeism they accept. If positive and negative controls are loose, so too will be the response from some employees. When the organization's culture and its control mechanisms are creating the message that there is no particular value to good attendance, that absences go unnoticed until they become extreme, or that only sporatic and uncertain monitoring exists, then the organization's culture can best be described as a major part of the problem rather than the solution. Clearly in these situations it is the organization itself that should begin addressing the problem by first examining and reforming its own structural and process controls before pointing to employees who are merely responding to what they are being given.

Poor attendance and absenteeism has been one of the most publicized, costly, and prevalent problems of American business for some years now. Studies show that nearly seven percent of the workforce fails to show up for work each week resulting in an estimated cost to employers of $20-25 billion annually. It is also tagged as one of the more disruptive forms of business productivity since most absences are unexpected, short term, and therefore a total loss of productivity, planning, and meeting work flow commitments.

To put matters into perspective, let's isolate the real problems of attendance and absenteeism. First, allow me to make a distinction between the two terms as follows:

1. Attendance means the frequency and length of absences from duty when the employee shows up. It includes late arrivals (tardy), early departures, extended break and meal periods, and their inattention to performance responsibilities (goofing off).

2. Absenteeism means the frequency and duration from duty when the employee fails to show altogether whether such absence was excused, unexcused, paid, or unpaid. It does not include absences due to vacation, industrial disability, or approved leave of absence.

From this distinction we can see that attendance problems are disruptive and unproductive, short term events, while absenteeism usually refers to the unexpected and complete absence of the employee for a day or more. So, if we wanted to compare the cost of productivity loss say between the United States average of seven sick leave days taken annually by the average worker as an absenteeism problem, to that of a common attendance problem of taking two 30 minute breaks during each day rather than the customary 15 minutes (ever timed employees?), we get the following lost hours.

Sick Leave: 7 days × 8 hours = 56 hours (7 days)
Breaks: ½ hr. per day × 244 workdays = 122 hours (15.25 days)

This would suggest that extended breaks, lunches, and other events of unproductive time *while at work* are twice as costly as the average sick leave usage, and both kinds of productivity absence are being paid by employers. Further, there exists in many organizations a serious contradiction between their policies on the most abused form of absenteeism—that of sick leave—and their control measures including discipline. For example, it makes little sense to have a sick leave policy allowing employees to be paid for up to 10 days per year for prescribed reasons (excused absences), and then threaten or terminate them for excessive absenteeism because they used what was available—even if they use it all each year and you can't prove improper use.

It is a further contradiction if you impose sanctions against an employee for excessive absences or poor attendance when each one of them has been approved, verbally or in writing, by the employee's supervisor. Union representatives enjoy these cases since it's a pretty sure bet what the arbitrator's conclusion will be. What situations like these suggest is that policy controls are lacking. Here are some ideas that you may want to consider to strengthen your control over sick leave abuse.

1. Monitor the use patterns of all employees and pay particular attention to high frequencies of single day use, use on first or last day of workweek, and day before/day after holidays, vacations, and payday.

2. Allow supervisors to use their discretion in requiring medical proof for an employee's absence, or to call or visit an employee who is allegedly, but perhaps questionably, at home ill.

3. Require employees to state the nature of their illness or other reason for their absence on a leave request form.

4. Provide paid absence only after the third consecutive day of illness.

5. Reduce the number of incidents (not days) to five per year.

6. Create incentives for non-use such as a bonus day off with pay, a higher merit pay increase in conjunction with the annual performance review, or allowing the banking of hours up to the qualifying period of a Long Term Disability plan.

So let's be honest. For those organizations who experience serious and widespread problems of attendance and absenteeism, the real problem is most likely to be one of poor control. Those organizations that experience more moderate levels of these problems have simply not spent the time to study and isolate the real problems so that specific measures to correct them can be implemented. The real problem is not those employees with periodic attendance problems or occasional sick leave use—we all have very real and legitimate reasons why we cannot be at work, can't get there exactly on time, need to leave early, or sometimes just need to goof off a little. The real problem employees are the misusers and chronic abusers.

• Problem misusers are those with erratic and high levels of absenteeism. They are frequently late to work with the proverbial 1,001 excuses, they are easily distracted when at work, and they have little attachment to organizational values of being a reliable employee. They will use sick leave primarily to their recreational advantage.

- Chronic abusers have the highest, most consistent pattern of absenteeism including unpaid absences. They may be good workers when in attendance, but they are also regularly late, take long breaks or meal periods even though they may rarely leave work early as a cover for other abuses.

With misusers and abusers, their absence is more of a conscious decision to not be at work, or perform work, than it is a conscious decision about the consequences upon either the organization or their job security. They either don't care or don't fear the consequences. In order for the manager to diagnose the possible cause (assuming the organization does, in fact, have adequate controls in place) and determine a corrective approach, here are some of the more common reasons the misusers and abusers develop problematic absences.

1. Job dissatisfaction or low morale in the work unit.
2. Alcoholism or drug dependency.
3. Poor health (physical or psychological).
4. Work pressure and/or results not going well.
5. Insufficient personal motivation and ambition.
6. Excessive self-indulgence (lack of work ethic or concern for effect on others).
7. Personal or family problems.
8. Child care or transportation problems.
9. Poor relationship with supervisor, an unskilled supervisor, or lack of organizational attention to absence problems.

There is simply no sure-fire, quick, or easy solution to absence problems. There are however specific kinds of controls that can, and should, be developed and practiced by every organization. Once in place, such structural and process controls should then be reinforced by regular evaluation of attendance and absenteeism patterns so that potential problems can be corrected (misusers), and particular problem solving measures taken with others (abusers) to stop their damaging and unproductive effect on performance. Evaluations should be done not only organization-wide, but by every manager over a work unit so that all attendance and absenteeism problems can be regularly identified, isolated, and dealt with in a suitable fashion that cures the cause and thereby eliminates its effect. Before disciplinary measures are taken, at least these questions should be examined.

- Is the employee's absenteeism well beyond the average of other employees?
- Was there a pattern of problem attendance or absenteeism?
- Was there a thorough investigation and documentation?
- Is it reasonable to conclude that the absence was not due to a continuing medical condition?

- Is there likelihood of improvement in the future?
- Was the attendance policy clear and communicated to the employee?
- Were there prior efforts to counsel and assist the employee in improving their attendance?

2.43 NEGLECT AND NEGLIGENCE OF DUTY

These similar sounding yet very different kinds of disciplinary cause of performance violations are not only quite serious, but they are also condition-specific based on their definitions within policy. *Neglect* of duty means that the employee's performance conduct is such that they fail to execute one or more essential aspects of their job. Their behavior is one of laxness, disregard, evasion, abandonment, and inattention with the result being a default in some visible, measurable, and explainable part of their performance. Failure to meet predetermined goals or deadlines without adequate reason is an example of neglect. It is a violation of omission and absence of contribution. *Negligence of duty*, on the other hand, is the careless or willful impropriety of an act where one knew what to do but chose not to, or knew what shouldn't be done but did it. Examples include the employee who knew the purpose and function of a safety guard on a machine but removed it during use of the machine, or the supervisor who coerced an employee to falsify documents.

As you can see, these are two different behavioral causes but both carry rather serious performance consequences. By the very words that describe neglect, we can readily see that there exists an underlying behavioral dysfunction that precipitates this form of misconduct. If we know the employee well enough to initially determine that this is not typical of their performance, then there is a good chance that something— perhaps an emotionally disturbing and work-distracting event—has happened recently. The quicker that source of changed behavior is known, the quicker its correction will be.

This situation calls for skilled and tactful counseling with the employee where their specific performance accountabilities are the focal point of the discussion. If the message is delivered too coldly or in a purely threatening way, the employee is not likely to expose their source of pain or any other troubles that they know are causing their deficient performance. If those sources are exposed (be ready for some unusual kinds of circumstances), your best approach is that of helping the employee solve their problem rather than you telling them what you're going to do with them (or how you think they should solve their problem).

Negligence of duty, however, almost always is the product of behavioral intent. Whether that intent is to look better on paper than truth would show, to avoid some aspect of work viewed as merely troublesome; or to pacify the possible scorn of superiors, it is an act of knowingly fraudulent performance and therefore a form of misconduct. The employee has failed to use due caution and/or exercise diligence and prudent judgment. There are only a few exceptions as to why an employee guilty of negligence of duty should not be terminated. These include where 1) the employee was ordered by, and was carrying out the instructions of a superior (fear of reprisal—the superior should be fired); 2) the act was not willful or with knowing intent; or, 3) the employee simply was never made aware of what to do, or not do, that caused their negligence. Most any other circumstance surrounding negligence of duty would be unacceptable performance and therefore should not be tolerated.

2.50 DEALING WITH CONFLICT AND OVERCOMING CONFRONTATION BARRIERS

What is probably most obvious by now is the fact that the workplace presents a vast array of opportunities for people to activate their behavioral and attitudinal differences in the course of work. Equally apparent should be the fact that organizations differ rather remarkably by their business type, philosophy and goals, operation methods, managerial styles, and problem solving approaches. When you add this arrangement of environmental diversity to the complex dynamics of human behavior, it becomes inevitable that varying degrees of conflict will result from time to time. Orchestrating people's differences toward common tasks and goals is clearly no easy task, and doing so in a harmonious fashion for an extended period of time is decidedly one of the greatest challenges faced by contemporary managers.

2.51 GETTING CONFLICT INTO PERSPECTIVE

The probability for conflict to occur in the workplace, particularly between employees and line managers, is an ever present condition. It becomes far more likely under certain circumstances such as when work conditions and relationships intensify. These are the events that energize emotions and set off many different types of behavioral chain reactions. One employee may be enthusiastically challenged, another burdened by additional pressure, and yet another wholly indifferent to new situations. For every action there is a reaction, but unlike physical science with its predictable consequences, the formula for successful management of people problems lies in our understanding of human behavior, using our knowledge to anticipate others, diagnosing each situation, and formulating a remedial approach that controls and corrects the situation in a suitable fashion to produce the most favorable outcome. It takes time to learn these skills, patience with their development, and practice in their execution. Don't expect to be right or successful every time—some people won't let you, but learn from these experiences too.

Within each organization there exists a number of sources of potential conflict. They exist in the structual arrangement of organizational officers, in roles and relationships, in policies and resultant practices, and in the ebb and flow of work processes.

As a matter of each organization's management control interests, organizations should routinely conduct an evaluation of their operations to determine if internal contributors to conflict exist. For example, policies should be evaluated to see if they are producing desired results; whether they are flexible enough to accommodate circumstantial handling of problem areas; and whether they are precise enough to be understood, and distinguishing between acceptable and unacceptable conditions.

Likewise, operational styles, methods, and practices should be evaluated periodically (and monitored routinely) to determine if leadership is congruent with organizational values, if clarity and consistency exists within each work unit, and whether ergonomic conditions are better than adquate. Given these kinds of internal evaluations that keep organizations functionally current, managers will be in a stronger position to then focus their attention on improved methods of solving individual and unique human resource problems.

Most conflicts in the workplace arise from interpersonal and role differences between two people. They will occur more frequently between employees, or between an employee and their supervisor, but more consequential to the organization when it occurs between managers. Conflicts range from minor tiffs that are eventually worked out between the feuding parties, to complex behavioral dysfunctions in which the parties struggle and someone eventually gets hurt. While not all conflict is negative, most of it has that potential because we have not yet conquered its management nor learned its control. For that reason, it invariably carries with it a probable damage to some aspect of organizational life however minor its form takes.

Ultimately, the responsibility to handle conflict falls upon each manager. The failure, inability, or avoidance to do so is quite simply shirking the responsibility; or put another way, neglect of duty. With that thought in mind, and knowing well that there are few of us who embrace every new opportunity to handle conflict, it may serve as a helpful conclusion to this chapter to examine some ways of overcoming our barriers to confrontation. If we can learn to overcome confrontation, we can go beyond merely surviving our dealings with conflict that so often accompanies disciplinary situations.

2.52 USING YOUR ROLE TO OVERCOME CONFRONTATION BARRIERS THAT IMPEDE PROBLEM SOLVING

Over the years I have observed countless interpersonal conflict situations in the work setting between different combinations of employees, supervisors, managers, and executives. Some I purely observed their development, progression, and handling, while others I played a more active role as facilitating or mediating its resolution. Many other situations created a variety of conflict scenarios in which I became a participant or the object of conflict—it goes with the territory of human resource management—and there were a number of other occasions in which someone would try desperately to pull me into their conflict situation. There are several things to be learned from personal experience, as well as observing others with respect to what works and what doesn't.

There are those in every workplace who enjoy personality games with others stemming from their own weaknesses, not the least of which is the need to feel a sense of personal power and importance. There are also the rule-benders and those that seem to insist on being a perpetual challenge in some respect to their manager. Just as there are so many behavioral conditions that can, and will, emerge between people at work, there is also an infinite number of approaches to dealing with such situations on an interactive level as each situation develops. These approaches represent both new knowledge and skills to be learned by managers as discussed thoughout this and the preceding chapters.

However, when behavioral conditions begin to turn toward a disciplinary problem solving approach, a new, more heightened sense of internal and intrapersonal conflict evolves. Our emotions become more involved which tends to obscure our rational thinking and conduct much like preparing for battle. We become more in touch with our personal self and less in touch with our role. When this happens there can be a powerful emotional force within the self that leads us to charge the confrontation assertively (or aggressively at the extreme). Second, we may confront the situation with anxiety thereby dealing uncomfortably and awkwardly with our conclusion and intended action. Third, we may avoid the confrontation altogether. Rarely will any of these three methods produce satisfactory results, and they are the product of allowing personal barriers to obstruct the kind of thinking (objective), observation (proper perspective), and conduct (mature and responsible) that is meant to be associated with sound managerial practice. No one truly relishes conflict other than those with psychological abnormalities, but confronting conflict situations is as necessary and as much of a managerial function as is planning the work of others.

Confronting disciplinary problem employees aggressively or with considerable anxiety will produce a definite result, or at least conclusion to the situation, even if it is the wrong one that ineffectively resolves the problem. These approaches will often cause escalation of a conflict. What never works is avoiding a confrontation with a disciplinary employee when it's required, since avoidance means no action, therefore no result, in altering the problem. Supervisors are the most guilty of avoiding these kinds of confrontations, and it is mostly management's fault when supervisors become debilitated by confrontation barriers. Here are some of the reasons for supervisorial avoidance.

- They are promoted into supervision without adequate training or evaluation of various "people" skills and abilities.

- Their role as a supervisor is not adequately distinguished from their personal role in terms of extending clear expectations, authority, and span-of-control guidelines.

- They work more directly and frequently with employees and so are more vulnerable to developing personal affiliations and allowing feelings to control relationships.

• There exists common uncertainty as to which role is appropriate for differing situations, since it is often unclear supervisors are employees or managers.

As Markowich aptly notes, confrontation avoidance can deepen or compound the eventuality of a conflict relationship between manager and employee.

> ...if a manager waits to "see what happens" when a performance problem is evident, the tables may get turned when the confrontation is finally held. That is, the employee may resist not only the manager's assessment of performance ("I think I'm doing a great job under the circumstances!"); he may also accuse the manager of inconsistency, since the past behavior seemed to have been condoned ("Besides, you've never said anything to me before. Why are you picking on me now?"). Thus, the manager ends up having to defend both the decision to confront, and the past decision not to confront.[4]

The result of avoidance and other preconditions frequently create the following kinds of confrontation barriers.

1. **Social Repercussions;** the fear they won't be liked, they don't want to hurt another's feelings, they don't want to be the one responsible for damaging another (letter in personnel file or job loss), they don't want to create an unpleasant experience, or they don't want to be seen by other employees as the "bad guy" or a fink.

2. **Organizational Repercussions;** they fear creating disharmony, they don't want to do anything that might reduce morale, and they become concerned about causing a reduction of performance with the employee or among co-workers.

3. **Loss of Credibility and Control;** they fear their ability to handle the situation properly, they are afraid of making a serious error, they are uncertain as to proper timing and facts needed to act, they are concerned about their objectivity and emotional feelings, and that they may lose the respect others.

4. **Physical Repercussions;** they fear the prospect of someone getting angry with them or even hostile or violent, they may have concern about an employee's physical retaliation, or they may not want to be the victim of their own physical anguish over confrontational circumstances.

As you can readily see, these barriers stem from one degree or another of different fears. Fears can only be overcome by each person gaining recognition of what theirs are (by ourselves or through the help of another person), developing the skills and

---

[4] M. Michael Markowich, etal; "Managing Your Achille's Heel". Personnel Administrator, June 1987, p. 144

confidence to deal with them, then forcing ourselves into those situations that create the fear so that we can gain the experience to diminish or eliminate its effect on us. It's not easy but it is necessary if we are to grow in our abilities to fulfill the confrontation role obligation.

The key to improving a manager's confrontation abilities lies in providing them with deeper knowledge and insights into human behavior including their own personality traits, teaching them more about workplace behavior situations, providing them with new skills to deal with these situations in the desired way, and coaching them through each new experience. Emphasis should be placed on:

- Staying in one's organizational role as a manager
- Remaining objective, including what to do when you can't
- Keeping performance and organizational interests as a prominent focus
- Maintaining a sense of responsibility to control the outcome of each event.

Here are a few basic guidelines to follow in dealing with confrontation situations:

1. Conduct your discussion with the other person in private, never in front of others or in a public place.

2. Determine the proper time and location of your meeting.

3. Gather and write down all of the facts and issues you wish to discuss; determine if each is objectively stated and relates to performance, job related behavior, and organizational interests.

4. Present the issues in emotional moderation, and be sensitive enough to the employee to allow them to tell their side.

5. Talk calmly and slowly, covering point by point, then be a good listener.

6. Be precise about disposing of an employee's excuses, faulty reasoning, vague responses, or other diversions; remember, you're there to confront and resolve a problem, not merely get through the experience.

7. If a discussion begins to get hostile, control it or break off the discussion and take it up again in a day or two when your superior can sit in.

8. Be alert to differences in perception and clarify them. Try to sway inaccurate perceptions using explanations and examples.

9. Determine how you want to conclude your discussion in terms of each issue, what has been concluded, where agreement is or is not, and what happens from here.

10. Document the discussion thoroughly.

11. Follow up to insure that things are going the way you intended.

When confronting problem employees for the purpose of effectuating a termination, not only should these guidelines be followed, but special consideration ought to be given to leaving the employee with a sense of dignity. So often I have found cases of botched handling of terminations on an interpersonal level due to the humanistic inadequacy of the manager's approach. Regardless of the offense or problem that gives rise to a termination decision, the manner in which it is carried out will have a dramatic impact on how it turns out. The manager should recognize that employment conditions elsewhere may be more suitable to the employee, and that the employee has a right to carry on with their life—the sooner they find other work, the better. They can only do that when they're intact as a worthy and resolved person over former employment.

Employees who are terminated abruptly, dishonestly, without adequate reason or explanation, and without a sense of their own contribution to the cause will not feel either worthy or resolved. They can become angry, offended, dejected, or feel many other emotional reactions to how the situation was handled, and thereby feel the retaliatory need to file discrimination claims or wrongful termination suits. Emotional consequences such as humilation, rejection, indignation, and the like can produce depression, weak confidence, and various states of withdrawal that will adversely affect not only the employee's personal state of well-being including family life, but their ability to make a good showing when trying to get another job. Also, the longer a terminated employee remains unemployed, the longer the organization continues its unemployment liability and vulnerability of damage awards should the employee prevail in a law suit—or decide to file one out of economic desperation.

Confronting most termination discussions should be looked at as more of a final counseling session, or at least a factual clarification session, than one of abrupt verdict and sentencing. Naturally, circumstances will vary widely, but when the opportunity exists the manager will get better overall results when: 1) the issues are clearly stated; 2) reason(s) for termination given; 3) prior action attempted to resolve the problem mentioned; 4) some reassurances given to the employee that they're not a horrible person (mention positive qualities); 5) why the organization (not you personally) feels that termination is the necessary recourse; and, 6) what their check-out procedure should be. Keep the situation as calm, positive, and pleasant as circumstances allow, but remain in control of the situation. If possible and appropriate, extend additional help to the departing employee such as out-placement counseling, resume assistance, and job placement services. If the employee asks to talk to someone higher about appealing your decision, make an appointment for them to do just that and apprise the higher manager on the situation before they meet with the employee. In short, follow the "golden rule"; do unto others as you would have them do unto you. When all else is said and done, we are left with our emotions and feelings of memorable experiences.

CHAPTER III: 3.0
PROBLEMS OF WORKPLACE CONTROL, PART I:
IMPROVING WEAKNESSES IN ORGANIZATIONAL
GOALS AND PERSONNEL POLICIES

In Chapters 1 and 2, an examination was made of many issues related to the behavioral causation of at least some troubling employees, and of using disciplinary correction methods to resolve these kinds of situations. Clearly, discipline is the least effective means of correcting behavioral problems. But, like other methods of dealing with difficult human problems that have been suggested, discipline has its purpose and place among workplace control mechanisms. What comes to the fore in situations where the resultant problem stems from the employee's own behavioral provacation is the manager's ability to diagnose or otherwise determine its causal source, and to then administer appropriate corrective measures. Diagnosing behavioral problems can be very illusive in many instances since not only is human behavior complex in itself, but also because it requires distinguishing between causal sources. This suggests that the manager should be able to ascertain, or at least examine possibilities, where problem behavior is created by the employee as part of their own makeup, or merely a reaction by the employee in response to external forces such as organizational sources of causation or provocation.

If we are to effectively resolve workplace problems by identifying and dealing with the source of their cause, we ought to be willing to examine all possibilities. This means going beyond judgments concerning employee idiosyncrasies and being willing to find, then correct, organizational sources of problem causation, or even its contribution to workplace problems. Chapters 3 and 4 set out to do precisely this. Among the sources of many workplace problems caused by inadequacies within the organization are such control mechanisms as the functional linkage between organizational goals, departmental objectives, personnel policies, performance appraisals, and other management activities that either impede or serve the interests of workplace productivity. Chapter 3 therefore points out the importance of linking goals, objectives, and personnel policies to creating effective workplace control systems, then goes on to solve problems particular to personnel policies. Chapter 4 carries on the theme of workplace control by addressing the weaknesses and solutions to performance appraisals as the yardstick by which productivity is measured.

Indeed, there are a number of human resource problems that emerge within the workplace not from purely abnormal behavior, personality clashes, or attitudinal proclivities, but from major weaknesses in the very controls that were intended to irradicate productivity problems. The more influential of these are the organization's goals, personnel policies, operations standards and rules, and the performance appraisal system. Other influential controls include organizational development, information flow, and structural changes that commonly occur in formal organizations. However, the emphasis of this chapter is to address those workplace controls that most directly affect human resource productivity, reactive behavior, and overall performance of our employees. Moreover, the underlying theme used throughout this chapter, as in those that precede it, is to recognize and use the three stages of human resource problem solving.

1. **Prevention;** to work toward proactive measures that resolve potential problems before they occur.

2. **Control;** to establish specific, realistic, and understandable standards that reinforce mutual needs between employees and the organization, and thereby reduce the likelihood of serious discontinuities.

3. **Correction;** to initiate timely, effective, and appropriate measures when deviations arise that might otherwise create a detrimental organizational consequence.

The ideal is of course prevention of human resource problems, and certainly there is much that needs to be done in the area of proactive management. We must first learn to eliminate and then prevent past problems, as well as to improve our skills at anticipating future problems by observing trends. However, managers are also inherently required to be realists. As a practical matter, we simply cannot prevent every conceivable problem. But we can use our experience and diligence to frame control measures. Creating practical controls serve as a guide to employees about the organization's expectations, to supervisors and managers as a decision making source, and to the organization itself as a system by which goals are achieved in the desired fashion. In the absence of control measures, the players will invaribly resort to their individual sense of propriety with the result being a myriad of operational dysfunctions.

3.10 ORGANIZATIONAL CONTROLS THAT GUIDE EFFECTIVE PRODUCTIVITY

As organizations grow, they invaribly become more formalized, departmentalized, and specialized in structure as well as the formality of relationships between those who participate in it. In this formalization process, managers will tend to absorb more general oversight functions and areas of responsibility, while departmental and work unit operations take on more specialty functions. For the manager, more controls now become necessary as a means of ensuring that proper planning, execution, evaluation, modification (correction), and desired results are achieved within prescribed standards of time, costs, resources, objectives, and other operations criteria.

Unit operations likewise become more complex and, with either growth and/or formalization of the organization, managers begin to be replaced at the operations level with work unit supervisors who then become responsible for line decision making, implementation of work, and orchestration of employees to produce the bottom line results, so to speak. Therefore, when management sets out to establish controls aimed at uniform guides to efficient productivity and methods of correcting human resource matters, attention ought to turn toward those devices that define work objectives, operational relationships, and methods of performing work—the basic accountabilities of each operation within the organization. Like writing a musical score, properly designed and applied workplace controls can guide all employees toward synchronized productivity; but absent, ill-conceived, or improperly used controls will yield only rehearsal activity.

It has been my experience as a management consultant that those organizations that encounter problems in such areas as productivity, morale, job satisfaction, grievances (or informal criticisms), and strained management-employee relations can most often trace these problems to their workplace control systems and the methods being used to apply those controls (i.e., policies, programs, structural relationships, communications and information flow, and leadership styles). The ability of each organization to identify, understand, and improve upon both the control mechanisms and their application methods is a crucial process by which the organization can maximize its potential for truly productive use of its human resources.

What we ought to recognize at the onset is that control measures can be established for virtually every business function. This is no less true for professional service organizations, governmental entities, or retail enterprise than it is for manufacturing companies. But too often this task falls victim by receiving a low priority, as do many other support measures, simply because it has been traditionally viewed as an extraneous, non-revenue or non-production activity for managers and supervisors who can be better utilized doing "real" work. There is always some price to pay for miscalculation of business decisions, and this kind of avoidance or cursory treatment of developing sound control mechanisms will prove just how costly it can be to the organization when management later begins to see evidence of organizational, human resource, and productivity problems. The longer such problems are left unattended, allowed to deepen, or treated with token reforms, the less likely it becomes for correction to produce meaningful solutions.

3.11 ORGANIZATIONAL INTEGRATION OF CONTROL STANDARDS

To be both integrated within and throughout the organization, and meaningful to those participating within its structure, control standards and processes must be connected from the top to the bottom of the organization regardless of its size. They should also be written in common, observable, and measurable terms. For example, I have found in numerous organizations that their goals or mission statements—intended to be the control catalyst for productivity objectives of all operating units—are phrased in rather abstract terms. Moreover, abstract goals tend not to be remembered by senior managers, and not understood by line managers and supervisors in any meaningful context of their operational responsibilities. In fact, with a few organizations for which I've performed consulting assignments, line managers were not even aware that corporate goals, missions, and philosophy statements existed much less the proposed manner in which these statements were intended to affect them. Little wonder why corporate and line managers were not getting expected results from each other.

To establish workable control standards each area of control must mesh vertically in the organization with special attention given to horizontal linkage with other controls. This is to say that such human resource controls as personnel policies, job descriptions, pay plans, and performance appraisal systems should not only stand alone as a sound instrument, but they should also result in a meaningful system of personnel operations between them (horizontal integration). Likewise, they should be equally effective in their purpose for employees up to top management (vertical integration). When fully integrated, such controls as these can and will produce a well orchestrated flow of work in a harmonious setting, assuming of course that their application is undertaken with the same degree of diligence with which the controls were designed. Communication will become clear, responsibilities easily understood, work becomes purposeful, and positive results produced. It's not theory, it works. If you doubt this fact, take a closer look at a few of your competitors who you know are doing things better than your organization (e.g., capturing greater market share), and I venture to speculate that you'll find your answer in their control mechanisms and application methods.

If we were to diagram some of the organizational control mechanisms in their vertical and horizontal relationships, they would look like the following.

Vertical Relationship Of Some Organizational Controls

Organization Unit	Structure	Policy	Productivity
Governing Body	Bylaws	Adoption	Mission
Corporate Admin.	Heirarchy Chart	Development	Goals Measures
Dept./Division	Functional Responsibilities	Implementation	Objectives
Work Unit	Work Plans & Flow	Enforcement	Operations Standards
Employees	Job Descriptions	Compliance	Performance Measures

Horizontal Relationship Of Some Human Resource Controls

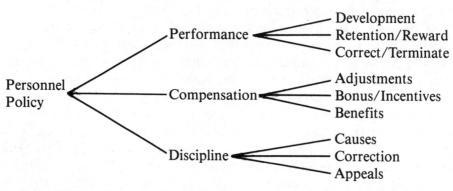

Another frequently encountered problem among many organizations is the belief by their managers that for control standards to be effective (or perhaps convincing) measures, the standard must be stated in quantifiable terms. Not so, and this has lingered too long as an excuse to avoid development of new standards that must be evaluated on the basis of qualitative measures because of the very nature of the activity under scrutiny. Consequently, the issue is not the presence or absence of quantifiable indexes or descriptive qualities. Rather, it is the ability to state standards in specific performance related terms that easily lend themselves to observations, evaluation, measurement, and correction—the fundamental elements of a control system!

3.12 CONTROL DISTINCTIONS AND SIGNS OF INADEQUACY

The relationship between individual jobs, and the people that occupy them, and the organization as an entity will of course vary depending on such characteristics as the organization's size, locations, goals and philosophies, industry type, diversity of operations and jobs, and its structural makeup. This is precisely why each organization becomes unique in the policies it chooses, people it hires, methods of operations used, and even the type of performance measurement system utilized. Yet each organization strives for many of the same things such as consistency, productivity, harmony, and goals achievement. The only way these can be realized is by integration of practical controls. If the chain of relationship between specific controls at different levels in the organization are broken, or don't match in an understandable way, a breakdown in that control system will result and proper diagnosis of this problem will be difficult due to the distracting complexity of resultant symptoms such as those indicated below.

Signs Of Inadequate Control

A critical first step in improving an organization's control system is determining the effectiveness of current methods. The need for more effective control is often indicated by:

- Frequently missed deadlines
- Declining or stagnant sales or profits
- Poor quality of goods or services
- Loss of leadership position within the company's industry
- Low employee morale and high absenteeism or turnover levels
- Inability to monitor employee performance and generate needed data
- Insufficient management/employee communications, written or verbal
- Excessive company debts or unpredictable borrowing requirements
- Adequate use of human and material resources, equipment, and facilities.[1]

To avoid such breakdowns, it is imperative for managers to carefully plan and design each control standard in ways that ensure its practicality and integration wherever it is to be applied within the organization. An effective way of accomplishing this is to use various (topical and systems) heirarcial task forces consisting of a senior manager, key department/division heads, and a couple of concerned and knowledgeable supervisors. Together, these individuals can bring a synergy to the process of identifying existing and potential problems, brainstorming needed elements of control, strategizing corrective and evaluative measures, and preparing control documents. Ultimately, each operations manager, supervisor, and employee affected by a control mechanism and its standards must be able to translate, implement, and evaluate each standard in the context of their own job responsibilities, work schedules, resources, and performance results.

Therefore, prior to implementation of new or revised controls it is advisable to review draft documents with those who will be most subject to their achievement and success. Employee input can be very helpful if properly involved to the refinement of standards since they and their supervisors are closest to the work, and success may well depend on their sense of the standards being fair, reasonable, purposeful, and achievable. Once implemented, however, we need to test our controls by watching for signs

---

[1] _____; "Controlling With Standards", p. 63.

of their effectiveness and areas needing further refinement through future modifications. This also means that no document having its purpose as a decision making or work process guide should be treated as a static, "leave well enough alone" device. Healthy organizations recognize the need for ongoing change, and they willingly confront them as both challenge and new opportunity for maintenance of their edge over others. As one such player, the choice is yours to take the initiative, or let others have the edge.

Taking proper corrective action to maintain those controls that have been put in place requires both the responsibility and authority to execute control measures, as well as having adequate time to stay in touch with those performing the work. In other words, we should not be so bogged down with our own work that we are not free enough to observe, help, and correct the work of subordinates. This has been a major mistake of American management practices. We tend to be more supportive of theory than of operational reality. Theory defines the functions of management, but in reality we do not give our operational managers sufficient time from their own assignments to practice the responsibilities of planning, organizing, controlling, actuating, and directing— then we criticize them for doing a marginal job at one or more of these functions. Perhaps it's time we reeaxmine our priorities in terms of the appropriate role for supervisors and line managers.

To control human resources within the context of work and the dynamics of organizational life, we need to have and exercise both process and structural controls. Process controls include such things as hiring the right people, providing them with good continuous training and supervision, having effective performance appraisal systems, developing sound information flow networks, and exercising prudent operations and management techniques. Structural controls are generally those that guide the entire organization or particular components of it. They include personnel policies, operating procedures, heirarchial relationships, job descriptions, proficiency standards, mission statements, strategic plans, and unit objectives and work plans.

3.13 ORGANIZATIONAL GOALS, POLICIES, AND OBJECTIVES AS CONTROL MECHANISMS

People in organizations have an understandable tendency to get caught up in their own realm of work and thereby develop a perspective of the organization only in the context of what is meaningful to their area of responsibility. It becomes easy to lose sight of the "big picture" even in those organizations who try to communicate and reinforce that picture. Organizations who are not diligent about keeping the organizational perspective in front of their employees are quite simply allowing that perspective to remain vague.

As managers, we all know that keeping in touch with our roles relative to the entire organization is important if the organization itself is to succeed. What success means is that fundamental goals are met, and to do so requires hard work, cooperation, dedication, and compromise—otherwise known as teamwork. Teams, of course, will only succeed where there exists willingness to dedicate effort to the benefit of the cause for which the team exists.

So what drives and guides the organization, and therefore each participant within it, are its goals. Most organizational goals are expressed in terms of short and long range economic, social, service, and other kinds of general achievements—depending on the type of organization—for which the organization is intended to serve (why it exists). For example, organizational goals are commonly phrased in very general terms such as the following illustrations, and there are any number of multiple goal statements that can be developed to express an organization's various interests.

1 . XYZ Corporation is dedicated to the development of innovative and high quality surgical instruments that are uniquely beneficial to the medical community, cost competitive to maintain or improve our market share, and profitable to shareholders to stimulate economic growth and employment opportunities.

2 . ABC Agency strives to provide the physically handicapped community and eligible clients with essential services, programs, and representation that fosters their integration into the workforce and mainstream into a more productive life. To the extent of available funding, A,B,C Agency places greatest emphasis on a full range of services to ensure that eligible clients can maximize their opportunity to obtain employment and other vital needs within the community.

There is nothing inherently wrong with these kinds of goal statements aside from the fact that they are rather operationally abstract and rather vague expressions of corporate philosophy. While they are necessary to help frame a sort of corporate big picture purpose for the organization itself, the statements in and of themselves do not tell managers, supervisors, or employees how to carry out these expectations. That task is the proper domain for top management to interpret and translate corporate goals into operational functions appropriate to each descending level in the organization. So, while it is important for managers and employees alike to keep the corporate, big picture goals in mind, they will only become meaningful if they are translated into functionally understandable expectations and accountabilities in the context of each person's job. To assume that managers and employees should merely act (instinctively) in an efficient manner solely on corporate goals without operational translation is an error of unrealistic overestimation of human nature—which is, to view things in the context of our individual work roles.

The first step in translating organizational goals into operational expectations and accountabilities is to write them into action statements that will ensure the delivery of specific results. These statements should be written as specific, short and long range goals for each major department which, in turn, translates each goal into more operationally specific objectives. Conversely, each work unit, within various departments, works with the department head to translate annual objectives into their work plans, operations procedures and standards, resource availability, and the like. The result thus becomes written work unit expectations and accountabilities that are realistic, achievable, and measurable in terms of each employee's performance. By following this sequence of translating general corporate goals into increasingly more specific goals, objectives, and work plans throughout operating units in the organization, goals turn into a control system. This chain of organizational controls should also be reinforced by such other structural controls as operating policies, procedural standards, and performance accountabilities.

Again by example, the following illustrates the translation of a corporate goal into one goal for a human resources department, then into a couple of specific objectives that are developed for the upcoming year—each of which happens to be a type of control mechanism that supports or guides organizational productivity.

Goal

To develop and maintain a contemporary system of human resource administration with respect to the company's personnel policies, procedures, practices, and programs that are responsive to both company interests and employee needs.

Objectives

1. Develop a new pay-for-performance program for sales personnel, and evaluate its effectiveness against established expectations and possible application to other positions.

2. Revise the performance appraisal instrument and compensation policy concerning sales personnel.

3. Research and prepare a report of findings, cost, benefits, and recommendations on the addition of an Employee Assistance Program in response to interests expressed in employee survey.

4. Prepare and conduct internal training for managers and supervisors in the subjects of:

   • Time Management
   • Communications And Teamwork
   • Advanced Interviewing Techniques
   • New Employment Laws And Effect On Operations

To complete this illustrated translation process and refine the development of both control mechanisms and individual performance accountabilities, these objectives would next be converted into work plans with specific staff assignments, timetables, and clearly defined expectations of the work and its results.

It was pointed out earlier that organizational goals are general statements of purpose, and it has been shown that departmental goals become function-specific statements in *direct* support of organizational goals; both of which are control systems, but at two different levels. Control mechanisms such as policies, standards, procedures, and programs become the product of these two control systems that progressively and systematically guide the organization, each operating unit, and performance accountabilities as diagrammed below.

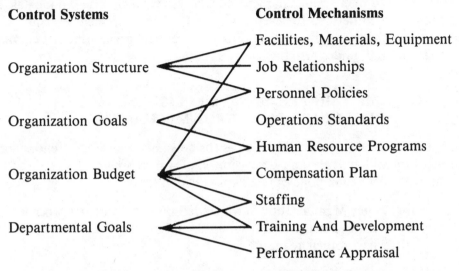

Control Systems   **Control Mechanisms**

Facilities, Materials, Equipment

Organization Structure   Job Relationships

Personnel Policies

Organization Goals   Operations Standards

Human Resource Programs

Organization Budget   Compensation Plan

Staffing

Departmental Goals   Training And Development

Performance Appraisal

Personnel policies, procedures, and compliance details serve as a control mechanism by way of delineating the organization's position on a particular topic, and they establish:

- intent
- what is, or is not, to be done
- how things work
- what is, or is not, available
- circumstances surrounding a topic

The purpose of policies, then, is to communicate uniform principles and provide a decision making, action-taking guide.

Operating standards, on the other hand, are usually distinguished from policies by virtue of being confined to either routine administrative matters not otherwise applicable to policy issues, or to specific department or work unit standard practices (i.e., using form 101A to reverse an error in a customer's open inventory account). With respect to enforcement, operations standards carry equal weight as policy, but to do so they need to be well communicated, be accompanied by adequate training, and preferably incorporated by reference into personnel policy. Both policy and operating standards can serve as valuable control mechanisms if properly written, disseminated, reinforced, and enforced.

Yet another control mechanism of some importance to human resource productivity and problem solving is the organization's performance appraisal system. It is important to view performance appraisal as a system because of its linkages to many other aspects of human resource decisions. In essence, performance appraisals are intended to serve as a program of collecting measurement information to determine productivity results. These measurements are made against prescribed tasks, behavior, methods, results, and many other characteristics of job performance. So long as these characteristics are well defined for each job, and their measurement executed under proper conditions, they will serve their purpose as a control mechanism that communicates expectations and guides resultant decisions.

3.20 USING PERSONNEL POLICIES AS A PRODUCTIVITY CONTROL MECHANISM

Personnel policies are the guiding sources for how an organization's entire human resource program will operate and deal with employment matters. The three most common ways for personnel policies to be embodied are:

1. **Personnel Policy Manual Only;** in which definitive policies and procedures are covered for use by managers and supervisors, but only available to employees for brief review at their request.

2. **Employee Handbooks Only;** in which only those basic topics of greatest interest to employees are described in brief, first-persons statements, bound in handy booklet form, and given to all employees at the time of hire or revision. This is the least desirable option.

3. **Manual and Handbook Combination;** where the manual is a comprehensive document used as a complete description and guide for management, and used as the basis for contents of the employee's handbook with referral on issues to the manual which is openly and readily available to any employee. Some smaller organizations will use their manual-only in this same open fashion.

Within the realm of human resource administration there is no stronger, absolute control mechanism than the policy manual, providing it is written with proper content coverage, clarity, and a writing style that accurately depicts the character of the organization. Communicating the character of the organization in personnel policy manuals can be even more impressionable to others than its provisions. In this regard I am reminded of Sir Adrian Cadbury's 1986 award-winning treatise on the ethics of management, in which he aptly points out:

> The character of a company is a matter of importance to those in it, to those who do business with it, and to those who are considering joining it...The ethical standards of a company are judged by its actions, not by pious statements of intent put out in its name.

What matters most, however, is where we stand as individual managers and how we behave when faced with decisions which require us to combine ethical and commercial judgments. In approaching such decisions, I believe it is helpful to go through two steps. The first is to determine, as precisely as we can, what our personal rules of conduct are. This does not mean drawing up a list of virtuous notions, which will probably end up as a watered-down version of the Scriptures without their literary merit. It does mean looking back at decisions we have made and working out from there what our rules actually are. The aim is to avoid confusing ourselves and everyone else by declaring one set of principles and acting on another. Our ethics are expressed in our actions, which is why they are usually clearer to others than to ourselves.

Once we know where we stand personally we can move on to the second step, which is to think through who else will be affected by the decision and how we should weight their interest in it. Some interests will be represented by well-organized groups; others will have no one to put their case.[2]

The principle function, then, of any personnel policy manual is to structure human resource operations, programs, and decision-making in varying degrees of specificity to guide consistent treatment of employees by the organization. Policy manuals certainly cannot address all possible situations, nor should such an attempt be made. To attempt doing so would likely alter language to imply conclusiveness. As a practical matter, being conclusive is often impossible due to the number of variables in many differing situations where circumstantial judgment is imperative to arrive at suitable resolution for those directly concerned, or those affected indirectly by precedent-setting decisions.

3.21 MAKING PERSONNEL POLICIES A POSITIVE CONTROL

The highly acclaimed management theorist Frederick Herzberg and others have found in their studies of motivational factors in the workplace that one of the least motivating was company policy. In fact, in Herzberg's Motivator-Hygiene Theory (1959) based on studies of professional and technical employees, he found that the number one item of discontent (hygiene factor) was company policy and administration—followed by supervision. I would speculate that a similar study performed among these and other employees would show only modest improvement in their regard for policy and its administrative application which, in itself, is a sad conclusion given three decades of opportunity to learn the errors of our ways.

This is not to say that all blame for the failing of policies to serve as a positive control mechanism rests with management in general, or those who write policies. Rather, the negativeness commonly associated with policy, and their attendant communication, interpretation, and application has been a combination of errors over this period. We need only look at the high rate of litigation, unionization, arbitration, and

---

[2] Sir Adrian Cadbury, "Ethical Managers Make Their Own Rules". Harvard Business Review. Sept.-Oct. 1987, p. 70.

other conflict-oriented effects policy has had on our employee-relations efforts to know this is true. These conflict-oriented situations may also be symptomatic of yet other conditions that have changed; some positive and some not so positive. For instance, a great deal has changed in the last 30 years; the way we do business, technology, management styles, employment laws, liberalization of social issues, and awareness of employees to equity matters to name only a few.

Clearly, these kinds of changes in work conditions has placed new and unusual burdens on the role of personnel policies as an effective organizational control mechanism, and where particular emphasis has been placed on employee performance. But, we should ask ourselves, what about management performance? Should we not expect—no require—ourselves as managers to be as abiding and subject to the sanctions of company policy as employees? And, don't most of our policies reinforce a sort of unnecessary chaste system that conveys to employees "what's good for the goose isn't necessary for the gander?" While there are indeed necessary (if not by legally required) separations of rights and authorities, let's be honest about the fact that some of our policies go too far in conveying our intent to operate as an "us and them" workplace society.

There are several ways in which we as operations managers and human resource practitioners can make policies more positive control mechanisms, and thereby improve their effectiveness as both an employee-relations and performance accountability device. These methods of improvement have to do with policy content and process.

POSITIVE CONTENT

Content has to do with what we say and how we say it. What we say communicates the provisions of the policy, procedure, and rules. How we phrase policy language communicates the underlying organizational philosophies and intended style of managing policy decisions. It may be an enlightening exercise to open your personnel policy manual to any page and read a page or two to see if you can depict these two communications characteristics. Then, evaluate your policy language against the following positive control elements.

1. **Use of Positive Language:** Control is not inherently synonymous with harsh or demanding language. While some topics need to be addressed in absolute terms, or where management exercises sole domain over an issue, there are ample areas in which various conditions, requirements, and standards can be expressed in positive (adult) language. Positive language explains purpose and intent of the policy, encourages, guides, shares power, and gives rights as well as obligations.

2. **Use of Two Way Language:** The nature of many, but not all, policies creates a tendency to write "you will do this" kinds of statements. Where appropriate,

change this kind of orientation to "this is what we are striving to achieve, and what we need and expect from you is..." Also include such statements as, "your supervisor is trained to help you in dealing with...," and where possible use references to "all employees." Care must be taken to avoid the inappropriate use of words or phrases that express or imply a contractual obligation, but the point here is to go through your policy manual to find opportunities for converting overly stringent one-way statements to two-way language that will give employees a sense of mutuality. This might even include adding a few management commitments and accountabilities, but be prepared to stick to them and ensure their enforcement.

3. **Be Clear and Specific About Performance and Conduct:** As a matter of policy each organization should articulate what standards of performance and conduct are expected, or discouraged, from all employees as well as the reasons for these standards. To be a positive source of information, these standards should be expressed in clear, specific (but not implying conclusiveness), and non-threatening language. An example of the latter might be to state:

> Management strives to prevent the use of disciplinary measures as a means of dealing with performance and conduct problems, but this is a shared responsibility between the company and its employees. Under most circumstances management will try to resolve these problems by informal means, but if any particular problem becomes so serious or remedial efforts do not provide satisfactory results, it may be necessary for the company to initiate formal proceedings.

4. **Allow Room for Discretionary Decisions:** In those policy areas that do not, of necessity, have to be one-and-only-one-way iron clad, provide operations managers and unit supervisors the discretion to use prudent judgment in making circumstantial decisions. Too often policies become negatively locked-in, restrictive, unfair in some situations, and forcing some of these decision makers to tell employees, "Sorry but that's the way the company says it has to be." You can be explicit in delineating parts of policy and still reserve some discretion in the decision making process. The major caution though is to make sure decision makers are thoroughly trained and given some fundamental guidelines including underlying principles of policy matters.

5. **Centralize Pre-Action Review of Negative Actions:** Many organizations embrace the advantages of decentralizing decisions and actions on personnel matters, but in some areas doing so is blind abandonment of the crucial need for assuring objectivity, consistency, and soundness of adverse actions. Without some form of centralized review prior to initiating an adverse action, policy decisions can easily gain a reputation as being personality contests, inconsis-

tent, without merit, and completely subjective—the message becomes, "so why even bother appealing it since the company apparently allows it to happen." There are also endless case law citations that could bear witness to the fact that using centralized pre-action reviews can eliminate an amazing variety of legal mistakes.

6 . **Offer a Legitimate Appeal Process:** This becomes a positive control because it shares power and instills a sense of earnest intent to be equitable; it says, "We may not always be right and we're willing to take another look at the situation to assure you of fair treatment." The policy language should reflect this principle, along with being simple, honest, and with timely treatment.

POSITIVE PROCESS
Process is a matter of how we carry out policy. It includes the methods used to develop, change, implement, and enforce policies, as well as the personal manner in which they are interpreted, conveyed, and applied. Therefore, policy process focuses on management practices in administering them, and on the way they are communicated.

1 . **Employee Involvement:** By nature, people do not tend to readily accept changes of which they were not a party to. Further, if the personnel policies are being examined for revision as opposed to newly developed, who would be better to ask about their effectiveness or weakness than those most subject to them? A desirable approach is the use of a properly structured survey questionnaire among all general employees to gain this information; and a separate questionnaire for line supervisors and operations managers aimed at interpretation, enforcement, and decision making applications of existing policy. Using the compiled results of these surveys, you are now in a stronger and more positive position to set up a working task force committee to undertake the project. Such a task force should consist of a senior manager, the human resource manager, key department heads, select supervisors, and a small cross-section of employees.

2 . **Opening Information Channels:** Another aspect of human nature is that people become suspicious, guarded, and skeptical when they feel important information is being withheld. Withholding information in organizational life is common, takes many forms, but is too often overplayed with regard to personnel policy matters. In fact, some organizations I've encountered would not allow employees to have access to their supervisor's copy of the personnel policies let alone have their own copies. Such a practice is rather absurd since it defies the very principle that employees need information to do their jobs and comply

with company practices if things are to run smoothly. Whatever management's fear is about a full and open disclosure of policy, it is largely unfounded and less realistic than the fear they should have about the reaction of employees who feel subject to information entrapment.

Employees should either be given their own copies of the organization's policy manual, or if this is too demanding by virtue of cost and effort, then at least let them know that they are welcome to read their supervisor's copy at any convenient time. What should accompany this approach is an annual training program that teaches employees such things as why these policies exist, how procedures are structured and why they must be followed, why it is in their best interest for management to exercise certain discretionary decisions, and answer any questions they are likely to have. It may come as a surprise to some of you, but there are some employees who actually believe that managers like to conspire in power dominant ways against employees—and even that some managers stay awake one extra hour each night to think of new ways to take advantage of them (that's why managers arrive at work later than employees).

3 . **Thorough Training of Managers and Supervisors:** One of the most harmful and negative things that can happen to an organization is to have good personnel policies and poor application of them. You might just as well have poor policies because, as Sir Adrian Cadbury was quoted earlier, people are more inclined to rely on what is done rather than what is said will be done. To ensure a more positive approach and lessen the organization's liability over errors, it is a worthy if not imperative endeavor to provide thorough training at regular intervals for *all* managers and supervisors on personnel policy matters. I do not mean simply a structured opportunity to go over policy language. Rather, what should be central to this kind of training is to impart comprehensive knowledge of the management, operational, and legal principles that underlie key policy areas; how each major policy was intended to be interpreted (importance of internal continuity); situational problem solving and decision making guidelines; and to answer questions that arise using the group opportunity to resolve common misconception.

3.30 THE CRUCIAL BUT LEGALLY VULNERABLE SIDE OF PERSONNEL POLICY

It probably comes as no surprise to find that those policies that tend to be nearest and dearest to management as a control mechanism and a discretionary decision making authority are also the very policies that have become the most legally vulnerable.

Why? Because crucial policies get acted on quicker, more frequently, more decisively, with greater subjectivity (inconsistency), and usually have the greatest potential for adverse effect on one or more employees. Hence, these policies and their attendant application tend to be the most likely to go before arbitrators, compliance agencies, and the courts for dispute resolution—whether or not the alleged impropriety has merit.

Part of the dilemma about policies being both crucial and vulnerable is the fact that policies are more than those official, written, and adopted statements we use in manuals and handbooks. Policies also mean unwritten rules that are carried out as a matter of practice, verbal statements expressed in official ways by one having some authority, and precedent actions of the organization established through past practices in dealing with any given situation. So, the issue of legal vulnerability becomes slightly more complex and difficult for employers to defend when extended to this broader definition of what constitutes "policy". It is not uncommon for the courts to acknowledge the existence of these kinds of formal/informal and written/unwritten policies, and then to treat them with equal esteem. The following, then, are those policy areas and topics that are both crucial sources of management decisions, as well as legally vulnerable to legal attack.

3.31 SENSITIVE POLICY AREAS AND THEIR CORRECTION

The following are frequently overlooked yet rather crucial issues that should be addressed in personnel policies.

1. **Revision Rights:** The right for management to revise policy as necessarily needed by changing conditions is essential to keeping the organization current in matters of human resource decisions, but some courts are construing this past discretionary power of management as a change in working conditions (which can be grounds for a breach of contract in those states holding that policy manuals are, or can be, contractual in nature). To protect the organization's interests in revising policy when deemed by management that it is appropriate to do so, the manual (or employee handbook) should contain a declaration reserving this right to management; where appropriate, management should make a good faith effort to obtain employee input prior to finalizing revisions; and management should ensure that each employee is formally notified of the revision(s). It may also be advisable to use a form for employees to sign acknowledging their receipt and acceptance of the revision.

2. **Equal Employment Opportunity:** Given the choice most employers would probably avoid including this area in their policy manual, but given laws and extremes in the values of some people, you need to deal with the subject in an open, honest, thorough, and forthright manner in order to fully state the orga-

nization's position. Address policy, prohibited activities, operational responsibilities, and the internal complaint procedure, but avoid making commitment statements predicated on future conditions.

3. **At-Will Employment:** Not to belabor the points raised in Chapter II, Parts 3 and 4, but employers can no longer assume (without written notice to employees) that employees know their employment is at-will unless covered by an employment contract. Such notice should be proclaimed in various parts of the manual (e.g., salary increases, performance, discipline, and other areas pertaining to longevity and continuation of employment), as well as a statement on the employment application form. Where such disclaimers exist, some state courts are rendering summary judgments for the employer thereby relieving the organization of the liability for creating a contractual obligation. Further, and as a precaution, references to "permanent" employee should be changed to "regular" employee where distinction is necessary from probationary employment.

4. **Behavioral Conduct Issues:** Similar to performance deficiencies, behavioral forms of (mis)conduct should likewise be addressed in policy including general statements of intent and purpose followed by illustrative examples of undesirable conduct related to the organization's legitimate interests (e.g., employee's execution of job responsibilities, effect on others, welfare and reputation of the organization, orderliness and harmony of the workplace setting, and the like). It should be pointed out to employees that while some conduct matters may be dealt with by informal remedial efforts, others may be subject to more formal discipline including immediate termination.

5. **Just Cause Termination:** Employers need to take great care to ensure and protect their right to terminate the employment of employees when there arises a reasonably legitimate reason to do so. Here, legal vulnerability exists in two areas: what constitutes reasonable and legitimate reasons for the termination action (i.e., can it be supported from an objective, business related decision); and, to what degree company policy language has committed the organization to terminate *only* for specified reasons (just cause).

Care must be taken throughout the policy manual to remind employees that corrective action can and will be taken under many circumstances when it is in the best interest of the organization to do so, including terminations, and such actions are not solely confined to matters of the employee's own performance and conduct. In other words, just cause for terminations should be both specifically defined by examples and broadly defined by purpose in terms of the organization's needs to deal with a diverse range of operational conditions.

6. **Confidentiality and Access:** Employees should be assured, and managers informed, that personnel matters are to be treated with the utmost confidentiality. This extends from virtually any written documents including forms pertinent to employment information to employment related discussions between supervisor and employee. Likewise, access to employee personnel files should be addressed in policy in support of the organization's interest to protect lawfully required confidentiality, and to inform employees of their right to know the contents of their file (see Chapter II, Part 2). Because employees do have a lawful right to review their personnel file, it is customary and prudent for each organization to charge their human resource office(r) with the responsibility to oversee the content of personnel files.

7. **Review and Appeal Mechanisms:** There are four common types of conflict situations that tend to arise at one time or another in most organizations, and the majority of them can be resolved easily by internal review if handled properly. The four situations to include in review and appeals mechanisms are:

    - Complaints of alleged discrimination
    - Performance evaluation disputes
    - Discipline and termination appeals
    - Working condition complaints

    By providing an honest and objective review and appeal mechanism(s) allowing employees to access progressively higher level evaluation of perceived problems, the organization can better identify and correct otherwise unknown problems. Too, such appeal mechanisms tend to build stronger morale, avert external involvements, and demonstrate their good faith effort in support of objective decision making. These are particularly important when you're called on to justify an employment action or decision. if required to defend an action.

8. **Interpretation and Creation of Policy:** What may otherwise seem an obvious right of management may not be that obvious to employees and the courts. Too often, the question of who does have the right or responsibility to interpret or create policy becomes a source of conflict not only between employees and supervision, but between managers themselves. Policy should reflect that supervisors and managers have the right to interpret and enforce policy, and that ultimate responsibility for questions and conflicts in interpretation matters rests with the human resource director (who may consult with the CEO prior to rendering final opinions). However, when it comes to declaring the organization's right to establish new policy in response to situations not addressed adequately in the existing manual, it should be the CEO who has this

sole authority, and who presumably enacts new policy under the advice of human resource and other affected managers.

9. **Permissive Versus Compulsory Words:** Words used to convey information to others creates impressions and connotations. Some organizations, in their effort to create a very positive impression of what a pleasant organization their's is, will too often avoid using absolute, controlling, or demanding words. Conversely, some over-controlling organizations use only absolute words. Absolute words are compelling with respect to the impressions they create, and compulsory in a legal sense of obligation; thereby compulsory words establish a liability for inaction or deviation. For example, compare these words:

Compulsory Words	*Permissive Words*
Must	May
Shall	Can
Will	Should

Whichever word is used, it should be applied to the situation with careful thought toward the desirability of creating a deliberate liability obligation, and the degree of need for absolute versus discretionary control. It may no longer be in the organization's best interest to say, "Employees *will* be formally evaluated annually on or near their employment anniversary date, at which time consideration *shall* be given to a merit pay increase." Compulsory words should be used only in conjunction with absolute control or commitment circumstances such as prohibited discriminatory activities.

3.32 SENSITIVE POLICY TOPICS AND THEIR CORRECTION

Policy topics that carry with them crucial decision making yet legal vulnerability are those specific employment issues where the organization takes a discretionary position (i.e., not necessarily regulated by statutory law), however the manner in which they are written or applied falls within the purview of legal scrutiny under prevailing case law. By way of summary and selected references, problem policy topics include the following.

1. **Accrued Time Payoffs:** paying employees for unused vacation, compensatory time, and sick leave upon employment separation (*Jones v. District Parking Management Co.,* 1970).

2. **Severence Pay:** paying employees an amount upon employment separation in consideration of their service length—as opposed to pay in lieu of advance termination notice—(*Ariganello v. Scott Paper Co.,* 1982).

3. **No Smoking:** complete prohibition of smoking within the entire company premises (non-accommodation remains a heavily debated issue of civil rights, selection validity, and Rehabilitation Act protections).

4. **Progressive Discipline:** *compelling* management to follow a prescribed seuence of more serious actions to correct a problem employee irrespective of the severity or circumstances (*Gray v. Superior Court,* CA 1986 et al.).

5. **Whistle Blowing Retaliation:** taking adverse action against an employee because of the employee's disclosure of an impropriety involving the use of funds, malfiescence of management, etc. (*Caplan v. St. Joseph's Hospital,* 1987 et al.).

6. **Repayments of Tuition Reimbursements:** requiring that employees repay company-paid tuition reimbursements if they leave the company within some lengthy, as opposed to short, duration after completion of the last course taken.

7. **Drug/Alcohol Testing:** the manner in which this information is held in confidence, disclosed, or dealt with and the potential for its defamatory effects (*O'Brian v. Papa Gino's of America,* 1986). See also Chapter II, Section 1.22.

8. **Protection of Trade Secrets and Non Competition:** the use of unreasonable kinds of restraints (policy, forms, written agreements, or provisions) that go beyond legitimate protection interests of the company's welfare and create unfounded hardships upon employees (*Tyler v. Tribune Publishing Co., Inc.,* 1986). See also Part II, Section 4.26.

9. **Confidentiality of Salary Rates:** prohibiting employees from divulging their own salary rate or that of others where the weight of free speech rights (First Amendment) becomes substantially greater than the soundness of company interests to insist on non-disclosure. There are other ways to maintain salary information confidentiality.

10. **Jury Duty:** avoiding harassment of employees who are empaneled to serve on a jury by summons which is a prohibited activity under the Jury System Improvement Act of 1978 (*Shea v. County of Rockland,* 1987).

11. **Antinepotism/No-Spouse Employment:** unreasonable prohibitions against the employment of spouses and/or relatives (*Thomas v. Metroflight, Inc.,* 1987 et al.). See also Part I, Section 3.31.

12. **Initial Versus Promotional Probationers:** the existence or absence of distinctions that would differentiate reasonable consideration for the continuation of employment rights and benefits between these two kinds of probationary status employees; e.g., probationers being the first to be laid off or having no grievance appeal rights (*Duldulao v. St. Mary of Nazareth Hospital Center,* 1987).

13. **Leave Return Rights:** under what kinds of reasons or circumstances employees are allowed to return to their same job, or otherwise guaranteed a return to employment with the organization, and the maximum durations for such kinds of absence without pay leaves.

14. **Use of Company Property:** allowing or prohibiting employee's personal use of company equipment, facilities, vehicles, materials, and other forms of property rather than disciplining or terminating an employee for breaking unwritten rules (and is practiced differentially in the organization).

15. **Dress and Grooming Standards:** insisting on standards that are rigid beyond circumstance and not reasonably related to occupational and business conditions where the result is (unintentional) sex or race discrimination (*Carroll v. Talman Federal Savings & Loan Assoc.,* 1979; and *EEOC v. Trailways,* 1981).

16. **Work Hours, Overtime, and Exempt Employees:** making adequate and lawful declarations of differences between part-time and full-time employees (hours, pay, benefits), work hour expectations of exempt and non-exempt employees, designating exempt positions, and qualifying eligibility and rates for overtime pay.

17. **Performance Appraisals:** avoiding reference to performance factors being the only condition of continued employment such as stating, "Employees who demonstrate at least satisfactory performance in their annual evaluation shall be retained and eligible for..." In states where policy manuals have been, or might be, held as an implied contract by virtue of the way statements are framed, a promise to conduct employee appraisals or consider pay increases after a specified time can be construed as evidence of an employment guarantee for at least the specified period (*Jones v. Intermountain Power Project,* 1986; *Eller v. Houstons Restaurants, Inc.,* 1984).

Also, whether or not policy allows managers to prepare supplemental appraisals at other discretionary times, and the manner of making appraisal-related decisions as a matter of company practice, which is discussed in greater detail later in this chapter.

3.40 PREPARATION OF PERSONNEL POLICY MANUALS

The framing of personnel policies, procedures, rules, and the like has become both art and science. It is art form with respect to the experience, creativity, anticipation of events and needs, and writing flare. Science is expressed by the imperatives for precision, thoroughness, and the implications they have on legal matters, operational significance, and propriety to the nature of employee-relations desired. Both characteristics should be brought to the task of developing a good personnel policy manual. Particular attention ought to be given to those conditions about and within the organization that set it apart, and make it a unique place of employment and opportunity. Consider how you would express such elements of the organization as:

1. Goals of the organization
2. Style of management
3. Functional relationships and the structural heirarchy
4. Values toward its human resources
5. Importance of human resource administation
6. Distinguishing between different types of jobs
7. The manner in which the organization wants to deal with employees
8. What is expected and needed of employees
9. What employees can expect from the organization
10. Which decisions are to be decentralized or centralized
11. The kinds of human resource programs and operational issues that best support organizational goals

Once these general elements of the organization and human resource operation are delineated as they relate to policy development, the next step is to begin outlining specifics of the manual itself. Here is where a small task force committee made up of key managers, supervisors, employees, and chaired by the human resource manager can be very useful. Well thought out decisions should be made with respect to such considerations as:

- **Format;** order of appearance and layout of purpose statements, policy, procedure, rule, etc.

- **Content;** which issues are to be presented in what order based on legal requirements, the clarity of legally oriented issues, the need to establish management principles, and how to provide decision making guidance?

- **Dissemination;** who is to review drafts before adoption or revision, and who is to receive final copies?

- **Communications;** what methods should be used to convey policy matters to employees, and how can we provide thorough training to supervisors, managers, and executives?

• **Implementation;** are there any other steps that should be taken to assure a smooth and orderly implementation of new or revised policies—will any of them represent radical changes where we may want to take six months/one year to grandfather in such changes?

• **Revisions and Evaluating Effectiveness;** how often should revisions be made when circumstances warrant (consider every six months for the first two years and annually thereafter); what methods are to be used to disseminate and communicate revisions; and is the format such that revised pages can be easily replaced? Also, who and by what means will policies be evaluated for their effectiveness in terms of producing desired results?

These and many other issues concerning personnel policy are likely to emerge in an organization giving consideration to the original preparation, or nearly any revision, to their policy manual. As a guidance and decision making document, personnel policy manuals will get daily use and close scrutiny by those effected. Therefore, if the document is to withstand the test of legal, thorough, practical, and sound policy, its development demands input and considerable work from multiple sources. Knowledgeable sources usually consist of internal task force members, human resource professionals, and human resource consultants experienced in policy and organizational matters. The use of qualified labor attorneys should be reserved to a draft review for any potentially vulnerable language relative to state and federal legal implications—not discretionary operation matters unless there is legal pertinence.

For those of you who might be considering what topics should be included in your policy manual, here is a list of topics you may want to draw from.[3]

ILLUSTRATIVE OUTLINE OF PERSONNEL POLICY MANUAL TOPICS

General Administration

    Purpose and Principles of the Personnel System
    Administration of the Personnel Program
    Application of Personnel Policies
    Amendment of Personnel Policy Manual
    Violation of Personnel Policy
    Reports and Records
    Departmental Operating Rules

---

[3] See also Chapters 1 & 2 in Levesque, Joseph D.; *Manual Of Personnel Policies, Procedures, And Operations.* Prentice-Hall, 1986.

Equal Employment Opportunity

   Equal Employment Policy
   Discrimination Prohibitions
   Program Responsibilities

Position Classification and Allocation Plan

   Preparation of Position Classification and Allocation Plan
   Amendment of Position Descriptions and Allocations
   Classification and Allocation of New Positions
   Position Reclassification

Compensation and Payroll Practices

   Preparation of Compensation Plan
   Structure and Advancement Within The Compensation Plan
   Exempt and Non Exempt Classifications
   Wage and Salary Reviews
   Part Time and Temporary Classifications
   Timekeeping, Pay Periods, and Time/Manner of Payment
   Overtime and Holiday Work Compensation
   Compensation Upon Promotion, Demotion, Transfer, or Reemployment/
      Reinstatement
   Compensation Upon Reclassification
   Compensation For Work Performed In A Higher Classification
   Compensation During Work Disability
   Attendance At Lectures, Meetings, and Out of Area Travel
   Compensatory Time Off Practices
   Payroll Deductions, Advances, and Deposits
   Compensation Upon Employment Separation

Employment Benefits, Leaves, and Holidays

   General Benefit Provisions and Applications
   Proration and Cost Sharing of Benefits
   Design, Implementation, and Modification of Benefits
   Health Care Benefits
   Disability and Death Benefits
   Workers' Compensation Benefits
   Vacations
   Holidays
   Sick Leave

Jury Duty
Military Leaves
Temporary Disability Leaves (incl. maternity)
Leaves of Absence

Hours of Work

General Hours of Work
Modification of Hours and Work Schedules
Reporting to Duty
Unauthorized Absence From Work
Meals and Rest Periods

Performance Appraisals and Promotion

Performance Policy and Standards
Intial Employment Performance Appraisals
Scheduled Performance Appraisals
Review With Employee
Distribution of Report
Discretionary Performance Appraisals
Effect of Performance Appraisals
Promotion Policy
Promotional Appraisals
Return of Promoted Employee to Former Position

Conditions of Employment and Employment Activities

General Conditions of Employment
Security and Confidentiality
Financial Affairs
Gifts and Gratuities
Unauthorized Visitors
Off Duty Employment and Conduct

Discipline and Grievances (Appeals)

Discipline Policy
General Employee Conduct
Causes For Discipline
Types and Progression of Discipline
Considerations and Procedures For Initiating Discipline
Disciplinary Notices and Reviews
Appeals Policy

Informal Appeals Procedure
Formal Appeals Procedure

Training and Safety

Purpose Of and Responsibility For Training
Off Duty Training and Development
Certification of Job Related Training
Safety Program Policy
Responsibility For Job Safety
General Safety Rules and Precautions
Reporting and Abating Hazardous Conditions
Reporting Job Injuries

Separation From Employment

Resignation
Dismissal
Layoff
Exit Interviews and Check Out Procedures

Definition of Terms

3.41 TAKING PRECAUTIONS WITH POLICY SAFEGUARDS

Two of the most serious implementation problems about the use of personnel policy manuals has been: 1) the reluctance of larger size organizations to commit themselves to all the assorted legal vulnerabilities of written policy, particularly in those states where manuals and handbooks are held as expressed or implied contracts; and 2) the honorable but imprudent desire of smaller size organizations to function informally, flexibly, and without all that cratic nonsense, as some view it—of restrictive written policy (a reflection of restrictive writing!). Both positions represent more of an emotional reaction based on "sour grapes" experience or perception where some flaw in policy backfired, or in some other way failed management's purpose leaving a soured feeling about the greater need and purpose for having personnel policies. Such documents will never be perfectly suited to every situation. They may eternally be riddled with legalistic war games, and they may at times demand temporary (until changed) rigidity where such was not intended. But, these are problems that can be reduced and should not overshadow the more imperative need to inform, control, and guide vital conditions of employment and human resource utilization decisions.

Using our business sense rather than emotional reaction, we need to confront these more objective managerial facts concerning personnel policy manuals:

- Our employees and decision makers have a legitimate need to know how things work in the organization, and conditions that affect them personally including proper adaptation to, and success in, the work setting.

- Anything in writing is vulnerable to misinterpretation, misapplication, and abuse—but we don't stop using this medium to communicate.

- Our business is a legal entity and, as such, is always vulnerable to the treachery of those less scrupulous than ourselves.

- Good policies can provide an essential and positive source of control in the organization as a means of assuring efficiency, order, and maximum productivity.

Given the current and ever-increasing legal vulnerability of personnel policies/ practices, there are some precautions that can be taken to lessen these kinds of risks. Some were mentioned earlier such as centralizing the review of negative actions, using an internal appeal mechanism, using clear and concise language to explain distinctions in employment categories and how situations will be dealt with, and the thorough training of those responsible for policy application. Additional measures that ought to be considered when preparing manuals with legal safeguards include the following elements.

1. **At-Will Employment Disclaimer:** Recent trends indicate that many courts are tiring of employees trying to abuse precedent legal theory concerning the forming of an implied contract from language contained in personnel manuals and employee handbooks. Moreover, these courts are beginning to grant summary judgments for the employer where the policy in question, or the manual itself, contains a specific disclaimer that employment is *not* for a fixed term nor does it carry with it any guarantees for continuance beyond that mutually desired. The case of *Dell v. Montgomery Ward & Co., Inc.* (1987) illustrates this point in which a supervisor of 12 years was fired for covering up a subordinate's underhanded conduct and brought suit because the employer did not follow its progressive discipline policy. The court rejected the employee's claim for breach of contract specifically because the employer's manual contained two at-will employment disclaims; one with regard to employment in general, and the other in connection to progressive discipline (others should be placed with policies on pay, pay increases, any earnings of benefits with continued employment, and performance appraisals). Here are the two disclaimers that prevailed in this case.

General Disclaimer

Employment at Montgomery Ward is for no definite period and may, regardless of the time and manner of payment of wages and salary, be terminated at any time by the company or by an employee, with or without cause, and without any previous notice.

Further, no organization manager or representative of Montgomery Ward, other than the President and Chief Executive Officer or the Executive Vice President of Human Resources, has the authority to enter into an agreement for employment for any specified period of time or to make any agreement contrary to the foregoing. This lack of guarantee or employment contract also applies to other benefits, working conditions, and privileges of employment at Montgomery Ward.

Progressive Discipline Disclaimer

Although employment with Montgomery Ward is not for a fixed term or definite period, and may be terminated at any time either by the employee or the Company, the Company has developed a procedure that it expects its supervisors to follow when exercising their right to either discipline employees or sever the employment relationship. This procedure does not form an employment contract.

2. **Supercedure and Consent Disclaimer:** Where courts continue to hold that manuals and handbooks carry a contractual liability, some cases (*Thompson v. King Entertainment Co.,* 1987) have raised the question as to whether revised policy forms a new contractual relationship that must then meet the standards of contract law which, among other conditions, requires the written consent of all affected parties (employees). Despite the fact that the well-known *Toussaint* case in 1980 clearly held that mere continuation of employment by employees after publication of a new policy created an implied consent to agree to the provisions of new policy, and that the employment relationship was not the same as customary contractual relationships, the entire issue of policy supercedure and consent by employees could become another snare.

To avoid this potential pitfall, it would be advisable to add to your manual a disclaimer that makes known not only the organization's right to revise policy, but that such revisions, additions, or deletions have the effect of rescinding and superceding related former policy upon publication (and notification) of such amendments. If extra caution is desired, you may wish to consider the use of a form for employees to sign acknowledging their receipt of, and consent to, these amendments in the same way that some employers are using manual/handbook receipt forms upon intial employment (or use a blanket form statement covering future amendments).

3. **Consistency/Coordination of Disclaimers:** Merely placing one or two disclaimers in the policy manual will not always exonerate the employer from potential contract liability, particularly where there is inconsistency in the meaning of other policy statements. For example, policy statements that declare or infer: employees will only be disciplined or terminated for prescribed

conditions of just cause; continuation of employment is based on satisfactory performance; or that the entire contents of the manual represent *the* conditions of continued employment are likely source statements of altering the at-will employment disclaimer (*Ferraro v. Koebach,* 1985; *Brooks v. TWA, Inc.,* 1983; *Longley v. Blue Cross and Blue Shield of Michigan,* 1984).

The point here is that policy manuals must be:

- Internally consistent in content to support and reinforce the principle of at-will employment, meaning the avoidance of conferring contradictory rights to employees, and stated in understandable terms.

- Coordinated between various employment documents meaning that manuals, handbooks, employment applications, performance appraisal forms, employment letters, and the like contain similar disclaimer statements.

4. **Legal Review:** While I have already committed myself to the unpopular position that attorneys should not be used by organizations to help write policy manuals, there is no substitute for their use in reviewing new or revised policies. Legal review of policy statements is a must if you are to have adequate safeguards. However, some caution should be exercised in selecting a truly qualified attorney so that you are certain they possess broad labor law experience, trial experience, and both statutory and case law knowledge in applicable state and federal laws as well as the emerging body of precedent trends in other states (anticipatory law). Further, because many judgment of damages against an employer are often paid—at least in part—by the employer's liability insurance carrier, you may be required to select an attorney from one of the larger law corporations since insurance companies often require the use of their greater resource pool as opposed to solo practitioners.

Once again, when requesting a labor attorney to review your policy, procedures, and practices, be clear about your desire for them to focus on legal issues only. Allow yourself to be the expert on how organizational, operational, and program matters are to be treated, but at the same time heed the advice of your legal counsel.

By now, some of you may be left with an uneasy feeling that use of these legalistic rituals will dampen your attempts to establish positive, informal, and humanistic relations with your employees. In this regard you may wish to know that there is no evidence supporting the contention that precautionary legal language contributes to lowered morale, nor increases insecurity among employees. Studies in this area of employee attitudes have found that employees react more to management's practices and actions than to the seeming harshness of written policy.

3.42 IMPROVEMENTS NEEDED TO SOLVE POLICY PROBLEMS

Those conditions that have become the moving forces to reshape American management practices has been evolving over the last 30 or so years, yet it is only in the last decade that sorely needed changes began to be implemented. It has taken time for American organizations to diagnose, and in other ways evaluate, the influence of external forces on their methods of human resource utilization. But, the time has come to make adjustments in a proactive, positive way using the experience of past changes and future insights to solve problems rather than allowing them to become obstacles. Now is the time to reexamine and make needed changes to the structure of our organizations, the content and purpose of jobs, our approaches to operations, and the management systems that are intended to support organizational goals. That is, if our businesses are to be efficient, productive, and opportunistic places of employment. Human resource management needs to place new emphasis on a reexamination of the ways in which workplace policy, programs, and operations reinforces or restrains organizational success—including that of its people as individuals.

Indeed, there are many organizations who are initiating several positive changes in the way they deal with human resource issues. Each, in their own way and industry circumstances, are bringing positive attention to their organizations through innovative approaches to solving problems, and hailed as industry leaders as well as good places to work. For example, Burlington Industries found that by decentralizing decisions to more employees and allowing them the freedom to make choices has created positive work relation results and greater support of the organization's product goals. Burlington's Director of Personnel Administration notes that more emphasis had to be placed on training employees in these new decision making opportunities as a means of adding the needed support to the organization's change in operational relationships and working methods.

Conversely, Tandy's Vice President of Human Resources notes that their organization has created a strong commitment to the value-added benefits derived from more intense selection, training, and development practices of its employees. Another change made by Tandy has been to place 75 percent of its managers on a compensation plan based on company profit and loss indexes.

The compensation and other human resource practices of First Interstate Bank are likewise changing because their industry is moving toward variable compensation (base pay plus incentives connected to results using new performance measurements for different jobs). Says their Senior Vice President of Human Resources, "It's part of our value system to foster employee growth and development...Our role is to help line management optimize its development of human assets. We do that through the design of strong, positive and professional personnel policies."

Even the federal Office of Personnel Management (OPM), with its 6,000 page (5 feet 2 inches high) personnel manual covering civil service employment regulations has been undergoing some reform since 1985. Since then, OPM's Director has been working diligently to simplify both those regulations that constrain sensible policy decisions and the meaningfulness of such personnel programs as compensation, performance, and retirement.

In other words, many of the reform measures taking place within various organizations and their management systems are aimed at value-added philosophies where their human resources will be better utilized, developed, and treated. Expressed in terms of a business practice, the goal is to achieve optimal use of our payroll dollars in contrast to needed returns. To complement this goal, we may need to retool many components of our human resource programs and practices to better fit the forces that are shaping changes in each industry's business environment.

A few of the improvements in human resource policy development and associated management practices that should be given immediate attention are:

1. Use policies and practices as a positive control mechanism and tie each one closely to the goals of the organization to create a cohesive control system.

2. Create positive policies and practices that reinforce desired outcomes for all jobs, operating conditions, objectives, and work relationships.

3. Build in economic, esteem, and other incentives that demonstrate visible opportunity for recognition and the value of good work.

4. Encourage and respond to the participative involvement of employees in problem solving, decision-making, and formulation of new ideas (reducing costs—gainsharing).

5. Allow opportunities for employees to develop and use new skills, then reward them for value-added results.

6. Place heavier emphasis (budgeted commitment) to employee training and the development of new skills, including preassessment and intensive training of new supervisors and managers.

7. Demand decisions that are fair and reasonable.

8. Be clear in communicating what you want and don't want concerning performance and conduct.

9. Use precautionary safeguard language to protect company interests from those who seek self-interest.

Having beckoned for these improvements to personnel policy and the management of our human resources, let's proceed with a more detailed examination of how performance appraisal systems should serve as a valuable control mechanism reinforcement of goals and policy, and specific ways in which to solve some lingering problems in their use.

CHAPTER III: 4.0
PROBLEMS OF WORKPLACE CONTROL, PART II: CHANGING WEAK PERFORMANCE APPRAISALS TO A PERFORMANCE CONTROL SYSTEM

As it was pointed out in the previous chapter, performance appraisal systems in conjunction with associated personnel policies represent an important productivity control mechanism for any organization; yet there is probably no other aspect of human resource administration that has had a stormier history than performance measurement programs. Why is performance measurement important, and how does it serve as a control of productivity? First, performance measurement is important because of its linkage to numerous and varied human resource decisions. It is also vital information to the organization as a means of measuring congruance with perform- ance related (personnel) programs and operations techniques intended to support and enhance organizational efficiency. If we were to diagram those features of perform- ance measurement that are important to individual employees as well as the organiza- tion, it would look as shown below.

	Individual	*Organization*
Performance Appraisal Control Mechanism	Feedback Coaching/Counseling Development Pay Increase/Incentives Promotion Retention Layoff	Goals & Objectives Achievement Production/Efficiency Policy Conformance Conduct Standards Job Descriptions Selection/Skills Validation Training Programs

The performance measurement process itself is also an important function for supervisors and managers alike. Despite being a dreaded task, and one met with both resistence and questionable results, the very process of attempting to measure individual employees forces supervisors and managers to more closely consider performance accountabilities. These may include routine tasks, skills needed, special aptitudes, behavioral traits, working conditions, situational adaptations, and other job conditions relative to the work setting. This process, then, provides an opportunity for the supervisor and manager to not only reflect on and compare each employee to prescribed performance measures, but also to associate those measures and resultant outcomes to work unit objectives; which, as you will recall from Chapter 13, are supposed to be direct translations of departmental goals.

4.10 PERFORMANCE APPRAISAL AS A CONTROL MECHANISM

Now to the second part of the question; how does performance measurement control productivity? To answer the question, we should understand what productivity means since it is a very broad term relating to several different aspects of performance. Fundamentally, productivity means producing—getting the work done with the most advantageous results using the best possible methods. Doing work and getting results is a measurement of *what* we do, while the methods used to carry out work is a measurement of *how* we conduct ourselves and our work transactions. Therefore, each job is represented by what is within the defined scope of the position (job description) in relation to others we work with, and how each job function is carried out. In brief but illustrative form, we can list them in the following categories.

Job Function Characteristics

What	*How*
Routine Tasks	Methods & Techniques
Projects	Processes & Procedures
Special Assignments	Behavior & Conduct
Traits & Skills	Adaptations

Performance Measurement Dimensions

Results	Efficiency & Economy
Quantity	Timeliness & Accuracy
Diversity	Quality
Proficiency	Work Habits

Performance measurement, then, becomes a powerful control of the organization's productivity, and each operating unit therein, when there exists a tightly meshed direct linkage between goals, objectives, work plans, job descriptions, personnel policy, valid and measurable performance standards, and support programs (supervision, selection, training, compensation, incentives, and promotional development and opportunities). When these linkages are not properly meshed, or there exists serious weakness in any one of them, productivity control becomes an illusive quest by upper management; a confusing concept by mid-management; a "stand-alone" assortment of standards to be tolerated by supervisors; and unrelated job requirements by employees.

The solution to these kinds of frequently encountered problems lies in creating necessary productivity linkages throughout the organization, and in eliminating technical weaknesses so often found within the performance appraisal program itself. The perpetuation of problems in performance appraisal programs continues to restrain their usefulness as a control mechanism through which productivity is intended to pass by means of measurement screens.

Performance appraisals also serve as other kinds of control when those dimensions of work represent the totality of an employee's job, not merely their tasks and methods within the narrow confines of a job description as some now believe. For example, if we were to stand back from looking at only the defined jobs we evaluate, we would quickly see that there are many other factors to be considered in relation to how any one employee's performance influences organizational needs that are indirectly tied to productivity. Here, we should begin seeing such factors as:

- Work relationships with others (cooperation, helpfulness, congeniality, inspiring, positive, etc.).

- Compliance with instructions, procedures, and rules.

- Flexibility in ways that accommodate, not resist, change.

- Contributions to the overall mission of the work unit or organization (innovative ideas, creativity, self-initiated projects, etc.).

These aren't the only "other factors" that should be brought into the scope of performance appraisal when considering the measurement of one's performance given the totality of employment conditions. Each different organizational type, setting, and conditions has its own set of other factors to measure, and they should be identified and incorporated into the measurement system. In so doing, we transform the more narrow connotation of performance (own job tasks) measurement to a more encompassing connotation of employment (total influence) measurement. By expanding measurement to include all aspects of one's employment performance, we gain a more accurate depiction of each employee's true organizational worth, and greater control over such conditions as interpersonal relations, compliance, adaptation, and special contributions.

In terms of actual measurement control, I recall a couple of client situations where they had at least one employee who was regarded as very good in many aspects of their job, including very positive customer relations, but was uncooperative and at times antagonistic toward co-workers. Other troublesome characteristics of the employee(s) consisted of resisting change, being a nonconformist, and in minor ways undermining peers and superiors. Management's inability to pin the employee down on these performance deficiencies was tied to their appreciation of the employee's excellent customer relations and the fact that the dimensions used to measure performance of these employees did not adequately include such "total job" factors. In short, management felt impeded to control undesirable characteristics of the employee's overall performance because of the weight given to customer relations, referred to as a "halo effect", and the absence of measurement dimensions that would properly bring out the true nature of deficiencies in view of the total scheme of employment requirements. Clearly, one's performance must be viewed in the context of all requirements and conditions of employment, not merely the manner in which individuals influence their own success.

4.11 PERFORMANCE MEASUREMENT AS A SYSTEM

Probably one of the greatest problems, and much of the cause for failure, of many performance appraisal programs has been tunnel-vision attention given to the form used to measure employee performance. It has been treated by human resource professionals as a design or redesign problem in terms of how best to incorporate a vast array of different jobs into common performance dimensions on one form that can be quickly and easily rated (not truly measured) by supervisors without alienating them for the time and effort the process may require. It is a problem for rating supervisors because the form never seems to have proper instructions, guidelines, defined standards, clarity of dimensions to specific jobs, narrative space, or other features that allow supervisors to bring out all pertinent detail of important, total job measures and information.

These limitations in measurement and forms design also limit the ways resultant information can be used by the organization relative to its linkage to other uses (goals, policy decisions, employee development, assignments, etc.). What we need to recognize is that the form used to measure performance is a tool like any other device used by management to record key information about the total performance of individual employees in specific jobs. Similar to survey questionnaires, the information on the form should be designed in such a way that it solicits all pertinent detail about the employee's performance in relation to the uses, conclusions, and decisions for which it purports to have purpose.

If our purpose is to consider pay raises, the process should allow us to make clear distinctions between performance levels reflecting on past activities of different employees. If we are to evaluate their relative efficiency in achieving or contributing toward work unit objectives, then the process should define efficiency standards and tie them to these objectives. And so it should proceed in the design of the overall process until all desired aspects of performance are matched to its purpose, or the totality of one's employment with respect to performance, in well defined and clearly measurable terms.

To be successful then, performance measurement must be treated as a complete system whose design must be fully integrated into the organization in such a way that it is clearly tied to its goals and policies; reflective of its philosophy and culture; and will create direct linkage to resultant decisions, actions, and information processing that will truly serve the organization's betterment. In this way, the appraisal system becomes both the yardstick by which the organization measures its productivity indexes, and a valuable control mechanism by which other human resource interests are served in the name of mutual productivity (employee feedback, supervisory relations, skills development, job design, rewards and incentives policy, planning, and the like). However, you should be prepared for at least some organizational repercussions.

In converting a "stand-alone" performance appraisal program to an organizationally integrated system—the process of which often takes two to three years—you may encounter isolated cases of sharp resistence. For example, top management will be looking for more precise results in measuring productivity, and it's not likely to be achieved by simplifying the measurement process. Given the fact that many supervisors and managers already view the process as an extraneous task compared to other job responsibilities, it may become difficult to reshape their attitudes when a more detailed or complex measurement process is introduced to them. When your best efforts fail to acquire the needed support and cooperation from a few obstinate hold-outs, it may ultimately become necessary to move those individuals out of the way for their failure to adapt. To do otherwise would be condoning a source of rejection for the new system, and thereby sending an unintentional message to employees, that upper management doesn't support the new system.

4.12 WEAK APPRAISAL SYSTEMS AND THEIR REFORM

There are three major weaknesses in appraisal systems that will continue to undermine their effectiveness until they become subject to diligent reform. These three areas consist of: 1) the lack of organizational integration and linkage to productivity purpose as previously mentioned; 2) the lack of validity in measuring the performance characteristics of different jobs; and, 3) the lack of attention given to the administration and management of appraisals, including inattention to precise skills development of performance evaluators (raters). In working with various organizations to help them improve their appraisal programs and systems, I have found that there are 14 common elements that are the most frequent contributors to weaknesses within their systems. They are as follows, and you may wish to compare your own system against these areas of weakness to determine the need for reforms.

1. Rating dimensions are so vague or ambiguous as to be meaningless.

2. Rating dimensions do not apply to particular jobs.

3. Rating dimensions are not weighted among differing jobs, and neither rating dimensions nor standards are sufficiently defined.

4. Rater training and instructional guidelines are absent.

5. Personnel policies associated with performance are absent or incongruent with the purpose and decisions connected to performance measurement.

6. Appraisals are not done on time and/or are done with only cursory detail.

7. Appraisals are used as a cumulative disciplinary tool.

8. Raters are not objective with all employees, or they show signs of such rating biases as "halo effect", "leniency", "central tendency", or a similar predisposition.

9. Rater fails to discuss the appraisal with employees.

10. Appraisal results are changed by higher department managers after the rater's discussion with the employee.

11. Employee not previously told about a performance deficiency.

12. Employee receives insufficient training (management problem) in a performance area and is rated low in that area.

13. Employee not given an adequate opportunity to comment on their own performance or views of rating results.

14. The appraisal process is an island—it stands alone without follow-up, decision making use, and consequence between distinctions of marginal and excellent performance.

Any number of horror stories about poor appraisal systems where low morale, defensive relationships, poor company credibility among employees, and even legal battles can be cited. What stands out among investigations into performance appraisal systems is that those organizations which treated problems as a serious threat to their employee relations program—meaning a visible sign of reduced productivity and market competitiveness—and chose to do something about it. Such was the case with Merck & Co., a leading pharmacy company in New Jersey, which recently revised both their performance appraisal and salary administration systems after obtaining extensive feedback from employees concerning their views on how the company could improve. Their new system gave greater financial and non-financial rewards to top performers, and fewer rewards to lesser performers. Result; a heightened sense of fair and equitable treatment of employees by the company and improved employee-supervisory relations.

Perhaps more economically pronounced is the case of Richway Stores' change to a performance management program at their distribution center in Morrow, Georgia where "management by exception" and autocratic leadership were concurrently changed to positive reinforcement, team building, and participation with employees relative to their performance. Result; a 30 percent increase in productivity as a direct result of the change in both the method of employee appraisals and style of management interaction over performance matters.

What begins to emerge after thorough examinations into the performance appraisal systems of Merck, Richway, and virtually hundreds of other organizations making drastic changes in their appraisal systems was the need to refine their philosophy, policies, methods, and rewards. True, there is usually some impetus connected with these reforms. Usually the impetus is reactionary in some respect, be it productivity slippage, reduced quality control, market share competition, employee morale problems, turnover, or litigation over some form of unfair treatment. However, the impetus to reform an appraisal system that is ineffective in some respect can also be through proactive management. Proactive management suggests that the development of a better system simply gives more meaning and use of the process, improves performance communications and human resource decisions, and gains more credibility as a management control mechanism.

4.13 WHAT PERFORMANCE APPRAISAL SYSTEMS SHOULD DO

It would be trite to say that performance appraisals are intended to measure performance, but this is the most common answer given to the question of what should performance appraisal systems do? Indeed, there are numerous reasons for the development of appraisal systems and conducting the process of individual employee appraisals as a means of data collection. To begin, each organization should start with a (re)examination of the purposes for its use of an appraisal system. Each purpose should be itemized and explained in terms of its meaning, linkage to business operations and human resource administration, and expectations as to how it will be carried out or used. Then, these collective purposes should be embodied into policy and procedure documents to establish proper linkages to policy as a supporting control mechanism, to procedures as an operational guide, to define the appraisal process, and to clarify decision making as a result of performance outcomes.

Once policies, procedures, and other linkages to the organization's purposes of having an appraisal system are developed, the performance appraisal instrument can be designed in conformance to both these linkages and improved methods of soliciting valid, accurate, fair, and measurable performance information. When we combine purposes with technical job differentiation detail (dimension and standards definitions, weights, etc.) in the construction of appraisal documents, the result will always be a much improved system for the organization and process for those subject to it. What this resultant system and process should do, then, is produce the following.

Productivity Measurement

- Measure the execution of routine and non-routine tasks carried out by employees based on their use of required skills, knowledge, and abilities.

- Measure work behavior and methods used by the employee to accomplish tasks and conform to prescribed rules, procedures, standards, objectives, expectations, and instructions.

- Measure key area and overall proficiency, productivity, and job progress.

- Measure initial employment adaptation or progress at milestones of long term assignments.

Performance Communications

- Provide the employee with performance feedback and strengthen the participative communication process between supervisors and employees concerning performance contributions, expectations, and needs.

- Convey to employees the need to correct or improve the development of deficiencies with respect to requisite skills, knowledge, abilities, behavior, and methods.

- Provide early discussion of performance weaknesses or potential problems before they lead to failure (emphasis on problem solving).

- Clarify performance expectations and distinctions between performance levels.

Training And Development

- Help supervisors recognize weaknesses in employee performance, causal sources of lowered productivity, and the identification of specific remedial measures to be taken.

- Utilize appraisal findings and results to assist employees in the development, and further strengthening, of their skills by coaching, inspiring, and providing individualized training.

- Identifying training needs by advising higher management, and the human resource department, of deficiency patterns and other performance conditions that should be addressed through group training programs.

Decision Making

- Provide a continuing record of each employee's performance history.

- Reward good performers in ways that are meaningful and distinctive to their performance level and service history.

- Serve as a guide to retention, promotion, layoff, and other personnel actions.

Human Resource Research

- Determine the validity of job qualification standards, recruitment and selection methods, and compensation programs.

- Verify the accuracy and currency of job content (job description detail).

- Ascertain the reasonableness of performance dimensions and standards.

These features of a performance appraisal system are no small order, but they can be achieved. Doing so should be the goal of every organization with an interest in productivity and effective employee relations. As managers, we can ill-afford to give only perfunctory attention to our appraisal systems while at the same time holding firmly to high expectations. It may sound like a cliche, but we should either give our full support and effort to the development of good appraisal systems, or abandoned poor ones until a better one can be constructed.

4.20 PROBLEMS WITH TRADITIONAL APPRAISAL METHODS

Few managers and human resource professionals would probably argue with the fact that traditional methods of employee performance appraisal fail to satisfy their intended purposes. But why should this surprise us given the further fact that 80 percent of all employers using appraisals have done little to modify the five traditional methods developed by the military during World War II and post-war industrial employers. The methods developed during these periods were essentially geared toward the measuring of two characteristics covering literally thousands of people, and the characteristics were efficiency and output for military personnel, and later changed to work quality and work quantity for factory workers. While these two characteristics remain valid for many employees today, they have a considerably different meaning in the contemporary workplace.

We are no longer an industrial society, but rather ours is an economy of diverse industries dominated by technological and service businesses. We employ an incredibly vast array of people with specialized skills and talents, and whose jobs are subject to rapid change and continuous diversification. So, while it may have once been easy to evaluate the work of a soldier or factory worker by the thousands, we are now in an era that must learn to cope with specialization, diversity, and acquiring more from performance measurement than mere production indexing.

The problems we currently face, then, lie in obsolete appraisal methods, the manner in which they are being used and not used, and in breaking away from the traditional factory worker mentality of viewing performance in light of production indexes so that these obsolete methods of appraisal can give way or be transformed to more accurate methods. A further examination of these obsolete methods and uses may help shed light on the essence of their problems, and why such appraisals have been problematic.

4.21 DESIGN AND APPLICATION WEAKNESSES OF TRADITIONAL METHODS

There are five traditional methods of performance appraisal that dominate the business community today. Over the years, these methods have been modestly reformed, combined, and in other ways given only cosmetic change so that we presently see thousands of different-looking forms, but they truly stem from one or more of the basic five. These five methods consist of:

1. Graphic Rating Scale
2. Ranking and Paired Comparison
3. Essay
4. Critical Incident
5. Forced Choice

With rapid changes in the nature of technical, professional, and managerial jobs during the 1960's and 1970's, two other methods emerged and are referred to as Behaviorally Anchored Rating Scale (BARS), and Management By Objectives (MBO). The BARS method is particularly useful among professional and technical jobs while MBO is almost exclusively a method applied to managerial jobs; yet both have encountered some serious problems related to the time, effort, and expense to develop as well as maintain.[1] A summary of the relative features of traditional and more recent appraisal methods in wide use is provided in the following table.

---

[1] An excellent review of the types of MBO methods and an analysis of why many have failed is presented by J.S. Kane and K.A. Freeman in "MBO And Performance Appraisal: A Mixture That's Not a Solution" (Parts 1 & 2), *Personnel,* December 1986/February 1987.

Summary of Appraisal Method Features

Evaluative base	Graphic rating scale	Forced choice	MBO	Essay	Critical incidents	Weighted checklist	BARS	Ranking	Paired comparison	Forced distribution	Performance test	Field review
Developmental cost	Moderate	High	Moderate	Low	Moderate	Moderate	High	Low	Low	Low	High	Moderate
Usage costs	Low	Low	High	High supervisory costs	High	Low	Low	Low	Low	Low	High	High
Ease of use by evaluators	Easy	Moderately difficult	Moderate	Difficult	Difficult	Easy	Easy	Easy	Easy	Easy	Moderately difficult	Easy
Ease of understanding by those evaluated	Easy	Difficult	Moderate	Easy	Easy	Easy	Moderate	Easy	Easy	Easy	Easy	Easy
Useful in promotion decisions	Yes	Yes	Yes	Not easily	Yes	Moderate	Yes	Yes	Yes	Yes	Yes	Yes
Useful in compensation and reward decisions	Yes	Moderate	Yes	Not easily	Yes	Moderate	Yes	Not easily	Not easily	Yes	Yes	Yes
Useful in counseling and development of employees	Moderate	Moderate	Yes	Yes	Yes	Moderate	Yes	No	No	No	Moderate	Yes

Now let's take a closer look at the basic five methods in terms of their advantages and disadvantages as applied to different organizations, business types, and diversity of jobs. Each method will be examined for their responsiveness to these and other features with sample illustrations so that at least some of their format and content become more visible in contrast to their respective value.

4.22 GRAPHIC RATING SCALE METHOD

This is one of the oldest methods and is best applied when evaluating the performance of a general group cf jobs where responsibilities are narrowly confined to a single occupational cluster such as laborers, tradesworkers, and clerical employees. It is relatively inexpensive to develop and can be used on a large number of employees provided they fall within narrowly defined, task-oriented jobs. Because graphic rating scale methods are task-based, they often fail to account for work methods, conditions, behaviors, and other essential elements of total job performance that are instrumental to the effective evaluation of an employee's overall results and related decision making.

The absence of total job evaluation elements, coupled with the fact that the usual performance dimensions in rating scale methods lack specific application to particular jobs, has the combined effect of rendering the graphic scale method legally vulnerable with respect to their validity. Too, individual employees often resent being evaluated against generic performance dimensions particularly when the dimensions are defined vaguely rather than peculiar to their jobs. So while supervisors may find the graphic rating scale easy to use and a quick method of *rating* employees, the method does not do an adequate job of *measuring* realistic performance characteristics, nor is it responsive to the development of a well integrated performance appraisal system.

4.23 RANKING AND PAIRED COMPARISON METHODS

Both the ranking and paired comparison methods evaluate employee performance relative to each other whether the group of employees is small or large, or similar or different in their jobs. Straight ranking requires that the rater arrange employees from highest to lowest performers for each performance dimension, while alternate ranking methods place employees in order by alternating between consecutively highest to lower, and lowest to higher performers for each dimension.

Obviously, the most serious problems with the ranking method is its subjectivity of standards by raters, the use of rather global dimensions, comparing employees to each other rather than against prescribed standards, and comparing employees who perform different jobs. Further, the results of ranking methods do not lend themselves to other uses of appraisal findings such as productivity indexing, achievement of operational objectives, valid retention and other personnel decisions, nor for matters important to human resource research that might lead to enhancements of organizational effectiveness.

Sample 1: Performance Appraisal and Development Plan (Partial)

Employee's Name: _____ Position Title: _____

Department: _____ Date Appointed to Present Position: _____

Covering Period From: _____ 19 _____ To: _____ 19 _____

Instructions: The purposes of the Performance Appraisal and Development Plan are to provide, as objectively as possible, a guided method for reviewing how well the employee listed above is performing in his job, to review accomplishments since his last review, to appraise his potential for possible greater responsibility, and to discuss a suggested development plan that will encourage him to strive toward improved performance.

Place a check mark in the middle of the block that best describes the performance level for each appraisal factor — or on the appropriate line between if appraisal on any item is intermediate. The comment portion is to be used to describe examples, facts, and accomplishments (or lack thereof) to support your judgment.

Appraise only those factors applicable

	Unsatisfactory	*Marginal Performance*	*More than Acceptable Performance*	*Acceptable Performance*	*Outstanding Performance*

Planning and Organizing   Demonstrated performance in anticipating needs, determining priorities, establishing courses of action, organizing and scheduling total activities so as to achieve desired objectives.

Comment

Economy   Actual results in meeting and reducing cost and expense objectives and exercising economy in the utilization of available resources contributing toward improved profit position.

Comment

Innovation   Demonstrated performance in exercising original thinking; ingenuity and initiative taken to introduce new ideas or courses of action. Consider creative, acceptable contributions to a project, products, new methods, techniques, and processes.

Comment

Source: Kahn, S.C.; *Personnel Director's Legal Guide,* 1987, p. 8-24.

Sample 2: Graphic Rating Scale Appraisal (Partial)

Name _____ Dept. _____ Date _____

	Out-standing	Good	Satis-factory	Fair	Unsatis-factory
Quantity of work Volume of acceptable work under normal conditions *Comments:* _____	☐	☐	☐	☐	☐
Quality of work Thoroughness, neatness and accuracy of work *Comments:* _____	☐	☐	☐	☐	☐
Knowledge of job Clear understanding of the facts or factors pertinent to the job *Comments:* _____	☐	☐	☐	☐	☐
Personal qualities Personality, appearance, sociability, leadership, integrity *Comments:* _____	☐	☐	☐	☐	☐
Cooperation Ability and willingness to work with associates, supervisors and subordinates toward common goals *Comments:* _____	☐	☐	☐	☐	☐
Dependability Conscientious, thorough, accurate, reliable with respect to attendance, lunch periods, reliefs, etc. *Comments:* _____	☐	☐	☐	☐	☐
Initiative Earnestness in seeking increased responsibilities. Self-starting, unafraid to proceed alone *Comments:* _____	☐	☐	☐	☐	☐

Source: Glueck, W.F.; *Personnel: A Diagnostic Approach,* 1978, p. 302.

Sample: Ranking Appraisal Method

Employees to be Ranked (Do not list more than 30)	Employee No.		
		1-Highest	
		2-Next Highest	
		3-Next Highest	
		4-Next Highest	
		5-Next Highest	
		6-Next Highest	
		7-Next Highest	
		8-Next Highest	
		9-Next Highest	
		10-Next Highest	
		11-Next Highest	
		12-Next Highest	
		13-Next Highest	
		14-Next Highest	
		15-Next Highest	
		15-Next Lowest	
		14-Next Lowest	
		13-Next Lowest	
		12-Next Lowest	
		11-Next Lowest	
		10-Next Lowest	
		9-Next Lowest	
		8-Next Lowest	
		7-Next Lowest	
		6-Next Lowest	
		5-Next Lowest	
		4-Next Lowest	
		3-Next Lowest	
		2-Next Lowest	
		1-Next Lowest	

Source: Adapted with permission of The Conference Board from R. Lazar & W. Wikstrom, Appraising Managerial Performance: Current Practices and Future Directions (The Conference Board, 1977).

Similarly, the paired comparison method requires that the rater pair employees with each other and evaluate them in these paired groups based on individual performance dimensions. The number of performers is determined by the total number of paired employees who must then be ordered from highest to lowest for each dimension.

Sample: Ordering of Pairs in Pair Comparison Appraisals

Pair Order	Number	Pair Names
1-2	1	Jack — Carolee
5-1	2	Libby — Jack
6-5	3	Ballard — Libby
5-7	4	Libby — Scott
2-5	5	Carolee — Libby
5-3	6	Libby — Charles
7-1	7	Scott — Jack
3-6	8	Charles — Ballard
3-7	9	Charles — Scott
2-3	10	Carolee — Charles
1-3	11	Jack — Charles
6-1	12	Ballard — Jack
7-6	13	Scott — Ballard
6-2	14	Ballard — Carolee
4-5	15	Claudia — Libby
2-7	16	Carolee — Scott
4-6	17	Claudia — Ballard
7-4	18	Scott — Claudia
4-2	19	Claudia — Carolee
3-4	20	Charles — Claudia
1-4	21	Jack — Claudia

Source: Myers, D. W.; *Human Resource Management: Principles and Practice,* 1986, p. 455.

One of the most immediately obvious problems with this method is the awkward and unwieldly number of comparisons for more than a very small group of employees being rated on several performance dimensions. As with other traditional appraisal methods, the major weakness is its lack of validity to each employee's job content. Validity is only slightly improved over the ranking method by virtue of having to pair employees which tends to reduce rater tendencies toward strong employee biases. Overly subjective and often bias judgment becomes the rule, and legitimacy weakens when individual discussions with employees cannot be supported by documented performance events. This method therefore has limited value with respect to employee feedback, clarity of distinctions between performance levels for pay increase and related determinations, and is only loosely tied to organizational and human resource evaluation of results.

4.24 ESSAY APPRAISAL METHODS

This appraisal method requires raters to write descriptive narratives that are intended to identify, discuss by illustration, and rate or measure the employee's performance in various aspects of their job. The structured essay method has preestablished performance dimensions and rating levels defined, and at least some instructional guidelines for rating supervisors. The unstructured essay method lacks these controls and merely requires the rater to write spontaneous free-form evaluative statements which usually turn out to be partial recollections of recent, and vaguely more prolonged memorable events.

Sample 1: Structured Free Lance Essay (Partial)

MEMO

Date: March 15, 1988
To: Michelle Dawson, Staff Analyst
From: J. Levins, Department Director
Re: Annual Performance Appraisal

Michelle, your overall performance in the most significant aspects of your job as precribed by the company have been above average. You are to be commended for these contributions and efforts to improve previous performance levels in assigned projects, and I am quite pleased with your demonstrated interest in developing more technical knowledge and writing skills. Specific to your assigned performance areas, you are evaluated as follows.

1. Analytic Skills: You completed one major assignment (Freeport account), three small projects, and began another large project (Medivac) during this appraisal period. Your Freeport findings were quite thorough with well organized and clearly illustrated presentations of support data. After only minimal discussion with you on May 9 and June 27 concerning the use and formating of raw data, you did a well above average job of preparing good illustrations, data interpretations, and pertinent discussion for your part of the final report that clearly synthesized important actions for the client to take. .

Sample 2: Unstructured Free Lance Essay (Partial)

Michelle, your performance for the last year has been very good. I was pleased with the efforts you put into the Freeport account and a couple of smaller projects you completed during this evaluation period. As you know, it is important for us to do a thorough job in the analysis of client work so that we can make factual and meaningful recommendations to them. Each of your projects were completed on time which enabled us to meet these deadlines. You are to be commended for your thoroughness, and I hope you will continue to put your best effort into the new Medivac project.

Sample 3: Structured Specific Dimension Essay (Partial)

These are areas of performance that tend to be of particular significance in most positions. You may add any applicable information to this assessment. Indicate your assessment of performance in terms of these items. Cite specific examples. When assessing supervisory personnel, orient remarks toward supervisory responsibilities of the position.

Technical Effectiveness
- Application of fundamentals and specialized techniques
- Awareness of recent developments
- Sensitivity to problems and facility for resolution
- Technical breadth and versatility
- Level of respect gained by technical decision-making
- Recent efforts to implement technical capability

Schedule Effectiveness
- Attitude toward importance of maintaining schedule
- Sensitivity to developments that may lead to delay

Cost Effectiveness
- Awareness of importance of cost in quality/schedule/cost cycle
- Direct contributions to cost-reduction effort

Comments and Observations:
(These should be made in consideration of established duties and responsibilities [(objectives]. Avoid discussion of traits or characteristics that are not related to objectives. Use specific examples, when possible, to prove points.

Source: Adapted with permission of The Conference Board from R. Lazar & W. Wikstron, Appraising Managerial Performance: Current Practices and Future Directions (The Conference Board, 1977).

Performance Development and Evaluation (Partial)

Employee's Name _____ Date of Hire _____

Job Title _____ Job Grade and Code _____

This evaluation covers the period from _____ to _____

Please be specific in answering the following:

1. What is your evaluation of this employee's ability to perform the technical aspects of his position as distinct from the factor listed in question 2?

_____

_____

_____

_____

_____

_____

2. What is your evaluation of his management skills? (His ability to plan, organize, delegate, develop and motivate subordinates; use time effectively; promote inter- and intradepartmental cooperation; improve systems and procedures; make decision.)

_____

_____

_____

_____

_____

_____

Source: Adapted with permission of The Conference Board from R. Lazar & W. Wikstron, Appraising Managerial Performance: Current Practices and Future Directions (The Conference Board, 1977).

As can easily be seen from these examples, the essay method can be very specific forms of appraisal and source of performance feedback when discussed in terms of particular dimensions, illustrated by examples of actual work situations, and distinguished by levels and expectations of performance relative to such conditions as the employee's job level and length of service (job progress). If written with care, essay appraisals provide useful feedback, constructive suggestions for further development, and other vital information for the organization upon which many decisions can be made. However, essays require dedicated time, effort, and good writing skills on the part of rating supervisors. They also require lengthy reading time by others in the organization to extract information of relevant interest to them. For these reasons, most organizations of any significant size avoid the use of the essay method, preferring to use more controlled and consistent methods even if the format or results are less job specific and thereby less valid.

4.25 CRITICAL INCIDENT METHOD

This method has a likeness to essay appraisals given that both require writing performance related narrative by raters, and in some critical incident methods these narratives are used in conjunction with other appraisal methods rather than as a singular method. Unlike essays however, the critical incident methods is not guided by predetermined dimensions of the employee's job and therefore tends to produce rather arbitrary conclusions about what raters perceive as critical performance events.

This method requires that supervisors either keep an ongoing log or write up individual accounts (with a copy to the employee) of significant performance events—negative or positive—as they occur. Such narratives are much the same as observed performance incidents referred to in this and other chapters as supervisory desk notes. However, the former is usually stated in more descriptive and conclusive detail with respect to each isolated incident while the latter is intended to document the event by describing what happened and leaving appraisal conclusions to a collective profile of various incidents over the performance year. In both cases, performance incidents that are deemed important or critical are dealt with openly as they occur, including commendations or disciplinary action, but their effect on performance is held for annual appraisal.

Sample 1: Critical Incident Narratives

1. You are to be commended for your recent handling of customer complaints. During the last two weeks, I have observed you cheerfully greet, calm, and resolve the problem of three customers who were upset over the quality or timeliness of our artwork. Your ability to satisfy their concerns by interested listening, expressing your understanding, and taking the initiative to immediately contact Ken in the layout department to get a priority and instructions on rework requests was very helpful in maintaining our customer image of quality work.

2. Karen, today was the third occasion of your late arrival to work in the last two weeks. You will recall that you did not arrive until 8:20 on Wednesday, March 3, and 8:55 on March 8. Your March 3 lateness was excused, but March 8 was not and I mentioned to you at that time that promptness was important due to the usual volume of order calls that start at 8:00. Today, March 12, you did not arrive until 8:15 and I must now remind you that any further deviations from your assigned work schedule, regardless of reason, could be grounds for disciplinary actions. I don't want to see this happen so please see to it that your attendance regularly conforms to the requirements of your job.

As you can see from these positive and negative examples of performance events, both can be considered critical incidents, but they are not clearly tied to all dimensions that are representative of the entire job or all significant characteristics of job performance. Other aspects of performance may not be drawn out by this method simply because they do not become visible as critical incidents during the appraisal year, yet such narratives can become valuable supporting documentation in conjunction with other methods to illustrate rating examples in various dimensions of job performance. For a slightly more structured approach, a form like the following example can be used to at least focus on specific dimensions in light of performance incidents, but if dimensions are used they should be given definition context to differing jobs.

Sample 2: Critical Incident Form

Name _____			Period Covered: From_____ To_____	
	Less Than Satisfactory		*Outstanding*	
Classification	Date	Incident	Date	Incident
1. Getting Along With People				
2. Initiative				
3. Reliability				
4. Response to Company Needs				
5. Productivity				
6. Judgment				
7. Learning and Comprehension				
8. Miscellaneous				

Source: William B. Wolf, Merit Rating as a Managerial Tool, Bureau of Business Research, College of Business Administration, University of Washington, 1958, p. 22. Reproduced with permission of the author.

4.26 FORCED CHOICE METHOD

In an attempt to reduce rater bias and achieve greater definition of performance dimensions among various jobs, the forced choice method requires raters to select one of four to six prewritten statements that best describes the type and level of performance in given categories. Some forced choice methods also require the rater to select the least performance statement thereby developing groups of both best and least performance statements in applicable dimensions.

Sample 1: Forced Distribution Method of Performance Appraisal

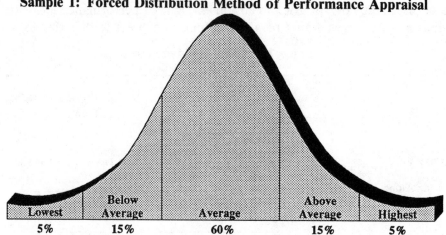

Lowest	Below Average	Average	Above Average	Highest
5%	15%	60%	15%	5%

Sample 2: Two Sample Clusters of Forced-Choice Checklist Items

Appraiser instructions: Read each of the four statements in a cluster and use a (✓) to denote the one item *most* descriptive of the employee. Next, mark the statement *least* descriptive of the employee.

Least   Most

☐   ☐   Notifies the office when unable to report
☐   ☐   Uses safety equipment when instructed
☐   ☐   Follows directions in completing work
☐   ☐   Researches work methods and accurately describes improvements

☐   ☐   Conducts vehicle safety inspections
☐   ☐   Completes route assignments before scheduled time
☐   ☐   Accepts work methods and procedures without complaining
☐   ☐   Promptly corrects errors when notified

Source for both samples: Myers, D.W.; Human Resource Management, 1986, p. 448-450.

Sample 3: Forced Choice Appraisal (Partial)

1. Limited foresight   —
    Can't deal with
    uncertainties   —
	10. Sometimes pompous or
	     overly formal —
	     Uncomfortable with
	     people he/she doesn't
	     know —
		19. Incisive thinker —
		     Experienced in chosen
		     field —

2. Needs supervision on
    most job assignments   —
    Does not provide enough
    job guidance to
    subordinates or peers   —
	11. Needs careful
	     supervision —
	     Manages own people
	     ineffectively —
		20. Anticipates problems —
		     Follows up on job as
		     needed —

3. Works at a slow pace   —
    Unimaginative   —
	12. Respected by most who
	     know him/her —
	     Technically competent —
		21. Deals effectively with
		     many assignments at
		     once —
		     A steadying influence —

4. Concedes too easily   —
    Tries to do the minimum
    possible job   —
	13. Intellectually agile —
	     Good business judgment —
		22. Creates a favorable
		     image —
		     Plans for the future
		     without sacrificing
		     today's efforts —

5. Uninspired   —
    Performance under
    stress is poor   —
	14. Effective in job —
	     Self-assured —
		23. A good person to check
		     with for help and ideas —
		     Explains position on
		     most matters quite
		     clearly —

6. Not straightforward   —
    Insensitive to the needs
    of others   —
	15. Self-activating —
	     Deals with abstract
	     concepts well —
		24. Accepts new
		     responsibilities easily —
		     Generally accepted by
		     most —

7. A follower rather than a
    leader   —
    Tends to resolve
    problems with routine
    approaches   —
	16. Inquisitive —
	     Gets the best out of
	     people —
		25. Sees and responds to
		     opportunities —
		     Distinguishes facts from
		     feelings —

8. Fails to consider
    consequences of
    decisions   —
    Narrow in outlook   —
	17. Generates enthusiasm —
	     Skillfull in dealing with
	     people —
		26. Innovative —
		     Contributes to resolving
		     problems —

9. Not really involved with
    work   —
    Works with uneven
    application of effort   —
	18. Persuasive —
	     Gives adequate balance
	     to long- and short-range
	     considerations —	

Source: Cherrington, D.J.; *Personnel Management*, 1983, p. 309.

Similar to other methods, the initial problem with forced choice appraisals is selecting and defining an adequate array of performance dimensions that appropriately represent each different job being evaluated. Second, the use of four to six prewritten performance statements are often viewed by raters as too restrictive inasmuch as they are frequently having to select a "nearest" statement that does not accurately depict the employee's true performance type or level—and both rater and employee know this which makes their discussion of the appraisal loosely tied to valuable feedback.

Forced choice methods may reduce some rater bias, but overall the method is very narrow in use. Dimensions are typically not weighted nor given point or even qualitative values, so it becomes difficult to determine clear distinctions among employees for various kinds of administrative decision making or meaningful evaluation of productivity indexing.

4.30 PROBLEMS OF RATER BIAS, CONFLICTING PERCEPTIONS AND LEGAL IMPLICATIONS OF APPRAISALS

So far, we have touched on rather broad administrative kinds of problems with appraisal systems and methods. These problems relate to the weaknesses and resultant dysfunctioning of performance appraisals because:

1. They often do not represent an understandable system of productivity measurement and employment decision making.

2. They do not serve as a control mechanism to assure the desired kinds and levels of performance because of weaknesses in the analysis, identification, and definition of both performance dimensions and standards.

3. These obsolete traditional methods do not adequately account for the "total job" in the context of performance, and they put more emphasis on rating than measuring employee performance.

There are yet other problems that permeate our attempts to find a suitable performance appraisal system. For example, virtually any appraisal method that requires one human being to eveluate another is inherently subject to rater bias. Too, since appraisals are used for different purposes by different people in the organization, it is common to experience conflicting perceptions of how results should be used by each person involved in the process and system. Finally, during the 1980's there has arisen several legal issues related to formal appraisals that are now creating some rather serious implications concerning employer and supervisor's liability in the use of performance appraisals. Given the developments in discrimination law during the 1960's through the 1970's, and wrongful discharge laws in the 1980's, the stage was set and should have been anticipated by managers that traditional and otherwise weak appraisal systems were eventually going to be held accountable in their use as an employment decision making device.

4.31 RATER BIAS PROBLEMS

It is probably not realistic to believe that performance appraisals will ever achieve complete objectively, so our goal ought to be to narrow the inherent amount of subjectivity of the measurement and evaluation process. Fundamentally, appraisal methods require the observation and evaluative judgment of one human being by another human being. Given the very nature of our human species, we all tend to see things a little differently, we have varying perceptions and values toward common situations, and our communications processes differ in rather complex ways. To reduce these and other differences that can stand in the way of achieving orderly work interactions and reliable productivity, we strive to create various control mechanisms. In appraisal methods, these control mechanisms become such things as predetermined and well defined performance dimensions, distinctively clear levels of performance, tangible objectives, job descriptions, and the like.

However, these controls do not appreciably eliminate the human tendency to use personal bias in interpreting actual versus perceived performance events or overall results between rater and employee. These biases are referred to as rater error, and are usually the product of some personal predisposition the rater has about an individual employee or other people in general. Some of the most common types of rater errors, or bias, are the following.

Halo Effect

The halo effect is the tendency of most raters to let the rating they assign to one characteristic excessively influence their rating on all subsequent traits. Many supervisors tend to give an employee approximately the same (artifically high) rating on all factors. The rating-scale technique is particularly susceptible to the halo effect. One way of minimizing its influence is to have the supervisor judge all subordinates on a single factor or trait before going on to the next factor. In this way the supervisor can consider all employees relative to a standard, or to each other on each trait.

Leniency Or Strictness

Some supervisors have a tendency to be either very liberal or strict in their ratings; that is, they assign consistently high or low values to their people. This is a very common error in performance ratings. Both of these trends can arise from varying standards of performance among supervisors and from different interpretations of what they observe in employee performance. It is due to the subjectiveness of humans. It can be partially overcome by holding meetings or training sessions for the raters so that they can reach common agreement on just what they expect of their employees. Of course, if the employees in Department A are consistently judged higher than those in Department B, it is difficult to determine whether this reflects true differences in their abilities and contributions or whether it simply reveals leniency on the part of one manager and strictness on the part of another.

Central Tendency

Some raters are reluctant to rate people at the outer ends of the scale. Quite frequently this central, or middle score rating, tendency is caused by lack of knowledge of the behavior of the persons being rated. Supervisors know that management policy dictates that they must appraise employees at periodic intervals. But if unfamiliar with some of the individuals, supervisors may play it safe by neither condemning nor praising. The supervisor would be hard pressed to substantiate such judgments. As we see under the heading Organizational Influences, the way in which appraisal information is handled by higher management sometimes induces supervisors to deliberately rate high, low, or down the middle.

Interpersonal Relations Bias

How a supervisor feels about each individual employee—whether the supervisor personally likes or dislike them—has a tremendous effect upon the supervisor's ratings of their performance. This is especially operative in those situations where objective measures of performance are either not available or difficult to develop.

Organizational Influences

Nowhere is the subjectivity of performance appraisals more glaring than when ratings change according to the way they are going to be used by management. Fundamentally, raters tend to take into consideration the end use of the appraisal data when they rate their subordinates. Perhaps this is only natural. For example, if they know that promotions and pay increases hinge on the ratings, they may tend to rate on the high side (they become lenient). After all, we're told that effective supervisors are supposed to go to bat for their employees. Besides it would look bad for a boss (and relations with subordinates would suffer) if other departments received higher pay increases than his/her group.

On the other hand, when appraisals are made principally for the development of employees, supervisors tend to emphasize weaknesses. The whole focus is upon what is wrong with these people and what they have to do to improve.

4.32 CONFLICTING PERCEPTIONS IN THE USE OF APPRAISALS

Much of the recent literature on performance appraisals has been trying to tackle the problem of various conflicts in how appraisals are perceived and used by those subject to them versus those who are responsible for their completion and use. In essence, the conflict arises out of mixed motives held by the parties to the appraisal process and resultant decisions and/or actions. The motives for having a performance appraisal system and conducting individual assessments is different for managers on behalf of organizational interests than are the motives of rating supervisors in carrying them out, as are the motives of effected employees who are often helplessly—and therefore defensively—subject to them.

You will recall from Chapter III.1.33 that perception is our fixed, preconceived way of viewing things and it is shaped or reshaped by our background, group affiliations and influences, and the experiences we encounter through life. Conflict, on the other hand, is the unresolved differences in perception held by two or more people. Consequently, we can do little to resolve perception conflicts until we can effectuate a mutual understanding and acceptance (you'll notice I didn't say agreement) between the parties and sources of conflict. If the sources of perceived conflict in the use of performance appraisals can be resolved, or at least dealt with in a more open and understandable way, then the people involved should have that much less to be in conflict about. Most sources of perception conflicts in performance appraisals are based in each person's, or group of persons', motives for the appraisal process. This includes expectations concerning appraisal results and decisional use. Let's look at some of these different motivational sources of conflict.

Organizational Motives

- Improve productivity and efficiency of work and operations.

- Develop a control and accountability system for performance.

- Create a measurable linkage between productivity related goals and the achievement of objectives through performance appraisal indexing.

- Identify the kinds of policies, programs, and management methods that will inspire and reinforce desirable performance results.

Departmental Manager Motives

- Compare and evaluate collective appraisal results against both departmental goals and the objectives of each work unit.

- Identify and correct performance deficiencies within work units through subordinate managers and supervisors as problems become apparent.

- Evaluate, anticipate, and act on employee development; or modify potential performance deficiencies.

- Determine and propose training, incentive, and other support programs needed to enhance performance goals.

- Evaluate results of appraisals for future promotional considerations, or approval of recommended administrative determinations by subordinate managers and supervisors (e.g., retention, merit increase, cautionary notice, etc.).

Work Unit Supervisor Motives

- Evaluate each employee against prescribed measurement standards based on their job, work unit objectives, and employment conditions.

- Develop employee skills and awareness of performance needs through coaching, counseling, appraisal, and development planning.

- Obtain ideas from employees about ways in which work can be accomplished better or more efficiently.

- Create an understanding of specific areas of each employee's performance needing more development, or further improvement, and establish new objectives for the forthcoming period.

- Recognize, acknowledge, and reward desirable performance results.

- Establish, through documented accounts, sufficient information upon which reliable decisions concerning such matters as retention, merit increases, and promotions can be based.

- Provide employees with honest, objective, comprehensive, and constructive feedback so they know where they stand and the reasoning behind resultant decisions and actions.

Employee Motives

- Eliminate any fear or anxiety that might be felt or associated with either the appraisal process, effects of the results (decisions and actions being proposed by supervisors), or how supervisors feel about them. Remember, to employees the appraisal process is a very personal experience.

- Obtain information that tells them where they stand; specifically, what they need to do to improve (and thereby get a larger merit increase or be in line for promotion), and whether or not they are being evaluated validly and objectively (i.e., they evaluate the credibility/integrity of management).

- Receive recognition, rewards, and bolster their self-esteem for those efforts or performance results they believe deserve special attention as significant contributions to either their job, other employees, the work unit, or the organization.

As you can see from the foregoing, there is a considerable mixture of motives held by different people in organizations about how performance appraisals should be used. In general, management, including supervisors, see it as a measurement and justification tool (looking downward through the work unit to employees), while employees tend to see it as an acknowledgement, reward, and validation tool (looking upward through their work unit to the organization). Because neither management nor employees have a sufficient understanding of each other's motives for performance systems or the appraisal process, clashes occur based on unharnessed perceptions rather than on efforts to create a mutual understanding, acceptance, and accommodation by each toward the other's interests. When these motivational sources of perception conflict are not dealt with as a dysfunctioning part of the appraisal system, four crucial problems will continue to plague the process, and consequently the achievement of intended results. They are:

1. **Synthesis:** individual appraisals lack sufficient detail to make clear conclusions or decisions on productivity, and therefore obscures related decision making; individual appraisals are not evaluated in terms of collective work unit or departmental results; and there is little if any synthesis of other performance related results such as for training program development, policy development and evaluation, selection reliability, job redesigns, and the like.

2. **Ambivalence:** lack of acceptance or support of the appraisal system, method, or process required by the organization when it is regarded as invalid, troublesome, unrealistic, adversarial, unsupported, uncertain in its purpose and consequence, and in other ways regarded as weak by employees, supervisors, or both.

3. **Avoidance:** when viewed by supervisors as time consuming, adversarial, and of limited or questionable value, they will tend to stall (procrastinate), apply minimal time and thought, and allow only cursory discussion with the employee as a means of avoiding the responsibility, particularly those not trained or skilled in dealing effectively with interpersonal situations.

4. **Defensiveness:** when viewed by employees as invalid, unfair, and/or inconsequential, they tend to react in defensive ways about ratings, judgmental narratives, and proposed actions. Also, because the process becomes personalized, employees often do not handle negative feedback well; they become defensive, or may blame other things for any judgment, about their shortcomings; and

they may even attack the rater's views, illustrative performance events, the applicability of particular performance dimensions, and even the comparative performance of other employees (transference of responsibility).

There is also some truth, as well as simple logic, to the fact that supervisors should not be put in the position of conflicting roles that are sometimes required in an appraisal process. These differing roles can create perception conflicts between the rating supervisor and employees. For example, in most organizations where a single annual appraisal is formally prepared on employees, the supervisor is put into the mixed role of *coach* that suggests "I'm here to help and show you ways to be successful;" of *judge* that suggests "I alone shall determine the merit and value of your existence;" and of *decision maker* that suggests "I will decide on the kinds of reform, reward, and other actions that are appropriate to your performance results." You will notice that each suggests "I" statements meaning there is little if any assumptions built in about shared power (participation) in the process.

The employee is thus at the mercy of the supervisor, and the natural product of such a relationship is conflict. Also, the coach role is mostly a positive, reinforcing, and assuring character, while the roles of judge and decision maker often evolve to negative characterizations for supervisors who frequently lack skills in dealing with judgment and decision making situations on an interpersonal level. When the judgment and decision maker roles are poorly handled, and thereby evoke negative characterization, conflict will occur with the employee over these roles alone, or as a contradiction to the supervisor's demonstration of a coach role suggesting that the supervisor can't be trusted.

4.33 LEGAL IMPLICATIONS: THE BACKLASH OF APPRAISALS

When performance appraisals are used for administrative (personnel transaction) decisions as retention, development, pay and promotion, and layoff, the entire appraisal system falls in the context of an employment test. As such, the system becomes subject to validity standards prescribed by the 1978 federal Uniform Guidelines On Employee Selection Procedures. These lengthy and complex standards describe statistical and procedural methods for determining whether evaluative tests that are administered to employees for decision making purposes are sufficiently valid for each job, or whether there exists some form of bias that has a discriminatory or otherwise arbitrary effect upon the job incumbent.

As they relate to performance appraisal, the fundamental purpose of the Guidelines is to require employers to use only the criteria and processes that can accurately measure applicable knowledge, skills, traits, and behavior essential to successful job performance (i.e., its validity). For most employers, validation study costs are prohibitive, and for very small businesses there are too few employees holding substantially similar jobs to gather statistically conclusive findings. Yet large and small employers are equally liable for maintaining invalid performance appraisal systems, methods, and processes.

Failure to use job and employment valid criteria as the basis of measuring and appraising employee performance—or failure to otherwise conduct the appraisal process in a reasonably careful, legitimate way—has been construed by compliance agencies, arbitrators, and the courts as acts of discrimination, breach of policy or good faith and fair dealing, and, yes, even negligence. The deficiencies found by legal authorities in appraisal systems have been costly for employers. Still, many employers have not been moved by the trends in legal scrutiny to reform their systems, if for no other reason than to reduce their prospective liability. Costs that have become commonly associated with deficient appraisal systems include litigation defense, administrative staff time, compensatory and punative damage awards, back pay awards, and reinstatement of terminated employees.

It is of little interest to legal authorities as to whether or not the discriminatory effect or other wrongdoing of the employer was unintentional. They are charged with fact-finding and judging the factual merit of alleged improprieties. If the facts point to discrimination, then employers will be held liable for the consequences which usually means damages that are theoretically aimed at making the wronged employee whole again.

Conversely, most courts have expressed their understanding of the subjective nature of the appraisal process itself, but even here such sentiment is usually confined to those cases where the appraisal method is supported by objective (observational rather than judgmental) behavior and other trait measurements relative to the actual job and the incumbent's results. Most condemnation from the courts has been where appraisal methods have not been developed from a systematic analysis of job factors, strong deviations from performance policies, the absence of training and instructional guidelines for raters, and the lack of honesty in the appraisal process.

Problem Scenarios

As you have probably surmised by now, there are a number of variables within appraisal systems that can and do lead to legal implications of employer liability. Likewise, there are numerous appraisal process situations that have found their way into one or more forms of legalistic scrutiny. The following, for example, are just a few scenarios where legal problems take shape within the appraisal process. Take heed and be forewarned!

1. An employee is demoted, laid off, or terminated due to some proported performance-related reason. The employee's attorney subpoena's the personnel file and finds an unblemished record of service (no prior warnings, evaluations,

or disciplinary action taken for performance reasons). Also, the file is full of appraisals with satisfactory or better ratings, and the employee has received one promotion and consistent pay raises. Your company's legal counsel sends you a copy of the summary case in *Bonura v. The Chase Manhatten Bank, N.A.* (1986) in which the employer lost and paid sizeable damages. How good is your documentation supporting your action?

2. An employee with good appraisals and regular pay increases is promoted. During the promotional probationary period the employee is fired due to alleged inadequate performance in the higher position. The questions asked of you by the employee's attorney while under oath on the witness stand are:

   • What methods, questions, and criteria was used to select this person for the position (particularly their attributes)?

   • What type of orientation, training, and support did you provide to this person to help assure their success?

   • In what way did you express your expectations of their work results; did you ever communicate with this person about their deficiencies (when, what said, etc.); and how much time did you allow for improvement?

   • Why wasn't this person reinstated to their former position?

   • What was the real reason this person was fired?

   Consider how legitimate, fair, and reasonable your answers would sound to a jury or review body composed of people who are employees just like the plaintiff.

3. An employee known to be consistently troublesome, but in minor irritating ways, is fired for simply "behavioral deficiencies" as noted on the appraisal form. Having received preliminary papers that a suit has been filed for wrongful discharge, you investigate the matter. Your findings are that the supervisor had not been counseling the employee nor writing performance narratives because the supervisor could not express the employee's behavioral and other trait inadequacies in objective, performance related terms; the supervisor did not want to demoralize the employee by engaging in a conflict discussion; and the supervisor felt it best just to wait until one really tangible event occurred so that the employee could be fired.

   Since it becomes clear to you that the situation over which the employee was fired does not stand on its own merit, the employee was never warned about their unacceptable behavior, and no supporting documentation exists to demonstrate the adversity of their performance effect, what is your course of action?

4. One employee is promoted over three others and prior performance appraisals were the deciding factor. When one of the three rejected competitors files a discrimination complaint with the state, you examine the files and find that the promoted employee's ratings are negligibly different, and in one or more cases lower than the other three employees.

    Knowing that use of prior appraisals for promotional considerations places considerable burden on the company's ability to defend the validity of performance criteria, the rating method, and supervisory judgments that lead to objective distinctions of performance levels among differing employees, how do you propose responding to the discrimination complaint?

5. An employee is fired for the legitimate reason of "consistent failure to comply with procedural policy" in their department, and told to go to Personnel at the end of the day to pick up their check. The employee arrives early and requests to examine their personnel file. Personnel allows the employee's lawful review of their file. Two weeks later you receive papers on the employee's lawsuit and, uncertain as to the nature of the action, you obtain the employee's file which you expect will be subpeoned. Among other questionable ratings and comments (unsupported by objective illustration) by the supervisor, you discover these written notations on the last three appraisals.

    > "The quality of your work is sometimes good and sometimes pathetic. When your work is poor, it is really lousy judgment which makes me wonder if you have the brains you were born with."

    > "I will no longer tolerate your lies. Despite your denials, I know that you are falsifying information on work orders and if I ever catch you, you'll lose your job."

    > "One more failure to follow our operating procedures and you can forget about using this company as a future employment reference. You wouldn't like what I would have to tell them, so shape up or ship out."

    You immediately send a copy of the legal papers you received and the employee's file to your company's legal counsel. One week later you receive a note from the company's attorney attached to two documents. The documents are summaries of two lawsuits (*Hewitt v. Grabicki*, 1986 and *DeMeo v. Goodall*, 1986) in which both plaintiffs won damages for defamation resulting from inappropriately stated critical comments about the employee on their appraisals. The attorney's note simply stated, "Thanks, I'll take it from here."

6. Two Senior Vice Presidents had become abrasive toward each other for some time. One wanted more power and spent a lot of time gaining the favor of the Executive Vice President who was recently appointed acting CEO until a replacement was found, while the other Senior Vice President merely wanted to do the best job possible. The power hungry V.P. consistently would find or create things in the more docile V.P.'s area of responsibility to criticize, complain, and otherwise harass the docile V.P. about. Power V.P. would also seize every opportunity to embellish on these situations when having coffee or playing golf with the Executive V.P. One day, Power V.P. marches into the Exec's office and says, "I've had it with that incompetent bitch, it's either her or me Charley." The Exec responds, "Okay Brutus, I've heard enough. Go downstairs and let her know she's through, but you better stop by the Personnel Office first and get rid of any performance appraisals that suggest she's done okay because we don't want a lawsuit out of this." Power V.P., Brutus, not only complies but also takes great pleasure when he walks into Docile's office and says, "You're through here. The old man says you've got ten minutes to clean out your desk and be out of the building." What Brutus didn't know was that Docile V.P. maintained a social relationship with the Personnel Officer who observed the removal of some documents from Docile's file by Brutus, and whose husband is a prominent attorney.

As the new CEO, you've just been briefed on this matter by your company's legal counsel whose handling the pending lawsuit. Your attorney also tells you that Docile's attorney is the husband of your Personnel Officer and old chums with the publisher of the metropolitan newspaper. Your attorney asks how you'd like this situation handled.

These situations, and many more just like them, are neither outrageous distortions nor unusual. They are out there in our work world and they happen every day. For most managers who can easily see the impropriety of these situations, one of the greatest problems is finding out about them after the fact, when the damage has been done, and little room seems to remain for correction. As untenable as they may seem (or be), the best course is usually an honest one rather than complicating matters further by trying to cover things up, or futilely defending facts that more than lean against the organization. Those who choose to take weak positions of fact as their defense into court merely create bad case law that casts legal skepticism upon the business community as a whole.

Legal actions brought by damaged and incensed employees point out serious weaknesses in appraisal systems. These actions can be extremely costly to an organization in more ways than just litigation. Any time litigation is involved, the expense goes up sharply—win or lose on the case itself—because many of these actions are being filed as civil suits alleging such actionable causes as (in order of the scenarios):

1) wrongful discharge and/or discrimination with infliction of emotional distress;

2) wrongful discharge under the theory of a breach of good faith and fair dealing and/or possible breach of company policy;

3) wrongful discharge based on pretextual and unsubstantiated reasons for the termination and/or possible negligence in the supervisor's duty to use reasonable care in conducting appraisals and communicating employee deficiencies;

4) discrimination based on the use of evaluative criteria known to be invalid;

5) defamation; and

6) wrongful discharge, fraud, and willful negligence.

Within the appraisal system, method, or process, there are other problems recognized by the courts in their findings and judgments in cases brought before them. Most have been won by plaintiff employees, however recent trends are beginning to show a small but increasing number of cases being won by employers. No doubt they, too, have been reading the kind of literature you're reading now, and learning from the unfortunate experiences of others. The following, then, are illustrations of problem areas that should be examined carefully by employers using performance appraisals, and corrections implemented promptly.

Subjective Criteria

Performance criteria refers to those factors or measures against which employees are being evaluated. This includes the dimensions of performance such as work quantity/quality, technical knowledge, leadership, cooperation, and the like, as well as performance standards, or rating levels, such as below satisfactory, satisfactory, and above satisfactory. Performance criteria can also mean the clarity, ambiguity, or absence to which dimensions and standards are defined.

Subjectivity in the context of performance criteria has to do with how clearly the criteria accurately depicts actual job functions of each different job being evaluated. This becomes a validity question of whether or not employees are being measured (tested) against performance dimensions that have a lot, only little, or are vaguely connected to those aspects and conditions of their respective job. More often than not, the courts are rejecting vague, ill defined, generic, and across-the-board applications of appraisal methods using such dimensions as illustrated in the cases of:

Rowe v. General Motors, 1972
Wade v. Mississippi Cooperative Extension Service, 1974
Albermarle Paper Co. v. Moody, 1975
Petterson v. American Tobacco Co., 1978
Pouncy v. Prudential Insurance Co., 1982 (criteria valid & reasonably
    measurable)
Capenter v. Stephen F. Antin State University, 1983
Martinez v. El Paso County, 1983
Segar v. Smith, 1984

Documenting Performance Events

Just as there is no substitute for well documented accounts of employee performance events, there is simply no excuse for supervisors who claim to be incapable or uncooperative about developing these narratives during evaluations. Somehow this weakness has been tolerated by managers concerning performance appraisal when the same managers would not even consider other business transactions without supporting documentation for the proposed action. Yet, for some years now companies have been granting pay increases, firing or promoting their people, and making other vital decisions on weak, and at times nonexistent, substantiation of facts to justify the action. The time has come to impress upon, if not demand, that each manager's and supervisor's job is to develop and present all pertinent matters of fact with each official request, position taken, recommendation, and act to which they are a party, and this specifically includes employment related documents.

Take the case of Sandra Coughlin, a promoted credit manager who had to be terminated due to reported insufficiency in her job progress over a two year period despite encouragement and help from her manager. After her termination, Coughlin alleged that sex discrimination and not job performance was the deciding factor in the company's action. Given Coughlin's allegation, the company will have to spend thousands of dollars to prepare a defense showing that the termination was justified on the basis of poor performance as a means of refuting the charge. The problem faced by the company is how to do this when all of her warnings, repeated instructions, and counseling sessions on deficiencies were verbal and never documented as they occurred. This is sort of a "whoever thought we'd have to let her go" posture that occurs all-too-frequently by and among managers who later are confronted with the consequences when the company attorney (or human resource professional) tells them "we have no defense... without proper documentation it's our word against hers and I don't want to test it with a jury."

To make matters worse, even the company's personnel manager openly confessed that the company's policies and system of performance appraisal weren't as strong as they should be. So this company, and many others just like it, will pay the price of having their operations challenged through a very time-consuming, expensive, wasteful, and painful legal process. This story has been told a hundred times, yet new ones like it occur everyday because of the existence of loose management practices, poor appraisal systems, and supervisors who fail to document performance events. See:

Marquez v. Ford Motor Co., 1971

EEOC v. Miller Brewing Co., 1986

Turner v. State Highway Commission of Missouri, 1982 (employer won; had documented evidence of several inadequate performance instances)

Johnson v. Fulton Sylphon Divis., Robertshaw Controls Co., 1977 (employer won; supervisor had objective documentation on employee's lack of diligence in areas of absenteeism, tardiness, inattention, personal problems, and inability to meet performance standards to support decision to not promote the employee).

Communicating Standards

Letting employees know what is expected of them in terms of not only their job tasks but also the performance dimensions and standards by which they'll be evaluated is of more than just casual importance. After all, it is only reasonable to expect good results from someone who has been fully appraised of what's expected of them. To do otherwise should produce no surprises for us. Think of it in terms of your own job when you started: how would you feel and possibly react if you received your first appraisal, rating you low in several categories, and only then were you told what the expectations and criteria were. Surprise! What shouldn't be a surprise is that employees are likely to be rather confused, disoriented, anxious and, later, paranoid about their jobs when they're asked to perform them without knowing the rules, game plan, or method of scoring.

If employees are to be held accountable for deficiencies in their performance, then they should first be told what performance expectations exist (job description detail, performance dimensions and standards, and associated policies), so say the courts. In addition to the court's finding of poor performance criteria in the previously cited *Rowe* case, the court further justified its decision favoring the plaintiff employee by noting that such criteria was not adequately communicated to employees. Conversely, in *Sell v. U.S.* (1979), the court concluded that appraisals were performed regularly, rating standards were adequately demonstrated, and performance criteria had been communicated to employees, and thereby relieved the employer of liability.

What does good communications of performance criteria constitute? At the very minimum it means giving employees copies of their job description and appraisal form, then explaining what kinds of job functions are evaluated against performance dimensions and standards. Better yet, employees should also receive a copy of company policies on all topics related to performance, conduct, working conditions, and disciplinary actions/appeals mechanism. Further, good communications means that dimensions and standards are well defined in writing for clarity among employees and supervisors, and communication exists through training and written guidelines from upper management to supervisors. Naturally, each of these communications events should be recorded as a matter of historical record-keeping like other important employment events.

Negligence/Duty To Use Reasonable Care

In the legal arena of employment law, negligence means the failure of a manager or supervisor to exercise their attendant duty to use reasonable care in discharging responsibilities that influence the lives of others. Constructive negligence infers that the superior knowingly failed to fulfill their duty to use reasonable care. As these kinds of negligence relate to performance appraisals, courts could go so far as to hold a supervisor negligent under such conditions as:

- Writing meaningless narratives, or not entering narrative comments appropriate to ratings given where provided on the appraisal form.

- Failing to give full consideration to all kinds of previous performance events as the basis of ratings and resultant decisions. This points to one more reason to maintain ongoing supervisory desk notes on performance events of employees.

- Failure to discuss results of the appraisal ratings or conclusions, and specifically failing to inform employees of the existence of any deficiencies.

Although employers are hoping that the case of *Chamberlain v. Bissell, Inc.* (1982) is an isolated exception rather than a precedent rule, consider these conditions from a legal perspective. Bissell, the defendent employer had a policy of just cause-only termination, and a policy requiring annual performance reviews. John Chamberlain, a sales manager with 22 years of unblemished service, according to prior appraisals, was terminated for incompetent performance. In his suit, Chamberlain alleges that the employer (his supervisor) did not use ordinary and reasonable care in conducting his last appraisal—which became the basis of the termination decision—by not advising him that he could be terminated, and such an action was not apparent from prior appraisals or experience with the company. The court agreed and concluded that company policy raised an expectation that employees would be told at least annually of their performance by comprehensive appraisal of how they were doing. To make a claim for negligence, the court articulated four things that must be proved:

1. A legal duty owed to an employee by the employer (e.g., conduct annual appraisals and advise employees of problems).

2. The employer's breach of that duty (e.g., failing to state the nature of deficient performance and possible actions).

3. Injury to the employee resulting from the employer's breach (e.g., loss of job, demotion, promotional rejection, etc.).

4. Damages suffered by the employee as a result of the employer's injury (e.g., lost wages, emotional distress, hardship, reputation, etc.).

Two other courts have more recently come to similar conclusions. For example, in *Flanigan v. Prudential Savings & Loan Assoc.* (1986), the Montana Supreme Court held that negligent appraisals can create a cause for wrongful discharge actions. Here, a 28 year service employee convinced the court that the employer's failure to consider prior performance and work history before making a termination decision constituted negligence.

Another case closely associated to the circumstances of Chamberlain was *Carver v. Sheller-Globe Corp.* (1986). Although the company headquarters are based elsewhere, the employee worked in Illinois where precedent decisions exist concerning the contractual nature of personnel policies in wrongful discharge suits. In this case, the employer's handbook required annual evaluations, and the employee claimed this imposed a duty to use ordinary and reasonable care. The employee further alleged that the employer failed to insure the accuracy of appraisals thereby breaching its duty. However, in this case the employer prevailed not on the basis of a faulty argument from the employee, but on the grounds that the policy did not form a contractual obligation. Similar conclusions were reached by the courts in *Prost v. F.W. Woolworth Co.* (1985) and in *Castiglione v. John Hopkins Hospital* (1986) who determined that:

1. There is no inherent obligation for an employer to conduct performance appraisals; and,

2. Their policy manuals contained adequate disclaimers of being contractual offers of employment conditions.

Supervisory Training

If you have been impressed with the fact that supervisors and anyone else conducting performance appraisals ought to be trained on the elements of negligence, communicating standards, and documentation of performance events, then I have succeeded in my attempt to reduce some of your liability in the use of appraisals. However, there is at least one more element that should be included, and that is providing raters with instructional guidelines. Such guidelines on the appraisal process should consist of all personnel policies related to performance, the process(es) used by the organization, the meaning of written dimension and standards definitions, how to complete the appraisal instrument, and techniques including skills-building of conducting the appraisal process.

So far, the courts and other legal authorities have not come right out in their decisions and said that employers must train raters in the elements just described. Rather, the essence of their decisions draw little other conclusion since some of the faultiness they cite points to subjectivity and irregularities of the process. This points apparent blame on raters when, in fact, most have not been adequately trained in this area of their job responsibility. This is particularly apparent in the cases involving rater negligence. It is doubtful that any supervisor would be wilfully negligent if they knew the conditions of negligent appraisals, and how it could affect their company generally and themselves for specific liability.

What the courts have said about supervisory (rater) training is that they should be given clear guidelines concerning the appraisal process, including how to use performance criteria, either verbally and/or in writing. It is preferable, more meaningful, and more defensible to do both. For example, in the previously mentioned *Carpenter* and *Rowe* cases, an additional weakness found by these courts in their appraisal process was the absence of clearly developed guidelines for supervisors. Without guidelines, the anticipated position of the courts is likely to be, "How can this or any other employee working for your company expect fairness in their appraisal when there is no form of control for the consistent interpretation of performance criteria for those who conduct the reviews?"

Consider the abusive use of appraisal guidelines in the case of *Mills v. Ford Motor Company* (1986). Here, a female employee was given low ratings shortly after the general announcement of impending layoffs. The employee brought suit and the court concluded that the supervisor's statements on the appraisal of counseling and other assistance provided to the employee did not conform to testimony. The employee was thusly reinstated to her job and awarded $100,000 in damages. Similarly, in *Miles v. MNC Corp.* (1985), the court rendered a decision in behalf of the employee due to the absence of appraisal guidelines and written standards, as well as the lack of sufficient supervisory observation of the employee's work to draw reasonable conclusions about the employee's performance. This case should provide due caution for those of you responsible for the oversight of employees who perform their work at locations other than yours. It also requires that you exercise diligence in observing their work sufficiently, or modifying your appraisal process to include the input of an on-site supervisor.

Interestingly enough, the much earlier case of *C.F. Crawford v. Western Electric Co.* (1980) determined that plaintiff employee was not discriminated against inasmuch as the company used written guidelines for supervisors, had developed descriptive performance criteria, required managerial review before discussion with employees, and had a written appeals mechanism for employees who felt their appraisals were unfair or faulty in some way. Perhaps we ought to pay more attention to both winners and loosers in legal contests!

4.40 SOLVING ORGANIZATIONAL, TECHNICAL, AND LEGAL PROBLEMS IN PERFORMANCE APPRAISAL SYSTEMS

Studies have shown that about 85 percent of the variables affecting productivity are internal to the organization; four-fifths can be changed by executive and managerial actions, while the remaining one-fifth is affected at the worker level. Most striking among productive organizations is the greater number of people who are involved and feel responsibility for solving problems—this requires participation! No one person is likely to solve an organization's performance problems. It takes the cooperation, support, and participation of several people, yet some one person must take the initiative to bring the problem to the forefront of the organization's priorities.

In review, there are six basic problems underlying the weakness or failure of most performance appraisal systems. They are:

1. The purpose and use of appraisals are ill-defined, have little linkage to operational problem-solving or human resource decisions, and are therefore of nominal value as a control mechanism.

2. Appraisals are only loosely tied to goals, policy, productivity indexing, and therefore do not function as an integrated system.

3. Performance dimensions are not accurate depictions of the total realm of individual job functions, nor are rating standards sufficiently distinguishing to separate performers, therefore rendering the appraisal method as invalid, inaccurate, and merely tolerated by its users.

4. Appraisals lack adequate guidelines to be instructive to raters and employees about their use, interpretation, processing, and consequences.

5. The performance system and its evaluative criteria is insufficiently communicated to those it affects most, therefore allowing each person to develop their own perception conflicts about the meaningfulness of both their performance and the appraisal system used to measure it.

6. Appraisals are conducted irregularly by raters; they are riddled with rater bias; raters provide inadequate documentation and narration; raters are not properly selected, trained, nor oriented toward the importance of this responsibility.

If these six problem areas within performance appraisal systems could be re-solved, or even significantly reduced, it is probable that all of the attendant legal vulnerabilities they currently possess would simply vanish. Moreover, the system itself would work better, meaning the organization could improve its tracking of produc-tivity; it would be seen as a fairer employer; it could rid itself of poor performers, make better performance related decisions, and experience much higher morale among all levels of employees. Let's look at some ways in which this can be achieved, and solutions to be used in resolving some of the problems.

4.41 SOLVING THE CONTROL MECHANISM PROBLEM BY DEVELOPING AN EFFECTIVE PERFORMANCE SYSTEM

Going back to the original problem of many performance appraisals not hanging together as a performance control mechanism, we should not be surprised to discover the absence of an apparent system; that is, clearly visible and defined linkages throughout the organization's operating documents where decisions are based on, and justified by, performance. To fully integrate a performance system into an organiza-tion, two components ought to be carefully developed: the control mechanism, and the performance delivery system.

Elements Of The Performance Control Mechanism

To develop a performance control mechanism that serves as the focus and cata-lyst of productivity and performance decision making, the organization needs to create strong linkages between four control elements, and they are:

1. **Organizational Goals:** Each organization should have clearly defined goals relating to various kinds of performance and what it strives to achieve as an entity. To become operative, these goals should be as specific as possible; they should require each department to generate more detailed goals for each one that is applicable to their function; and they should require each operating unit to develop clearly defined, measurable, and obtainable objectives associ-ated with each departmental goal as discussed in Part III, Chapter 3. While organizational goals may infrequently or never change due perhaps to concep-tual language, departmental goals and unit objectives should be reviewed an-nually to assure consistent updating with the kind of progress desired.

2. **Performance System Purposes:** To amplify and give meaning to intended lin-kages within the performance system, each organization should articulate the reasons or purposes for the existence of such a system. This is simply a way of saying why we do appraisals and how they are used. Typically, the statements of purpose are contained in the organization's personnel policy manual as an introductory subject of the performance system, but these purposes can be re-

stated or referenced in other organizational documents such as departmental goals and performance plans.

3. **Personnel Policy:** To be a worthy control, performance ought to be one of the more prolific subjects of the organization's personnel policy and procedure manual. It is here that the organization needs to give careful attention to capturing all pertinent detail of performance, and it should address general expectations, conduct, system provisions, support programs, and procedural guidelines. It is likely that the subject of performance will appear in numerous, different sections of a comprehensive personnel manual. It is important to assure that each reference is linked to every other reference under a common theme—"we want and reward good performance; we will try to help and correct marginal performance; and we reject poor and uncooperative performance."

4. **Operational Philosophy:** Some of the attitudes and behavior of many managers and supervisors may have to be changed to develop a well integrated, reliable performance control mechanism. But one thing is certain, there must be some reasonable degree of consistency of leadership styles throughout the organization. The style most conducive to positive performance results is leadership that is knowledgeable, participative, decisive, objective, and fair. Such consistency is best achieved by good selection practices, regular management development programs, statements and support of corporate leadership from the top, and retention decision making based on individual adaptation to the desired leadership style, meaning it becomes part of every manager's performance measurement.

Elements Of The Performance Delivery System

Next comes the performance system itself including how it is delivered or carried out as both a routine and long range administrative function. Routine delivery involves the processing of individual appraisals and the resultant short term decisions and actions. The long range administration of performance involves the collection, analysis, conclusions, and modification actions of performance results so that the organization can make necessary and timely adjustments that will improve its efficiency of performance, and therefore its competitiveness in its industry. Before either routine or long range administration of a performance system can occur, the system itself must be carefully developed among four elements requiring linkage. They are:

1. **Support Programs:** These are the various programs, provisions, and procedures that reinforce the recognition/reward of good performance, the correc-

tion of marginal performance, and the rejection of poor performance. Such program descriptions, including specific provisions and procedures, are usually prescribed in the organization's personnel policy manual under these subject headings:

- Merit pay increases
- Performance recognition awards
- Distinguished performance pay
- Performance bonuses
- Suggestion incentive awards
- Employee training and development
- Consequences of marginal performance
- Evaluation of initial and promotional performance
- Consequences of unacceptable performance
- Causes of discipline and other corrective actions

Not all support programs should or need to be provided in the personnel policy manual, particularly in those states where manuals are likely to be construed by the courts as contractural in nature. For example, if the organization wants to develop a special performance incentive pay program with discretionary latitude, it may be too lengthy and binding if placed in the manual. Rather, such special program descriptions might better serve the intended purpose by being prepared as a separate document with some form of cross-reference to performance policy so that linkage is maintained. Another approach is to describe the program generally in policy, then reference the availability of the more complete program document.

2. **Performance Appraisal Methods:** Next comes the analysis and detailed design of those performance appraisal instruments, guidelines, processes, and policies for the routine conducting of employee appraisals. As a technical set of problems, in and of itself, specific solutions will be presented in the next section. However, in the context of sequentially developing the performance system, you should be aware that the particular kinds of performance methods to be used ought to be developed at this stage.

Although specific and technical detail involved in the design of various parts of the appraisal method(s) should be assigned to human resource professionals, the use of a task force composed of a cross-section of internal staff can be instrumental to overall success of the project. For example, the task force can help deal with the following:

- Current problems and weaknesses.
- Review and suggest ideas on appraisal formats.

- Help refine various performance policies and procedures.
- Recommend support programs.
- Actively participate in the implementation stages.
- Help conduct rater training programs.
- Identify various clusters of jobs that should be subject to different appraisal methods.

Some organizations have continued the use of its performance task force by subsequently having it serve as an appeal review body. To be effective, each task force member should:

- Be knowledgeable about the organization and/or a major subunit such as a department, including organizational policy, procedures, performance problems, and an array of differing jobs.

- Possess objective problem identification and solving skills.

- Be an active participant and interested in the project.

- Be familiar with the various purposes, uses, and underlying principles of performance appraisal systems.

- Possess a linear perspective of an appraisal system ranging from organizational goals, departmental functions, operating conditions, and the diversity of jobs.

- Be allowed time to devote attention and work on the task force project, rather than expected to absorb their involvement into their usual work schedule.

3. **Management Support:** Once the method components are designed and fully developed, the system will now require the support of *all* managers and supervisors. This means that the system as a whole and each of its elements must be thoroughly communicated, explained, understood, and accepted as both a legitimate interest of the organization, as well as a high priority responsibility for its success by each manager. There are two formats that are best to deliver this information: one is to prepare a formal management training program, and videotape it for future use by new managers and supervisors; while the other format is small, informal meetings to discuss these issues as a singular topic (starting with executive, then an executive meets with department heads, and so forth down through the organization).

Ultimately, the goal is to achieve complete support for the system, so a certain amount of selling will be necessary to overcome possible objections. However, this is also a worthy time to flush out legitimate objections and modify the system accordingly. Likewise, it is a good time to reassure management staff that any serious deficiencies of the system will be part of organization's ongoing efforts to refine the system where needed in order to be more responsive to its intended purposes.

4. **Employee Communications:** It would not be prudent to simply adopt a new appraisal system without adequate implementation measures. Nor is it a prudent practice to hold employees retroactively accountable for what may be new, or entirely different, performance criteria. A smooth and orderly implementation of revised appraisal methods should be scheduled for each employee, while other elements of the appraisal system can be installed on any given date as a matter of organizational changes.

To assure that each employee understands the system and how the new appraisal method will affect them, each operating manager and supervisor should be required to conduct thorough employee communication sessions to explain these details:

- Hand out copies of the appraisal form, new or revised policies, and any other associated information.

- Specify the effective dates.

- Have employees sign an acknowledgement form.

- Answer any questions they may have.

Again, a certain amount of selling the new system may be necessary, and this can best be achieved by the manager's demonstration of enthusiasm and support for its improvements over the former appraisal program.

In other words, the only adequate way to gain control over performance is to treat it as an entire system. It must be developed in this way, and it must operate as such. Setting up such a system may sound confusing, but really it isn't. It is a matter of creating the effort as a priority, getting the right people to help, taking enough time to be thorough, and coordinating each sequential step as previously described. Graphically depicted, a good performance system would look as follows.

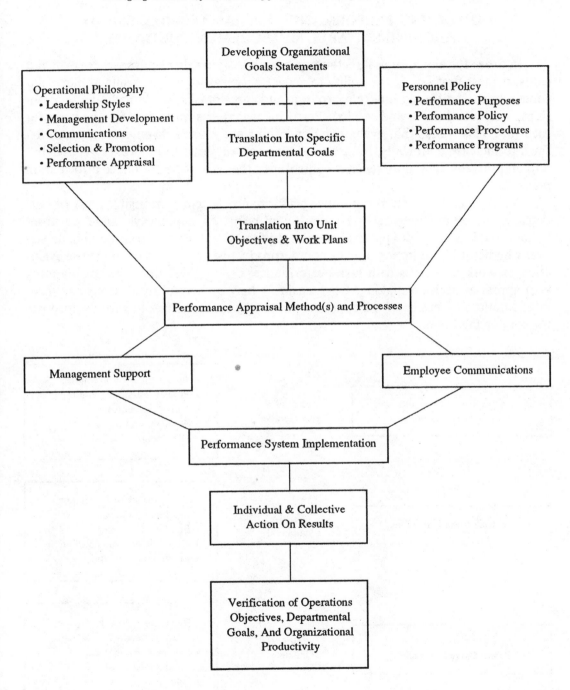

4.42 SOLVING PERFORMANCE APPRAISAL PROBLEMS BY DESIGNING SUITABLE MEASUREMENT METHODS

In order for any appraisal method to begin satisfying those purposes for which it exists, it must first satisfy the ability to accurately measure worker traits in particular context to their differing jobs (e.g., routine and special tasks, work methods, relationships, work conditions, and results). Performance criteria must therefore be valid for each job. This means that evaluative dimensions and standards ought to be well defined to increase uniformity, reduce rater bias and subjectivity (interobserver reliability), and thereby gain more realistic control over the type of performance information being processed.

We also need to keep in mind that performance systems, through the use of particular appraisal methods, serve many different purposes. Not always can all purposes be captured in a singular appraisal method. In fact, there remains considerable debate over whether it is conflicting or even counterproductive practice to combine the evaluation of work objectives with task performance, or employee development planning with appraisal decision making. Once again, it may be helpful to illustrate the three most common functions of the appraisal process by their linkages to various purposes for conducting them.

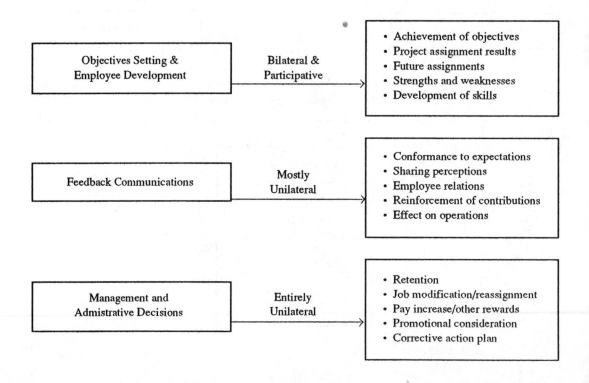

It should become apparent from this diagram that not all aspects of appraisals are measured the same, used the same, nor acted upon with the highest degree of consistent "theme". Some of the process is bilaterial, some unilateral, some positive (motivational), and some of it may be negative (correctional). Each person will vary in their performance and how such results affect them, or how results are used by the organization to make decisions. I'm not certain as to what truly valuable purpose would be served by separating the functions of the appraisal process merely because they are at times at odds with each other for some employees. That just happens to be the nature of management, and good management requires skill at handling a variety of situations daily. Be that as it may, the design of appraisal methods that will lead to more reliable performance measurement, decisions, and problem solving should proceed as follows.

Developing Valid Performance Criteria

This is no doubt one of the more universal problems of appraisal methodologies cited by legal authorities. That is, an employer's use of generic and ill-defined performance dimensions (in particular, and rating standards in general) which are then applied to a diverse range of jobs. Here, the meaning of dimensions inherently vary, and among which some dimensions simply don't apply to many jobs. Even in some court cases where performance dimensions have been acceptable for purposes of validity to the job in question, the appraisal itself has been held to be invalid because each dimension was not weighted for the job with respect to a realistic distribution of work responsibility. In essence, what the courts are saying with regard to weighted performance is that it is more realistic to assume that not all functions performed by a worker are of equal value—a point well made—and that employers ought to first determine what weighted value should be assigned to each dimension of each job, then evaluate the incumbent's performance accordingly. Using a matrix to illustrate how various jobs might be matched to applicable, job valid performance dimensions and weighted according to such factors as time, importance, consequences, or the like, the performance distribution control sheet would look like the following.

Performance Dimension	Chief Engineer	Project Engineer	Associate Engineer I	Associate Engineer II	Sales & Coordination	Engineering Technician
1. Research & Data Collection	5		15	10	60	15
2. Preparation of Technical Reports & Illustrations	10	5	10	55	25	75
3. Coordination of Projects	20	10	20	15	10	
4. Scheduling & Materials Handling		40	15	10		10
5. Customer/Vendor Relations	5	30	40	10	5	
6. General Administration	60	15				

As you can see from this example, some of these jobs have performance dimensions in common even though the nature of their work means different things and is weighted differently, yet they do not have all dimensions in common. Each dimension, then, should be described (defined) in the context of what measures of performance are appropriate to the jobs possessing that dimension. By separating dimensions in this way, and weighting them according to each different job, you are able to maximize the validity of performance measurement, minimize subjectivity, obtain more reliable productivity indexing, and provide employees with more meaningful feedback. This is not a purely conceptualized methodology that makes sense only for intellectual purposes of illustration. I've developed this method, used it with clients, and it works with remarkable accuracy of results. Employees like it too since it focuses on exactly what they do. Obviously, there is more to the method than what is depicted here as an illustration, but the point remains that we must move away from the use of generic, broadly applied dimensions to measure the performance of vastly different jobs. The process by which more valid performance criteria can be developed is by following these steps.

1. **Job Analysis:** A formal job analysis should be conducted on each job in the organization, exempt and non-exempt, in such a manner as to elicit the major areas of each job's responsibility (dimension), prioritized tasks within each dimension (used to define the dimension), and percentage weight assigned to the dimension (as agreed by the employee and supervision). Results are analyzed and compiled on a Performance Distribution Control Sheet such as that shown in the above illustration.

2. **Writing Dimension Definitions:** Dimension definitions are then taken from the prioritized task statements on the job analysis questionnaires. Such definitions should be worded in such a way as to be clear and concise, representative of the dimension, and measurable through observation.

If you prefer to use more conventional dimensions to a broad range of jobs, you should do at least two things: one, avoid weak and vulnerable dimension terms; and, two provide thorough definitions of those dimensions you use in terms of job related characteristics and worker traits. With respect to the former point, you should consider changing the following weak dimensions to more job related dimensions.

Weak Dimension		**Job Related Dimension**
• Loyalty	→	• Adaptation To Work Conditions
• Dependability	→	• Reliability For Thorough & Timely Work
• Health	→	• Appearance & Demeanor
• Attendance	→	• Attendance To Duties
• Intelligence	→	• Job Knowledge & Skills
• Promotability	→	• Job Progress
• Attitude	→	• Behavior
• Risk Taking	→	• Judgment & Decision Making
• Results	→	• Achievement Of Established Goals

In defining performance dimensions, you should also focus on combining or including both statements of task (what is done) and behavior (how things are done). The latter seems to be more difficult for most of us to get in touch with. Nevertheless, writing combined task, method, and results performance definitions can be done with a little analytical thought, and this should be done since many performance failures result from behavioral deficiencies in workers. To identify behavior measures of performance, we might take the first job related dimension listed above and define it in this way.

Dimension	**Expectation**	**Undesirable**
Adaptation to Work Conditions	• Complies with policies, rules, directions, and assignments	• Ignores, bends, or avoids compliance standards
	• Offers useful and positive suggestions for improvements	• Does not contribute ideas nor show interest in the organization
	• Is pleasant and cooperative with others	• Selectively pleasant and cooperative with others
	• Is not disrupted by changes in work priorities	• Becomes ineffective when work priorities change
	• Adapts easily to new situations	• Is resistent to changing conditions

3. **Writing Measurement (Rating) Definitions:** Once we have identified the what and how, or task and behavior dimensions of jobs, we must then determine the performance standards against which these dimensions will be measured and evaluated. This can be done in one of two ways: either by lengthy descriptions of performance in each dimension according to each different level of performance as in the following format;

Dimension	Below Standards	Meets Standards	Exceeds Standards
Adaptation to Work Conditions	(description)	(description)	(description)

or, you can use generalized definitions of the rating levels. If this approach is used, the rating level definitions should be sufficiently descriptive to create a clear *distinction* between each level. For that reason, you should use no less than three, nor more than five, rating levels. If you wish to quantify results of the appraisal process, merely give each rating level a numerical range of value—such as 0-3 for below standards, 4-6 for meets standards, and 7-9 for exceeds standards—which can then be used to multiply the weight given to each dimension to arrive at weighted scoring.

Formating The Appraisal Instrument

This step in the appraisal development process is easier said than done when we consider the amount of information that needs to be presented on the form. On the one hand, we don't want it to appear so awesome for raters that it immediately discourages the desired amount of time and attention for their completion. On the other hand, we want to capture all pertinent detail in order to apply its results toward those purposes for which appraisals are intended to serve. However sensitive we are to both concerns, it is time we required the latter to outweigh the former concern. Notwithstanding the need for accuracy and detail, we do need to remain mindful of the form's length and format out of respect for the effort required of raters to do a good job in completing it. The generally accepted formating sequence of appraisal detail is as follows.

1. **Employee Data:** This identification detail is needed for personnel recordkeeping and processing decisional results of appraisals. Employee data includes the employee's name, position title, department and/or work location, payroll number, hire date, length of service in the position, date of last appraisal review, and present pay rate. Other data included in this section often includes the type of report (probationary, annual, or supplemental), position status (exempt/non-exempt, part-time/full-time, etc.), and other information relevant to the business or appraisal purposes.

2. **Rater Instructions:** Succinctly stated instructions should be provided on the form to raters indicating how the form is to be used and processed. Special emphasis should be placed on the rater's consideration of the entire evaluation period, all applicable dimensions of performance, and the use of narratives to illustrate or highlight the more notable aspects of the employee's performance. However, such instructions are not adequate, in and of themselves, to provide reasonable guidelines on how to do appraisals. These guidelines should be more fully developed through the use of a written document and a formal training program.

3. **Performance Criteria:** Next comes a listing of the actual performance dimensions and measurement, or rating, standards against which the employee is to be evaluated. Here is where the rating supervisor is to enter—whether by essay, check mark, or numeric value—how the employee has performed in each dimension overall (i.e., on an average that reflects all performance events in the category).

4. **Narratives:** Sufficient room on the form should be made for the rater and employees' use of comprehensive narratives about specific aspects of performance, elaboration or illustrations on particular ratings, achievement of objectives, and noteworthy deficiencies. Employees, too, ought to have room to state their position or rebuttal when disagreement between the two is not resolved between them. Because narrative space can absorb a considerable amount of the form, some organizations alternatively advise raters and employees to attach separate pages, but this creates a sense that narratives are optional rather than essential documentation intended to support ratings and resultant actions.

5. **Proposed Actions:** Appraisals should have a section that deals with the consequences of performance results. These should be stated or provided for in the context of specific actions that are being proposed by the rating supervisor. Examples of proposed actions include such things as a recommended or denied merit increase, deficiency improvement or follow-up plan, reevaluation of particular performance areas at a prescribed date, and advancement from probationary to regular status. What should not be addressed in this or other sections of the appraisal is the employee's promotability. Normally, higher level jobs consist of different or more acute dimensions of performance that may or may not be strongly related to the employee's present job, thus rendering inferences about promotability generally invalid. Nowhere else is this more apparent than in the promotion of line employees (task based jobs) to that of supervisor (judgment and decision based jobs) where past performance

in one capacity—even if they are considered "good workers" is not necessary valid criteria for presuming success in a higher job.

6. **Approvals:** This final section should provide a sign-off statement and require the date and signatures of authorized parties to the appraisal. It is highly adviseable for supervisors to first review their written appraisal with departmental management to assure agreement prior to discussing it with the employee. Such approval statements and signatures should include:

Employee: I acknowledge discussion and receipt of a copy of this evaluation and I ☐ wish ☐ do not wish to discuss it further with departmental management.

Supervisor: The foregoing appraisal represents my considered evaluation of this employee's performance during the entire appraisal period, and I have discussed it with him/her.

Department Head: I have reviewed this appraisal and I concur with its findings/recommendations.

Personnel Office: Received, processed, and placed in the employee's personnel file.

Depending on the distribution of copies—remember, this is a confidential document—you may want to have the form printed on self copying paper, but always be sure to file the original copy in the employee's file. Also, if merit increases are processed by the Payroll Office by means of the authorities on this form, be sure that the copy sent to them omits all appraisal information—payroll staff only needs to know what the pay increase is, when effective, and that it's been approved by a duly authorized person.

Preparing Support Documents And Rater Training

Now that your appraisal method and form has been developed, you're almost ready for its implementation. Three important steps remain if you are to achieve a smooth, well understood transition into the new or revised appraisal process, and they are:

1. **Review Personnel Policies:** By a thorough review of existing personnel policies you should insure that each policy is congruent with the appraisal process. You might look for such detail as any change in terms used to refer to rating levels, consequences of low ratings, references to merit increases, and the presence of a disclaimer to the effect that satisfactory or better performance is not to be construed as an implied guarantee of continued employment.

You may also wish to consider at this point whether it is timely and fitting to prepare new policies on methods of employee performance recognition programs.

2. **Prepare Rater Guidelines:** Ideally, these guidelines should be written in thorough, concise language about the following details:

- Use and importance of the organization's performance system.
- How it serves as a productivity control mechanism.
- The use of supervisory desk notes; how to avoid rater bias.
- Understanding the performance criteria in the context of individual jobs.
- How to complete the form.
- Suggested tips for conducting the appraisal interview.

This document may get rather lengthy, which is okay, given the fact that some want this detail, you may have it scrutinized by legal sources some day, and its detail can be a valuable source in preparing your rater's training program.

3. **Formalize Rater Training:** Don't just prepare written guidelines and distribute them with the new appraisal form and a memo telling people when it all goes into effect—this is usually a fatal error. The responsibility to prepare appraisals is too important and misunderstood to be dealt with in such a meaningless way. Formal training of all those who will be using the performance system should be included in a personalized, but required, training session. In addition to the content items mentioned above, the training program should include discussion periods, the answering of all questions, the presentation of legal issues, and skills-building exercises (such as role plays) in evaluating performance behaviors, eliminating rater bias, conducting the appraisal interview, situational decision making, and action planning.

As a time-saving measure, and an effective means of continuing an ongoing program of rater training, you should videotape the initial training session so that new managers and supervisors can become equally advantaged, and those already trained can review it as desired.

So there you have it; a fully developed performance appraisal system that serves the organization as a well integrated productivity control mechanism; a comprehensive system that makes sense to managers for purposes of their human resource decisions; an appraisal method that is legally valid and more realistic to employees and supervisors alike; and a process that should insure more useable results throughout the organization. Assuredly, being thorough takes more time than not, but we should bear in mind that the absence of thoroughness in the appraisal of our employees' performance has cost our organizations even more dearly in the way of turnover, malingerers and malcontents, reduced morale, inappropriate decision making, and I hasten to add the dreaded but very real likelihood of legal defense costs. Clearly, the cost for prevention is small in comparison, and its results will be far more beneficial to any organization's productivity indexes. Again, the choice is yours.

CHAPTER III: 5.0
SOLVING WORKPLACE PROBLEMS WITH THE HELP
OF CONSULTANTS AND OTHER PROFESSIONALS

One of the most valuable and effective ways to resolve workplace problems is to engage the help of those professionals specifically trained for diagnostic and problem solving work. However, not all who claim this kind of expertise are right for the assignment or your organization. To get the best and most desirable results in the use of consultants and other professionals skilled at handling problem situations, care must be exercised to use the right person for the right job. This chapter will greatly assist you in these kinds of determinations.

Of all those professionals actively immersed in the resolution of countless business problems, consultants have long been the focal resource of problem solving processes. They have also been historically one of the most maligned by the general business community. Why has this malignity developed? There are many reasons contributing to a negative perception of persons making themselves known as "consultants"; some reasons are myth, some obsolete information about the growth and professionalization of the field occurring in recent years, and some reasons remain fact such as the continued existence of charlatans that crop up from time to time. But let's be frank, we have charlatans in every profession, and the consulting field is no exception.

Like so many other professions, there is no minimum or qualifying licensing or other regulatory mandate that would ensure at least a known threshold of competence for consultants, except for certification standards and code of ethics required by some national and international professional associations. Like other professionals, legitimate consultants are the first and most outspoken to oppose those that bring disrepute to the profession by engaging in the practice with less than what the profession demands and clients deserve. In the words of Elsevier Science Publishers:

Management consulting is still an emerging profession. There are no universally accepted standards concerning what constitutes acceptable performance, technically or ethically...Professional development to achieve and maintain acceptable performance standards is the only thing that distinguishes a true management consultant from people who merely earn fees by giving advice...[1]

The private practice of consultancy is not much different than such other professional entrepreneurs as physicians, lawyers, and accountants. There are good ones, and there are bad ones. Some are very expensive, some will do almost any work for a sliding scale price. When it comes to management consultants, there seems to persist a few common objections and misconceptions about their ability to withstand the tests of truly qualified and worthy resource professionals, and these include:

MYTH #1: Consultants are nothing more than displaced managers who cannot find another job, or are green post-graduate students striving for independence.

ANSWER: These individuals are negligible in number; they will not stay "in business" long due to the high cost and endurance required for business development; and they do not qualify for admittance into professional consulting associations.

MYTH #2: Consultants are too expensive with fees often over $100 per hour. Even our highest paid people don't make that kind of money.

ANSWER: Consultant work should be viewed in the context of cost/benefit comparisons and not superficial relationships to the compensation of others in the organization. Qualified consultants can almost always save their client substantially more than their fees by generating new ways to produce revenue or development of preventative measures to avoid the probability of extensive liability. Benefits derived from use of consultants can also be measured in terms of indirect dollar savings such as higher efficiency, productivity, morale, lower turnover, better decision making, or a more effective way of operating.

Another often underestimated point is the consultant's cost of being in business. Operating expenses of consultants go as high as 60 percent or more of revenue. Such costs include office space, office equipment and support services, payroll expenses, self employment taxes, insurances, travel, lodging and meals, association memberships and professional development, subscription services, marketing costs, and the like. Not all consultants operate out of a spare bedroom using their spouse to do errands and help with client projects!

---

[1] _____; Journal Of Management Consulting, Elsevier Science Publishing, Amsterdam. Vol. 4, No. 1, 1988.

MYTH #3: Consultants don't present themselves well in appearance, verbal or writing skills, nor do they demonstrate a suitable understanding of our business or the nature of our problem.

ANSWER: You have (or had) the misfortune of hiring the wrong consultant for your needs. It's a common problem but the answer lies in improving your selection methods rather than condemning all consultants because your past choices didn't meet your expectations. Like hiring a good employee, the process requires some effort to find the right person, not left to luck of the draw.

Because problems in many organizations calling for the help of consultants can be either technical to a particular field or industry-based, you should first decide which it is, and then seek a consultant with the appropriate background. It is important for every consultant to *understand* the nature of each client's business to assure practical solutions to problems, but only when the problem is industry-based do you require a consultant with *industry experience*.

MYTH #4: Consultants don't do a thorough job, and they take too long to produce their results.

ANSWER: The quickest and most certain way of avoiding either of these situations is to conduct thorough reference checks on any consultant you are intending to engage. The thoroughness and timeliness of results, along with other traits of your prospective consultant, should be subject to careful investigation even more-so than the importance given to employee reference checks. Normally, checking the references of consultants is easier in terms of obtaining complete, uncensored information about their work than employees since consultants are retained under a contractual rather than employment relationship, and there is less concern by the reference source for defamation liability.

The issues of consultants taking too long and producing incomplete results can and should also be addressed early in the engagement. This is best accomplished by both parties agreeing to acceptable schedules of work activities and outcomes; doing so also helps to clarify expectations, and this should include a method of dealing with unforeseen or uncontrollable delays.

MYTH #5: Results produced by consultants don't adequately fit our needs or resolve the problem situation.

ANSWER: One or both parties were quilty of insufficient identification or disclosure of the real problem, its sources, or those elements and influences that affect solution development. In order to effectuate workable solutions to any problem, the first part of a consultant's engagement ought to include detailed discussions of the problem, and the kind of outcome sought by means of a collaborative client-consultant approach (see Section 5.40-5.44). Then, the consultant should undertake a complete fact-finding process that may include some sensitive situations and questions. If problems were all easy, you wouldn't need consultants; so consultants need to be prepared to probe into sensitive and difficult situations, and the client ought to be prepared to support the effort. When this is not done, or the client psychologically or in other ways resists the validity of the consultant's results, then rejection, disappointment, or "shelving" these results are likely to occur. This simply points out the need for client and consultant to establish a solid, formal, and clearly delineated business relationship early in the engagement.

Indeed, there are numerous types of consultants who offer the business community many valuable services in all parts of the United States and abroad. The field is rapidly becoming international throughout the free world, and many consultants are spending considerable travel time annually in service of their clientelle. Far greater is the importance of having the right consultant come to you with the proper experience, credentials, and services, than it is to acquire the lowest bidder.

As you will learn in the sections to follow, there is a right way and a wrong way to use consultants and other professionals in dealing with workplace problems. The points that are raised should help you make the right choices and thereby produce the most desirable results.

5.10 TYPES OF CONSULTANTS AND THEIR SERVICES

Since many consultants, particularly solo practitioners, do not join professional consulting associations, it is difficult to determine exactly how many are in business at any one time. Rough estimates project about 45,000 such firms are in business throughout the United States. Among these firm, it is believed that the specialty areas of consulting services are as follows in order of the number of firms:

1. General Management
2. Human Resources
3. Marketing
4. Organizational Planning
5. Manufacturing

6. Staff Development
7. Strategic Planning
8. Administration
9. Finance Accounting
10. Marketing Strategy

If we use the term consultant in a broader sense to mean professional advisors external to the organization whom we rely on in a contractual or similar fee basis, we are likely to see that there is an array of specialized talent available. This remains true even when we narrow the field of consultants to those engaged in professions whose services focus on various kinds of human resource problem solving. For example, the specialty professions listed below provide services with a focus of reducing or eliminating particular problems that relate to each organization's human resource assets and liabilities.

- Human Resource Consultants
- Labor Relations Consultants
- General Management, Organizational, and Administration Consultants
- MIS and Financial Consultants
- Organizational Development and Training Consultants
- Risk Management Consultants
- Medically Related Consultants

Some consulting firms will overlap in their services depending on the diversity and depth of background of their staff, while some firms or individual consultants are very specialized by their service or the type of industry they serve. This is illustrated by the fact that most human resource consultants are diversified in both services and industry types due to the interrelatedness of their functional areas, whereas labor relations and risk management consultants tend to be highly specialized in their services, and sometimes among certain industry types. A closer examination of the services offered by these workplace problem solving consultants might serve as an important guide in your determination of who to select for any given assignment.

5.11 HUMAN RESOURCE CONSULTANTS

Presuming the consultants engaged in this field have a well developed background of practitioner experience, proper academic training, and remain professionally current, they can offer a wealth of expertise, objective insight, and creative problem solving to just about any organization. Their services tend to be diverse given that the nature of the profession and kinds of exposure received as a practitioner in contemporary organizations give them this background. Their services can include any of the following.

- Organizational and operational audits
- Human resource programs and operations audits
- Classification (job analysis) and position control studies
- Compensation analysis (job evaluation) and salary plan design
- Employee benefit studies
- Personnel manual and employee handbook development
- Labor and employee relations program design
- Employee attitude surveys
- Recruitment, examination, and selection process development

- Performance appraisal system design
- Organizational (management) development programs
- Management planning retreats and team building
- Mid management and supervisory development programs
- General advisor on vulnerable or sensitive issues
- Third party dispute resolution (arbitration or mediation) facilitator

5.12 LABOR RELATIONS CONSULTANTS

In most circumstances this is a specialty service whereby consultants are selected to handle some aspect of an organization's labor relations program in a unionized environment, or one that is pending unionization. Oftentimes, labor attorneys are used for this purpose but, depending on circumstances, doing so may raise more intense reaction from employees who then feel that they need equivalent representation, and escalation of the issues can ensue. Whether the consultant is an attorney or other suitably credentialed consultant, the services provided typically consist of these.

- Evaluation and training on maintaining a non-unionized environment
- Counter-unionizing campaign advice and assistance
- Chief negotiator and/or advisor during collective bargaining sessions
- Strategy and issues advisor on collective bargaining issues
- Contract clause writer
- Contract administration (clause/issue interpretation) advisor
- Dispute resolution (grievance) advisor
- Employer representative to hearing bodies on unfair practice, strike, and related events

5.13 GENERAL MANAGEMENT, ORGANIZATIONAL, AND ADMINISTRATION CONSULTANTS

The theme or focus of these consultants, like human resource consultants, is those issues pertaining to the organization as a whole or some major subunit thereof. They are the "big picture" people who key in on those problems and other conditions that affect the structure, order, flow, assignments, objectives, and relationships of the organization's key players, top managers, and boards of directors. Frequently used services consist of the following.

- Organizational (upper management) audits
- Strategic planning programs and development
- Board of Directors advisor
- Goals and objectives planning
- Management team building programs
- Competency and efficiency evaluations
- Executive management advisor

Usually these consultants are industry specific because of the kind and amount of detail involved in dealing with the upper echelon issues of a business. These matters are no place for the novice or meek.

5.14 MANAGEMENT INFORMATION SYSTEMS (MIS) AND FINANCIAL CONSULTANTS

At first glance, these consultants may seem remote to what we normally consider human resource problem issues, but they can be crucial to solving problems that become directly or indirectly a causal source. Without the proper kind and timing of information, people become functionally disabled and everyone suffers. Likewise, the manner in which each organization uses its financial resources and recordkeeping (payroll) systems will have a profound effect upon each and every person in the organization. A few of these consultants' services are as follows.

- Analysis of business transaction and information useage
- Software and hardware development and applications to MIS needs
- Staff training in MIS useage
- Business change modifications to MIS
- Financial recordkeeping and accountabilities development
- Payroll systems evaluation and installations
- Personnel systems evaluation and installation
- Internal MIS and financial staff advisor
- Competency and effectiveness evaluations

5.15 ORGANIZATIONAL DEVELOPMENT AND TRAINING CONSULTANTS

According to the American Society for Training and Development (ASTD) there are some 80,000 consultants offering services in this area, and in 1987, employers spent approximately 13 billion dollars for training and development programs. Presumably because about 85 percent of all U.S business is small, with under 500 employees, a great many of these programs are sponsored by independent training firms and trade associations whose attendance is composed of people from several organizations. However, it has consistently been shown that more customized, internal training programs are more cost and learning effective—whether developed and conducted by internal staff or external consultants—than "open market" training programs.

Additionally, organizational development firms usually offer a broader array of services than just training. These other services usually consider programmatic kinds of problem identification and resolution. Organizational development and training consultants offer these kinds of services.

- Developmental needs assessment and planning
- Employee skills assessment and development planning
- Employment orientation program development
- Company training program planning
- Training program development and implementation
- Management skills development programs
- Succession and technological change planning

5.16 RISK MANAGEMENT CONSULTANTS

These consultants can range from those offering bona fide, technical, and objective services in safety, product liability, hazards control, and indemnification strategies to insurance agents merely wanting to sell their particular product under the guise of service to the client as a consultant. The key difference among various kinds of risk management situations is whether or not the consultant has both the appropriate technical background, and does not personally gain benefit (conflict of interest) from their analysis or recommendations (e.g., to purchase the insurance plan the consultant underwrites). If, for example, you wish to determine the effectiveness of your workers' compensation administrator, or consider the advantages of self-insuring one of your more costly benefit programs, then you may wish to retain an independent auditor with experience in the type of program being evaluated rather than the consultant, administrator, or other party actually handling the program. Here are some of the more commonplace services of risk management firms.

- Conduct audits of workers' compensation, healthcare, and other risk-oriented benefit programs

- Perform cost/benefit analyses on methods of benefit and liability cost-containment measures

- Conduct field inspections and prepare reports on job hazard risks, compliance standards, and correction methods

- Conduct self-insurance studies and assist with claims administrator selection

- Assist in the preparation of equipment bid specifications

- Prepare annual injury loss reports

5.17 MEDICALLY RELATED CONSULTANTS

There are a host of medically related professionals that all organizations should identify and have available to assist in various workplace problems and situations, but with one common thread; these advisors should be familiar with your workplace, the nature of different jobs, and they should have particular background in industrial or organizational treatment. The most frequently used medical and allied professionals are industrial physicians, specialized doctors such as cardiologists, physical therapists, chiropractors, and organizational psychologists. Countless human resource problems could be averted if these consultants were more thoroughly used in these service areas:

- Validating and conducting pre-employment physicals

- Resumption of work, or modified duty assignments for employees following disability

- Work methods advice to avoid physical disability, fatigue, and job stress conditions

- Workers' compensation injury evaluation and treatment

- Evaluation and treatment of special condition employees

- Employee Assistance Program development and services

- Diet and fitness (wellness) program development

- Job stress and burnout counseling/therapy

5.18 LEGAL ADVISORS AND REPRESENTATIVES

Without much doubt, one of the most apparent trends in employment during the last two or so decades is that statutory and case law has had profound influence on shaping workplace issues related to the management of our human resources. Given the ever-present visibility and potential impact on an organization of these legal/legislative matters, it is imperative for each employer—including their management representatives—to maintain at least fundamental knowledge of legal issues and new events. Equally imperative is the need for every employer to select and have readily available an attorney who specializes in labor law with trial experience in both state and federal employment matters. Preferably, these attorneys should also possess some experience in working within organizational structures for purposes of having some operations insight. The kinds of valuable services offered by labor attorneys include the following:

- Preparing such legal contracts as employment, non-disclosure, trade secret, and separation agreements

- Reviewing and advising on personnel policy for legal compliance

- Providing advice on vulnerable employment actions

- Preparing a defense and representing the employer at administrative hearings and in litigated cases.

Let us not forget, too, that legislative representatives should be contacted and fully appraised of the effect that their action on a pending bill will have on our business operations, and thereby thwart bad laws.

Obviously, this is only a partial listing of the kinds of consulting professionals and their services available to the business community. Yes, they can be expensive, but these costs are almost always small compared to the actual costs when such preventative or efficiency-improving measures are not taken. Part of the key to getting the best dollar value from the use of consultants lies in the ability to identify a suitable need, selecting the right one, and developing a sound business relationship, each of which are discussed in the sections that follow.

5.20 DETERMINING THE NEED FOR A CONSULTANT

Determining the need for a consultant may sound easier than it actually should be, and there is a difference between purpose and need. There may be innumerable purposes which companies can identify that could require the services of a consultant but, when evaluated more carefully, the need may not be fully developed. A useful exercise that will become helpful, if and when you do meet with a consultant, is to first write down the basic problem, situation, or issue you feel might be appropriate to engage the services of a consultant. Next, break this problem down into existing, known, or perceived subparts such as causal sources, effects, influences, and the like. Here's an example taken from the previous chapter topic—performance appraisal systems.

Problem:
- Does not provide adequate productivity indexing
- Supervisors resist use
- Insufficient documentation to support related decisions
- Criteria not valid for differing jobs
- System not adequately linked to related decisions and actions

Sub Issues:
- Legal vulnerability
- Reduced management credibility on decisions
- Policies questioned by employees for incongruences
- Supervisory orientation and training on this responsibility
- Employee morale
- Sufficiency of performance incentive

This initial process of writing down your problem or issue that need to be addressed will be of tremendous help in clarifying whether a real need exists, and where at least preliminary attention should be given. It may also identify certain goals that should be achieved once the work is done. Now you're ready to examine other aspects of the need for a consultant.

5.21 EVALUATING THE EIGHT FACTORS OF NEED

There are eight factors you should now evaluate in determining both the need for, and propriety of, using a consultant to help deal with workplace issues. Depending on the actual situation at hand, any one of these factors may serve as sufficient justification to engage a consultant. If the decision rests with a higher level manager to whom you report, then you may want to consider the ways in which each of these factors would appeal to that decision maker. It may be up to you to make the need more apparent by showing more than one way the need exists and benefits will result.

1. **Staff Supplement:** Many smaller companies lack highly skilled administrative staff to deal effectively with the many complex areas of human resource and workplace problem solving. Consultants often serve as a sort of adjunct human resources director, advisor on critical situations, on special projects, or simply because additional staff resources are needed to work on a collaborative basis to accomplish some task. Where the latter approach is used, the company staff can benefit by learning new methods, procedures, or techniques brought in by the consultant.

2. **Expertise:** As opposed to eminent authority, the term expert is relative and carries the meaning that the person has substantial, well recognized experience, insight, skills, and approach (methodology) as in dealing with particular issues or areas. If an issue requires more of these characteristics than is available within the organization, then the need exists to find a consultant who matches the expertise prerequisites. When the right one is found, they can be of immense value in guiding the issue toward its proper course and conclusion.

3. **Creativity:** By nature, most professional consultants tend to be creative sorts—and that's probably a major reason why they don't work for someone else! Sometimes creativity may be needed with an issue by virtue of just bringing a fresh look to it; an experienced or respected point-of-view that is not too close or influenced by it; or because the issue truly needs a whole new and fresh approach. Because consultants are professionally required to keep up with trends and ideas, and because they're exposed to such a variety of organizations and operational situations, many of them can offer rather unique opportunities for their clients to delve into wholly new ways of doing things.

4. **Objectivity:** This is singularly the most frequently cited reason companies hire consultants. When there exists an honest need for the untouched objectivity of a qualified professional, then consultants are the way to go. However, true objectivity is also accompanied by true independence, and this means that the

consultant should not be placed in the position of undue influence in fact-finding, methods, conclusions, and recommendations.

There does arise occasions in which some companies want to use a consultant like a pawn which is highly objectionable to professional consultants and counterproductive to the realization of any legitimate benefit. Conversely, there is nothing inherently sacrilegious about engaging a consultant to disclose the obvious, then take the blame for the outcome rather than company officers; so long as the obvious result surfaces by means of the consultant's objectivity, independence, and professional integrity in tact.

5. **Timeliness:** With many workplace issues, problems, or projects, timeliness can be essential to advantageous results. Time can be associated with limited internal staff resources, their ongoing commitments, and/or their level of experience with an issue. The need, then, can be to either supplement existing staff by absorbing much of the more time consuming phases of the work, to draw upon a larger but temporary pool of resource professionals, or to deal promptly with a priority issue in a highly responsive manner.

6. **Confidentiality:** Sometimes issues or problems in an organization surface that are highly sensitive, delicate, or have the potential to become vulnerably damaging to those within the organization. The need thus becomes one of proper handling with an emphasis on discretion, confidentiality, accuracy, thoroughness, and independent objectivity. Examples of the confidentiality need includes such matters as sexual harassment and other types of discrimination complaints, evaluations of serious discipline or termination cases, competency evaluations, and conduct investigations.

7. **Quality/Quantity:** The need for quality and/or quantity measures of some efforts can become important ingredients in determining the prospect of using consultants. These factors can vary considerably depending on the nature of the assignment. These assignments usually carry some element of efficiency, effectiveness, productivity, cost reduction, revenue production, or liability containment. Special skills, methods, or industry expertise of consultants can respond favorably to these needs, including such costly human resource problems as turnover, absenteeism, poor internal relationships, theft, work injuries, and termination litigation.

8. **Cost:** There are two aspects of cost when consultant need is being considered; how much are we willing (able to spend) for a consultant to help with the problem or issue, and how much are we going to spend if the situation isn't addressed properly? This is a question of prevention or treatment versus specu-

lative risk. In other words, you're gambling with potentially high stakes by inaction and a continuation or deepening of the problem. Yet another aspect of cost is how much can we save or reduce costs, directly or indirectly, by using a consultant where this need exists. Examples of such actions might involve downsizing, reorganization, production method changes, job restructures, and computerization.

5.22 THE NEED FOR MULTIPLE CONSULTANTS

No man is an island—no one person stands alone with all the answers—is perhaps the best way to view the potential need for multiple consultants in various situations that call for differing kinds of expertise. I, myself, have worked in tandem with labor attorneys, doctors, psychologists, benefit administrators, computer experts, and other professional consultants on client projects where this need existed, and where clients ultimately benefitted from such combined talent.

The use of multiple consultants can, of course, be slightly more awkward than working with just one. This is natural since two or more independent people with experience in any given area will likely have differing ideas, perceptions, and methods to accomplish the task. The easiest way to overcome prospective breakdowns between consultants—although you should bear in mind that some differences can be very healthy to the assignment—is to select your primary consultant with whom you know and respect, and who is to serve as the project leader, then allow your primary consultant to subcontract with any other consultants you mutually identify as needed for the project.

If your primary consultant does not know of the kind(s) of consultant(s) that are needed, then you both should seek out and jointly select from among the unknowns that are solicited. In this case it is likely that your primary consultant will not want to subcontract with an unfamiliar consultant since a poor outcome can damage the primary's reputation and cause considerable aggravation during the assignment. Since you and your primary consultant will both be working with other consultants, it is important that you share in the selection process, but contract with them separately when these other consultants are unknown—even though you check them out thoroughly.

The next step is to orient other consultants toward the project at hand by going over all details, phases, steps, probable conditions, and the particular timing and roles to be carried out by each consultant. Clarity of roles and expectations is imperative early in the assignment if it is to proceed smoothly.

5.30 FINDING AND SELECTING QUALIFIED CONSULTANTS

Consultants can be found within the environs of every major and some lesser cities. In larger cities they are usually in abundant supply. Wherever your location, and whatever your business need entails, there is a good consultant out there, some-where, for you. But, merely because there is a consultant or two in your vicinity who offers the services you need, they may or may not be the best person for the assign-ment or prevailing conditions—it merely means they live in your area. In fact, the more qualified and sought after consultants spend a considerable amount of time traveling to client locations even though there may be no shortage of business opportu-nities in their own home town. The margin of cost for a distant consultant to a local one can be small, particularly when added talent may travel with distance.

On the other hand, you may find just what you need in the way of consultant talent locally, and thereby avoid the added costs of travel and some inconveniences associated with distance. Whether local or distant, the crucial issue is that you acquire the right consultant for the assignment, and this may take some looking. They may have tried to knock on your door before but you may not have been interested at the time. Hopefully, you at least kept their business card and literature in a retrievable place now that it would be handy to have!

5.31 USING PROFESSIONAL SOURCES TO LOCATE CONSULTANTS

If you want your consultant to be a professional in both their field of expertise and their business of consultancy, then your search should focus primarily on profes-sional sources of information about consultants. If, on the other hand, your need is for someone good, but not necessarily a top gun, to handle a routine assignment then your search will be more confined and less involved. You may even know of such a consultant already, heard other business associates speak about using a consultant, or perhaps even find a good one in the telephone book or through your local chamber of commerce.

Those consultants who attach themselves to their profession and the business of consultancy are more likely to be found through professional channels. By having acquired more years of experience in their profession and in business, they often discard the more speculative sources of promoting their services, preferring instead to become more heavily involved with their industry, field, particular clientelle, and deeper in-volvement with professional associations and other consultants. When seeking out these consultants, you should contact these excellent sources of information and re-ferral.

- Make inquiries of other managers in your own organization about their knowl-edge of the kind of consultant sought. Also, check with your human resources manager to see if a file has been kept on consultants, or see if your company maintains a file on consultants' newsletters.

- Make similar inquiries to your colleagues in other organizations.

• Check the membership directory to professional or trade associations to which you belong, or call other associations specific to the nature of the assignment.

• Look in trade magazines for consultant ads or articles written by consultants, then call the magazine's editor to get the consultant's address and phone number.

• Call or write to these associations who have members in diverse fields of consulting specialities:

1. Institute of Management Consultants (IMC)
   19 West 44th Street, Suite 810
   New York, NY 10036
   (212) 921-2885

   Request Association Of Managing Consultants Directory

2. Consultant News 17 Templeton Road
   Fitzwilliam, NH 03447

   Request Directory Of Management Consultants

• When your need for a consultant pertains to human resource matters, you should additionally contact these sources for referral information, including how to contact their local affiliates:

1. American Society For Personnel Administration (ASPA)
   606 North Washington Street
   Alexandria, VA 22314
   (203) 548-3440

   Mostly Private Sector

2. International Personnel Management Association (IPMA)
   1850 K Street, N.W., Suite 870
   Washington, D.C. 20006
   (202) 833-5860

   Mostly Public Sector

3. American Society For Training And Development (ASTD)
   1630 Duke Street, Box 1443
   Alexandria, VA 22313
   (703) 683-8170

5.32 SOLE SOURCE SELECTION VERSUS REQUEST FOR PROPOSALS

Professional consultants known in their field, industry, and/or geographic area are usually engaged as a sole source selection be it by referral, reputation, or return engagement. There often evolves a certain kind of comfortable reliability and organizational familiarity between sole source consultants and their clients.

Another form of sole source selection emanates from the specialized nature of the assignment to which there is one known person or firm who has developed the needed kind of expertise, methods, processes, or materials. In these situations, there usually exists a very explicit organizational need. What and how the client organization wants simply points to a sole source provider, so client and consultant simply go about negotiating details of the assignment. A slightly different version of this type of sole source selection is in the case of a very few competing consultants who offer very similar specializations that are suitable to the client's needs. Here, the client may wish to make its selection from among these few solicited competitors.

The other frequently used method of selecting consultants is the Request For Proposal (RFP). This method is normally used only in those cases where the client organization has not had prior experience in dealing with a suitable consultant of the type needed, does not wish to rely on the strength of a referral, and wishes to identify what is believed to be the best consultant through this competitive process among those consultants providing the same or similar service. Here, I would remind you that there is much more to the selection of a consultant who can create valuable results than merely cost. One only needs to see the condition of many city streets to question the value of lowest bidders!

Most busy consultants won't respond to RFPs; they don't need to and the process is usually viewed as a waste of time or too speculative at best. It is often seen as a guessing game in terms of what the client really wants, has preferences or predispositions towards, and how much or little has been budgeted to get the job done. However, if the proposal process is made simple and straightforward, you're more likely to get better response from those who might not otherwise participate. One way to do this is to request a letter proposal rather than thick, verbose, fluffy, and impressively bound proposals that no one wants to wade through anyway. After all, one of the things you want to evaluate about a consultant is if they can get to the point in a thorough yet concise manner. In addition to the value that might be derived in using an RFP for consultant selection, the document can become a beneficial attachment to a general contract or letter of engagement once the selection is made.

The contents of client-prepared RFPs vary depending on the nature of the issue, desired processes or methodologies, and other conditions of the assignment. In those circumstances where the organization knows what it wants done—usually expressed in terms of tasks and results—but is open to, or unclear about, the methods and processes to be used, the organization may ask solicited consultants to describe their approach to the tasks and how it is beneficial to producing prescribed results. Doing so also communicates to the consultant that either the client organization has no experience in this area, or the client is knowledgeable but in search of some fresh, innovative ideas. Nevertheless, a few of the more common content topics used in RFPs are:

1. **Project Statement;** in which the consultant is to articulate their understanding of the nature of the assignment; its background, conditions, and requirements; deadlines, and desired results.

2. **Work Methodology;** providing background on the consultant's techniques, processes, and methods of performing the work of each different phase; resources needed or to be used; and products that will result.

3. **Project Schedule;** giving a description or illustration of start/completion dates of each phase of the project and delivery of the final product/report.

4. **Fees and Expenses;** in which the consultant provides a breakdown of fees and expenses, total project cost (or estimated ranges), and their required method of fee payment (billings).

As a selection device then, the RFP serves as a tool to screen down to a few of the better proposal writers who are asked to undergo further evaluation such as interviews, reference checks, and negotiating contract details.

5.33 CONSULTANT INTERVIEWS AND REFERENCE CHECKS

Like any other important selection process, the selection of a consultant should include an interview conducted by key executives of the client organization followed by at least a few reference checks. Remember, you're interviewing professionals so the process demands that you use only top level professionals to conduct the interview. In fact, once a selection is made, many consultants will insist on a private interview or meeting with the company's CEO or president for the purpose of determining whether or not the assignment is mutually acceptable in all respects, and the likelihood of a positive outcome for both parties.

In conducting your consultants' interview, you should notify each firm by telephone of their appointed time, the date, location, and where they can find parking. Allow sufficient time for a lengthy discussion of questions and issues, but stay on schedule. Before the interviews, you should meet briefly with those conducting it to assure that they are prepared to review issues, and to go over basic questions that will be asked of each consultant. This will lead to a more orderly and time-efficient process. You may wish to consider asking some of the following questions.

- How long has the firm been in business and what were the prior backgrounds of its principals?

- Who is to be directly involved in handling this project, what are their backgrounds, and what roles will they play?

- What other types of projects has the firm performed, and for what kinds of organizations?

- With whom in the organization will the consultant (team) interact?

- What is the projected cost (if not already quoted), method of fee calculation, and estimated completion time for the project. Has a work schedule been developed? What, if any, additional expenses are foreseen?

- Under what circumstances has the consultant rejected or broken-off client relationships?

- To which professional associations does the consultant belong, and do principles or other staff possess any professional certifications?

- What is the firm's operating philosophy, and by what code of ethics does it abide by?

- Have any staff taught college courses, delivered formal speeches, published technical articles, or held association officer positions?

- How does the firm stay abreast of developments in the field?

- What methods of quality control are used by the firm?

- What percentage of the firm's clients are repeat business, and what percentage of the firm's recommendations have been implemented with successful results?

In addition to your interviewer's evaluative assessment of these and more project-specific questions, there are other important characteristics of a consultant to be considered. For the most part they are qualitative in nature, and they have to do with how the consultant "fits" your organization and/or the circumstances surrounding the project. Such qualitative characteristics include the consultant's:

- Honesty
- Sincerity
- Integrity
- Insightfulness
- Confidence
- Maturity
- Practicality
- Demeanor
- Personality

After concluding interviews, the panel should discuss the relative strengths and weaknesses of each, then reach a consensus opinion on who is to be selected after a reference check. The reference evaluation should be completed promptly and, if results are satisfactory, the other competing consultants notified as to your decision.

If not already available to you, a request should be made of your selected consultant to provide a list of client references. This should include a contact person, their position title, company name, address, telephone number, and type of work performed. You may wish to request only those clients where the consultant has performed the same or similar work, but this may limit an accurate picture of the consultant's diversity or success with other kinds of work. Yet another approach is to request three to five present or recent client references and a similar number with which the consultant no longer does work (and try to learn why this is so).

When contacting the consultant's references, you should consider following these steps:

1. Identify yourself by name, title, company, and the nature of the project for which this consultant is under consideration.

2. Inform the contact person that their name has been given to you by the consultant as a reference, and ask them to provide you with an overview of the consultant's work and relationship with people in their organization.

3. If not addressed during this general discussion, key in on these points.

   • Did the consultant do what they said they were going to do and what you wanted them to do?

   • How did they handle themselves with others in your organization? Were there any special situations or sensitive conditions involved and, if so, how were these handled?

   • Were all time commitments met including meetings, progress milestones, and the submission of reports?

   • How would you rate their technical competence and methods?

   • Were any problems encountered with this consultant during or after their work for you? Do you, or would you, continue to use their services?

   • Were the consultant's results worth the cost of the project?

   • Would you do anything differently in managing your project or working with this consultant if you had it to do over again?

   • Do you recommend that we use them for our project and, if so, do you have any advice about working with them?

5.34 ENTERING INTO A FORMAL AGREEMENT

There are a vast number of assignment situations for which consultants are engaged ranging from an informal task of a few hours to highly formalized, complex, and long term projects involving substantial resources and details. The manner in which these relationships are entered into can be equally diverse. The norm is to develop some sort of formal, written agreement that addresses pertinent details of the engagement and business relationship. It is perhaps one of the most critical steps in the relationship and outcome of the work to be done, since its purpose is to define various elements of the entire transaction between the parties. An early and clear agreement on these elements is essential if problems and misunderstandings are to be avoided.

The three most commonly used methods of formal agreements are the project (proposal) letter, the general services agreement, and the project agreement. All are considered contractual with respect to binding the parties to the terms specified, but they vary in degrees of formality, length, and specificity of detail as illustrated below.

1. **Project Letter:** This is the shortest and least formal of the three methods because it is in letter form and categorically specifies only pertinent details of the project work itself. It typically covers such elements as the project statement (purpose and intended results); the delivery methods (what is to be done by whom and by what means); the work schedule (starting, milestones, and completion dates); and costs (including payment schedule and billing methods).

   A consultant's proposal letter can be used as an attachment to the client's letter of engagement which, in addition to accepting the proposal, clarifies any elements such as starting date, fees, or other details needing redress or amplification. If consultant's proposal letter is insufficient in detail for purposes of an engagement agreement, then the project letter may have to be redrafted to reflect more explicit details of the work and other understandings between the parties.

   Project letters are a particularly useful agreement method on short, routine, straightforward, and simple projects. They are also commonly used for slightly longer, more involved projects with consultants well known to the client organization where mutual trust and ethical familiarity has developed over a period of time working together.

2. **General Services Agreement:** Some organizations need and like the idea of having one or more consultants available on an ongoing, as-needed basis to perform different kinds of services offered by their firm. This is particularly true of, and popular with, smaller organizations who do not have (or perhaps yet need) internal resource expertise to handle certain situations. For example, many organizations do not consider hiring human resource professionals until they reach 100+ employees. But, the absence of such a professional does not lessen their legal or administrative need to develop and manage numerous operational functions. In these cases, technical expertise is needed in the areas of policy, pay and benefits, job descriptions, recordkeeping, training, perform-

ance appraisal, planning, advice to management, problem solving, and so forth.

The general services agreement responds to this need for ongoing and diversified services. The agreement is a formal contract—usually renewable from year-to-year—sets forth the kinds of services provided by the consultant which can be accessed by the client, addresses other contractual detail relative to the consultant-client relationship, and usually requires the advance payment of a retainer fee against which the consultant deducts time (hours) or amounts (rates) as services are used that are documented in monthly or periodic statements. If developed and used properly, it can be a very effective method of establishing a clear, yet flexible, means of using a consultant's services without going through a lot of repetitive transaction paperwork each time these services are needed. You merely need to call the consultant to arrange different assignments or, better yet, draft the details of each engagement in a brief assignment letter.

3. **Project Agreement:** This is the most common form of a consultant services contract when a singular or very specific set of services are to be provided to the client. Its use suggests that there is no present intent to use the consultant for anything outside the prescribed scope or other detail of the contractual project arrangement. Some of the issues that should be addressed in such agreements are:

a) The *nature, purpose, and desired results* of the project (what is to be done and why the consultant is being engaged).

b) The specific *scope and objectives* of the project (details of who is going to do what, how it is to be done, and what particular results are to be achieved—stated in measurable terms).

c) A description of *staffing and reporting* relationships (how many and what kind of staff is consultant to use, use of subcontractors, involvement of client staff, project coordinators, consultant and staff as independent contractors).

d) The *role and responsibilities* of both parties (a further description of any necessary distinctions between client and consultant in terms of who is to do what, authorities, obligations, and the means of resolving conflicts).

e) The *work schedule* (when each part or phase is to be completed, progress report dates and methods, final results deadline, mutual obligation for timely response, unforeseen delays).

f) Relevant issues in conjunction with *records access, confidentiality, and working papers* (who, what, and under what conditions will the consultant be able to access company records, assurances concerning the strict maintenance of confidentiality and no reuse of protected company information, turning consultant's working papers over to client upon completion).

g) Details of the *project cost, contingencies, billings, and schedule of payment.*

Some of the most frequently used contract clauses for project agreements which are used to embody the above descriptive detail are the following. Remember though, because the document legally binds the parties to good faith performance, it is important that each clause be mutually agreeable to both parties, and that they seek the review and advice of their respective legal counsels.

- Parties Involved
- Services Rendered
- Start/Completion Dates
- Additional Work
- Support Services
- Work Delegation
- Contingencies
- Advertising
- Employment Status

- Reimbursement
- Expenses
- Late Payment Penalty
- Confidentiality
- Product Ownership
- Legal Process
- Stop Work
- Termination
- Signatures[2]

5.40 WORKING WITH CONSULTANTS AND DEALING WITH THEIR RESULTS

Working with consultants can be quite different than the normal relationship that usually evolves between professionals. Unlike working with internal professionals, consultants are independent; detached from those conditions that create the organization's "culture"; they are not bound by any of the policies or rituals; and the relationship is contractual with very specific, if not limited, purpose. Frequently, however, the relationship can quickly become a close one in which mutual trust, respect, and appreciation develops. When it occurs, it is usually because of the shared experiences attached to working through and resolving a tough problem.

To dispel a common myth about professional consultants, they may enjoy the advantages of not being attached to the kinds of problems and familiarities that internal managers have to live with daily, but that doesn't mean that consultants are im-

---

[2] _____; "Corporate Services Consultants Directory", Winter/Spring 1987, Small Business Report, p. 23.

mune and unaffected by the conditions being encountered by their clients. Quite the contrary would be closer to the truth. Most professional consultants are not merely chasing a buck and trying to escape the rigidity of bureaucratic life. Rather, they truly want to make a difference with their client problems by creating workable solutions. Their fee is to sustain them and their business, but the real payoff for these consultants is creating change that works—contributing something valuable toward the client's success and receiving an appreciative handshake when the job is done.

When you or your organization sign a contract with a consultant, you're not likely to be handed a booklet entitled, "Suggestions About The Installation And Care Of Your New Consultant." After all, consultants are just people hired on a temporary basis to do a job, so no big deal, right? Wrong; it is precisely that attitudinal assumption that has contributed to many failed consultant-client relationships, and therefore *mutual* results. If you want any business transaction to be successful, diligent effort must be put forth. In bringing new people into an organizational setting, this is no less true for consultants than it is for new employees. Because consultants are normally experienced professionals, they adapt quickly but they still need your help and involvement throughout their stay to bring their purpose to a fruitful conclusion. The following, then, might serve you well as just such an instructional guide to working with consultants for the purpose of creating success.

5.41 WHY CLIENT-CONSULTANT RELATIONSHIPS SOMETIMES FAIL

From time to time the representative of a client organization and their consulting firm find themselves in a chasm. They may not even be certain as to how their relationship or respective position on issues got that way, but what is apparent is that they are far apart and deeply entrenched in their differences from what was expected and desired. The usual result is either a sort of polite conflict where the client makes a diplomatic stab at getting the consultant to reexamine some issue(s) (as evidenced by those fearful clients who ask for preliminary reports); or the consultant's work gets "shelved" due to the client's disdain for the consultant personally, their findings and recommendations (sometimes because they're painfully accurate), or that results just don't fit the organization's needs or character. I, myself, have met many business people who've become disillusioned about the use of consultants, not just because of their insufficient background, but because of such things as their blind autonomy process, methods used, self-righteousness, their occasional vigilante orientation, or a preoccupation with concept that never quite touches the reality of the situation.

Consultants, too, have their own picture of failed client relationships but, as human nature would have it, it is usually attributable to some fault of the client. Such conditions include the client's inability, or benevolent blindness to see and accept that which has been made obvious and right by the consultant; stubborn attachment to a wrong position, behavior, or course of action; unwillingness to face facts and act accordingly; and the client's overindulgent insistence on trying to influence particular results.

Like any other kind of business relationship there will probably always exist reasons for, and stories about, client-consultant failures. Hopefully they will lessen in number and frequency as the consulting profession continues its present course toward increasing sophistication, and the difficulties of staying in business as a consultant drives the meek and marginally suited consultants into other endeavors. Meanwhile, organizational managers are learning that not all consultants are alike, and that it is no more appropriate to give up on the usefulness of all consultants than it would be to "throw the baby out with the washwater," despite this tendency as a solution when one is on the buying end of services.

What causes most failures in client-consultant relationships, and the work product that results, is the use of traditional work relation transactions rather than collaborative planning and problem solving transactions. In traditional client-consultant transactions the consultant is choosen from some selection process—usually predicated more on task and cost criteria. The consultant then acquires background information from the client representative (problem identification and possibly causal sources), disappears to independently study the situation, and later (in isolation of countless internal factors) comes up with their findings and recommendations. When traditional selection processes work it's usually where the assignment inherently lends itself to an isolated process (i.e., is not influenced nor affected by other organizational factors); it is unnecessary for the consultant to interact with others in the organization, or the outcome is only relevant in a specialized or technical sense to one small part of the organization. Admittedly, such a qualification eliminates many workplace problem situations for which consultants are hired, and therefore points to the fact that the traditional approach may not work very well absent these qualifications.

What is far more appropriate to most organizational problem-solving situations where mutual satisfaction is most likely to occur, is in using the collaborative work relationship approach. The collaborative approach recognizes at the onset that the client representative is both a technical and organizational expert in the sense of such matters as:

- The nature of any given problem(s).

- Possible sources of organizational or other influences.

- The nature of the organization itself including its people, processes, styles of decision making, and the like.

- Resource people available and sources of information.

- Perceptions, ideas, and/or conclusions as to how the situation should be dealt with and expectations of the outcome(s).

The consultant, on the other hand, is recognized for their qualities, characteristics, and expertise such as:

- Technical, managerial, and organizational background.

- Subject and process experience.

- Problem identification, fact finding, and creative problem solving abilities as a result of repetitive dealing with the situation in a variety of settings.

- Objectivity inherent in personal detachment from the influences or effects of the situation.

These respective characteristics of both client and consultant representatives are essential ingredients of a successful work relationship and project conclusion. They should be discussed and recognized openly as well as early in their association. Doing so not only has the advantage of establishing mutual rapport, but also contributes to the necessary defining of roles, clarification of issues, and the surfacing of any prevailing predispositions, fallacious views, unlikely events, and untenable solutions or expectations. Collectively, there are three steps in achieving a collaborative client-consultant relationship and these consist of getting the relationship started, working together, and dealing with results as discussed in the following sections.

5.42 GETTING STARTED ON THE RIGHT FOOT

Effective relations that are to be the prelude of a successful working and results association between client and consultant must be mutually desired, and a conscious effort of both parties. One person cannot develop nor sustain a relationship. Since it is the client who chooses the consultant, and the consultant who accepts preliminary conditions of the assignment, then the courtship so to speak has begun. Therein may lie the reason we use the term engagement to depict this business relationship.

Collaboration means the mutually sharing of information, resources, talent, and energy toward some common goal by means of help, cooperation, and assistance. It is rarely achieved without some form of acknowledgement of a mutual desire or need for its existence, the characteristics each brings to it, or the presence of commitment towards its development. That may sound more inspirational than actual fact, but evidence consistently reminds us that it is the inability to communicate, or the allowing of communication barriers, that causes most breakdowns in various kinds of relationships. So, the initial step in developing an effective client-consultant relationship is to get started on the right foot by using the collaborative approach to establish two-way communications between client and consultant. Naturally, emphasis will be placed on problem identification, process planning, and problem solving of the issue(s) at hand, but the establishment of a successful relationship will be built upon accomplishing these conditions as a result of initial meetings.

1. Seek Rapport Based on Trust and Respect

Aside from getting to know each other on a diplomacy and personal(ity) level, it is helpful for both parties to gain more insight into each other's professional background, experiences, attitudes, and styles of dealing with business matters. A casual meeting away from the work setting, such as having lunch in conjunction with a business meeting, is a good way to delve into this kind of familiarity.

What should also be disclosed is what each wants or doesn't want, will or won't do, and needs from the other person—or persons to be involved. The conversation need not be brutally frank, merely honest, polite, and to the point. The goal, of course, is to let each other know where you stand as a person and professional in your respective roles, as well as ways in which you can rely on each other. By opening up to each other, both gain valuable insight in terms of how best to work together and accomplish the task at hand. Each should quickly learn to trust and respect the other from this sort of initial transaction.

2. Share Sensitive Information and Difficult Situations

Many people have difficulty even admitting to the existence of a problem let alone the ability to cope with the process of unearthing it. As you might expect, there aren't too many workplace problems that are absent some degree of sensitivity or peculiar difficulty of the situation. If client and consultant are to be effective in dealing with realities, then there must be a mutual willingness, or agreement, to deal with these conditions in an open manner. However, in order to gain the client's confidence that these matters will be properly handled, the consultant should be prepared to offer some concrete assurances that confidentiality, discretion, and other ethical standards will be maintained including the consultant's willingness to sign nonuse/non-disclosure kinds of documents.

There are any number of very sensitive kinds of information and awkward situations that occur in the workplace. So whether the issue is competency, illegality, or behavior dysfunction within the client organization, or the emergence of a delicate issue within the consultant's operation, both parties must be willing to share the full extent of the situation with each other and then agree on a course of action.

3. Provide Support

Client and consultant should let each other know about their willingness and respective abilities, limitations, and conditions for providing support. The kind of support needed in any given assignment can vary considerably, so it may also be helpful to identify them. With respect to conducting the work, support may mean access to documents, cooperation from other managers and employees, availability of facilities and equipment, scheduling needs, or perhaps clerical tasks.

Yet other kinds of support can be even more instrumental to the client-consultant relationship. These include such things as exchanging assurances to keep each other informed of developments (frequent contact), being responsive to each other's requests (and phone calls), providing regular feedback to each other, working through differences that arise, and keeping their respective principals accurately appraised of what has, is, or will happen during the course of the project. This is a good way to control rumor, speculation, and false impressions.

With these kinds of initial discussions and agreements the collaborative client-consultant relationship is ready to take on more of a functional form. Subsequent meetings and contact will then apply this base of understandings to planning, execution, and conclusion phases of the project.

5.43 MANAGING THE PROJECT TOGETHER

The collaborative approach places emphasis on key opportunities to work together rather than dealing with the conditions of a project in isolation of each other. One of these key opportunities is the project background and planning meeting. Here, client and consultant representatives' respective areas of expertise come sharply into play. Each one approaches this meeting from the perspective of the characteristic strengths of their roles, and with a partnership orientation toward the entire project. The order and results of this business meeting should be as follows.

1. **Backgrounding the Project**

   This is the opportunity for the consultant to gain important details, insight, and a thorough overview of the project, and a time for the client to tell all. These aspects of any given workplace problem should be fully addressed:

   - History of the issue(s) and particular detail as to how it evolved to present conditions

   - What exactly is the present condition, and what are the suspected causal sources and known effects?

   - How are these effects defined as adverse?

   - Who are the people that are directly or indirectly involved—who has what responsibilities?

- What documents or materials exist relevant to the issue(s)?

- What are the expected or desired outcomes of this situation?

2. **Planning the Work Process**

In many cases much of this detail will already be addressed in consultant's proposal response. However, sometimes that detail can be rather general and this is the time to jointly lay out, discuss, and come to an understanding about the entire work process. The issues to be covered here include:

- The different phases of each part of the project and their estimated start/ completion dates.

- The specific work plan and processes to be used in each phase.

- Consultant and client staff resources needed in each phase, and what their respective roles and responsibilities are to be.

- The clarifying of roles of the client and consultant representatives in each phase, what is needed from each other, when are progress reports or meetings to occur, and how problems are to be addressed.

One of the more important roles for the client and consultant representatives to play is to help each other coordinate events, ensure that responsibilities are being carried out, keep each other posted on events and progress, and be willing to make any necessary adjustments as the work unfolds.

3. **Gathering and Verifying Information**

Nearly all problems relating to the workplace and its human resources will involve some sort of information gathering process. For this reason the consultant must be adept at knowing what kind of information is germane to any given set of circumstances. The consultant must have sufficient experience to know what kinds of questions to ask or processes to use to uncover all the right information that will point to the causal source of the problem. The consultant must be equally skilled in how to become quickly familiar with the organization so that a meaningful solution can be developed to fit the combined conditions of problem and solution (or treatment).

The only way this is likely to occur—or occur with any reasonable degree of accuracy—is for the client and consultant representatives to consciously collaborate on this vital phase since it usually becomes the foundation of conclusions and recommendations (i.e., supporting evidence). The process itself requires planning, concentrated thought, and the cooperative effort of anyone who has access to relevant information.

For example, when I am confronted with a difficult or perhaps obscure client situation, I will ask my client counterpart to set up a meeting with any other internal people who are connected to the issue in an important way. I will ask them to give advance thought to the issue by jotting down and bringing notes. I do the same, but my notes include given facts or speculation on the nature of the issue as well as a preliminary set of questions I want to ask the group when we meet. In this meeting I will ask each person to articulate their views, interject questions, encourage a free-flow discussion once everyone has addressed the issue, and ask my prepared questions. Simultaneously I am taking notes. Based on the kind of information that emerges from this multiple source, I will give them a summary review, seek their concurrence or modification, identify what I need from them in the way of documents or other supporting information, and proceed accordingly with a better prospect of enlisting their further cooperation if needed at a later time.

Other workplace problem situations may require a more "clinically pure" information gathering process such as competency or behavioral evaluations, or matters dealing with perceptual differences within the organization as in the dysfunctioning of a management team. In these situations a more appropriate process by the consultant would be to key in on one internal resource person who is personally unattached to the players, collaborate with that resource person, then go about gathering separate information from each person connected to the problem. This process will require more than the usual amount of cross-reference verification of information that is gathered from each person involved, since the underlying nature of the problem is their attachment to their own truth and reality.

When client and consultant representatives mutually share in the backgrounding, planning, and execution of the project there is likely to be few (if any) surprises, delays, misunderstandings, or internal misconceptions about what is going on. Such a relationship is also more likely to ensure a smoother, more orderly, and accurate undertaking of any process applied to a workplace situation. Once the process is completed, it is time to deal with the bottom line—results!

5.44 DEALING JOINTLY WITH RESULTS

When all is said and done, it is up to the consultant to produce results for the client. This can be the toughest part of the relationship—to come up with a suitable, useable, and worthy plan of action that leaves the client organization in a substantially better position than it was at the onset of the engagement. Where the traditional approach is used, this means that the consultant would scurry off to their office for a couple of weeks where they assemble and write their final report, and proudly put it in the mail along with their final billing—another job well done! Wrong; the most important part of the engagement has only begun.

Let's replay the same tape using the collaborative approach. Picking up where the consultant scurries off to prepare their report, we might find the consultant contacting the client once or twice during the report preparation to verify information, clarify some final issues, or to use the client as a "sounding board" for a new idea—these can occur frequently during the big-picture development of a comprehensive report. Some fairly novel solutions can result, but they may not fit well if it isn't checked out.

The consultant then produces their semi-final results, be it a full report, just findings and recommendations, or new documents and information. Rather than binding and sending off as a final result, the collaborative consultant mails this draft to their client contact person for review. At the same time, the consultant calls to notify this person of the mailing and arranges a meeting date to go over the results. In this meeting they jointly review each part to ensure its clarity, accuracy and thoroughness, applicability to real issues, and the propriety of results.

It is this last item that should receive the most attention since all else simply is in support of the results, and results are what the client is most interested in having. Here is where the communication skills and integrity of their relationship will be tested because it is a time for candor. If the consultant's results are shallow, both should discuss how results can be strengthened; if the proposed results won't quite fit conditions within the organization, these issues and alternative approaches should be explored; and if the results are suitable and satisfy the objective(s), then the consultant should be acknowledged for their work.

Before this meeting is concluded, the collaborative client-consultant relationship will discuss a final, usually critical subject; that being implementation. Both parties should realize that the job isn't truly done until the goal is achieved, and that can only be accomplished by implementing some course of action based on consultant's results. Regrettably, this step is a common oversight by many consultants who forget this fact because they're unaffected by the client organization's action. The collaborative consultant will, however, recognize the importance of implementation as well as realize that clients may agree with the results but feel uncertain as to how best to implement them. Discussing various features and approaches to implementation of results is much the same as any work planning process. But, when implementation involves the solving of workplace problems, due consideration needs to be given to maximizing the goal and minimizing adversities. Here are just a few of the elements to be discussed and worked out in this meeting concerning implementation.

- What information is confidential or sensitive, and requires restraint from other?

- Who should receive what information, and what should they be asked to do?

- Which people in the organization should have, or be included in, what kinds of decisions and actions?

- Will there be any type of resistence and, if so, from whom about what; how can this be overcome?

- What are reasonable time frames to attach to each part of the implementation, and who will/should be responsible for each part?

- Are there any special preparations or processes that should be used with any part of the implementation plan (e.g., training program, departmental meetings, a grievance procedure, etc.)?

- Is there a particularly useful role for the consultant during implementation?

At the conclusion of this meeting, the consultant is in a much improved position to make any final modifications to their results, thereby assuring that the goals of each have been accomplished—a client that is pleased with the work, and a solution that fits and will work in the client's best interest. The consultant also has the advantage now of proposing a particular course of action for the client's implementation of results. In other words, the final report should now contain *what* should be done (results), and *how* it should be done (implementation).

When consultant's findings or recommendations are of a particularly sensitive nature (e.g., perhaps bordering on defamation of a client employee), then the client and consultant representatives should agree on one of two ways to handle this information.

1. Omit this kind of information from the report because it may inadvertently fall into the wrong hands later when the presence of such information may have been forgotten, but provide it verbally or in a separate document to the organization's top executive and marked "confidential."

2. Include this information in proper context of the report but qualify it as "privileged and confidential" information. Most state courts are likely to hold harmless consultants and similar advisors who deal with sensitive information in the interest of a client; provided reasonable safeguards and good faith efforts are present to protect the exchange of information. Such was the finding of the California Appeals Court in *Los Angeles Airways, Inc. v. Davis* (1982) when the court determined that an advisor's conduct is privileged under California law if it is motivated in part by a desire to benefit his principal.

Once the final report is submitted to the client, and enough time allowed for its digesting, the collaborative approach should follow-up with a meeting of the client-consultant representatives and the organization's top executive. This meeting is held to review and conclude the issues, and seek direction on a course of action.

REFERENCES

PART I. SOLVING PROBLEMS INVOLVING DISCRIMINATORY ACTIONS

Chapter 1.0 Problems Characterized By Workforce Age And Age Discrimination

Bentell, Nicholas J.; "Managing The Older Worker." Personnel Administration, Aug. 1983.

Blocklyn, Paul L.; "The Aging Workforce." Personnel, August 1987.

Carlson, Elliot; "Longer Work Life." Modern Maturity, June-July 1985.

Challenger, James E.; "Older Managers Are Making A Resurgence." Personnel Journal, July 1986.

Foley, Robt. H., et al.; "Age Discrimination And Personnel Psychology: A Review And Synthesis Of The Legal Literature With Implications For Future Research." Personnel Psychology, 1984, No. 37.

Friedman, Dana E.; "Eldercare: The Employee Benefit Of The 1990's". Across The Board, June 1986.

Jones, Edward W. Jr.; "What It's Like To Be A Black Manager." Same

Kahn, Steven C. et al.; *Personnel Director's Legal Guide* [Supplemented]. N.Y.: Warren, Gocham & Lamont, 1986.

Kieffer, Jarold; "New Roles For Older Workers." Aging, Feb.-March 1984.

Levesque, Joseph D.; *Manual Of Personnel Policies, Procedures, And Operations.* N.J.: Prentice-Hall, 1986.

Levinson, Harry; "On Being A Middle Age Manager." *In The Executive Dilemma: Handling People Problems At Work.* N.Y.: Howard Business Review, 1985.

Murphy, B.S., Barlow, W.E. & Hatch, D.D. eds.; "Manager Newsfront." Personnel Journal, 1984-1988.

Schrank, Robert; "Two Women, Three Men On A Raft." Same

Snyder, Robt. A. and Brandon, B.; "Riding The Third Wave: Staying On Top Of ADEA Complaints." Personnel Administrator, Feb. 1983. "ADEA Update: Case Law And Cost As A Defense." Personnel Administration, Feb. 1985.

_____; "EEOC Reports 16,000 Age Discrimination Charges Nationwide." Aging, Feb.-March 1984.

_____; "Job Commission Releases New Studies On Older Workers." Aging, Feb.-March 1984.

_____; Personnel Managers Legal Reporter, 1985-1988.

_____; "Benefits Important In Costs Of Employing Elderly." Employee Benefit Plan Review, March 1985.

Chapter 2.0 Problems Based On The Race, Color, Or National Origin Of Employees

Agege, Chas. O.; "Employment Discrimination Against Aliens: The Constitutional Implications." Labor Law Journal, February 1985.

Almquist, Elizabeth McTaggart; *Minorities, Gender, and Work*. Lexington, Mass.: Lexington Books, 1979.

Berry, D.P. and Appleman, J.T.; "Policing The Hiring Of Foreign Workers: Employers Get The Job." Personnel, March 1987.

Bowen, David; *The Struggle Within: Race Relations In The United States*. New York: W.W. Norton & Company, 1965.

Burnstein, Paul; *Discrimination, Jobs, and Politics: The Struggle for Equal Employment Opportunity in the United States Since the New Deal*. Chicago, Ill.: University of Chicago Press, 1985.

Gossett, Thomas F.; *Race: The History Of An Idea In America*. New York: Schocken Books, 1965.

Jones, Edward W. Jr.; "What It's Like To Be A Black Manager." In *The Executive Dilemma: Handling People Problems At Work*. New York: Harvard Business Review, 1985.

Kahn, Steven C. et al.; *Personnel Director's Legal Guide* [Supplemented]. Boston: Warren, Gorham & Lamont, 1986.

Levesque, Joseph D.; *Manual of Personnel Policies, Procedures, And Operations*. New Jersey: Prentice-Hall, 1986.

Loye, David; *The Healing of a Nation*. New York: W.W. Norton & Company, 1971.

Manley, Marisa; "Coping With The New Immigration Law." INC., August 1987.

May, Bruce D.; "Law Puts Immigration Control In Employers' Hands." Personnel Journal, March 1987.

Norback, Craig T.; *The Human Resources Yearbook*. New Jersey: Prentice-Hall, 1986.

Shaeffer, Ruth G.; *Nondiscrimination In Employment: Changing Perspectives, 1963-1972*. A Research Report from The Conference Board (no date).

Sisneros, Antonio; "Early Application Of Contemporary Race-Conscious Law In The Lower Federal Courts." Labor Law Journal, 1986.

Soshnick, Julian; "Lawful Employment Of Aliens." Employment Relations Today, Winter 1985-86.

Steinfield, Melvin; *Cracks In The Melting Pot: Racism and Discrimination in American History*. Beverly Hills, CA: Glencoe Press, 1970.

Yin, Robert K.; *Race, Creed, Color, or National Origin: A Reader on Racial and Ethnic Identities in American Society*. Washington, D.C.: M.I.T., 1973.

_____; *Legislature History of Titles VII and XI of Civil Rights Act of 1964*. Washington, D.C.: Equal Employment Opportunity Commission (no date).

_____; *Equality In Respect of Employment Under Legislation and Other National Standards*. Geneva, Switzerland: La Tribune De Geneve, 1967.

Chapter 3.0 Problems In A Mixed Workforce Part I: Gender Discrimination and Sexual Harassment

Bernokraitis, Nijole V. and Feagin, J.R.; *Modern Sexism: Blatant, Subtle, And Covert Discrimination*. N.J.: Prentice-Hall, 1986.

Collins, Eliza G.C. and Blodgett, Timothy B.; "Sexual Harassment...Some See It... Some Won't" in *The Executive Dilemma: Handling People Problems At Work*. N.Y.: Harvard Business Review, 1985.

Feldman, Diane; "Sexual Harassment: Policies And Prevention." Personnel, September 1987.

Freeman, Patricia; "Sexual Harassment: How To Spot It In The Workplace, How To Stop It." Los Angeles, California Business Magazine, Oct. 1986.

Garvey, Margaret S.; "The High Cost Of Sexual Harassment Suits." Costa Mesa: Personnel Journal, Jan. 1986.

Gutek, Barbara A.; *Sex And The Workplace*. S.F.: Jossey-Bass, 1985.

Kahn, Steven C. et al.; *Personnel Director's Legal Guide* [Supplemented]. Boston: Warren, Gorham, Lamont, 1986.

Kohl, John P. and Stephens, David B.; "Expanding The Legal Rights Of Women." Personnel, May 1987.

Levesque, Joseph D.; *Manual of Personnel Policies, Procedures, And Operations*. N.J.: Prentice-Hall, 1986.

Manley, Marisa; "Dealing With Sexual Harassment." Inc. Magazine, May 1987.

McEnery, Jean; "Sexual Harassment in Blue-Collar Jobs—A Problem Unresolved." Employment Relations Today, 1984.

Norback, Craig T.; *The Human Resources Yearbook*. N.J.: PrenticeHall, 1986.

Oshiro, Sandra S.; "Discrimination: It's Not Just Based On Race." The Honolulu Advertiser, Feb. 17, 1987.

Rowe, Mary P.; "Dealing With Sexual Harassment" in *The Executive Dilemma: Handling People Problems At Work*. N.Y.; Harvard Business Review, 1985.

Shaeffer, Ruth G.; *Nondiscrimination In Employment: Changing Perspectives, 1963-1972*. A Research Report From The Conference Board.

Strayer, Jacqueline F. and Rapoport, Sandra E.; "Sexual Harassment, 2: Limiting Corporate Liability." American Management Association, Personnel, April 1986.

Sullivan, Frederick L.; "Sexual Harassment: The Supreme Court's Ruling." AMA, Personnel, Dec. 1986.

Terpstra, David E. & Cook, Susan E.; "Complaint Characteristics And Reported Behaviors And Consequences Associated With Formal Sexual Harassment Charges." Personnel Psychology, 1985.

Thornton, Terry; "Sexual Harassment, 1: Discouraging It in the Work Place." American Management Association, Personnel, April 1986.

Torrey, Jane W.; "A Psychologist's Look At Women" in Sutermeister, Robt. A; *People And Productivity*. N.Y.: McGraw-Hill, 1976.

Woodworth, Margaret and Warner; "The Female Takeover: Threat or Opportunity" in Beach, Dale S.; *Managing People At Work*, Third Ed. N.Y.: MacMillan Pub. Co., 1980.

———; Personnel Manager's Legal Reporter. 1983-1987.

Chapter 4. Problems In A Mixed Workforce, Part II: Romance Between Employees, Pregnancy Discrimination, And Accommodating Child Care Needs

Anderson, C. & Hunsaker, P.; "Why There's Romancing At The Office And Why It's Everybody's Problem." Personnel, February 1985.

Burud, Sandra et al.; *Employer-Sponsored Child Care: Investing In Human Resources*. Mass.: Auburn House, 1985.

Chapman, Fern; "Executive Guilt: Who's Taking Care Of The Children?" Fortune, February 16, 1987.

Clawson, James G. & Dram, Kathy E.; "Managing Cross-Gender Mentoring." Business Horizons, May-June 1984.

Collins, Eliza G.C.; "Managers And Lovers', in *The Executive Dilemma: Handling People Problems At Work*. N.Y.: Harvard Business Review, 1985.

Fenn, Donna; "Kid Stuff: How To Create Affordable Alternatives To On-Site Day Care." INC., September 1987.

Ford, Robert; "Nepotism". Personnel Journal, September 1985.

Friedman, Dana; "Corporate Financial Assistance For Child Care." The Conference Board, Research Bulletin No. 177. (undated).

Horn, P. & Horn, J.; *Sex In The Office: Power And Passion In The Workplace*. Reading, Mass: Addision-Wesley, 1982.

Jamison, Kaleel; "Managing Sexual Attraction In The Workplace." AMA, Personnel Administrator, August 1983.

Jamison, Kaleel; "Sexual Attraction and Productivity." The Executive Female, July-August, 1984.

Johnson, Theresa; "The Legal Background And Implications Of Pregnancy Benefits." Labor Law Journal, June 1984.

Kohl, J.P. and Greenlaw, P.S.; "The Pregnancy Discrimination Act: Compliance Problems." Personnel, November-December 1983.

MacKay, Kathleen; "Corporate Orphans." Los Angeles: California Business Magazine, April 1987.

Magid, Renee Y.; "When Mothers And Fathers Work: How Employers Can Help." Personnel, December 1986.

Mainiero, Lisa A.; "A Review and Analysis of Power Dynamics in Organizational Romances." Academy of Management Review, Vol. 11, No. 4, 1986.

Mason, Jan; "Corporate Kids', Life Magazine, April 1986.

Meredith, Dennis; "Day Care, The Nine-To-Five Dilemma." Psychology Today, February 1986.

Miller, Joyce D.; "Family And Work." Labor Law Journal, August 1986.

Miller, Thomas I.; "The Effects Of Employer-Sponsored Child Care On Employee Absenteeism, Turnover, Productivity, Recruitment Or Job Satisfaction: What Is Claimed And What Is Known." Personnel Psychology, No. 37, 1984.

Mondy, R. Wayne & Premeaux, Shane R.; "People Problems: The Workplace Affair." Management Solutions, November 1986.

Newton, Margaret M.; "Child Care: The Employee Benefit Of The 1990's?" National Underwriter, April 12, 1986.

Pottenger, Dennis; "Sex At The Office." Sacramento Magazine, April 1987. Quinn, Robt. E.; "Coping With Cupid: The Formation, Impact, And Management of Organizational Romance." Administrative Science Quarterly, March 1977.

Powell, Gary N.: "What Do Tomorrow's Managers Think About Sexual Intimacy in the Workplace?" Business Horizons, July-August 1986.

Quinn, Robt. E. & Lees, Patricia L.; "Attraction and Harassment: Dynamics of Sexual Politics in the Workplace." Organizational Dynamics, Autumn 1984.

Smith, Larry; "Corporate-Funded Day Care." Employment Relations Today, Autumn 1985.

Turk, Harry N. & Strauss, Robt. K.; "Can Companies Regulate Marriage And Work? A Look At Antinepotism Policies In Corporate America." Employment Relations Today, Winter 1984-1985.

References

Warfield, Andrea; "Co-Worker Romances: Impact On The Work Group And On Career-Oriented Women." Personnel, May 1987.

———; "Child Care: Get Your Boss To Help." Changing Times Magazine, October 1986.

———; "Changes In The Workplace: Child Care Is Now An Item On The National Agenda." Newsweek Magazine, March 31, 1986.

———; "Love At Work." Personnel Management, January 1986.

Chapter 5.0 Problems Where The Worker Is Physically Handicapped Or A Religious Observer

Burgdorf, Robert L., Jr. ed.; The Legal Rights Of Handicapped Persons. Baltimore: Paul H. Brookes Publishers, 1980.

Carrell, M.R. and Heavin, W.T.; "The 'Handi-Capable' Employee: An Untapped Resource." Personnel, August 1987.

Condon, Susan Goff; "Hiring The Handicapped Confronts Cultural Uneasiness." Personnel Journal, April 1987.

Dansky, Howard; "Hiring The Disabled." Venture, Vol. 5, October 1983.

Emer, Wm. H. & Frink, Catherine B.; "Hiring The Handicapped—What Every Employee Should Know". Employment Relations Today, 1984.

Helburn, I.B. and Hill, John R.; "The Arbitration Of Religious Practice Grievances". The Arbitration Journal, Vol. 39, No. 2, June 1984.

Hull, Kent; The Rights Of Physically Handicapped People. N.Y.: Avon Books, 1979.

Hyner, G.C. and Melby, C.L.; Priorities For Health Promotion & Disease Prevention. Dubuque: Eddie Bowers Publishing Co., 1987.

Kahn, Steven C. et al.; Personnel Directors' Legal Guide [Supplemental]. Boston: Warren, Gorham & Lamont, 1986.

Landry, Judy; "Employment Rights Of The Handicapped: A Survey Of The Developments". International Personnel Management Association, Public Employee Relations Counsellor, No. 1, Vol. 3, 1979.

Lester, R.A. and Caudill, D.W.; "The Handicapped Worker: Seven Myths." Training and Development Journal, August 1987.

Levesque, Joseph D.; Manual Of Personnel Policies, Procedures, And Operations. N.J.: Prentice-Hall, 1986.

Macleod, Jennifer S.; "Integrating Handicapped People Into The Workforce". Employment Relations Today, Autumn 1984.

Manager's Newsfront; Personnel Journal, 1985-1988.

Masi, Dale A.; "AIDS In The Workplace: What Can Be Done?" Personnel, July 1987.

Matusewitch, Eric; "Employment Discrimination Against The Overweight". Personnel Journal, June 1983.

Murphy, Michael J. et al.; *Beyond Paternalism: Local Governments And Rights Of The Disabled*. Washington: ICMA Management Information Service, Report No. 9, December 1981.

Norback, Craig T. ed.; *The Human Resources Yearbook, 1986 Edition*. N.J.: Prentice-Hall, 1986.

Personnel Manager's Legal Reporter; published by Business & Legal Reports; Madison, CT. 1985-1988.

Remmers, Cynthia L.; "Dealing With The Unproductive Employee: With Special Emphasis On Age And Handicap Discrimination". A position paper presented February 24, 1987 through the Council On Education In Management.

Schulnick, Michael W.; "Handicap Discrimination—Guidelines For Alleviating Employer Concerns". Employment Relations Today, Winter 1984-85.

Scott, Richard S.; *From Good Will To Civil Rights: Transforming Federal Disability Policy*. Philadelphia: Temple University Press, 1984.

Stevens, George E.; "Exploding The Myths About Hiring The Handicapped". Personnel, December 1986.

Turk, Harry N.; "EEO Questions—And Answers". Employment Relations Today, Summer 1985 & Winter 1985/86.

Zimmer, Arno B.; *Employing The Handicapped: A Practical Compliance Manual*. N.Y.: Amacom, 1981.

_____; "Section 504 Of The Rehabilitation Act Of 1973—Requirements". Federal Grants Management Handbook, April 1984.

_____; "AIDS Triggers Painful Legal Battles". U.S. News & World Report, March 24, 1986.

_____; "Covering AIDS: A Handbook For Journalists." University of Oregon School of Journalism, September 1987.

_____; *AIDS: Employers Rights And Responsibilities*. Chicago: Commerce Clearing House, 1985.

_____; *AIDS: The Workplace Issues*. New York: American Management Association, 1985.

REFERENCES

PART II. SOLVING PROBLEMS RELATED TO EMPLOYMENT RIGHTS

Chapter 1.0 Problems Concerning Workplace Privacy: Legal Overviews, Drugs/Alcohol Control, And Health Rights Of Employees
—and—
Chapter 2.0 Problems With The Privacy Of Personnel Files And Employment Records

Cook, Suzanne H.; "Privacy Rights: Whose Life Is It Anyway?" Personnel Administration, April 1987.

Duffy, D. Jan; "Conducting Work-Place Investigations: Potential Liabilities For Employers." Employment Relations Today, Spring 1985.

Duffy, D. Jan; "Privacy In The Workplace: Tortious Invasion Of Privacy." Employment Relations Today, Winter 1983-84.

Duffy, D. Jan; "Privacy In The Workplace: Constitutional Restrictions On Employers." Employment Relations Today, Autumn 1984.

Duffy, D. Jan; "Statutory Restrictions On Employers." Employment Relations Today, Spring 1984.

Harris, Donald; "A Matter Of Privacy: Managing Personnel Data In Company Computers." Personnel; February, 1987.

Hoyt, David W. et al.; "Drug Testing In The Workplace—Are Methods Legally Defensible?" Journal of the American Medical Association, Vol. 258, No. 4, 1987.

In Personnel Administrator, March 1988:
   Fraze, James; "Changing Times, Charging Values."
   Fraze, James and Finney, Martha I.; "Employee Rights Between Our Shores."

Kendall, Daniel W.; "Rights Across The Waters."

Kohn, Joseph P.; "When Bad Management Becomes Criminal." INC. Magazine, March 1987.

Mendelsohn, S.R. and Morrison, K.K.; "The Right To Privacy In The Workplace, Part 1: Employee Searches." Personnel, July 1988.

Munchus, George; "An Update On Smoking: Employee's Rights and Employer's Responsibilities." Personnel, August 1987.

Pattison, Robert M. & Shea, Mary J.; "The Secret Truth About Inspection Of Personnel Files." California Labor & Employment Law Quarterly; Vol. 5, No. 5, Spring 1987.

Westin, Alan F.; "The Problem Of Employee Privacy Still Troubles Management"; in Beach, Dale S., Managing People At Work. NY: Macmillan, 1975.

_____; "Employee Drug Screening." National Institute On Drug Abuse, U.S. Department of Health and Human Services, 1986.

_____; "Drugs In The Workplace: Solution For Business And Industry." Bureau of Business Practices, 1987.

_____; "Personnel Manager's Legal Reporter." Business & Legal Reports. Madison, CT, 1986 - 1988.

_____; "Personnel Management - Policies & Practices." Prentice-Hall Information Services. Paramus, N.J.

_____; "Privacy In The Workplace: When Employer-Employee Rights Collide." Modern Business Reports, Alexander Hamilton Institute. NY, 1987.

Chapter 3.0 Problems Of Wrongful Discharge, Part 1: Why Employees Sue, Legal Background, And Firing For Good Cause
-and—
Chapter 4.0 Problems Of Wrongful Discharge, Part 2: Diagnosing Management's Violation Of Employee Rights And Finding Solutions

Dowdle, J.L. and Eide, S.R.; "Avoiding Severance Pay Disputes." Personnel, November 1987.

Fitzgerald, James F.; "Helping Departing Employees Find Another Job." Personnel, August 1987.

Heshizer, Brian; "The New Common Law Of Employment: Changes In The Concept Of Employment At-Will". Labor Law Journal, February 1985.

Heshizer, Brian & Okocha, Nivabueze; "Wrongful Discharge In Britain: Lessons For The United States". The Arbitration Journal, '1 (3), 1986.

Holley, Wm. H. and Wolters, Roger S.; "An Employment At-Will Vulnerability Audit". Personnel Journal, April 1987.

Howard, Cecil G.; "Strategic Guidelines For Terminating Employees." Personnel Administrator, April 1988.

Klotchman, Janisse & Neides, Linda L.; "EEO Alert: Watch Out For Discrimination In Discharge Decisions". Personnel, January-February 1983.

Levesque, Joseph D.; Manual Of Personnel Policies, Procedures, And Operations, N.J.: Prentice Hall, 1986.

Levesque, Joseph D.; "Sound Personnel Operations Are No Mistake(s)".

Lorber, Laurence Z.; "Basic Advice On Avoiding Employment-At-Will Trouble". Personnel Administrator, ²9 (1), 1985.

Richey, P. Jerome; "Signed Waivers With Pay Protect Discharge Process". Personnel Journal, May 1987.

Sculnick, Michael W.; "Respect for Employee Perspective Grows". Employment Relations Today, Spring 1985.

St. Antoine, Theodore J.; "The Revision Of Employment At-Will Enters A New Phase". Labor Law Journal 6 (8), 1985.

_____; "Employee Terminations Law Bulletin", Boston: Quinlan Pub. Co., 1986-1988.

_____; "Personnel Manager's Legal Report". 1986-1988.

_____; "Personnel Practice Ideas". 1986-1988.

REFERENCES

PART III. SOLVING PROBLEMS INVOLVING DIFFICULT EMPLOYEES AND THE ADEQUACY OF WORKPLACE CONTROLS

Chapter 1.0 Problems Concerning Workplace Behavior: Understanding The Nature of Human Behavior Before Attempting Its Control Or Correction
—and—
Chapter 2.0 Problems With Disciplinary Employees: Approaches To Correcting Undesirable Behavior And Performance

Axline, Larry L.; "Identifying And Helping The Troubled Executive". Personnel, November 1987.

Bula, R. J.; "Absenteeism Control". Personnel Journal, June 1984.

Burns, David D.; "The Perfectionist's Script For Self-Defeat". Psychology Today, November 1980.

Caudill, Donald W.; "Some Less Recognized Forms Of Employee Theft". Management Solutions, October 1987.

Davis, Keith; Human Behavior At Work. N.Y.: McGraw-Hill, 1977.

Donnelly, Katherine Fair; "Returning To Work After The Loss Of A Loved One". Personnel, August 1986.

Flynn, W.R. and Stratton, W. E.; "Managing Problem Employees". Human Resource Management, Summer 1981.

Giacolone, R. A. and Knouse, S. B.; "Reducing The Need For Defensive Behavior". Management Solutions, September 1987.

References

Griffith, T. J.; "Understanding the Work Personality". Supervisory Management, February 1986.

Hellriegel, Don and Slocum, John W.; Management. Third Ed. Mass: Addison-Wesley Pub. Co., 1982.

In Beach, Dale S.; Managing People At Work. 3rd Ed. N.Y.: Macmillan, 1980.
Eli Ginzberg, "Man And His Work"
Jack Barbash, "Humanizing Work—A New Ideology"
M. R. Cooper, et al., "Changing Employee Values: Deepening Discontent."
Frederick Herzberg, "One More Time: How Do You Motivate Employees?"

In Collins, Eliza G. C. ed.; The Executive Dilemma: Handling People Problems At Work. N.Y.: John Wiley & Sons, 1985.
Manfred F. R. Kets de Vries, "Managers Can Drive Their Subordinates Mad"
Harry Levinson, "The Abrasive Personality"
Mary P. Rowe, "Are You Hearing Enough Employee Concerns"
Abraham Zoleznik, "The Dynamics Of Subordinacy"

Lees-Haley, Paul R.; "How to Detect Malingerers In The Workplace". Personnel Journal, July 1986.

Levesque, Joseph D.; Manual Of Personnel Policies, Procedures, And Operations. N.Y.: Prentice-Hall, 1986.

Long, J. and Ormsby, J. G.; "Stamp Out Absenteeism". Personnel Journal, November 1987.

Macleod, Jennifer S.; "The Work Place As Prison". Employment Relations Today, Autumn 1985.

Markowich, M. Michael and Farber, JoAnna; "Managing Your Achilles' Heel". Personnel Administrator, June 1987.

Matejka, J. Kenneth, et al; "Managing Difficult Employees: Challenge Or Curse?" Personnel, July 1986.

McCulloch, Kenneth; "Alternative Dispute Resolution Techniques: Pros And Cons". Employment Relations Today, Autumn 1984.

McEwan, Bruce; "Mediating Between Disputing Employees". Supervisory Management, May 1984.

Mitchell, Terence R.; People In Organizations: Understanding Their Behavior. N.Y.: McGraw-Hill, 1978.

Myers, Donald W.; Human Resources Management: Principles and Practices. Wash., D.C.: Commerce Clearing House, Inc., 1986.

Pitone, Louise; Absence & Lateness: How To Reduce It, How To Control It. Madison, CT: Business & Legal Reports, 1986.

Premeaus, Shane R., et al; "Supervising The Office Socializer". Management Solutions, August 1987.

Sandwith, Paul; "Absenteeism: You Get What You Accept". Personnel Journal, November 1987.

Schlotzhauer, D. and Rossee, I.; "A Five Year Study Of A Positive Incentive Absence Control Program". Personnel Psychology, Vol. 38, 1985.

Scott, Dow and Markham S.; "Absenteeism Control Methods: A Survey of Practices And Results". Personnel Administrator, June 1982.

Sculnick, Michael W.; "Discipline For Off Site Conduct". Employment Relations Today, Summer 1985.

Sheppard, I. Thomas; "Managing Those You Don't Like". Management Solutions, September 1987.

Sherman, V. Clayton; "Eight Steps To Preventing Problem Employees". Personnel, June 1987.

Snyder, Peg; "The First Steps In Solving People Problems". Management Solutions, November 1987.

Sparber, Andrew G.; "The Hazards Of Managing The Emotionally Handicapped". Personnel Journal, October 1987.

Taylor, Robert R.; "A Positive Guide to Theft Deterence". Personnel Journal, August 1986.

Terry, George R. and Franklin, Stephen G.; Principles of Management. Eighth Ed. Illinois: Richard D. Irving, Inc., 1982.

Chapter 3.0 Problems Of Workplace Control, Part 1: Improving Weaknesses In Organizational Goals And Personnel Policies
—and—
Chapter 4.0 Problems Of Workplace Control, Part 2: Changing Weak Performance Appraisals To a Performance Control System

Bartunek, John N.; "What To Do When Your Employees Plateau." Supervisory Management, July 1984.

Beer, Michael; "Performance Appraisal: Dilemmas And Possibilities." Organizational Dynamics, Winter 1981.

Burchett, S.R. and DeMeuse, K.P.; "Personnel Appraisal And The Law." Personnel, July 1985.

Butler, R.J. and Yorks, Lyle; "A New Appraisal System As Organizational Change: GE's Task Force Approach." Personnel, January-February 1984.

Carroll, S.J. and Schneier, C.E.; Performance Appraisal And Review Systems. Glenview, Illinois: Scott Foresman, 1982.

Cherrington, David J.; Personnel Management. Dubuque, Iowa: William C. Brown Co. Publishers, 1983.

References

Cocheu, Ted; "A Case In Points: Performance Appraisal." Personnel Journal, September 1986.

Fletcher, Clive; "What's New In Performance Appraisal?" Personnel Management, February 1984.

Glueck, William F.; Personnel: A Diagnostic Approach. Revised ed. Dallas: Business Publishers Inc., 1978.

Kane, Jeffrey S. & Freeman, K.A.; "MBO And Performance Appraisal: A Mixture That's Not A Solution, Parts 1 & 2." Personnel, December 1986/February 1987.

Kaye, Beverly L.; "Performance Appraisal And Career Development: A Shotgun Marriage." Personnel, March-April 1984.

Martin, David C.; "Performance Appraisal, 2: Improving the Rater's Effectiveness". Personnel, August 1986.

McConkey, Dale D.; How To Manage By Results, Fourth Ed. New York: AMACOM, 1983.

McTague, Michael; "Productivity Is Shaped By Forces Beneath Corporate Culture." Personnel Journal, March 1986.

Myers, Donald W.; Human Resource Management: Principles And Practice. Washington, D.C.: Commerce Clearing House, Inc., 1986.

Perry, Manuel; "Does Your Appraisal System Stack Up?" Personnel Journal, May 1987.

Phillips, Kenneth R.; "Red Flags In Performance Appraisal." Training and Development Journal, March 1987.

Reed, P.R. and Kroll, M.J.; "A Two-Perspective Approach To Performance Appraisal." Personnel, October 1985.

Riley, Mary & Noland, Richard; "Beyond Performance Reviews." Management Solutions, October 1987.

Sashkin, Marshall; "Appraising Appraisal: Ten Lessons From Research For Practice." Organizational Dynamics, Winter 1981.

Schmidt, Frank L. et al.; "Impact Of Job Experience And Ability On Job Knowledge, Work Sample Performance, And Supervisory Ratings Of Job Performance." Journal of Applied Psychology, 1986 (Vol. 71, No. 3).

Schneier, Craig E. et al.; "Performance Appraisals: No Appointment Needed." Personnel Journal, November 1987.

Shaw, James B. & Weekley, Jeff A.; "The Effects Of Objective Work-Load Variations of Psychological Strain and Post-Work-Load Performance." Journal of Management, 1985 (Vol. 11, No. 1).

Terry, John; "In Praise Of Appraisals." Canadian Business, December 1984.

Wagel, William H.; "Performance Appraisal With A Difference." Personnel, February 1987.

Wertzel, William; "How To Improve Performance Through Successful Appraisals." Personnel, October 1987.

Chapter 5.0 Solving Workplace Problems With The Help Of Consultants And Other Professionals

Barbour, George Jr.; "How To Get The Most Out Of Your Consultant". Public Management, ICMA, April 1981, Vol. 63, No. 4.

Craig, Robert L. ed.; Training And Development Handbook: A Guide To Human Resource Development, 2nd Ed. New York: McGraw-Hill, 1976.

Farr, Cheryle; "Free Advice From 30 Consultants: The Manager's Role In Enhancing Client-Consultant Relationships". Public Management, ICMA, April 1981, Vol. 63, No. 4.

Holtz, Herman; The Consultant's Guide To Proposal Writing. New York: John Wiley & Sons, 1986.

In Journal Of Management Consulting, Vol. 3, No. 4, 1987:

　　Metzger, Robet O.; "The Changing Paradigm Of Consulting"

　　Tagiuri, Renato; "Of Change And The Consultant"

　　Lundberg, Craig C.; "Consulting Through The Looking Glass"

　　Sabath, Robert E.; "From Our Roots To Our Future: An Irreverent Look At Management Consulting"

Olsen, Raymond; "Managing Consultants On The Job". Public Management, ICMA, April 1981, Vol. 63, No. 4.

Sussman, Lyle and Kuzmits, Frank; "The HRD Professional As In-House Consultant". Personnel, June 1987.

_____; "Corporate Services Consultants Director". Small Business Report, Winter/ Spring 1987, Vol. 1.

INDEX

Index

INDEX OF COURT CASES

About the Author

Joseph D. Levesque is the managing director of Personnel Systems Consultants, a human resource and organizational management consulting firm based in Sacramento, California. He is the author of the *Manual of Personnel Policies, Procedures, and Operations* and *The Complete Hiring Manual: Policies, Procedures, and Practices.*